VIVA_AMERICA

That's right, it's me: America Chavez, exile of the Utopian Parallel and student at Sotomayor U. And I'm not new. I'm Teen Brigade, Young Avengers, and the Ultimates certified. You don't need to see I.D. I've got my own solo series now, *oíste?*

BEAMCHAT

AMERICA CHAVEZ
Following • Beamz • Profile

subscribe

message   ...

LAST PLAYED:

So a while back, I started college with my old friend Prodigy. Sotomayor University, baby!

But then some luchador-looking *vieja* showed up using *my* portals as her calling card.

I met up with my girl Kate Bishop to help me sort out my life…

…and ended up fighting to save an old crush, courtesy of the Midas Corporation.

By the time lady luchador showed up again, I was ready to listen.

Check this: She's my *grandmother.* Madrimar is family, y'all. I have an *abuela.* And she's taking me *home.*

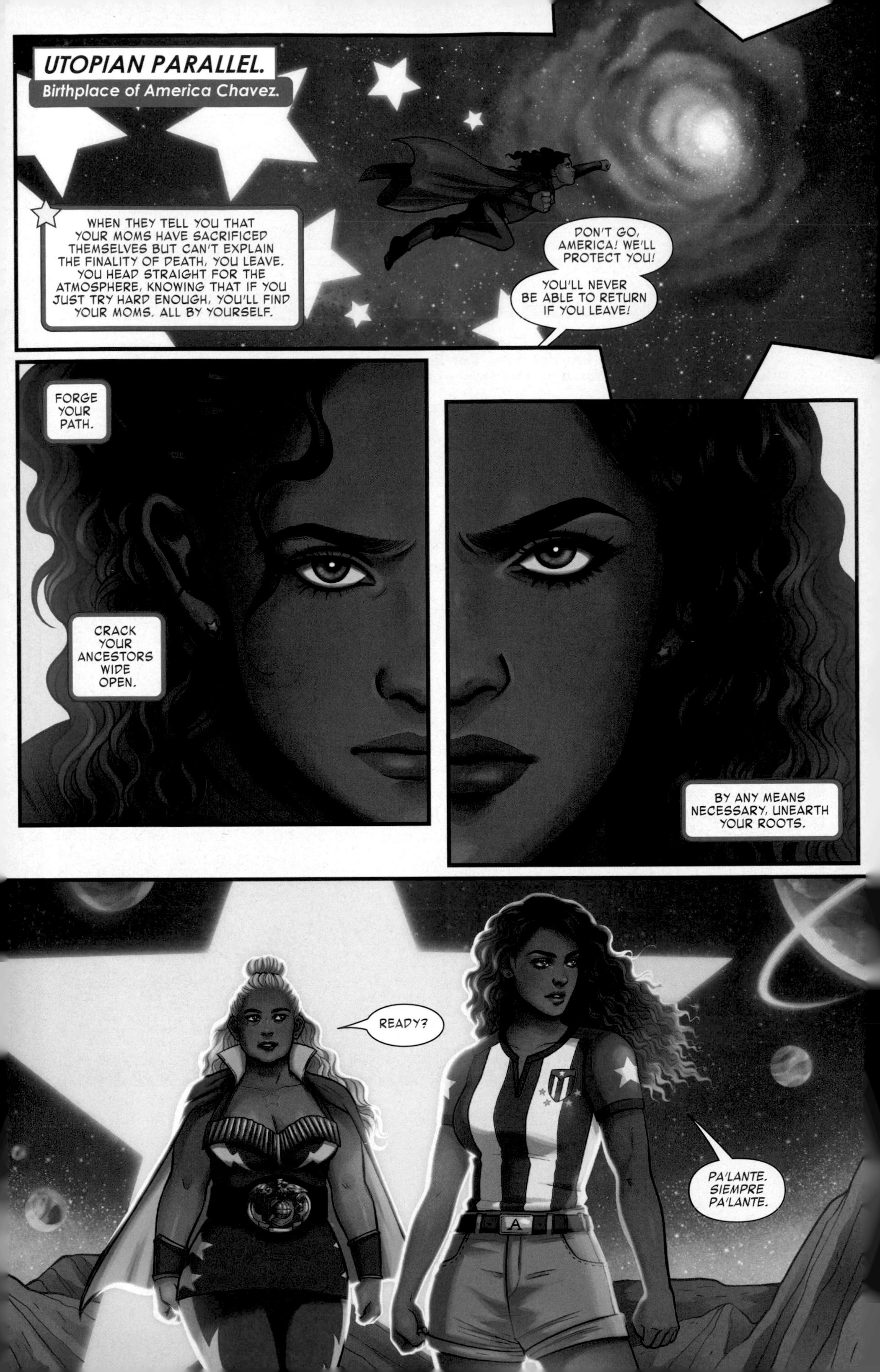
UTOPIAN PARALLEL.
Birthplace of America Chavez.
WHEN THEY TELL YOU THAT YOUR MOMS HAVE SACRIFICED THEMSELVES BUT CAN'T EXPLAIN THE FINALITY OF DEATH, YOU LEAVE. YOU HEAD STRAIGHT FOR THE ATMOSPHERE, KNOWING THAT IF YOU JUST TRY HARD ENOUGH, YOU'LL FIND YOUR MOMS. ALL BY YOURSELF.
DON'T GO, AMERICA! WE'LL PROTECT YOU!
YOU'LL NEVER BE ABLE TO RETURN IF YOU LEAVE!
FORGE YOUR PATH.
CRACK YOUR ANCESTORS WIDE OPEN.
BY ANY MEANS NECESSARY, UNEARTH YOUR ROOTS.
READY?
PA'LANTE. SIEMPRE PA'LANTE.

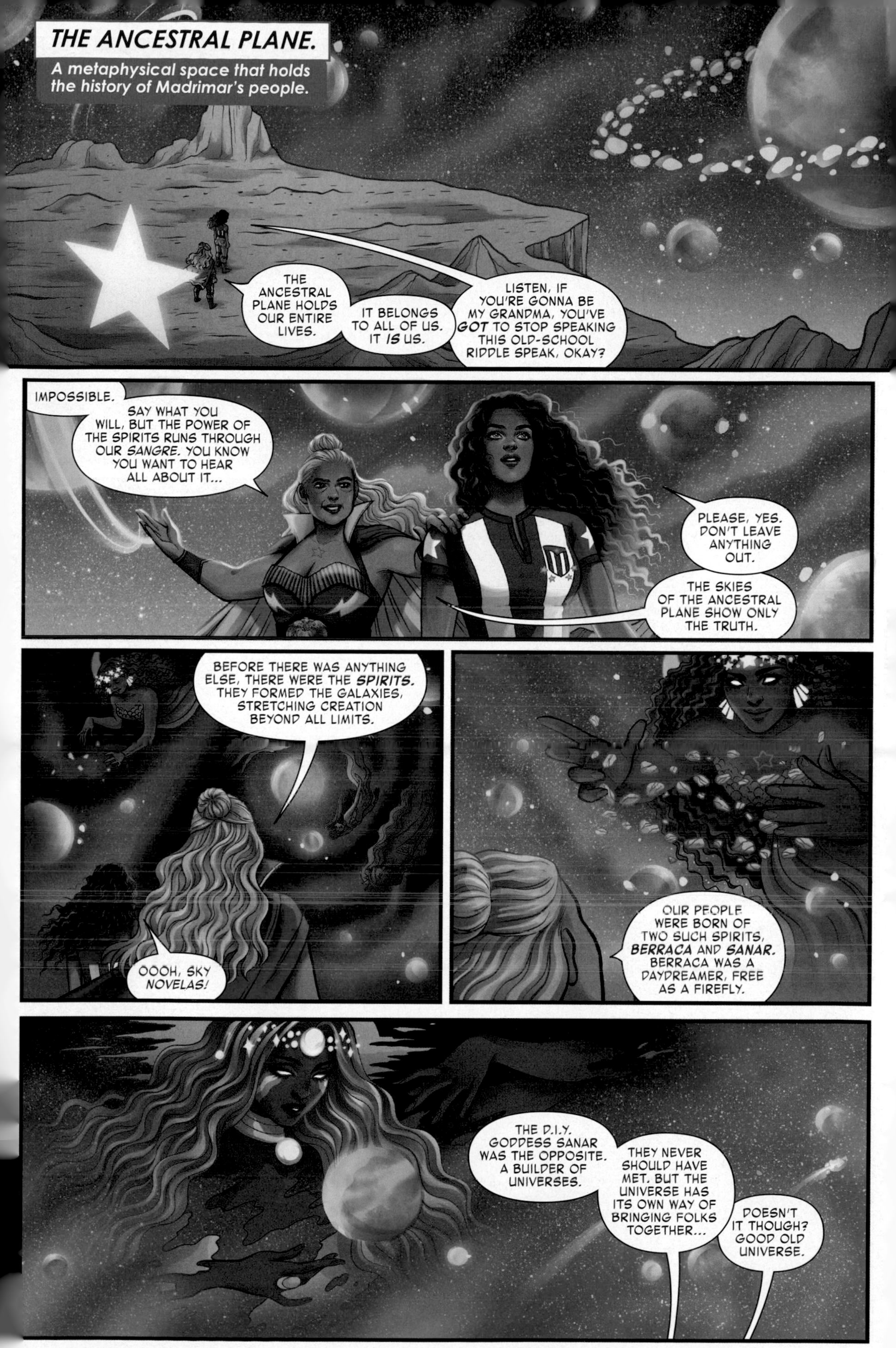
THE ANCESTRAL PLANE.
A metaphysical space that holds the history of Madrimar's people.
THE ANCESTRAL PLANE HOLDS OUR ENTIRE LIVES.
IT BELONGS TO ALL OF US. IT IS US.
LISTEN, IF YOU'RE GONNA BE MY GRANDMA, YOU'VE GOT TO STOP SPEAKING THIS OLD-SCHOOL RIDDLE SPEAK, OKAY?
IMPOSSIBLE.
SAY WHAT YOU WILL, BUT THE POWER OF THE SPIRITS RUNS THROUGH OUR SANGRE. YOU KNOW YOU WANT TO HEAR ALL ABOUT IT...
PLEASE, YES. DON'T LEAVE ANYTHING OUT.
THE SKIES OF THE ANCESTRAL PLANE SHOW ONLY THE TRUTH.
BEFORE THERE WAS ANYTHING ELSE, THERE WERE THE SPIRITS. THEY FORMED THE GALAXIES, STRETCHING CREATION BEYOND ALL LIMITS.
OOOH, SKY NOVELAS!
OUR PEOPLE WERE BORN OF TWO SUCH SPIRITS, BERRACA AND SANAR. BERRACA WAS A DAYDREAMER, FREE AS A FIREFLY.
THE D.I.Y. GODDESS SANAR WAS THE OPPOSITE. A BUILDER OF UNIVERSES.
THEY NEVER SHOULD HAVE MET. BUT THE UNIVERSE HAS ITS OWN WAY OF BRINGING FOLKS TOGETHER...
DOESN'T IT THOUGH? GOOD OLD UNIVERSE.

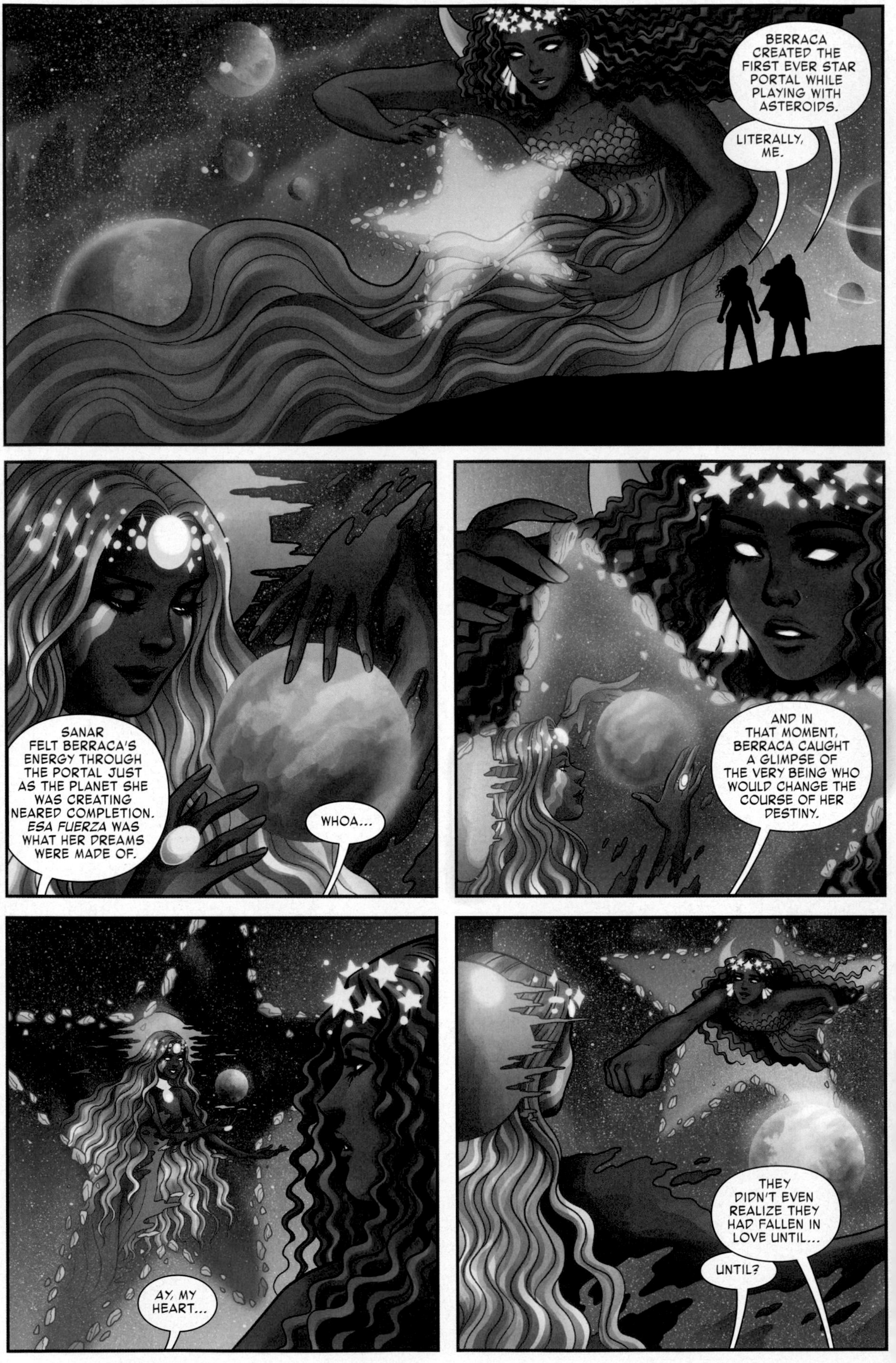
BERRACA CREATED THE FIRST EVER STAR PORTAL WHILE PLAYING WITH ASTEROIDS.
LITERALLY, ME.
SANAR FELT BERRACA'S ENERGY THROUGH THE PORTAL JUST AS THE PLANET SHE WAS CREATING NEARED COMPLETION. *ESA FUERZA* WAS WHAT HER DREAMS WERE MADE OF.
WHOA...
AND IN THAT MOMENT, BERRACA CAUGHT A GLIMPSE OF THE VERY BEING WHO WOULD CHANGE THE COURSE OF HER DESTINY.
AY, MY HEART...
THEY DIDN'T EVEN REALIZE THEY HAD FALLEN IN LOVE UNTIL...
UNTIL?

AMERICA

★ FAST AND FUERTONA ★

GABBY RIVERA
WRITER

─── ★ ISSUE #7 ★ ───

JEN BARTEL (PP. 1-4), **ANNIE WU** (PP. 5-9), **MING DOYLE** (PP. 10-14),
AUD KOCH (PP. 15-19) & **JOE QUINONES** WITH **JOE RIVERA** (P. 20)
ARTISTS

JEN BARTEL (PP. 1-4), **RACHELLE ROSENBERG** (PP. 5-19) & **JORDAN GIBSON** (P. 20)
COLOR ARTISTS

─── ★ ISSUE #8 ★ ───

JOE QUINONES
PENCILER

JOE RIVERA
INKER

JORDAN GIBSON
COLOR ARTIST

─── ★ ISSUE #9-10 ★ ───

FLAVIANO WITH **JEN BARTEL** (#10)
ARTISTS

JORDAN GIBSON WITH **CHRIS O'HALLORAN** (#10)
COLOR ARTISTS

─── ★ ISSUE #11 ★ ───

STACEY LEE WITH **FLAVIANO**
ARTISTS

JORDAN GIBSON WITH **CHRIS O'HALLORAN**
COLOR ARTISTS

─── ★ ISSUE #12 ★ ───

STACEY LEE, ANNIE WU & **FLAVIANO**
ARTISTS

JORDAN GIBSON WITH **CHRIS O'HALLORAN**
COLOR ARTISTS

VC'S TRAVIS LANHAM
LETTERER

JOE QUINONES
COVER ART

SARAH BRUNSTAD & **WIL MOSS**
EDITORS

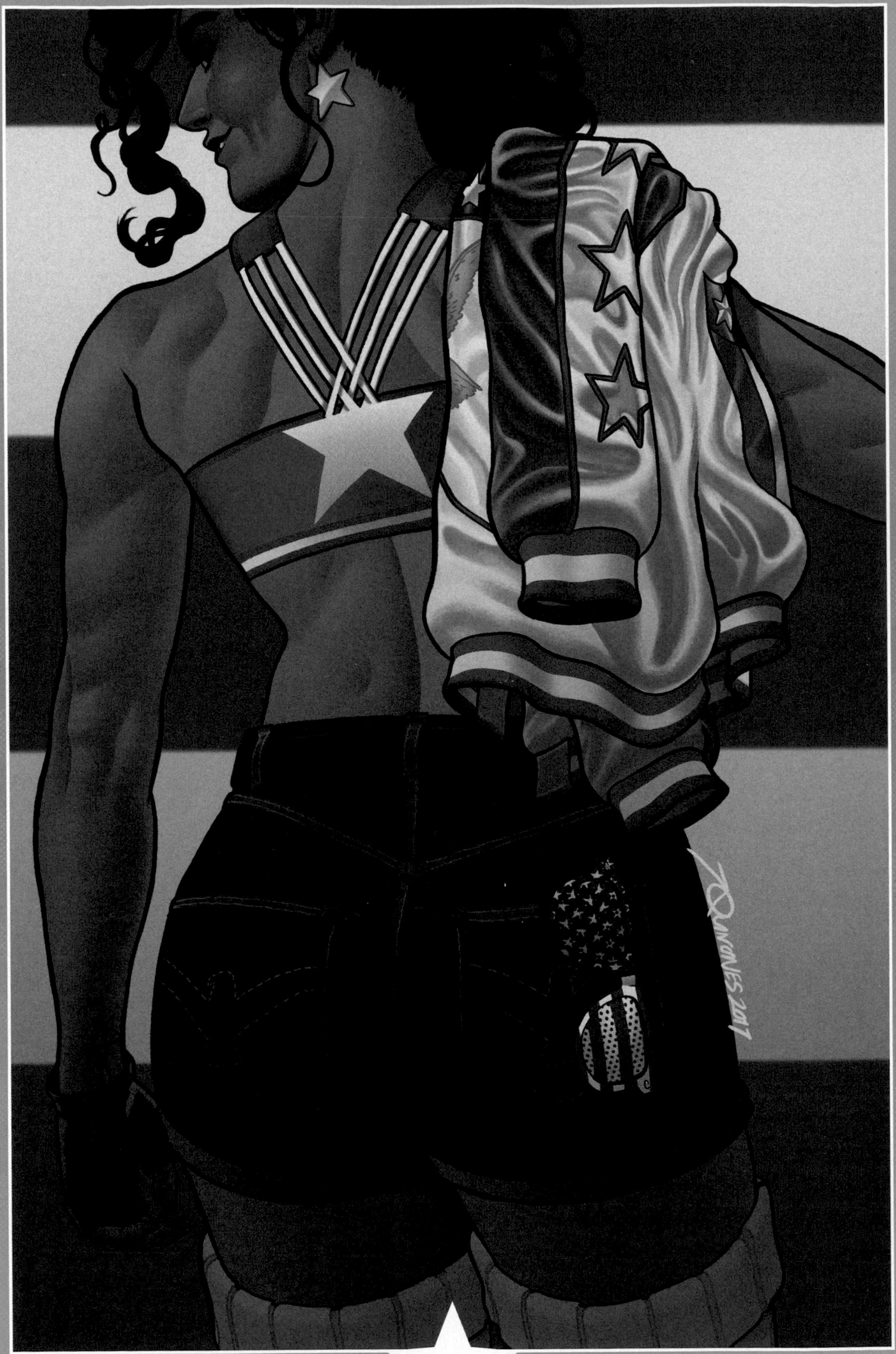

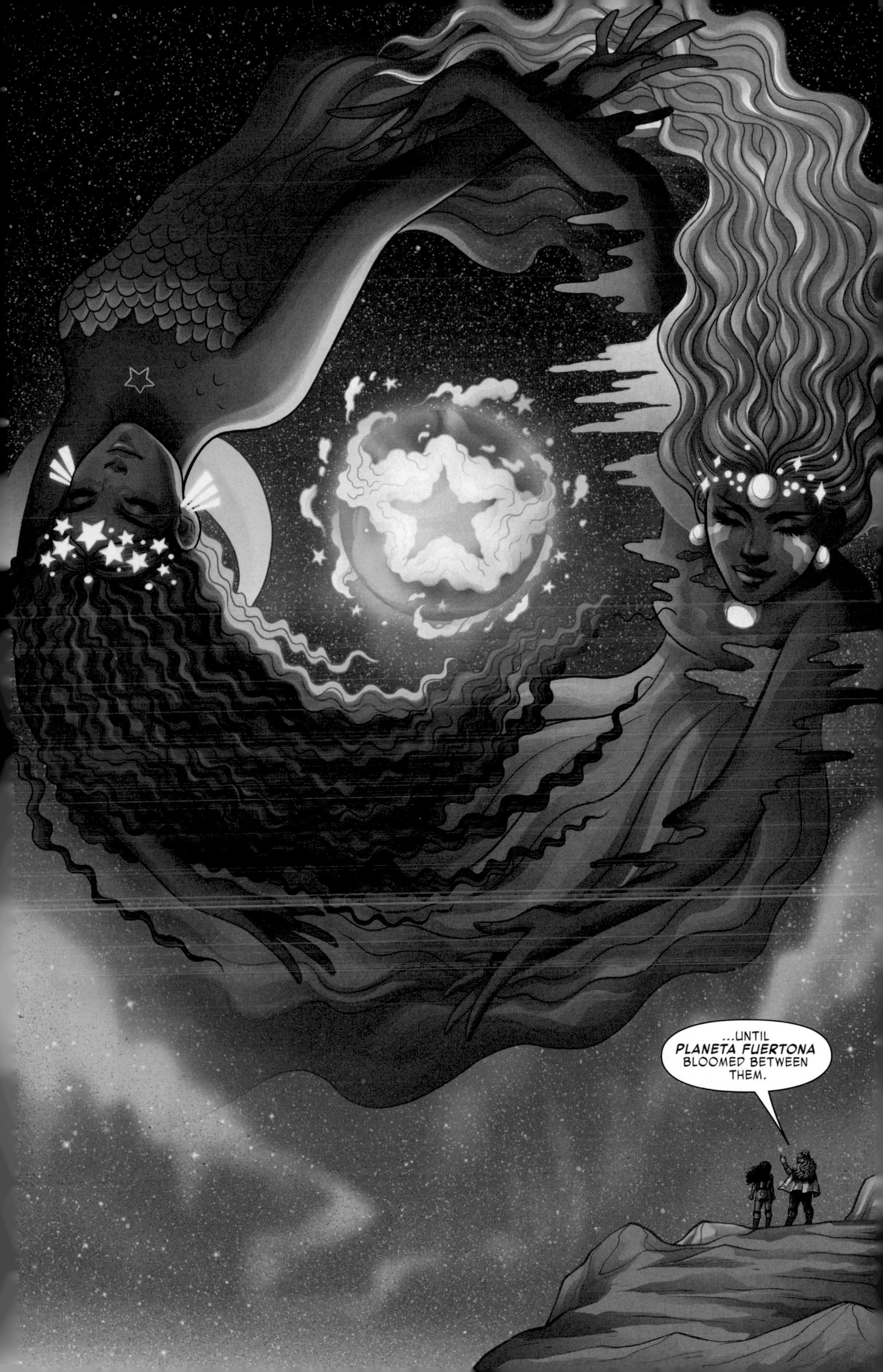
...UNTIL *PLANETA FUERTONA* BLOOMED BETWEEN THEM.

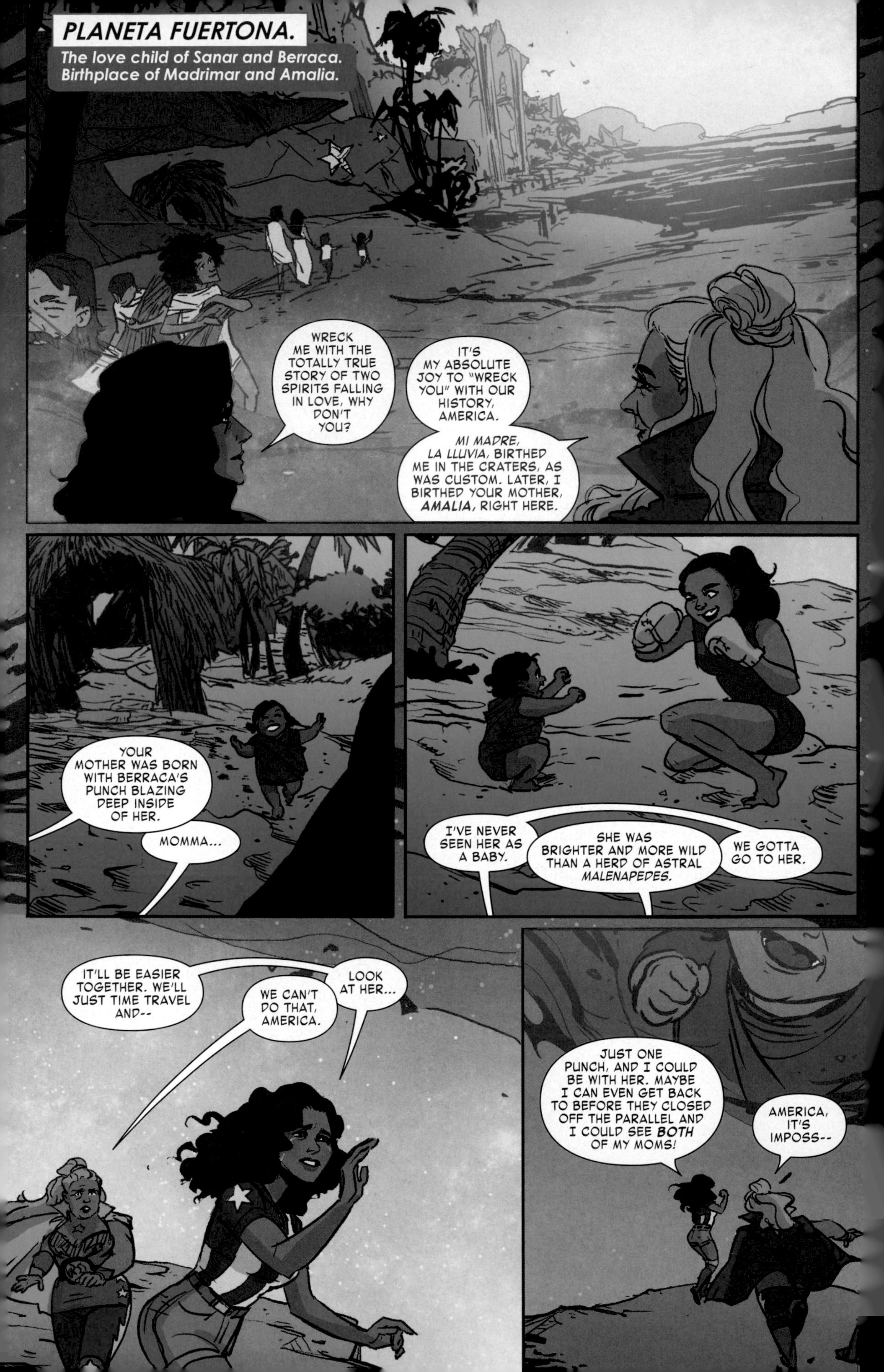
PLANETA FUERTONA.
The love child of Sanar and Berraca. Birthplace of Madrimar and Amalia.
WRECK ME WITH THE TOTALLY TRUE STORY OF TWO SPIRITS FALLING IN LOVE, WHY DON'T YOU?
IT'S MY ABSOLUTE JOY TO "WRECK YOU" WITH OUR HISTORY, AMERICA.
MI MADRE, LA LLUVIA, BIRTHED ME IN THE CRATERS, AS WAS CUSTOM. LATER, I BIRTHED YOUR MOTHER, AMALIA, RIGHT HERE.
YOUR MOTHER WAS BORN WITH BERRACA'S PUNCH BLAZING DEEP INSIDE OF HER.
MOMMA...
I'VE NEVER SEEN HER AS A BABY.
SHE WAS BRIGHTER AND MORE WILD THAN A HERD OF ASTRAL MALENAPEDES.
WE GOTTA GO TO HER.
IT'LL BE EASIER TOGETHER. WE'LL JUST TIME TRAVEL AND--
LOOK AT HER...
WE CAN'T DO THAT, AMERICA.
JUST ONE PUNCH, AND I COULD BE WITH HER. MAYBE I CAN EVEN GET BACK TO BEFORE THEY CLOSED OFF THE PARALLEL AND I COULD SEE BOTH OF MY MOMS!
AMERICA, IT'S IMPOSS--

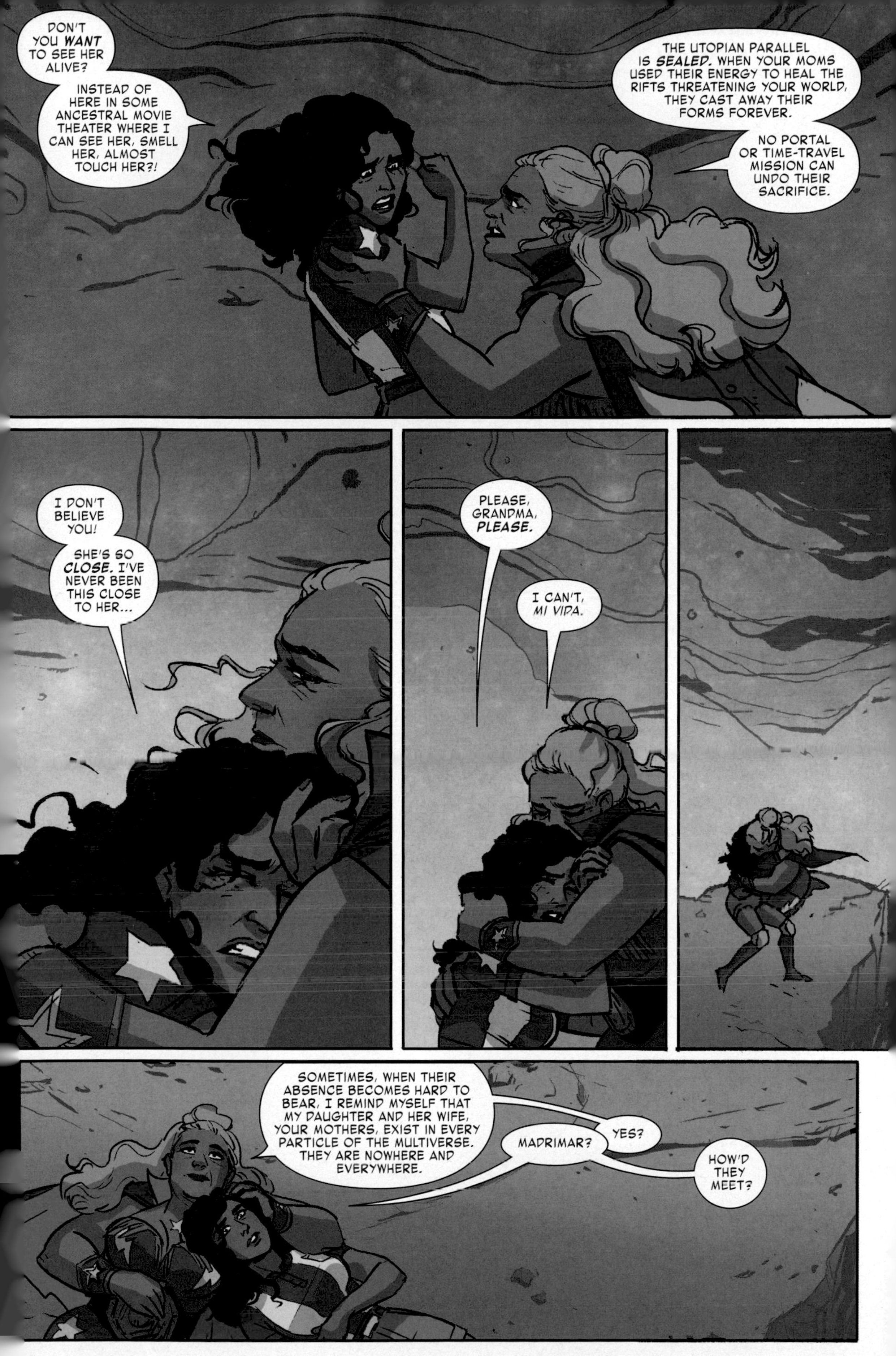
DON'T YOU *WANT* TO SEE HER ALIVE?
INSTEAD OF HERE IN SOME ANCESTRAL MOVIE THEATER WHERE I CAN SEE HER, SMELL HER, ALMOST TOUCH HER?!
THE UTOPIAN PARALLEL IS *SEALED.* WHEN YOUR MOMS USED THEIR ENERGY TO HEAL THE RIFTS THREATENING YOUR WORLD, THEY CAST AWAY THEIR FORMS FOREVER.
NO PORTAL OR TIME-TRAVEL MISSION CAN UNDO THEIR SACRIFICE.
I DON'T BELIEVE YOU!
SHE'S SO *CLOSE.* I'VE NEVER BEEN THIS CLOSE TO HER...
PLEASE, GRANDMA, *PLEASE.*
I CAN'T, *MI VIDA.*
SOMETIMES, WHEN THEIR ABSENCE BECOMES HARD TO BEAR, I REMIND MYSELF THAT MY DAUGHTER AND HER WIFE, YOUR MOTHERS, EXIST IN EVERY PARTICLE OF THE MULTIVERSE. THEY ARE NOWHERE AND EVERYWHERE.
MADRIMAR?
YES?
HOW'D THEY MEET?

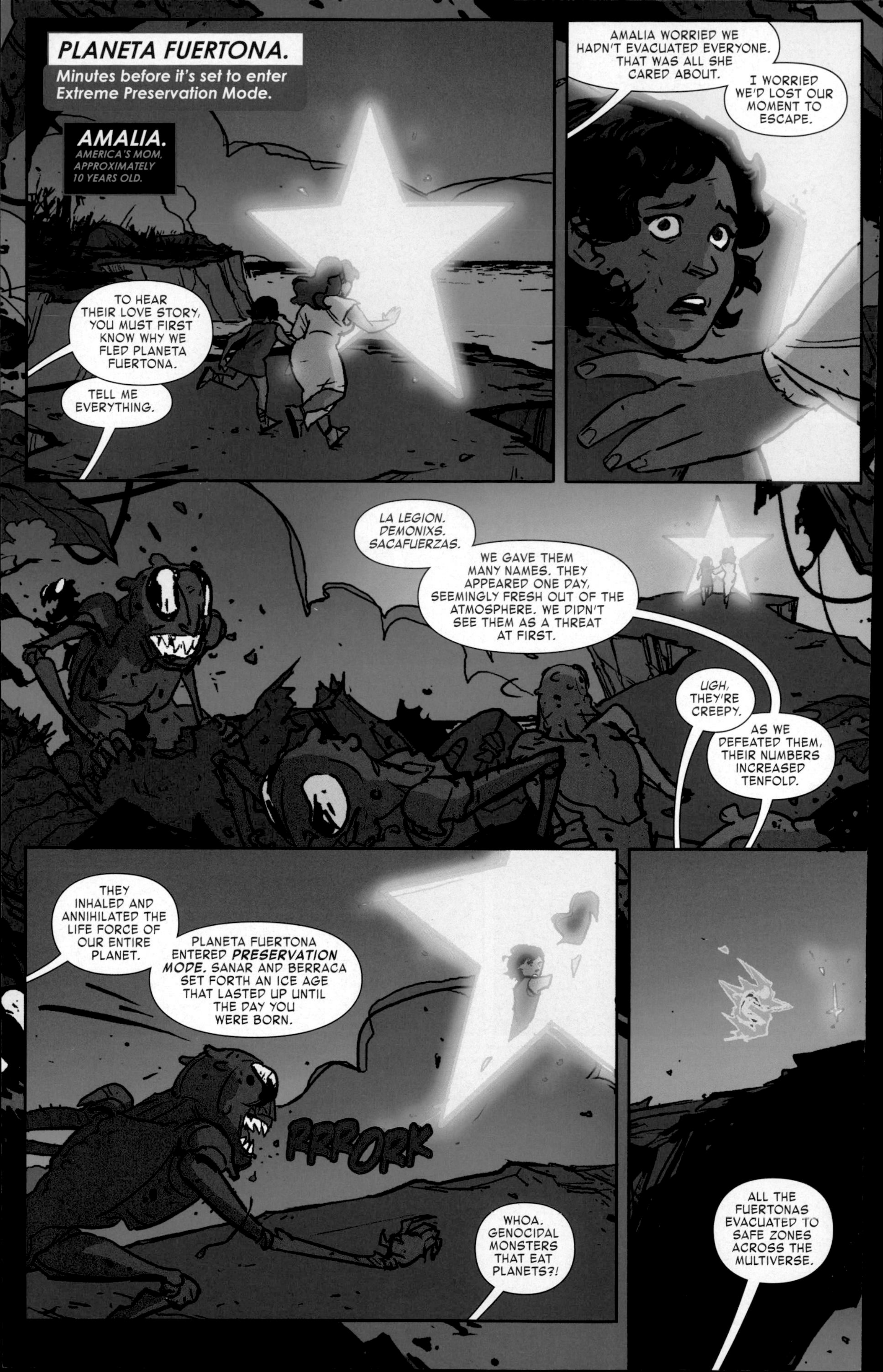
PLANETA FUERTONA.
Minutes before it's set to enter Extreme Preservation Mode.
AMALIA.
AMERICA'S MOM, APPROXIMATELY 10 YEARS OLD.
TO HEAR THEIR LOVE STORY, YOU MUST FIRST KNOW WHY WE FLED PLANETA FUERTONA.
TELL ME EVERYTHING.
AMALIA WORRIED WE HADN'T EVACUATED EVERYONE. THAT WAS ALL SHE CARED ABOUT.
I WORRIED WE'D LOST OUR MOMENT TO ESCAPE.
LA LEGION. DEMONIXS. SACAFUERZAS.
WE GAVE THEM MANY NAMES. THEY APPEARED ONE DAY, SEEMINGLY FRESH OUT OF THE ATMOSPHERE. WE DIDN'T SEE THEM AS A THREAT AT FIRST.
UGH, THEY'RE CREEPY.
AS WE DEFEATED THEM, THEIR NUMBERS INCREASED TENFOLD.
THEY INHALED AND ANNIHILATED THE LIFE FORCE OF OUR ENTIRE PLANET.
PLANETA FUERTONA ENTERED PRESERVATION MODE. SANAR AND BERRACA SET FORTH AN ICE AGE THAT LASTED UP UNTIL THE DAY YOU WERE BORN.
RRRORK
WHOA. GENOCIDAL MONSTERS THAT EAT PLANETS?!
ALL THE FUERTONAS EVACUATED TO SAFE ZONES ACROSS THE MULTIVERSE.

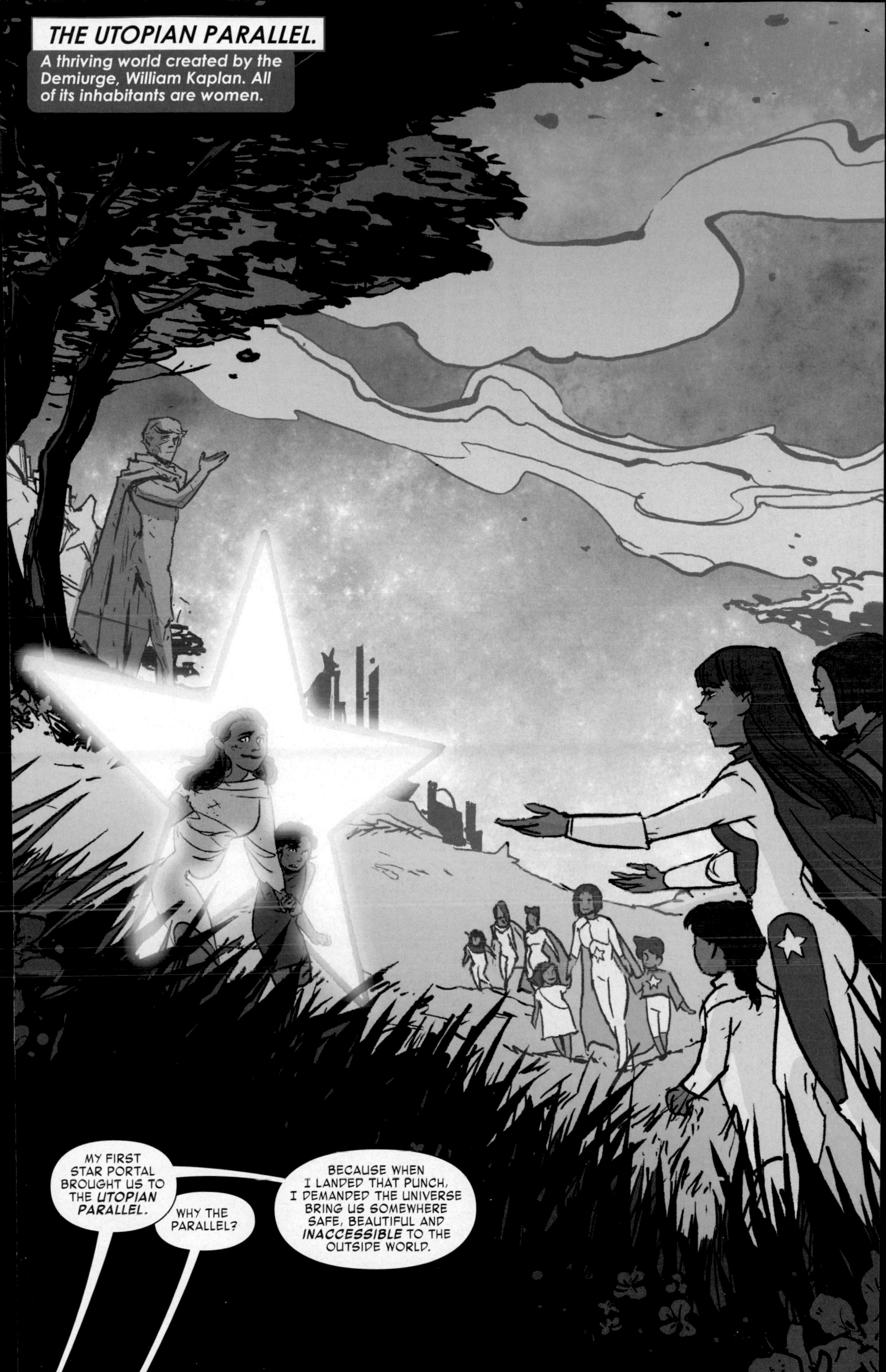
THE UTOPIAN PARALLEL.
A thriving world created by the Demiurge, William Kaplan. All of its inhabitants are women.
MY FIRST STAR PORTAL BROUGHT US TO THE UTOPIAN PARALLEL.
WHY THE PARALLEL?
BECAUSE WHEN I LANDED THAT PUNCH, I DEMANDED THE UNIVERSE BRING US SOMEWHERE SAFE, BEAUTIFUL AND INACCESSIBLE TO THE OUTSIDE WORLD.

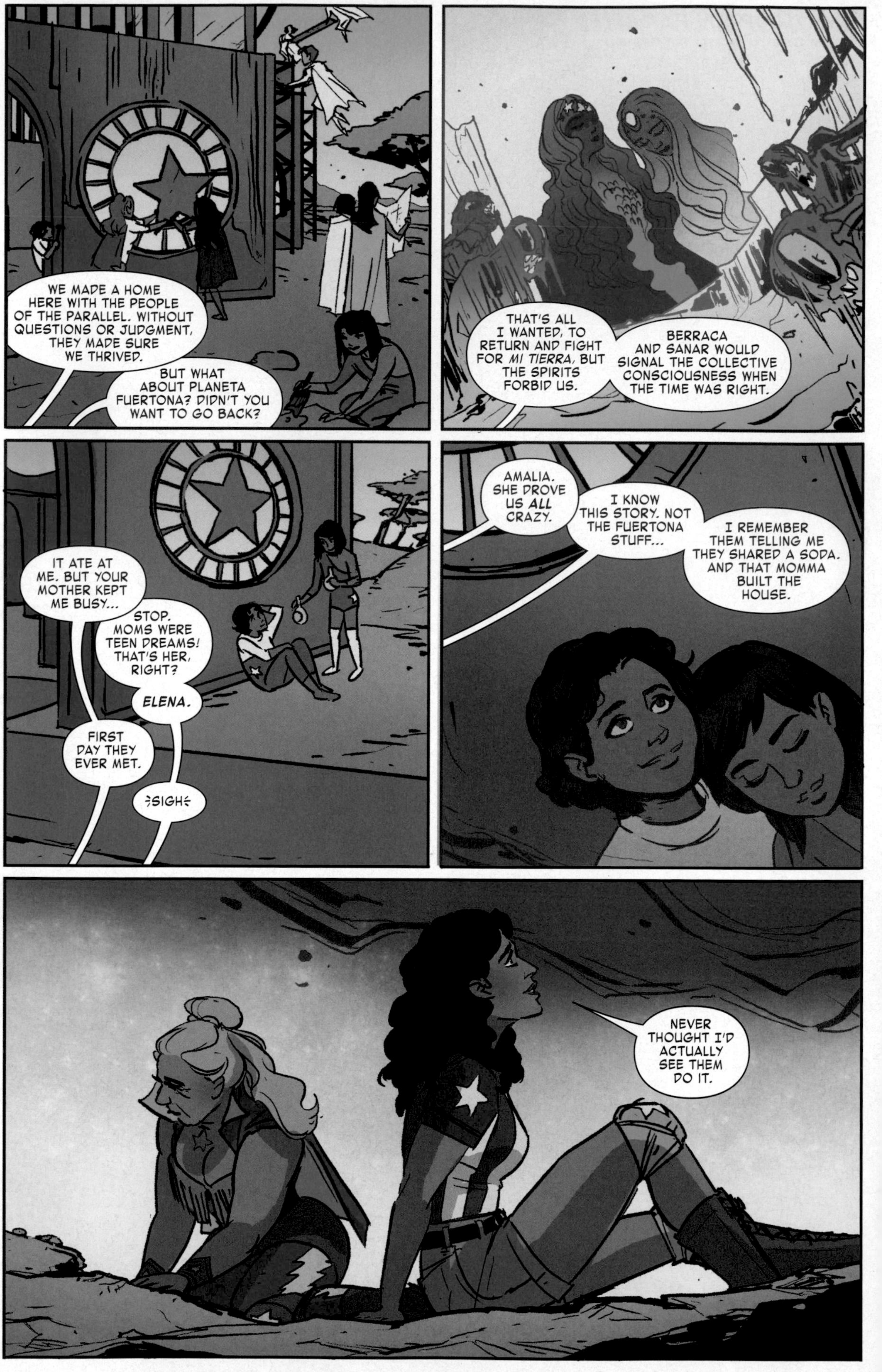
WE MADE A HOME HERE WITH THE PEOPLE OF THE PARALLEL. WITHOUT QUESTIONS OR JUDGMENT, THEY MADE SURE WE THRIVED.
BUT WHAT ABOUT PLANETA FUERTONA? DIDN'T YOU WANT TO GO BACK?
THAT'S ALL I WANTED, TO RETURN AND FIGHT FOR *MI TIERRA*, BUT THE SPIRITS FORBID US.
BERRACA AND SANAR WOULD SIGNAL THE COLLECTIVE CONSCIOUSNESS WHEN THE TIME WAS RIGHT.
IT ATE AT ME. BUT YOUR MOTHER KEPT ME BUSY...
STOP. MOMS WERE TEEN DREAMS! THAT'S HER, RIGHT?
ELENA.
FIRST DAY THEY EVER MET.
SIGH
AMALIA. SHE DROVE US *ALL* CRAZY.
I KNOW THIS STORY. NOT THE FUERTONA STUFF...
I REMEMBER THEM TELLING ME THEY SHARED A SODA. AND THAT MOMMA BUILT THE HOUSE.
NEVER THOUGHT I'D ACTUALLY SEE THEM DO IT.

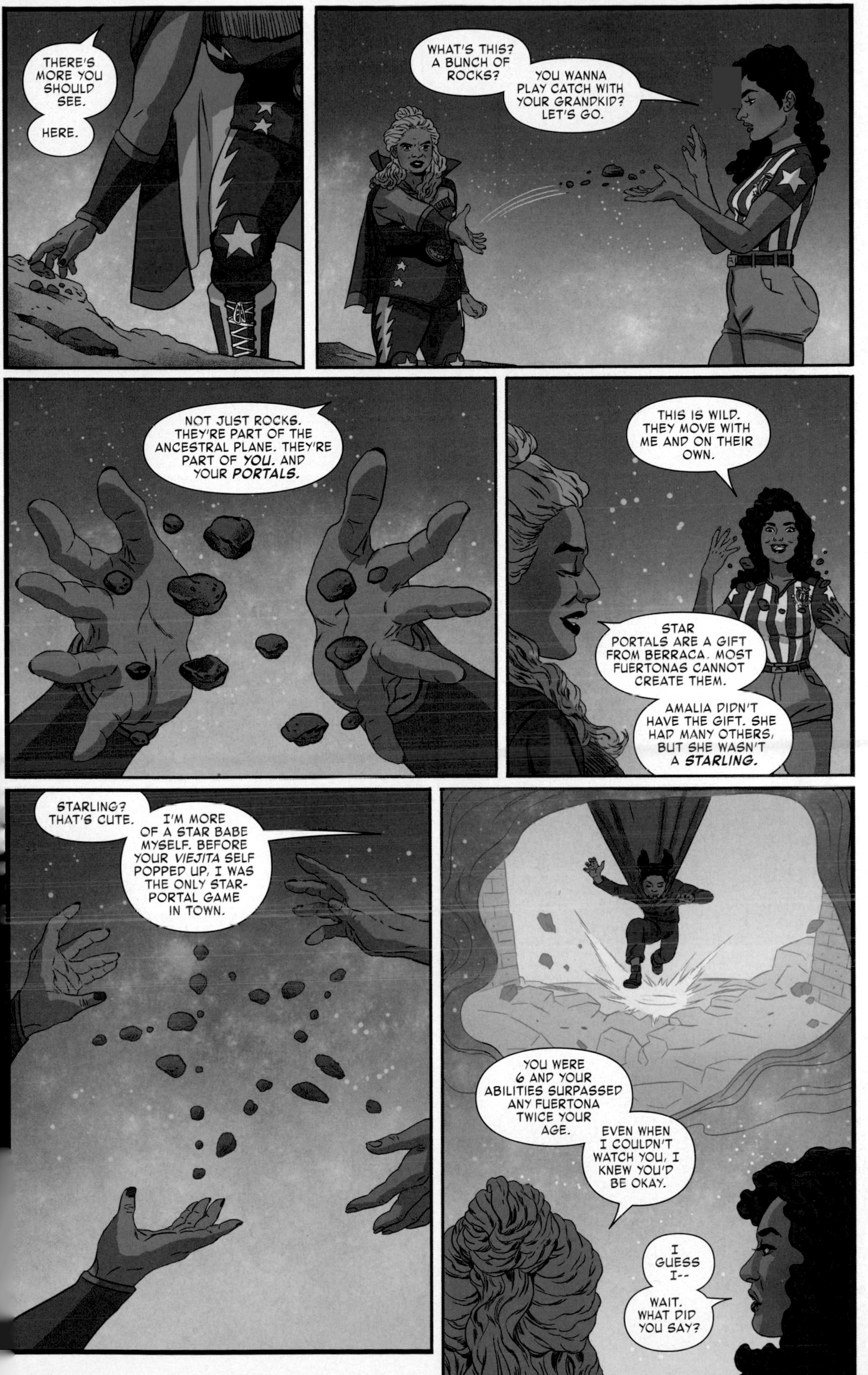
THERE'S MORE YOU SHOULD SEE.
HERE.
WHAT'S THIS? A BUNCH OF ROCKS?
YOU WANNA PLAY CATCH WITH YOUR GRANDKID? LET'S GO.
NOT JUST ROCKS. THEY'RE PART OF THE ANCESTRAL PLANE. THEY'RE PART OF YOU. AND YOUR PORTALS.
THIS IS WILD. THEY MOVE WITH ME AND ON THEIR OWN.
STAR PORTALS ARE A GIFT FROM BERRACA. MOST FUERTONAS CANNOT CREATE THEM.
AMALIA DIDN'T HAVE THE GIFT. SHE HAD MANY OTHERS, BUT SHE WASN'T A STARLING.
STARLING? THAT'S CUTE.
I'M MORE OF A STAR BABE MYSELF. BEFORE YOUR VIEJITA SELF POPPED UP, I WAS THE ONLY STAR-PORTAL GAME IN TOWN.
YOU WERE 6 AND YOUR ABILITIES SURPASSED ANY FUERTONA TWICE YOUR AGE.
EVEN WHEN I COULDN'T WATCH YOU, I KNEW YOU'D BE OKAY.
I GUESS I--
WAIT. WHAT DID YOU SAY?

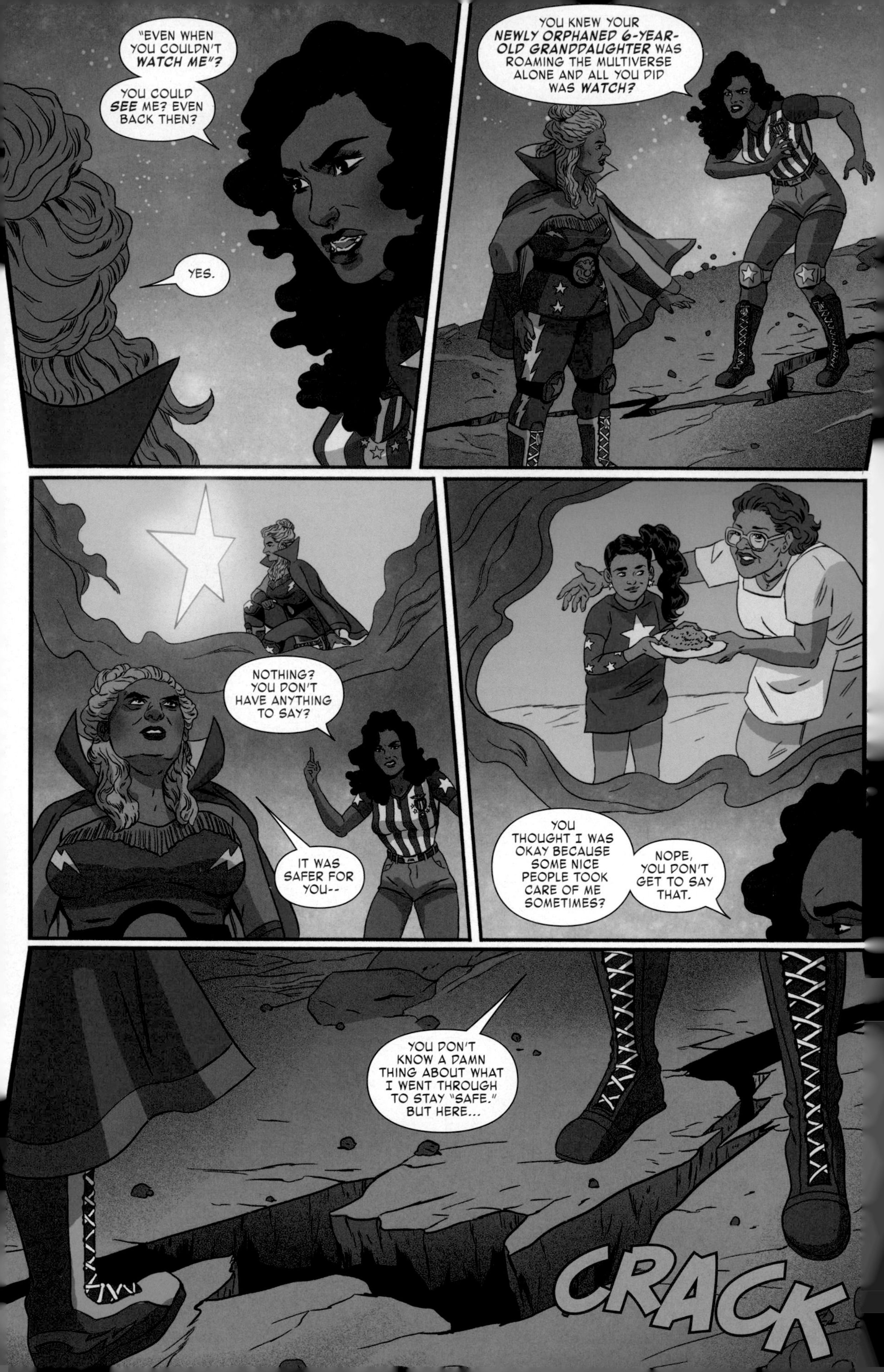

"EVEN WHEN YOU COULDN'T WATCH ME"?
YOU COULD SEE ME? EVEN BACK THEN?
YES.
YOU KNEW YOUR NEWLY ORPHANED 6-YEAR-OLD GRANDDAUGHTER WAS ROAMING THE MULTIVERSE ALONE AND ALL YOU DID WAS WATCH?
NOTHING? YOU DON'T HAVE ANYTHING TO SAY?
IT WAS SAFER FOR YOU--
YOU THOUGHT I WAS OKAY BECAUSE SOME NICE PEOPLE TOOK CARE OF ME SOMETIMES?
NOPE, YOU DON'T GET TO SAY THAT.
YOU DON'T KNOW A DAMN THING ABOUT WHAT I WENT THROUGH TO STAY "SAFE." BUT HERE...
CRACK

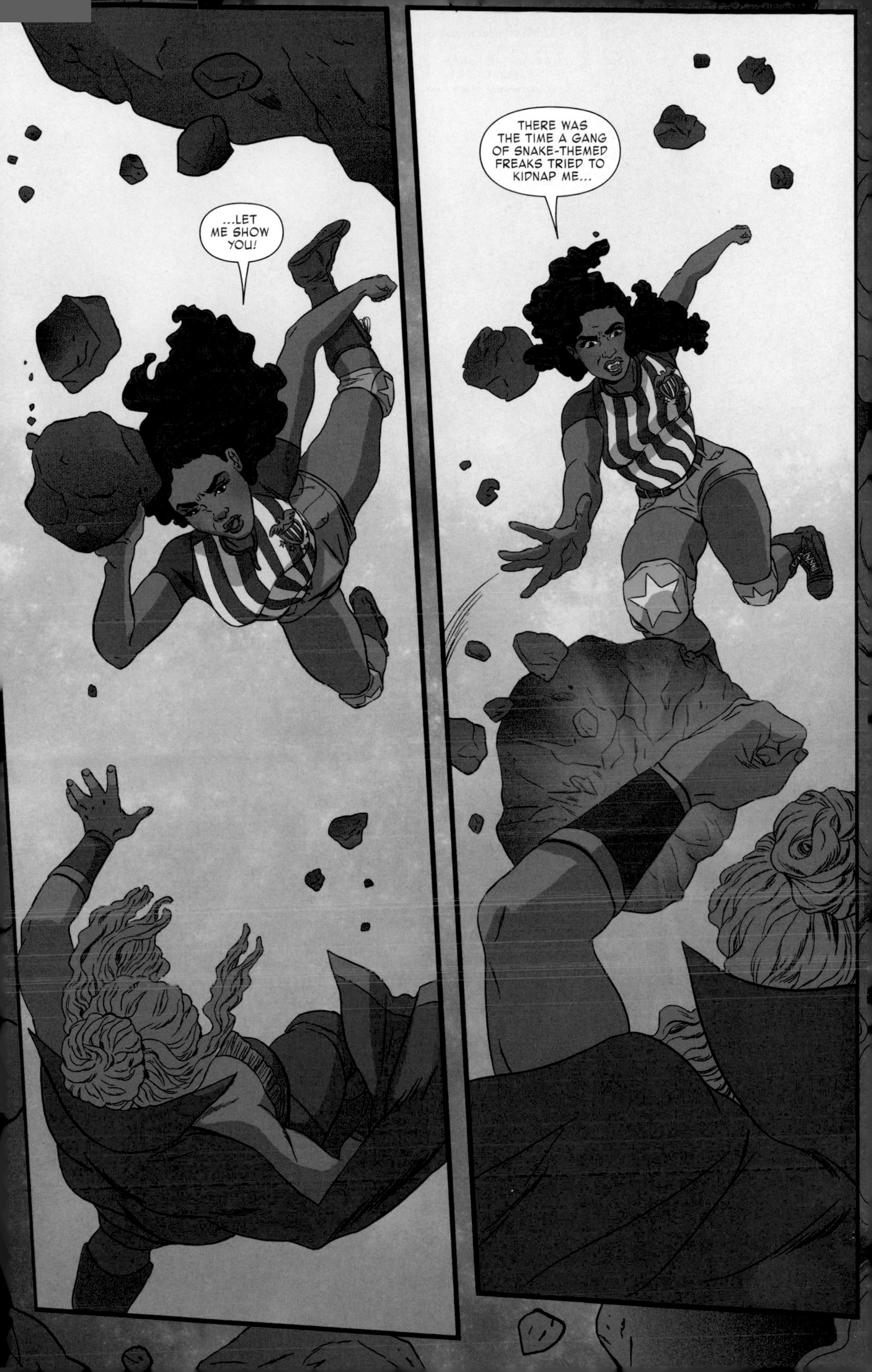
...LET ME SHOW YOU!
THERE WAS THE TIME A GANG OF SNAKE-THEMED FREAKS TRIED TO KIDNAP ME...

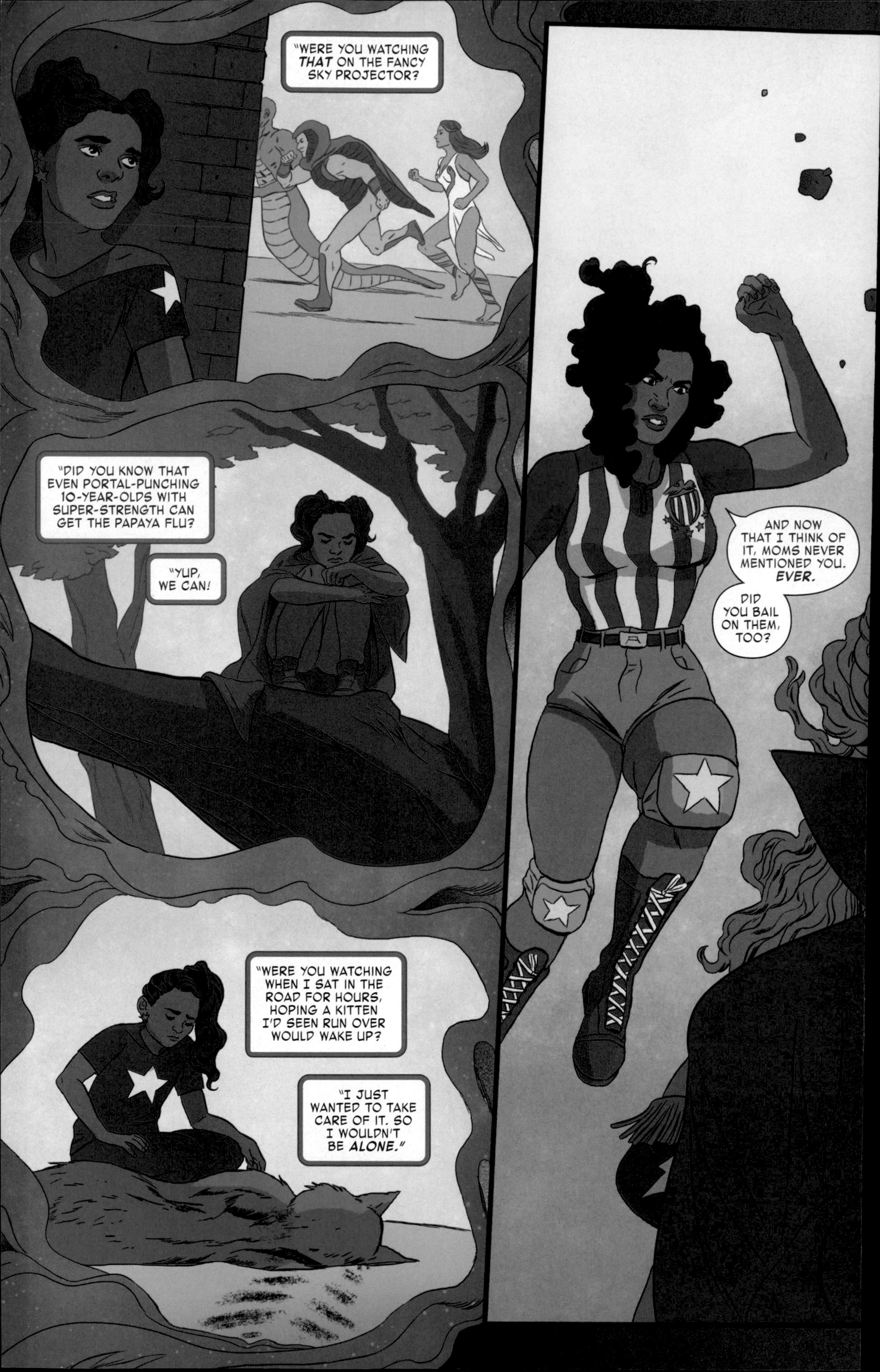
"WERE YOU WATCHING THAT ON THE FANCY SKY PROJECTOR?
"DID YOU KNOW THAT EVEN PORTAL-PUNCHING 10-YEAR-OLDS WITH SUPER-STRENGTH CAN GET THE PAPAYA FLU?
"YUP, WE CAN!
"WERE YOU WATCHING WHEN I SAT IN THE ROAD FOR HOURS, HOPING A KITTEN I'D SEEN RUN OVER WOULD WAKE UP?
"I JUST WANTED TO TAKE CARE OF IT. SO I WOULDN'T BE ALONE."
AND NOW THAT I THINK OF IT, MOMS NEVER MENTIONED YOU. EVER.
DID YOU BAIL ON THEM, TOO?

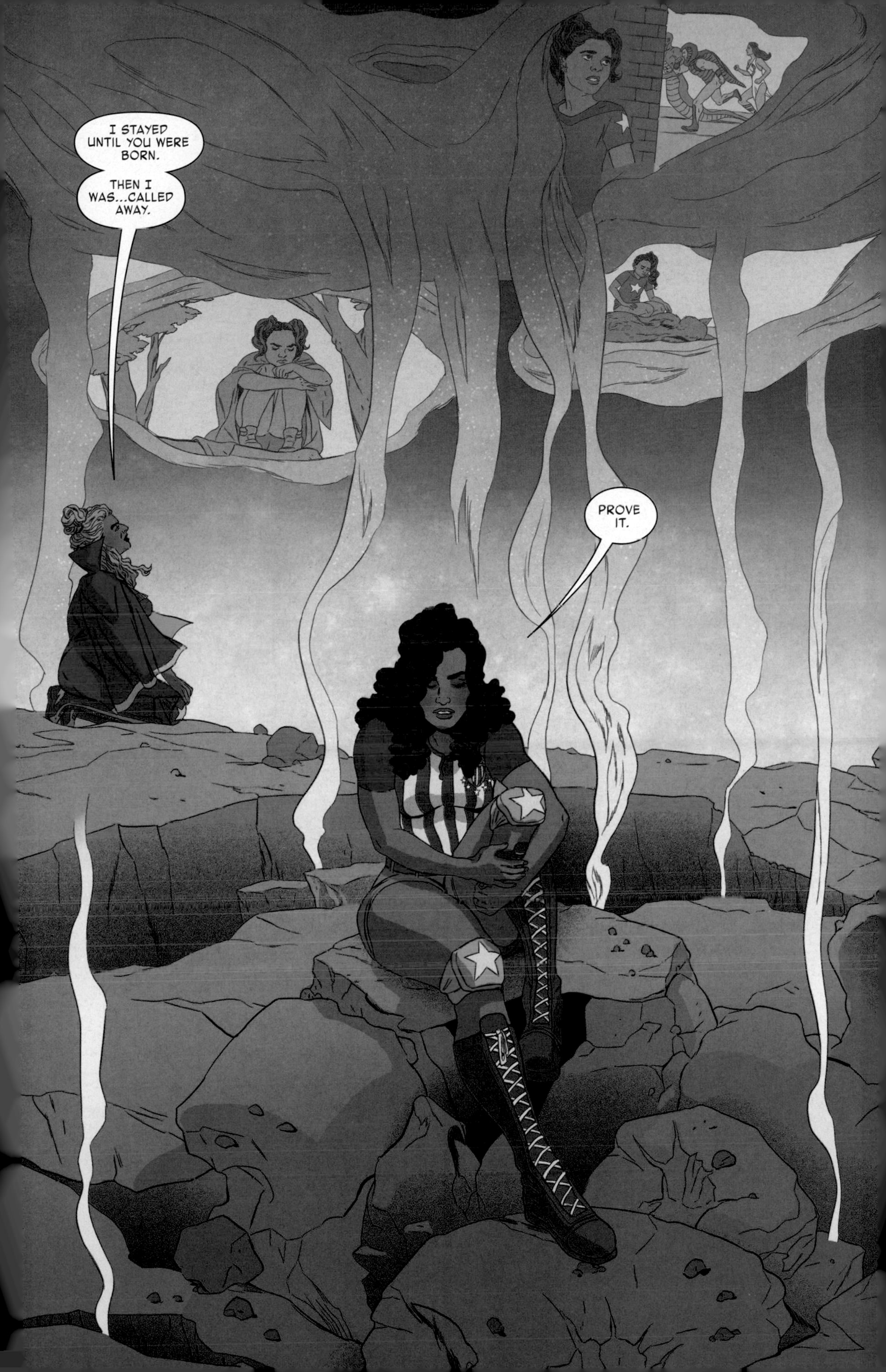
I STAYED UNTIL YOU WERE BORN.
THEN I WAS...CALLED AWAY.
PROVE IT.

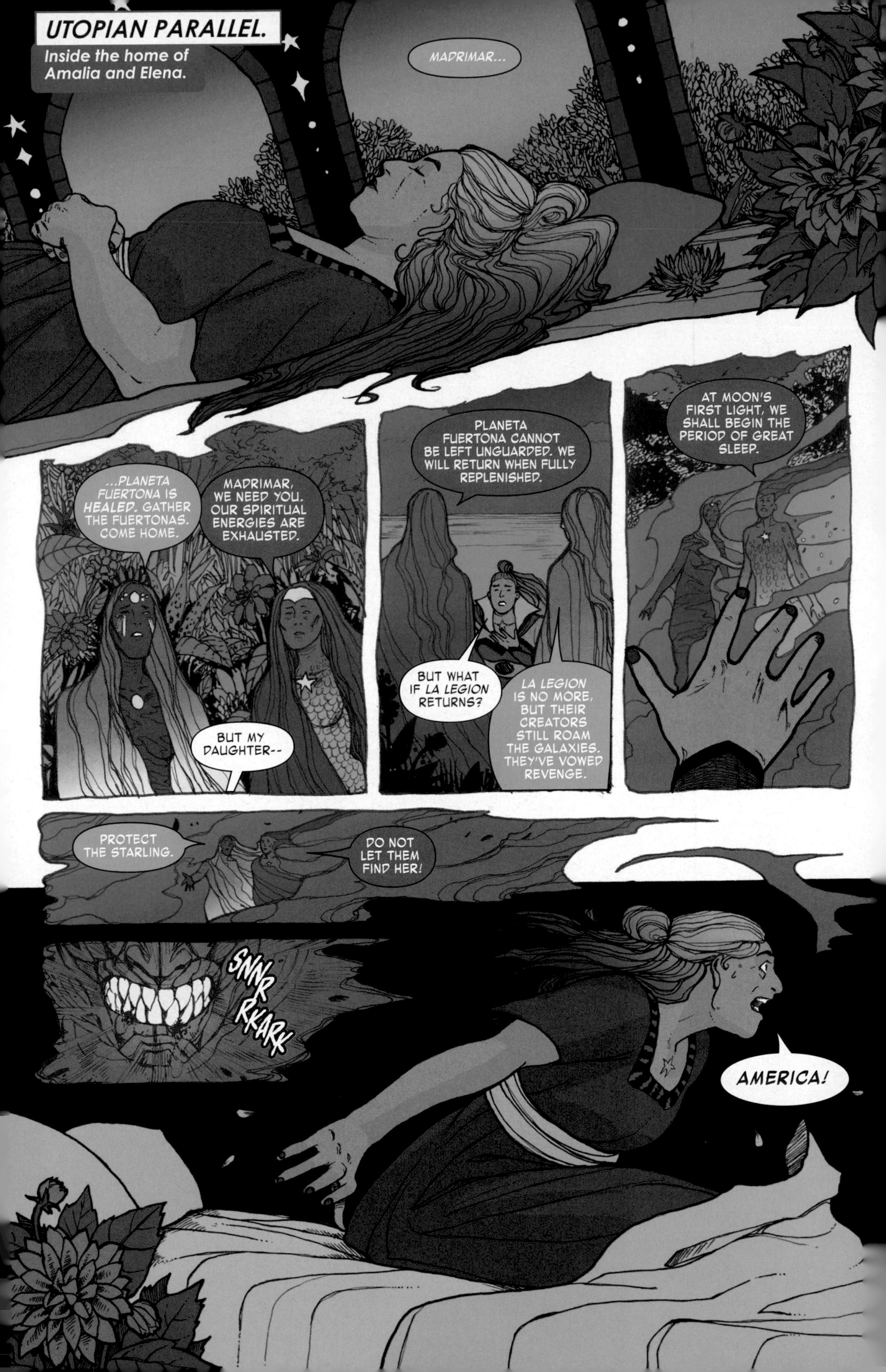
UTOPIAN PARALLEL.
Inside the home of Amalia and Elena.
MADRIMAR...
...PLANETA FUERTONA IS HEALED. GATHER THE FUERTONAS. COME HOME.
MADRIMAR, WE NEED YOU. OUR SPIRITUAL ENERGIES ARE EXHAUSTED.
BUT MY DAUGHTER--
PLANETA FUERTONA CANNOT BE LEFT UNGUARDED. WE WILL RETURN WHEN FULLY REPLENISHED.
BUT WHAT IF LA LEGION RETURNS?
LA LEGION IS NO MORE, BUT THEIR CREATORS STILL ROAM THE GALAXIES. THEY'VE VOWED REVENGE.
AT MOON'S FIRST LIGHT, WE SHALL BEGIN THE PERIOD OF GREAT SLEEP.
PROTECT THE STARLING.
DO NOT LET THEM FIND HER!
SNNR RKARK
AMERICA!

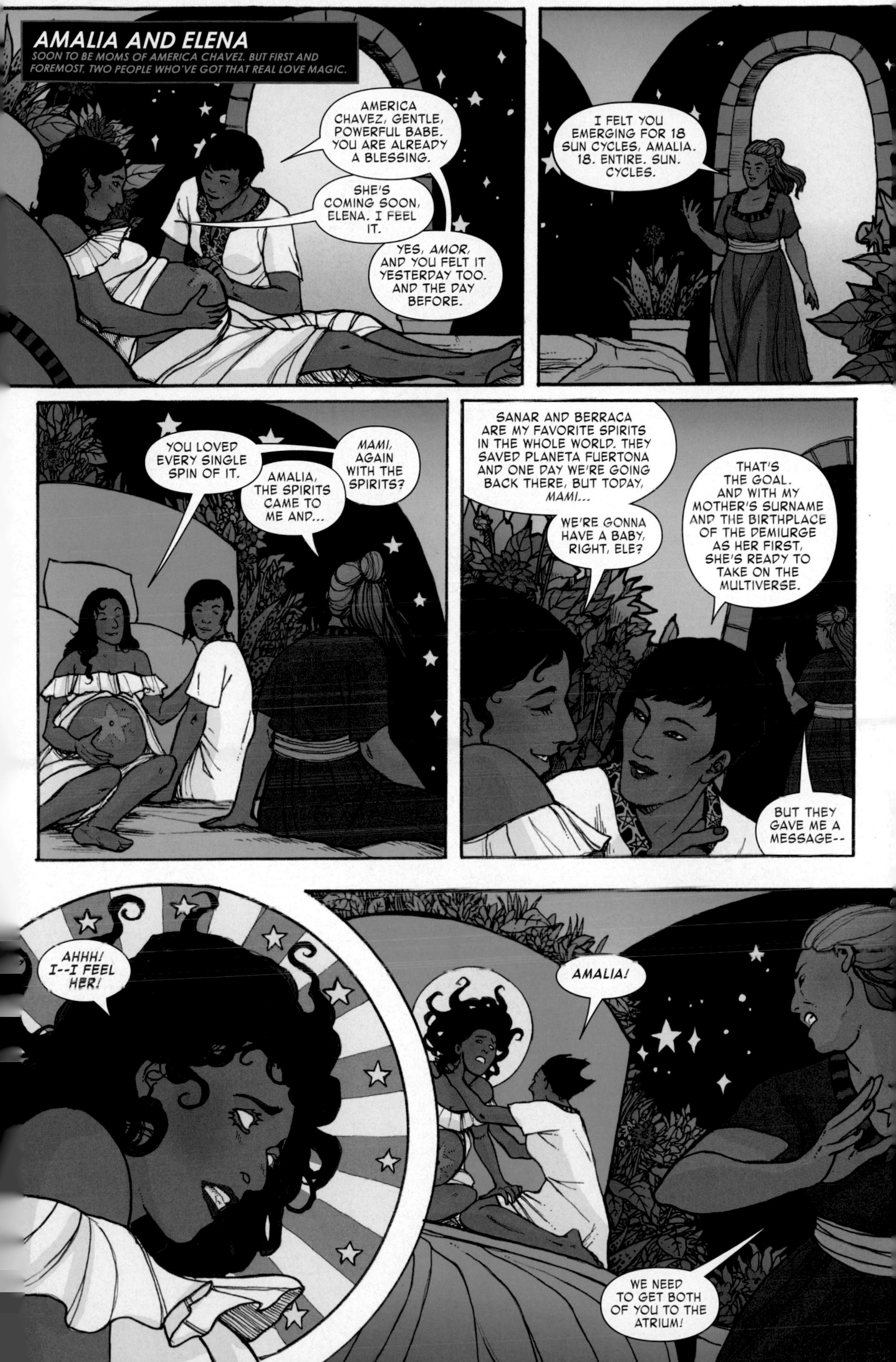
AMALIA AND ELENA
SOON TO BE MOMS OF AMERICA CHAVEZ. BUT FIRST AND FOREMOST, TWO PEOPLE WHO'VE GOT THAT REAL LOVE MAGIC.
AMERICA CHAVEZ, GENTLE, POWERFUL BABE. YOU ARE ALREADY A BLESSING.
SHE'S COMING SOON, ELENA. I FEEL IT.
YES, AMOR, AND YOU FELT IT YESTERDAY TOO. AND THE DAY BEFORE.
I FELT YOU EMERGING FOR 18 SUN CYCLES, AMALIA. 18. ENTIRE. SUN. CYCLES.
YOU LOVED EVERY SINGLE SPIN OF IT.
MAMI, AGAIN WITH THE SPIRITS?
AMALIA, THE SPIRITS CAME TO ME AND...
SANAR AND BERRACA ARE MY FAVORITE SPIRITS IN THE WHOLE WORLD. THEY SAVED PLANETA FUERTONA AND ONE DAY WE'RE GOING BACK THERE, BUT TODAY, MAMI...
WE'RE GONNA HAVE A BABY, RIGHT, ELE?
THAT'S THE GOAL. AND WITH MY MOTHER'S SURNAME AND THE BIRTHPLACE OF THE DEMIURGE AS HER FIRST, SHE'S READY TO TAKE ON THE MULTIVERSE.
BUT THEY GAVE ME A MESSAGE--
AHHH! I--I FEEL HER!
AMALIA!
WE NEED TO GET BOTH OF YOU TO THE ATRIUM!

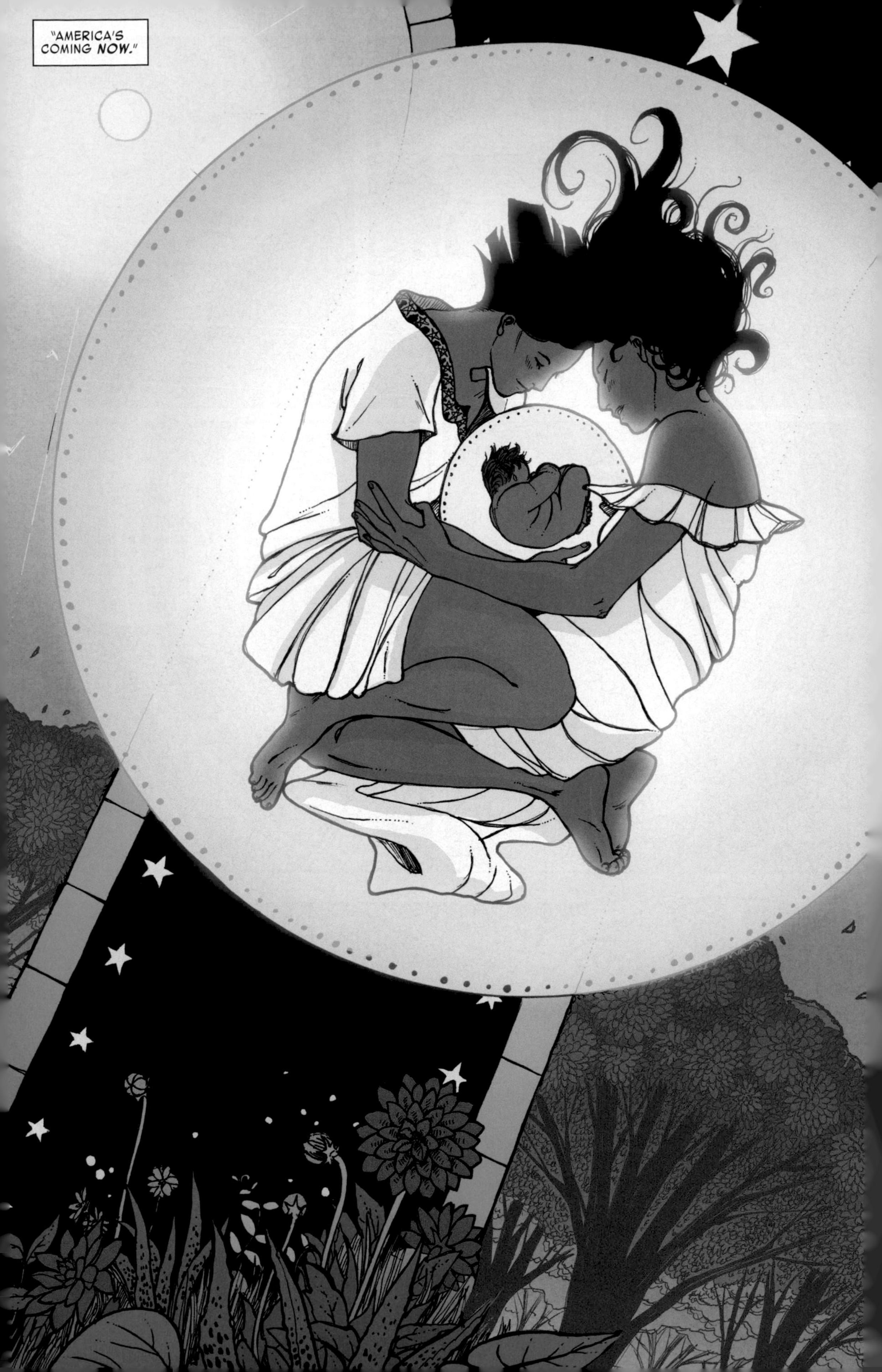
"AMERICA'S COMING NOW."

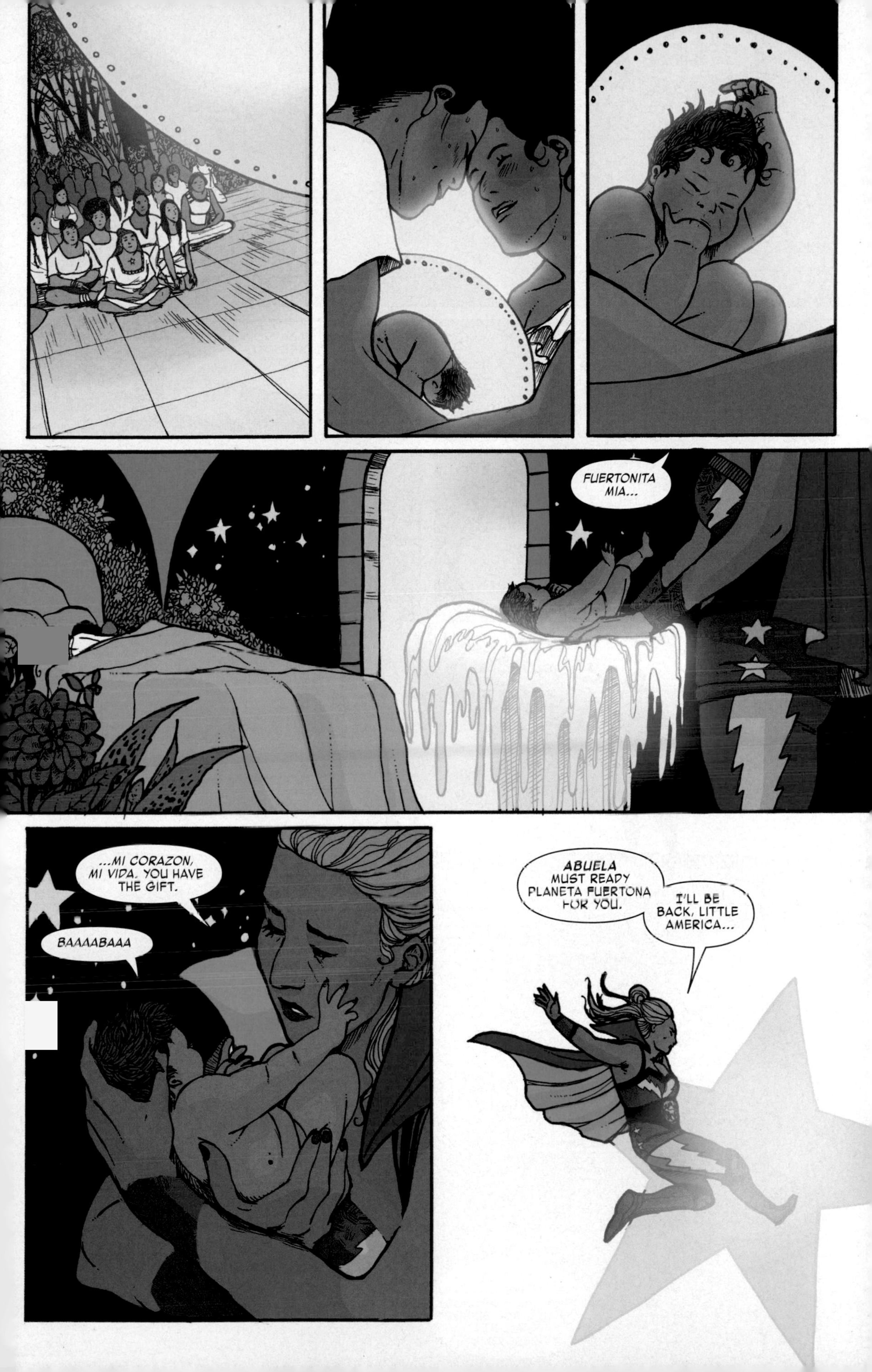

FUERTONITA MIA...
...MI CORAZON, MI VIDA. YOU HAVE THE GIFT.
BAAAABAAA
ABUELA MUST READY PLANETA FUERTONA FOR YOU.
I'LL BE BACK, LITTLE AMERICA...

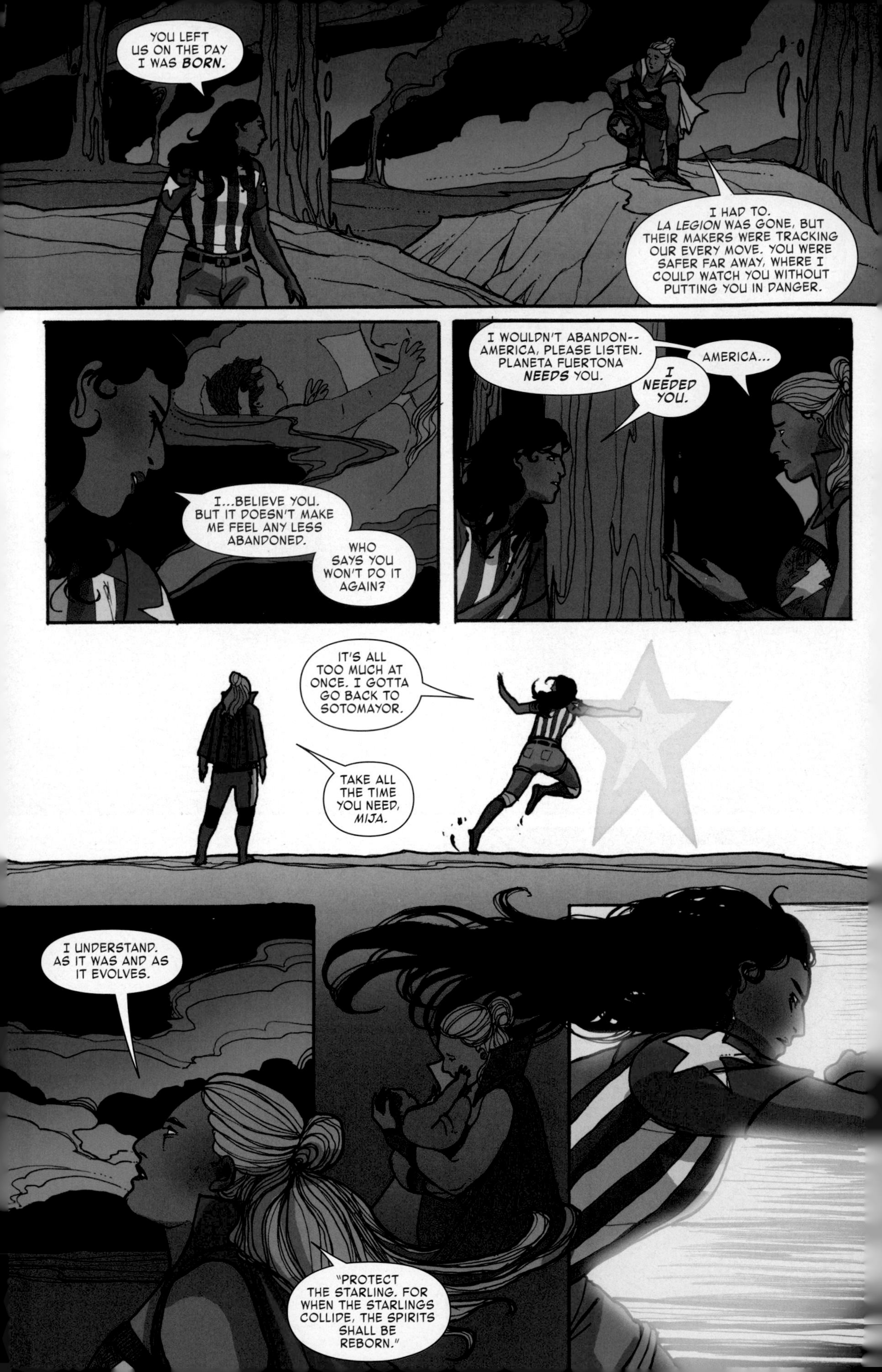
YOU LEFT US ON THE DAY I WAS BORN.
I HAD TO. LA LEGION WAS GONE, BUT THEIR MAKERS WERE TRACKING OUR EVERY MOVE. YOU WERE SAFER FAR AWAY, WHERE I COULD WATCH YOU WITHOUT PUTTING YOU IN DANGER.
I...BELIEVE YOU. BUT IT DOESN'T MAKE ME FEEL ANY LESS ABANDONED.
WHO SAYS YOU WON'T DO IT AGAIN?
I WOULDN'T ABANDON-- AMERICA, PLEASE LISTEN. PLANETA FUERTONA NEEDS YOU.
I NEEDED YOU.
AMERICA...
IT'S ALL TOO MUCH AT ONCE. I GOTTA GO BACK TO SOTOMAYOR.
TAKE ALL THE TIME YOU NEED, MIJA.
I UNDERSTAND. AS IT WAS AND AS IT EVOLVES.
"PROTECT THE STARLING. FOR WHEN THE STARLINGS COLLIDE, THE SPIRITS SHALL BE REBORN."

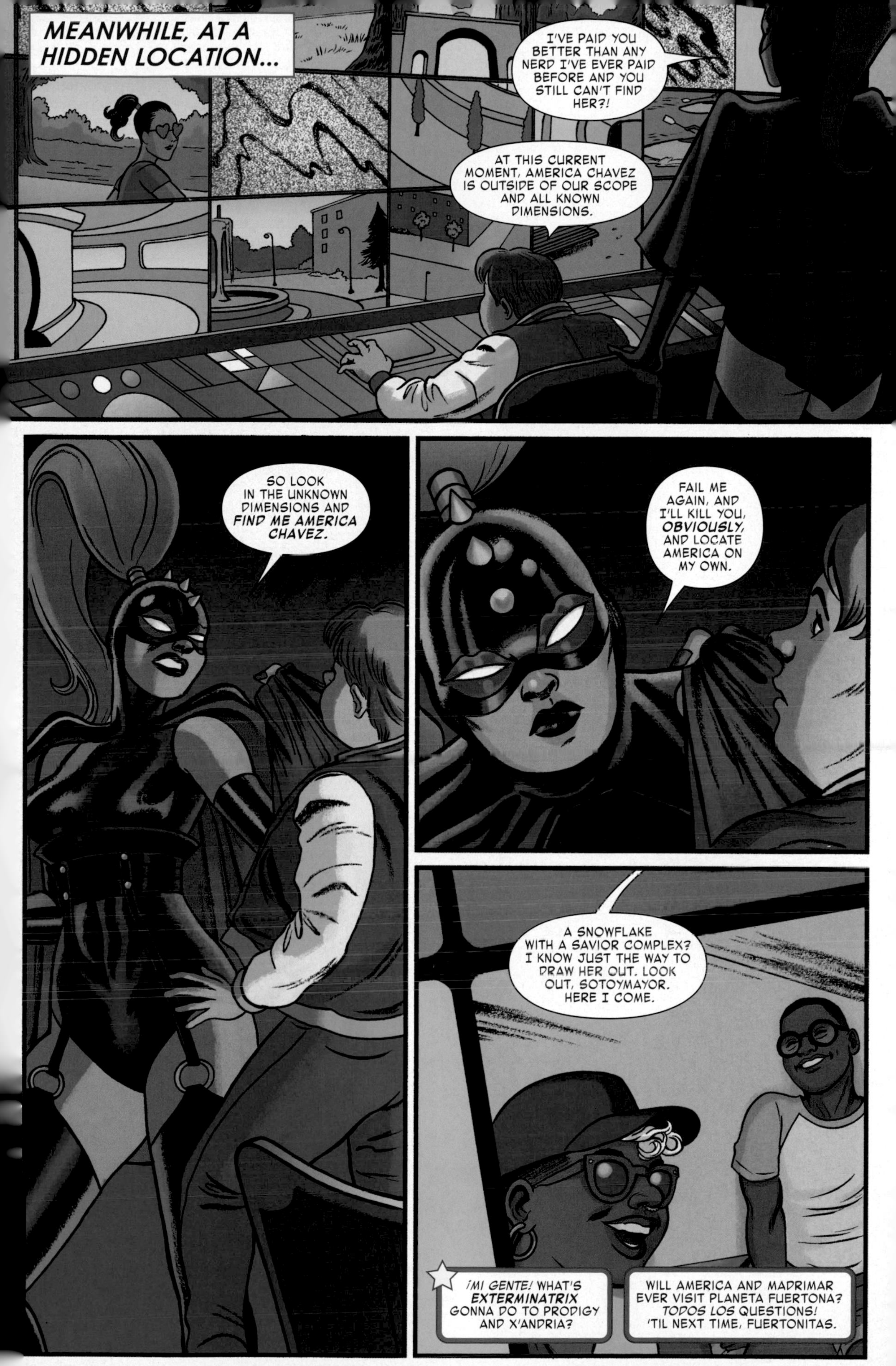
MEANWHILE, AT A HIDDEN LOCATION...
I'VE PAID YOU BETTER THAN ANY NERD I'VE EVER PAID BEFORE AND YOU STILL CAN'T FIND HER?!
AT THIS CURRENT MOMENT, AMERICA CHAVEZ IS OUTSIDE OF OUR SCOPE AND ALL KNOWN DIMENSIONS.
SO LOOK IN THE UNKNOWN DIMENSIONS AND FIND ME AMERICA CHAVEZ.
FAIL ME AGAIN, AND I'LL KILL YOU, OBVIOUSLY, AND LOCATE AMERICA ON MY OWN.
A SNOWFLAKE WITH A SAVIOR COMPLEX? I KNOW JUST THE WAY TO DRAW HER OUT. LOOK OUT, SOTOYMAYOR. HERE I COME.
¡MI GENTE! WHAT'S EXTERMINATRIX GONNA DO TO PRODIGY AND X'ANDRIA?
WILL AMERICA AND MADRIMAR EVER VISIT PLANETA FUERTONA? TODOS LOS QUESTIONS! 'TIL NEXT TIME, FUERTONITAS.

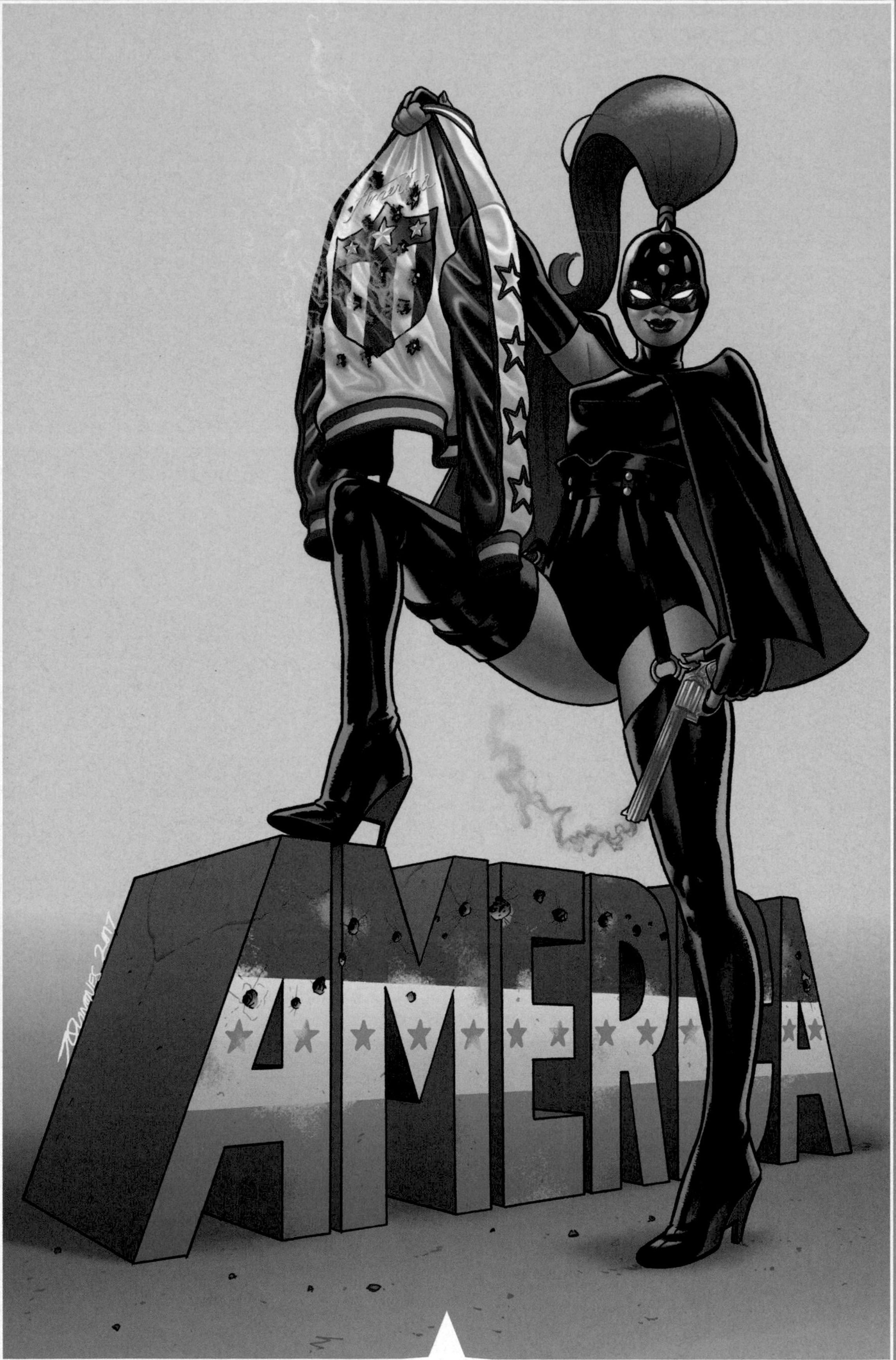

8

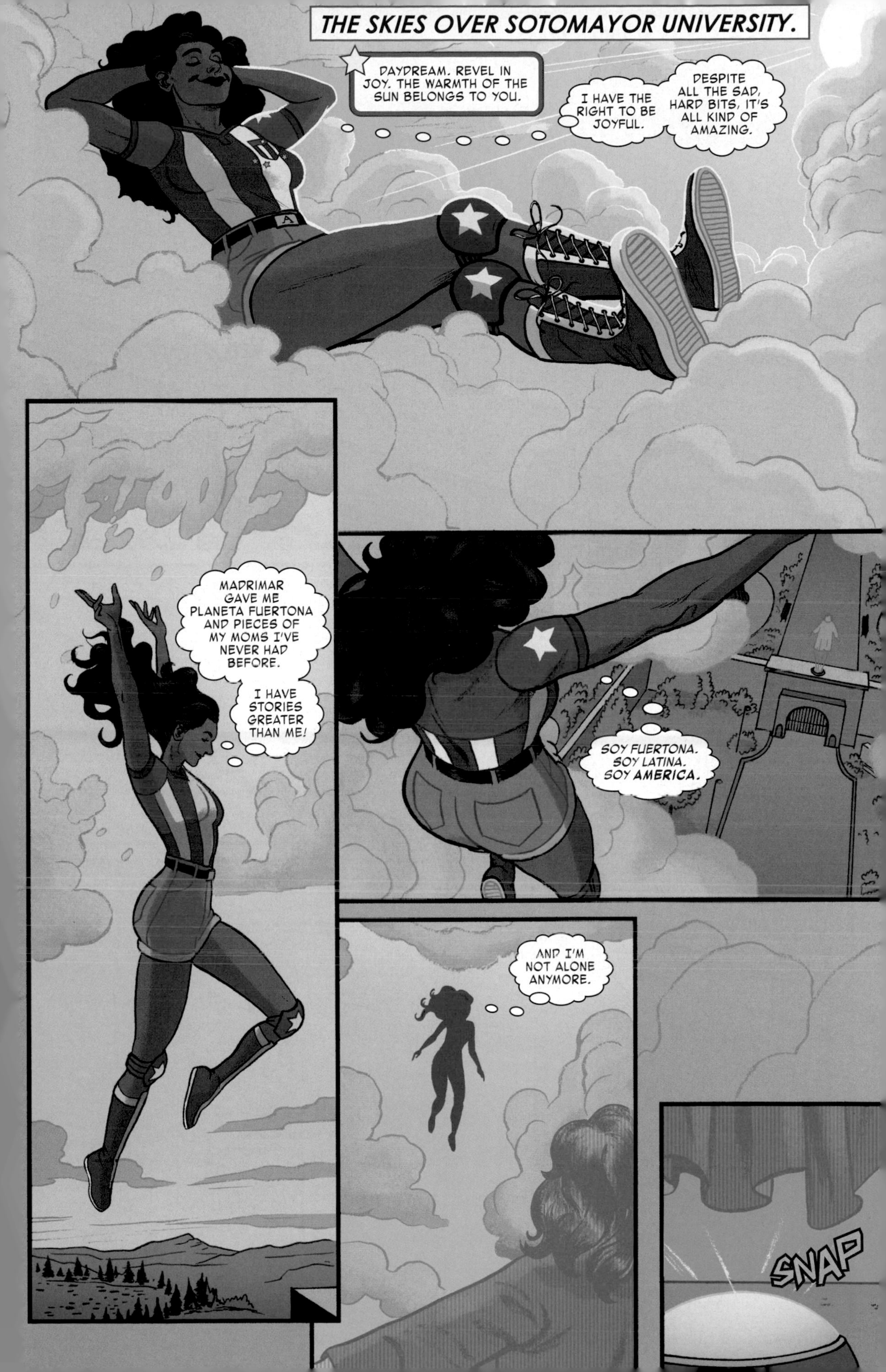

THE SKIES OVER SOTOMAYOR UNIVERSITY.
DAYDREAM. REVEL IN JOY. THE WARMTH OF THE SUN BELONGS TO YOU.
I HAVE THE RIGHT TO BE JOYFUL.
DESPITE ALL THE SAD, HARD BITS, IT'S ALL KIND OF AMAZING.
MADRIMAR GAVE ME PLANETA FUERTONA AND PIECES OF MY MOMS I'VE NEVER HAD BEFORE.
I HAVE STORIES GREATER THAN ME!
SOY FUERTONA. SOY LATINA. SOY **AMERICA.**
AND I'M NOT ALONE ANYMORE.
SNAP

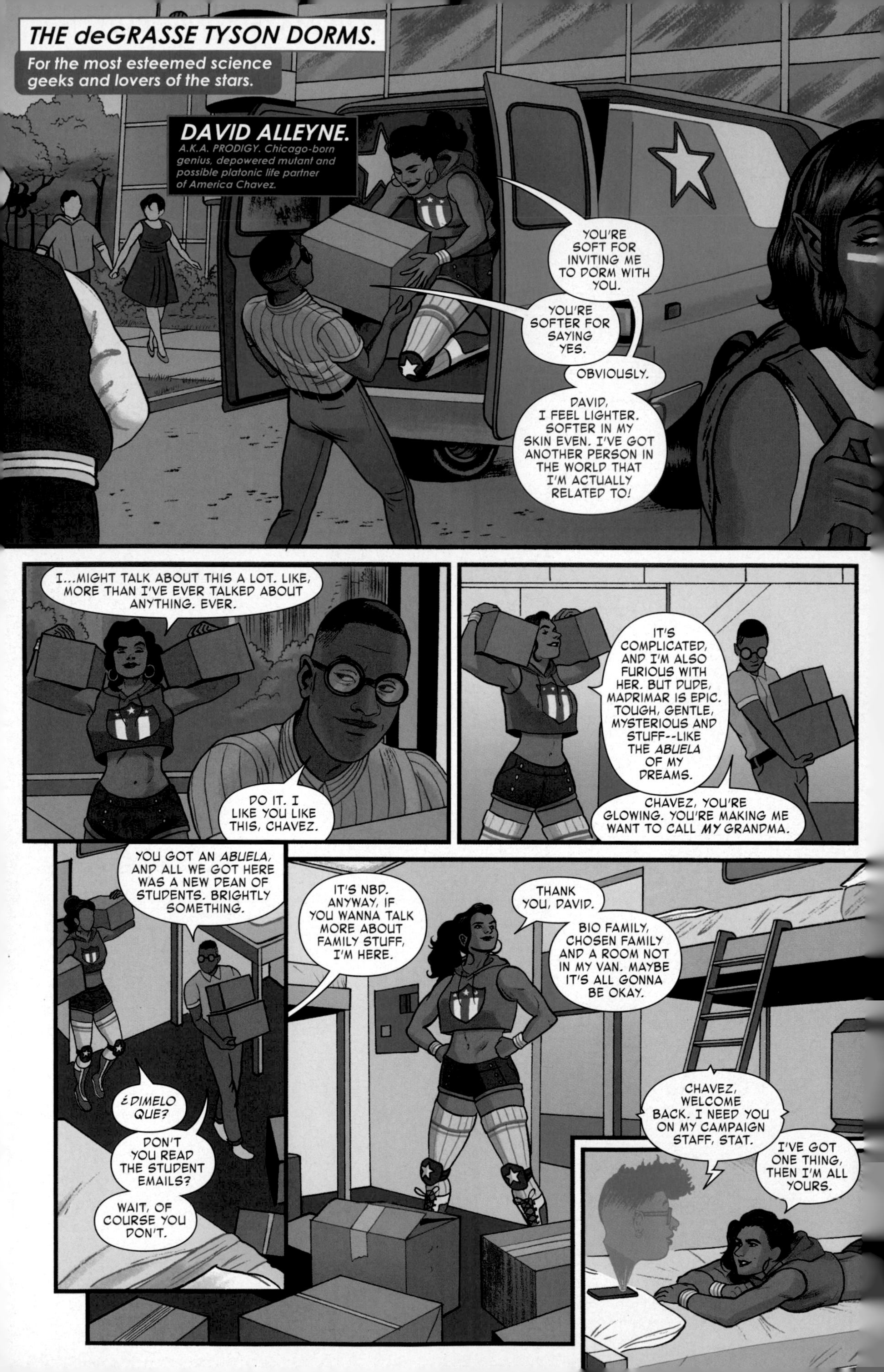
THE deGRASSE TYSON DORMS.
For the most esteemed science geeks and lovers of the stars.
DAVID ALLEYNE.
A.K.A. PRODIGY. Chicago-born genius, depowered mutant and possible platonic life partner of America Chavez.
YOU'RE SOFT FOR INVITING ME TO DORM WITH YOU.
YOU'RE SOFTER FOR SAYING YES.
OBVIOUSLY.
DAVID, I FEEL LIGHTER. SOFTER IN MY SKIN EVEN. I'VE GOT ANOTHER PERSON IN THE WORLD THAT I'M ACTUALLY RELATED TO!
I...MIGHT TALK ABOUT THIS A LOT. LIKE, MORE THAN I'VE EVER TALKED ABOUT ANYTHING. EVER.
DO IT. I LIKE YOU LIKE THIS, CHAVEZ.
IT'S COMPLICATED, AND I'M ALSO FURIOUS WITH HER. BUT DUDE, MADRIMAR IS EPIC. TOUGH, GENTLE, MYSTERIOUS AND STUFF--LIKE THE *ABUELA* OF MY DREAMS.
CHAVEZ, YOU'RE GLOWING. YOU'RE MAKING ME WANT TO CALL *MY* GRANDMA.
YOU GOT AN *ABUELA*, AND ALL WE GOT HERE WAS A NEW DEAN OF STUDENTS. BRIGHTLY SOMETHING.
¿DIMELO QUE?
DON'T YOU READ THE STUDENT EMAILS?
WAIT, OF COURSE YOU DON'T.
IT'S NBD. ANYWAY, IF YOU WANNA TALK MORE ABOUT FAMILY STUFF, I'M HERE.
THANK YOU, DAVID.
BIO FAMILY, CHOSEN FAMILY AND A ROOM NOT IN MY VAN. MAYBE IT'S ALL GONNA BE OKAY.
CHAVEZ, WELCOME BACK. I NEED YOU ON MY CAMPAIGN STAFF, STAT.
I'VE GOT ONE THING, THEN I'M ALL YOURS.

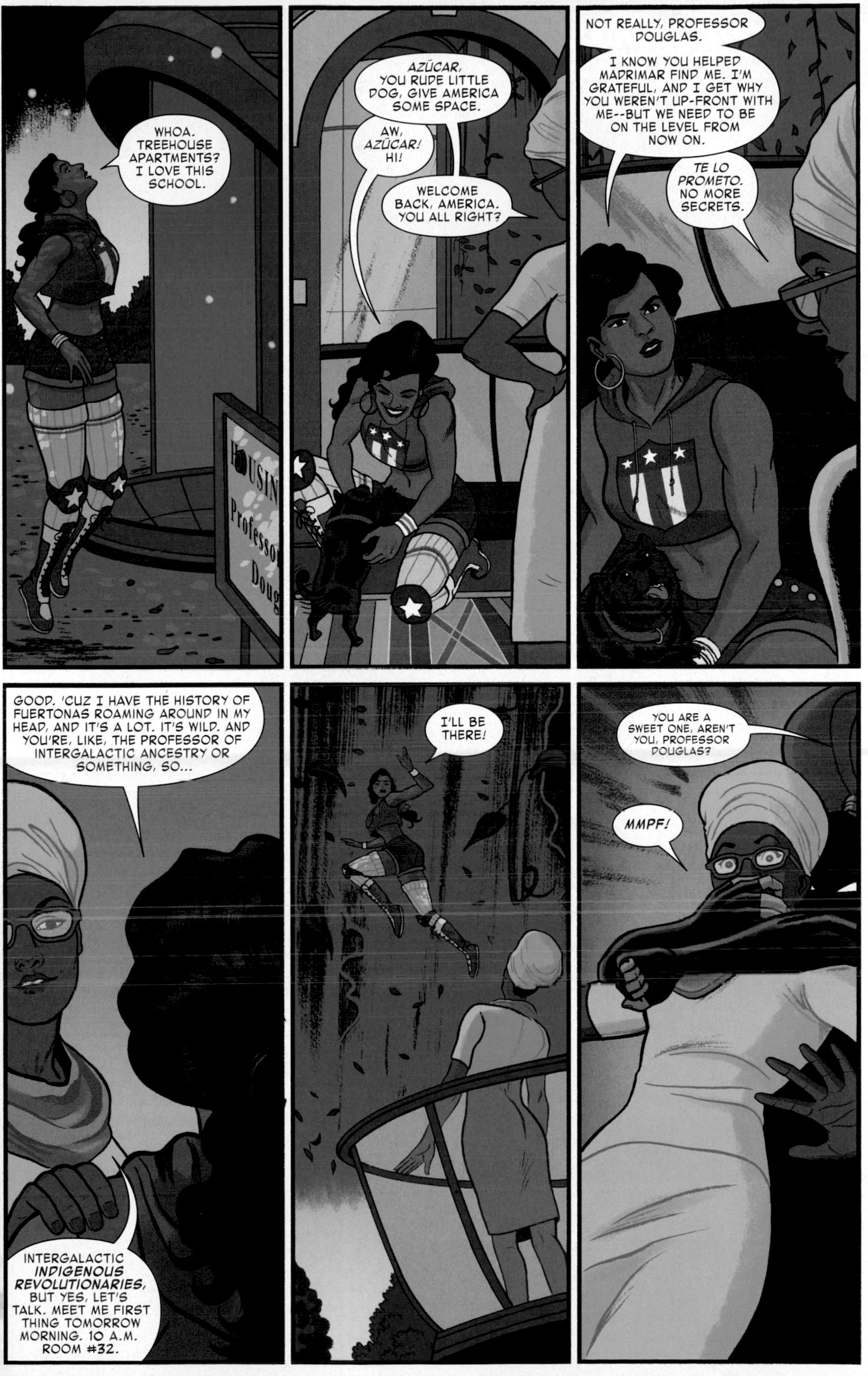
WHOA. TREEHOUSE APARTMENTS? I LOVE THIS SCHOOL.
HOUSING Professor Doug
AZÚCAR, YOU RUDE LITTLE DOG, GIVE AMERICA SOME SPACE.
AW, AZÚCAR! HI!
WELCOME BACK, AMERICA. YOU ALL RIGHT?
NOT REALLY, PROFESSOR DOUGLAS.
I KNOW YOU HELPED MADRIMAR FIND ME. I'M GRATEFUL, AND I GET WHY YOU WEREN'T UP-FRONT WITH ME--BUT WE NEED TO BE ON THE LEVEL FROM NOW ON.
TE LO PROMETO. NO MORE SECRETS.
GOOD. 'CUZ I HAVE THE HISTORY OF FUERTONAS ROAMING AROUND IN MY HEAD, AND IT'S A LOT. IT'S WILD. AND YOU'RE, LIKE, THE PROFESSOR OF INTERGALACTIC ANCESTRY OR SOMETHING, SO...
INTERGALACTIC INDIGENOUS REVOLUTIONARIES, BUT YES, LET'S TALK. MEET ME FIRST THING TOMORROW MORNING. 10 A.M. ROOM #32.
I'LL BE THERE!
YOU ARE A SWEET ONE, AREN'T YOU, PROFESSOR DOUGLAS?
MMPF!

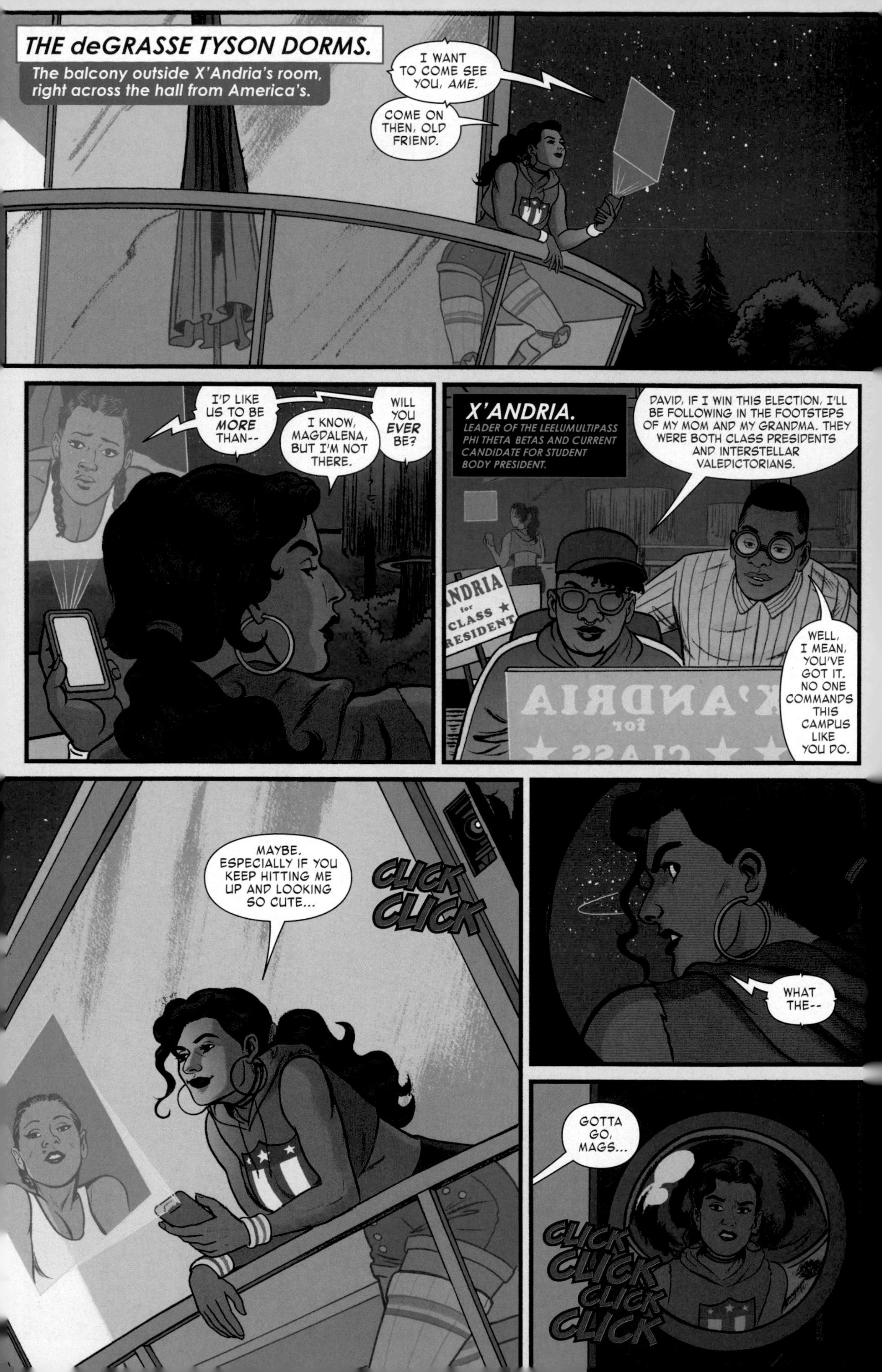

THE deGRASSE TYSON DORMS.
The balcony outside X'Andria's room, right across the hall from America's.
I WANT TO COME SEE YOU, AME.
COME ON THEN, OLD FRIEND.
I'D LIKE US TO BE MORE THAN--
I KNOW, MAGDALENA, BUT I'M NOT THERE.
WILL YOU EVER BE?
X'ANDRIA.
LEADER OF THE LEELUMULTIPASS PHI THETA BETAS AND CURRENT CANDIDATE FOR STUDENT BODY PRESIDENT.
DAVID, IF I WIN THIS ELECTION, I'LL BE FOLLOWING IN THE FOOTSTEPS OF MY MOM AND MY GRANDMA. THEY WERE BOTH CLASS PRESIDENTS AND INTERSTELLAR VALEDICTORIANS.
ANDRIA for CLASS ★ PRESIDENT
WELL, I MEAN, YOU'VE GOT IT. NO ONE COMMANDS THIS CAMPUS LIKE YOU DO.
MAYBE. ESPECIALLY IF YOU KEEP HITTING ME UP AND LOOKING SO CUTE...
CLICK CLICK
WHAT THE--
GOTTA GO, MAGS...
CLICK CLICK CLICK CLICK

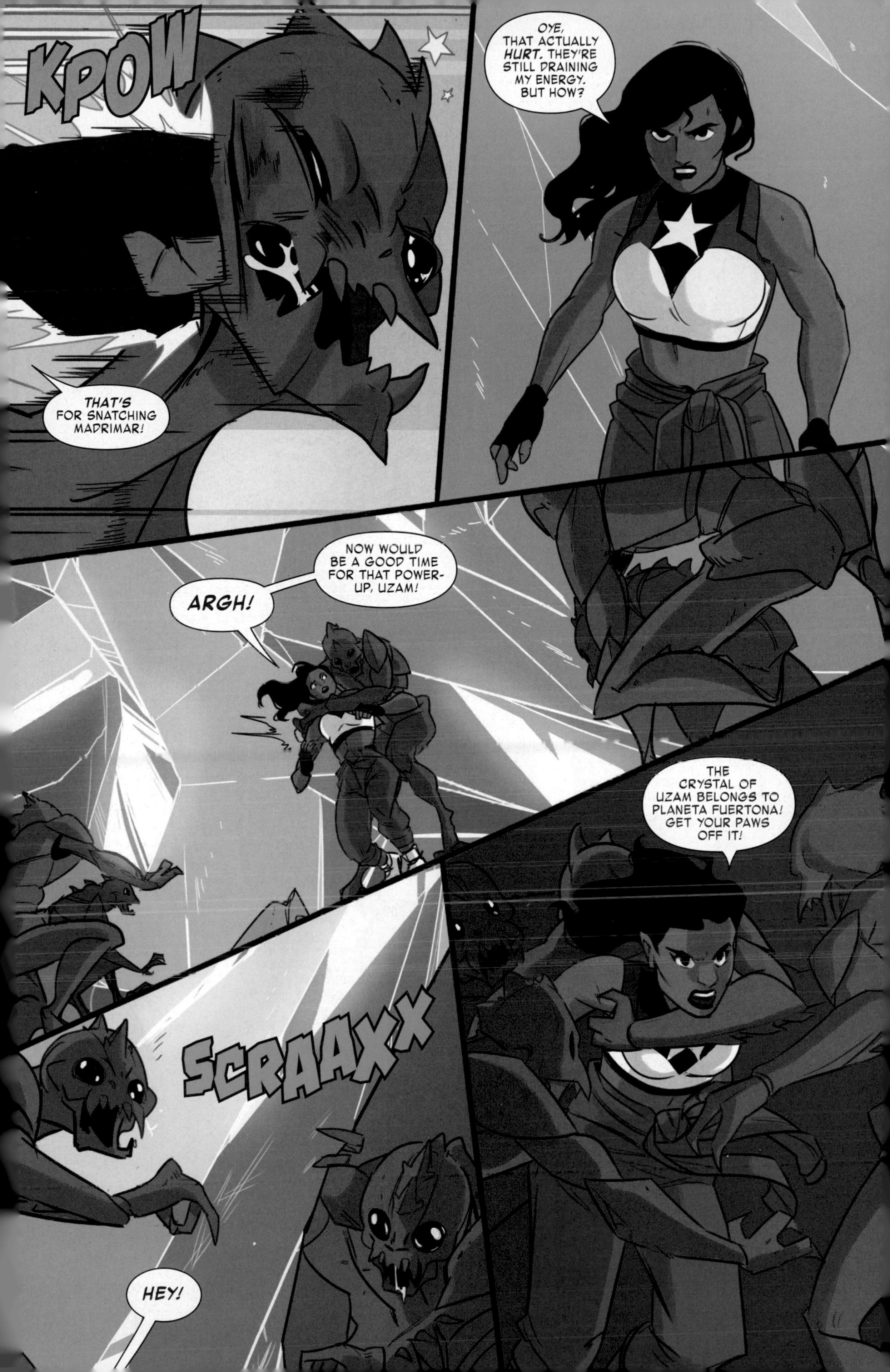
KPOW
THAT'S FOR SNATCHING MADRIMAR!
OYE, THAT ACTUALLY HURT. THEY'RE STILL DRAINING MY ENERGY. BUT HOW?
ARGH!
NOW WOULD BE A GOOD TIME FOR THAT POWER-UP, UZAM!
THE CRYSTAL OF UZAM BELONGS TO PLANETA FUERTONA! GET YOUR PAWS OFF IT!
SCRAAXX
HEY!

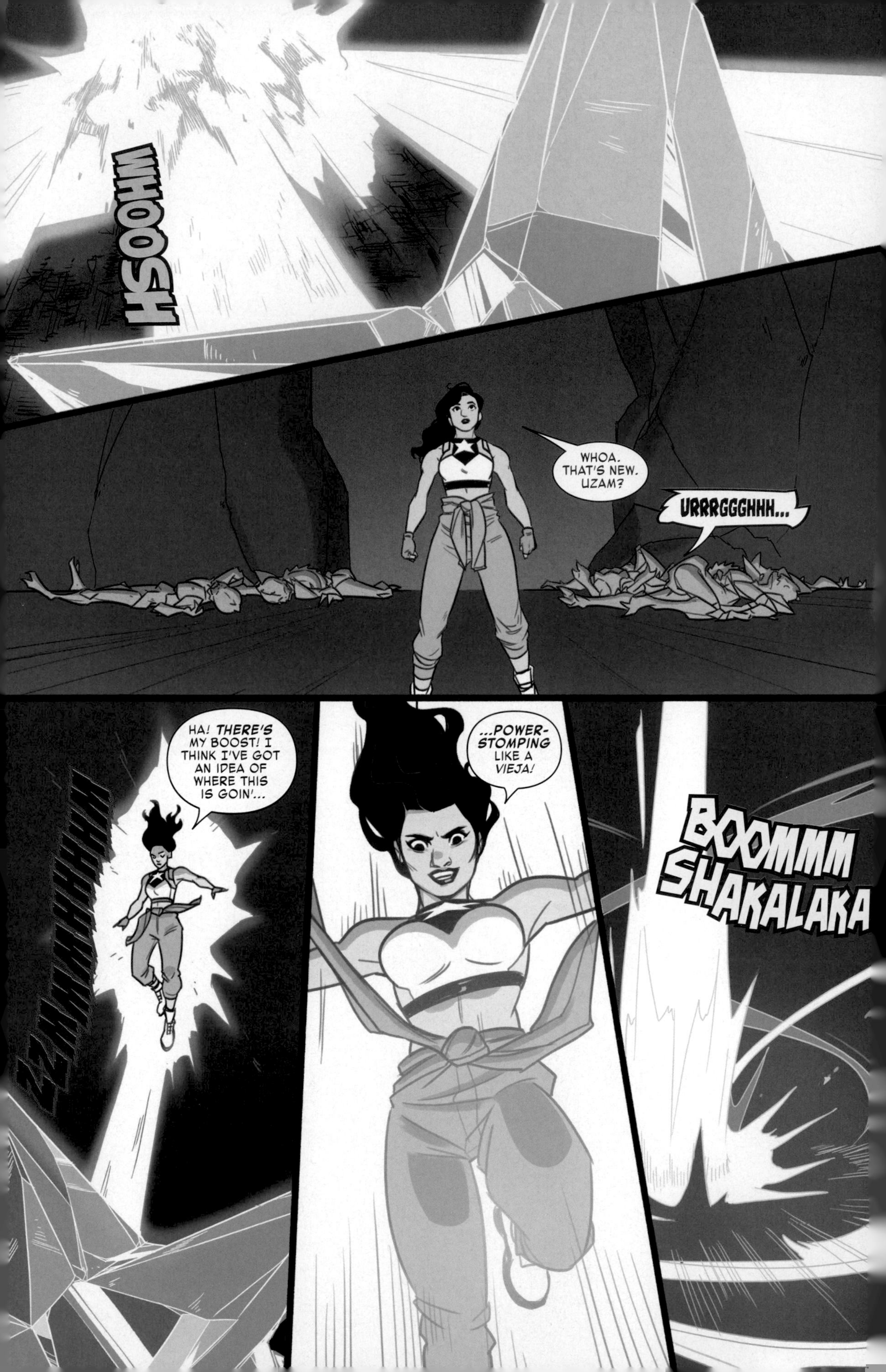
WHOOSH
WHOA. THAT'S NEW. UZAM?
URRRGGGHHH...
HA! THERE'S MY BOOST! I THINK I'VE GOT AN IDEA OF WHERE THIS IS GOIN'...
...POWER-STOMPING LIKE A VIEJA!
BOOMMM SHAKALAKA

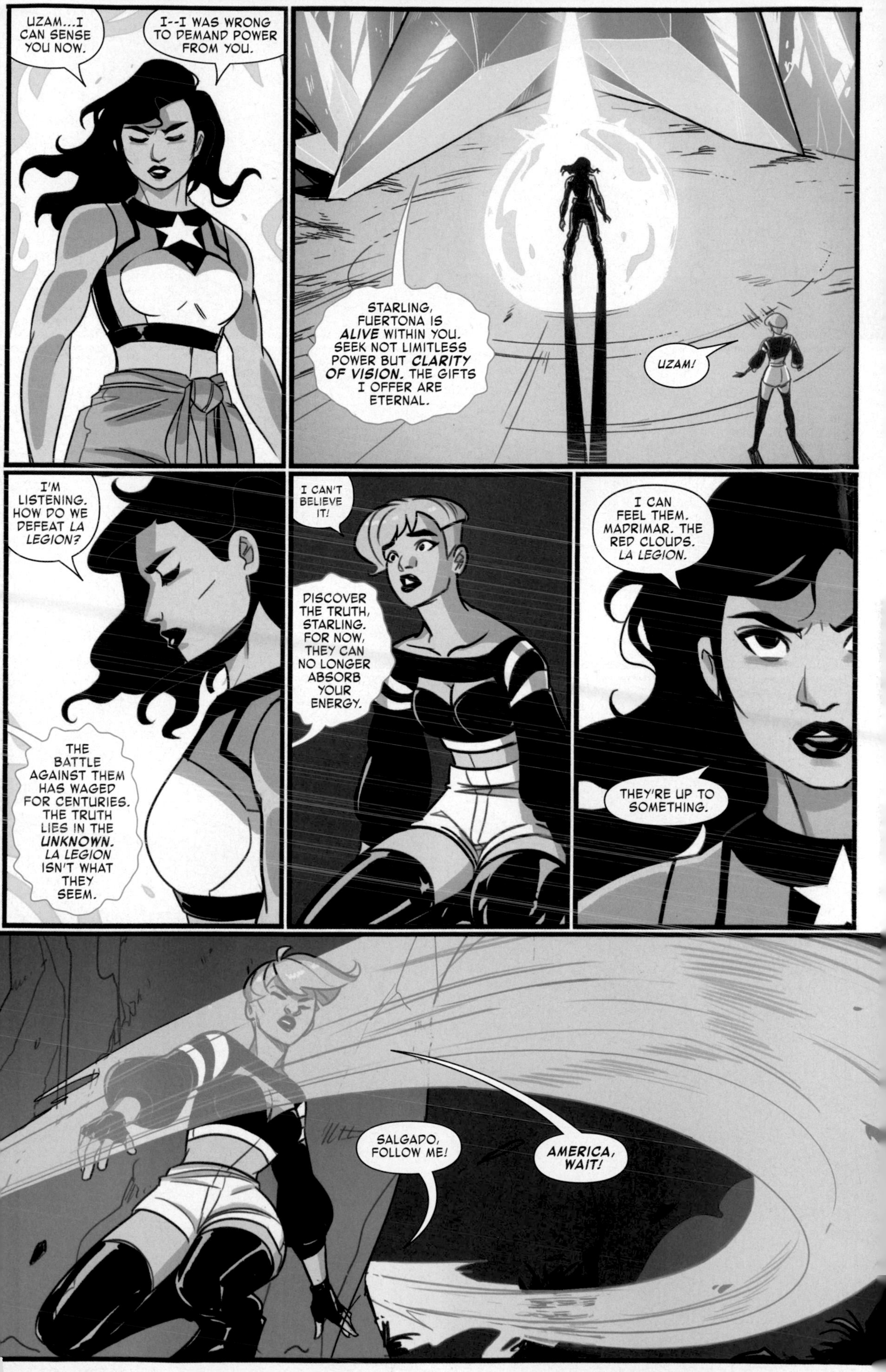

UZAM...I CAN SENSE YOU NOW.
I--I WAS WRONG TO DEMAND POWER FROM YOU.
STARLING, FUERTONA IS *ALIVE* WITHIN YOU. SEEK NOT LIMITLESS POWER BUT *CLARITY OF VISION.* THE GIFTS I OFFER ARE ETERNAL.
UZAM!
I'M LISTENING. HOW DO WE DEFEAT *LA LEGION?*
THE BATTLE AGAINST THEM HAS WAGED FOR CENTURIES. THE TRUTH LIES IN THE *UNKNOWN. LA LEGION* ISN'T WHAT THEY SEEM.
I CAN'T BELIEVE IT!
DISCOVER THE TRUTH, STARLING. FOR NOW, THEY CAN NO LONGER ABSORB YOUR ENERGY.
I CAN FEEL THEM. MADRIMAR. THE RED CLOUDS. *LA LEGION.*
THEY'RE UP TO SOMETHING.
SALGADO, FOLLOW ME!
AMERICA, WAIT!

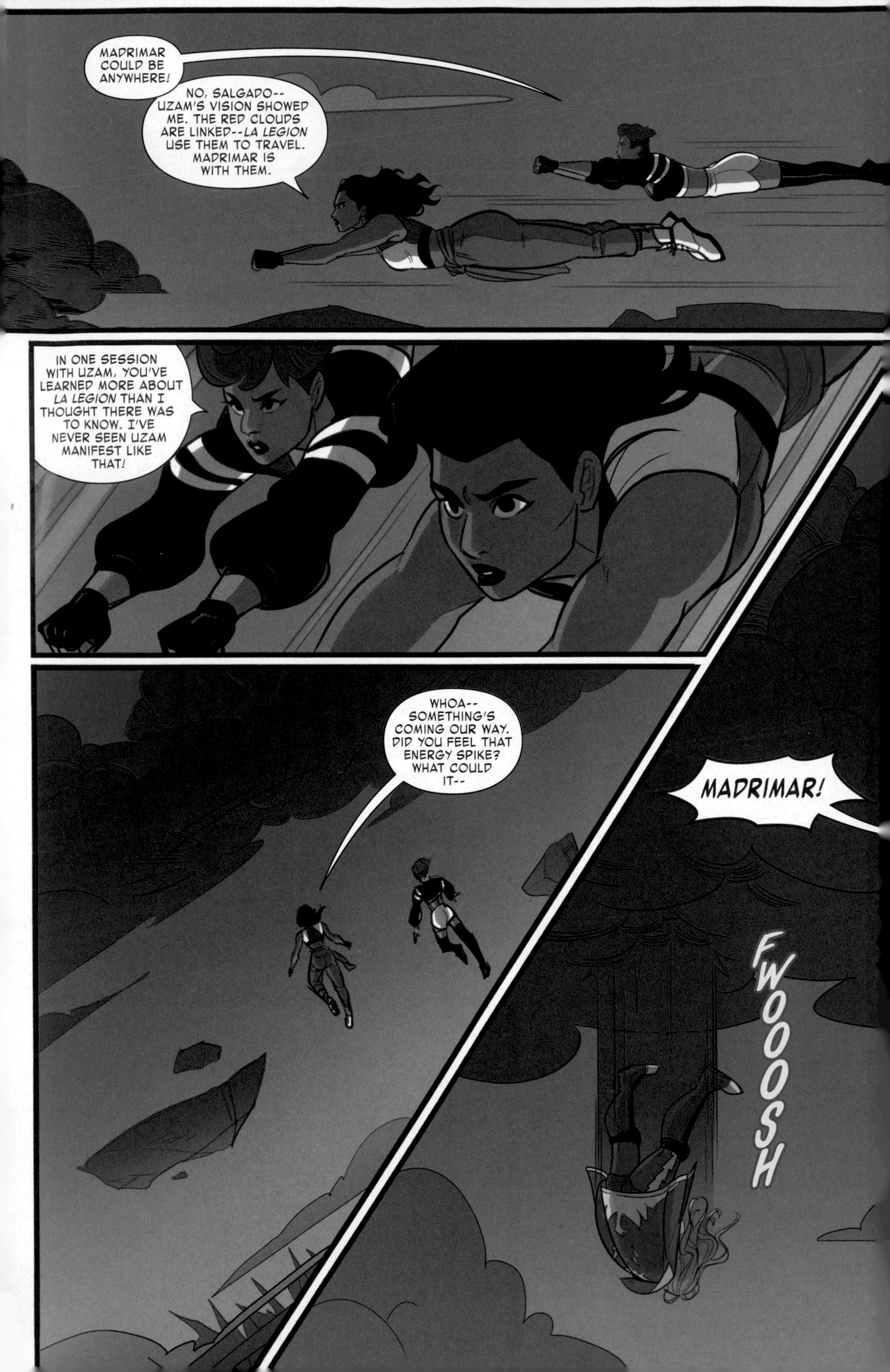
MADRIMAR COULD BE ANYWHERE!
NO, SALGADO-- UZAM'S VISION SHOWED ME. THE RED CLOUDS ARE LINKED--*LA LEGION* USE THEM TO TRAVEL. MADRIMAR IS WITH THEM.
IN ONE SESSION WITH UZAM, YOU'VE LEARNED MORE ABOUT *LA LEGION* THAN I THOUGHT THERE WAS TO KNOW. I'VE NEVER SEEN UZAM MANIFEST LIKE THAT!
WHOA-- SOMETHING'S COMING OUR WAY. DID YOU FEEL THAT ENERGY SPIKE? WHAT COULD IT--
MADRIMAR!
FWOOOOSH

F.I.S.T. AND CYBORG AMERICA DESIGNS BY JOE QUINONES

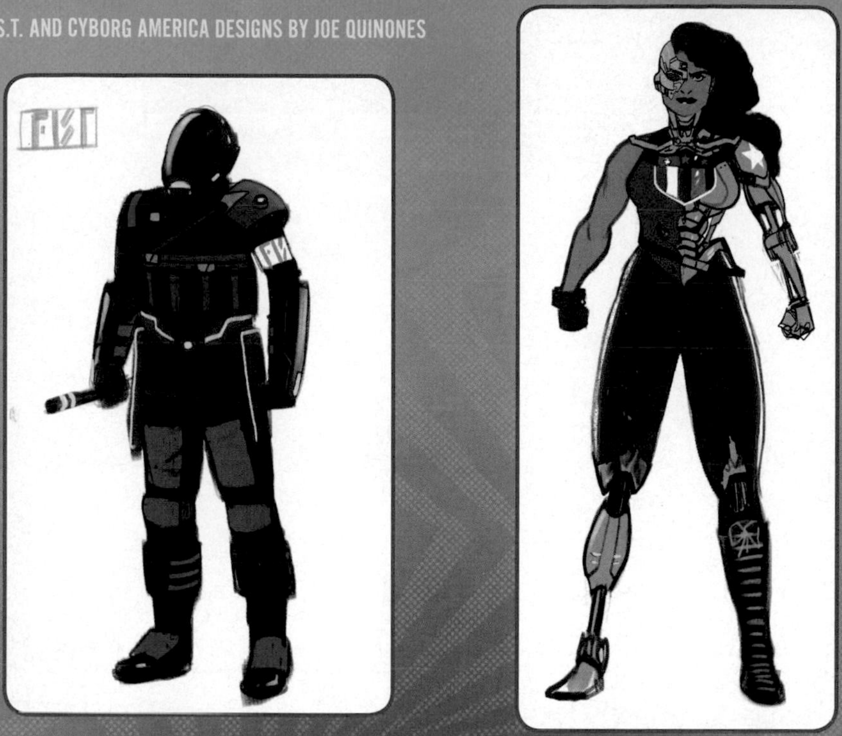

FUERTONAS CLOTHING DESIGNS BY FLAVIANO

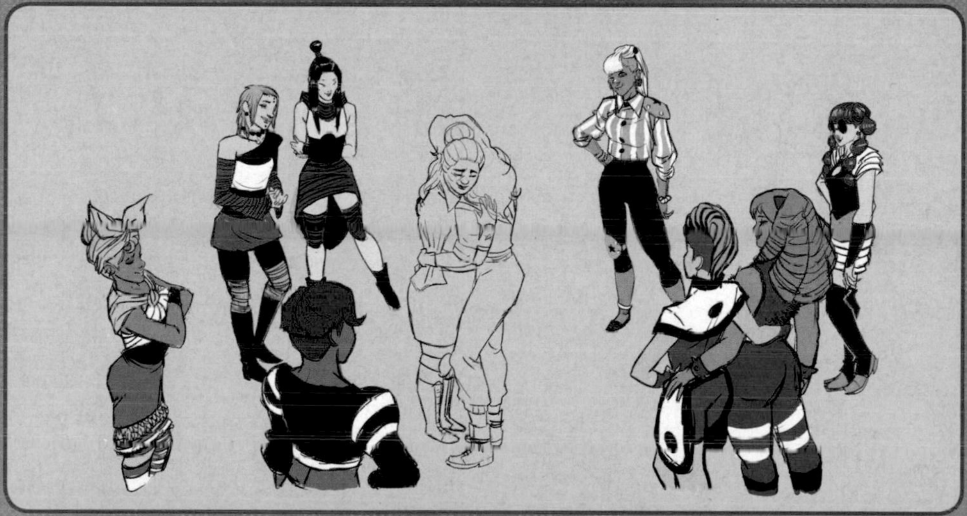

AMERICA'S FLIGHT SUIT AND SALGADO DESIGNS BY STACEY LEE

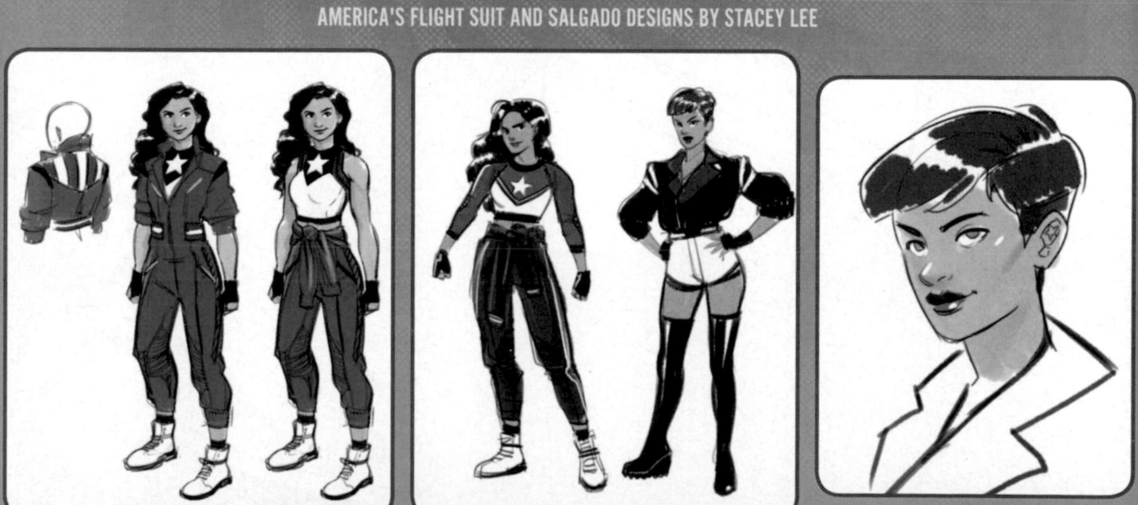

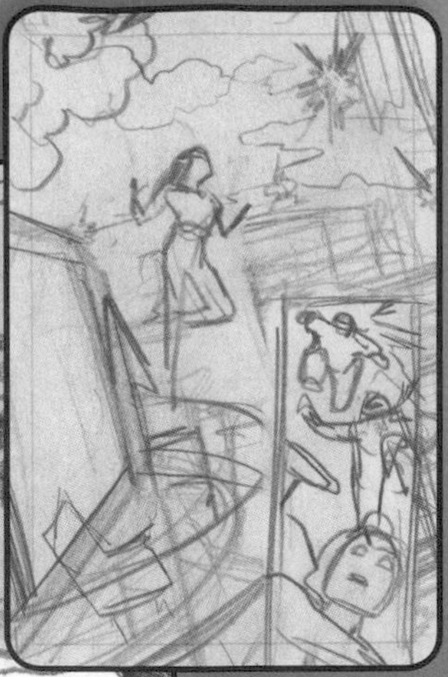

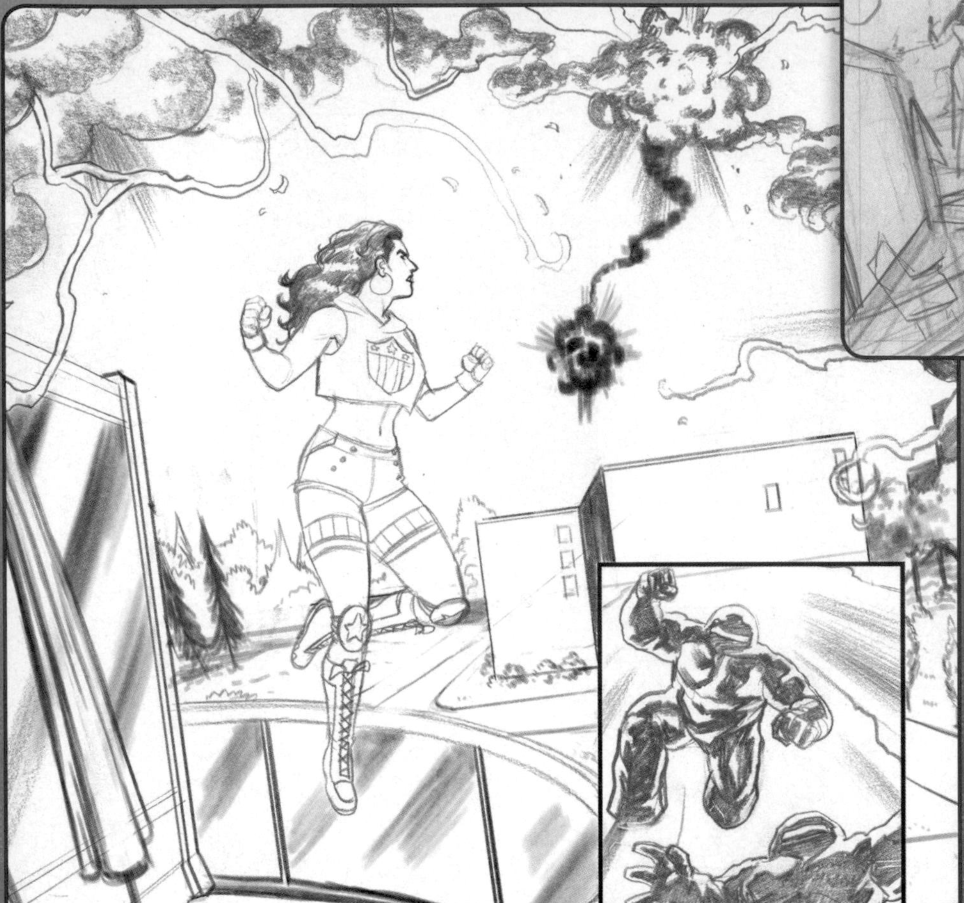

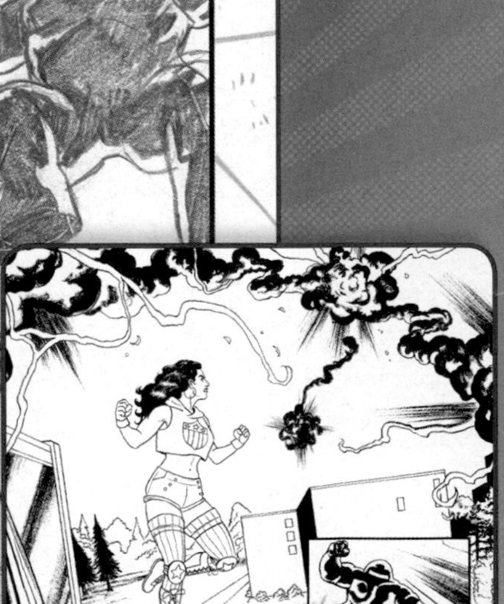

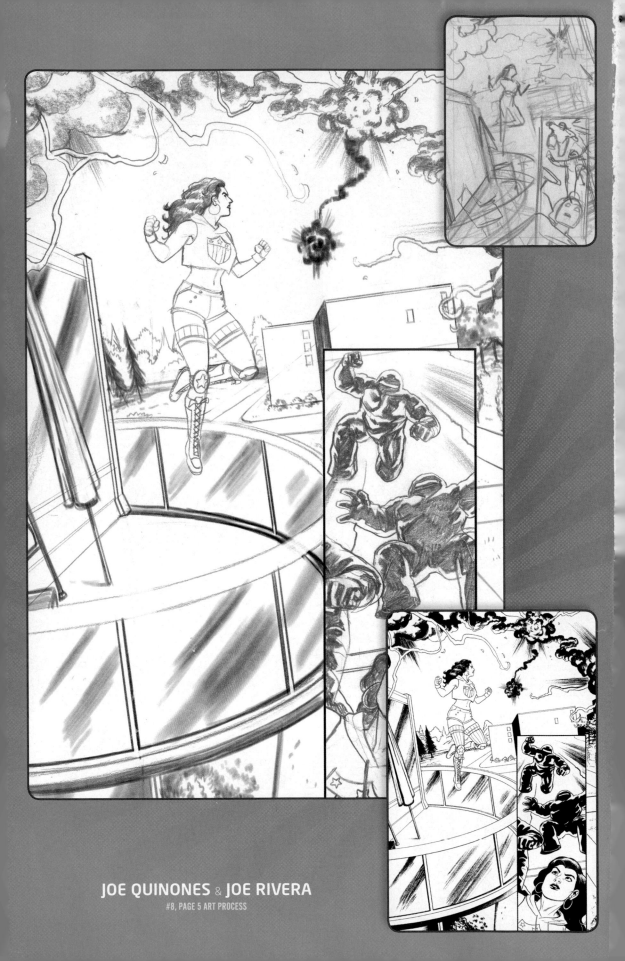

JOE QUINONES & JOE RIVERA

#8, PAGE 5 ART PROCESS

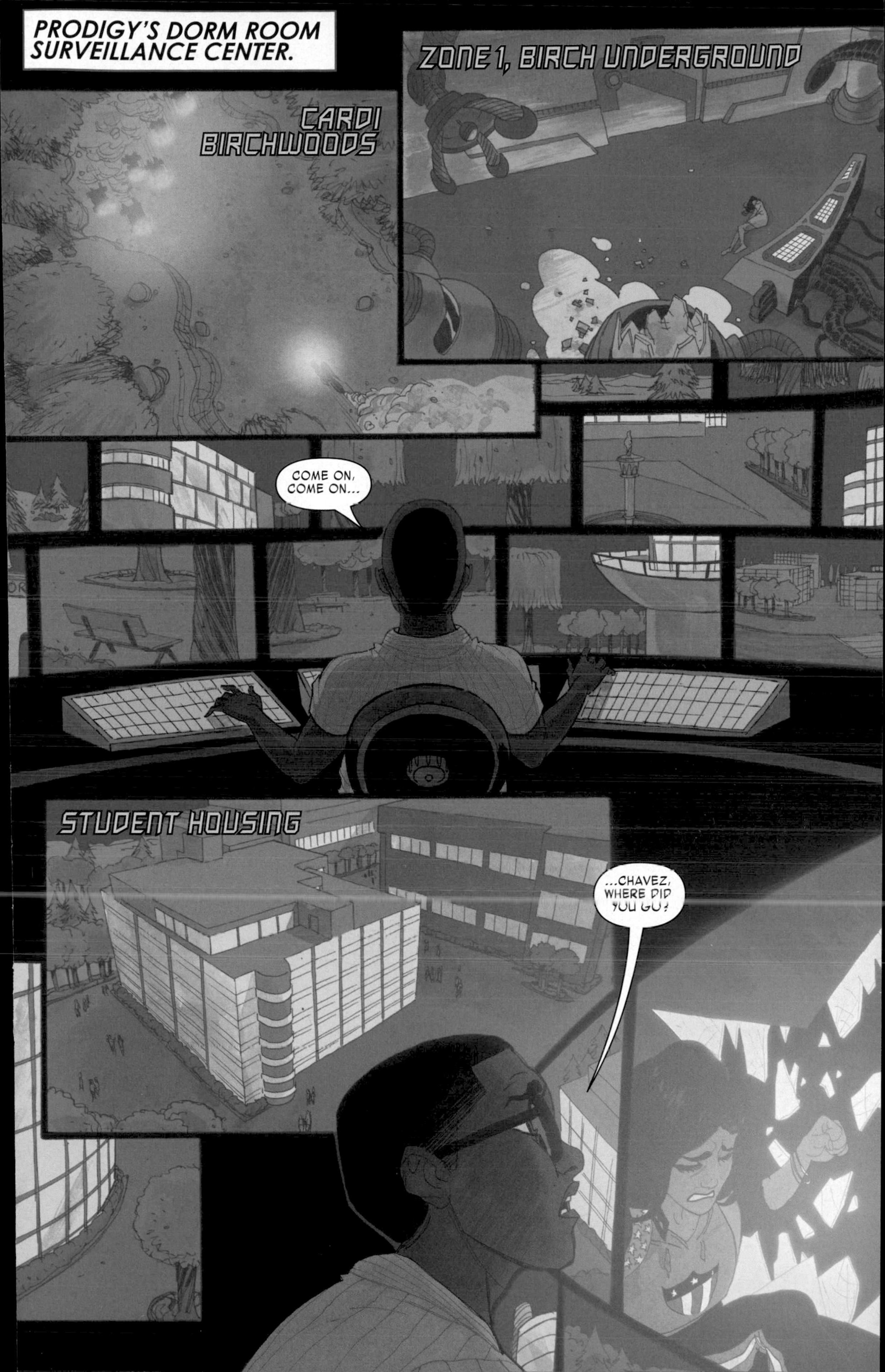
PRODIGY'S DORM ROOM SURVEILLANCE CENTER.
ZONE 1, BIRCH UNDERGROUND
CARDI BIRCHWOODS
COME ON, COME ON...
STUDENT HOUSING
...CHAVEZ, WHERE DID YOU GO?

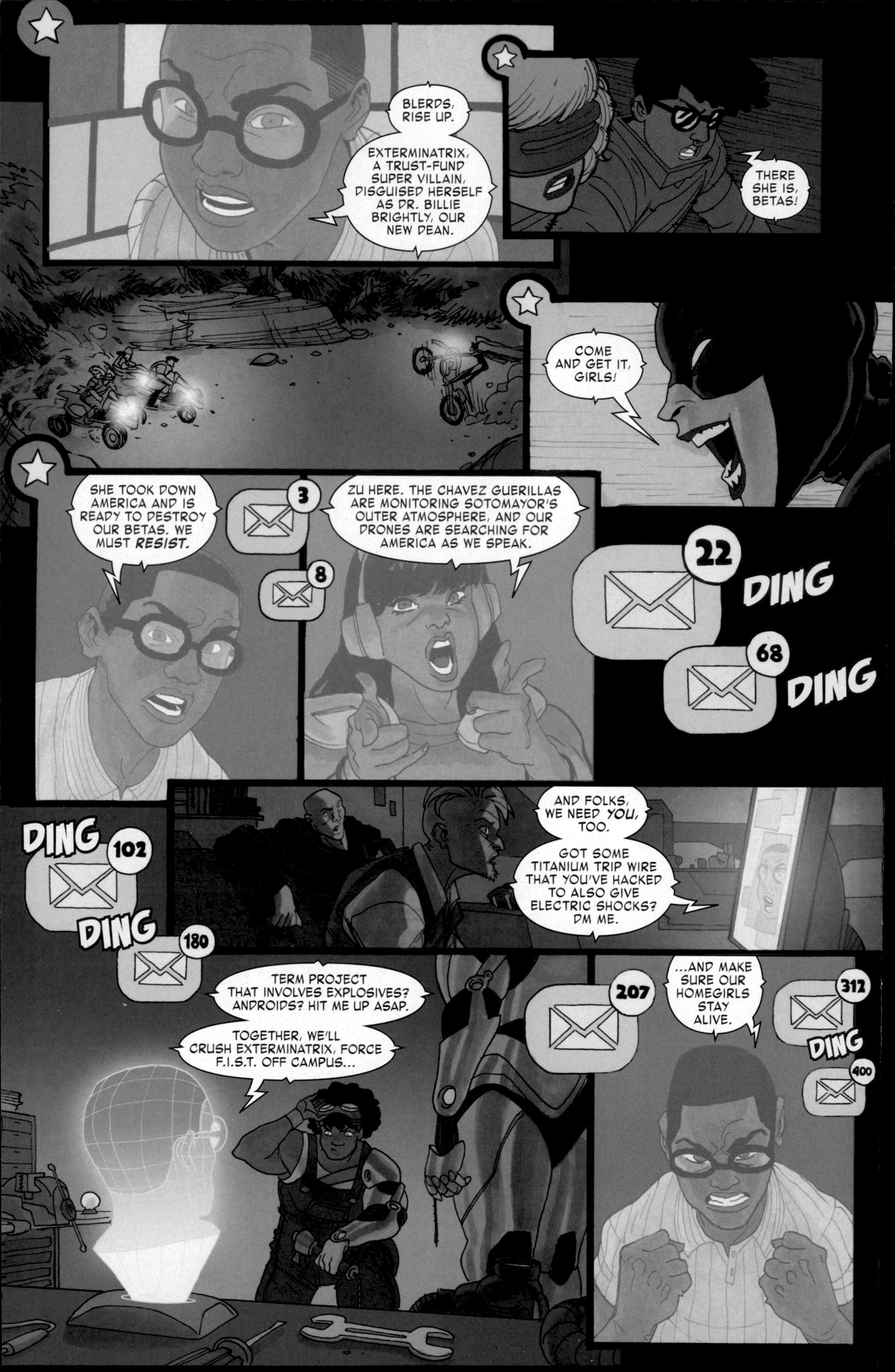
BLERDS, RISE UP.
EXTERMINATRIX, A TRUST-FUND SUPER VILLAIN, DISGUISED HERSELF AS DR. BILLIE BRIGHTLY, OUR NEW DEAN.
THERE SHE IS, BETAS!
COME AND GET IT, GIRLS!
SHE TOOK DOWN AMERICA AND IS READY TO DESTROY OUR BETAS. WE MUST RESIST.
3
8
ZU HERE. THE CHAVEZ GUERILLAS ARE MONITORING SOTOMAYOR'S OUTER ATMOSPHERE, AND OUR DRONES ARE SEARCHING FOR AMERICA AS WE SPEAK.
22
DING
68
DING
DING
102
DING
180
AND FOLKS, WE NEED YOU, TOO.
GOT SOME TITANIUM TRIP WIRE THAT YOU'VE HACKED TO ALSO GIVE ELECTRIC SHOCKS? DM ME.
TERM PROJECT THAT INVOLVES EXPLOSIVES? ANDROIDS? HIT ME UP ASAP.
TOGETHER, WE'LL CRUSH EXTERMINATRIX, FORCE F.I.S.T. OFF CAMPUS...
207
...AND MAKE SURE OUR HOMEGIRLS STAY ALIVE.
312
DING
400

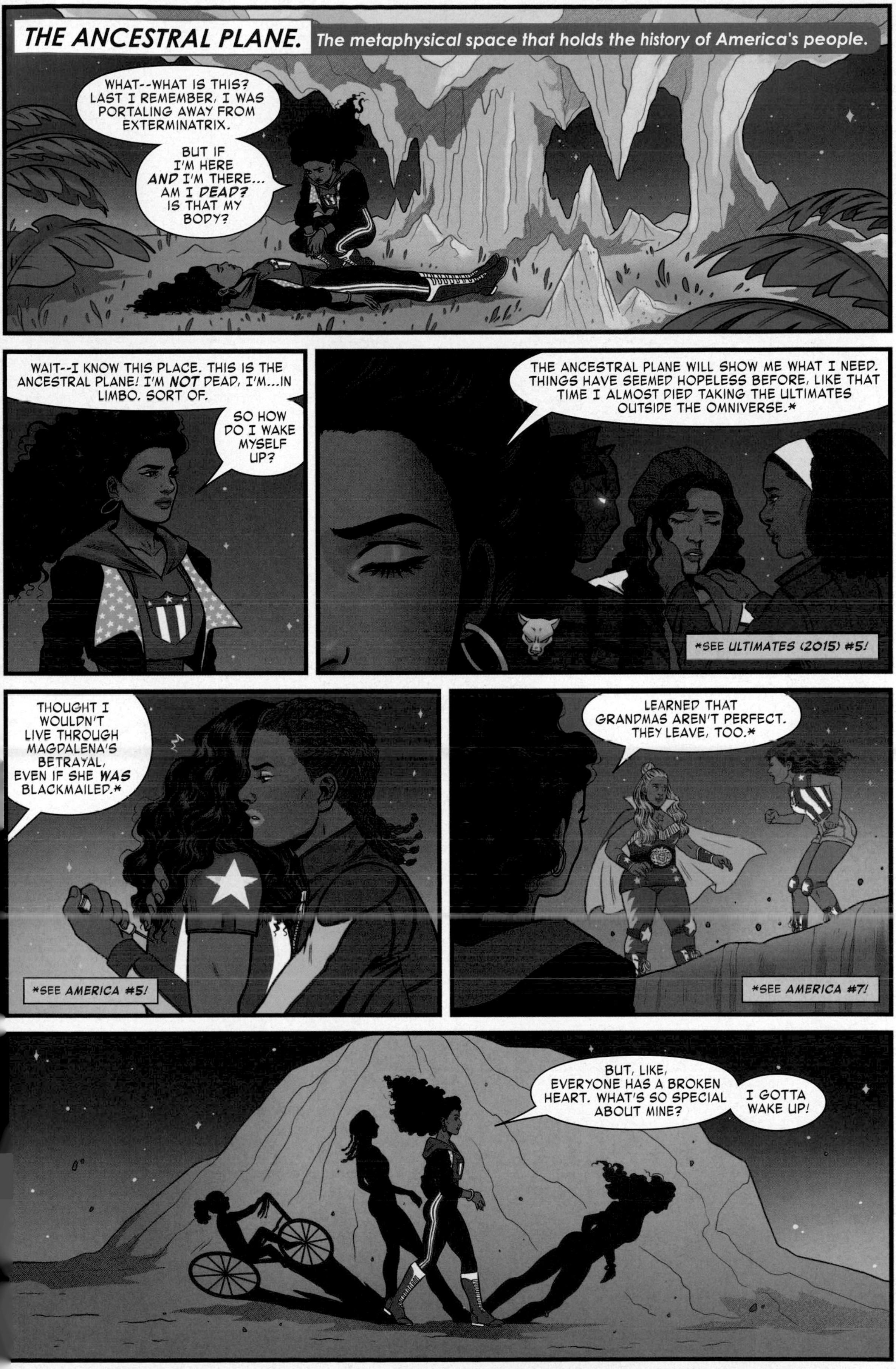
THE ANCESTRAL PLANE. The metaphysical space that holds the history of America's people.
WHAT--WHAT IS THIS? LAST I REMEMBER, I WAS PORTALING AWAY FROM EXTERMINATRIX.
BUT IF I'M HERE AND I'M THERE... AM I DEAD? IS THAT MY BODY?
WAIT--I KNOW THIS PLACE. THIS IS THE ANCESTRAL PLANE! I'M NOT DEAD, I'M...IN LIMBO. SORT OF.
SO HOW DO I WAKE MYSELF UP?
THE ANCESTRAL PLANE WILL SHOW ME WHAT I NEED. THINGS HAVE SEEMED HOPELESS BEFORE, LIKE THAT TIME I ALMOST DIED TAKING THE ULTIMATES OUTSIDE THE OMNIVERSE.*
*SEE ULTIMATES (2015) #5!
THOUGHT I WOULDN'T LIVE THROUGH MAGDALENA'S BETRAYAL, EVEN IF SHE WAS BLACKMAILED.*
*SEE AMERICA #5!
LEARNED THAT GRANDMAS AREN'T PERFECT. THEY LEAVE, TOO.*
*SEE AMERICA #7!
BUT, LIKE, EVERYONE HAS A BROKEN HEART. WHAT'S SO SPECIAL ABOUT MINE?
I GOTTA WAKE UP!

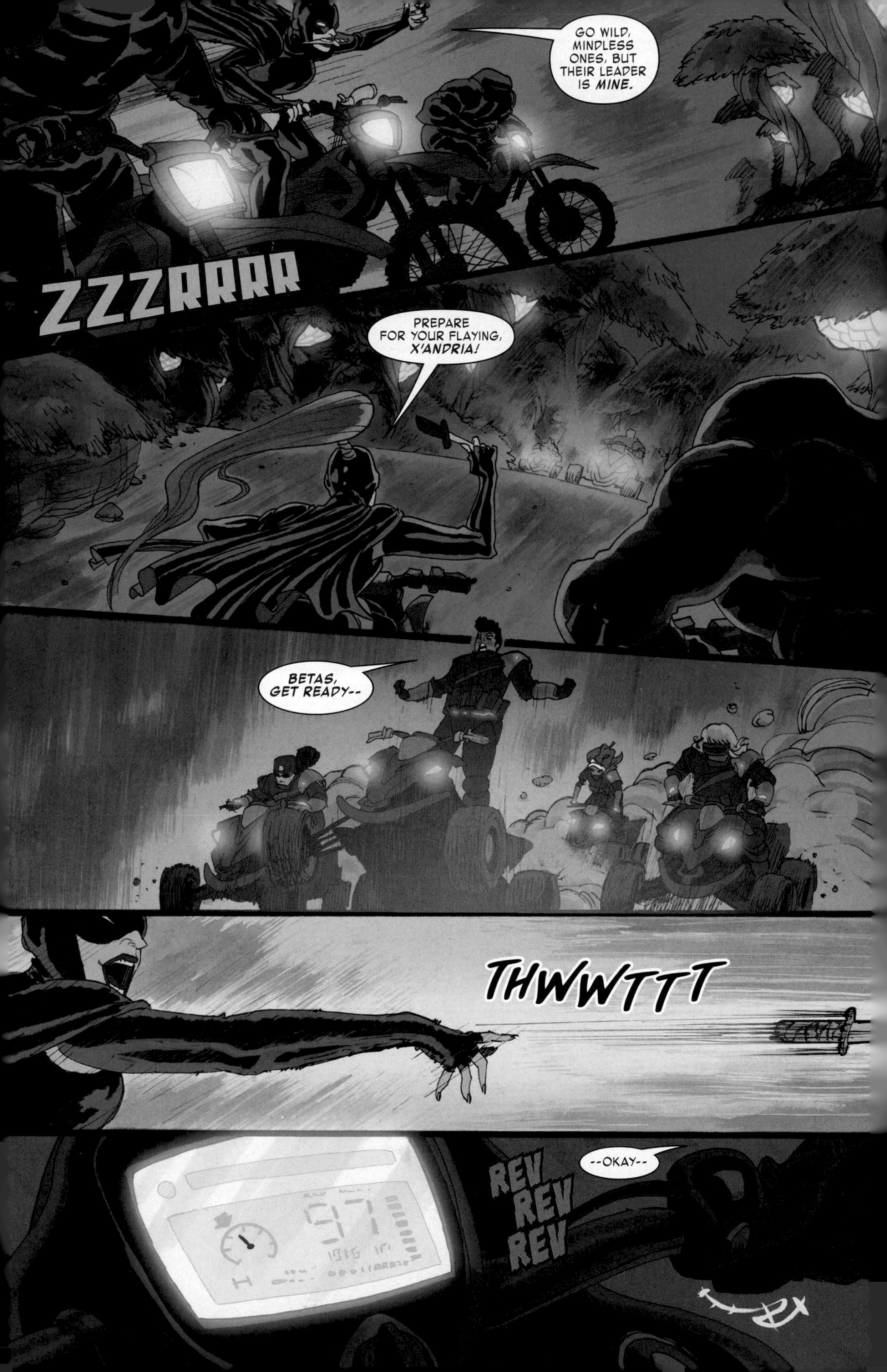
GO WILD, MINDLESS ONES, BUT THEIR LEADER IS *MINE.*
ZZZRRRR
PREPARE FOR YOUR FLAYING, *X'ANDRIA!*
BETAS, GET READY--
THWWTTT
--OKAY--
REV REV REV

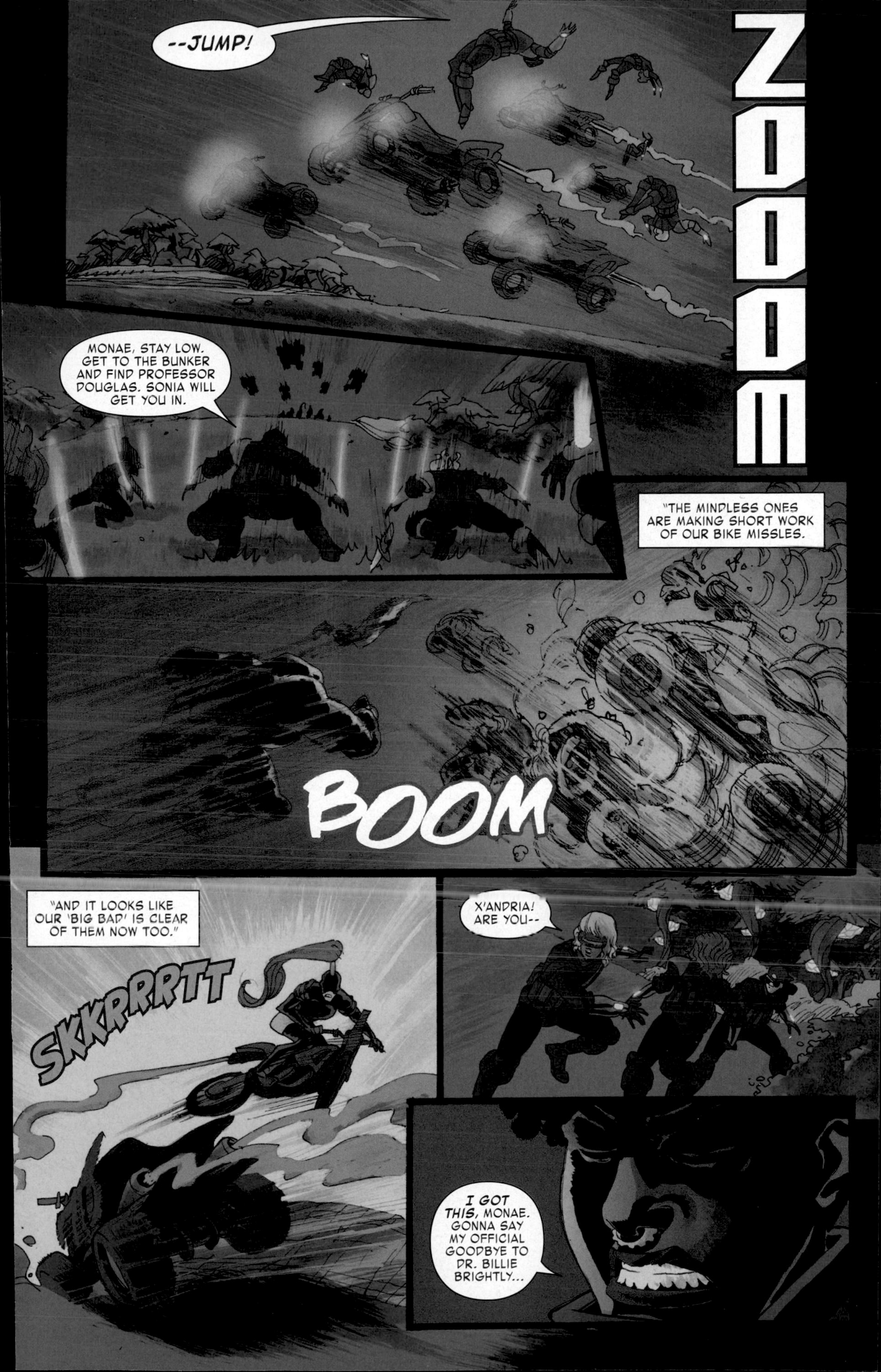

--JUMP!
ZOOOOM
MONAE, STAY LOW. GET TO THE BUNKER AND FIND PROFESSOR DOUGLAS. SONIA WILL GET YOU IN.
"THE MINDLESS ONES ARE MAKING SHORT WORK OF OUR BIKE MISSLES.
BOOM
"AND IT LOOKS LIKE OUR 'BIG BAD' IS CLEAR OF THEM NOW TOO."
SKKRRRTT
X'ANDRIA! ARE YOU--
I GOT THIS, MONAE. GONNA SAY MY OFFICIAL GOODBYE TO DR. BILLIE BRIGHTLY...

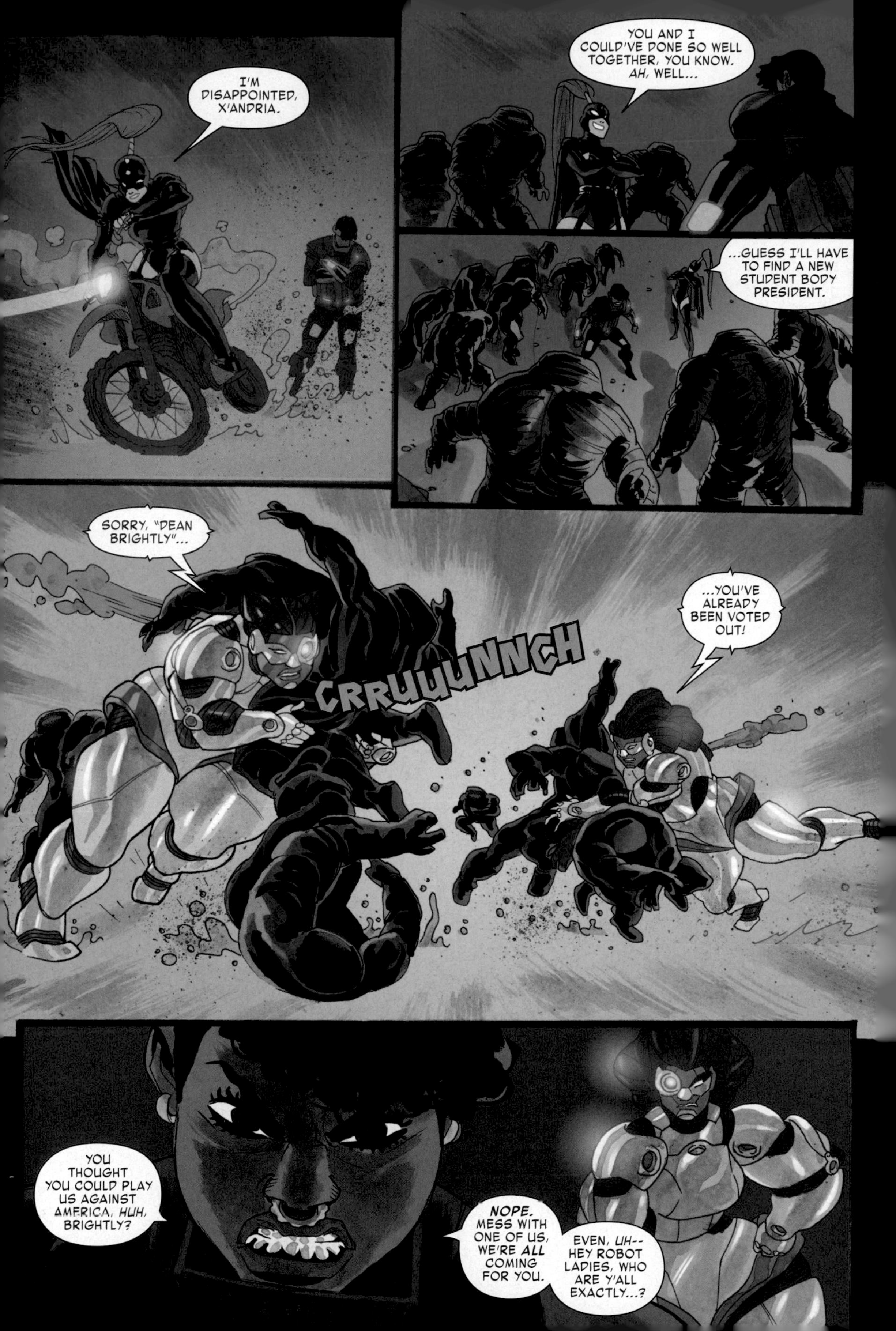
I'M DISAPPOINTED, X'ANDRIA.
YOU AND I COULD'VE DONE SO WELL TOGETHER, YOU KNOW. AH, WELL...
...GUESS I'LL HAVE TO FIND A NEW STUDENT BODY PRESIDENT.
SORRY, "DEAN BRIGHTLY"...
...YOU'VE ALREADY BEEN VOTED OUT!
CRRUUUNNCH
YOU THOUGHT YOU COULD PLAY US AGAINST AMERICA, HUH, BRIGHTLY?
NOPE. MESS WITH ONE OF US, WE'RE ALL COMING FOR YOU.
EVEN, UH-- HEY ROBOT LADIES, WHO ARE Y'ALL EXACTLY...?

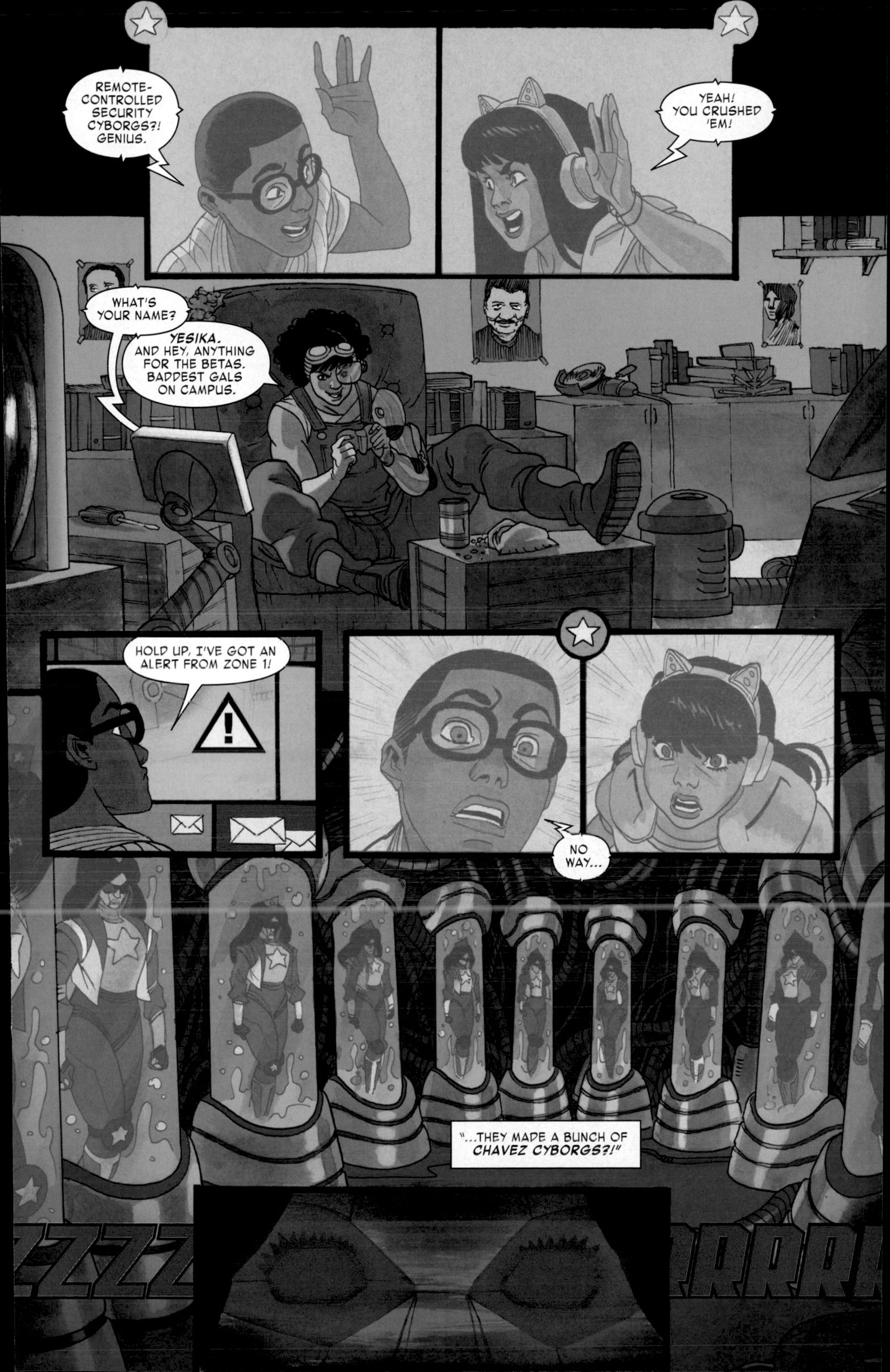
REMOTE-CONTROLLED SECURITY CYBORGS?! GENIUS.
YEAH! YOU CRUSHED 'EM!
WHAT'S YOUR NAME?
YESIKA. AND HEY, ANYTHING FOR THE BETAS. BADDEST GALS ON CAMPUS.
HOLD UP, I'VE GOT AN ALERT FROM ZONE 1!
NO WAY...
"...THEY MADE A BUNCH OF CHAVEZ CYBORGS?!"
ZZZZ
RRRR

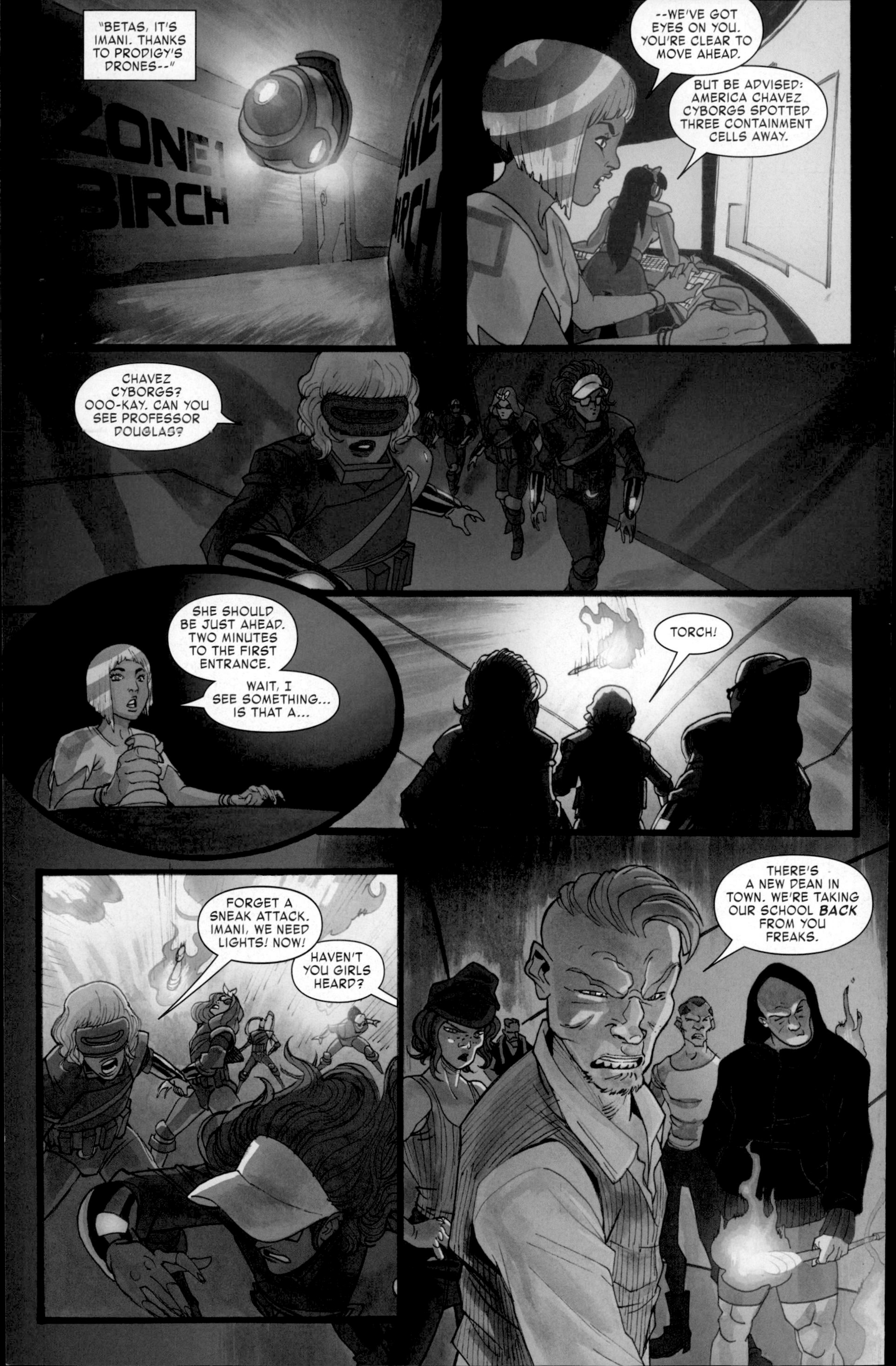
"BETAS, IT'S IMANI. THANKS TO PRODIGY'S DRONES--"
ZONE 1 BIRCH
--WE'VE GOT EYES ON YOU. YOU'RE CLEAR TO MOVE AHEAD.
BUT BE ADVISED: AMERICA CHAVEZ CYBORGS SPOTTED THREE CONTAINMENT CELLS AWAY.
CHAVEZ CYBORGS? OOO-KAY. CAN YOU SEE PROFESSOR DOUGLAS?
SHE SHOULD BE JUST AHEAD. TWO MINUTES TO THE FIRST ENTRANCE.
WAIT, I SEE SOMETHING... IS THAT A...
TORCH!
FORGET A SNEAK ATTACK. IMANI, WE NEED LIGHTS! NOW!
HAVEN'T YOU GIRLS HEARD?
THERE'S A NEW DEAN IN TOWN. WE'RE TAKING OUR SCHOOL BACK FROM YOU FREAKS.

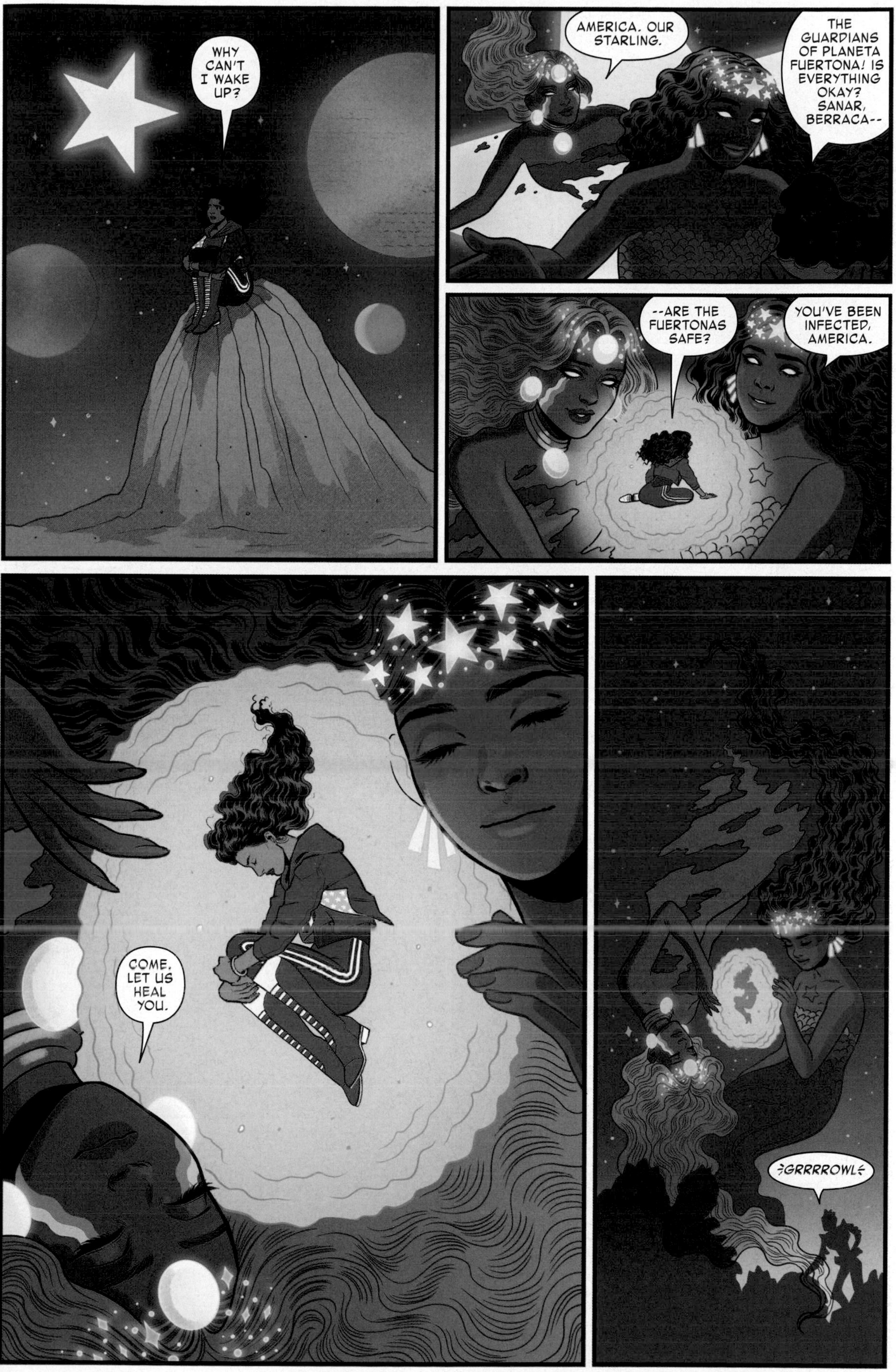
WHY CAN'T I WAKE UP?
AMERICA. OUR STARLING.
THE GUARDIANS OF PLANETA FUERTONA! IS EVERYTHING OKAY? SANAR, BERRACA--
--ARE THE FUERTONAS SAFE?
YOU'VE BEEN INFECTED, AMERICA.
COME. LET US HEAL YOU.
GRRRROWL

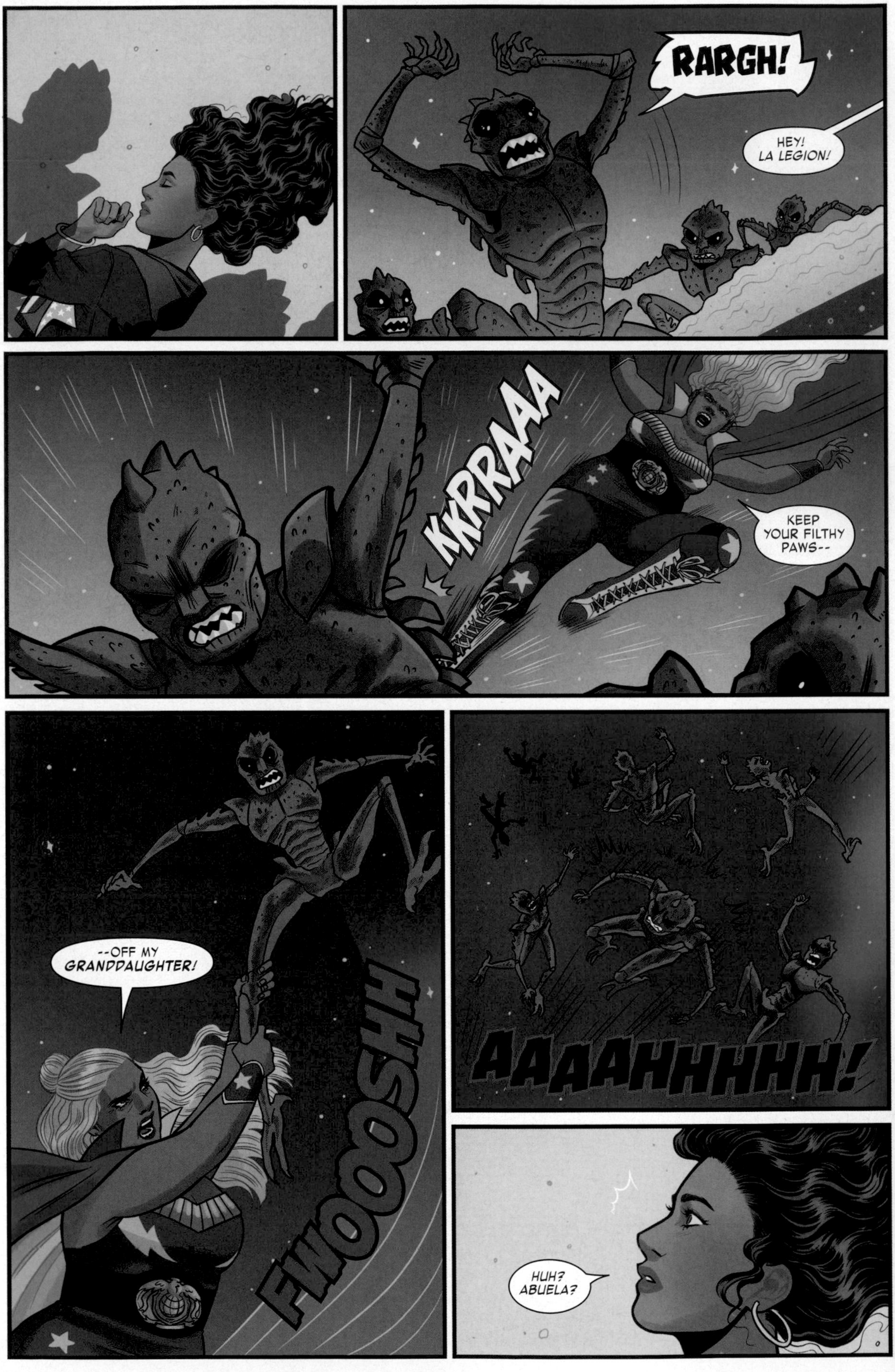
RARGH!
HEY! LA LEGION!
KKRRAAA
KEEP YOUR FILTHY PAWS--
--OFF MY GRANDDAUGHTER!
FWOOOSHH
AAAAHHHHH!
HUH? ABUELA?

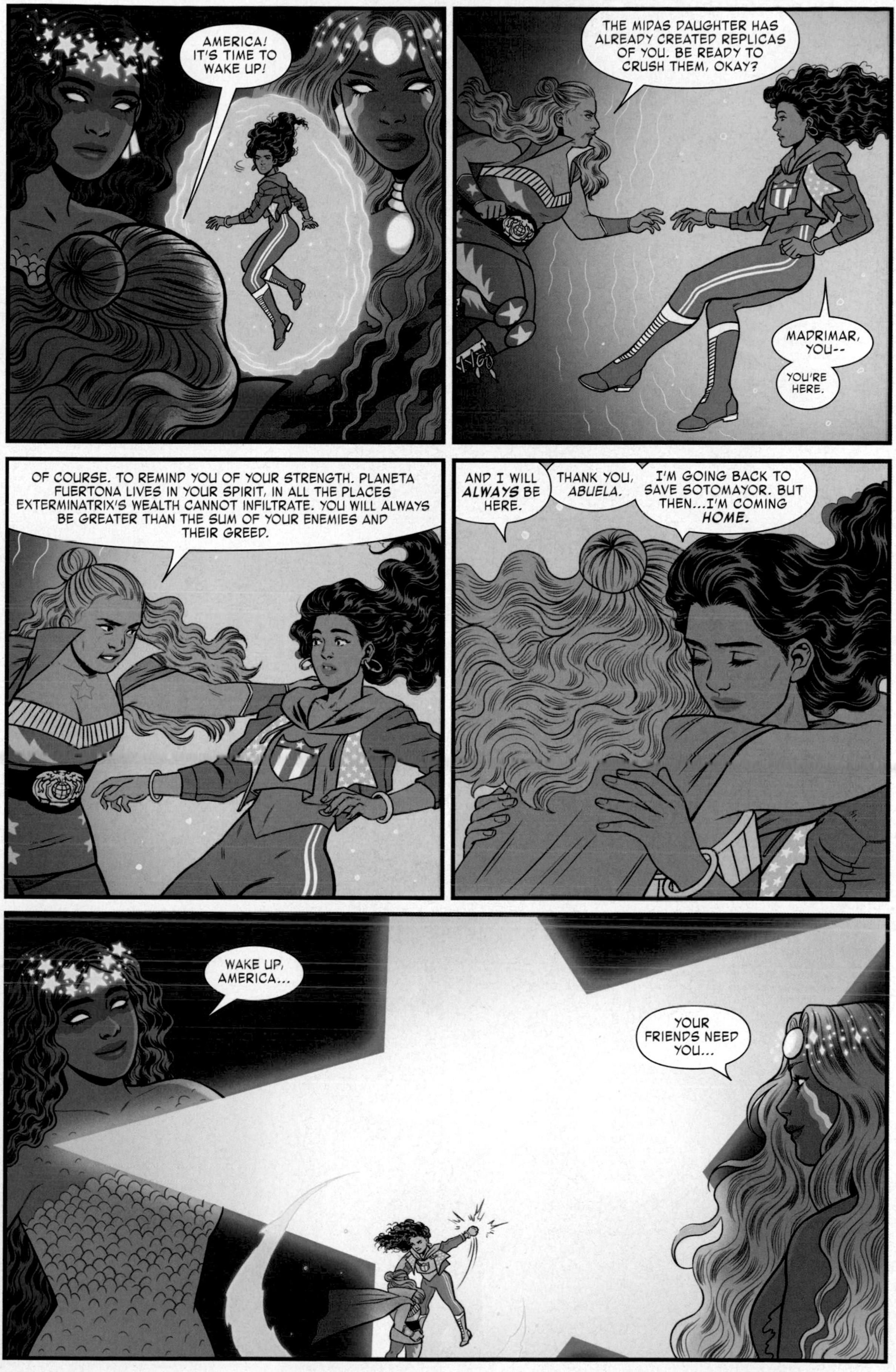
AMERICA! IT'S TIME TO WAKE UP!
THE MIDAS DAUGHTER HAS ALREADY CREATED REPLICAS OF YOU. BE READY TO CRUSH THEM, OKAY?
MADRIMAR, YOU--
YOU'RE HERE.
OF COURSE. TO REMIND YOU OF YOUR STRENGTH. PLANETA FUERTONA LIVES IN YOUR SPIRIT, IN ALL THE PLACES EXTERMINATRIX'S WEALTH CANNOT INFILTRATE. YOU WILL ALWAYS BE GREATER THAN THE SUM OF YOUR ENEMIES AND THEIR GREED.
AND I WILL ALWAYS BE HERE.
THANK YOU, ABUELA.
I'M GOING BACK TO SAVE SOTOMAYOR. BUT THEN...I'M COMING HOME.
WAKE UP, AMERICA...
YOUR FRIENDS NEED YOU...

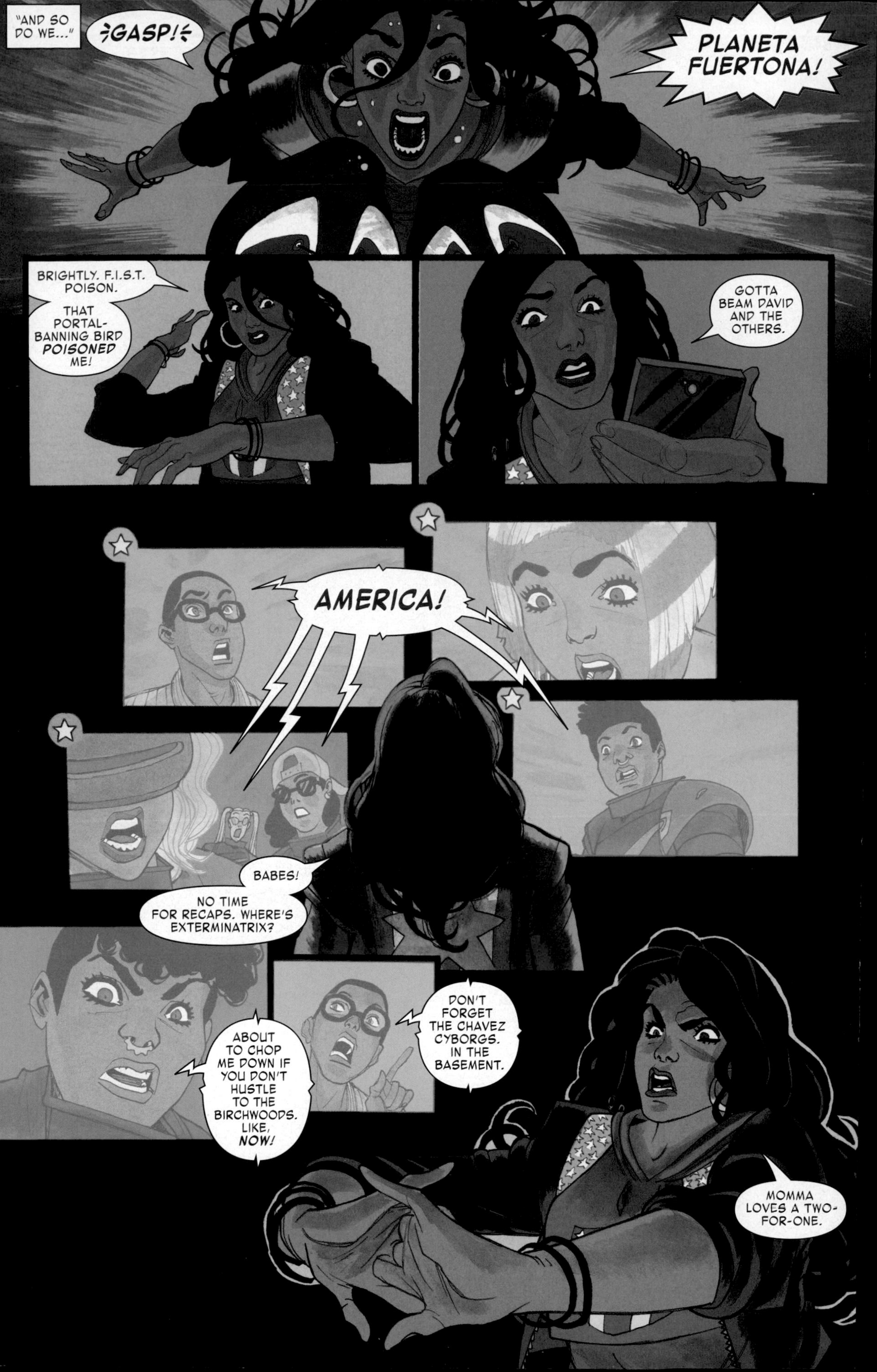
"AND SO DO WE..."
GASP!
PLANETA FUERTONA!
BRIGHTLY. F.I.S.T. POISON.
THAT PORTAL-BANNING BIRD POISONED ME!
GOTTA BEAM DAVID AND THE OTHERS.
AMERICA!
BABES!
NO TIME FOR RECAPS. WHERE'S EXTERMINATRIX?
ABOUT TO CHOP ME DOWN IF YOU DON'T HUSTLE TO THE BIRCHWOODS. LIKE, NOW!
DON'T FORGET THE CHAVEZ CYBORGS. IN THE BASEMENT.
MOMMA LOVES A TWO-FOR-ONE.

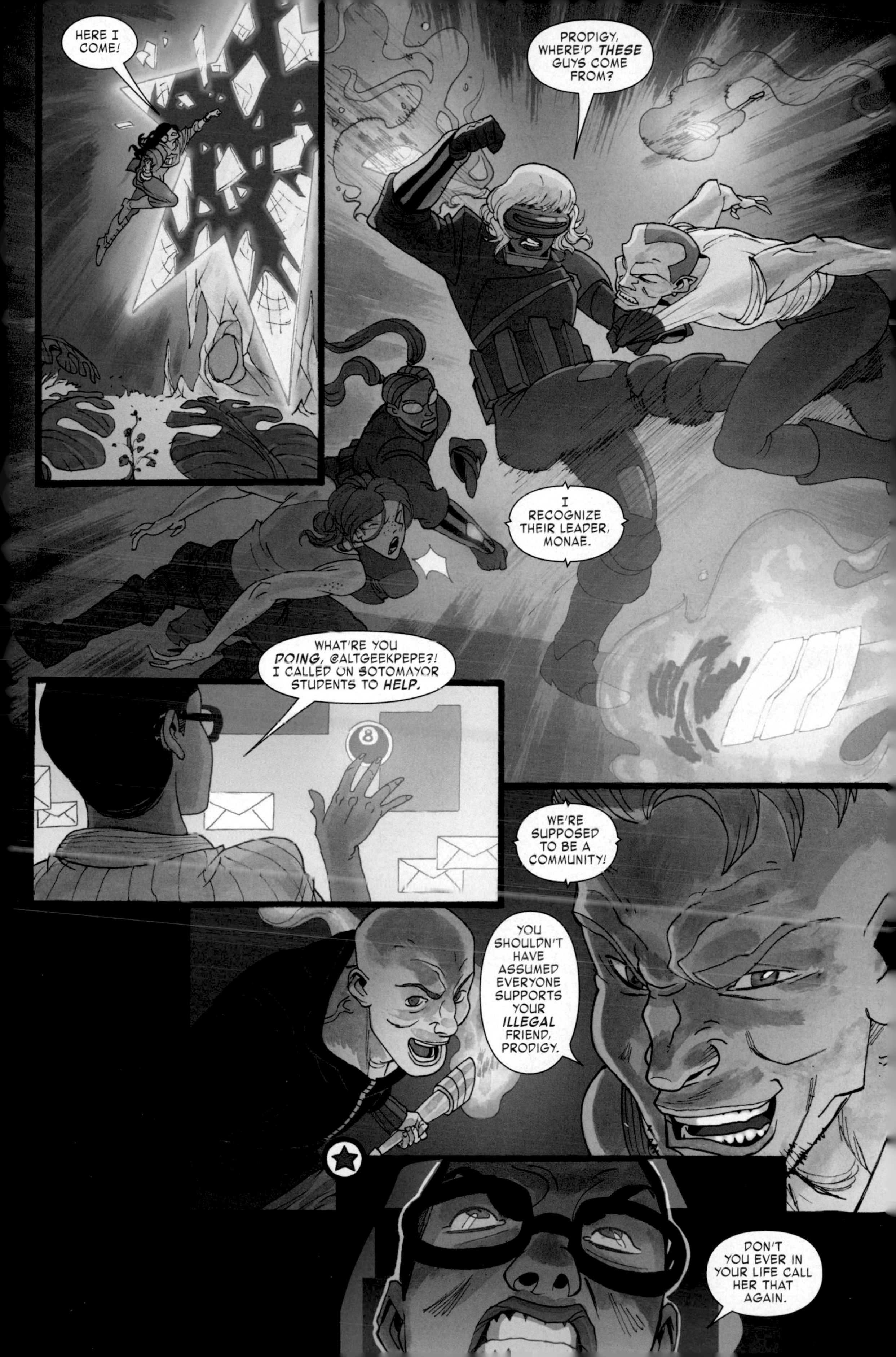
HERE I COME!
PRODIGY, WHERE'D THESE GUYS COME FROM?
I RECOGNIZE THEIR LEADER, MONAE.
WHAT'RE YOU DOING, @ALTGEEKPEPE?! I CALLED ON SOTOMAYOR STUDENTS TO HELP.
WE'RE SUPPOSED TO BE A COMMUNITY!
YOU SHOULDN'T HAVE ASSUMED EVERYONE SUPPORTS YOUR ILLEGAL FRIEND, PRODIGY.
DON'T YOU EVER IN YOUR LIFE CALL HER THAT AGAIN.

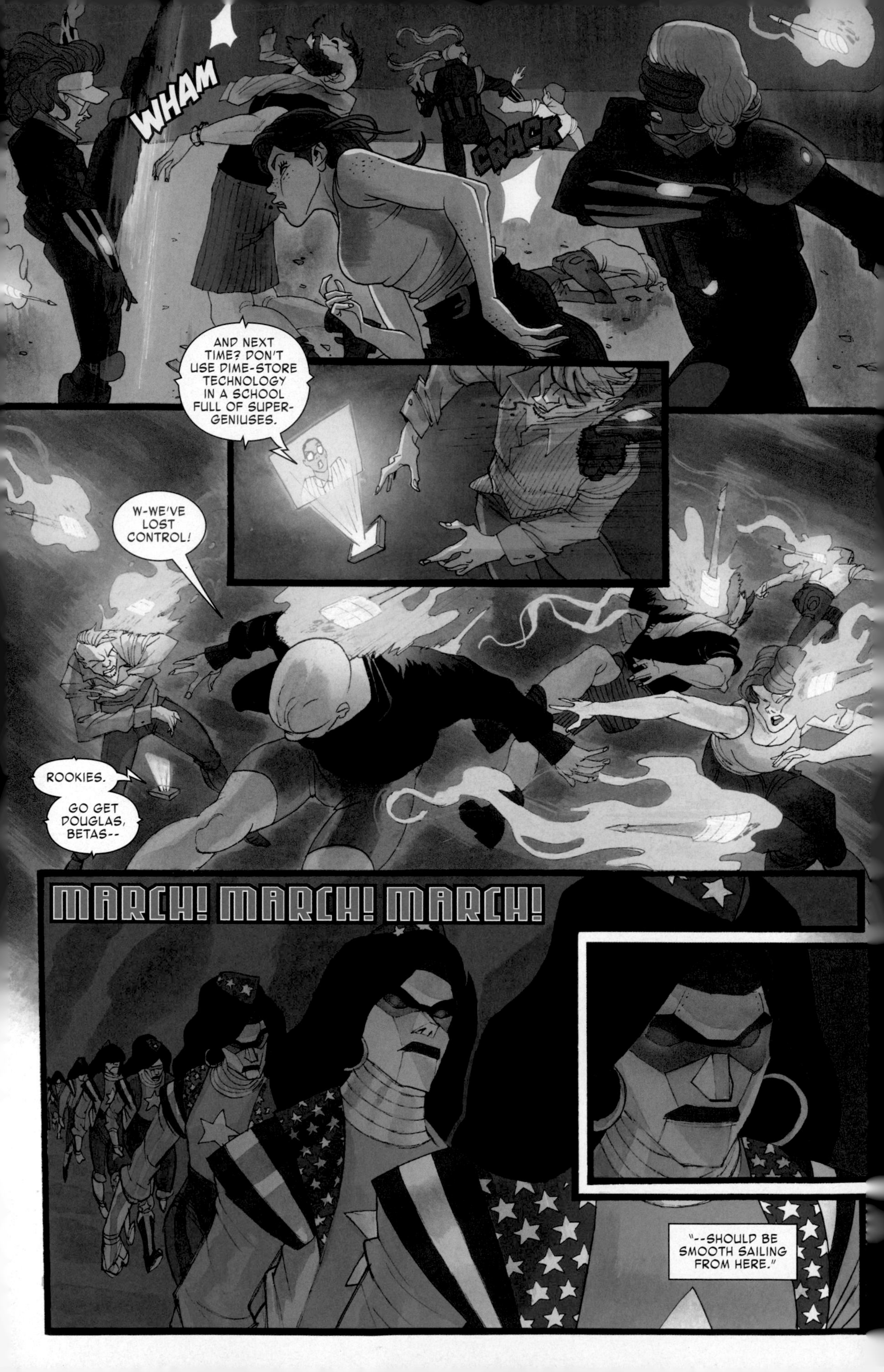
WHAM
CRACK
AND NEXT TIME? DON'T USE DIME-STORE TECHNOLOGY IN A SCHOOL FULL OF SUPER-GENIUSES.
W-WE'VE LOST CONTROL!
ROOKIES.
GO GET DOUGLAS, BETAS--
MARCH! MARCH! MARCH!
"--SHOULD BE SMOOTH SAILING FROM HERE."

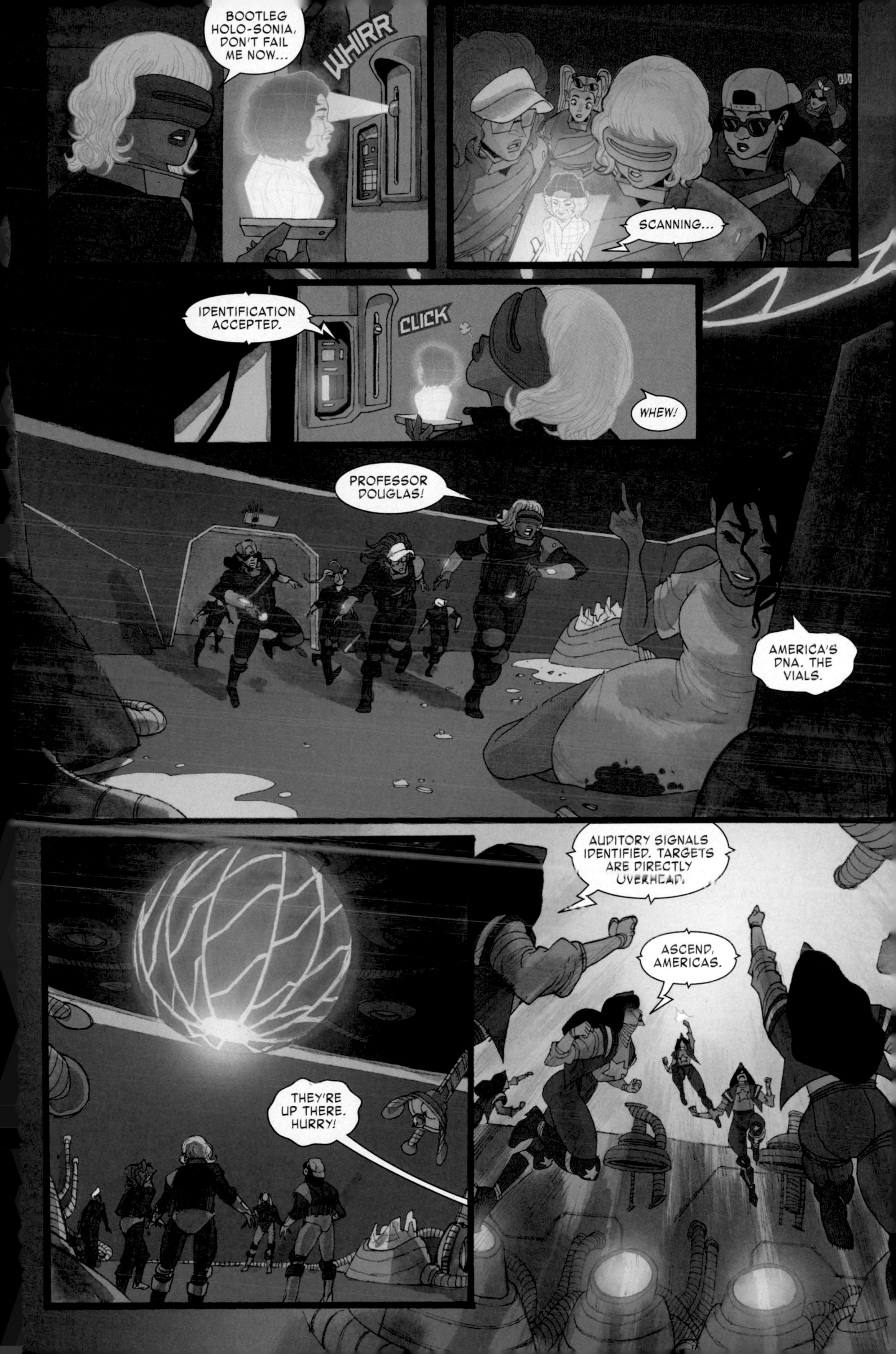
BOOTLEG HOLO-SONIA, DON'T FAIL ME NOW...
WHIRR
SCANNING...
IDENTIFICATION ACCEPTED.
CLICK
WHEW!
PROFESSOR DOUGLAS!
AMERICA'S DNA. THE VIALS.
THEY'RE UP THERE. HURRY!
AUDITORY SIGNALS IDENTIFIED. TARGETS ARE DIRECTLY OVERHEAD.
ASCEND, AMERICAS.

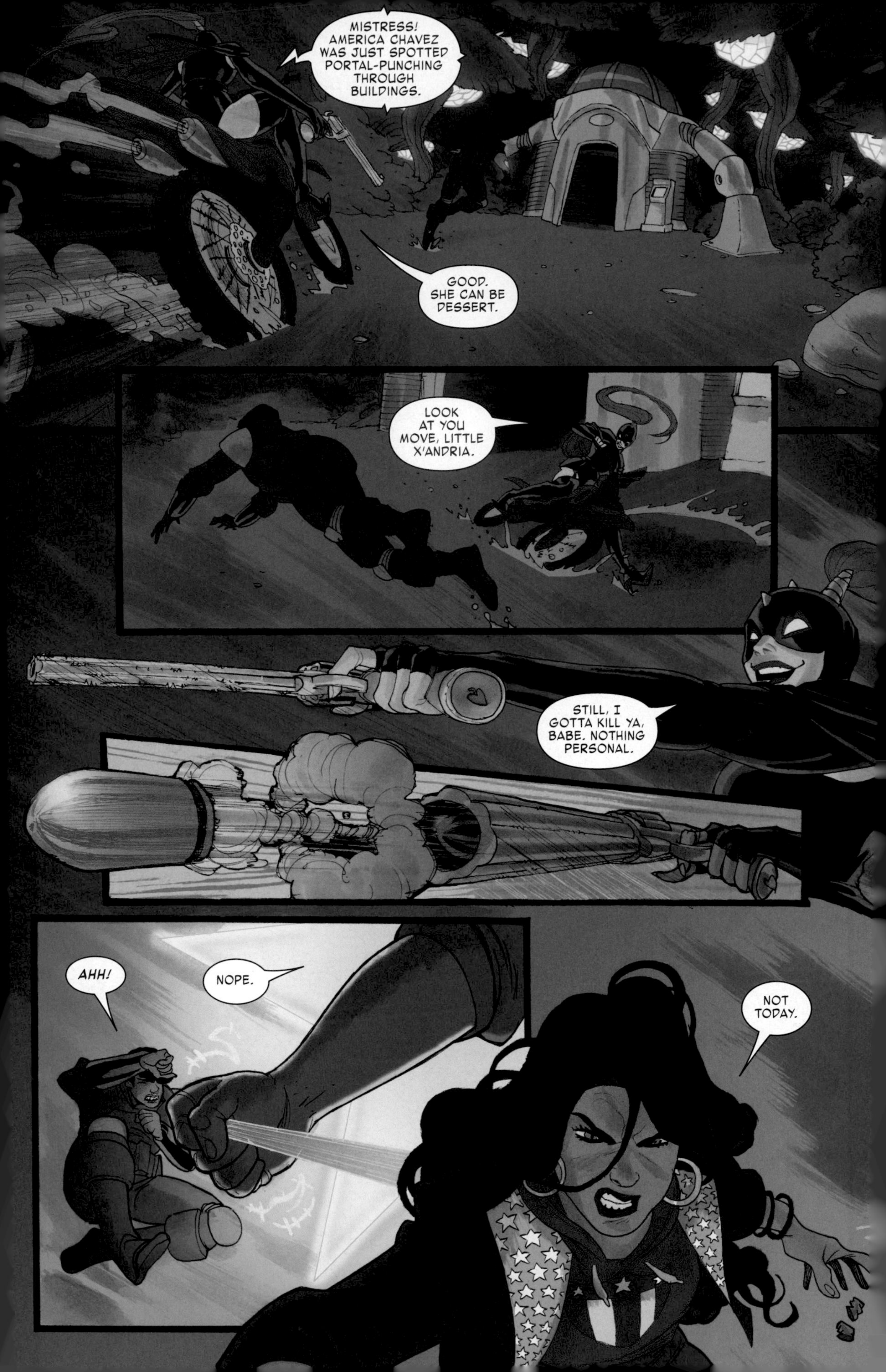
MISTRESS! AMERICA CHAVEZ WAS JUST SPOTTED PORTAL-PUNCHING THROUGH BUILDINGS.
GOOD. SHE CAN BE DESSERT.
LOOK AT YOU MOVE, LITTLE X'ANDRIA.
STILL, I GOTTA KILL YA, BABE. NOTHING PERSONAL.
AHH!
NOPE.
NOT TODAY.

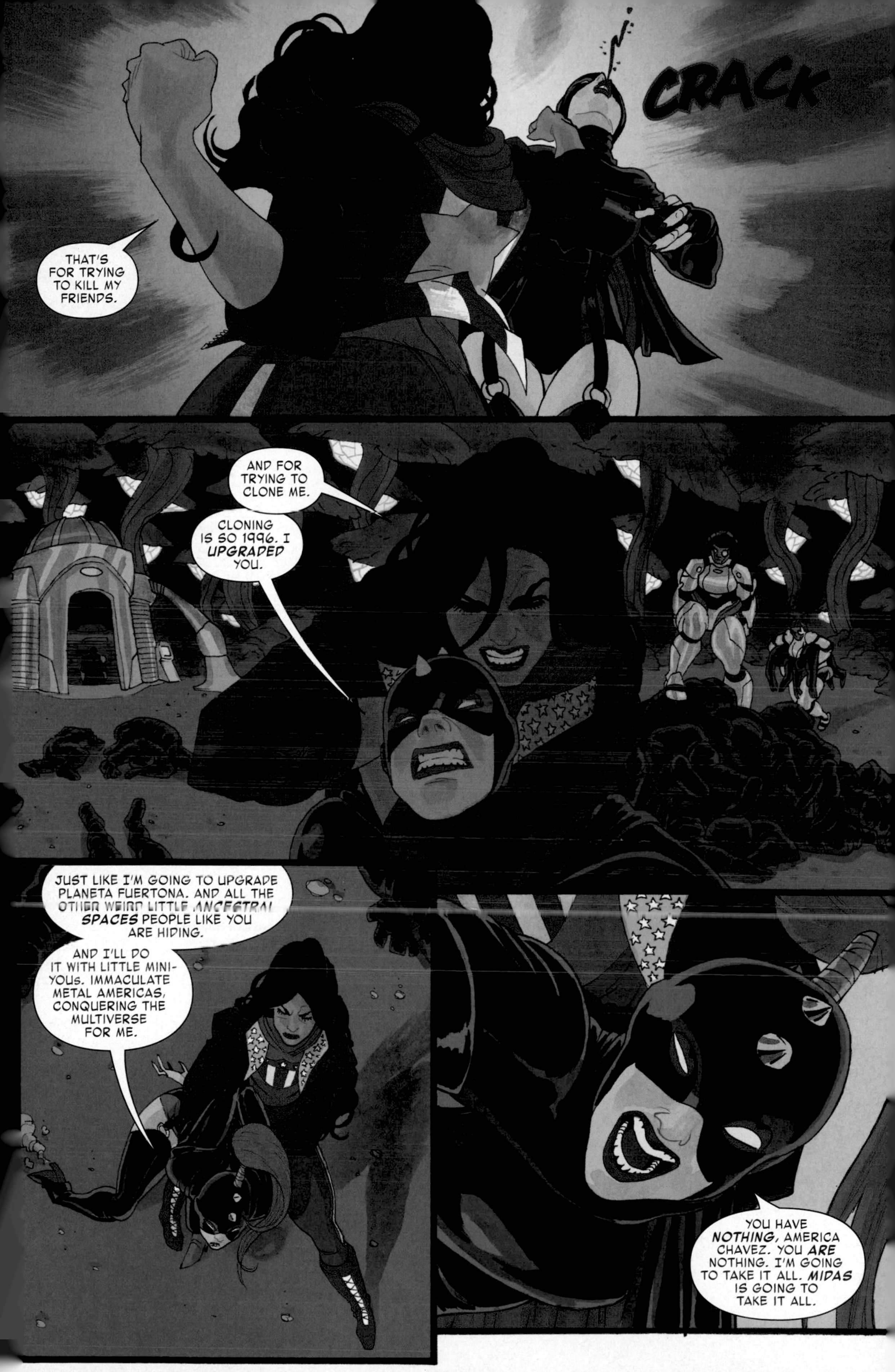
CRACK
THAT'S FOR TRYING TO KILL MY FRIENDS.
AND FOR TRYING TO CLONE ME.
CLONING IS SO 1996. I *UPGRADED* YOU.
JUST LIKE I'M GOING TO UPGRADE PLANETA FUERTONA. AND ALL THE OTHER WEIRD LITTLE *ANCESTRAL SPACES* PEOPLE LIKE YOU ARE HIDING.
AND I'LL DO IT WITH LITTLE MINI-YOUs. IMMACULATE METAL AMERICAS, CONQUERING THE MULTIVERSE FOR ME.
YOU HAVE *NOTHING*, AMERICA CHAVEZ. YOU *ARE* NOTHING. I'M GOING TO TAKE IT ALL. *MIDAS* IS GOING TO TAKE IT ALL.

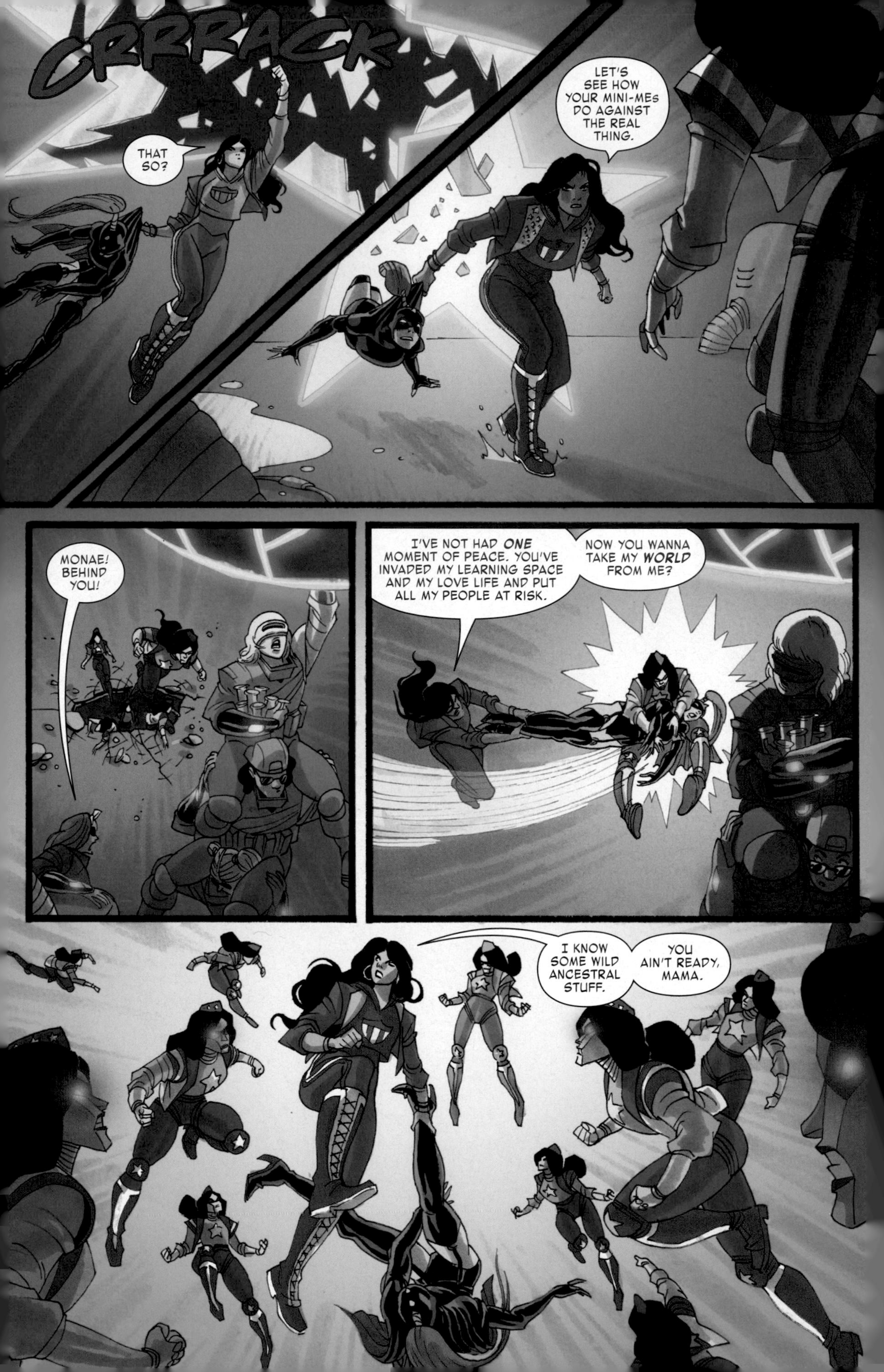
CRRRACK
THAT SO?
LET'S SEE HOW YOUR MINI-MEs DO AGAINST THE REAL THING.
MONAE! BEHIND YOU!
I'VE NOT HAD ONE MOMENT OF PEACE. YOU'VE INVADED MY LEARNING SPACE AND MY LOVE LIFE AND PUT ALL MY PEOPLE AT RISK.
NOW YOU WANNA TAKE MY WORLD FROM ME?
I KNOW SOME WILD ANCESTRAL STUFF.
YOU AIN'T READY, MAMA.

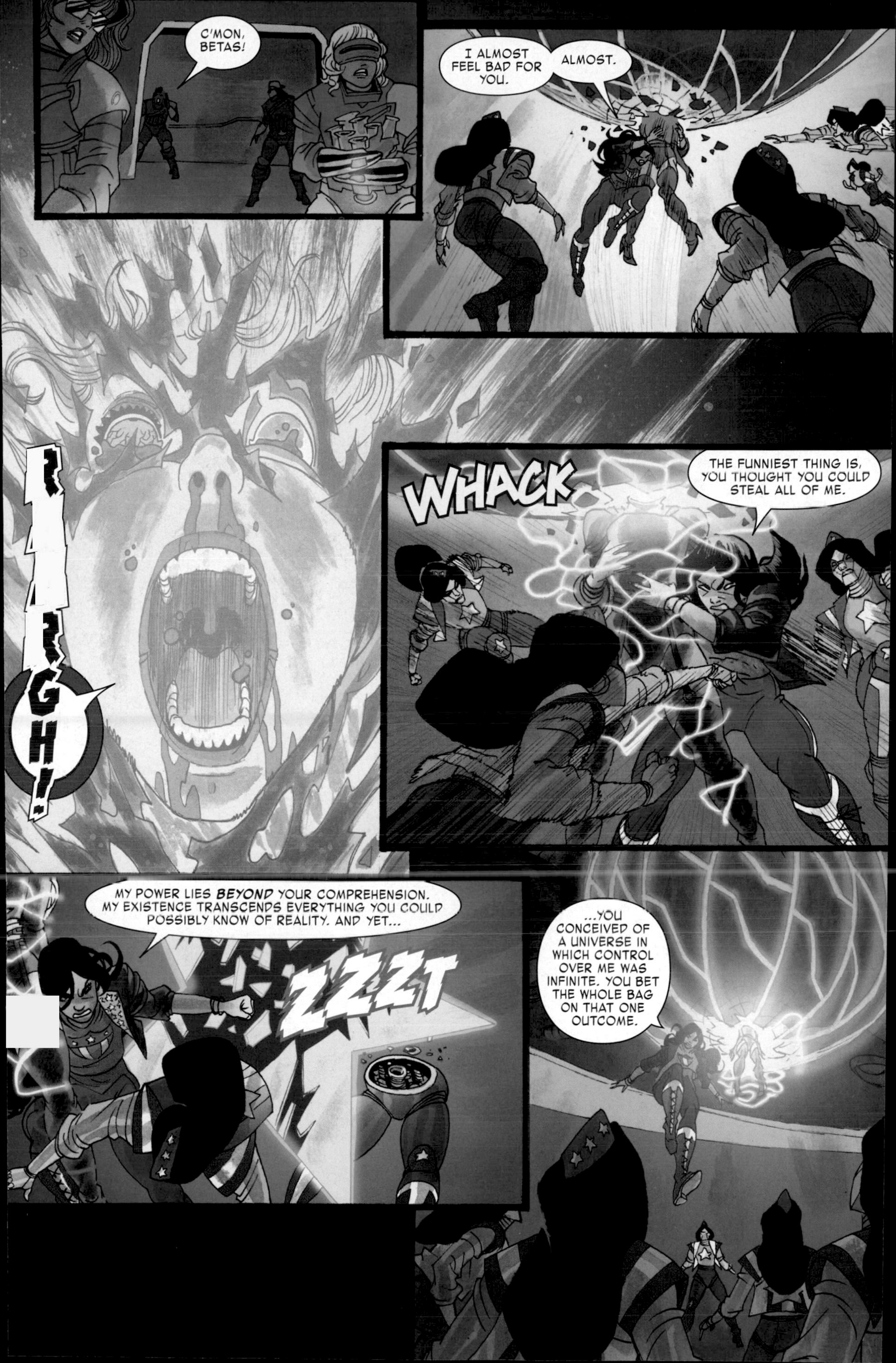
C'MON, BETAS!
I ALMOST FEEL BAD FOR YOU.
ALMOST.
WHACK
THE FUNNIEST THING IS, YOU THOUGHT YOU COULD STEAL ALL OF ME.
MY POWER LIES BEYOND YOUR COMPREHENSION. MY EXISTENCE TRANSCENDS EVERYTHING YOU COULD POSSIBLY KNOW OF REALITY. AND YET...
ZZZT
...YOU CONCEIVED OF A UNIVERSE IN WHICH CONTROL OVER ME WAS INFINITE. YOU BET THE WHOLE BAG ON THAT ONE OUTCOME.

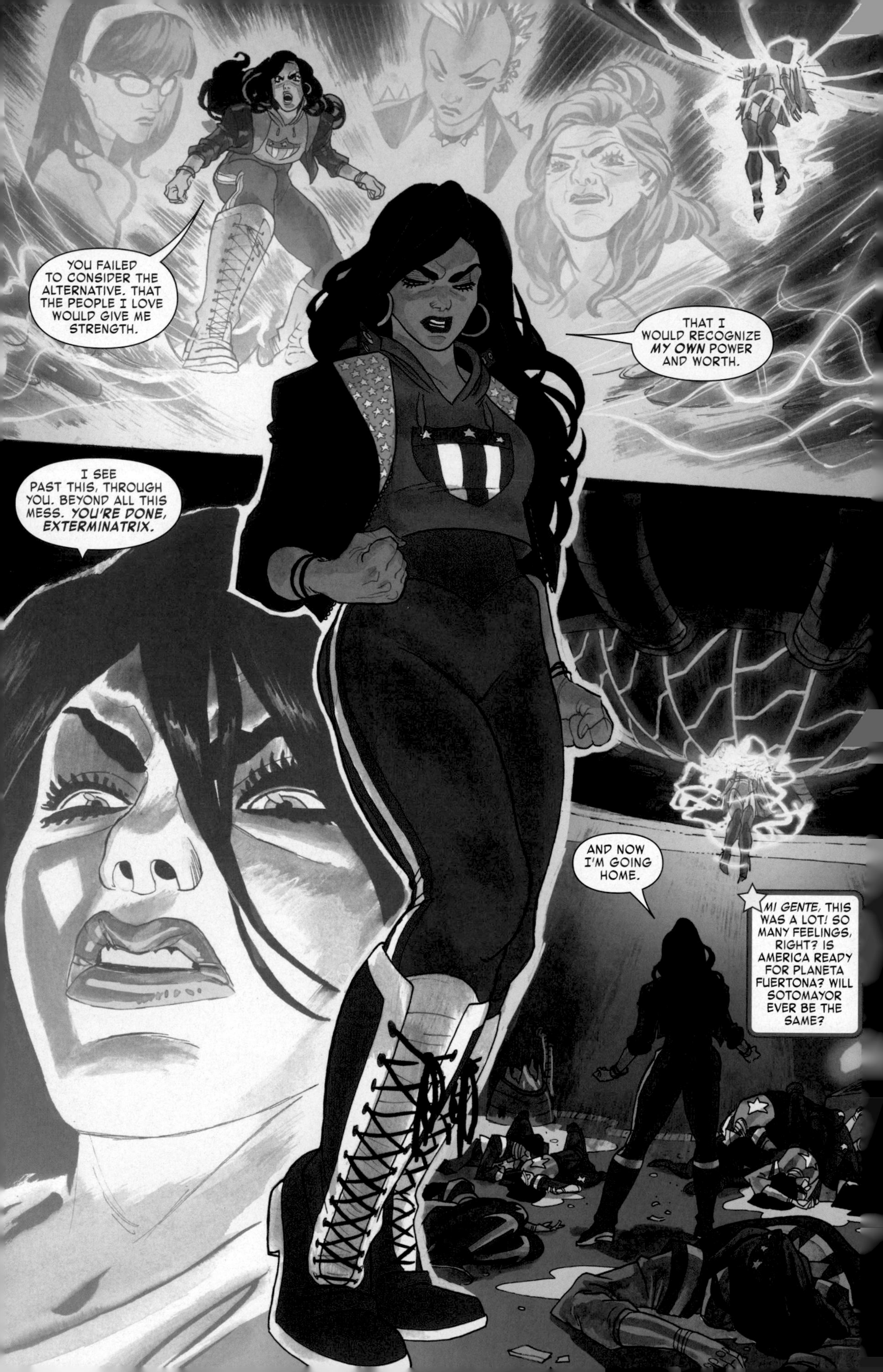

YOU FAILED TO CONSIDER THE ALTERNATIVE. THAT THE PEOPLE I LOVE WOULD GIVE ME STRENGTH.
THAT I WOULD RECOGNIZE *MY OWN* POWER AND WORTH.
I SEE PAST THIS, THROUGH YOU. BEYOND ALL THIS MESS. *YOU'RE DONE, EXTERMINATRIX.*
AND NOW I'M GOING HOME.
MI GENTE, THIS WAS A LOT! SO MANY FEELINGS, RIGHT? IS AMERICA READY FOR PLANETA FUERTONA? WILL SOTOMAYOR EVER BE THE SAME?

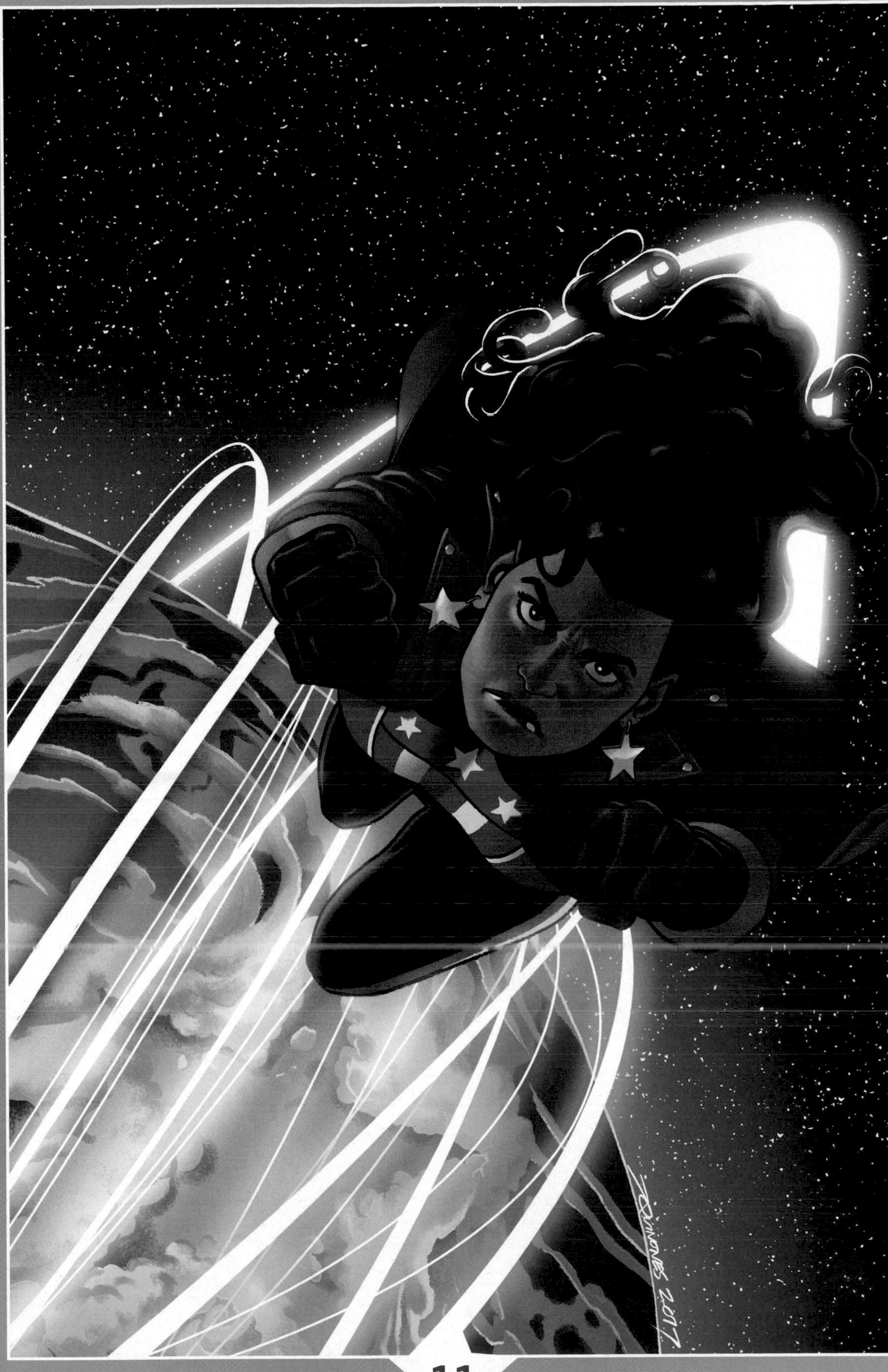

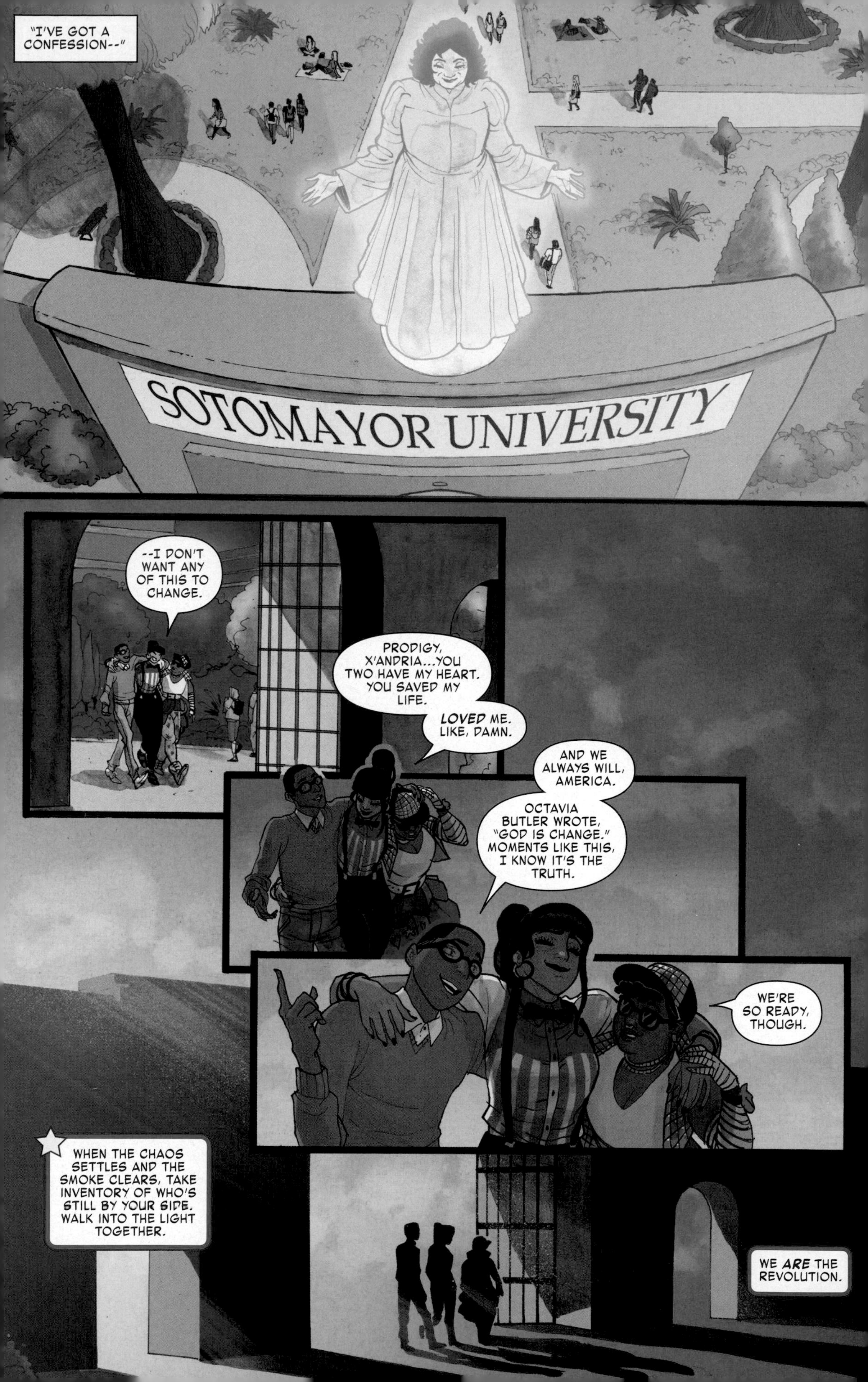
"I'VE GOT A CONFESSION--"
SOTOMAYOR UNIVERSITY
--I DON'T WANT ANY OF THIS TO CHANGE.
PRODIGY, X'ANDRIA...YOU TWO HAVE MY HEART. YOU SAVED MY LIFE.
LOVED ME. LIKE, DAMN.
AND WE ALWAYS WILL, AMERICA.
OCTAVIA BUTLER WROTE, "GOD IS CHANGE." MOMENTS LIKE THIS, I KNOW IT'S THE TRUTH.
WE'RE SO READY, THOUGH.
WHEN THE CHAOS SETTLES AND THE SMOKE CLEARS, TAKE INVENTORY OF WHO'S STILL BY YOUR SIDE. WALK INTO THE LIGHT TOGETHER.
WE ARE THE REVOLUTION.

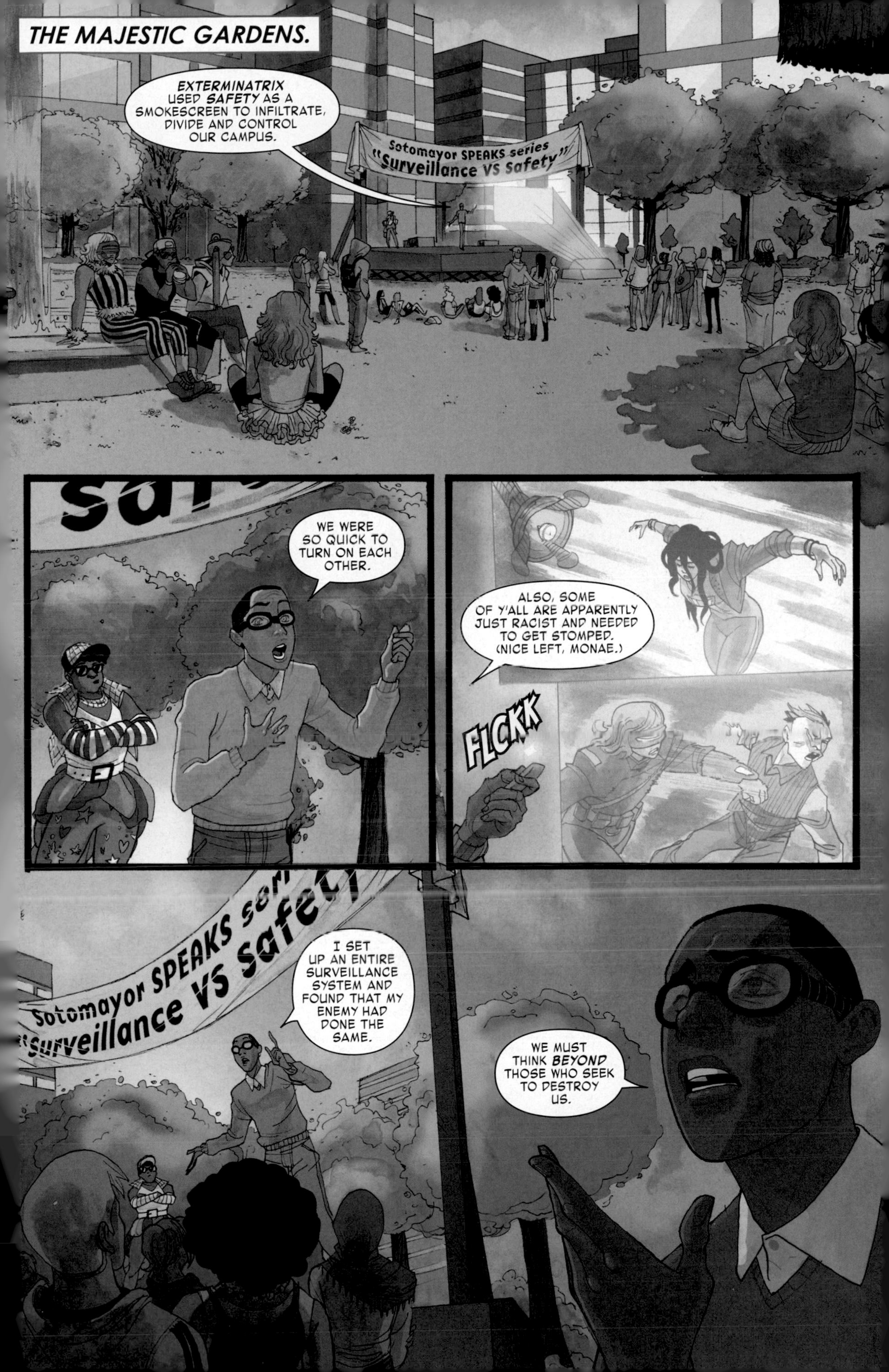
THE MAJESTIC GARDENS.
EXTERMINATRIX USED SAFETY AS A SMOKESCREEN TO INFILTRATE, DIVIDE AND CONTROL OUR CAMPUS.
Sotomayor SPEAKS series "Surveillance VS Safety"
WE WERE SO QUICK TO TURN ON EACH OTHER.
ALSO, SOME OF Y'ALL ARE APPARENTLY JUST RACIST AND NEEDED TO GET STOMPED. (NICE LEFT, MONAE.)
FLCKK
I SET UP AN ENTIRE SURVEILLANCE SYSTEM AND FOUND THAT MY ENEMY HAD DONE THE SAME.
WE MUST THINK BEYOND THOSE WHO SEEK TO DESTROY US.

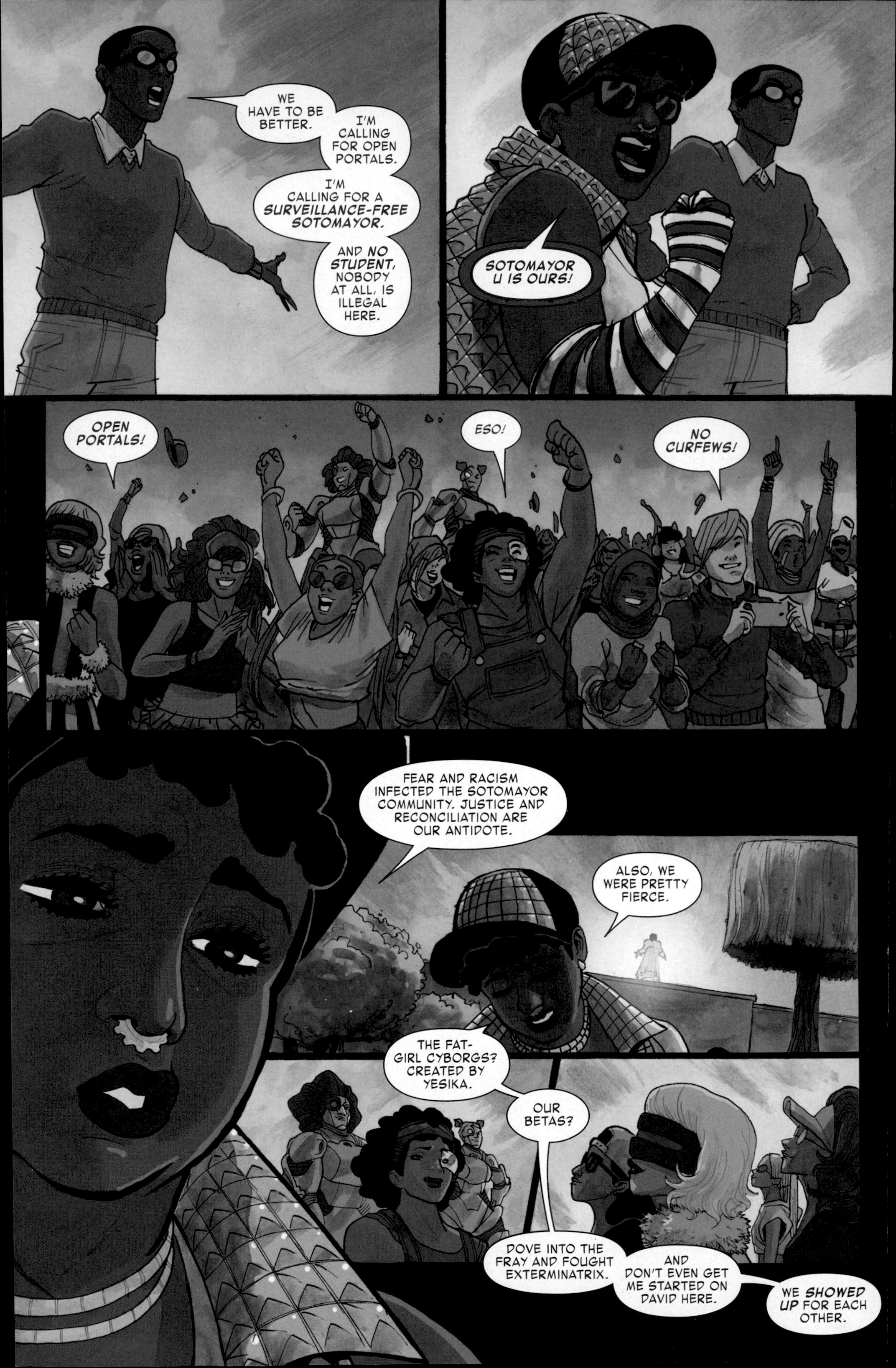
WE HAVE TO BE BETTER.
I'M CALLING FOR OPEN PORTALS.
I'M CALLING FOR A SURVEILLANCE-FREE SOTOMAYOR.
AND NO STUDENT, NOBODY AT ALL, IS ILLEGAL HERE.
SOTOMAYOR U IS OURS!
OPEN PORTALS!
ESO!
NO CURFEWS!
FEAR AND RACISM INFECTED THE SOTOMAYOR COMMUNITY. JUSTICE AND RECONCILIATION ARE OUR ANTIDOTE.
ALSO, WE WERE PRETTY FIERCE.
THE FAT-GIRL CYBORGS? CREATED BY YESIKA.
OUR BETAS?
DOVE INTO THE FRAY AND FOUGHT EXTERMINATRIX.
AND DON'T EVEN GET ME STARTED ON DAVID HERE.
WE SHOWED UP FOR EACH OTHER.

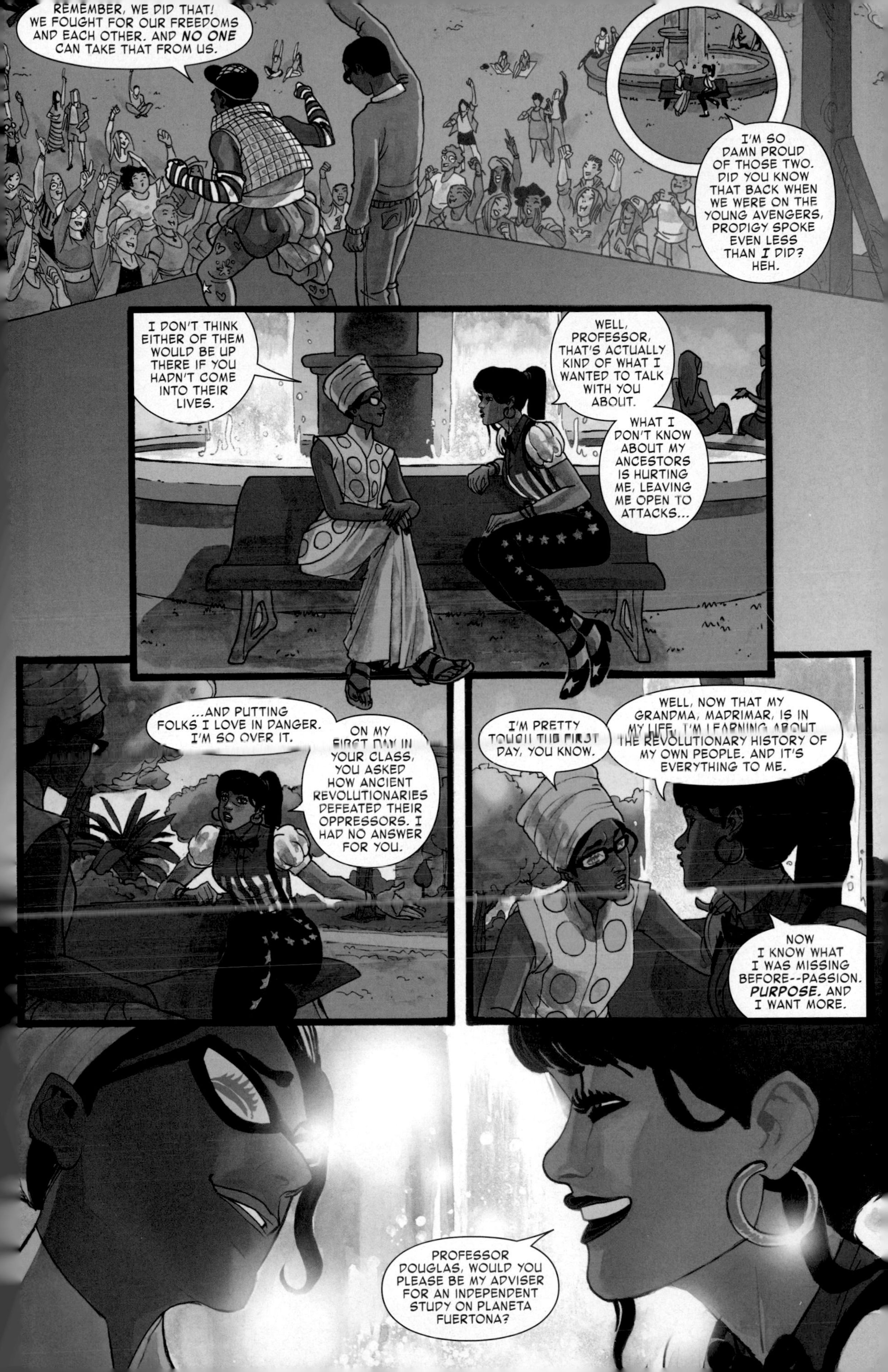

REMEMBER, WE DID THAT! WE FOUGHT FOR OUR FREEDOMS AND EACH OTHER. AND NO ONE CAN TAKE THAT FROM US.
I'M SO DAMN PROUD OF THOSE TWO. DID YOU KNOW THAT BACK WHEN WE WERE ON THE YOUNG AVENGERS, PRODIGY SPOKE EVEN LESS THAN I DID? HEH.
I DON'T THINK EITHER OF THEM WOULD BE UP THERE IF YOU HADN'T COME INTO THEIR LIVES.
WELL, PROFESSOR, THAT'S ACTUALLY KIND OF WHAT I WANTED TO TALK WITH YOU ABOUT.
WHAT I DON'T KNOW ABOUT MY ANCESTORS IS HURTING ME, LEAVING ME OPEN TO ATTACKS...
...AND PUTTING FOLKS I LOVE IN DANGER. I'M SO OVER IT.
ON MY FIRST DAY IN YOUR CLASS, YOU ASKED HOW ANCIENT REVOLUTIONARIES DEFEATED THEIR OPPRESSORS. I HAD NO ANSWER FOR YOU.
I'M PRETTY TOUGH THE FIRST DAY, YOU KNOW.
WELL, NOW THAT MY GRANDMA, MADRIMAR, IS IN MY LIFE, I'M LEARNING ABOUT THE REVOLUTIONARY HISTORY OF MY OWN PEOPLE. AND IT'S EVERYTHING TO ME.
NOW I KNOW WHAT I WAS MISSING BEFORE--PASSION. PURPOSE. AND I WANT MORE.
PROFESSOR DOUGLAS, WOULD YOU PLEASE BE MY ADVISER FOR AN INDEPENDENT STUDY ON PLANETA FUERTONA?

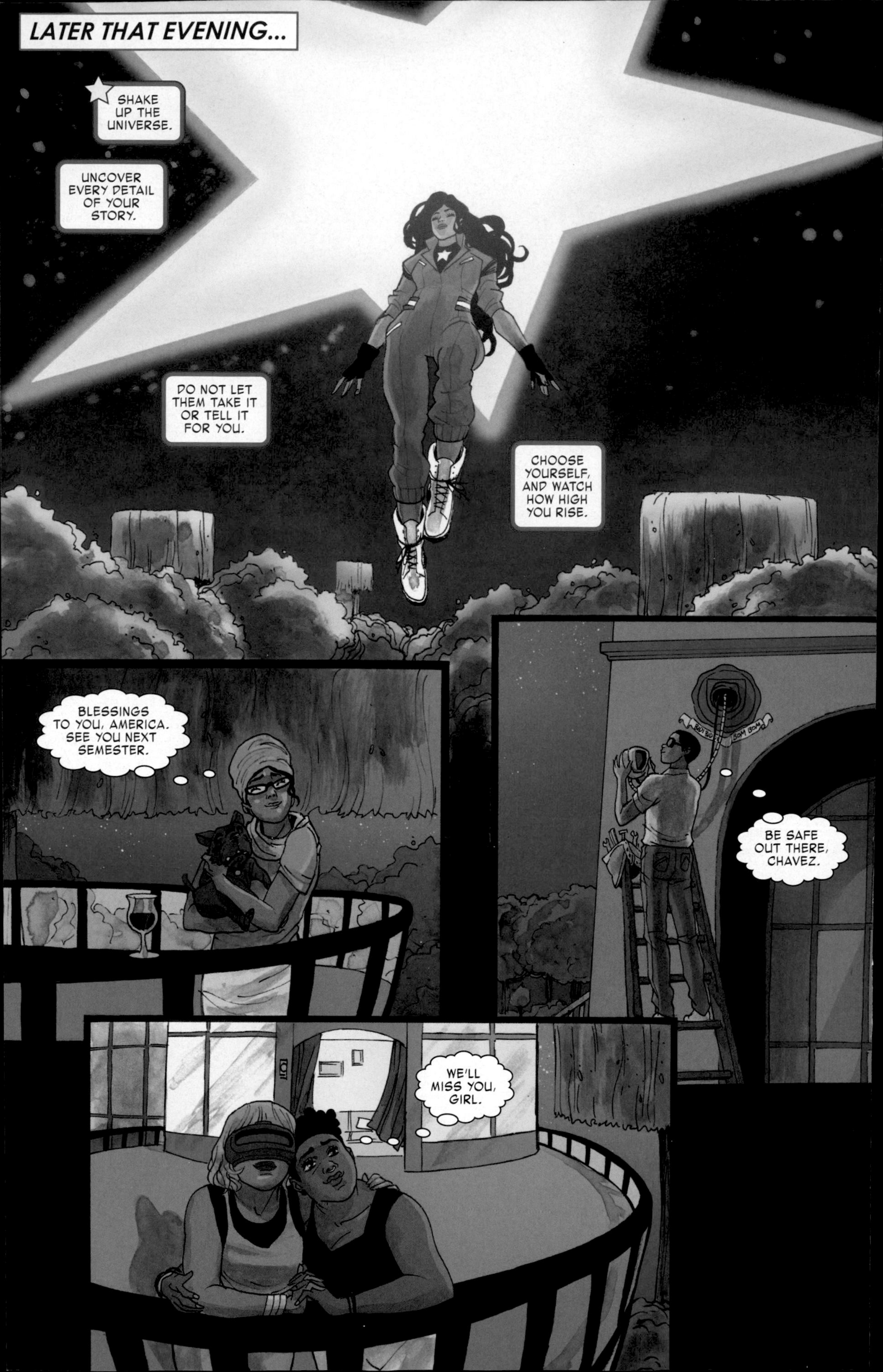
LATER THAT EVENING...
SHAKE UP THE UNIVERSE.
UNCOVER EVERY DETAIL OF YOUR STORY.
DO NOT LET THEM TAKE IT OR TELL IT FOR YOU.
CHOOSE YOURSELF, AND WATCH HOW HIGH YOU RISE.
BLESSINGS TO YOU, AMERICA. SEE YOU NEXT SEMESTER.
BE SAFE OUT THERE, CHAVEZ.
WE'LL MISS YOU, GIRL.

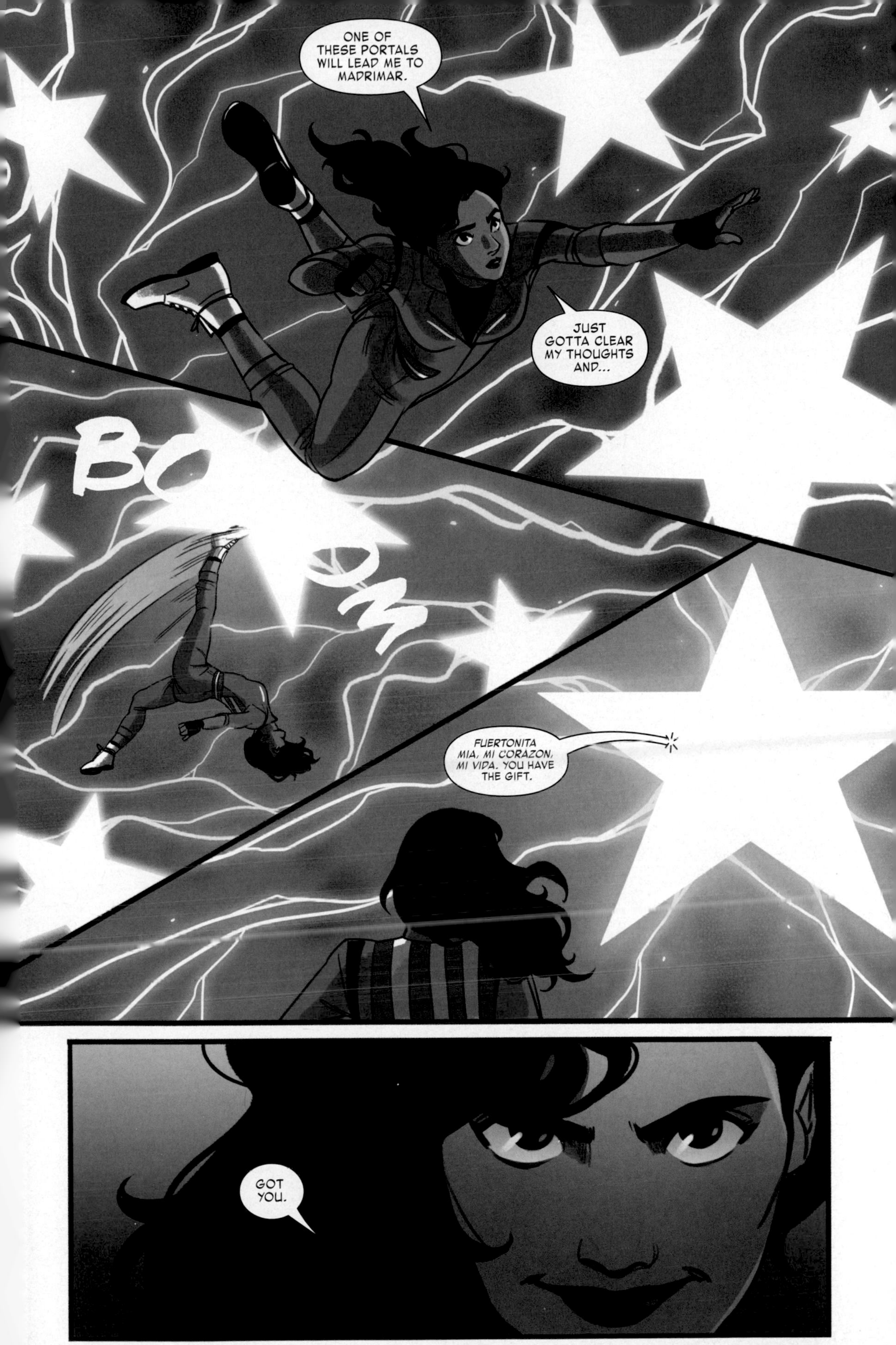

ONE OF THESE PORTALS WILL LEAD ME TO MADRIMAR.
JUST GOTTA CLEAR MY THOUGHTS AND...
FUERTONITA MIA, MI CORAZON, MI VIDA. YOU HAVE THE GIFT.
GOT YOU.

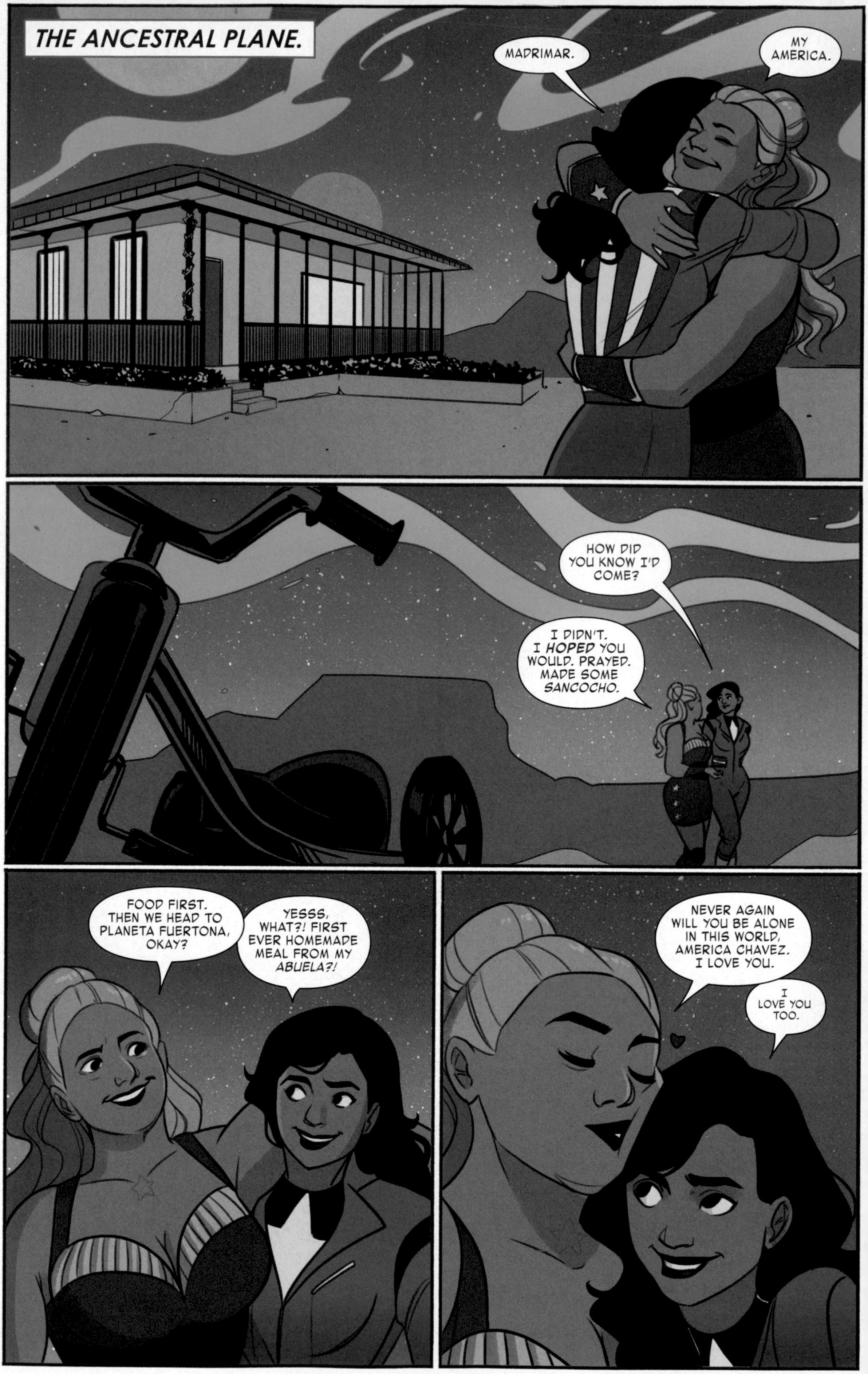
THE ANCESTRAL PLANE.
MADRIMAR.
MY AMERICA.
HOW DID YOU KNOW I'D COME?
I DIDN'T. I *HOPED* YOU WOULD. PRAYED. MADE SOME *SANCOCHO.*
FOOD FIRST. THEN WE HEAD TO PLANETA FUERTONA, OKAY?
YESSS, WHAT?! FIRST EVER HOMEMADE MEAL FROM MY *ABUELA?!*
NEVER AGAIN WILL YOU BE ALONE IN THIS WORLD, AMERICA CHAVEZ. I LOVE YOU.
I LOVE YOU TOO.

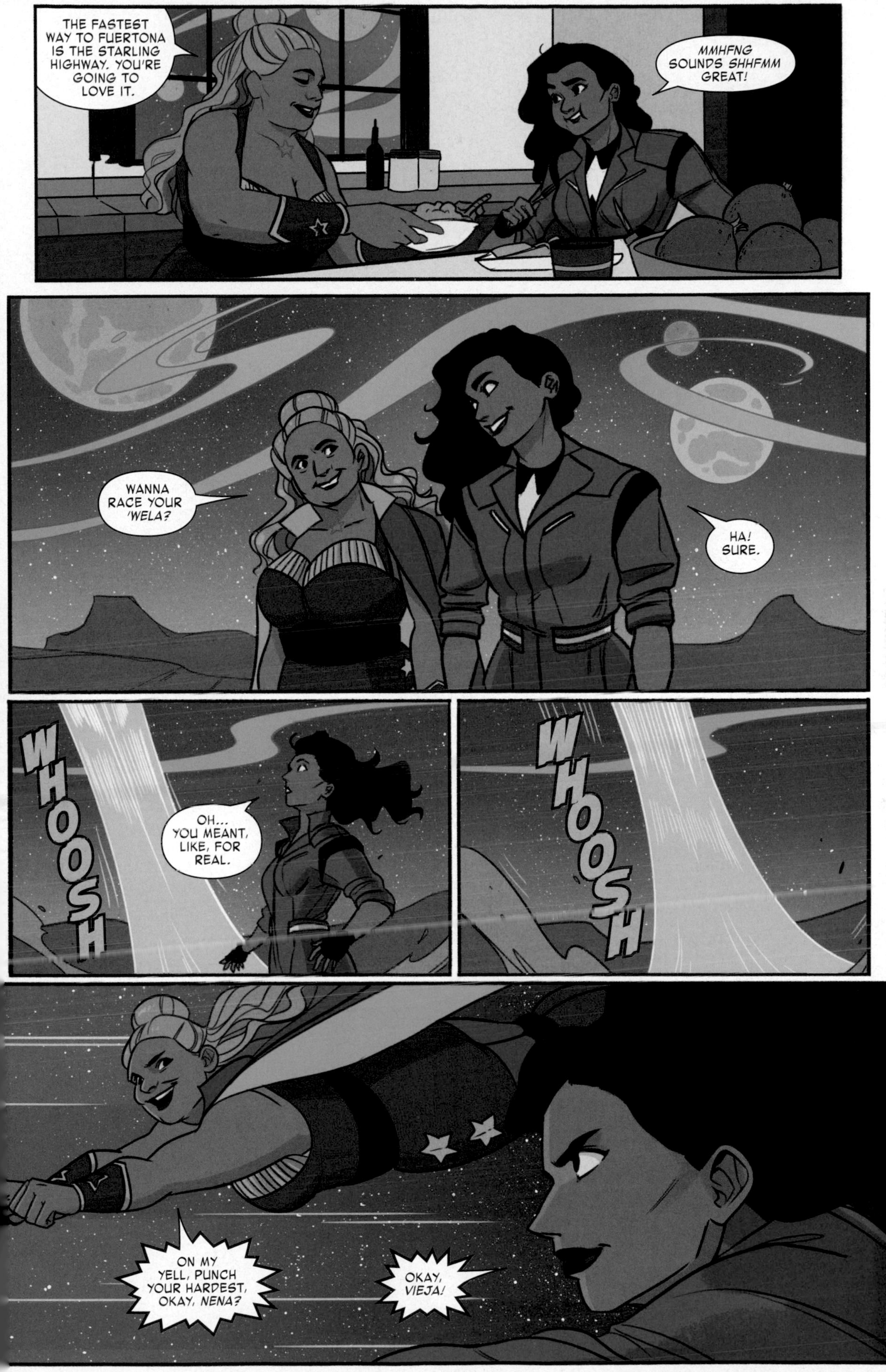
THE FASTEST WAY TO FUERTONA IS THE STARLING HIGHWAY. YOU'RE GOING TO LOVE IT.
MMHFNG SOUNDS SHHFMM GREAT!
WANNA RACE YOUR 'WELA?
HA! SURE.
WHOOSH
OH... YOU MEANT, LIKE, FOR REAL.
WHOOSH
ON MY YELL, PUNCH YOUR HARDEST, OKAY, NENA?
OKAY, VIEJA!

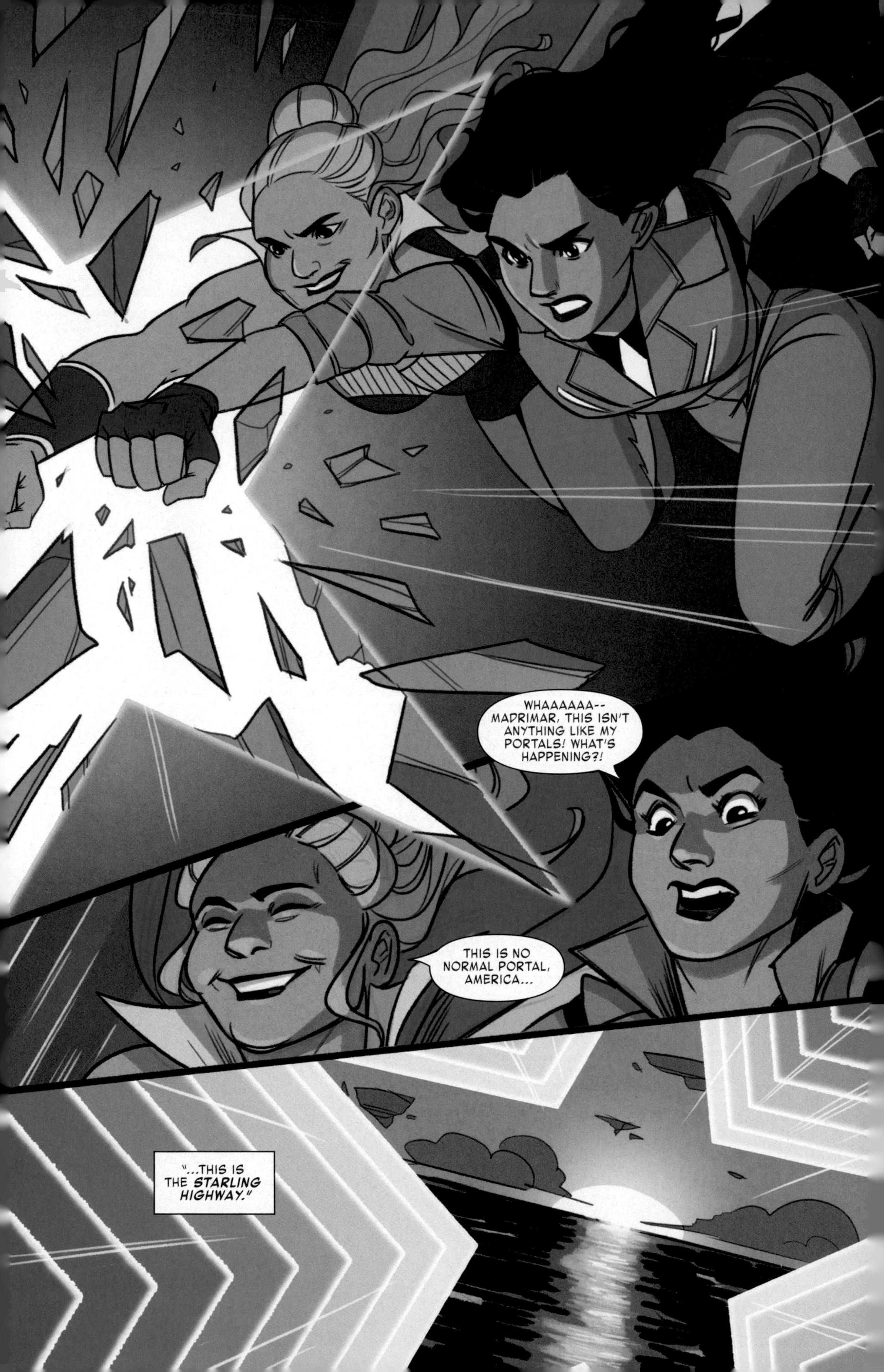
WHAAAAAA-- MADRIMAR, THIS ISN'T ANYTHING LIKE MY PORTALS! WHAT'S HAPPENING?!
THIS IS NO NORMAL PORTAL, AMERICA...
"...THIS IS THE STARLING HIGHWAY."

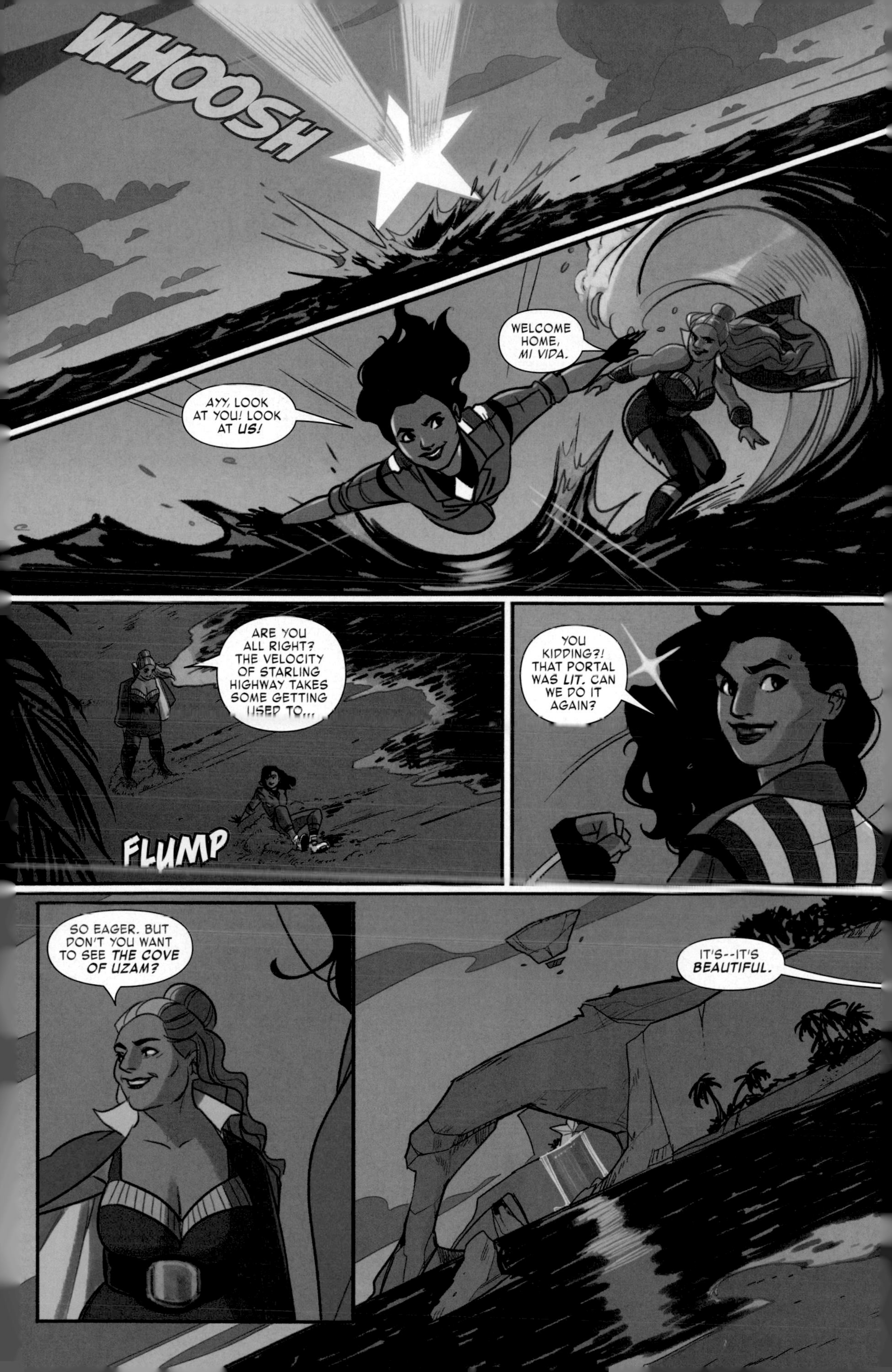
WHOOSH
WELCOME HOME, MI VIDA.
AYY, LOOK AT YOU! LOOK AT *US!*
ARE YOU ALL RIGHT? THE VELOCITY OF STARLING HIGHWAY TAKES SOME GETTING USED TO...
FLUMP
YOU KIDDING?! THAT PORTAL WAS *LIT.* CAN WE DO IT AGAIN?
SO EAGER. BUT DON'T YOU WANT TO SEE *THE COVE OF UZAM?*
IT'S--IT'S *BEAUTIFUL.*

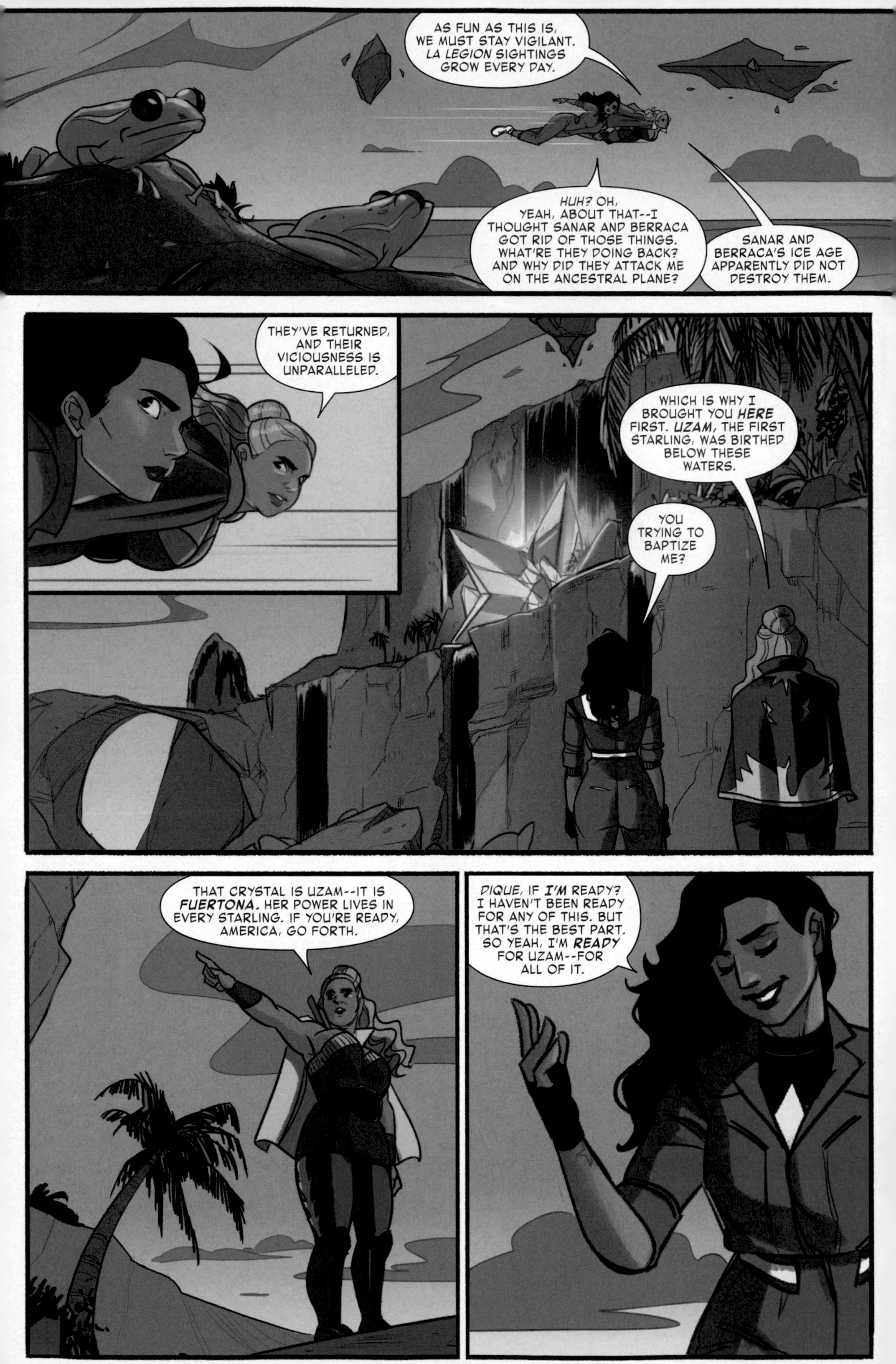
AS FUN AS THIS IS, WE MUST STAY VIGILANT. LA LEGION SIGHTINGS GROW EVERY DAY.
HUH? OH, YEAH, ABOUT THAT--I THOUGHT SANAR AND BERRACA GOT RID OF THOSE THINGS. WHAT'RE THEY DOING BACK? AND WHY DID THEY ATTACK ME ON THE ANCESTRAL PLANE?
SANAR AND BERRACA'S ICE AGE APPARENTLY DID NOT DESTROY THEM.
THEY'VE RETURNED, AND THEIR VICIOUSNESS IS UNPARALLELED.
WHICH IS WHY I BROUGHT YOU HERE FIRST. UZAM, THE FIRST STARLING, WAS BIRTHED BELOW THESE WATERS.
YOU TRYING TO BAPTIZE ME?
THAT CRYSTAL IS UZAM--IT IS FUERTONA. HER POWER LIVES IN EVERY STARLING. IF YOU'RE READY, AMERICA, GO FORTH.
DIQUE, IF I'M READY? I HAVEN'T BEEN READY FOR ANY OF THIS. BUT THAT'S THE BEST PART. SO YEAH, I'M READY FOR UZAM--FOR ALL OF IT.

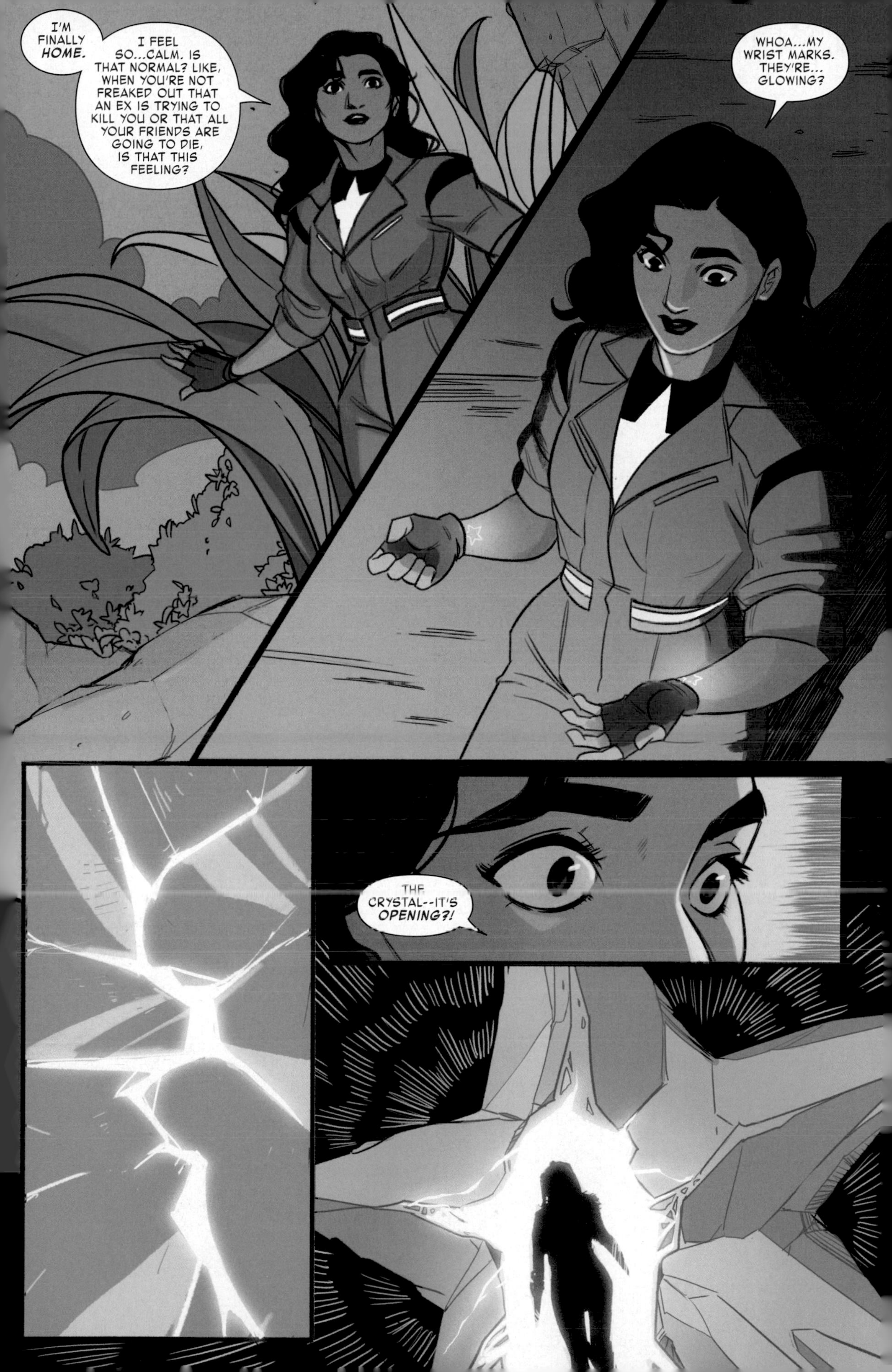
I'M FINALLY HOME.
I FEEL SO...CALM. IS THAT NORMAL? LIKE, WHEN YOU'RE NOT FREAKED OUT THAT AN EX IS TRYING TO KILL YOU OR THAT ALL YOUR FRIENDS ARE GOING TO DIE, IS THAT THIS FEELING?
WHOA...MY WRIST MARKS. THEY'RE... GLOWING?
THE CRYSTAL--IT'S OPENING?!

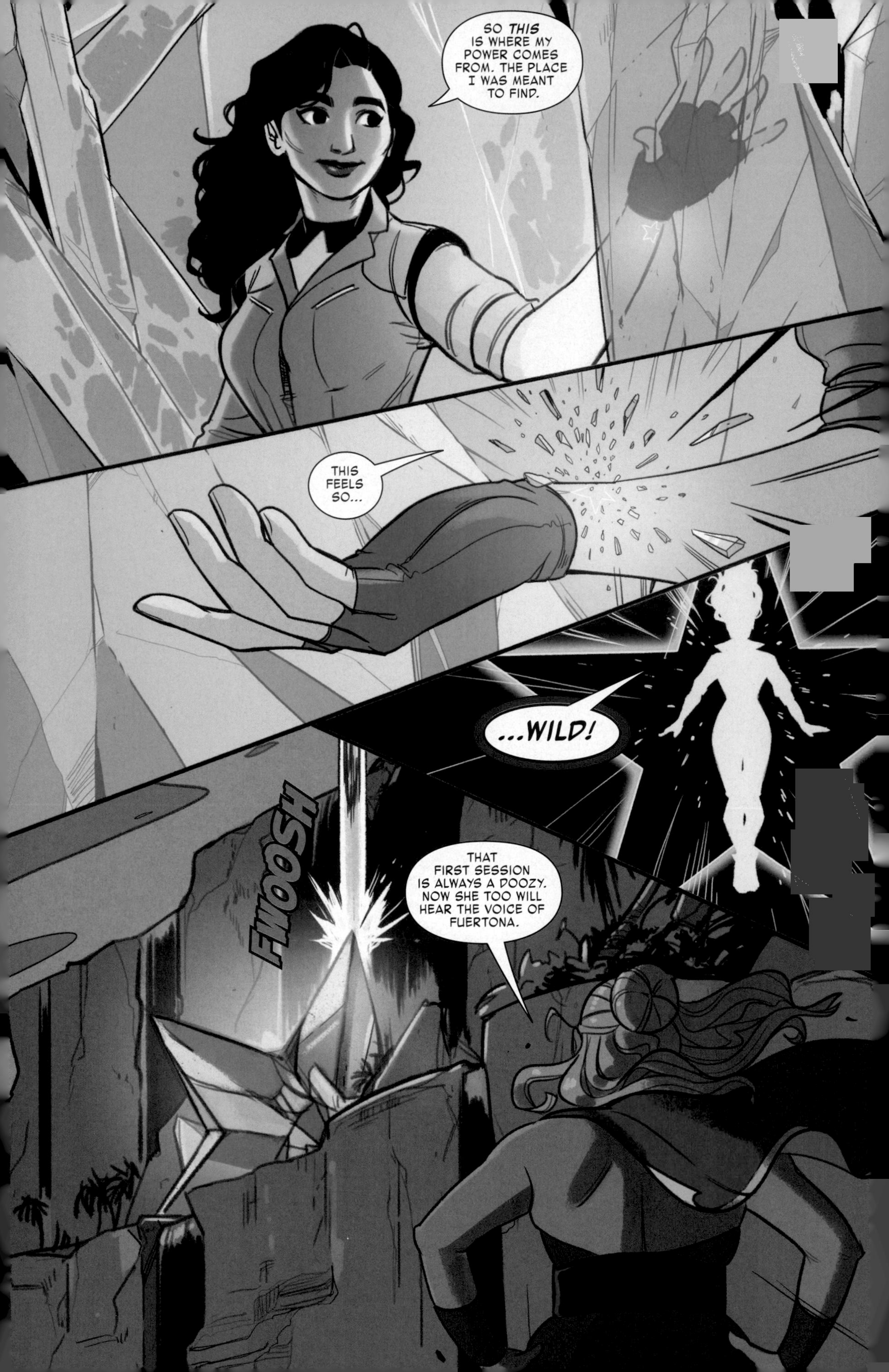
SO *THIS* IS WHERE MY POWER COMES FROM. THE PLACE I WAS MEANT TO FIND.
THIS FEELS SO...
...WILD!
FWOOSH
THAT FIRST SESSION IS ALWAYS A DOOZY. NOW SHE TOO WILL HEAR THE VOICE OF FUERTONA.

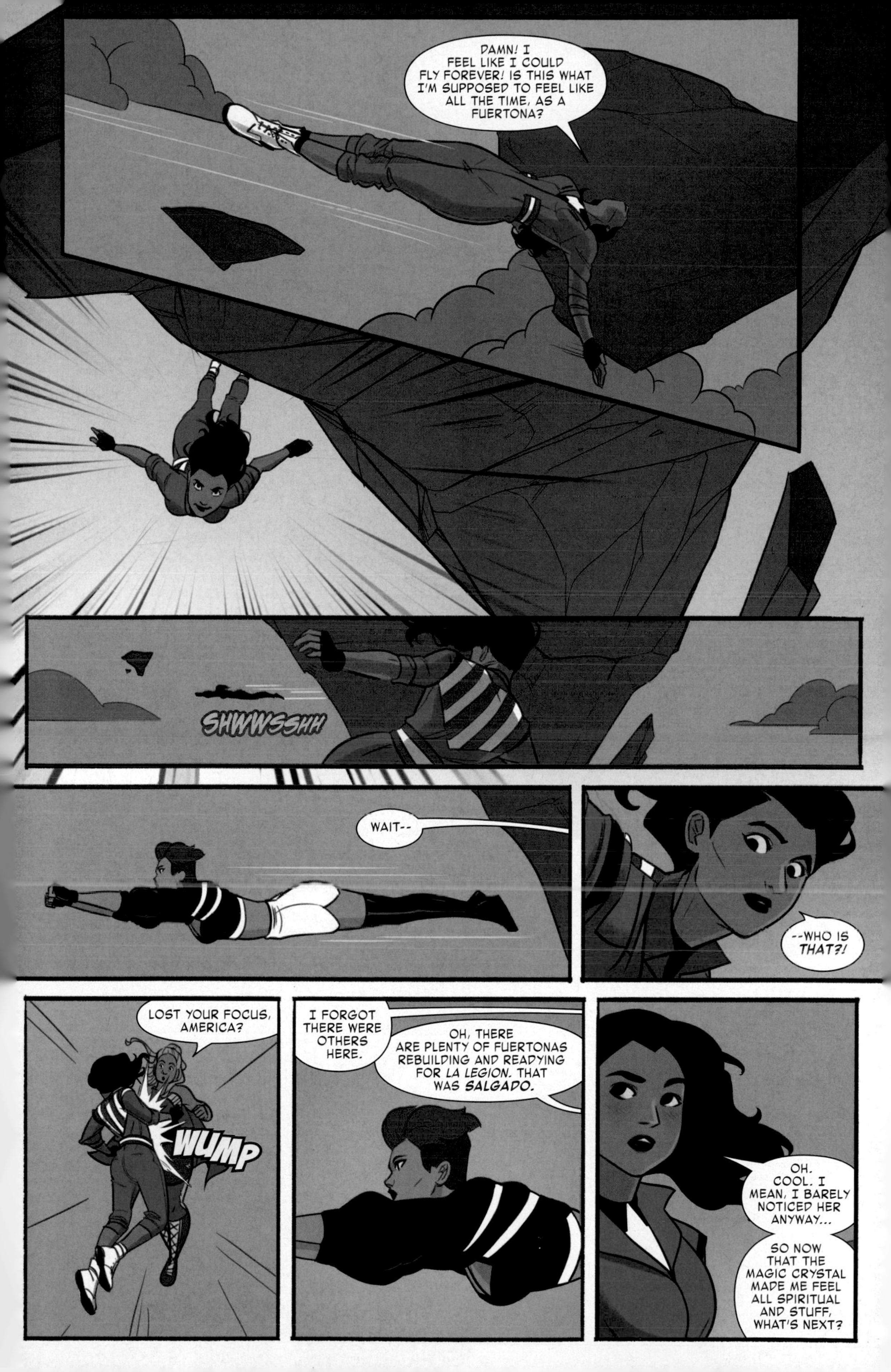
DAMN! I FEEL LIKE I COULD FLY FOREVER! IS THIS WHAT I'M SUPPOSED TO FEEL LIKE ALL THE TIME, AS A FUERTONA?
SHWWSSHH
WAIT--
--WHO IS THAT?!
LOST YOUR FOCUS, AMERICA?
WUMP
I FORGOT THERE WERE OTHERS HERE.
OH, THERE ARE PLENTY OF FUERTONAS REBUILDING AND READYING FOR LA LEGION. THAT WAS SALGADO.
OH. COOL. I MEAN, I BARELY NOTICED HER ANYWAY...
SO NOW THAT THE MAGIC CRYSTAL MADE ME FEEL ALL SPIRITUAL AND STUFF, WHAT'S NEXT?

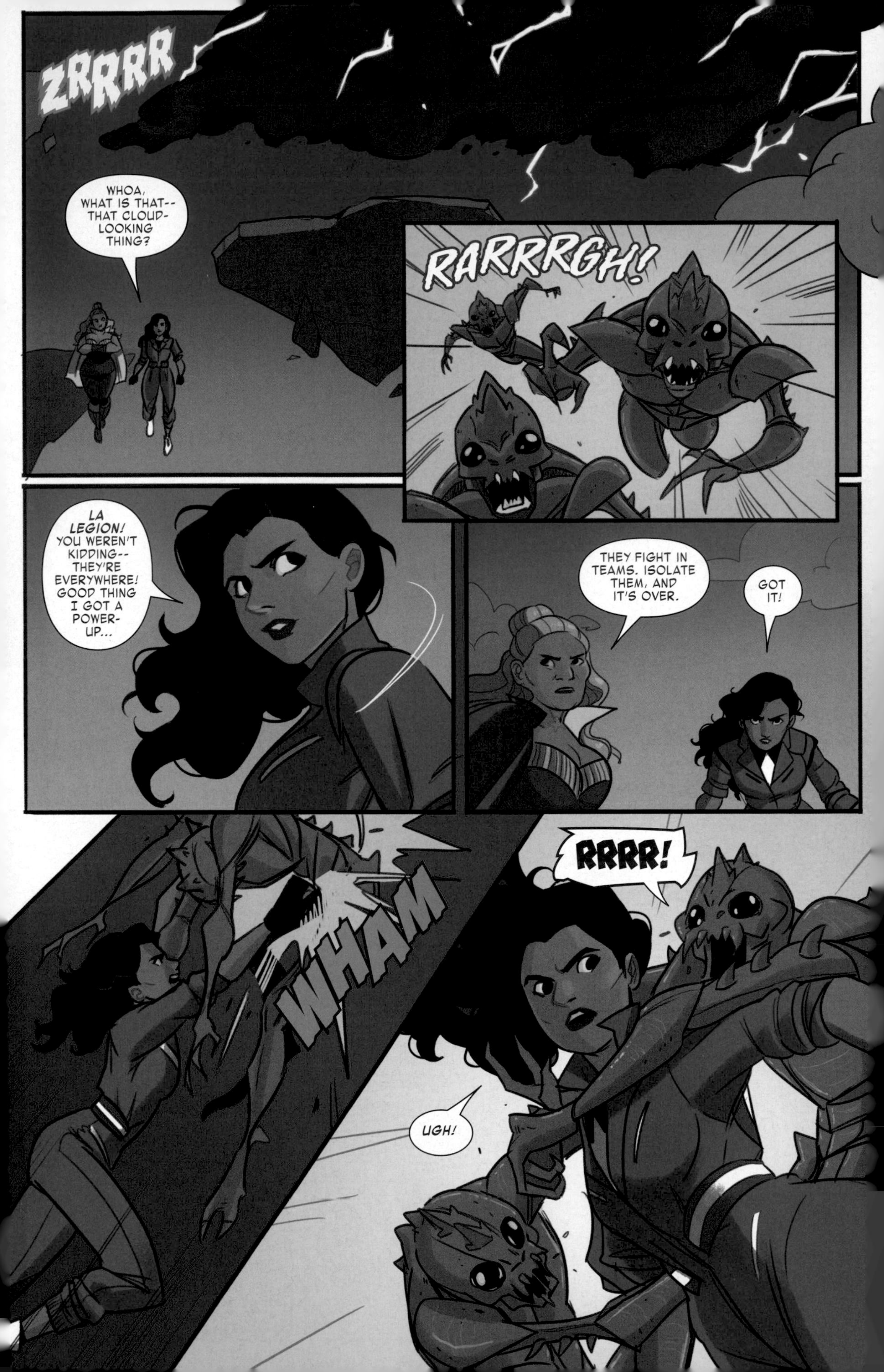
ZRRRR
WHOA, WHAT IS THAT-- THAT CLOUD-LOOKING THING?
RARRRGH!
LA LEGION! YOU WEREN'T KIDDING-- THEY'RE EVERYWHERE! GOOD THING I GOT A POWER-UP...
THEY FIGHT IN TEAMS. ISOLATE THEM, AND IT'S OVER.
GOT IT!
WHAM
RRRR!
UGH!

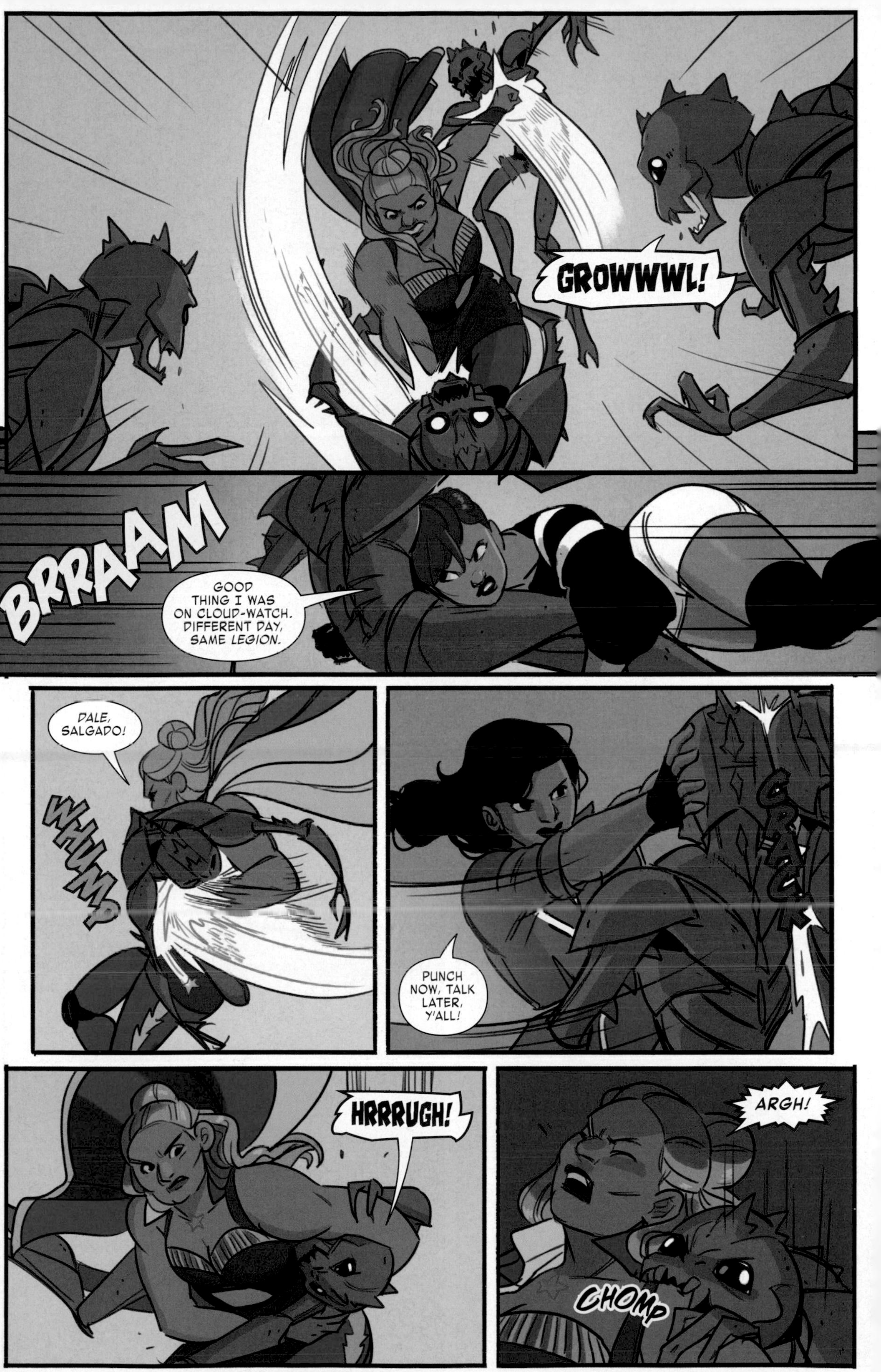
GROWWWL!
BRRAAM
GOOD THING I WAS ON CLOUD-WATCH. DIFFERENT DAY, SAME LEGION.
DALE, SALGADO!
WHUMP
CRACK
PUNCH NOW, TALK LATER, Y'ALL!
HRRRUGH!
ARGH!
CHOMP

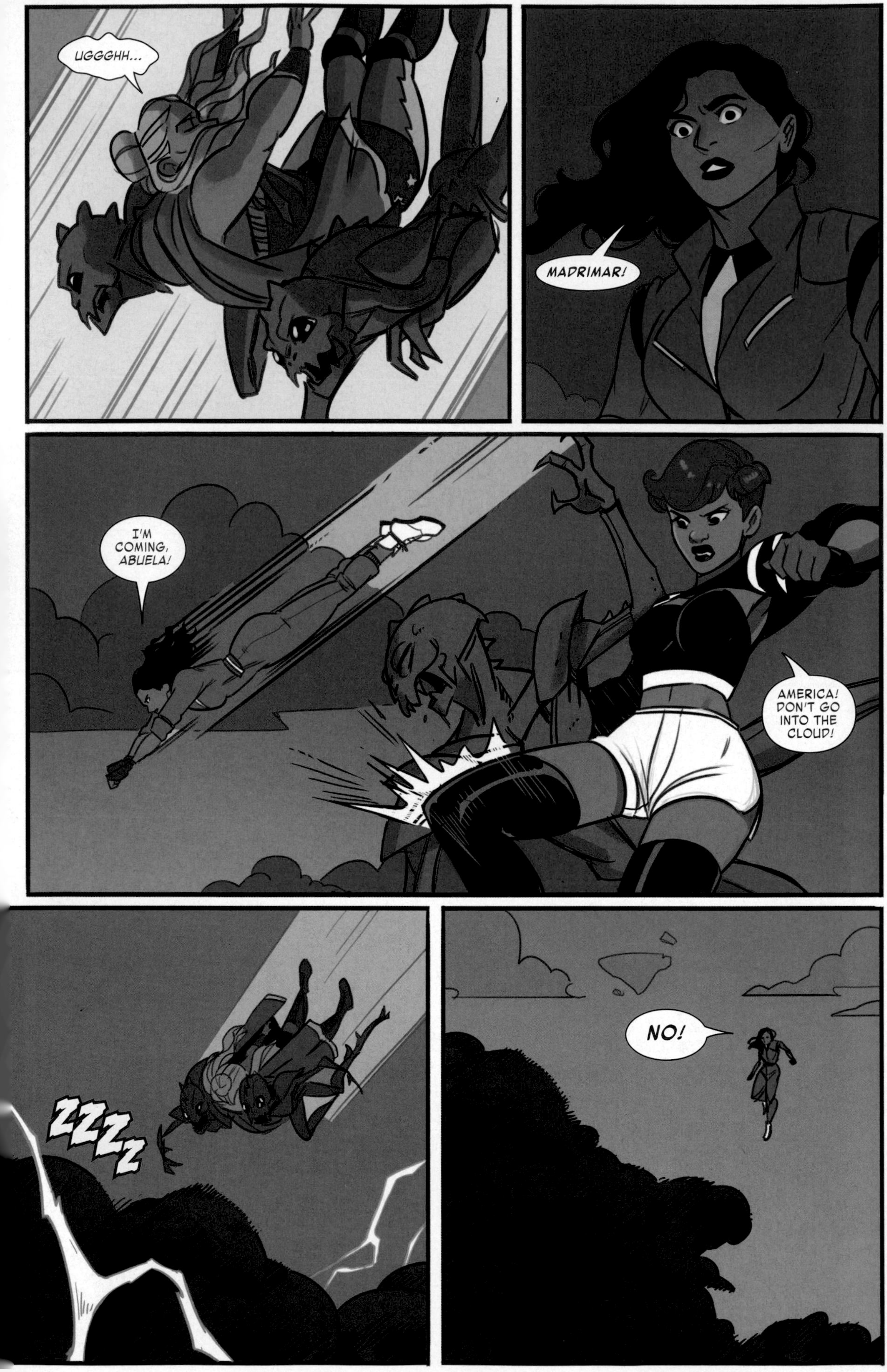
UGGGHH...
MADRIMAR!
I'M COMING, ABUELA!
AMERICA! DON'T GO INTO THE CLOUD!
ZZZZ
NO!

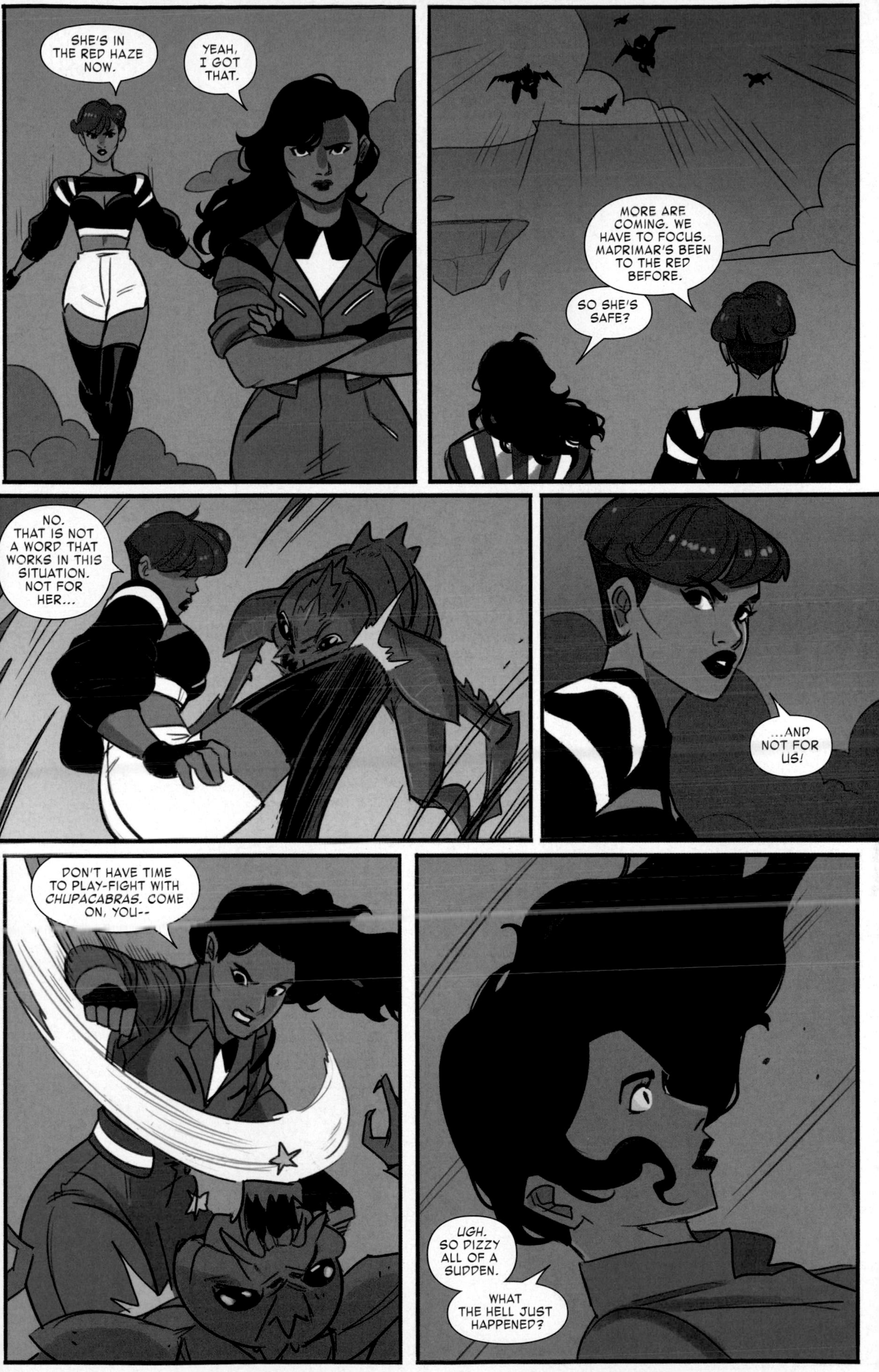
SHE'S IN THE RED HAZE NOW.
YEAH, I GOT THAT.
MORE ARE COMING. WE HAVE TO FOCUS. MADRIMAR'S BEEN TO THE RED BEFORE.
SO SHE'S SAFE?
NO. THAT IS NOT A WORD THAT WORKS IN THIS SITUATION. NOT FOR HER...
...AND NOT FOR US!
DON'T HAVE TIME TO PLAY-FIGHT WITH *CHUPACABRAS.* COME ON, YOU--
UGH. SO DIZZY ALL OF A SUDDEN.
WHAT THE HELL JUST HAPPENED?

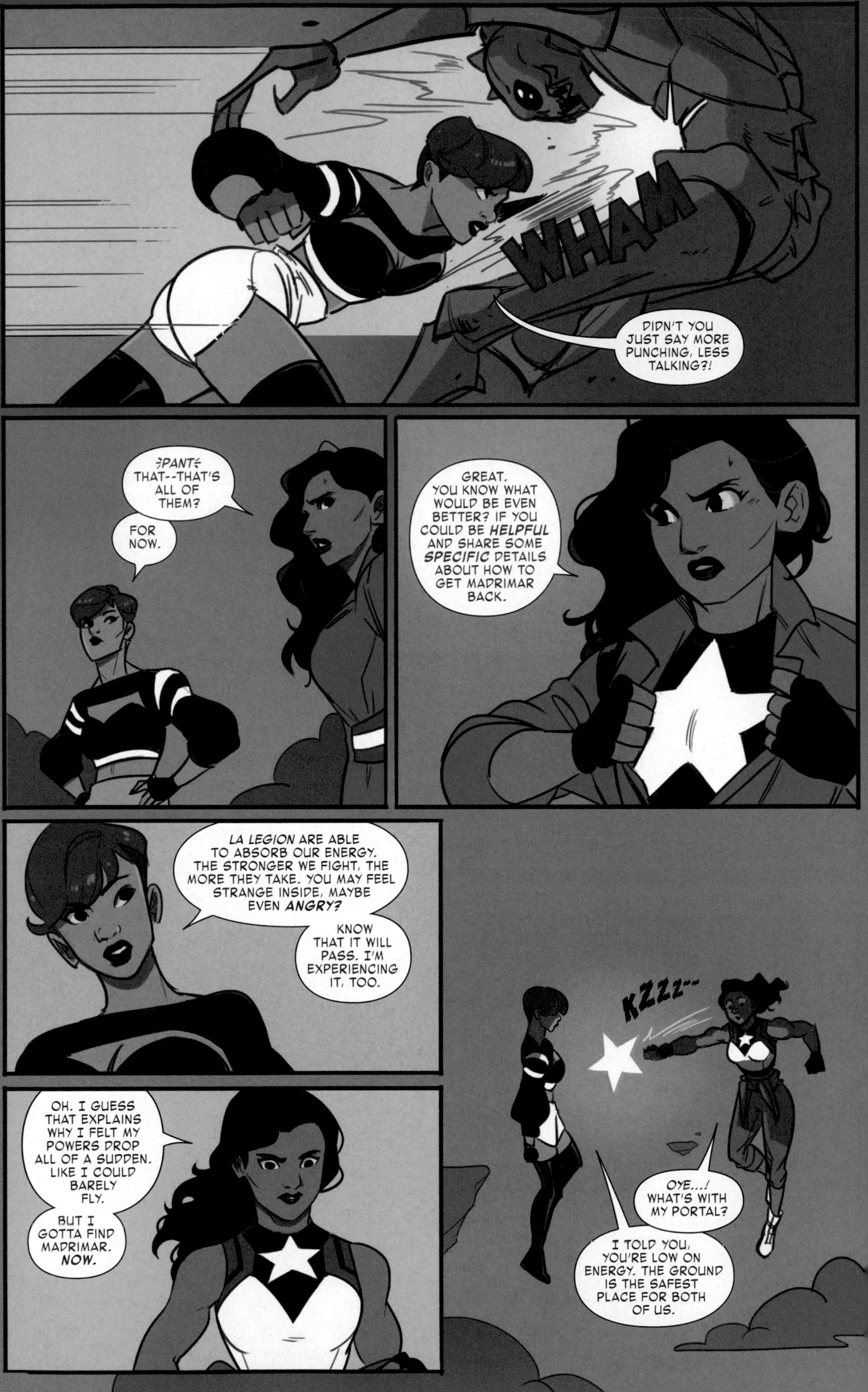
WHAM
DIDN'T YOU JUST SAY MORE PUNCHING, LESS TALKING?!
PANT THAT--THAT'S ALL OF THEM?
FOR NOW.
GREAT. YOU KNOW WHAT WOULD BE EVEN BETTER? IF YOU COULD BE *HELPFUL* AND SHARE SOME *SPECIFIC* DETAILS ABOUT HOW TO GET MADRIMAR BACK.
LA LEGION ARE ABLE TO ABSORB OUR ENERGY. THE STRONGER WE FIGHT, THE MORE THEY TAKE. YOU MAY FEEL STRANGE INSIDE, MAYBE EVEN *ANGRY?*
KNOW THAT IT WILL PASS. I'M EXPERIENCING IT, TOO.
OH. I GUESS THAT EXPLAINS WHY I FELT MY POWERS DROP ALL OF A SUDDEN. LIKE I COULD BARELY FLY.
BUT I GOTTA FIND MADRIMAR. *NOW.*
KZZZ--
OYE...! WHAT'S WITH MY PORTAL?
I TOLD YOU, YOU'RE LOW ON ENERGY. THE GROUND IS THE SAFEST PLACE FOR BOTH OF US.

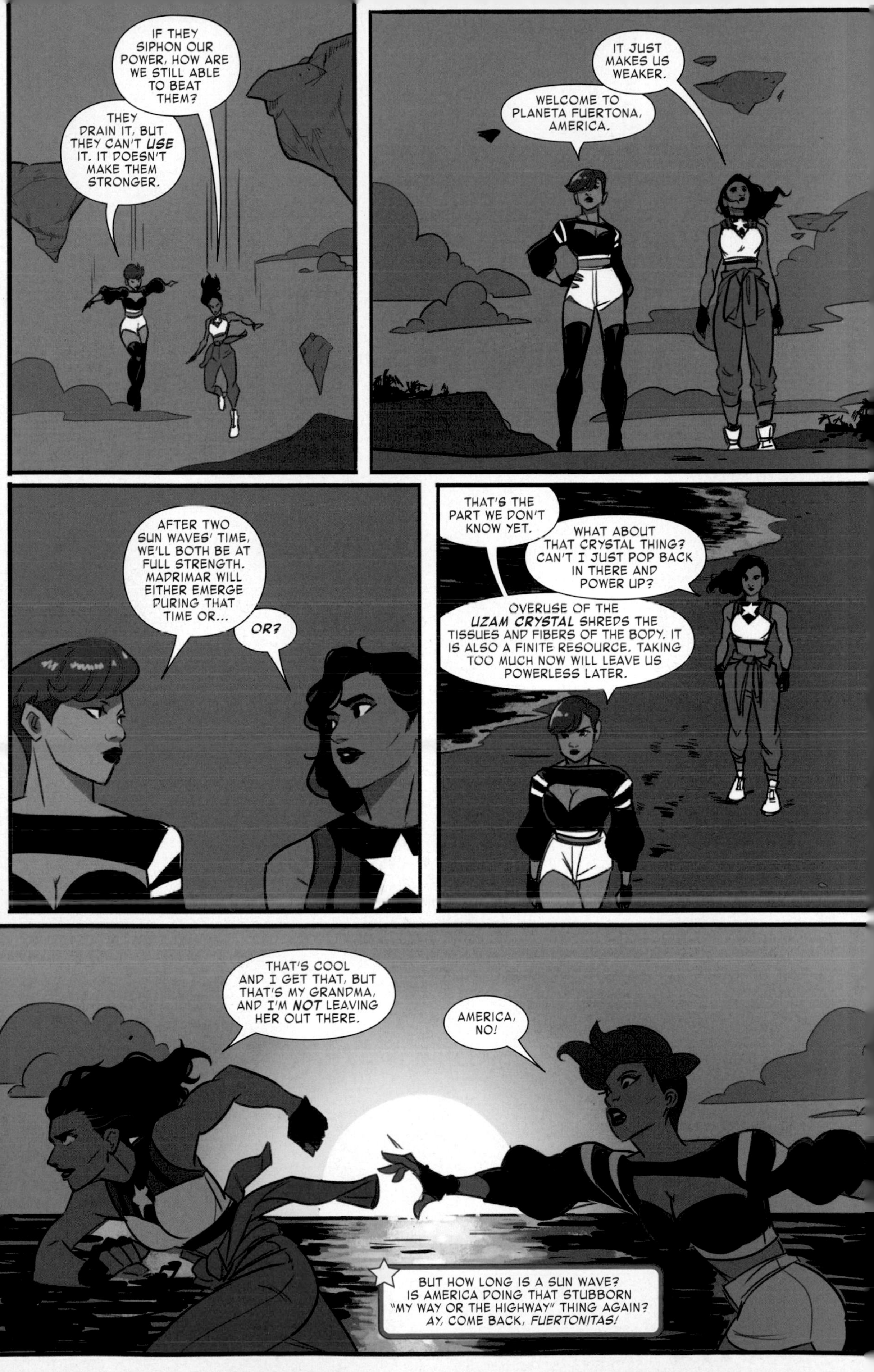

IF THEY SIPHON OUR POWER, HOW ARE WE STILL ABLE TO BEAT THEM?
THEY DRAIN IT, BUT THEY CAN'T *USE* IT. IT DOESN'T MAKE THEM STRONGER.
IT JUST MAKES US WEAKER.
WELCOME TO PLANETA FUERTONA, AMERICA.
AFTER TWO SUN WAVES' TIME, WE'LL BOTH BE AT FULL STRENGTH. MADRIMAR WILL EITHER EMERGE DURING THAT TIME OR...
OR?
THAT'S THE PART WE DON'T KNOW YET.
WHAT ABOUT THAT CRYSTAL THING? CAN'T I JUST POP BACK IN THERE AND POWER UP?
OVERUSE OF THE *UZAM CRYSTAL* SHREDS THE TISSUES AND FIBERS OF THE BODY. IT IS ALSO A FINITE RESOURCE. TAKING TOO MUCH NOW WILL LEAVE US POWERLESS LATER.
THAT'S COOL AND I GET THAT, BUT THAT'S MY GRANDMA, AND I'M *NOT* LEAVING HER OUT THERE.
AMERICA, NO!
BUT HOW LONG IS A SUN WAVE? IS AMERICA DOING THAT STUBBORN "MY WAY OR THE HIGHWAY" THING AGAIN? AY, COME BACK, *FUERTONITAS!*

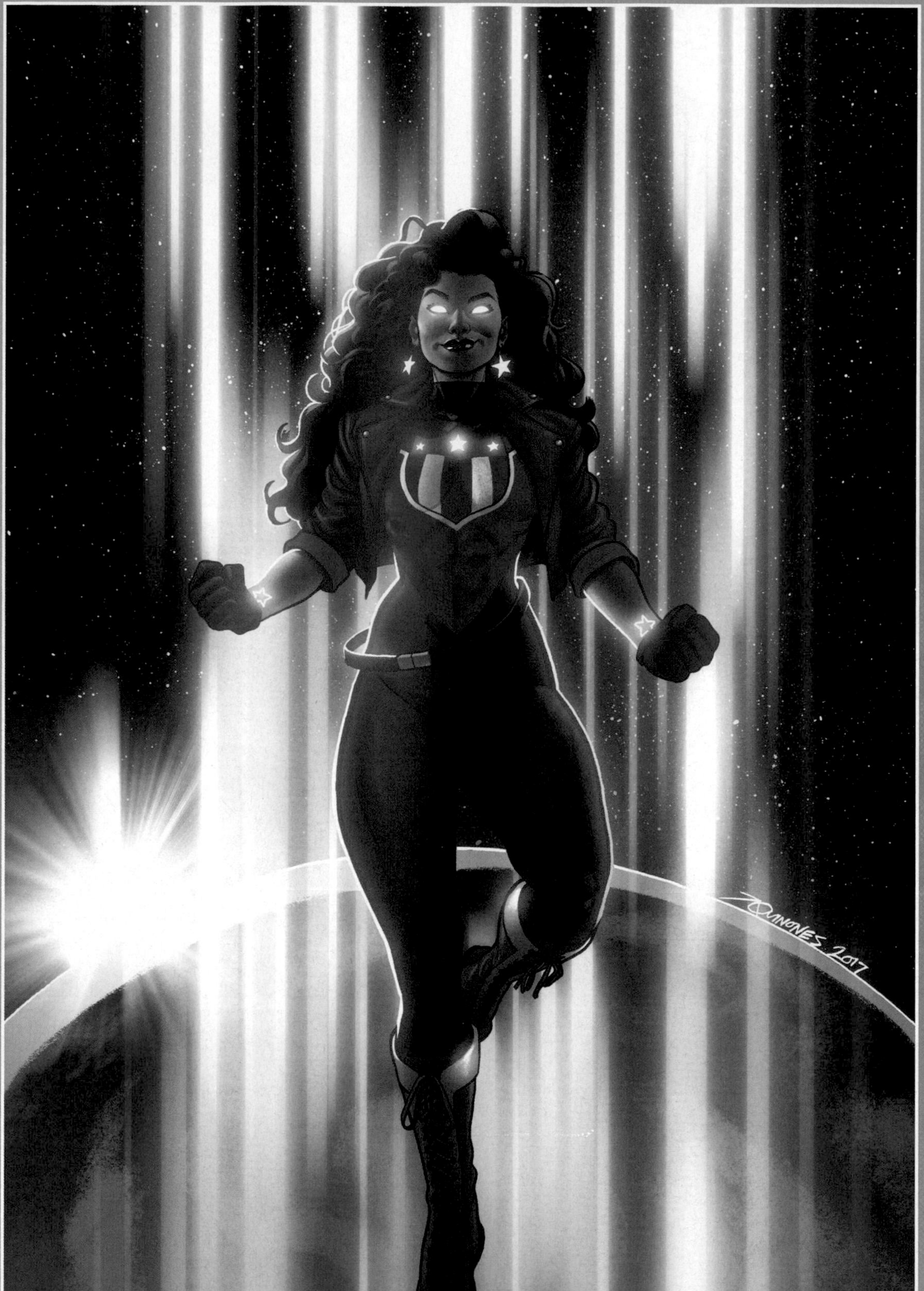
QUINONES 2017

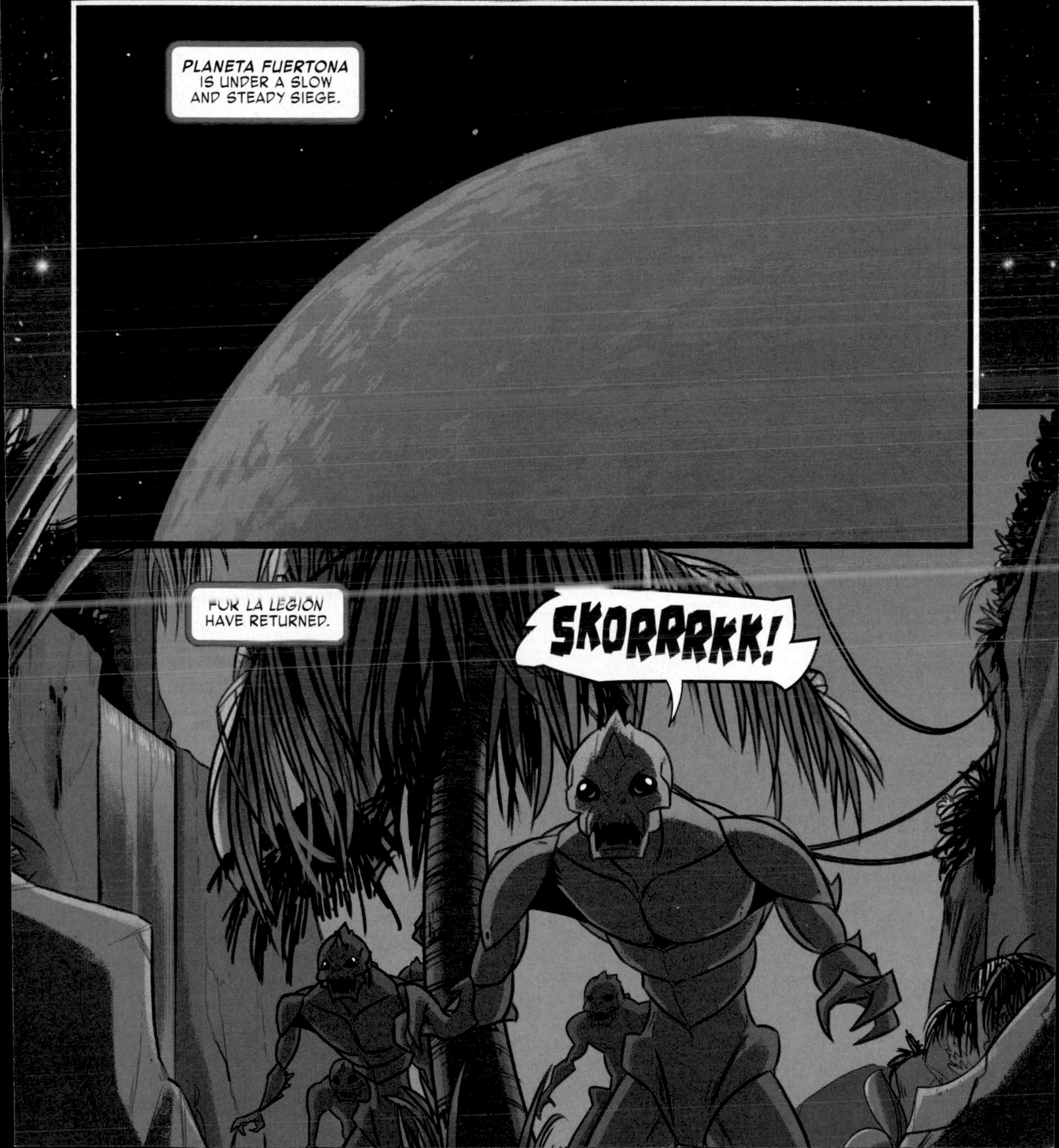
PLANETA FUERTONA IS UNDER A SLOW AND STEADY SIEGE.
FUR LA LEGION HAVE RETURNED.
SKORRRKK!

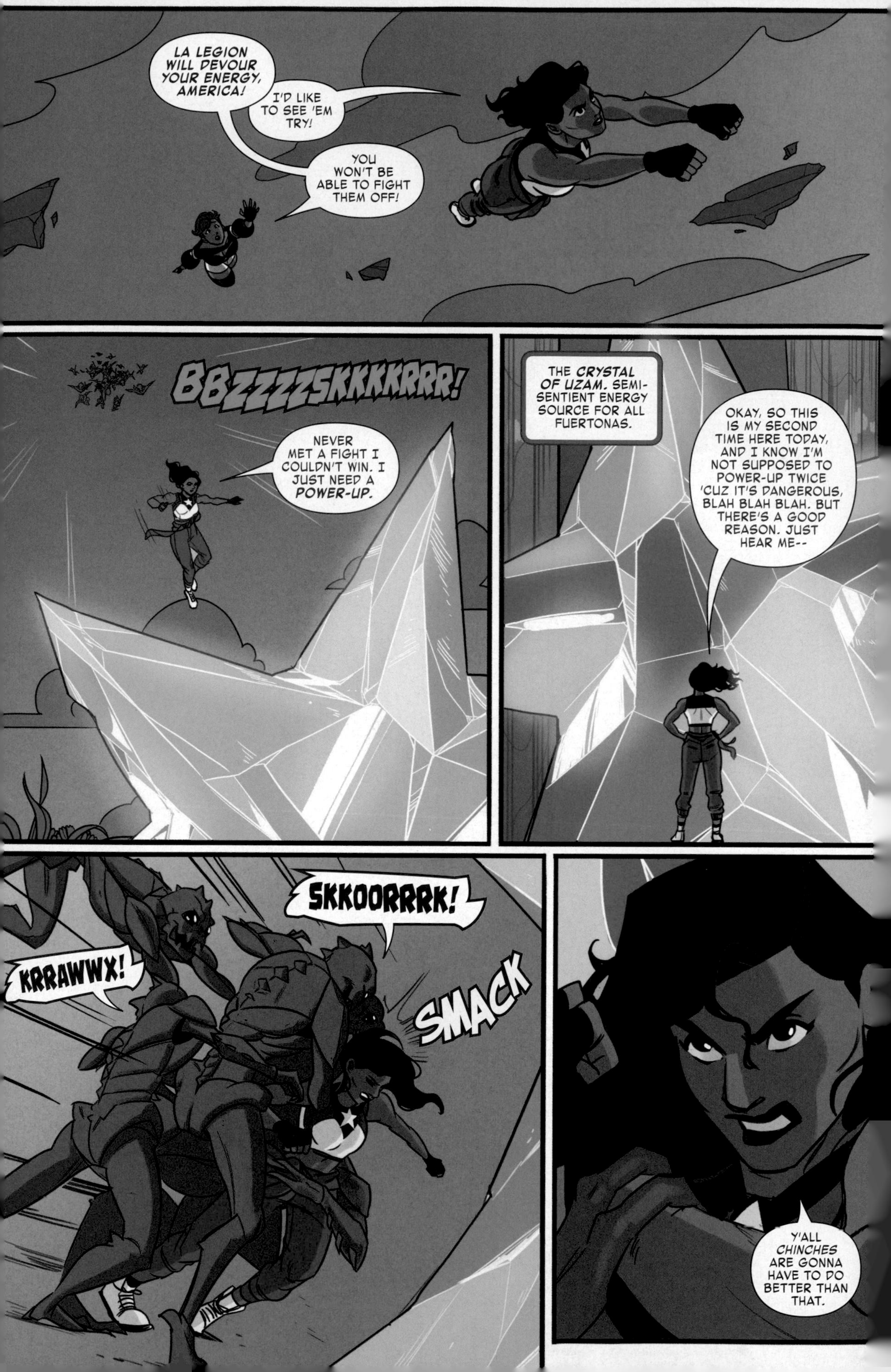
LA LEGION WILL DEVOUR YOUR ENERGY, AMERICA!
I'D LIKE TO SEE 'EM TRY!
YOU WON'T BE ABLE TO FIGHT THEM OFF!
BBZZZZSKKKKRRR!
NEVER MET A FIGHT I COULDN'T WIN. I JUST NEED A POWER-UP.
THE CRYSTAL OF UZAM. SEMI-SENTIENT ENERGY SOURCE FOR ALL FUERTONAS.
OKAY, SO THIS IS MY SECOND TIME HERE TODAY, AND I KNOW I'M NOT SUPPOSED TO POWER-UP TWICE 'CUZ IT'S DANGEROUS, BLAH BLAH BLAH. BUT THERE'S A GOOD REASON. JUST HEAR ME--
SKKOORRRK!
KRRAWWX!
SMACK
Y'ALL CHINCHES ARE GONNA HAVE TO DO BETTER THAN THAT.

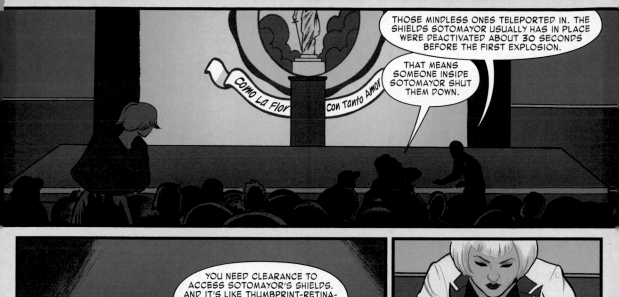

THOSE MINDLESS ONES TELEPORTED IN. THE SHIELDS SOTOMAYOR USUALLY HAS IN PLACE WERE DEACTIVATED ABOUT 30 SECONDS BEFORE THE FIRST EXPLOSION.

THAT MEANS SOMEONE INSIDE SOTOMAYOR SHUT THEM DOWN.

Como La Flor *Con Tanto Amor*

YOU NEED CLEARANCE TO ACCESS SOTOMAYOR'S SHIELDS. AND IT'S LIKE THUMBPRINT-RETINA-SCAN-DNA-SWAB-LEVEL TYPE OF CLEARANCE, SO THEIR TECH PLAN MUST BE SUPER TIGHT.

WE GOTTA FIND PROFESSOR DOUGLAS, TOO. IF SHE DOESN'T SHOW UP FOR THIS, THERE'S GONNA BE A PROBLEM.

AHEM.

STUDENTS OF SOTOMAYOR UNIVERSITY, THIS IS NOT HOW I WAS SUPPOSED TO MEET ALL OF YOU, BUT GIVEN THE CIRCUMSTANCES, IT'S BETTER WE MOVE FAST. I'M DR. BILLIE BRIGHTLY, NEWLY APPOINTED DEAN OF STUDENTS.

TONIGHT'S ATTACK HIGHLIGHTS SOTOMAYOR'S INABILITY TO KEEP ITS STUDENTS SAFE. I'M HERE TO CHANGE THAT.

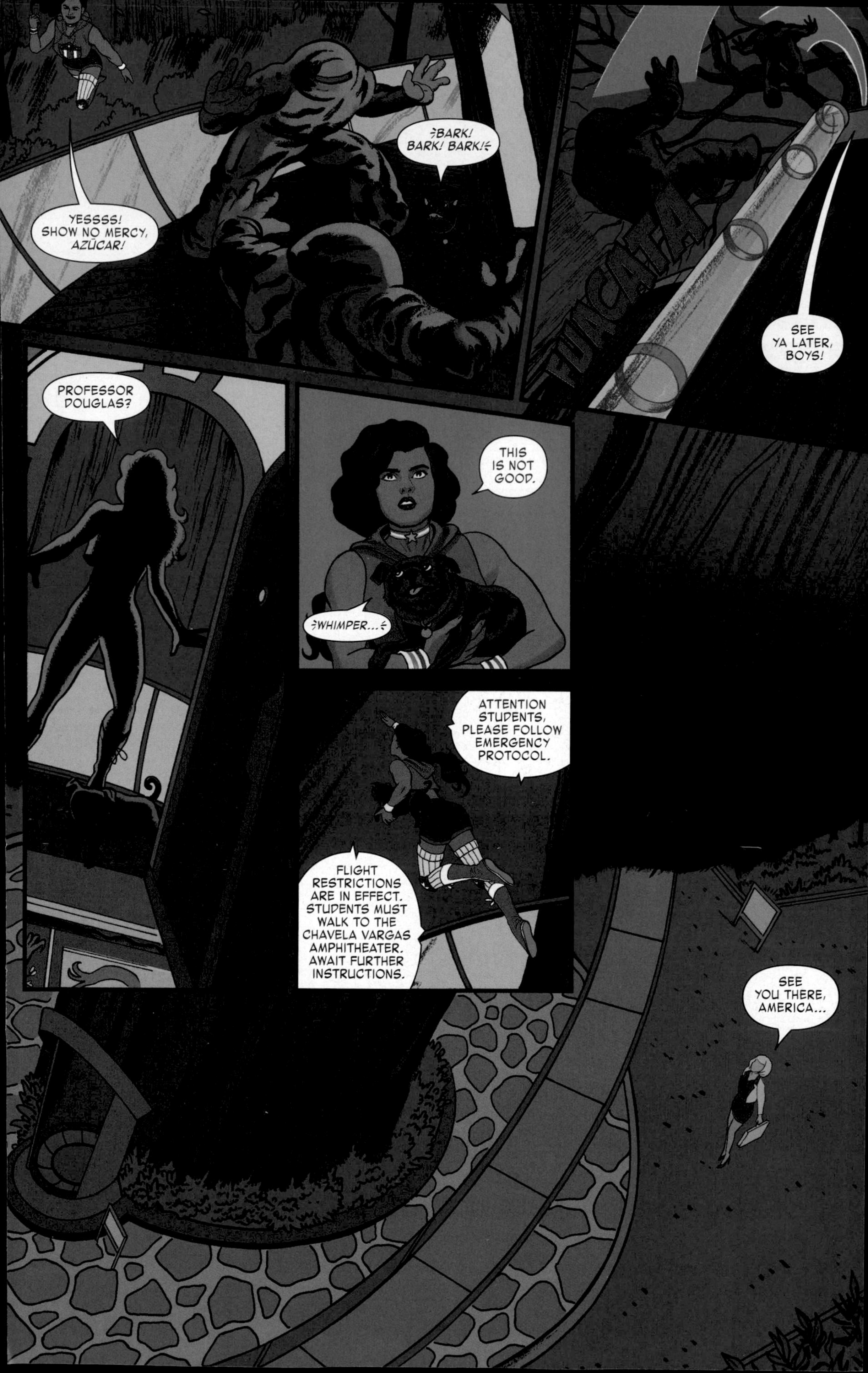
YESSSS! SHOW NO MERCY, AZÚCAR!
BARK! BARK! BARK!
FUNCATA
SEE YA LATER, BOYS!
PROFESSOR DOUGLAS?
THIS IS NOT GOOD.
WHIMPER...
ATTENTION STUDENTS, PLEASE FOLLOW EMERGENCY PROTOCOL.
FLIGHT RESTRICTIONS ARE IN EFFECT. STUDENTS MUST WALK TO THE CHAVELA VARGAS AMPHITHEATER. AWAIT FURTHER INSTRUCTIONS.
SEE YOU THERE, AMERICA...

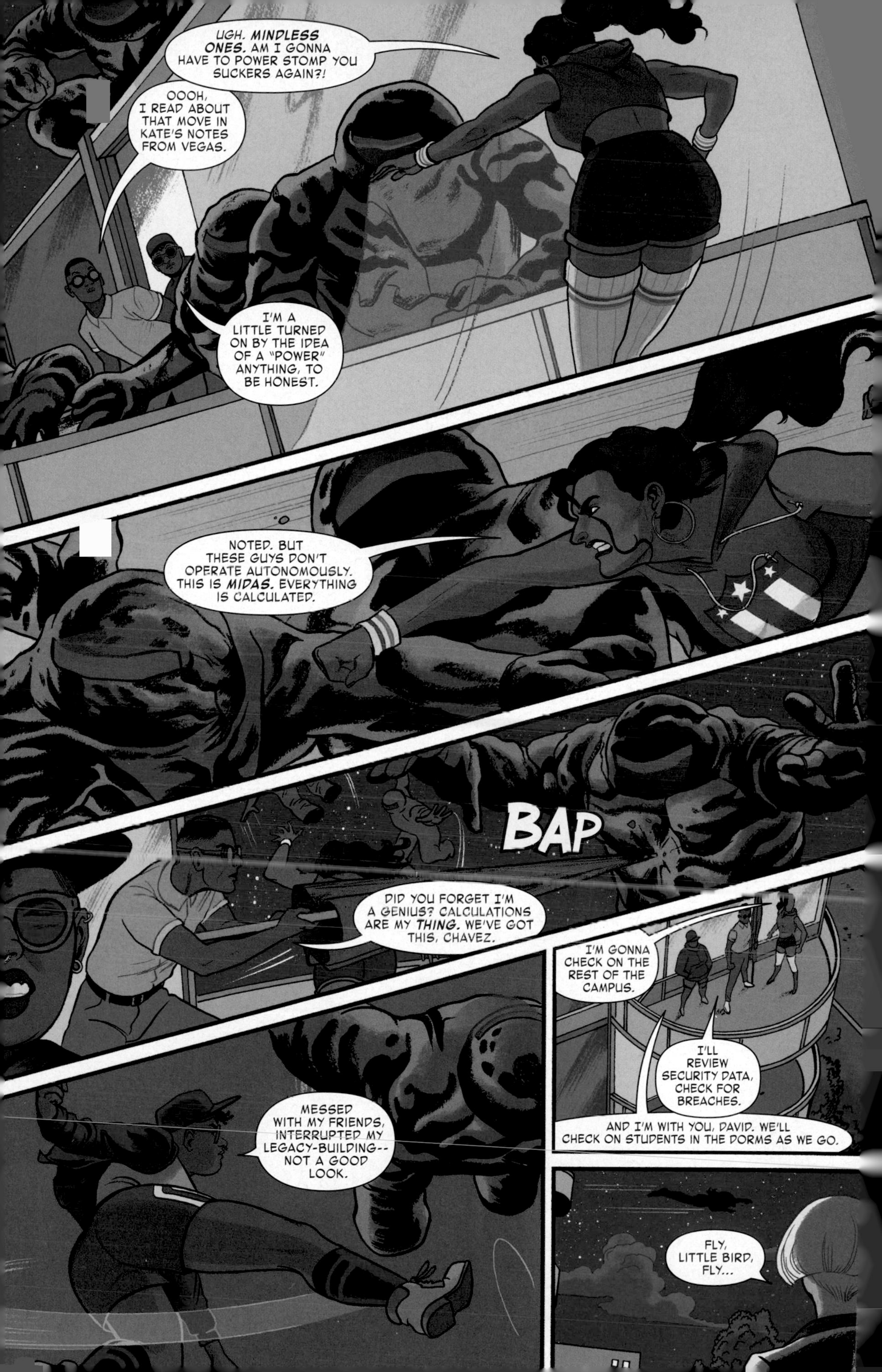
UGH. MINDLESS ONES. AM I GONNA HAVE TO POWER STOMP YOU SUCKERS AGAIN?!
OOOH, I READ ABOUT THAT MOVE IN KATE'S NOTES FROM VEGAS.
I'M A LITTLE TURNED ON BY THE IDEA OF A "POWER" ANYTHING, TO BE HONEST.
NOTED. BUT THESE GUYS DON'T OPERATE AUTONOMOUSLY. THIS IS MIDAS. EVERYTHING IS CALCULATED.
BAP
DID YOU FORGET I'M A GENIUS? CALCULATIONS ARE MY THING. WE'VE GOT THIS, CHAVEZ.
I'M GONNA CHECK ON THE REST OF THE CAMPUS.
I'LL REVIEW SECURITY DATA, CHECK FOR BREACHES.
AND I'M WITH YOU, DAVID. WE'LL CHECK ON STUDENTS IN THE DORMS AS WE GO.
MESSED WITH MY FRIENDS, INTERRUPTED MY LEGACY-BUILDING-- NOT A GOOD LOOK.
FLY, LITTLE BIRD, FLY...

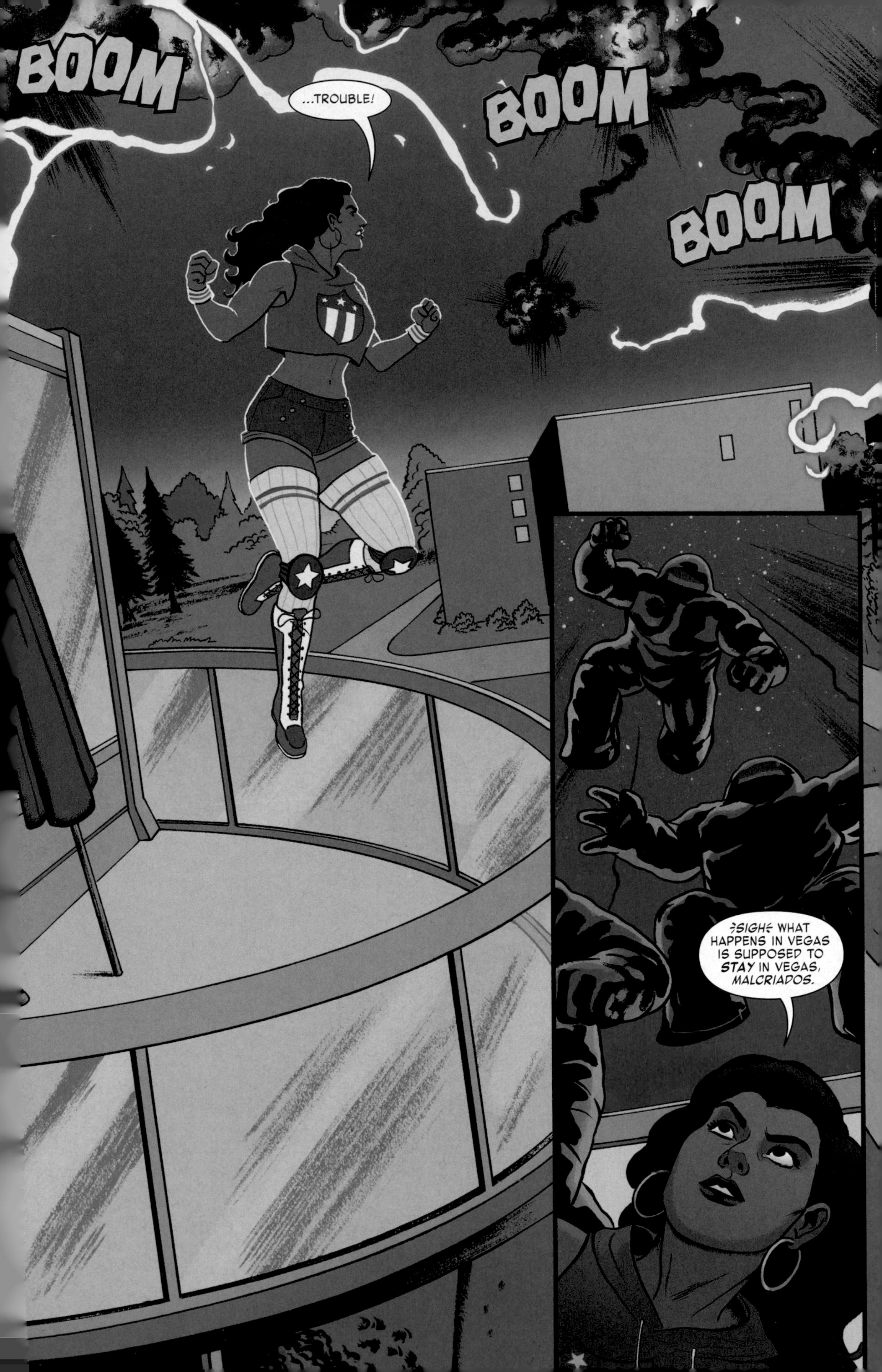
BOOM
...TROUBLE!
BOOM
BOOM
SIGH WHAT HAPPENS IN VEGAS IS SUPPOSED TO STAY IN VEGAS, MALCRIADOS.

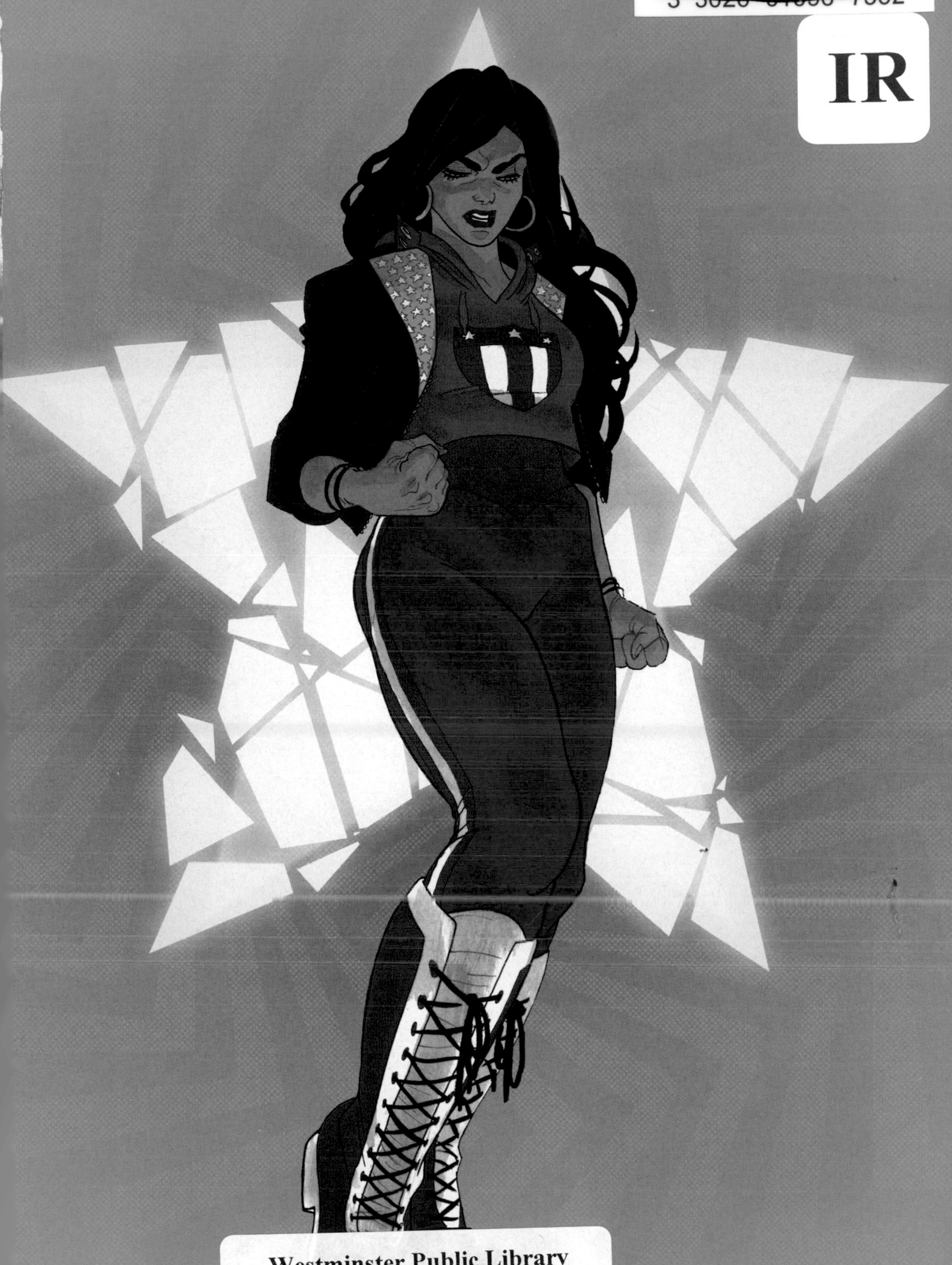

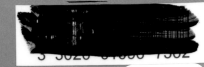

JENNIFER GRÜNWALD
COLLECTION EDITOR

CAITLIN O'CONNELL
ASSISTANT EDITOR

KATERI WOODY
ASSOCIATE MANAGING EDITOR

MARK D. BEAZLEY
EDITOR, SPECIAL PROJECTS

JEFF YOUNGQUIST
VP PRODUCTION & SPECIAL PROJECTS

DAVID GABRIEL
SVP PRINT, SALES & MARKETING

ADAM DEL RE
BOOK DESIGNER

C.B. CEBULSKI
EDITOR IN CHIEF

JOE QUESADA
CHIEF CREATIVE OFFICER

DAN BUCKLEY
PRESIDENT

ALAN FINE
EXECUTIVE PRODUCER

AMERICA VOL. 2: FAST AND FUERTONA. Contains material originally published in magazine form as AMERICA #7-12. First printing 2018. ISBN 978-1-302-90882-9. Published by MARVEL WORLDWIDE, INC., a subsidiary of MARVEL ENTERTAINMENT, LLC. OFFICE OF PUBLICATION. 135 West 50th Street, New York, NY 10020. Copyright © 2018 MARVEL No similarity between any of the names, characters, persons, and/or institutions in this magazine with those of any living or dead person or institution is intended, and any such similarity which may exist is purely coincidental. **Printed in Canada.** DAN BUCKLEY, President, Marvel Entertainment; JOHN NEE, Publisher; JOE QUESADA, Chief Creative Officer; TOM BREVOORT, SVP of Publishing; DAVID BOGART, SVP of Business Affairs & Operations, Publishing & Partnership; DAVID GABRIEL, SVP of Sales & Marketing, Publishing; JEFF YOUNGQUIST, VP of Production & Special Projects; DAN CARR, Executive Director of Publishing Technology; ALEX MORALES, Director of Publishing Operations; SUSAN CRESPI, Production Manager; STAN LEE, Chairman Emeritus. For information regarding advertising in Marvel Comics or on Marvel.com, please contact Vit DeBellis, Custom Solutions & Integrated Advertising Manager, at vdebellis@marvel.com. For Marvel subscription inquiries, please call 888-511-5480. **Manufactured between 2/16/2018 and 3/20/2018 by SOLISCO PRINTERS, SCOTT, QC, CANADA.**

10 9 8 7 6 5 4 3 2 1

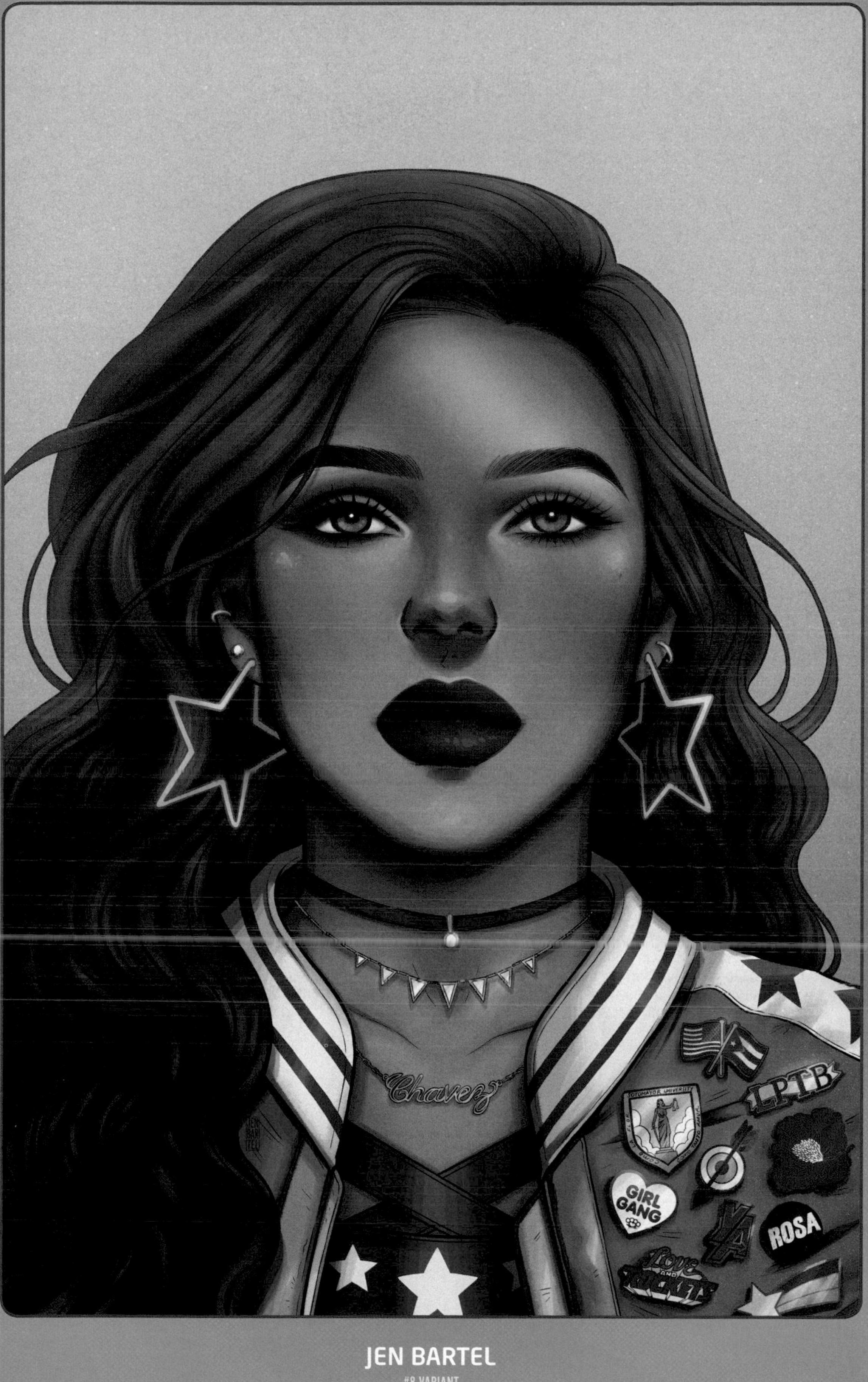
Chavez
LPTB
GIRL GANG
ROSA

JEN BARTEL

#8 VARIANT

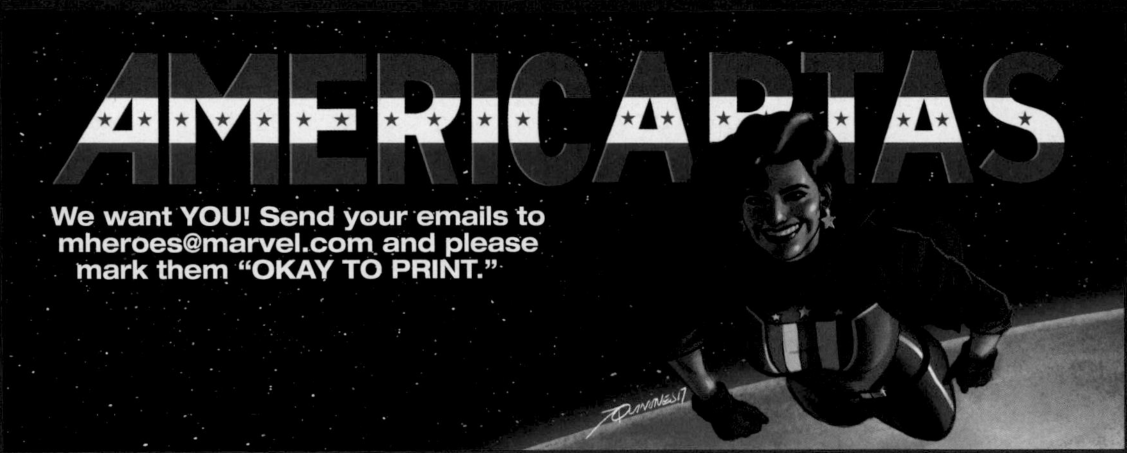
AMERICARTAS
We want YOU! Send your emails to mheroes@marvel.com and please mark them "OKAY TO PRINT."

Fuertona Familia, A.K.A. Seeds of the Resistance,

Abrazos. You've made it to the final issue of AMERICA. And now, just like her, you're ready to take on the ultimate powers of the galaxy and forge entire worlds in your image.

Not bad for a first-time solo run for our girl America Chavez, huh?

Listen, I came into her world not knowing too much about her. She was a Latina from outer space, and we just rocked with that. What a dope concept! Her original creators, Joe Casey and Nick Dragotta, shrouded her origins in mystery. She left the Utopian Parallel at age six, but then what? Did she ever have a childhood crush? Why was she always so ready to punch stuff? There were a million things to explore about her, and I was so excited to let her lead us into all of them and then some.

Also, she was essentially an orphan, so exploring grief and the loss of connection to family were huge to me, as well. We wanted to make sure she found family. Brown, space-alien, Spanglish-speaking, *abuelita*-style family. 'Cuz we deserve to exist and thrive in all corners of the galaxy.

So she got a grandma, Madrimar, a road trip with her best friend, Kate Bishop, and so many star-portal miles that she can fund a trip to the end of the universe if she wants! Also, she attended the most prestigious Sotomayor University, and we watched as Prodigy, X'Andria and America saved it from the corporate greed and corruption of Midas.

May their bravery in the face of fascism inspire all of us to protect each other, no matter what, and to continue the relentless fight for justice.

With Wil Moss and Sarah Brunstad as editors in chief of AMERICA, and our founding artist Joe Quinones, along with Jen Bartel, Ramon Villalobos, Ming Doyle, Stacey Lee, Flaviano and a slew of other mega-talented artists, inkers and colorists, AMERICA dazzled y'all with stunning backdrops and ultra-fresh outfits.

America Chavez has changed my entire life. I know she's done the same for all of you.

So carry on, *mi gente. Sigue pa'lante, siempre pa'lante.*

Much respect and love,
G. Rivera

P.S.: Bring on all of your stunning America Chavez cosplay at 2018's New York Comic Con and all the cons to come!

As a final goodbye, we'd like to send some love to Mallarie Chavez, who wrote to Gabby personally about how much AMERICA meant to her. Mallarie, we owe you and everyone else who wrote in and bought this book and told their friends about it a tremendous debt. You are the reason this book exists.

So thank you to Mallarie and all you AMERICA fans out there. Don't go away. We need you around.

Dear Gabby Rivera,

Hello! My name is Mallarie Chavez and I'm 15 years old. I just wanted to say congrats on how well the AMERICA series is going. She is my favorite Marvel character ever. I just couldn't wait till she got her own series, and I'm so happy with your writing!

The reason that America is my favorite is mainly because of how much I can relate to her personally. We act and look alike, and if that's not cool enough, we have matching initials: MAC. I'm known for my brown curly hair and earrings and style, and for how sarcastic I can be, and my sense of humor. Then when I did some research on America, and after reading the comics, it's creepy cool how alike we are. (My mother thinks that America is actually based off me. Haha.)

Again, your work with this series is AMAZING and I love it. I look forward to your future works. Have a great day!

Sincerely,
Mallarie Chavez

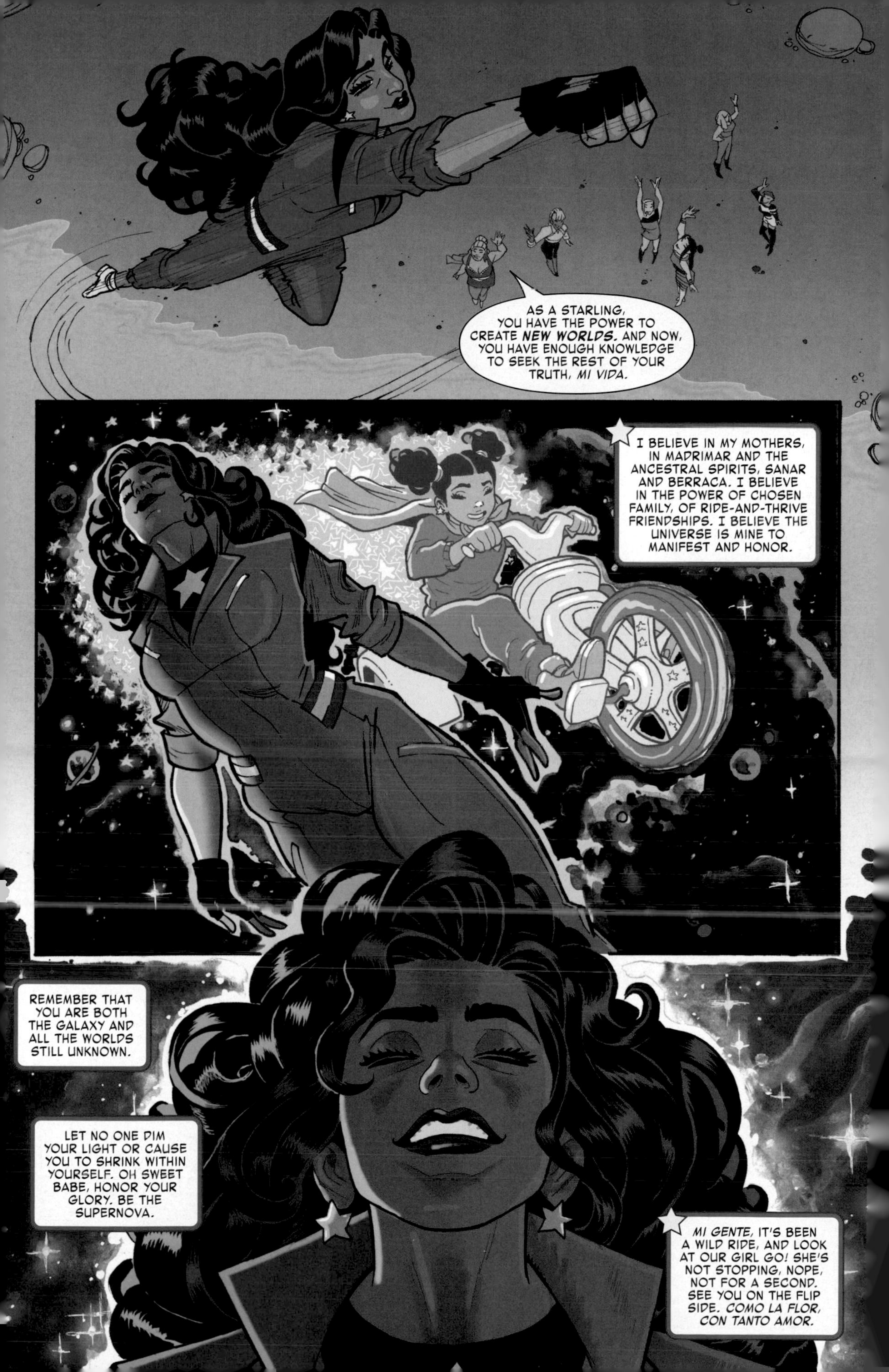
AS A STARLING, YOU HAVE THE POWER TO CREATE **NEW WORLDS.** AND NOW, YOU HAVE ENOUGH KNOWLEDGE TO SEEK THE REST OF YOUR TRUTH, *MI VIDA.*
I BELIEVE IN MY MOTHERS, IN MADRIMAR AND THE ANCESTRAL SPIRITS, SANAR AND BERRACA. I BELIEVE IN THE POWER OF CHOSEN FAMILY, OF RIDE-AND-THRIVE FRIENDSHIPS. I BELIEVE THE UNIVERSE IS MINE TO MANIFEST AND HONOR.
REMEMBER THAT YOU ARE BOTH THE GALAXY AND ALL THE WORLDS STILL UNKNOWN.
LET NO ONE DIM YOUR LIGHT OR CAUSE YOU TO SHRINK WITHIN YOURSELF. OH SWEET BABE, HONOR YOUR GLORY. BE THE SUPERNOVA.
MI GENTE, IT'S BEEN A WILD RIDE, AND LOOK AT OUR GIRL GO! SHE'S NOT STOPPING, NOPE, NOT FOR A SECOND. SEE YOU ON THE FLIP SIDE. *COMO LA FLOR, CON TANTO AMOR.*

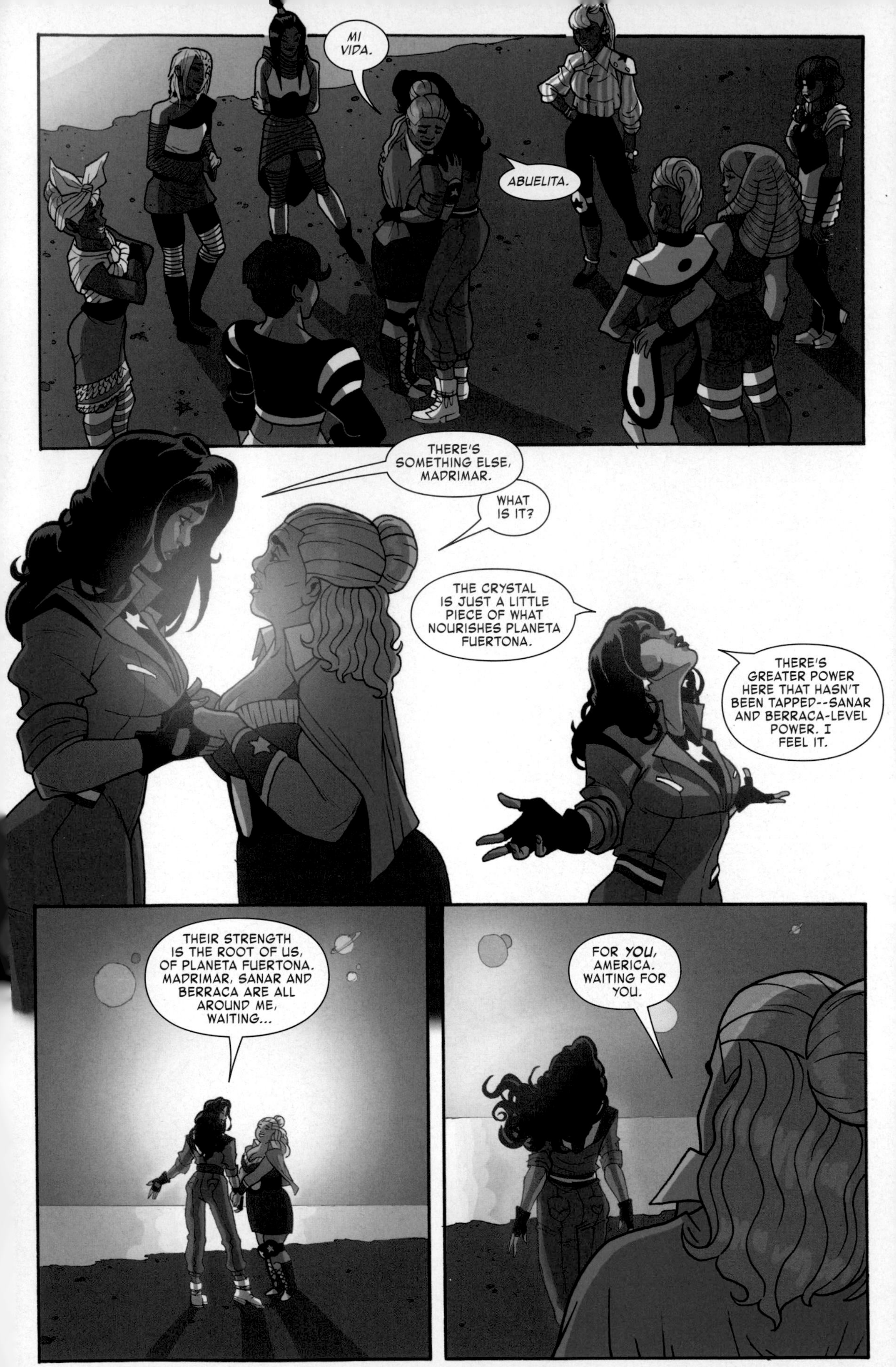
MI VIDA.
ABUELITA.
THERE'S SOMETHING ELSE, MADRIMAR.
WHAT IS IT?
THE CRYSTAL IS JUST A LITTLE PIECE OF WHAT NOURISHES PLANETA FUERTONA.
THERE'S GREATER POWER HERE THAT HASN'T BEEN TAPPED--SANAR AND BERRACA-LEVEL POWER. I FEEL IT.
THEIR STRENGTH IS THE ROOT OF US, OF PLANETA FUERTONA. MADRIMAR, SANAR AND BERRACA ARE ALL AROUND ME, WAITING...
FOR YOU, AMERICA. WAITING FOR YOU.

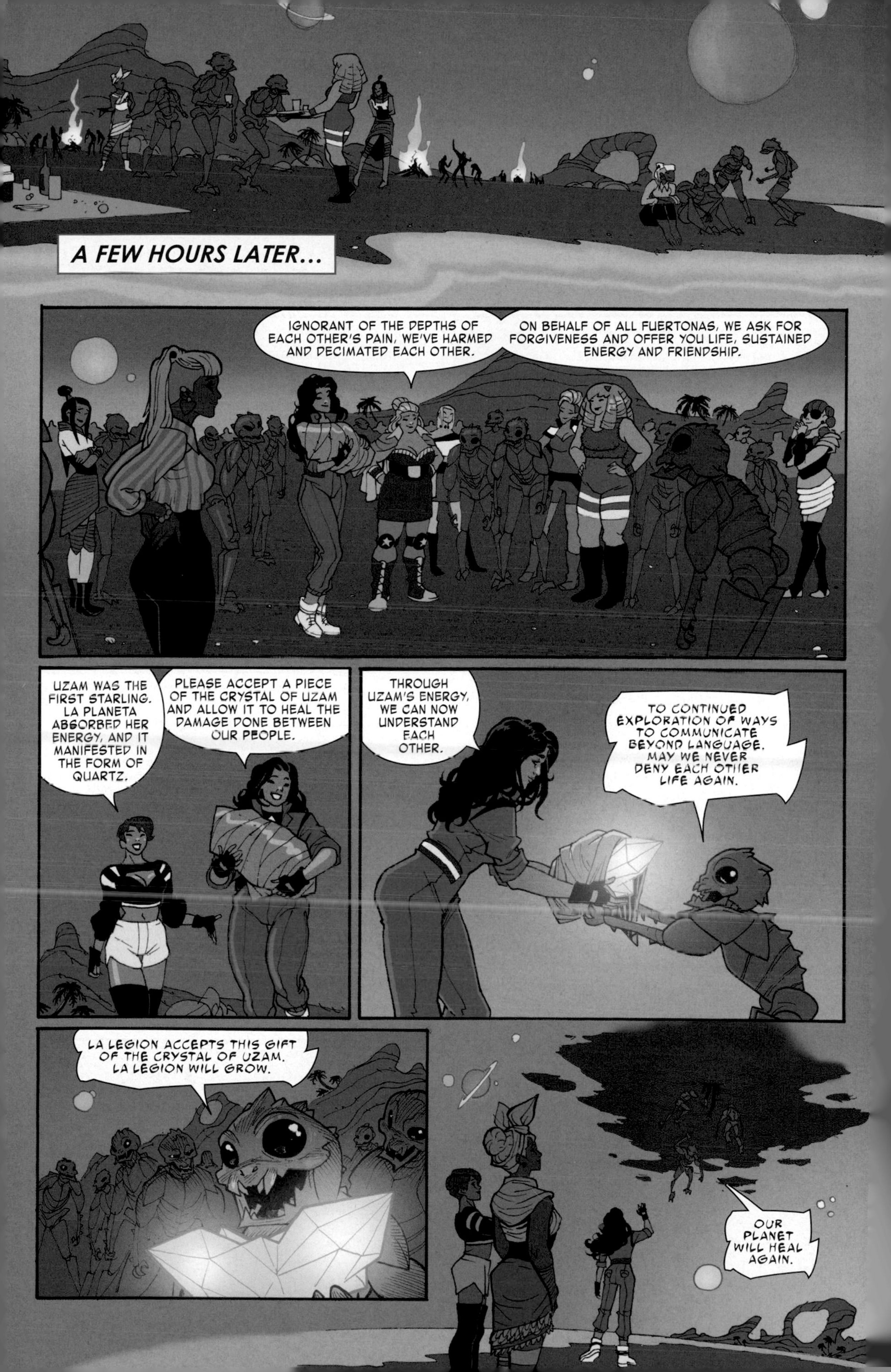
A FEW HOURS LATER...
IGNORANT OF THE DEPTHS OF EACH OTHER'S PAIN, WE'VE HARMED AND DECIMATED EACH OTHER.
ON BEHALF OF ALL FUERTONAS, WE ASK FOR FORGIVENESS AND OFFER YOU LIFE, SUSTAINED ENERGY AND FRIENDSHIP.
UZAM WAS THE FIRST STARLING. LA PLANETA ABSORBED HER ENERGY, AND IT MANIFESTED IN THE FORM OF QUARTZ.
PLEASE ACCEPT A PIECE OF THE CRYSTAL OF UZAM AND ALLOW IT TO HEAL THE DAMAGE DONE BETWEEN OUR PEOPLE.
THROUGH UZAM'S ENERGY, WE CAN NOW UNDERSTAND EACH OTHER.
TO CONTINUED EXPLORATION OF WAYS TO COMMUNICATE BEYOND LANGUAGE. MAY WE NEVER DENY EACH OTHER LIFE AGAIN.
LA LEGION ACCEPTS THIS GIFT OF THE CRYSTAL OF UZAM. LA LEGION WILL GROW.
OUR PLANET WILL HEAL AGAIN.

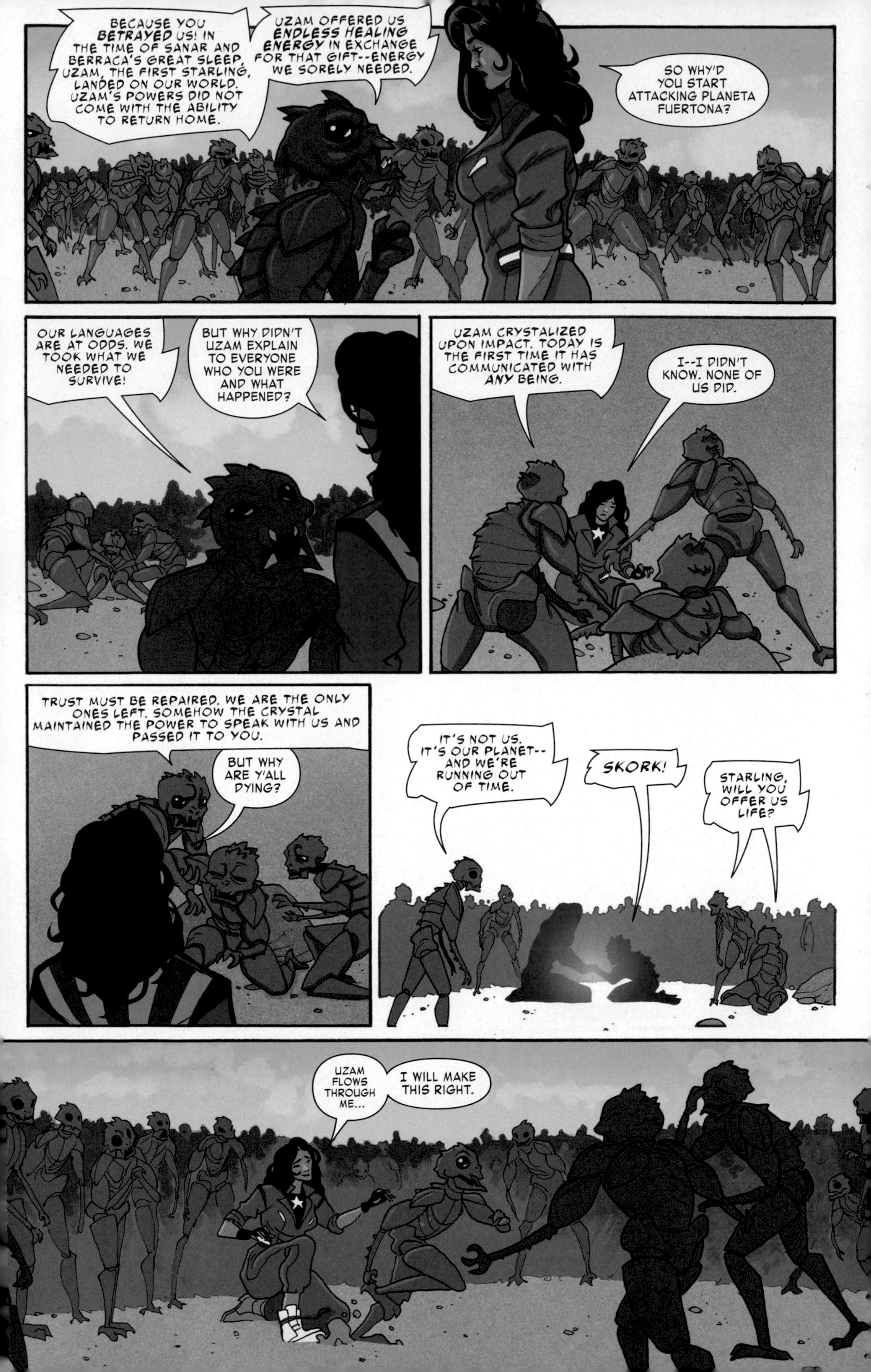
BECAUSE YOU BETRAYED US! IN THE TIME OF SANAR AND BERRACA'S GREAT SLEEP, UZAM, THE FIRST STARLING, LANDED ON OUR WORLD. UZAM'S POWERS DID NOT COME WITH THE ABILITY TO RETURN HOME.
UZAM OFFERED US ENDLESS HEALING ENERGY IN EXCHANGE FOR THAT GIFT--ENERGY WE SORELY NEEDED.
SO WHY'D YOU START ATTACKING PLANETA FUERTONA?
OUR LANGUAGES ARE AT ODDS. WE TOOK WHAT WE NEEDED TO SURVIVE!
BUT WHY DIDN'T UZAM EXPLAIN TO EVERYONE WHO YOU WERE AND WHAT HAPPENED?
UZAM CRYSTALIZED UPON IMPACT. TODAY IS THE FIRST TIME IT HAS COMMUNICATED WITH ANY BEING.
I--I DIDN'T KNOW. NONE OF US DID.
TRUST MUST BE REPAIRED. WE ARE THE ONLY ONES LEFT. SOMEHOW THE CRYSTAL MAINTAINED THE POWER TO SPEAK WITH US AND PASSED IT TO YOU.
BUT WHY ARE Y'ALL DYING?
IT'S NOT US. IT'S OUR PLANET--AND WE'RE RUNNING OUT OF TIME.
SKORK!
STARLING, WILL YOU OFFER US LIFE?
UZAM FLOWS THROUGH ME...
I WILL MAKE THIS RIGHT.

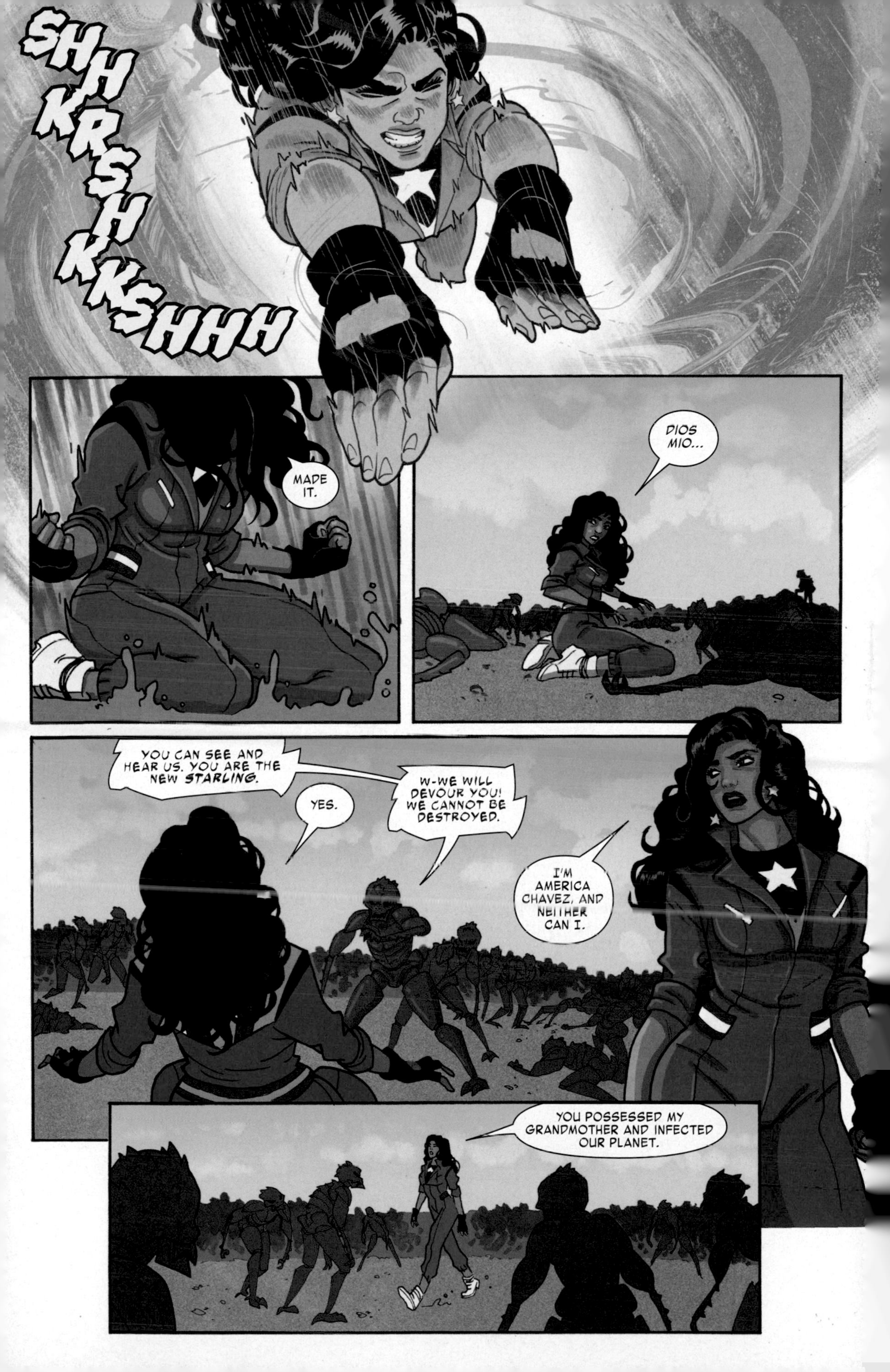
SHHKRSHKKSHHH
MADE IT.
DIOS MIO...
YOU CAN SEE AND HEAR US. YOU ARE THE NEW STARLING.
YES.
W-WE WILL DEVOUR YOU! WE CANNOT BE DESTROYED.
I'M AMERICA CHAVEZ, AND NEITHER CAN I.
YOU POSSESSED MY GRANDMOTHER AND INFECTED OUR PLANET.

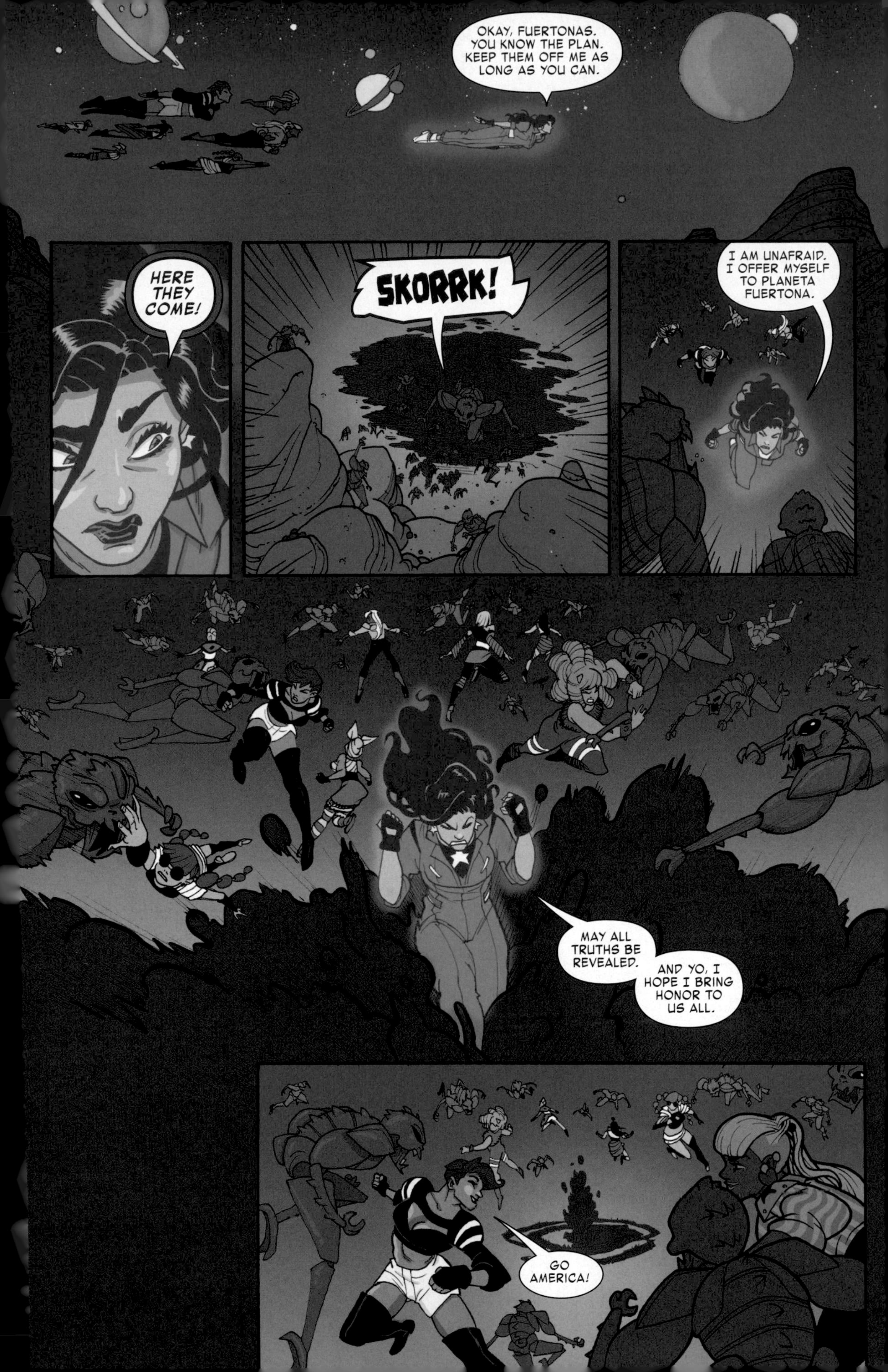
OKAY, FUERTONAS. YOU KNOW THE PLAN. KEEP THEM OFF ME AS LONG AS YOU CAN.
HERE THEY COME!
SKORRK!
I AM UNAFRAID. I OFFER MYSELF TO PLANETA FUERTONA.
MAY ALL TRUTHS BE REVEALED.
AND YO, I HOPE I BRING HONOR TO US ALL.
GO AMERICA!

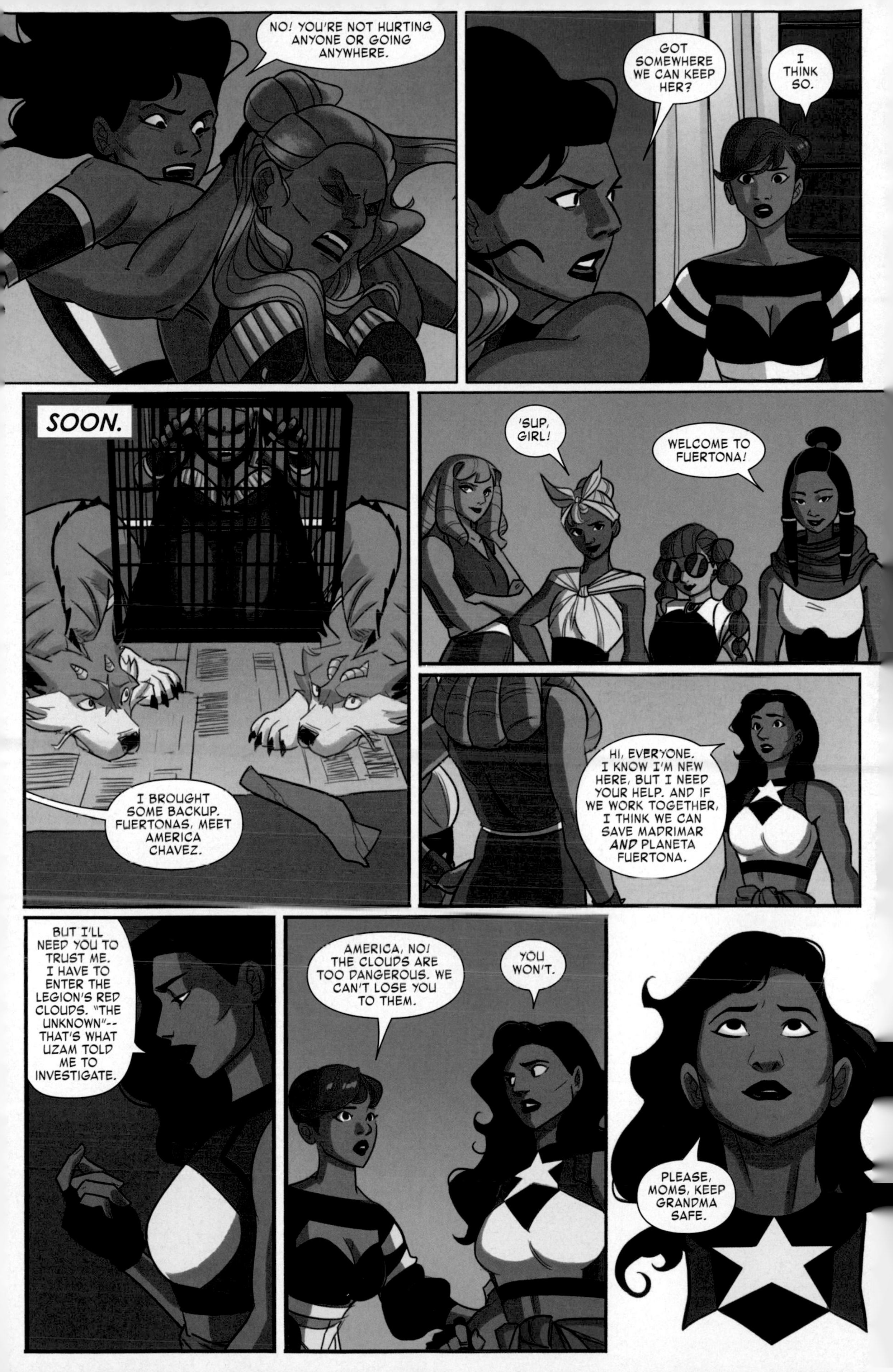

NO! YOU'RE NOT HURTING ANYONE OR GOING ANYWHERE.
GOT SOMEWHERE WE CAN KEEP HER?
I THINK SO.
SOON.
'SUP, GIRL!
WELCOME TO FUERTONA!
I BROUGHT SOME BACKUP. FUERTONAS, MEET AMERICA CHAVEZ.
HI, EVERYONE. I KNOW I'M NEW HERE, BUT I NEED YOUR HELP. AND IF WE WORK TOGETHER, I THINK WE CAN SAVE MADRIMAR AND PLANETA FUERTONA.
BUT I'LL NEED YOU TO TRUST ME. I HAVE TO ENTER THE LEGION'S RED CLOUDS. "THE UNKNOWN"-- THAT'S WHAT UZAM TOLD ME TO INVESTIGATE.
AMERICA, NO! THE CLOUDS ARE TOO DANGEROUS. WE CAN'T LOSE YOU TO THEM.
YOU WON'T.
PLEASE, MOMS, KEEP GRANDMA SAFE.

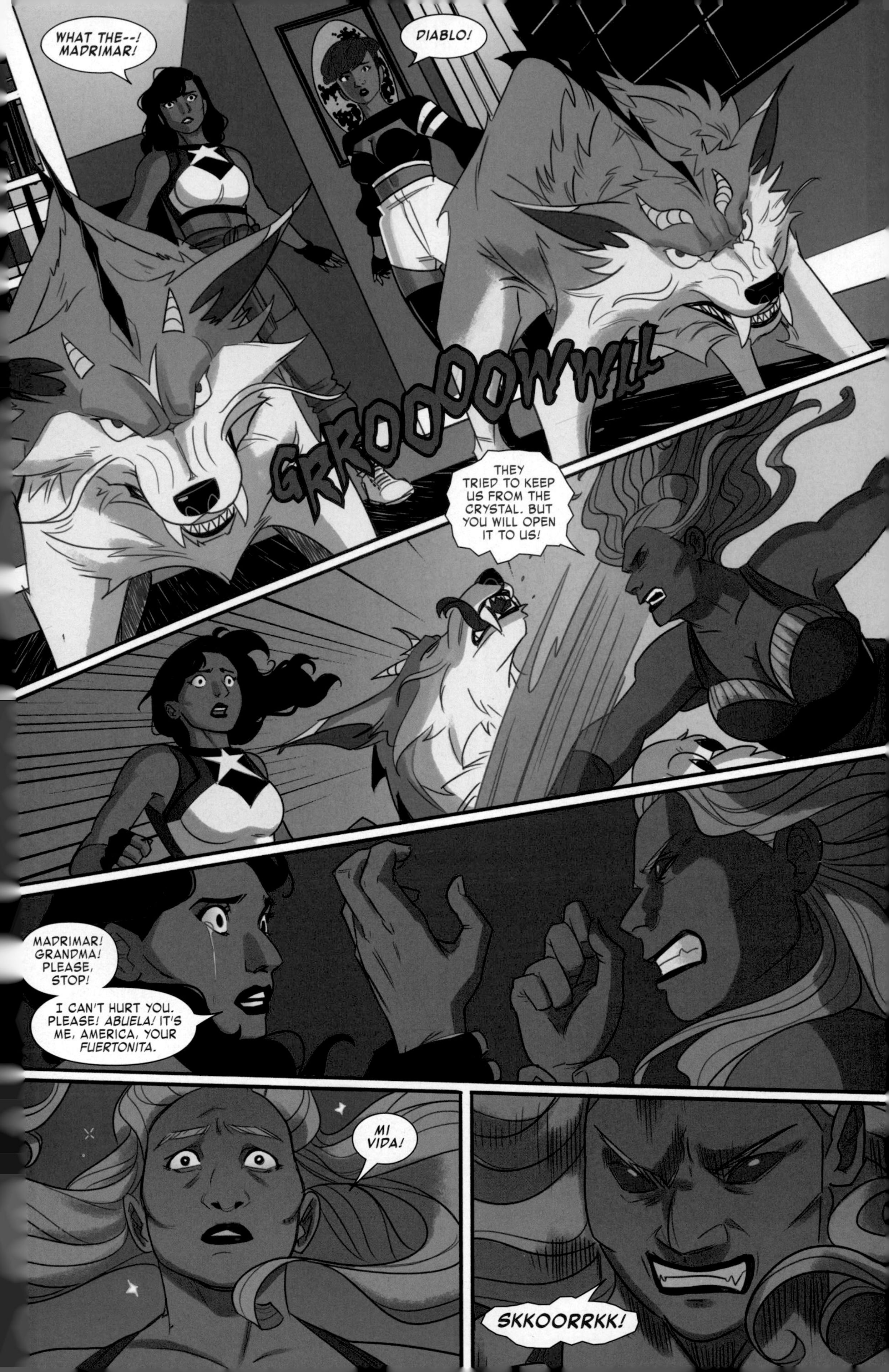
WHAT THE--! MADRIMAR!
DIABLO!
GRROOOOOWWL!
THEY TRIED TO KEEP US FROM THE CRYSTAL. BUT YOU WILL OPEN IT TO US!
MADRIMAR! GRANDMA! PLEASE, STOP!
I CAN'T HURT YOU. PLEASE! ABUELA! IT'S ME, AMERICA, YOUR FUERTONITA.
MI VIDA!
SKKOORRKK!

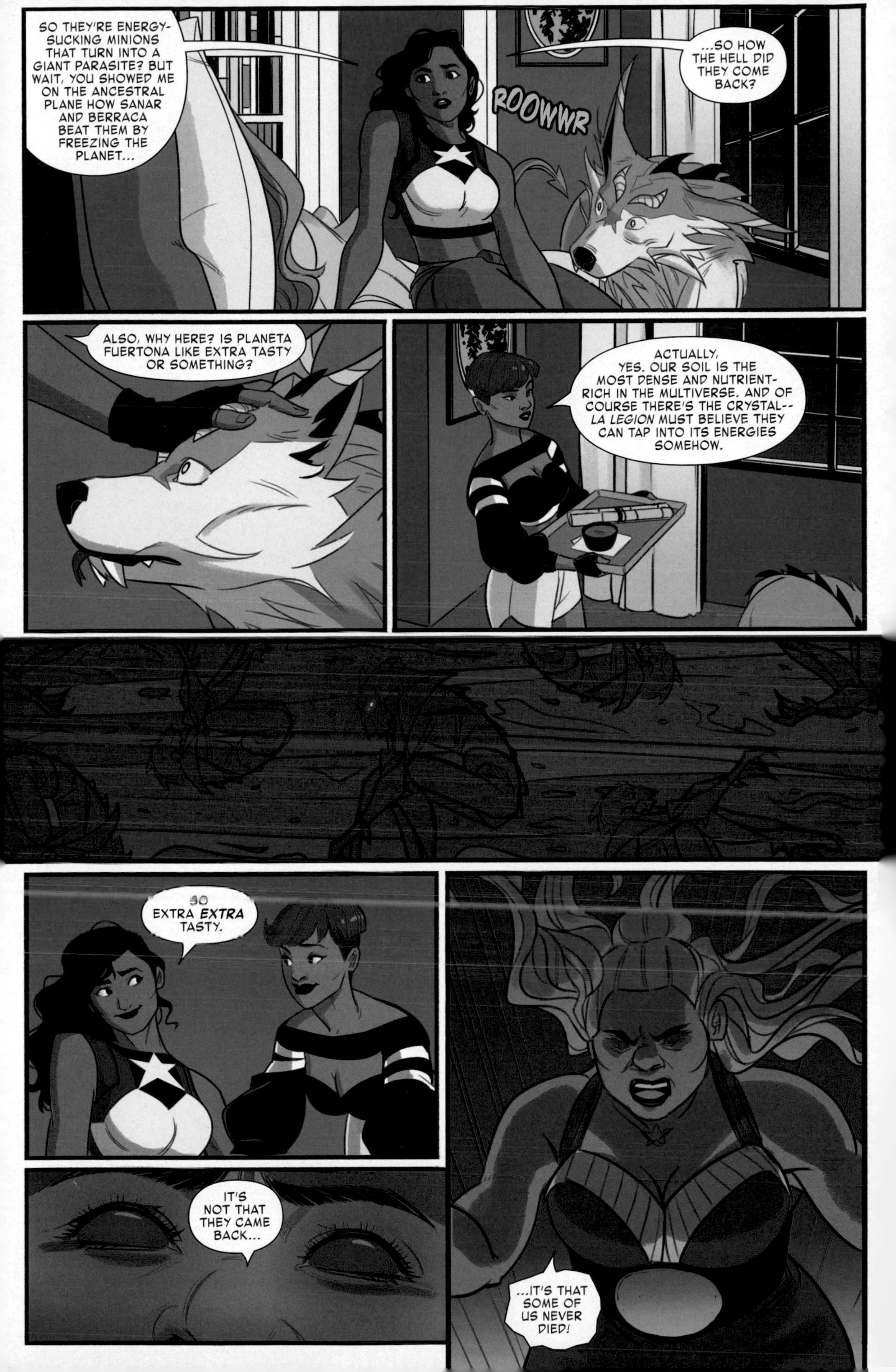
SO THEY'RE ENERGY-SUCKING MINIONS THAT TURN INTO A GIANT PARASITE? BUT WAIT, YOU SHOWED ME ON THE ANCESTRAL PLANE HOW SANAR AND BERRACA BEAT THEM BY FREEZING THE PLANET...
ROOWWR
...SO HOW THE HELL DID THEY COME BACK?
ALSO, WHY HERE? IS PLANETA FUERTONA LIKE EXTRA TASTY OR SOMETHING?
ACTUALLY, YES. OUR SOIL IS THE MOST DENSE AND NUTRIENT-RICH IN THE MULTIVERSE. AND OF COURSE THERE'S THE CRYSTAL-- *LA LEGION* MUST BELIEVE THEY CAN TAP INTO ITS ENERGIES SOMEHOW.
SO EXTRA **EXTRA** TASTY.
IT'S NOT THAT THEY CAME BACK...
...IT'S THAT SOME OF US NEVER DIED!

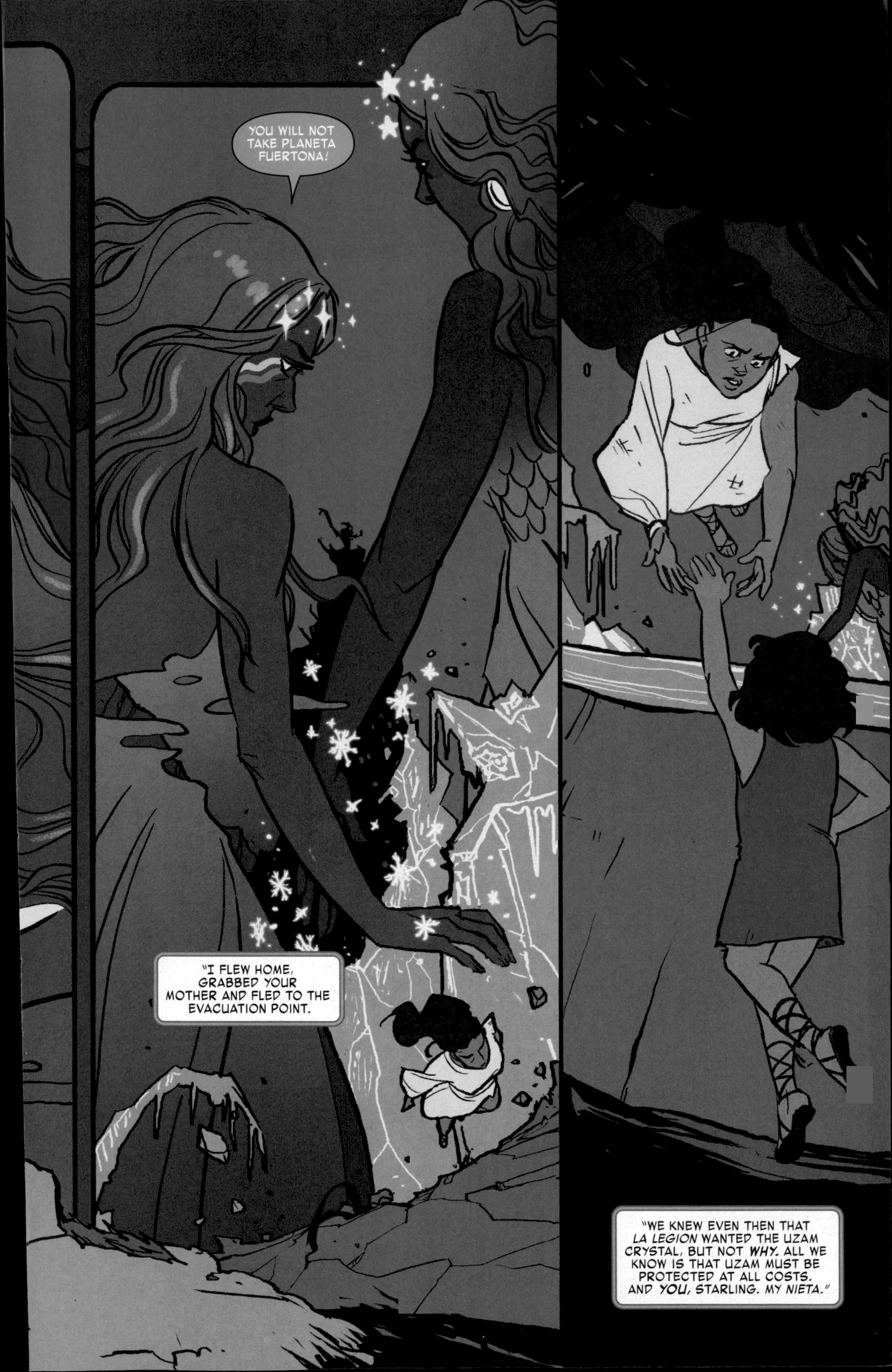
YOU WILL NOT TAKE PLANETA FUERTONA!
"I FLEW HOME, GRABBED YOUR MOTHER AND FLED TO THE EVACUATION POINT.
"WE KNEW EVEN THEN THAT *LA LEGION* WANTED THE UZAM CRYSTAL, BUT NOT ***WHY.*** ALL WE KNOW IS THAT UZAM MUST BE PROTECTED AT ALL COSTS. AND ***YOU,*** STARLING. MY *NIETA.*"

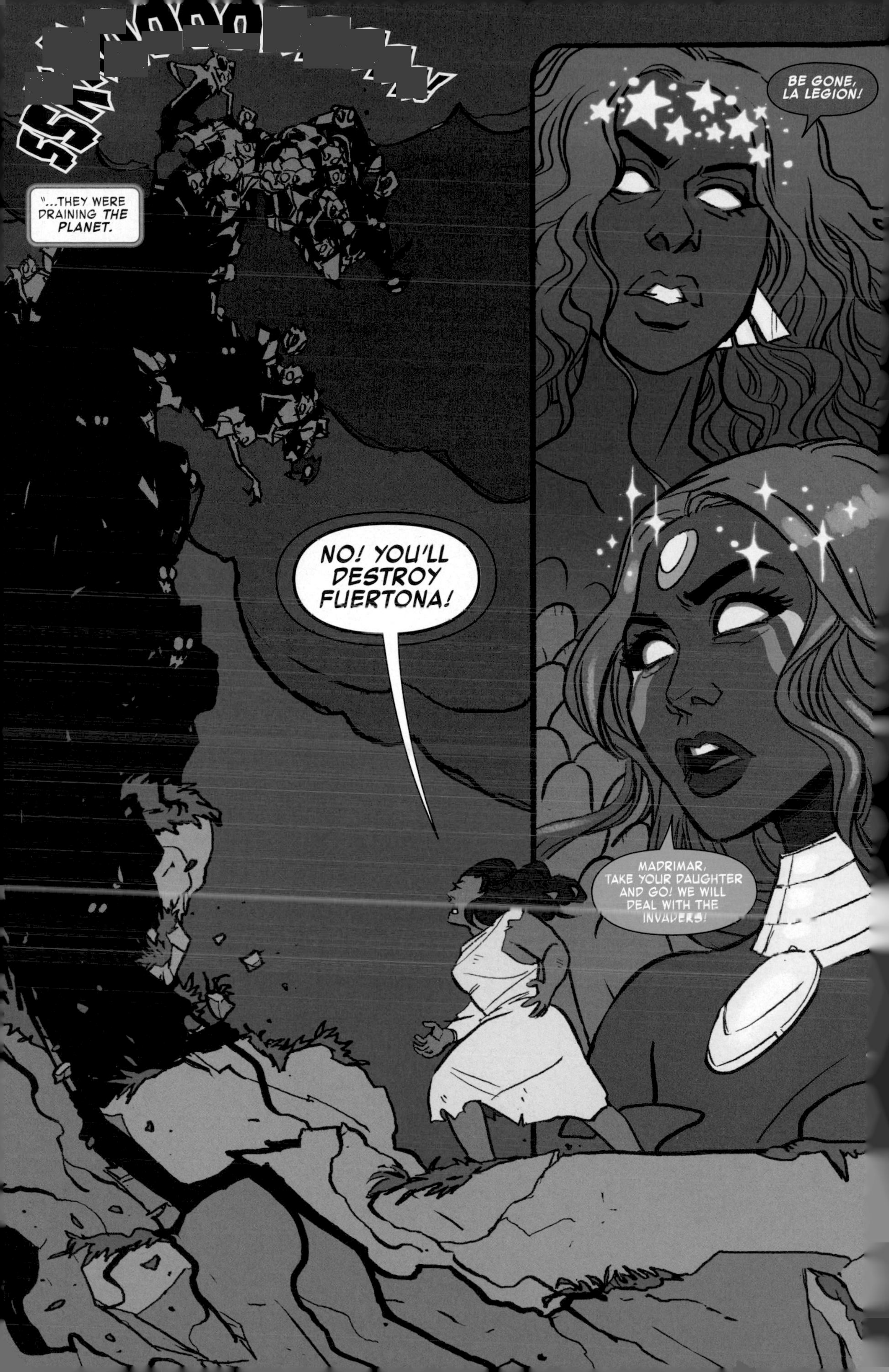
[redacted]
"...THEY WERE DRAINING THE PLANET.
BE GONE, LA LEGION!
NO! YOU'LL DESTROY FUERTONA!
MADRIMAR, TAKE YOUR DAUGHTER AND GO! WE WILL DEAL WITH THE INVADERS!

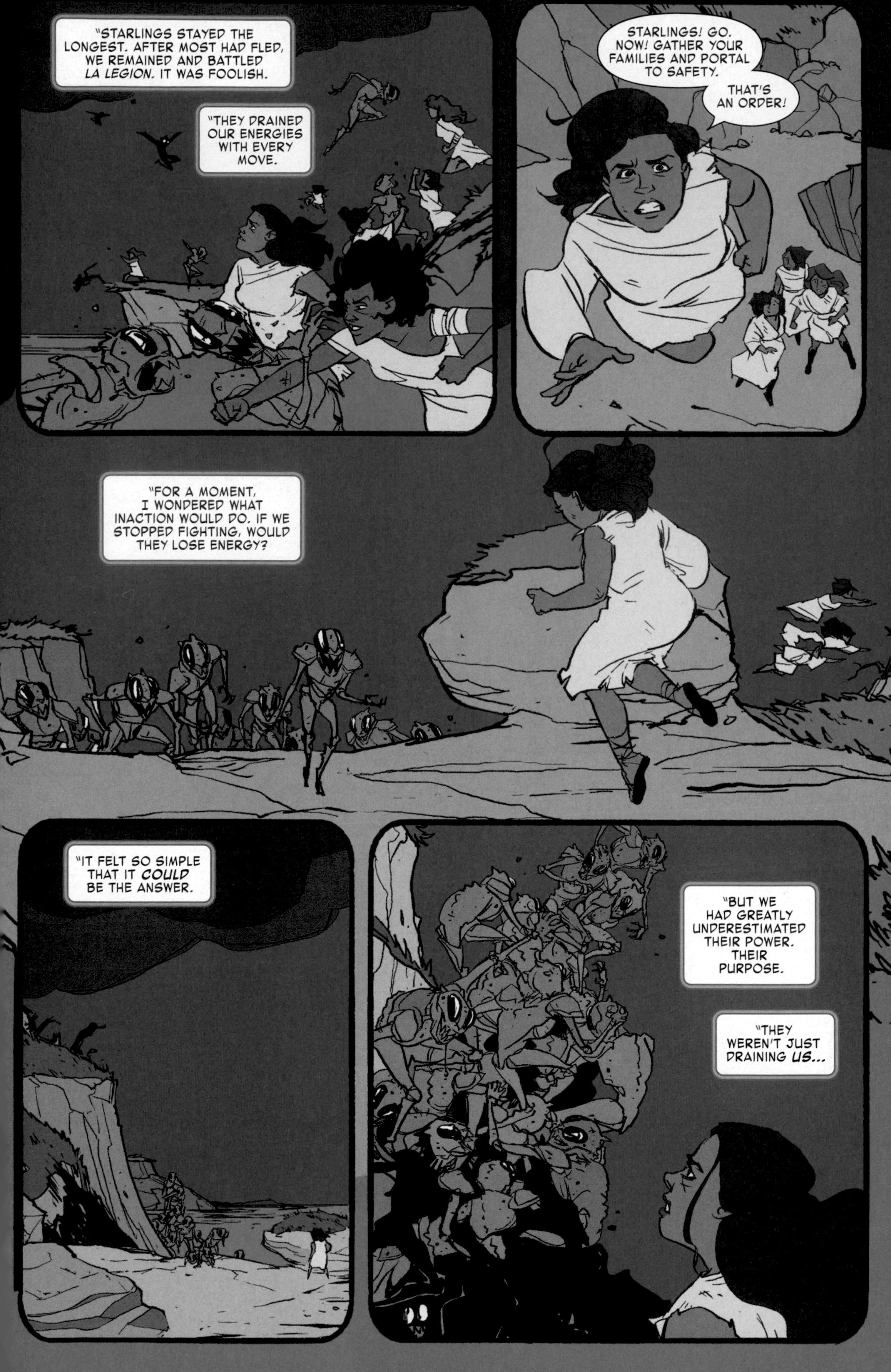
"STARLINGS STAYED THE LONGEST. AFTER MOST HAD FLED, WE REMAINED AND BATTLED *LA LEGION*. IT WAS FOOLISH.
"THEY DRAINED OUR ENERGIES WITH EVERY MOVE.
STARLINGS! GO. NOW! GATHER YOUR FAMILIES AND PORTAL TO SAFETY.
THAT'S AN ORDER!
"FOR A MOMENT, I WONDERED WHAT INACTION WOULD DO. IF WE STOPPED FIGHTING, WOULD THEY LOSE ENERGY?
"IT FELT SO SIMPLE THAT IT ***COULD*** BE THE ANSWER.
"BUT WE HAD GREATLY UNDERESTIMATED THEIR POWER. THEIR PURPOSE.
"THEY WEREN'T JUST DRAINING ***US...***

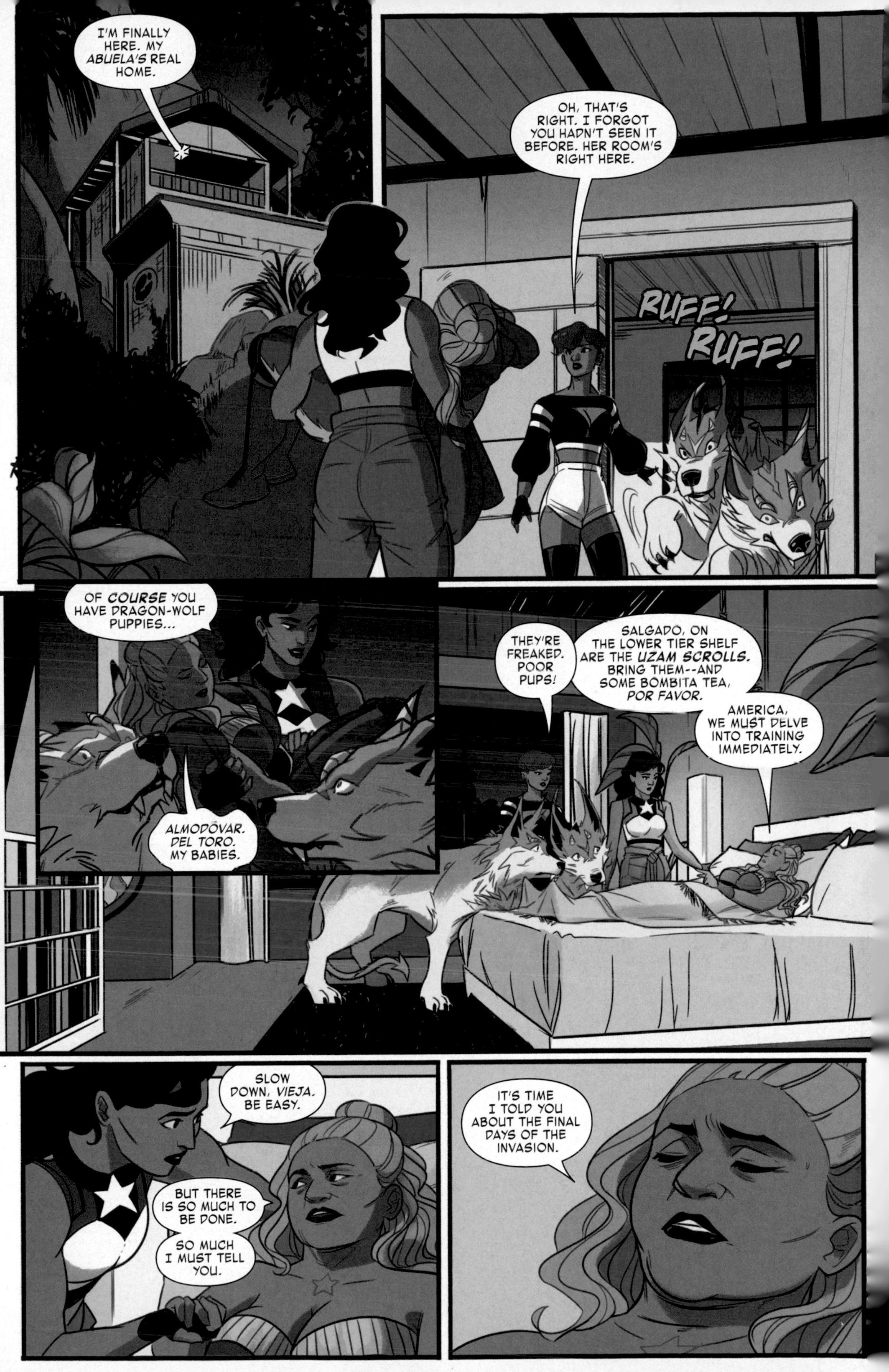
I'M FINALLY HERE. MY *ABUELA'S* REAL HOME.
OH, THAT'S RIGHT. I FORGOT YOU HADN'T SEEN IT BEFORE. HER ROOM'S RIGHT HERE.
RUFF! RUFF!
OF **COURSE** YOU HAVE DRAGON-WOLF PUPPIES...
ALMODOVAR. DEL TORO. MY BABIES.
THEY'RE FREAKED. POOR PUPS!
SALGADO, ON THE LOWER TIER SHELF ARE THE ***UZAM SCROLLS.*** BRING THEM--AND SOME BOMBITA TEA, *POR FAVOR.*
AMERICA, WE MUST DELVE INTO TRAINING IMMEDIATELY.
SLOW DOWN, *VIEJA.* BE EASY.
BUT THERE IS SO MUCH TO BE DONE.
SO MUCH I MUST TELL YOU.
IT'S TIME I TOLD YOU ABOUT THE FINAL DAYS OF THE INVASION.

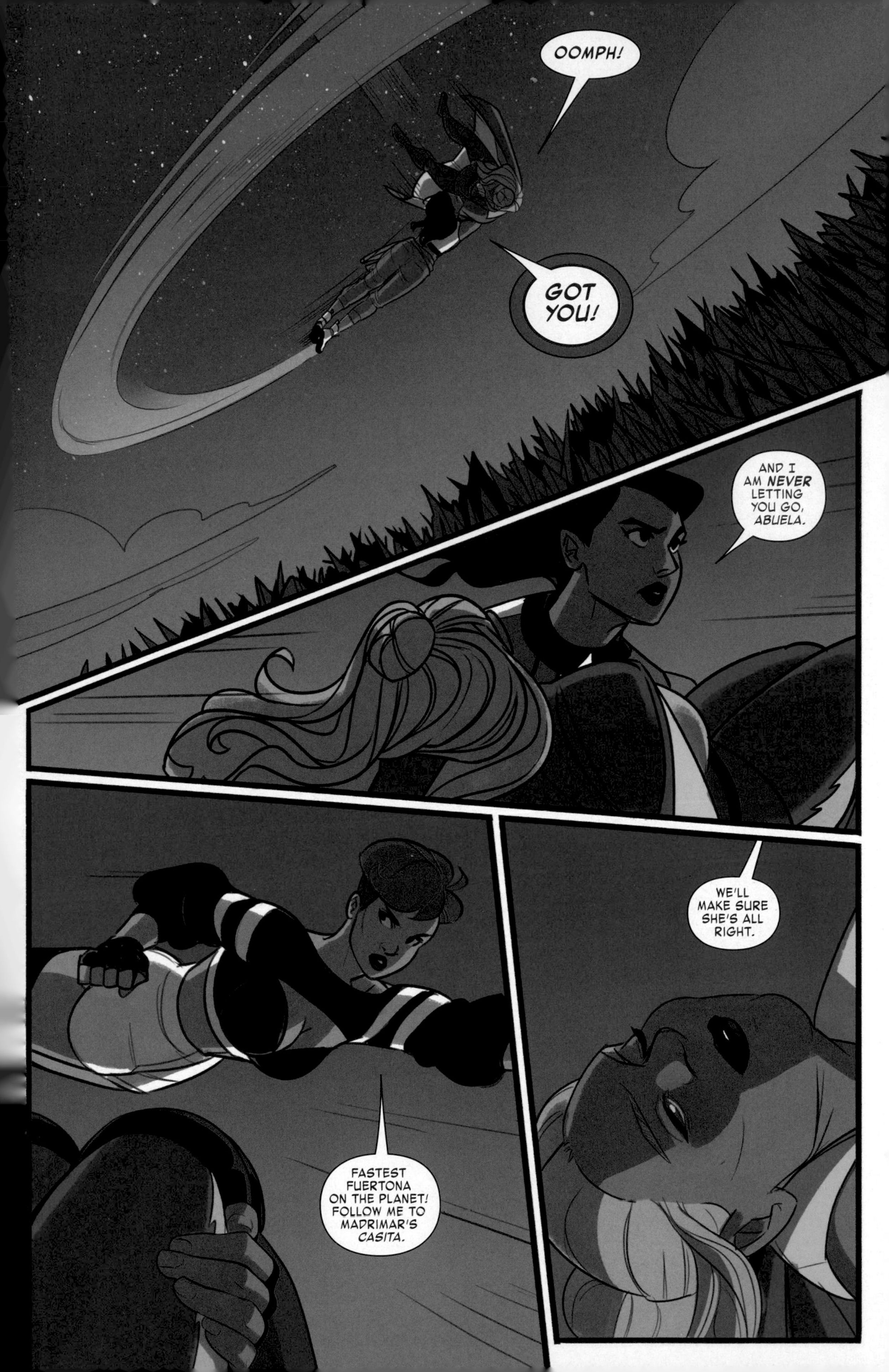
OOMPH!
GOT YOU!
AND I AM NEVER LETTING YOU GO, ABUELA.
FASTEST FUERTONA ON THE PLANET! FOLLOW ME TO MADRIMAR'S CASITA.
WE'LL MAKE SURE SHE'S ALL RIGHT.

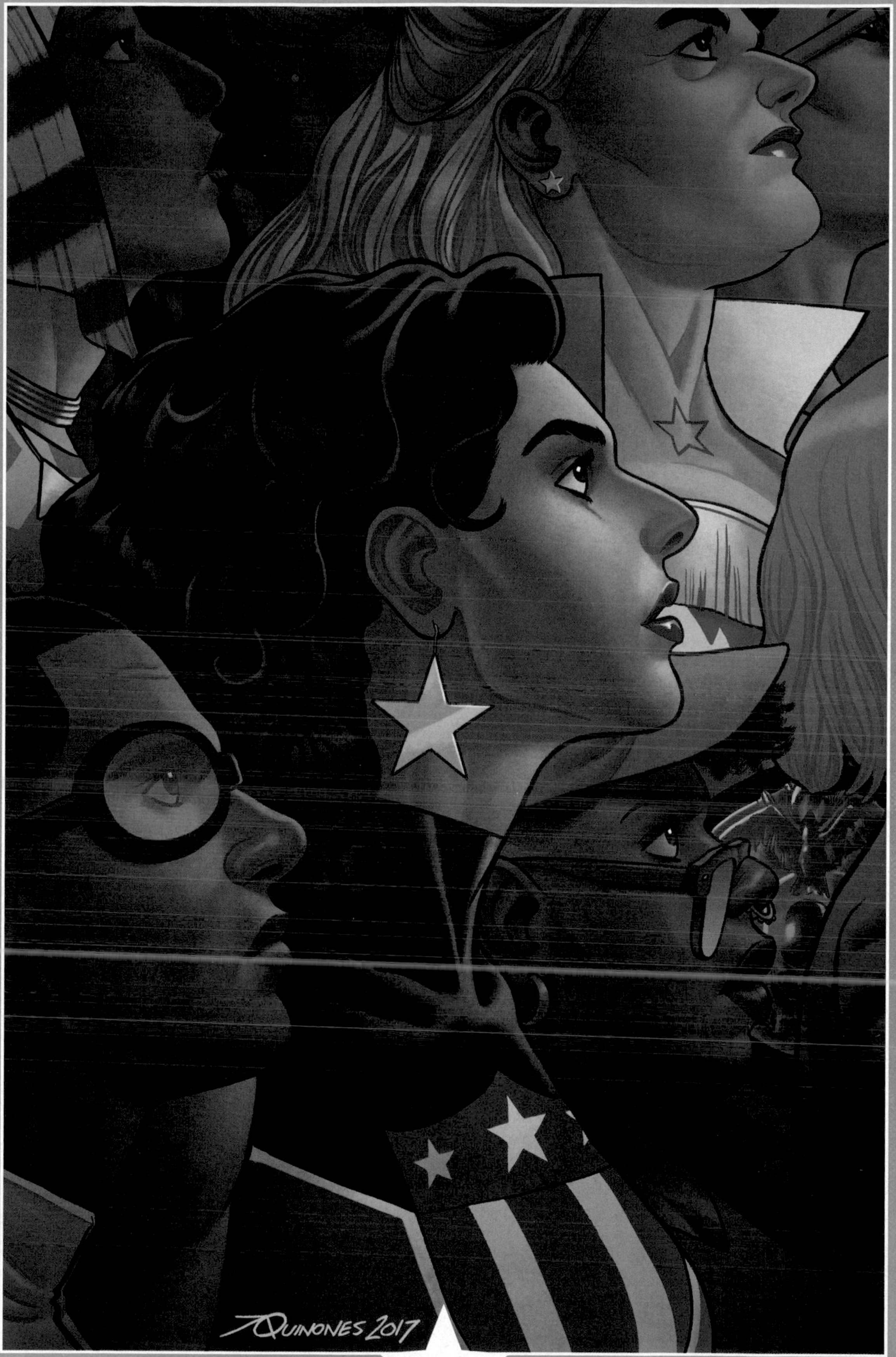
JQUINONES 2017

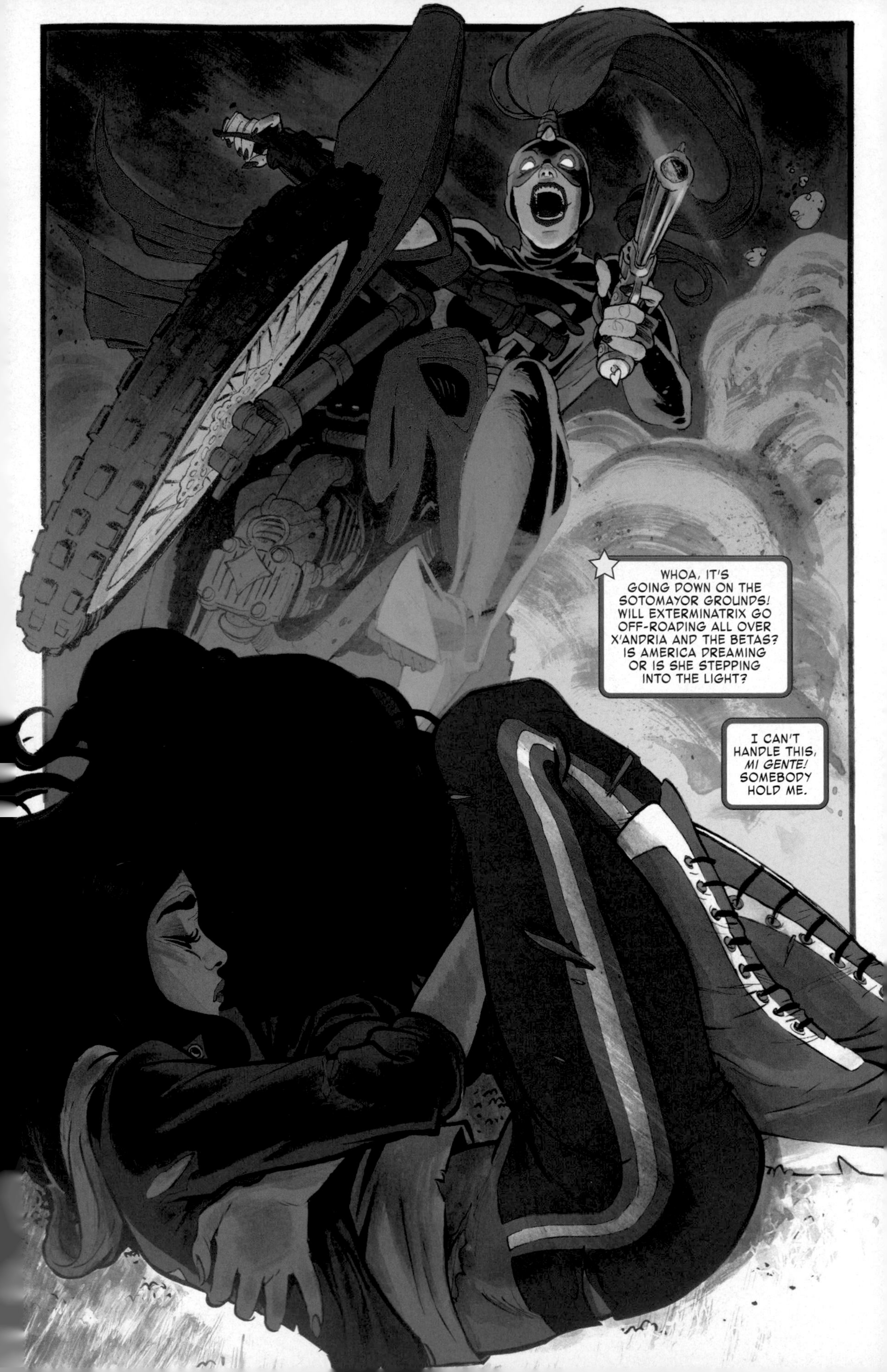
WHOA, IT'S GOING DOWN ON THE SOTOMAYOR GROUNDS! WILL EXTERMINATRIX GO OFF-ROADING ALL OVER X'ANDRIA AND THE BETAS? IS AMERICA DREAMING OR IS SHE STEPPING INTO THE LIGHT?
I CAN'T HANDLE THIS, *MI GENTE!* SOMEBODY HOLD ME.

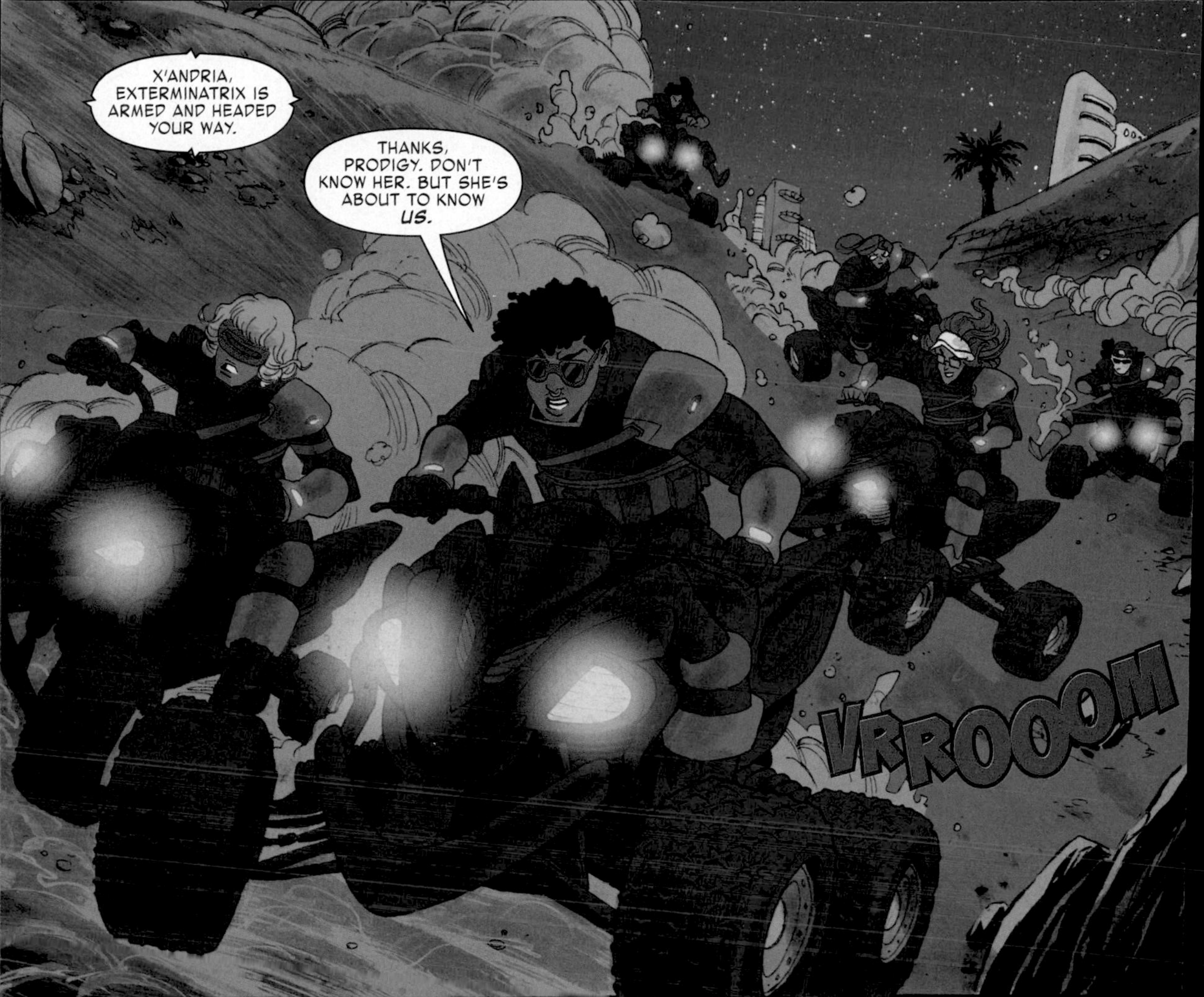
X'ANDRIA, EXTERMINATRIX IS ARMED AND HEADED YOUR WAY.
THANKS, PRODIGY. DON'T KNOW HER. BUT SHE'S ABOUT TO KNOW *US.*
VRROOOM

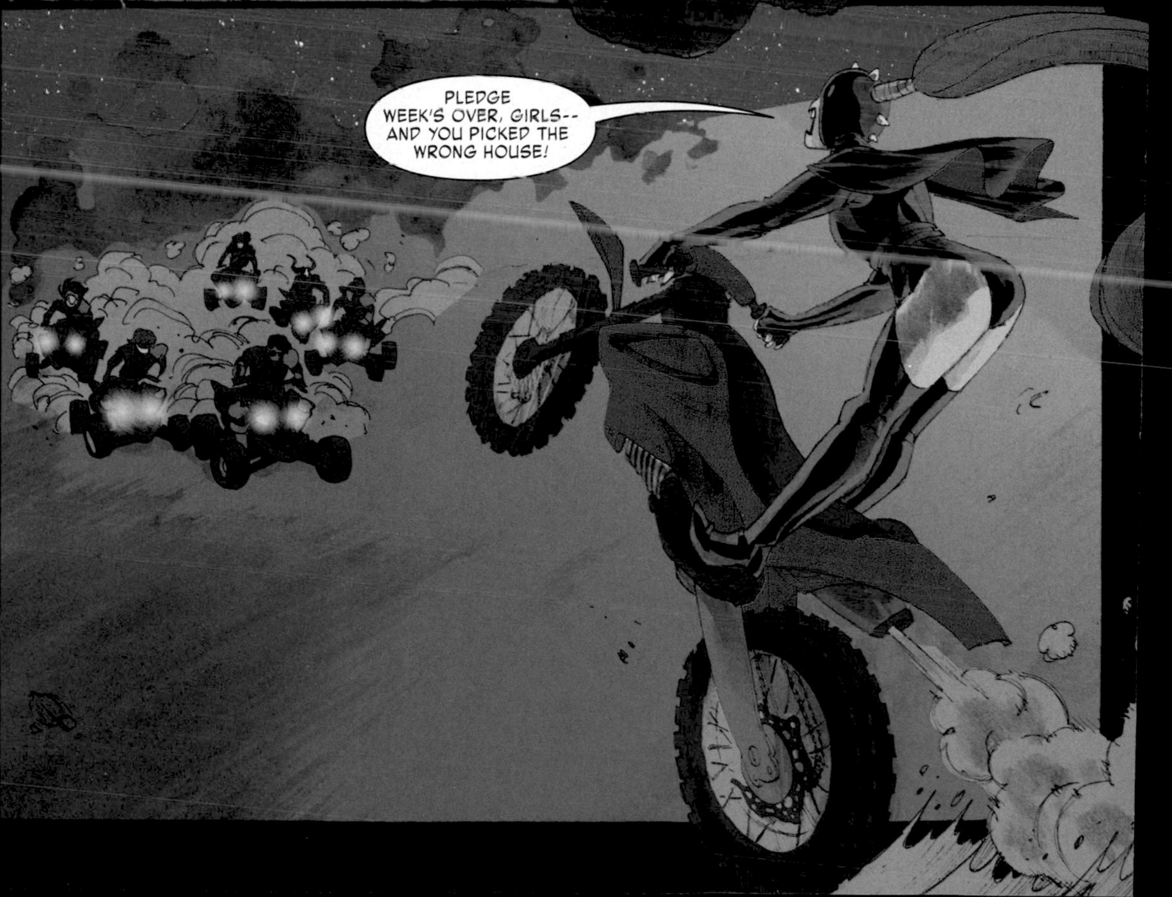
PLEDGE WEEK'S OVER, GIRLS-- AND YOU PICKED THE WRONG HOUSE!

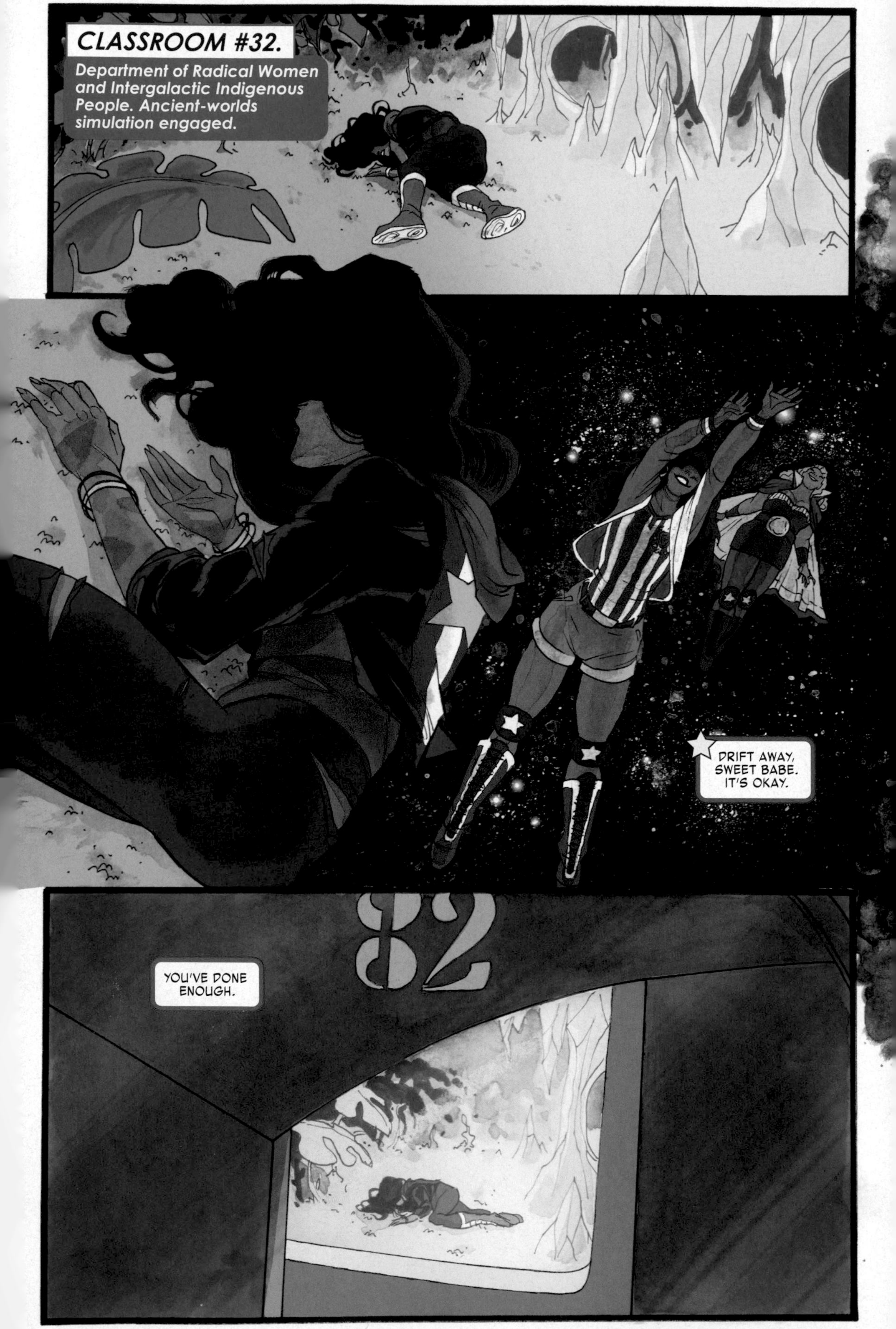
CLASSROOM #32.
Department of Radical Women and Intergalactic Indigenous People. Ancient-worlds simulation engaged.
DRIFT AWAY, SWEET BABE. IT'S OKAY.
82
YOU'VE DONE ENOUGH.

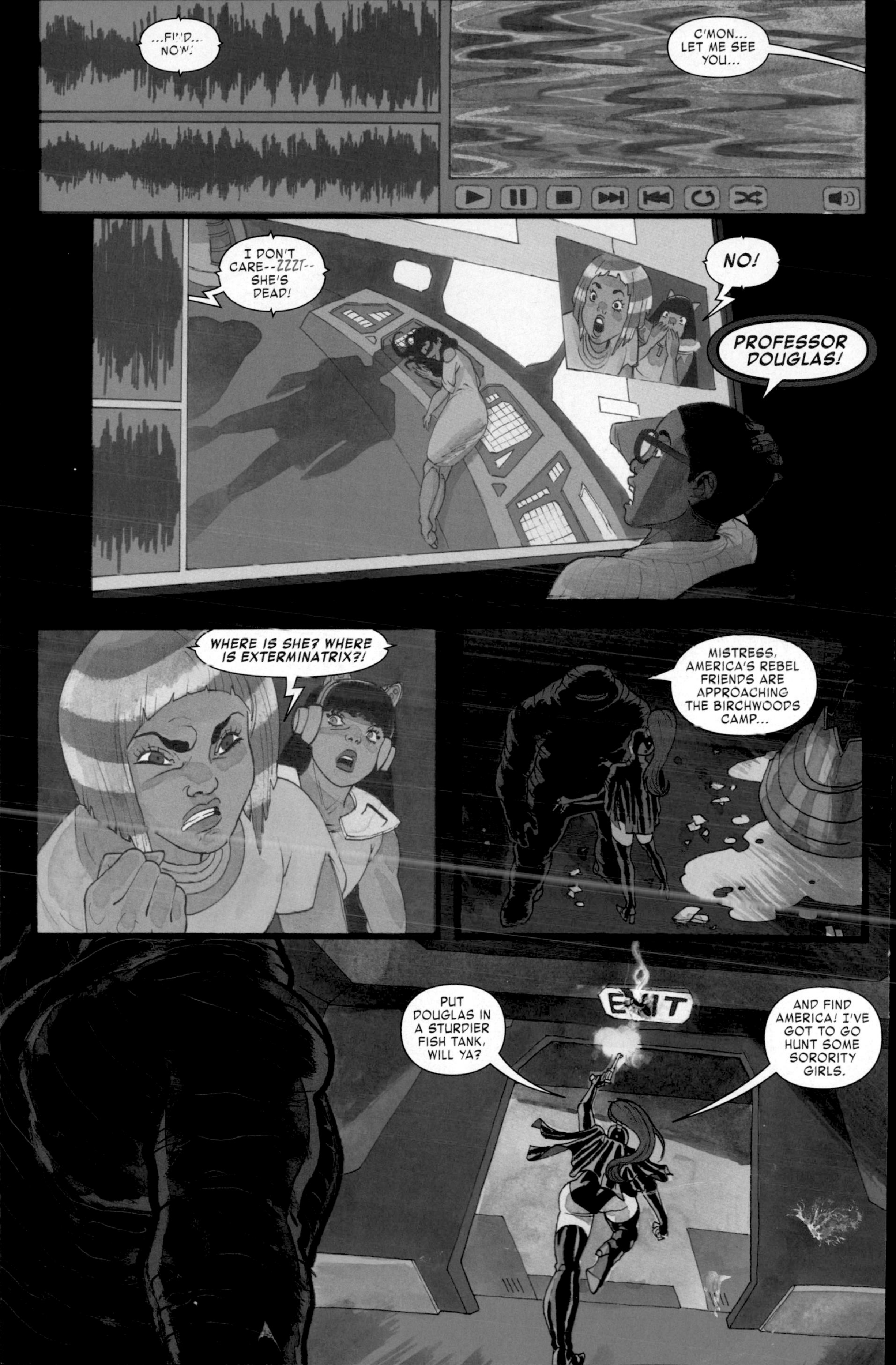
...FI'D... NOW.
C'MON... LET ME SEE YOU...
I DON'T CARE--ZZZT--SHE'S DEAD!
NO!
PROFESSOR DOUGLAS!
WHERE IS SHE? WHERE IS EXTERMINATRIX?!
MISTRESS, AMERICA'S REBEL FRIENDS ARE APPROACHING THE BIRCHWOODS CAMP...
EXIT
PUT DOUGLAS IN A STURDIER FISH TANK, WILL YA?
AND FIND AMERICA! I'VE GOT TO GO HUNT SOME SORORITY GIRLS.

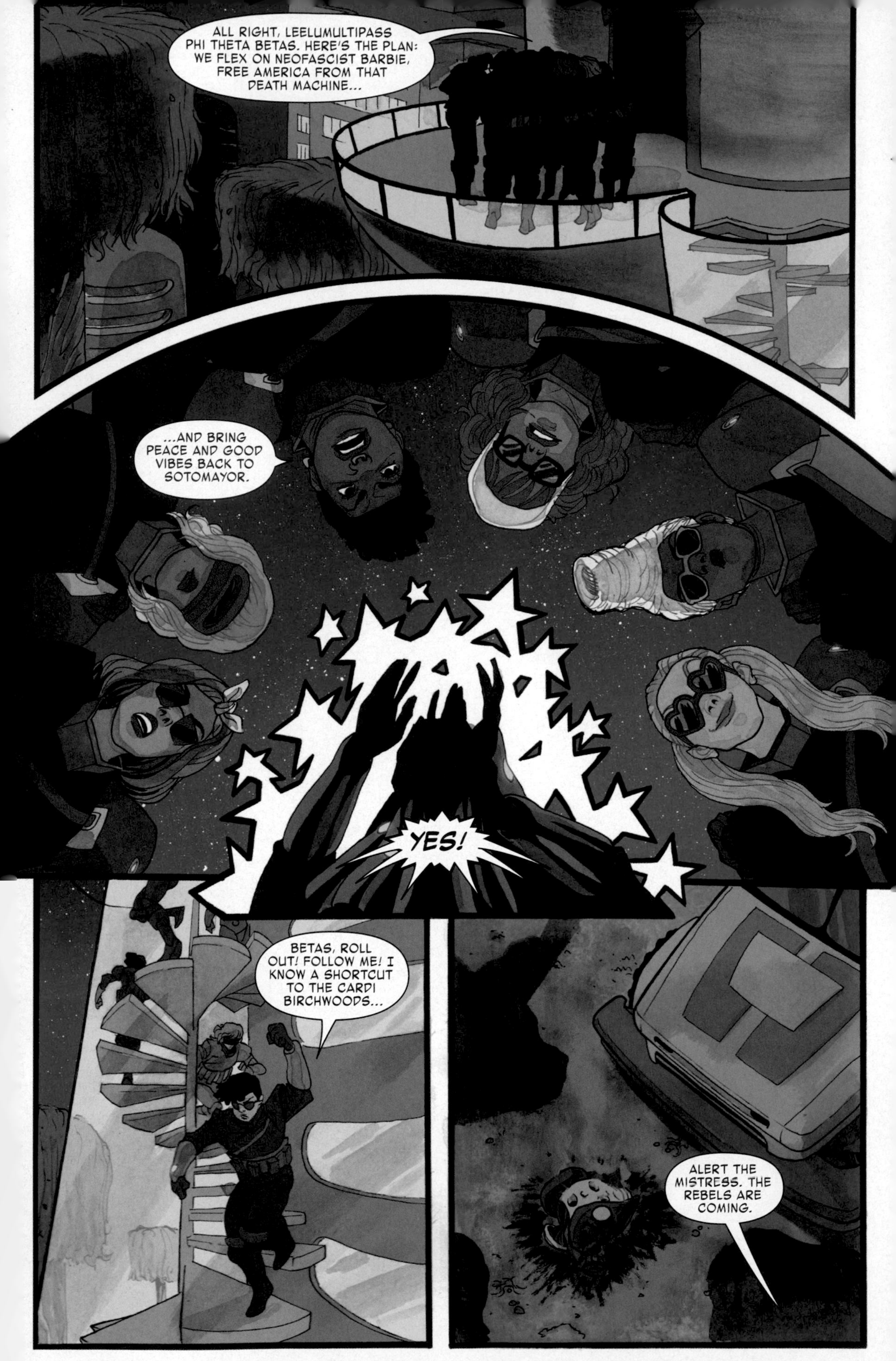
ALL RIGHT, LEELUMULTIPASS PHI THETA BETAS. HERE'S THE PLAN: WE FLEX ON NEOFASCIST BARBIE, FREE AMERICA FROM THAT DEATH MACHINE...
...AND BRING PEACE AND GOOD VIBES BACK TO SOTOMAYOR.
YES!
BETAS, ROLL OUT! FOLLOW ME! I KNOW A SHORTCUT TO THE CARDI BIRCHWOODS...
ALERT THE MISTRESS. THE REBELS ARE COMING.

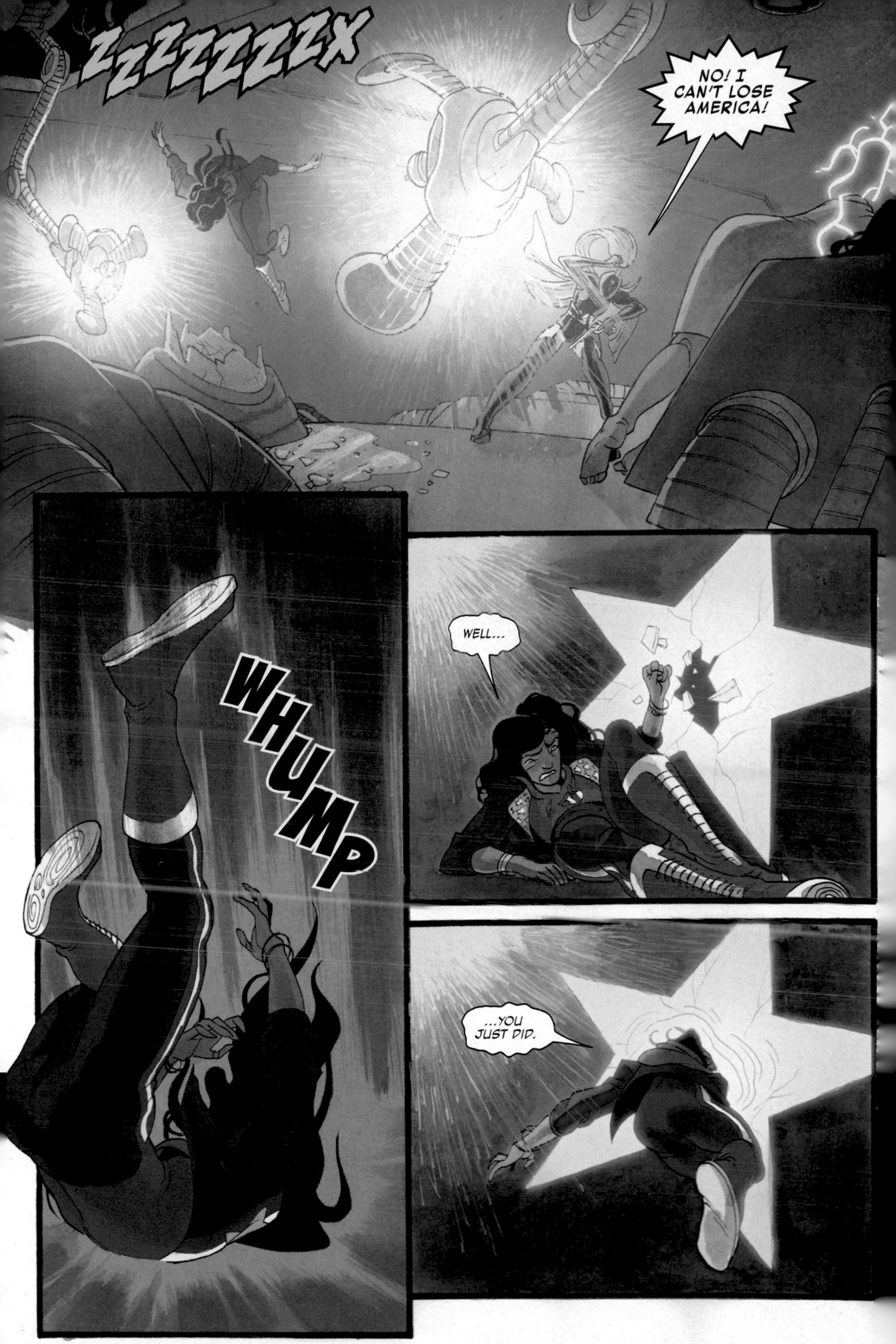
ZZZZZZZZX
NO! I CAN'T LOSE AMERICA!
WHUMP
WELL...
...YOU JUST DID.

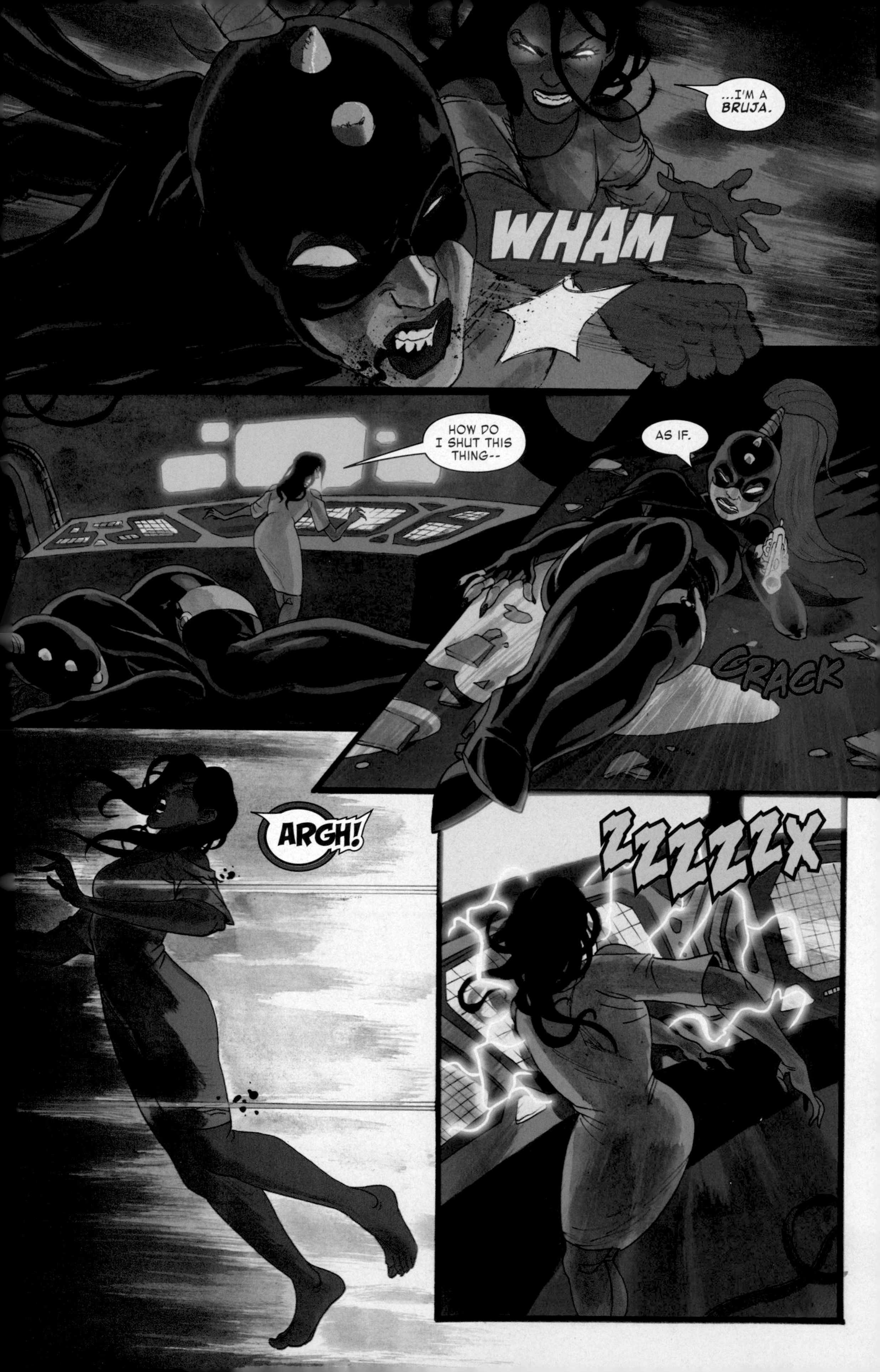
...I'M A BRUJA.
WHAM
HOW DO I SHUT THIS THING--
AS IF.
CRACK
ARGH!
ZZZZZX

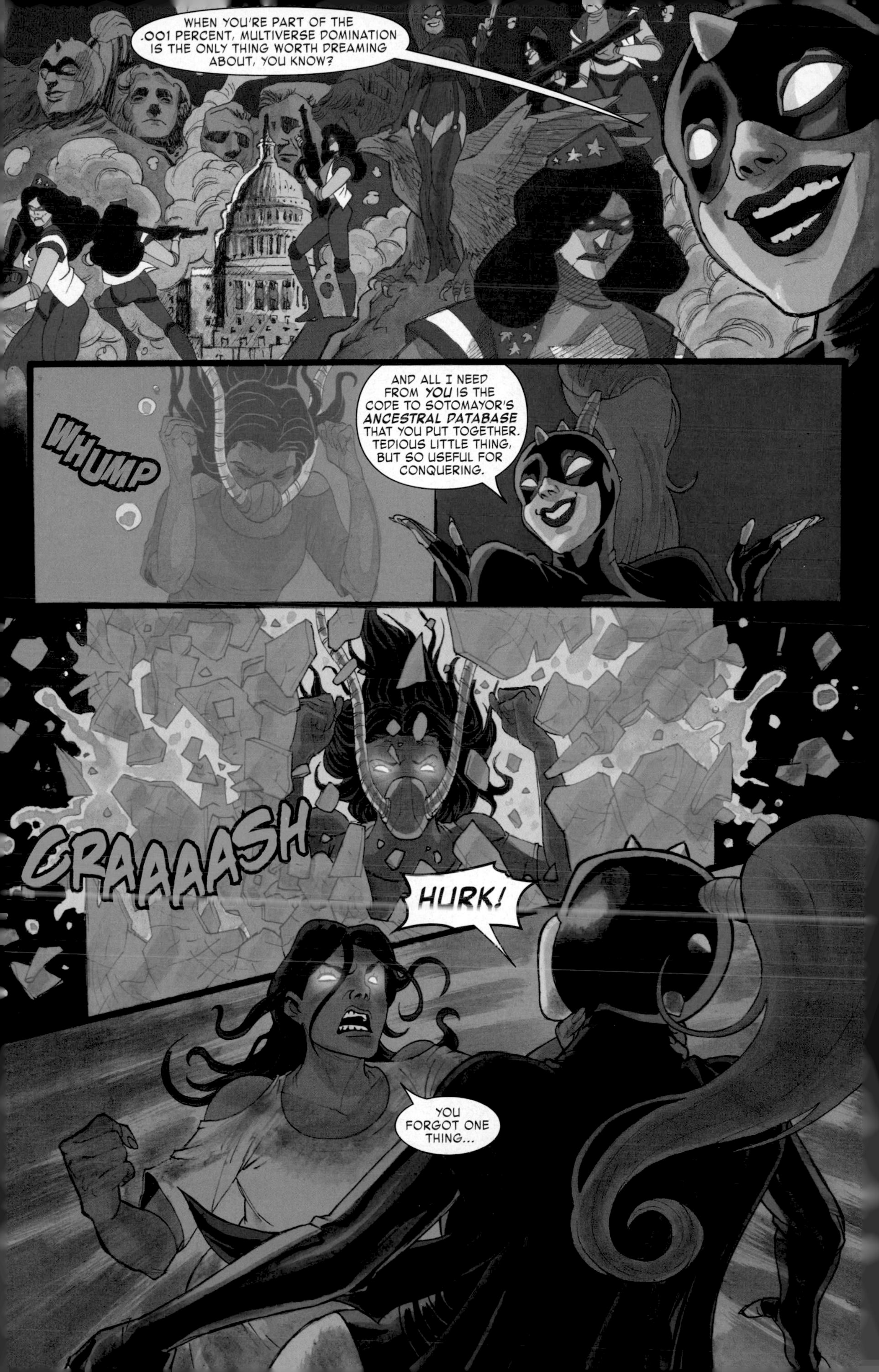
WHEN YOU'RE PART OF THE .001 PERCENT, MULTIVERSE DOMINATION IS THE ONLY THING WORTH DREAMING ABOUT, YOU KNOW?
WHUMP
AND ALL I NEED FROM YOU IS THE CODE TO SOTOMAYOR'S ANCESTRAL DATABASE THAT YOU PUT TOGETHER. TEDIOUS LITTLE THING, BUT SO USEFUL FOR CONQUERING.
CRAAAASH
HURK!
YOU FORGOT ONE THING...

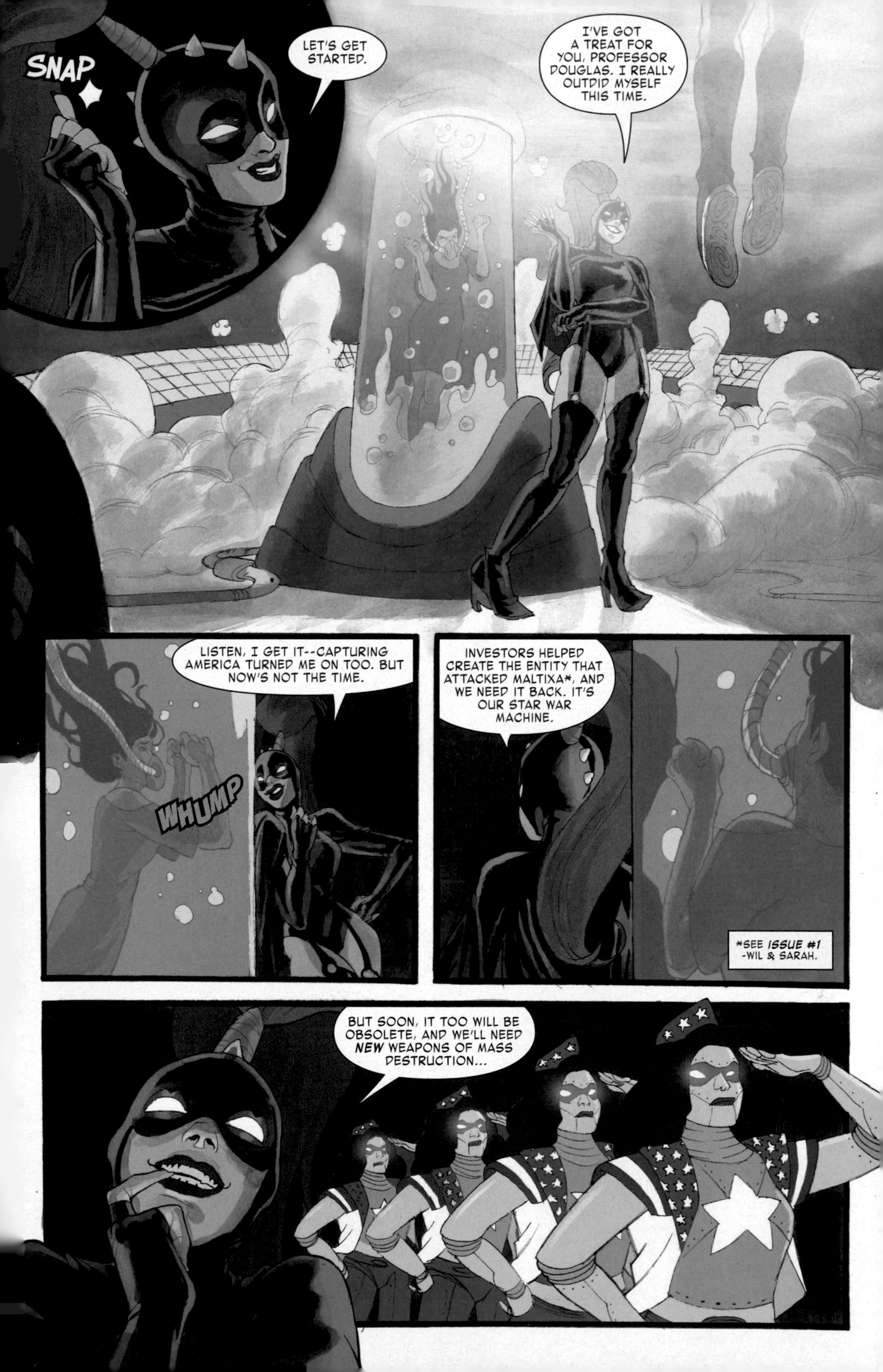
SNAP
LET'S GET STARTED.
I'VE GOT A TREAT FOR YOU, PROFESSOR DOUGLAS. I REALLY OUTDID MYSELF THIS TIME.
LISTEN, I GET IT--CAPTURING AMERICA TURNED ME ON TOO. BUT NOW'S NOT THE TIME.
WHUMP
INVESTORS HELPED CREATE THE ENTITY THAT ATTACKED MALTIXA*, AND WE NEED IT BACK. IT'S OUR STAR WAR MACHINE.
*SEE ISSUE #1 -WIL & SARAH.
BUT SOON, IT TOO WILL BE OBSOLETE, AND WE'LL NEED NEW WEAPONS OF MASS DESTRUCTION...

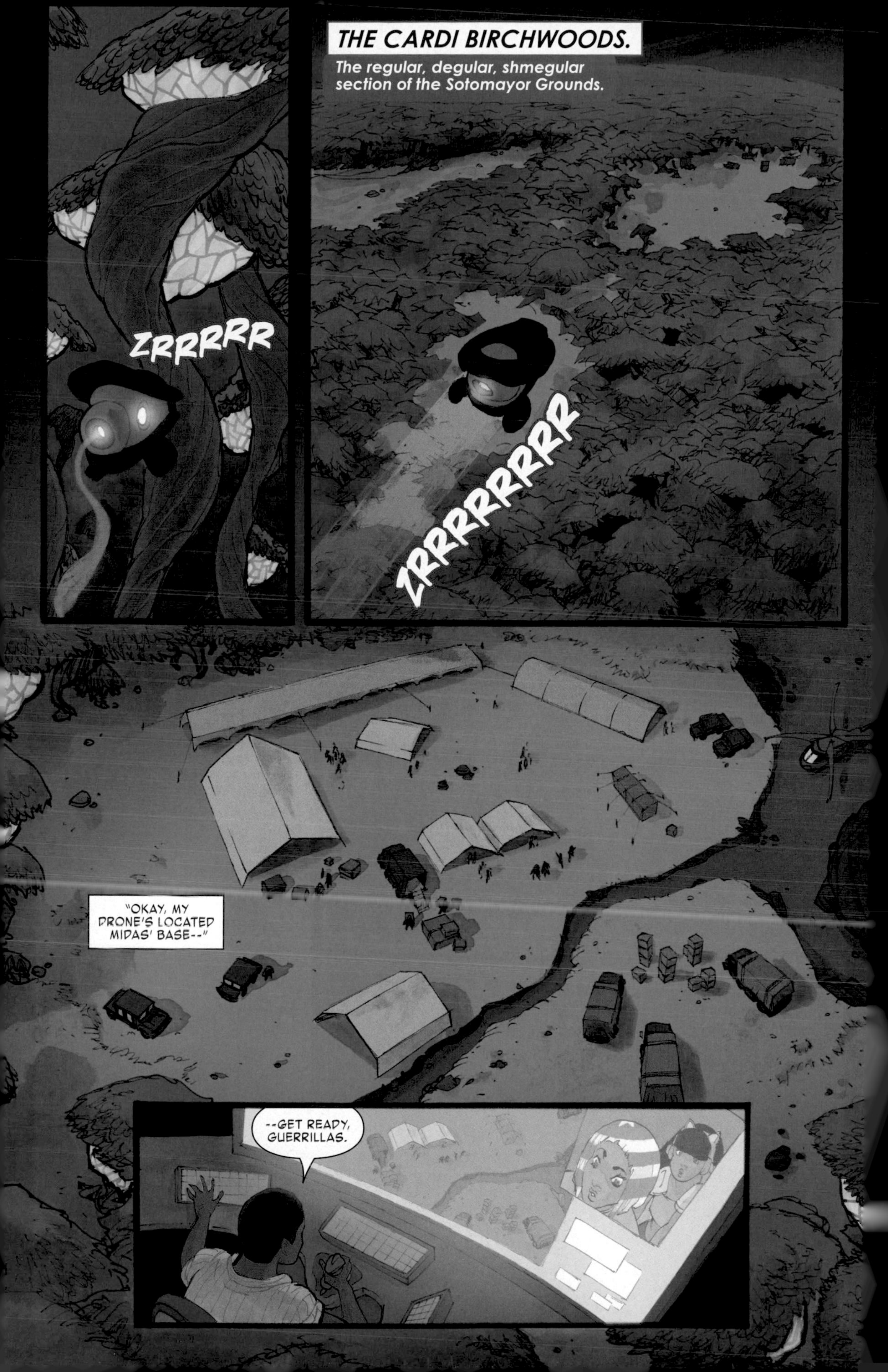
THE CARDI BIRCHWOODS.
The regular, degular, shmegular section of the Sotomayor Grounds.
ZRRRRR
ZRRRRRRRR
"OKAY, MY DRONE'S LOCATED MIDAS' BASE--"
--GET READY, GUERRILLAS.

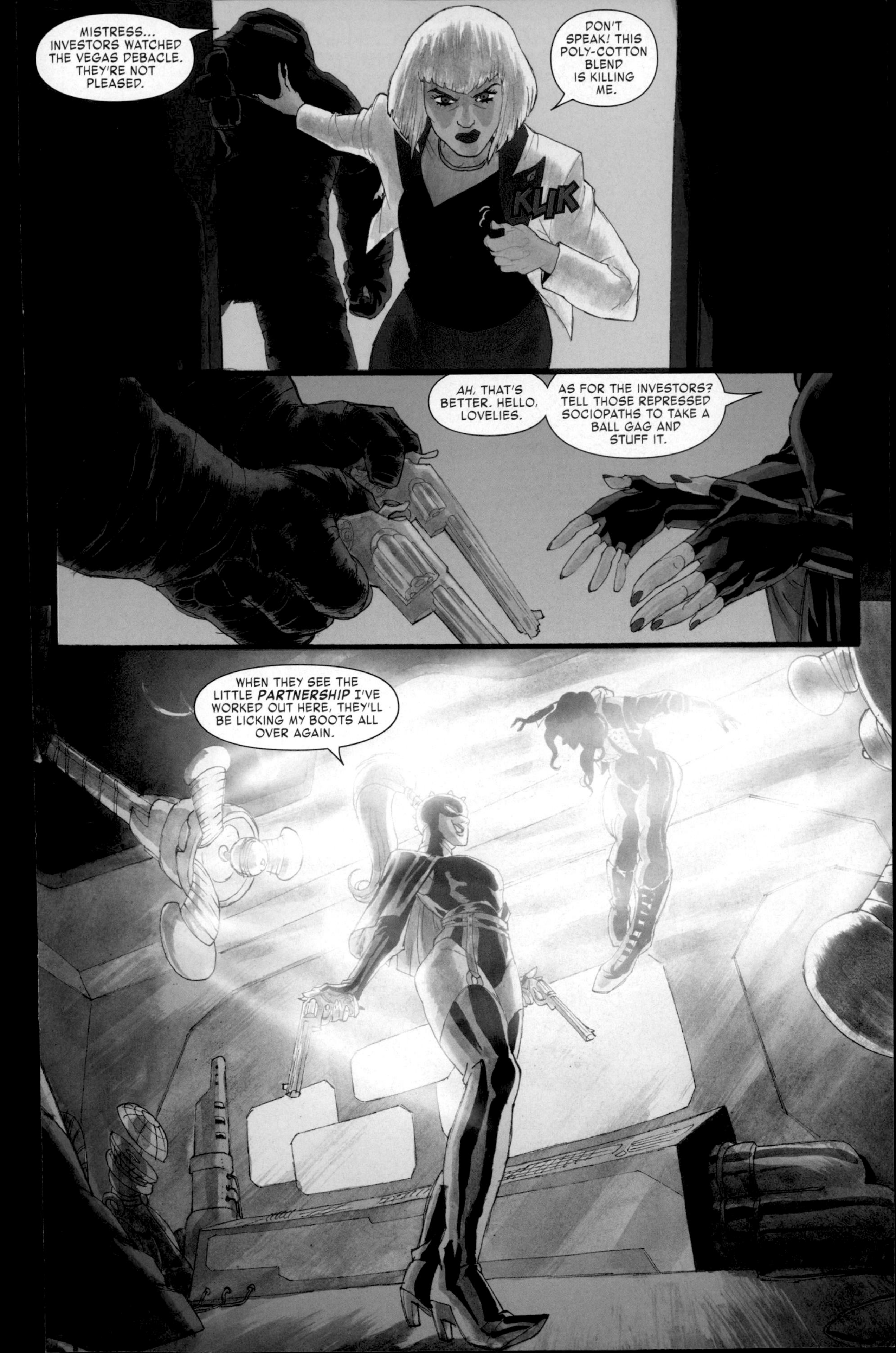
MISTRESS... INVESTORS WATCHED THE VEGAS DEBACLE. THEY'RE NOT PLEASED.
DON'T SPEAK! THIS POLY-COTTON BLEND IS KILLING ME.
KLIK
AH, THAT'S BETTER. HELLO, LOVELIES.
AS FOR THE INVESTORS? TELL THOSE REPRESSED SOCIOPATHS TO TAKE A BALL GAG AND STUFF IT.
WHEN THEY SEE THE LITTLE PARTNERSHIP I'VE WORKED OUT HERE, THEY'LL BE LICKING MY BOOTS ALL OVER AGAIN.

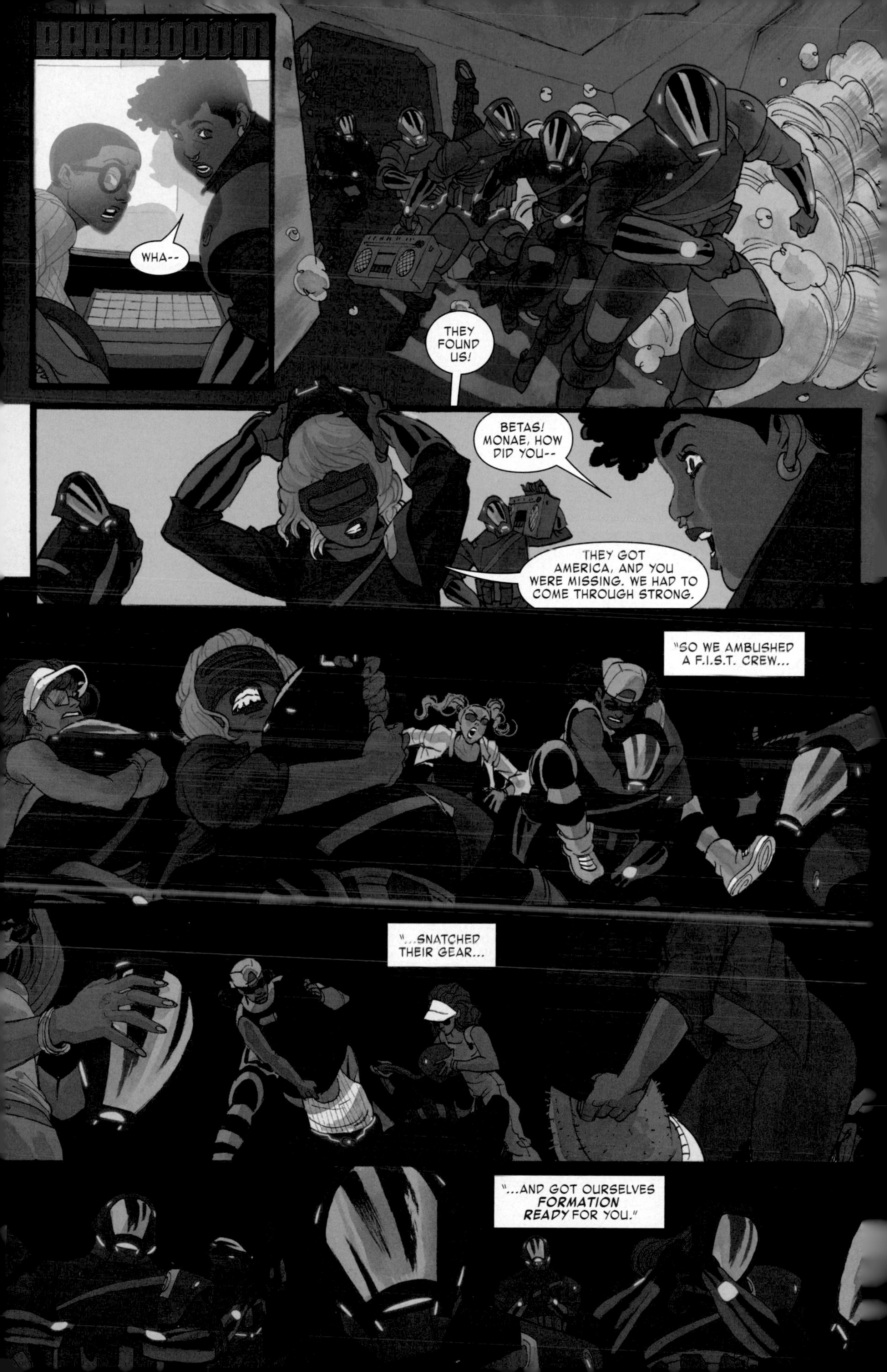
BRRABOOOM
WHA--
THEY FOUND US!
BETAS! MONAE, HOW DID YOU--
THEY GOT AMERICA, AND YOU WERE MISSING. WE HAD TO COME THROUGH STRONG.
"SO WE AMBUSHED A F.I.S.T. CREW...
"...SNATCHED THEIR GEAR...
"...AND GOT OURSELVES FORMATION READY FOR YOU."

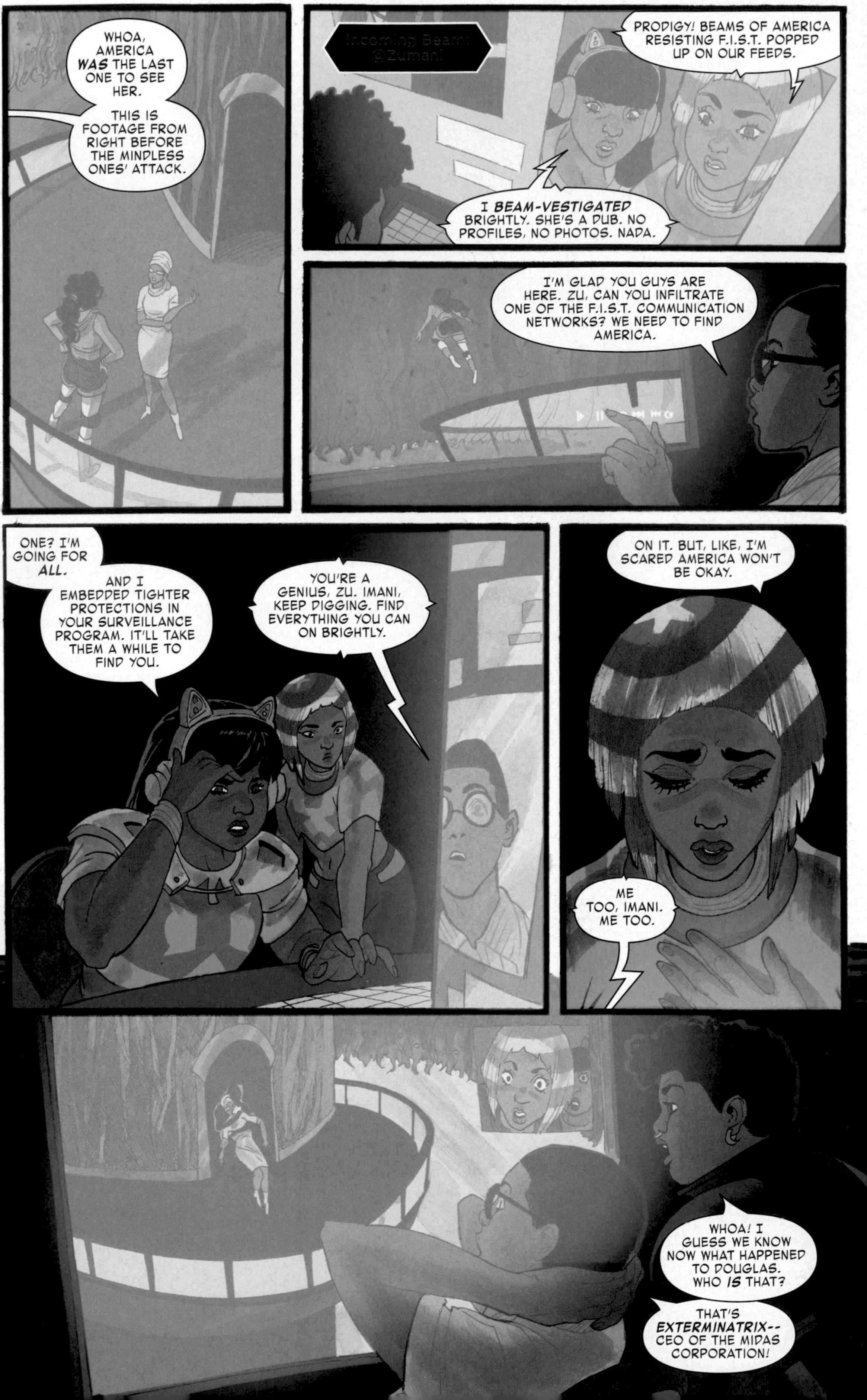
WHOA, AMERICA WAS THE LAST ONE TO SEE HER.
THIS IS FOOTAGE FROM RIGHT BEFORE THE MINDLESS ONES' ATTACK.
Incoming Beam: @Zumani
PRODIGY! BEAMS OF AMERICA RESISTING F.I.S.T. POPPED UP ON OUR FEEDS.
I BEAM-VESTIGATED BRIGHTLY. SHE'S A DUB. NO PROFILES, NO PHOTOS. NADA.
I'M GLAD YOU GUYS ARE HERE. ZU, CAN YOU INFILTRATE ONE OF THE F.I.S.T. COMMUNICATION NETWORKS? WE NEED TO FIND AMERICA.
ONE? I'M GOING FOR ALL.
AND I EMBEDDED TIGHTER PROTECTIONS IN YOUR SURVEILLANCE PROGRAM. IT'LL TAKE THEM A WHILE TO FIND YOU.
YOU'RE A GENIUS, ZU. IMANI, KEEP DIGGING. FIND EVERYTHING YOU CAN ON BRIGHTLY.
ON IT. BUT, LIKE, I'M SCARED AMERICA WON'T BE OKAY.
ME TOO, IMANI. ME TOO.
WHOA! I GUESS WE KNOW NOW WHAT HAPPENED TO DOUGLAS. WHO IS THAT?
THAT'S EXTERMINATRIX-- CEO OF THE MIDAS CORPORATION!

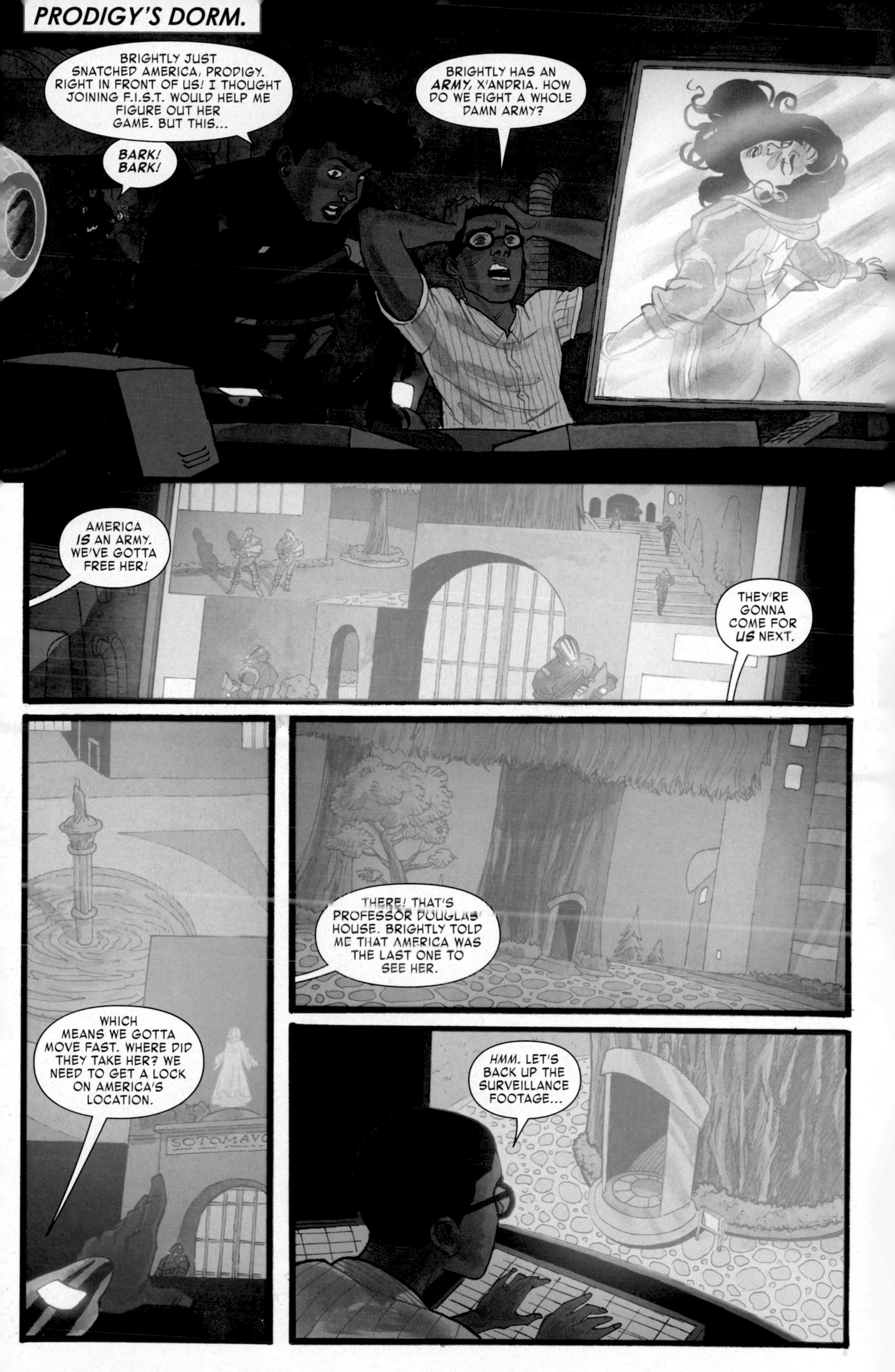
PRODIGY'S DORM.
BRIGHTLY JUST SNATCHED AMERICA, PRODIGY. RIGHT IN FRONT OF US! I THOUGHT JOINING F.I.S.T. WOULD HELP ME FIGURE OUT HER GAME. BUT THIS...
BARK! BARK!
BRIGHTLY HAS AN *ARMY*, X'ANDRIA. HOW DO WE FIGHT A WHOLE DAMN ARMY?
AMERICA *IS* AN ARMY. WE'VE GOTTA FREE HER!
THEY'RE GONNA COME FOR *US* NEXT.
THERE! THAT'S PROFESSOR DOUGLAS' HOUSE. BRIGHTLY TOLD ME THAT AMERICA WAS THE LAST ONE TO SEE HER.
WHICH MEANS WE GOTTA MOVE FAST. WHERE DID THEY TAKE HER? WE NEED TO GET A LOCK ON AMERICA'S LOCATION.
SOTOMAYO
HMM. LET'S BACK UP THE SURVEILLANCE FOOTAGE...

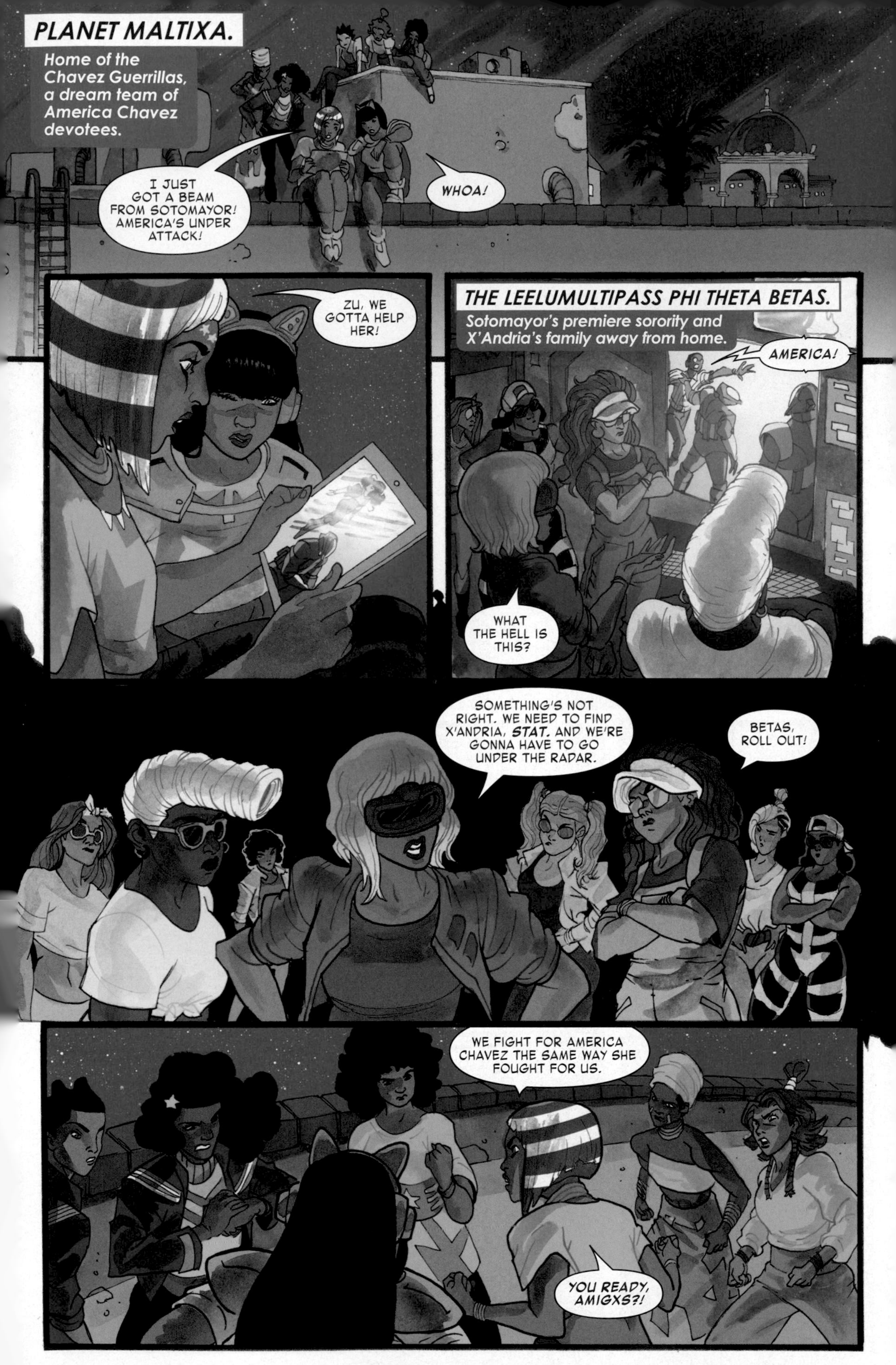
PLANET MALTIXA.
Home of the Chavez Guerrillas, a dream team of America Chavez devotees.
I JUST GOT A BEAM FROM SOTOMAYOR! AMERICA'S UNDER ATTACK!
WHOA!
ZU, WE GOTTA HELP HER!
THE LEELUMULTIPASS PHI THETA BETAS.
Sotomayor's premiere sorority and X'Andria's family away from home.
AMERICA!
WHAT THE HELL IS THIS?
SOMETHING'S NOT RIGHT. WE NEED TO FIND X'ANDRIA, STAT. AND WE'RE GONNA HAVE TO GO UNDER THE RADAR.
BETAS, ROLL OUT!
WE FIGHT FOR AMERICA CHAVEZ THE SAME WAY SHE FOUGHT FOR US.
YOU READY, AMIGXS?!

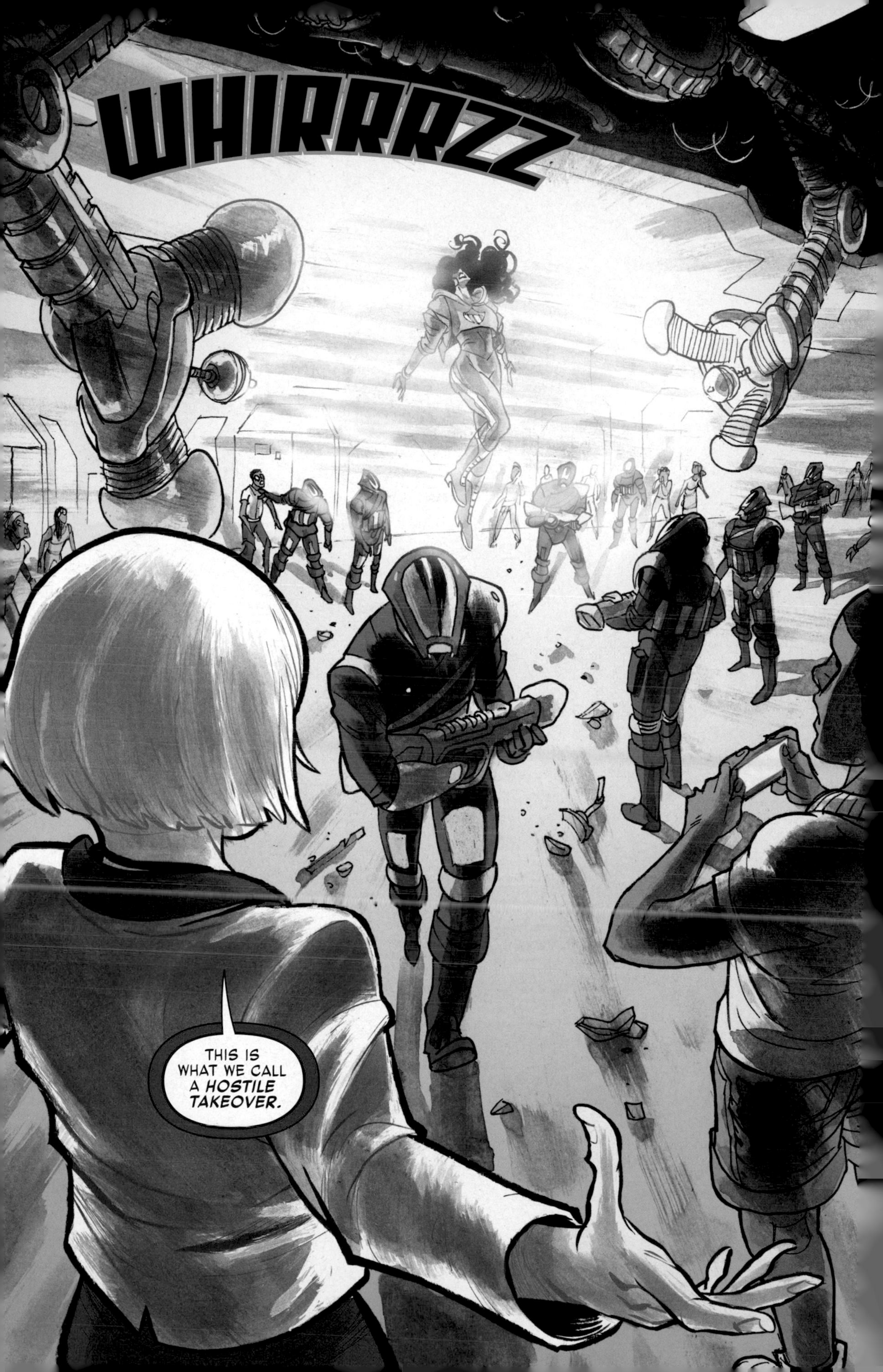
WHIRRRZZ
THIS IS WHAT WE CALL A *HOSTILE TAKEOVER.*

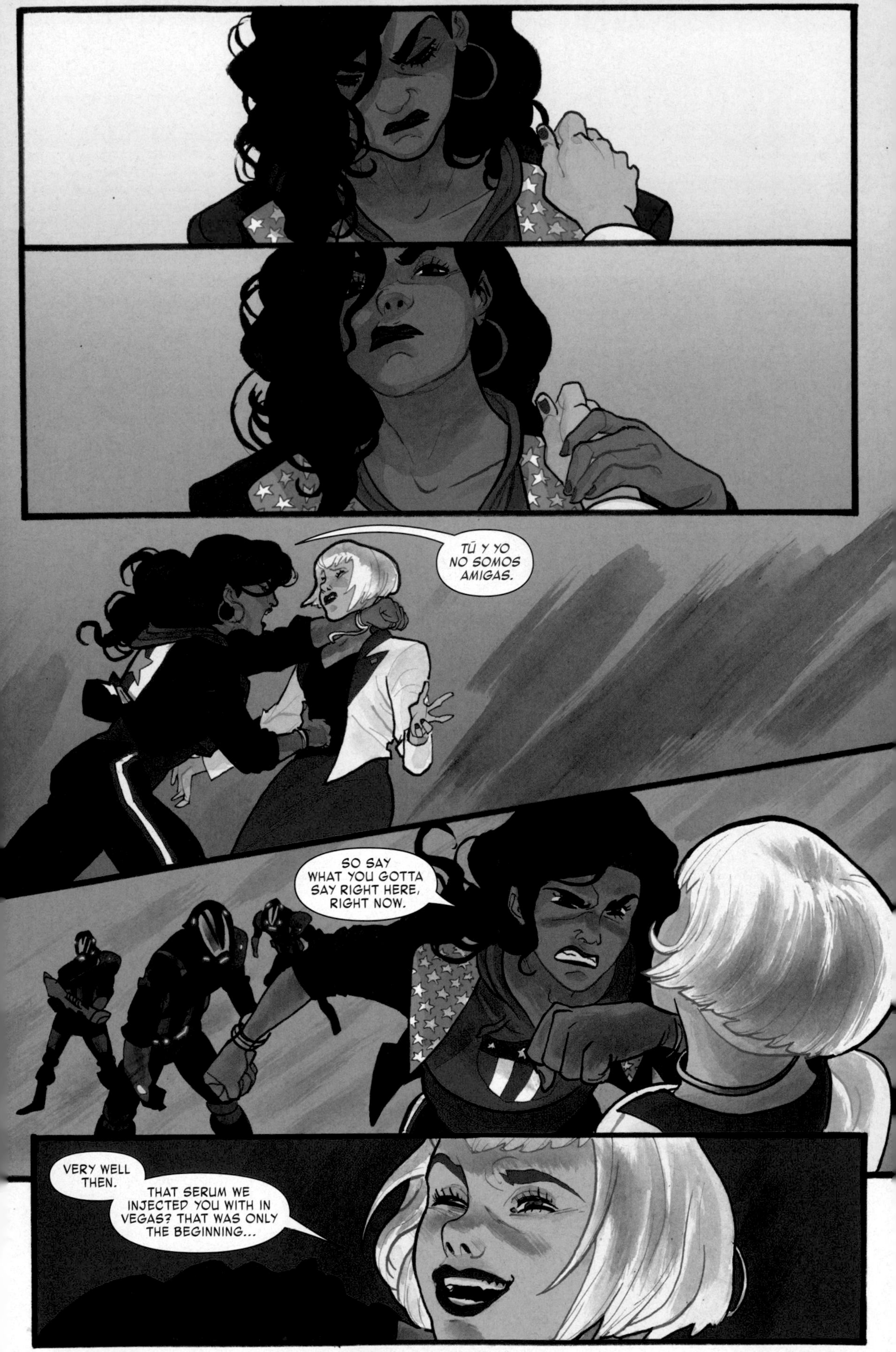
TÚ Y YO NO SOMOS AMIGAS.
SO SAY WHAT YOU GOTTA SAY RIGHT HERE, RIGHT NOW.
VERY WELL THEN.
THAT SERUM WE INJECTED YOU WITH IN VEGAS? THAT WAS ONLY THE BEGINNING...

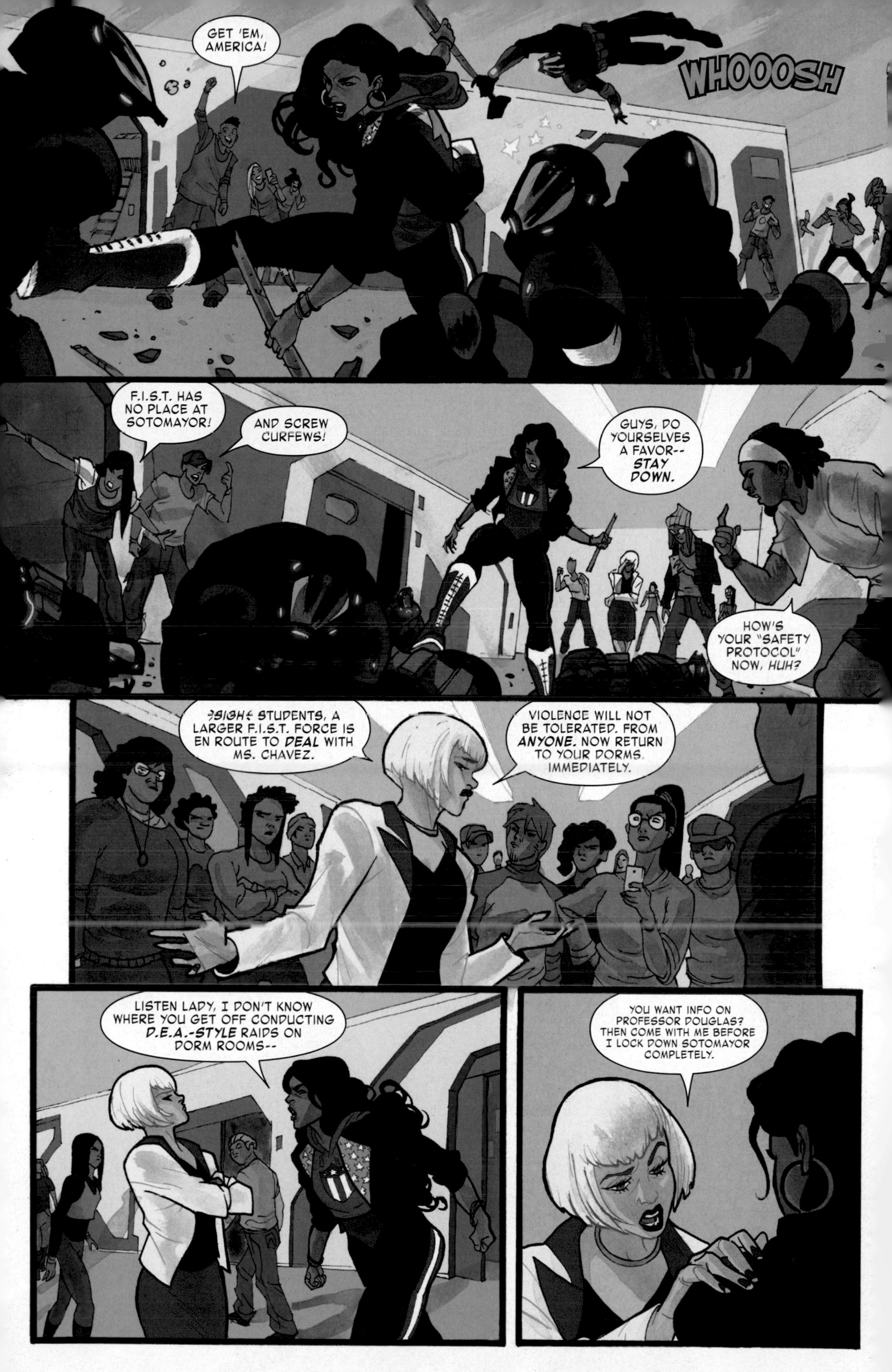
GET 'EM, AMERICA!
WHOOOSH
F.I.S.T. HAS NO PLACE AT SOTOMAYOR!
AND SCREW CURFEWS!
GUYS, DO YOURSELVES A FAVOR-- STAY DOWN.
HOW'S YOUR "SAFETY PROTOCOL" NOW, HUH?
SIGH STUDENTS, A LARGER F.I.S.T. FORCE IS EN ROUTE TO DEAL WITH MS. CHAVEZ.
VIOLENCE WILL NOT BE TOLERATED. FROM ANYONE. NOW RETURN TO YOUR DORMS. IMMEDIATELY.
LISTEN LADY, I DON'T KNOW WHERE YOU GET OFF CONDUCTING D.E.A.-STYLE RAIDS ON DORM ROOMS--
YOU WANT INFO ON PROFESSOR DOUGLAS? THEN COME WITH ME BEFORE I LOCK DOWN SOTOMAYOR COMPLETELY.

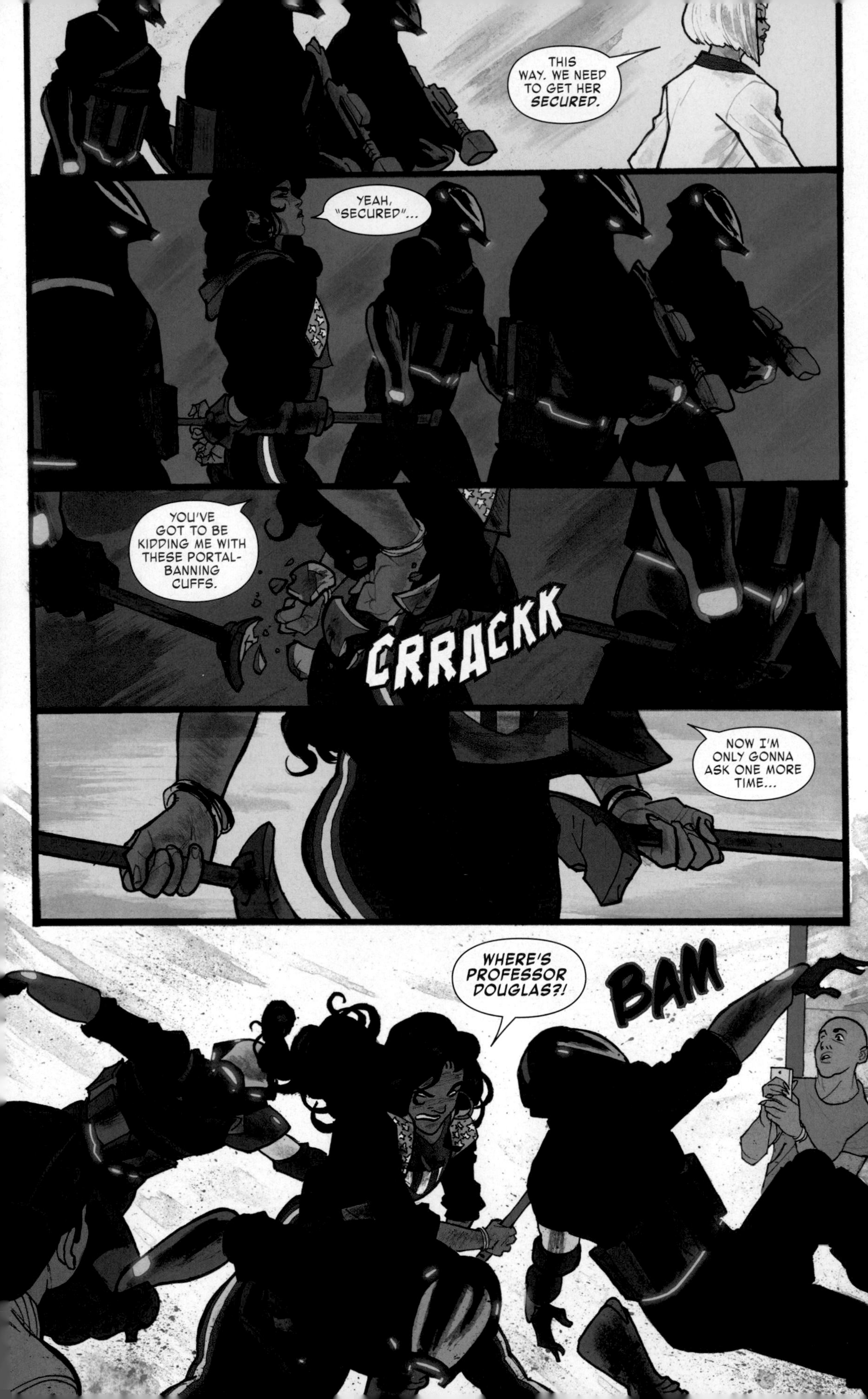

THIS WAY. WE NEED TO GET HER SECURED.
YEAH, "SECURED"...
YOU'VE GOT TO BE KIDDING ME WITH THESE PORTAL-BANNING CUFFS.
CRRACKK
NOW I'M ONLY GONNA ASK ONE MORE TIME...
WHERE'S PROFESSOR DOUGLAS?!
BAM

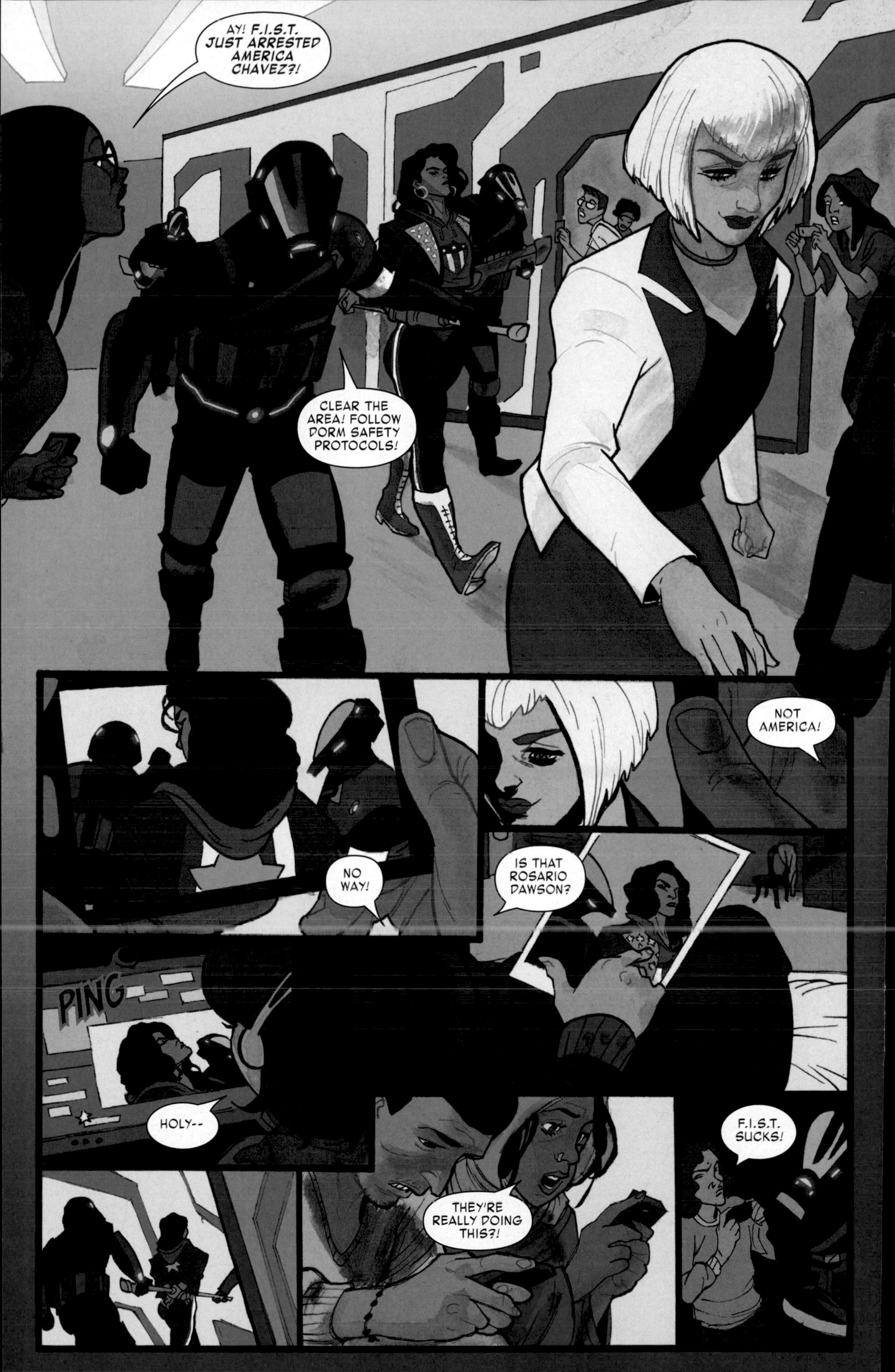
AY! F.I.S.T. JUST ARRESTED AMERICA CHAVEZ?!
CLEAR THE AREA! FOLLOW DORM SAFETY PROTOCOLS!
NOT AMERICA!
NO WAY!
IS THAT ROSARIO DAWSON?
PING
HOLY--
F.I.S.T. SUCKS!
THEY'RE REALLY DOING THIS?!

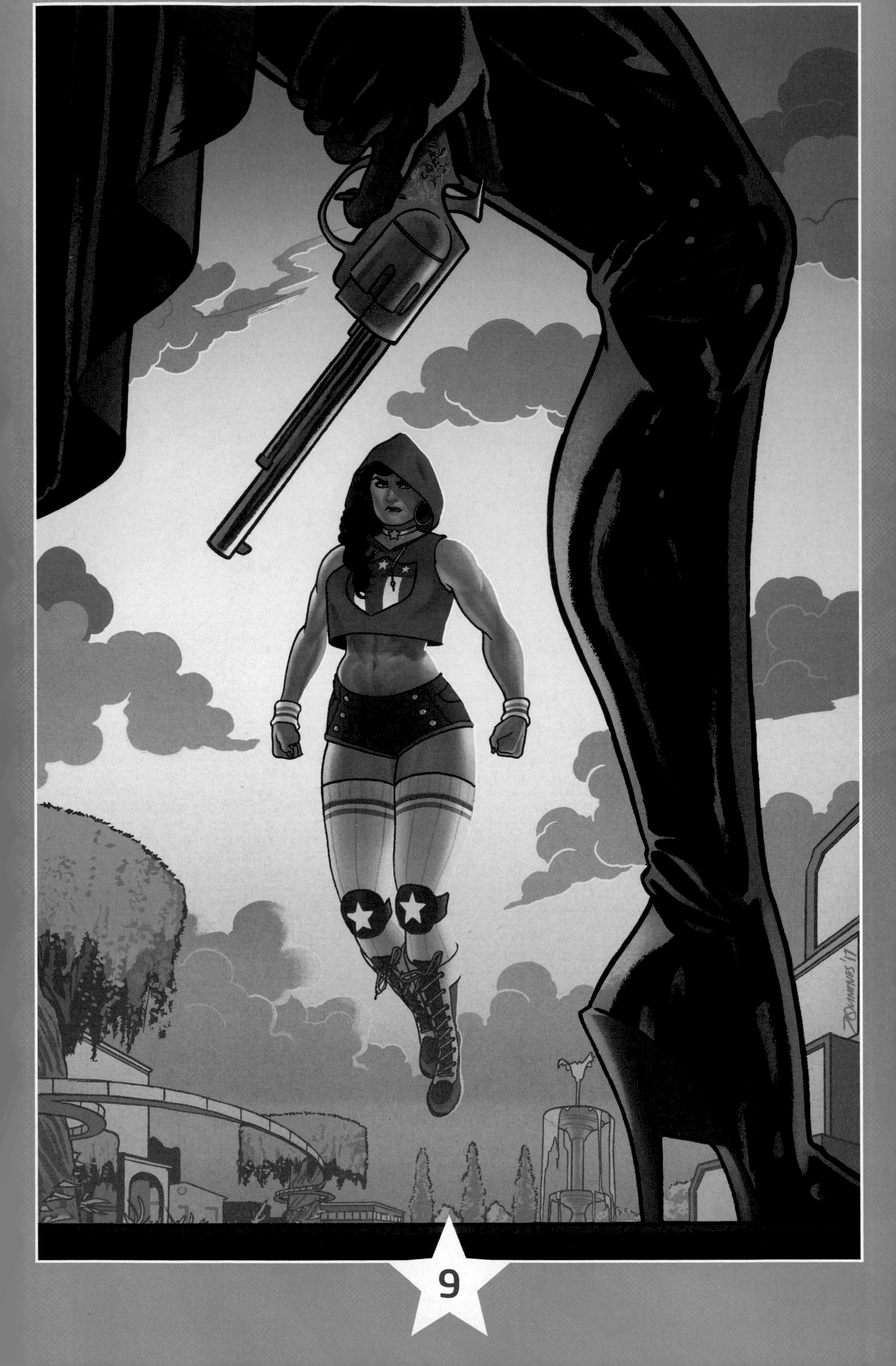

9

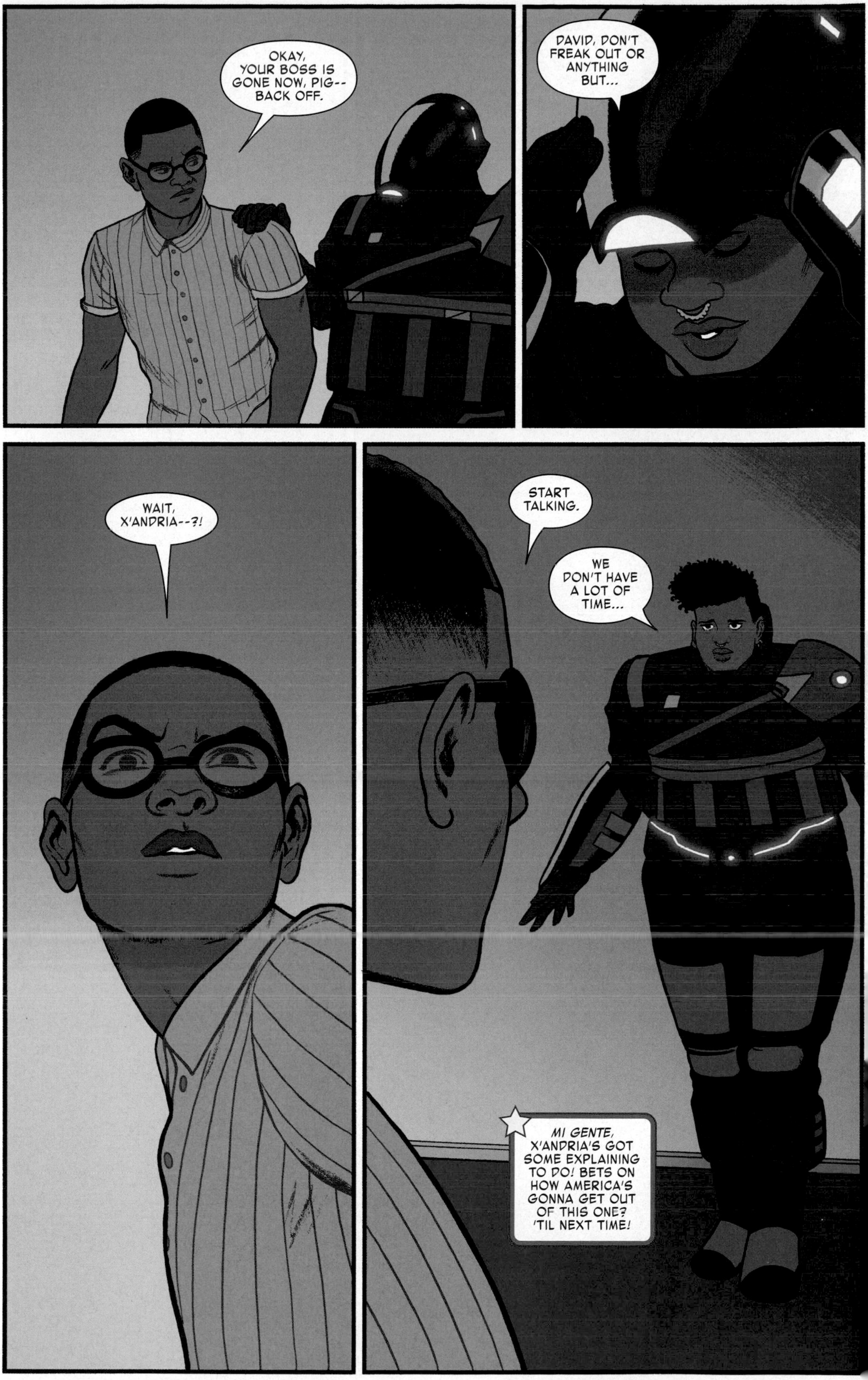
OKAY, YOUR BOSS IS GONE NOW, PIG-- BACK OFF.
DAVID, DON'T FREAK OUT OR ANYTHING BUT...
WAIT, X'ANDRIA--?!
START TALKING.
WE DON'T HAVE A LOT OF TIME...
MI GENTE, X'ANDRIA'S GOT SOME EXPLAINING TO DO! BETS ON HOW AMERICA'S GONNA GET OUT OF THIS ONE? 'TIL NEXT TIME!

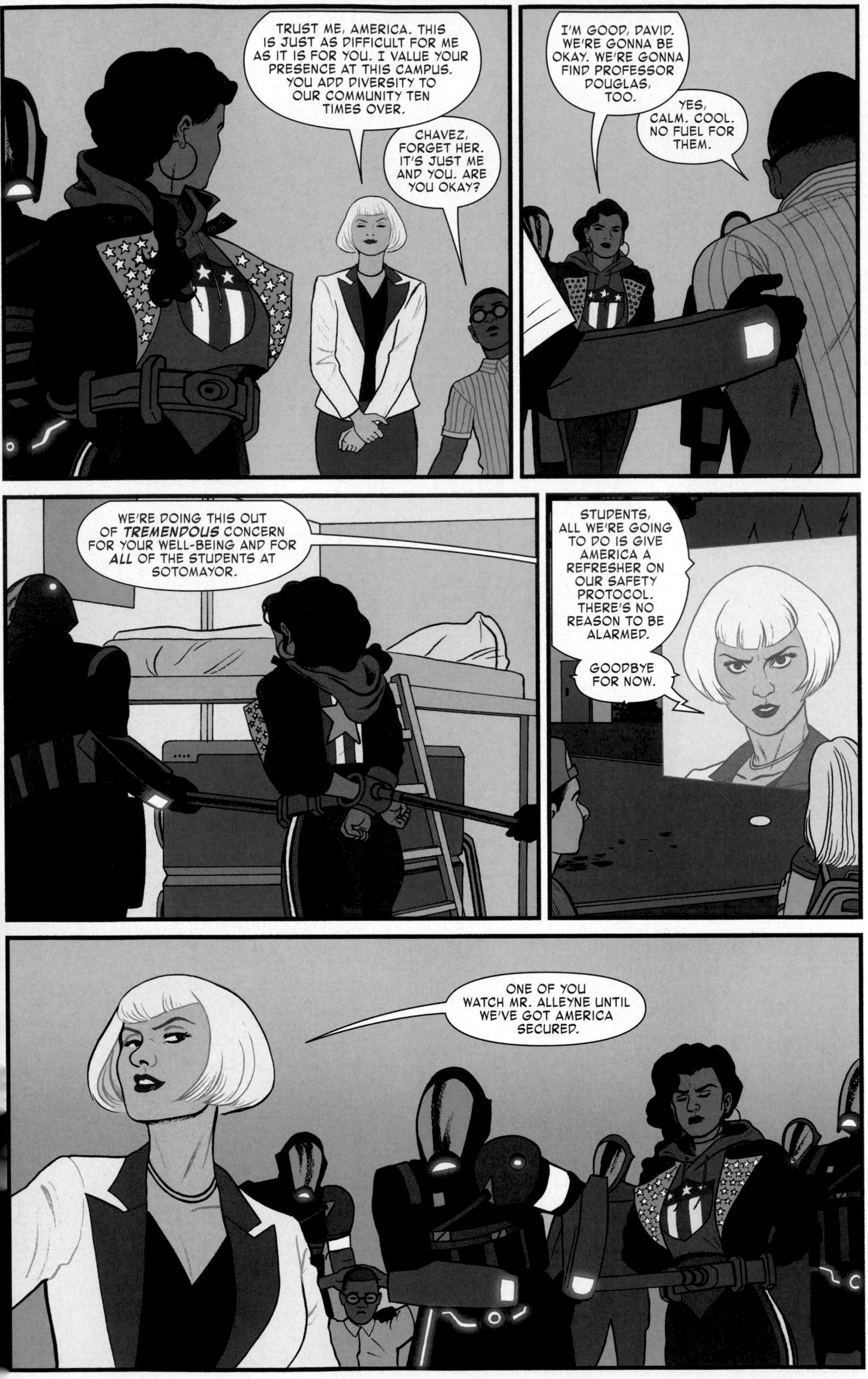
TRUST ME, AMERICA. THIS IS JUST AS DIFFICULT FOR ME AS IT IS FOR YOU. I VALUE YOUR PRESENCE AT THIS CAMPUS. YOU ADD DIVERSITY TO OUR COMMUNITY TEN TIMES OVER.
CHAVEZ, FORGET HER. IT'S JUST ME AND YOU. ARE YOU OKAY?
I'M GOOD, DAVID. WE'RE GONNA BE OKAY. WE'RE GONNA FIND PROFESSOR DOUGLAS, TOO.
YES, CALM. COOL. NO FUEL FOR THEM.
WE'RE DOING THIS OUT OF TREMENDOUS CONCERN FOR YOUR WELL-BEING AND FOR ALL OF THE STUDENTS AT SOTOMAYOR.
STUDENTS, ALL WE'RE GOING TO DO IS GIVE AMERICA A REFRESHER ON OUR SAFETY PROTOCOL. THERE'S NO REASON TO BE ALARMED.
GOODBYE FOR NOW.
ONE OF YOU WATCH MR. ALLEYNE UNTIL WE'VE GOT AMERICA SECURED.

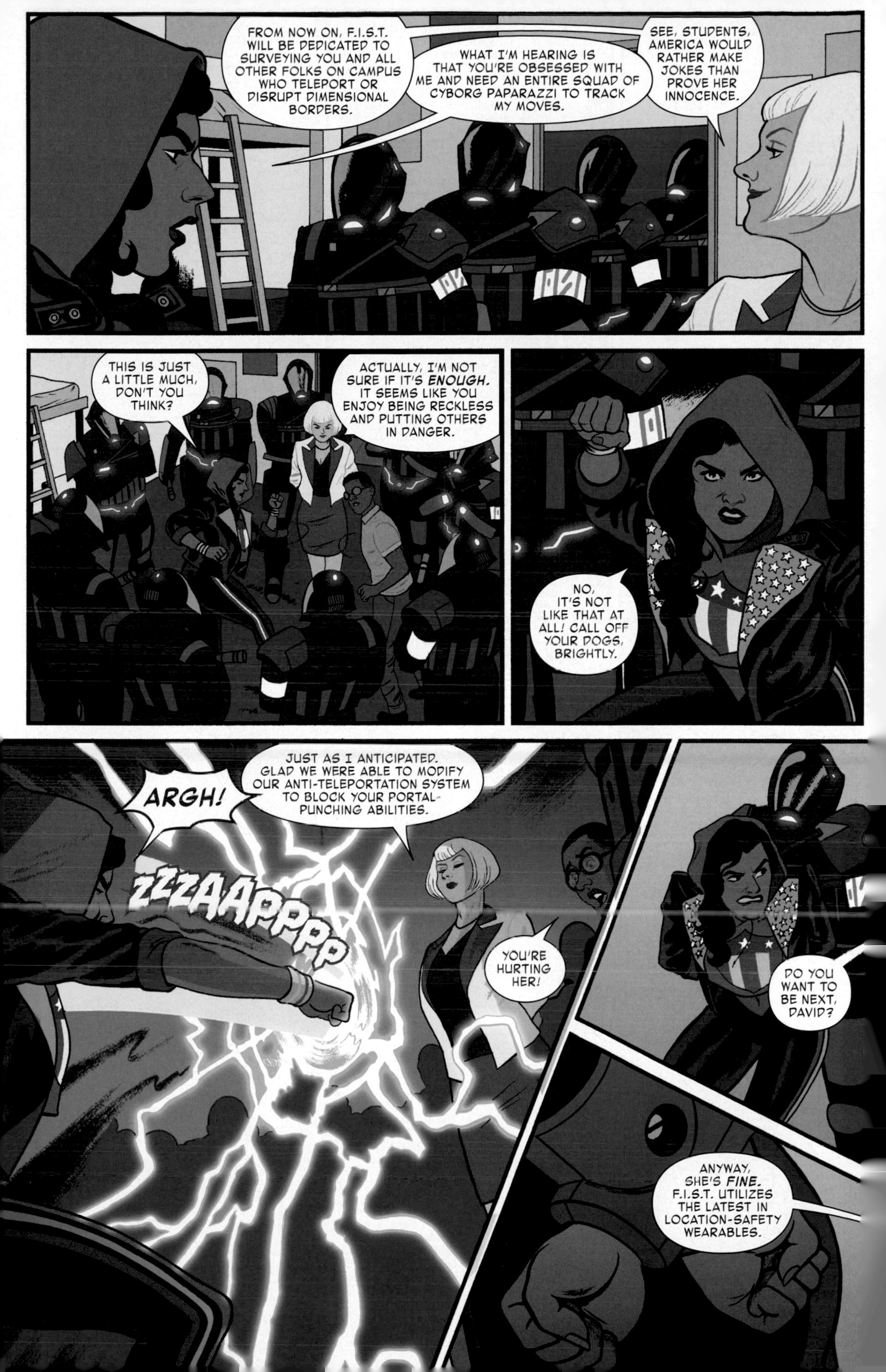
FROM NOW ON, F.I.S.T. WILL BE DEDICATED TO SURVEYING YOU AND ALL OTHER FOLKS ON CAMPUS WHO TELEPORT OR DISRUPT DIMENSIONAL BORDERS.
WHAT I'M HEARING IS THAT YOU'RE OBSESSED WITH ME AND NEED AN ENTIRE SQUAD OF CYBORG PAPARAZZI TO TRACK MY MOVES.
SEE, STUDENTS, AMERICA WOULD RATHER MAKE JOKES THAN PROVE HER INNOCENCE.
THIS IS JUST A LITTLE MUCH, DON'T YOU THINK?
ACTUALLY, I'M NOT SURE IF IT'S *ENOUGH.* IT SEEMS LIKE YOU ENJOY BEING RECKLESS AND PUTTING OTHERS IN DANGER.
NO, IT'S NOT LIKE THAT AT ALL! CALL OFF YOUR DOGS, BRIGHTLY.
ARGH!
JUST AS I ANTICIPATED. GLAD WE WERE ABLE TO MODIFY OUR ANTI-TELEPORTATION SYSTEM TO BLOCK YOUR PORTAL-PUNCHING ABILITIES.
ZZZAAPPPPP
YOU'RE HURTING HER!
DO YOU WANT TO BE NEXT, DAVID?
ANYWAY, SHE'S *FINE.* F.I.S.T. UTILIZES THE LATEST IN LOCATION-SAFETY WEARABLES.

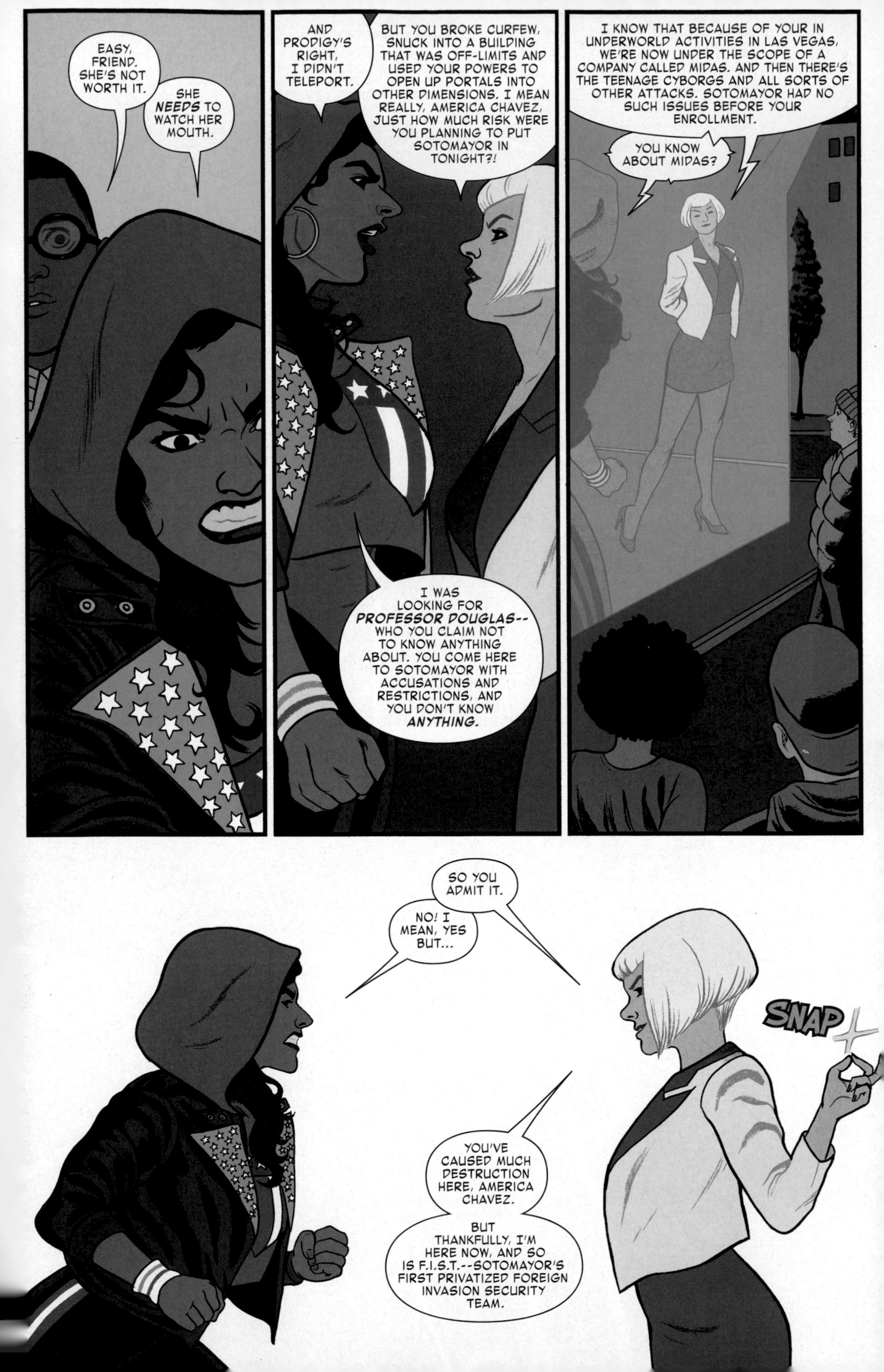
EASY, FRIEND. SHE'S NOT WORTH IT.
SHE NEEDS TO WATCH HER MOUTH.
AND PRODIGY'S RIGHT, I DIDN'T TELEPORT.
BUT YOU BROKE CURFEW, SNUCK INTO A BUILDING THAT WAS OFF-LIMITS AND USED YOUR POWERS TO OPEN UP PORTALS INTO OTHER DIMENSIONS. I MEAN REALLY, AMERICA CHAVEZ, JUST HOW MUCH RISK WERE YOU PLANNING TO PUT SOTOMAYOR IN TONIGHT?!
I WAS LOOKING FOR PROFESSOR DOUGLAS-- WHO YOU CLAIM NOT TO KNOW ANYTHING ABOUT. YOU COME HERE TO SOTOMAYOR WITH ACCUSATIONS AND RESTRICTIONS, AND YOU DON'T KNOW ANYTHING.
I KNOW THAT BECAUSE OF YOUR IN UNDERWORLD ACTIVITIES IN LAS VEGAS, WE'RE NOW UNDER THE SCOPE OF A COMPANY CALLED MIDAS. AND THEN THERE'S THE TEENAGE CYBORGS AND ALL SORTS OF OTHER ATTACKS. SOTOMAYOR HAD NO SUCH ISSUES BEFORE YOUR ENROLLMENT.
YOU KNOW ABOUT MIDAS?
SO YOU ADMIT IT.
NO! I MEAN, YES BUT...
SNAP
YOU'VE CAUSED MUCH DESTRUCTION HERE, AMERICA CHAVEZ.
BUT THANKFULLY, I'M HERE NOW, AND SO IS F.I.S.T.--SOTOMAYOR'S FIRST PRIVATIZED FOREIGN INVASION SECURITY TEAM.

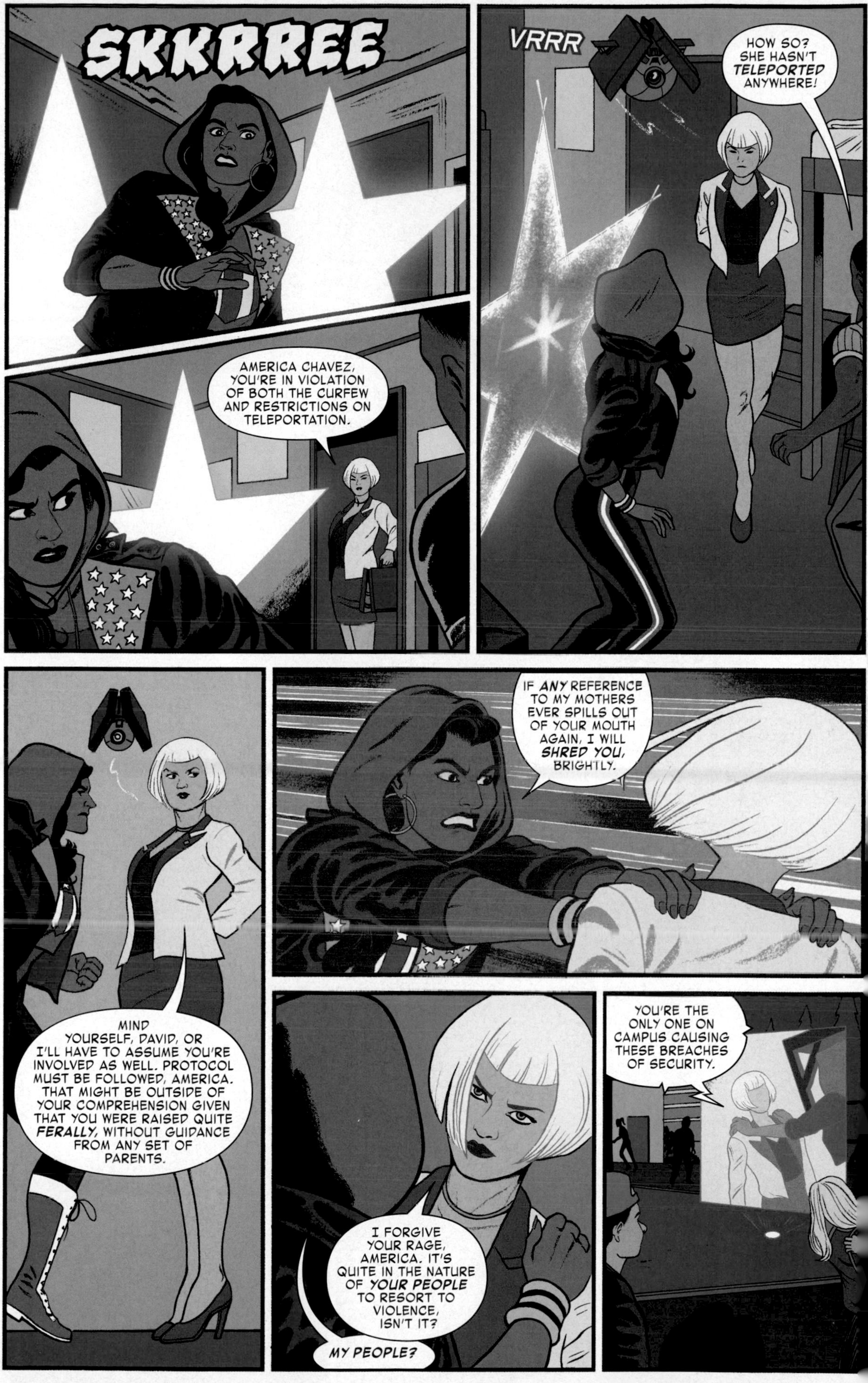
SKKRREE
AMERICA CHAVEZ, YOU'RE IN VIOLATION OF BOTH THE CURFEW AND RESTRICTIONS ON TELEPORTATION.
VRRR
HOW SO? SHE HASN'T TELEPORTED ANYWHERE!
MIND YOURSELF, DAVID, OR I'LL HAVE TO ASSUME YOU'RE INVOLVED AS WELL. PROTOCOL MUST BE FOLLOWED, AMERICA. THAT MIGHT BE OUTSIDE OF YOUR COMPREHENSION GIVEN THAT YOU WERE RAISED QUITE FERALLY, WITHOUT GUIDANCE FROM ANY SET OF PARENTS.
IF ANY REFERENCE TO MY MOTHERS EVER SPILLS OUT OF YOUR MOUTH AGAIN, I WILL SHRED YOU, BRIGHTLY.
I FORGIVE YOUR RAGE, AMERICA. IT'S QUITE IN THE NATURE OF YOUR PEOPLE TO RESORT TO VIOLENCE, ISN'T IT?
MY PEOPLE?
YOU'RE THE ONLY ONE ON CAMPUS CAUSING THESE BREACHES OF SECURITY.

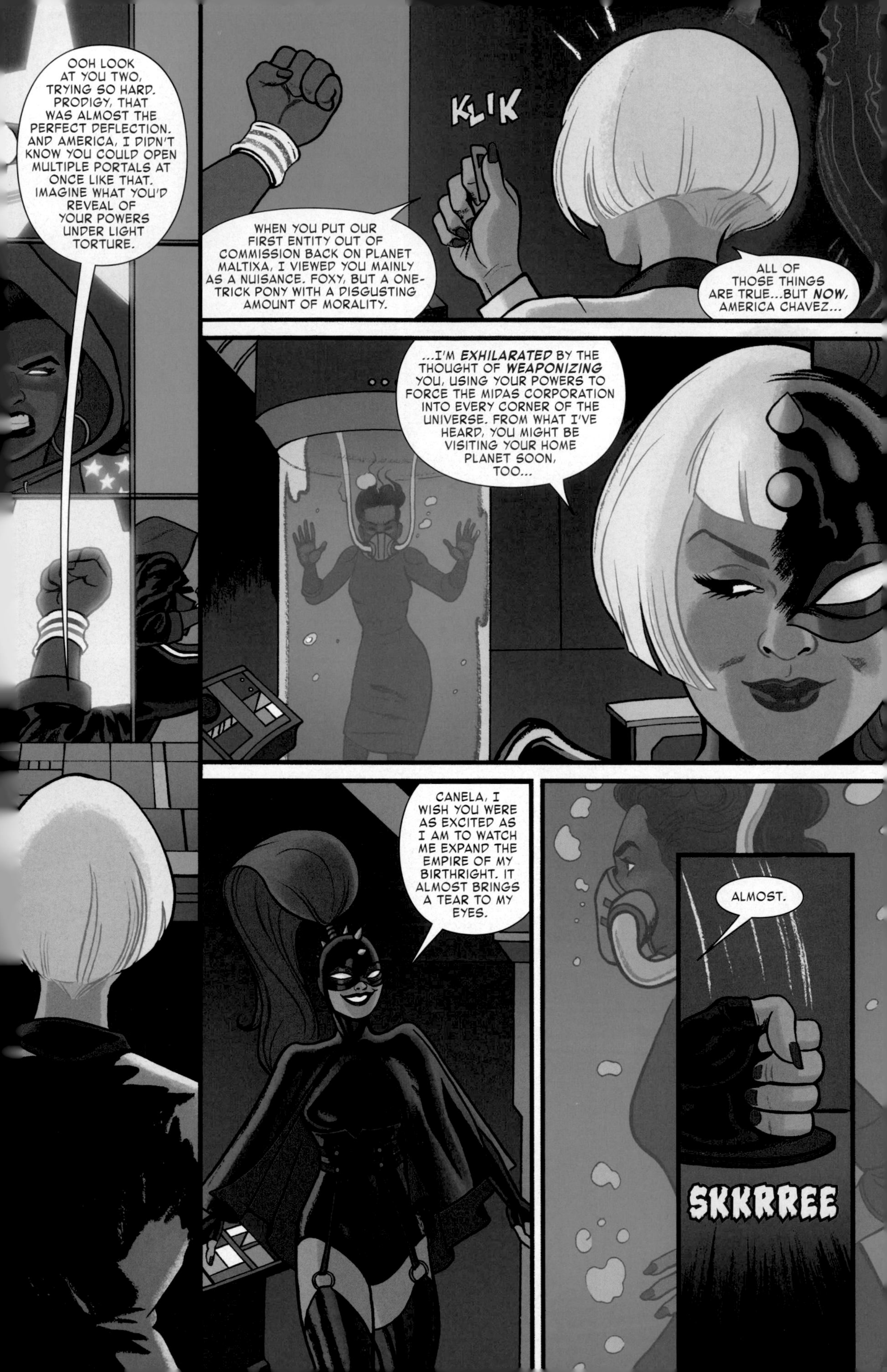
OOH LOOK AT YOU TWO, TRYING SO HARD. PRODIGY, THAT WAS ALMOST THE PERFECT DEFLECTION. AND AMERICA, I DIDN'T KNOW YOU COULD OPEN MULTIPLE PORTALS AT ONCE LIKE THAT. IMAGINE WHAT YOU'D REVEAL OF YOUR POWERS UNDER LIGHT TORTURE.
WHEN YOU PUT OUR FIRST ENTITY OUT OF COMMISSION BACK ON PLANET MALTIXA, I VIEWED YOU MAINLY AS A NUISANCE. FOXY, BUT A ONE-TRICK PONY WITH A DISGUSTING AMOUNT OF MORALITY.
KLIK
ALL OF THOSE THINGS ARE TRUE...BUT NOW, AMERICA CHAVEZ...
...I'M EXHILARATED BY THE THOUGHT OF WEAPONIZING YOU, USING YOUR POWERS TO FORCE THE MIDAS CORPORATION INTO EVERY CORNER OF THE UNIVERSE. FROM WHAT I'VE HEARD, YOU MIGHT BE VISITING YOUR HOME PLANET SOON, TOO...
CANELA, I WISH YOU WERE AS EXCITED AS I AM TO WATCH ME EXPAND THE EMPIRE OF MY BIRTHRIGHT. IT ALMOST BRINGS A TEAR TO MY EYES.
ALMOST.
SKKRREE

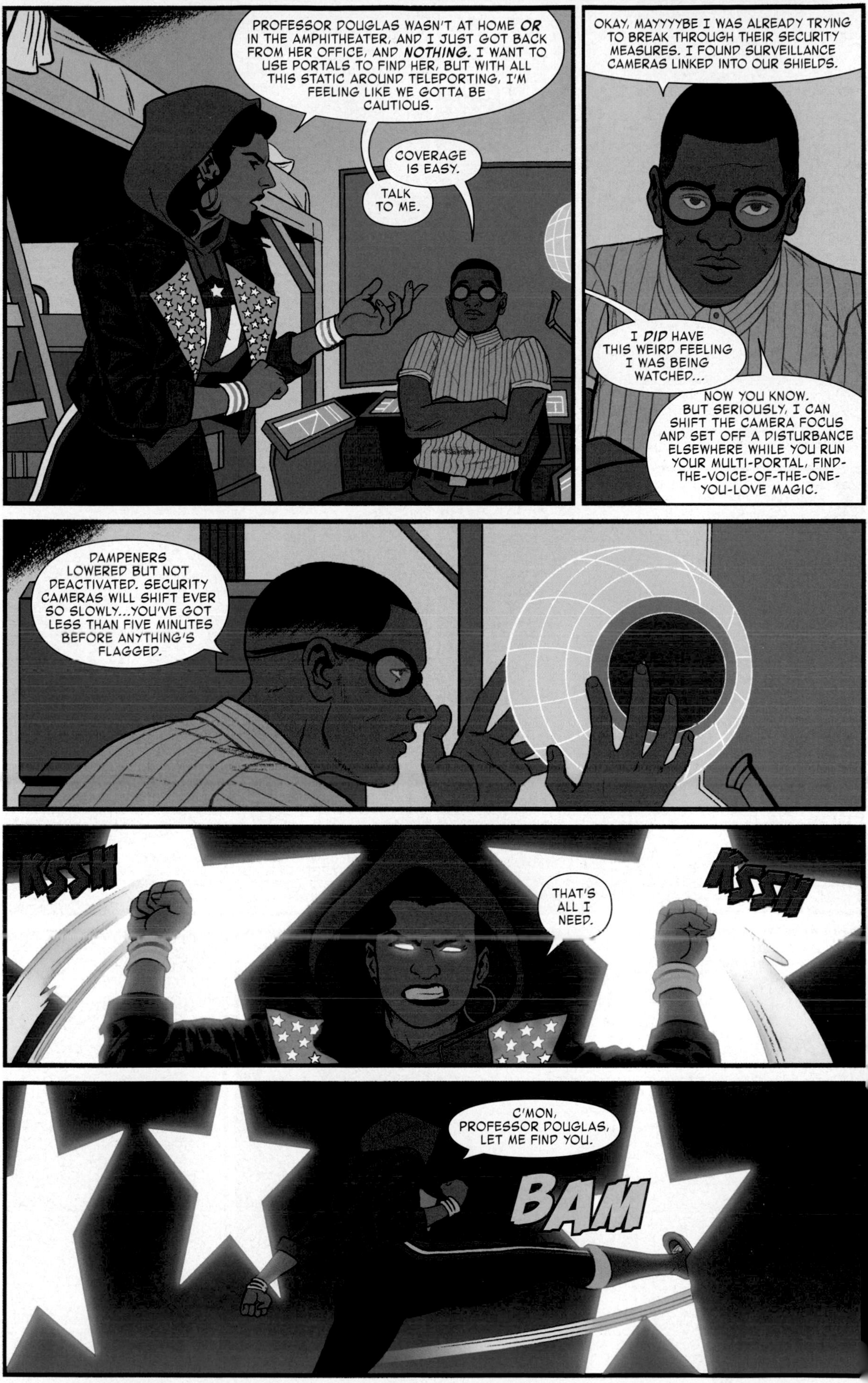
PROFESSOR DOUGLAS WASN'T AT HOME OR IN THE AMPHITHEATER, AND I JUST GOT BACK FROM HER OFFICE, AND NOTHING. I WANT TO USE PORTALS TO FIND HER, BUT WITH ALL THIS STATIC AROUND TELEPORTING, I'M FEELING LIKE WE GOTTA BE CAUTIOUS.
TALK TO ME.
COVERAGE IS EASY.
OKAY, MAYYYYYBE I WAS ALREADY TRYING TO BREAK THROUGH THEIR SECURITY MEASURES. I FOUND SURVEILLANCE CAMERAS LINKED INTO OUR SHIELDS.
I DID HAVE THIS WEIRD FEELING I WAS BEING WATCHED...
NOW YOU KNOW. BUT SERIOUSLY, I CAN SHIFT THE CAMERA FOCUS AND SET OFF A DISTURBANCE ELSEWHERE WHILE YOU RUN YOUR MULTI-PORTAL, FIND-THE-VOICE-OF-THE-ONE-YOU-LOVE MAGIC.
DAMPENERS LOWERED BUT NOT DEACTIVATED. SECURITY CAMERAS WILL SHIFT EVER SO SLOWLY...YOU'VE GOT LESS THAN FIVE MINUTES BEFORE ANYTHING'S FLAGGED.
KSSH
THAT'S ALL I NEED.
KSSH
C'MON, PROFESSOR DOUGLAS, LET ME FIND YOU.
BAM

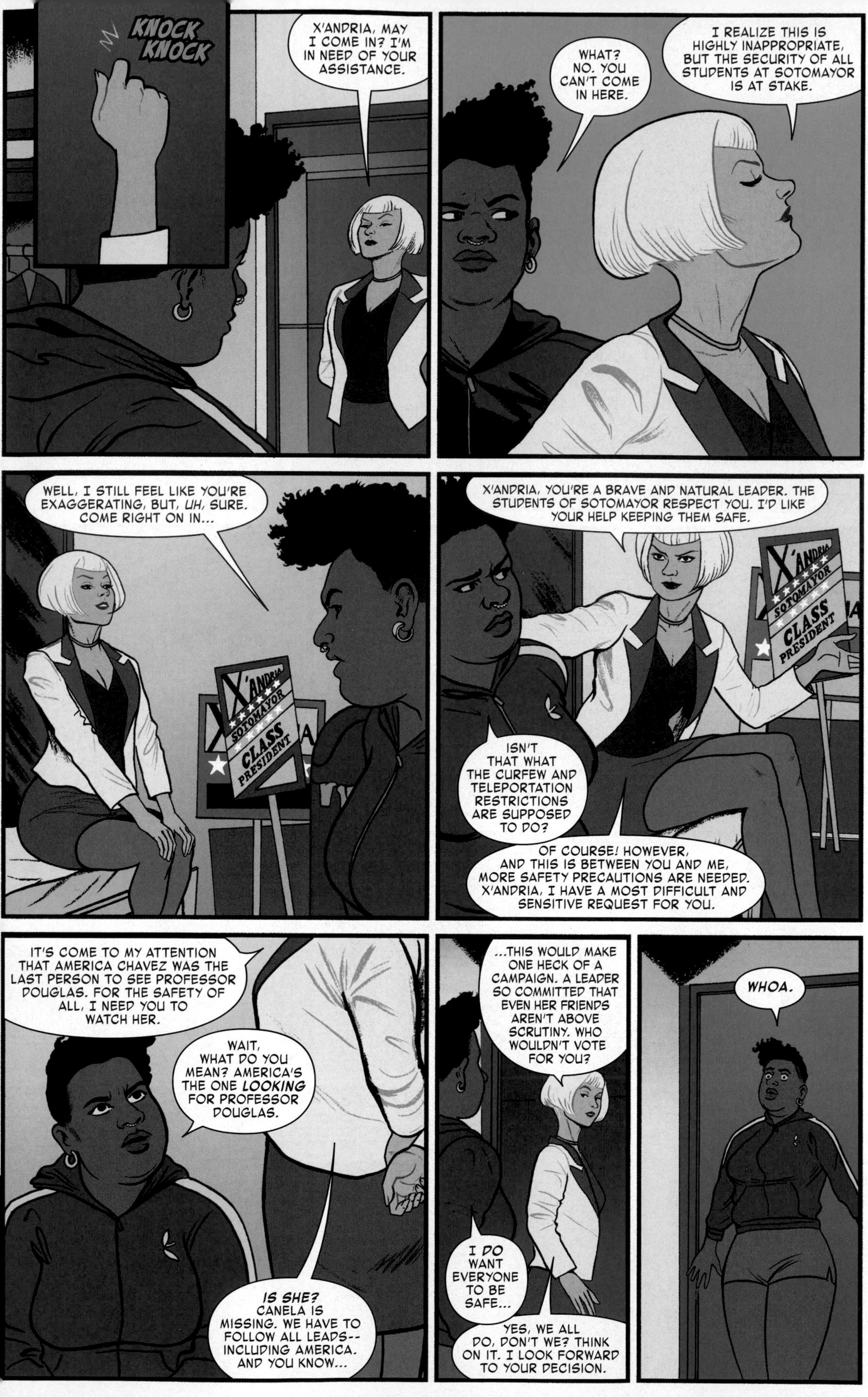
KNOCK KNOCK
X'ANDRIA, MAY I COME IN? I'M IN NEED OF YOUR ASSISTANCE.
WHAT? NO. YOU CAN'T COME IN HERE.
I REALIZE THIS IS HIGHLY INAPPROPRIATE, BUT THE SECURITY OF ALL STUDENTS AT SOTOMAYOR IS AT STAKE.
WELL, I STILL FEEL LIKE YOU'RE EXAGGERATING, BUT, *UH*, SURE. COME RIGHT ON IN...
X'ANDRIA SOTOMAYOR CLASS PRESIDENT
X'ANDRIA, YOU'RE A BRAVE AND NATURAL LEADER. THE STUDENTS OF SOTOMAYOR RESPECT YOU. I'D LIKE YOUR HELP KEEPING THEM SAFE.
X'ANDRIA SOTOMAYOR CLASS PRESIDENT
ISN'T THAT WHAT THE CURFEW AND TELEPORTATION RESTRICTIONS ARE SUPPOSED TO DO?
OF COURSE! HOWEVER, AND THIS IS BETWEEN YOU AND ME, MORE SAFETY PRECAUTIONS ARE NEEDED. X'ANDRIA, I HAVE A MOST DIFFICULT AND SENSITIVE REQUEST FOR YOU.
IT'S COME TO MY ATTENTION THAT AMERICA CHAVEZ WAS THE LAST PERSON TO SEE PROFESSOR DOUGLAS. FOR THE SAFETY OF ALL, I NEED YOU TO WATCH HER.
WAIT, WHAT DO YOU MEAN? AMERICA'S THE ONE *LOOKING* FOR PROFESSOR DOUGLAS.
IS SHE? CANELA IS MISSING. WE HAVE TO FOLLOW ALL LEADS-- INCLUDING AMERICA. AND YOU KNOW...
...THIS WOULD MAKE ONE HECK OF A CAMPAIGN. A LEADER SO COMMITTED THAT EVEN HER FRIENDS AREN'T ABOVE SCRUTINY. WHO WOULDN'T VOTE FOR YOU?
I *DO* WANT EVERYONE TO BE SAFE...
YES, WE ALL DO, DON'T WE? THINK ON IT. I LOOK FORWARD TO YOUR DECISION.
WHOA.

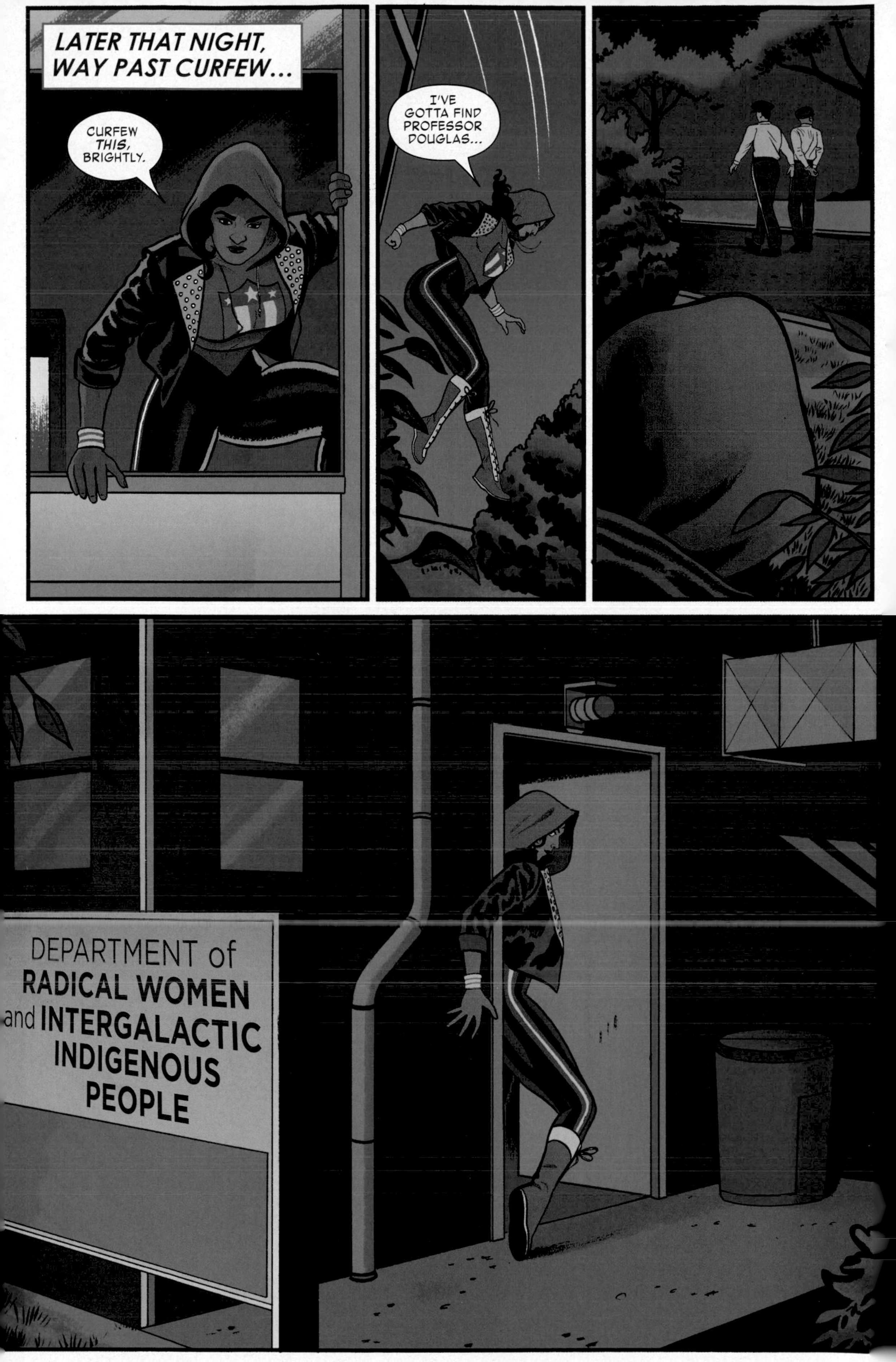
LATER THAT NIGHT, WAY PAST CURFEW...
CURFEW THIS, BRIGHTLY.
I'VE GOTTA FIND PROFESSOR DOUGLAS...
DEPARTMENT of RADICAL WOMEN and INTERGALACTIC INDIGENOUS PEOPLE

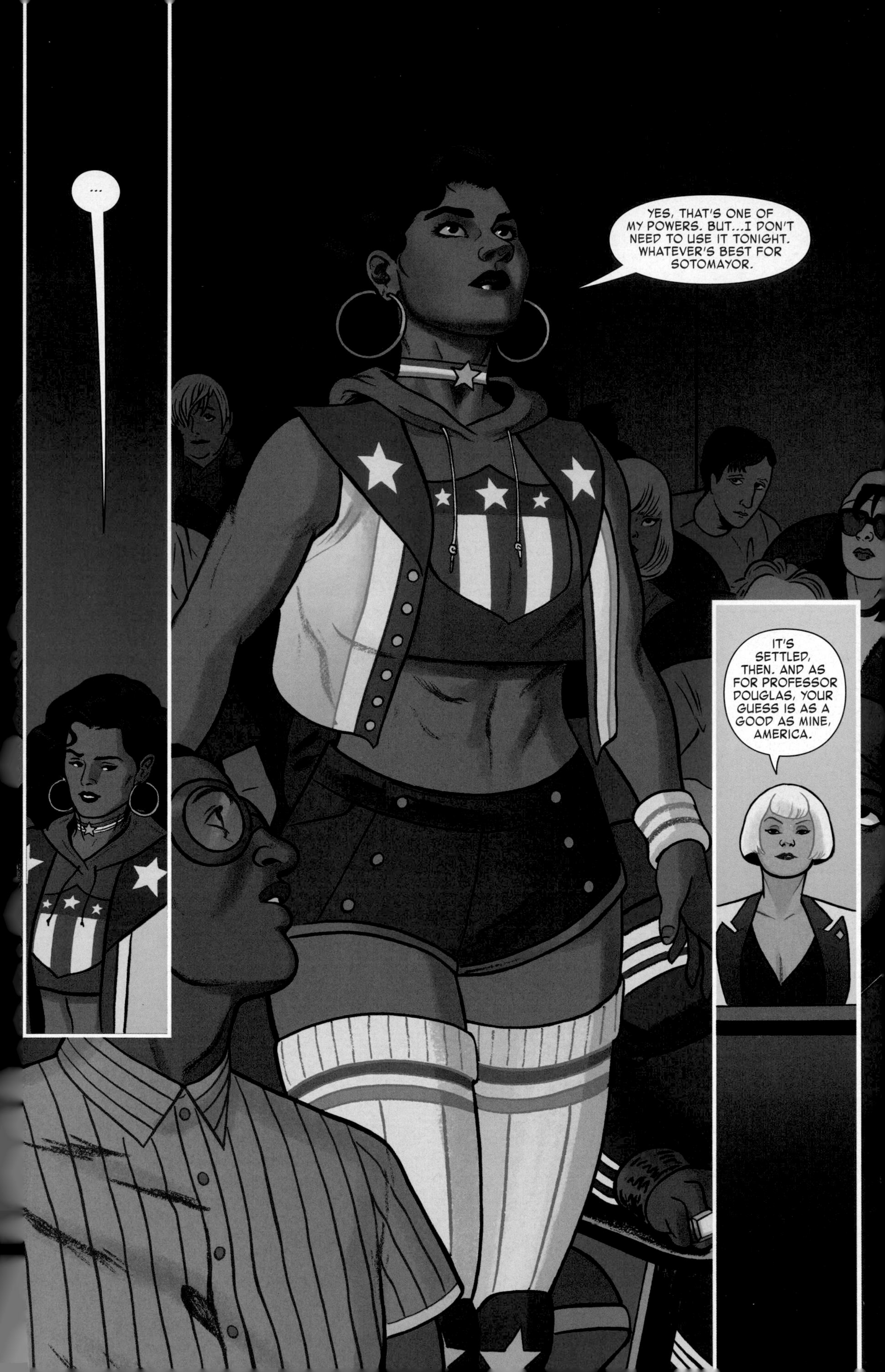
...
YES, THAT'S ONE OF MY POWERS. BUT...I DON'T NEED TO USE IT TONIGHT. WHATEVER'S BEST FOR SOTOMAYOR.
IT'S SETTLED, THEN. AND AS FOR PROFESSOR DOUGLAS, YOUR GUESS IS AS A GOOD AS MINE, AMERICA.

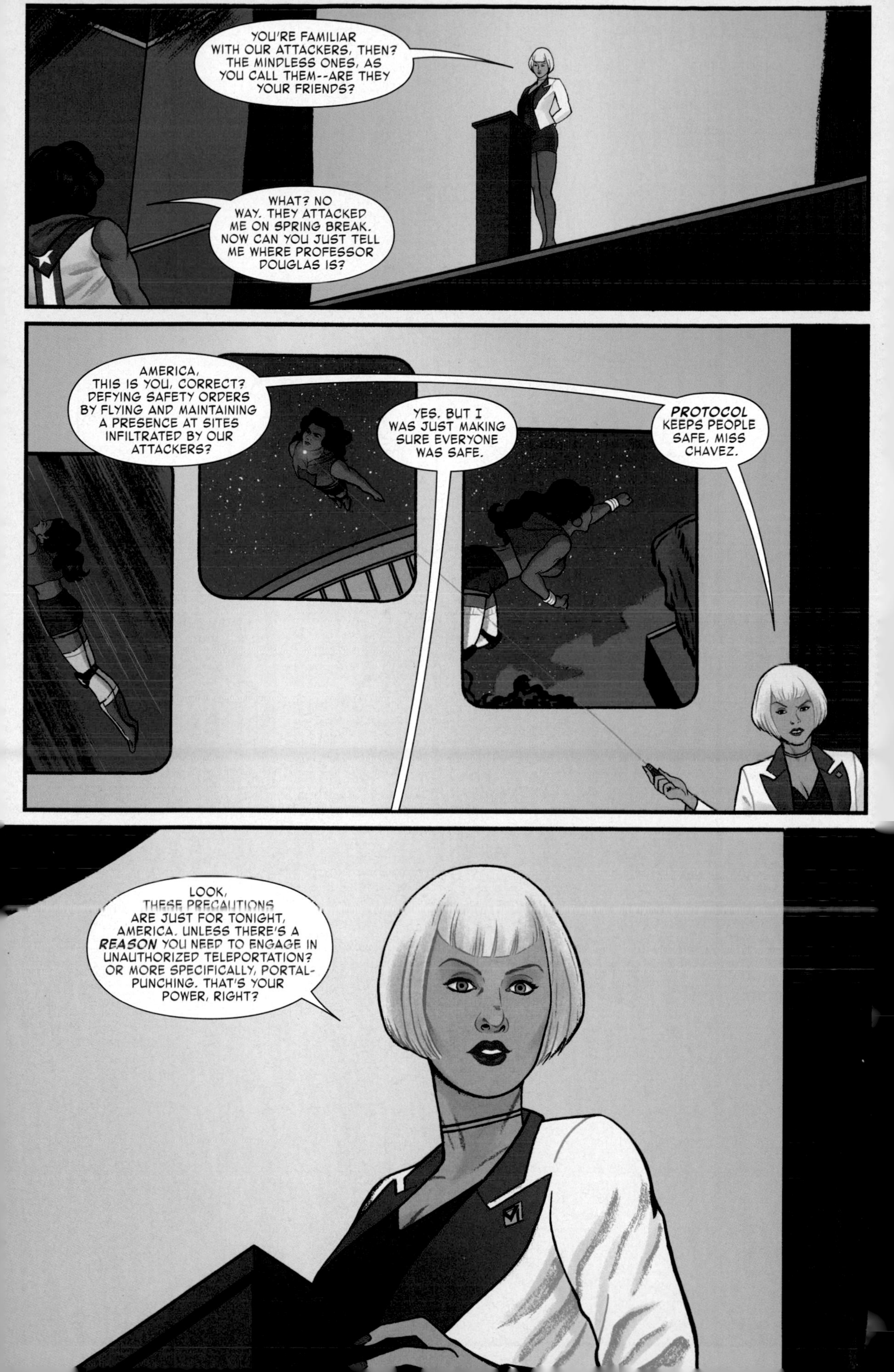
YOU'RE FAMILIAR WITH OUR ATTACKERS, THEN? THE MINDLESS ONES, AS YOU CALL THEM--ARE THEY YOUR FRIENDS?
WHAT? NO WAY. THEY ATTACKED ME ON SPRING BREAK. NOW CAN YOU JUST TELL ME WHERE PROFESSOR DOUGLAS IS?
AMERICA, THIS IS YOU, CORRECT? DEFYING SAFETY ORDERS BY FLYING AND MAINTAINING A PRESENCE AT SITES INFILTRATED BY OUR ATTACKERS?
YES. BUT I WAS JUST MAKING SURE EVERYONE WAS SAFE.
PROTOCOL KEEPS PEOPLE SAFE, MISS CHAVEZ.
LOOK, THESE PRECAUTIONS ARE JUST FOR TONIGHT, AMERICA. UNLESS THERE'S A REASON YOU NEED TO ENGAGE IN UNAUTHORIZED TELEPORTATION? OR MORE SPECIFICALLY, PORTAL-PUNCHING. THAT'S YOUR POWER, RIGHT?

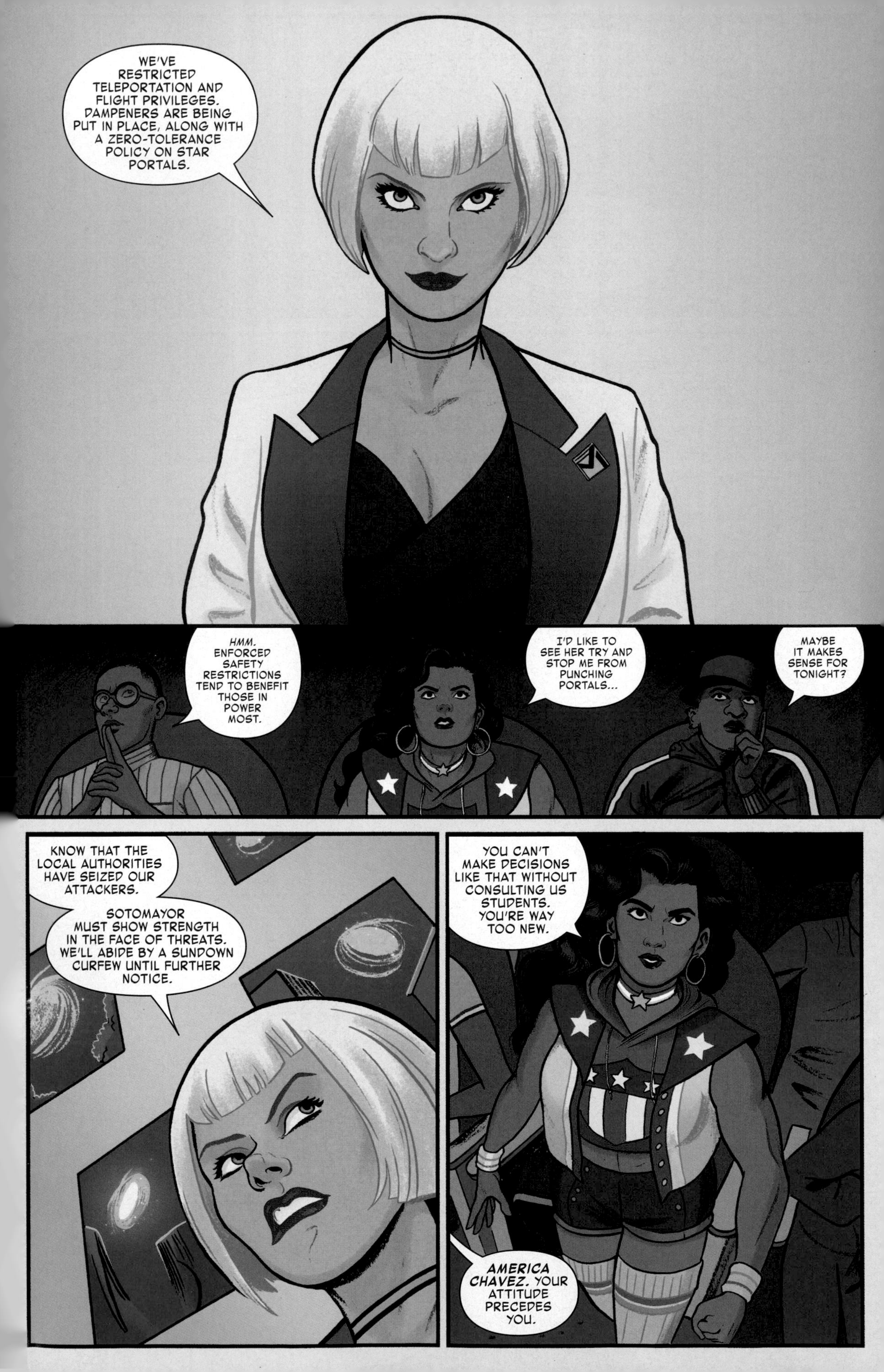
WE'VE RESTRICTED TELEPORTATION AND FLIGHT PRIVILEGES. DAMPENERS ARE BEING PUT IN PLACE, ALONG WITH A ZERO-TOLERANCE POLICY ON STAR PORTALS.
HMM. ENFORCED SAFETY RESTRICTIONS TEND TO BENEFIT THOSE IN POWER MOST.
I'D LIKE TO SEE HER TRY AND STOP ME FROM PUNCHING PORTALS...
MAYBE IT MAKES SENSE FOR TONIGHT?
KNOW THAT THE LOCAL AUTHORITIES HAVE SEIZED OUR ATTACKERS.
SOTOMAYOR MUST SHOW STRENGTH IN THE FACE OF THREATS. WE'LL ABIDE BY A SUNDOWN CURFEW UNTIL FURTHER NOTICE.
YOU CAN'T MAKE DECISIONS LIKE THAT WITHOUT CONSULTING US STUDENTS. YOU'RE WAY TOO NEW.
AMERICA CHAVEZ. YOUR ATTITUDE PRECEDES YOU.

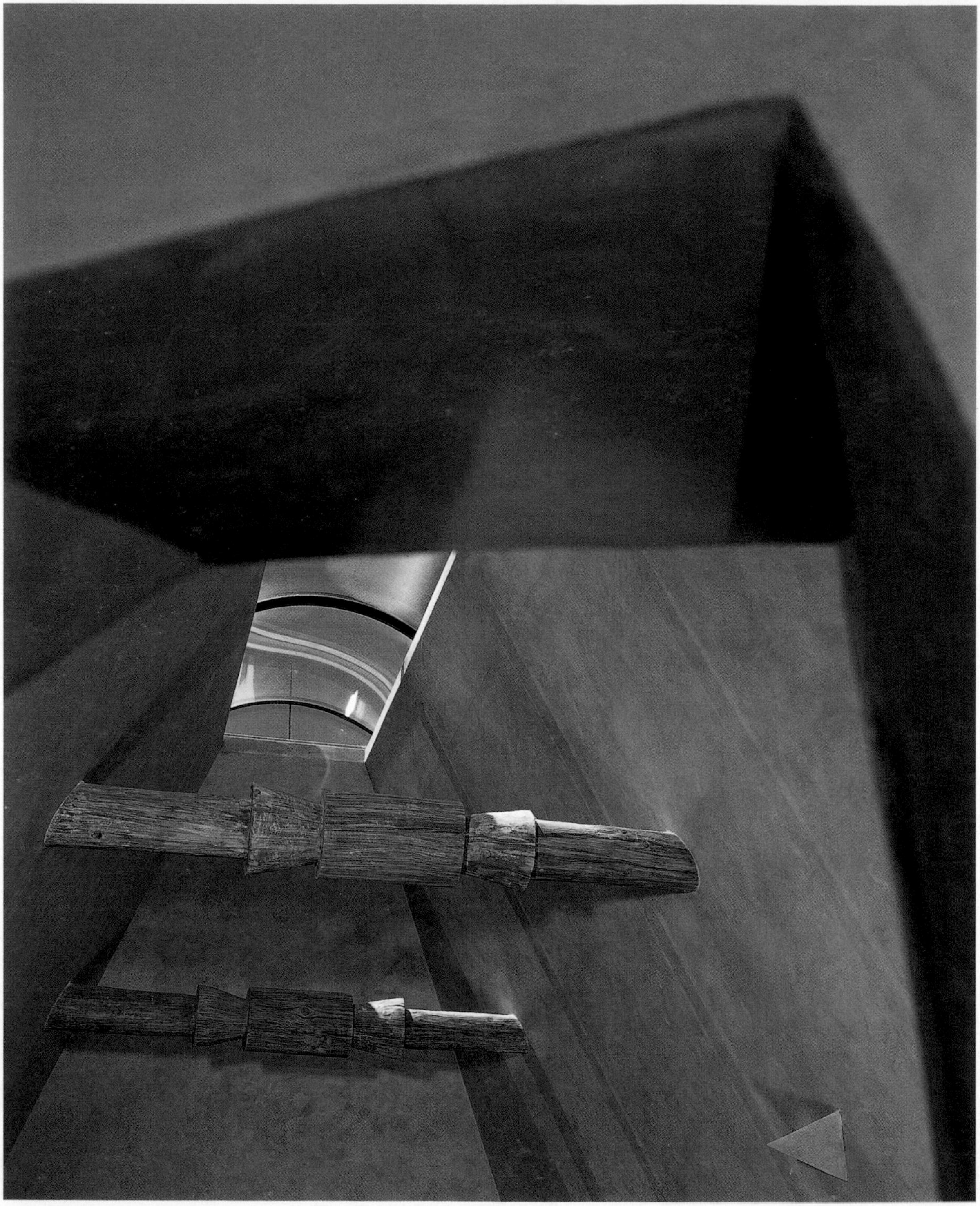

Behind
Adobe Walls

*The Hidden
Homes and Gardens
of Santa Fe and Taos*

by LANDT DENNIS   *Photographs by* LISL DENNIS

CHRONICLE BOOKS
SAN FRANCISCO

Library of Congress Cataloging-in-Publication
Data available.

ISBN 0-8118-1164-6

Printed in Hong Kong.

Book and cover design: Jim Drobka

Distributed in Canada by
Raincoast Books
8680 Cambie Street
Vancouver, B.C. V6P 6M9

10 9 8 7 6 5 4

Chronicle Books
85 Second Street
San Francisco, California 94105

www.chroniclebooks.com

Page 2. A hall in the Markinson house, Santa Fe.
Above. The living/dining room of the Martha Wallis house, Santa Fe.

CONTENTS

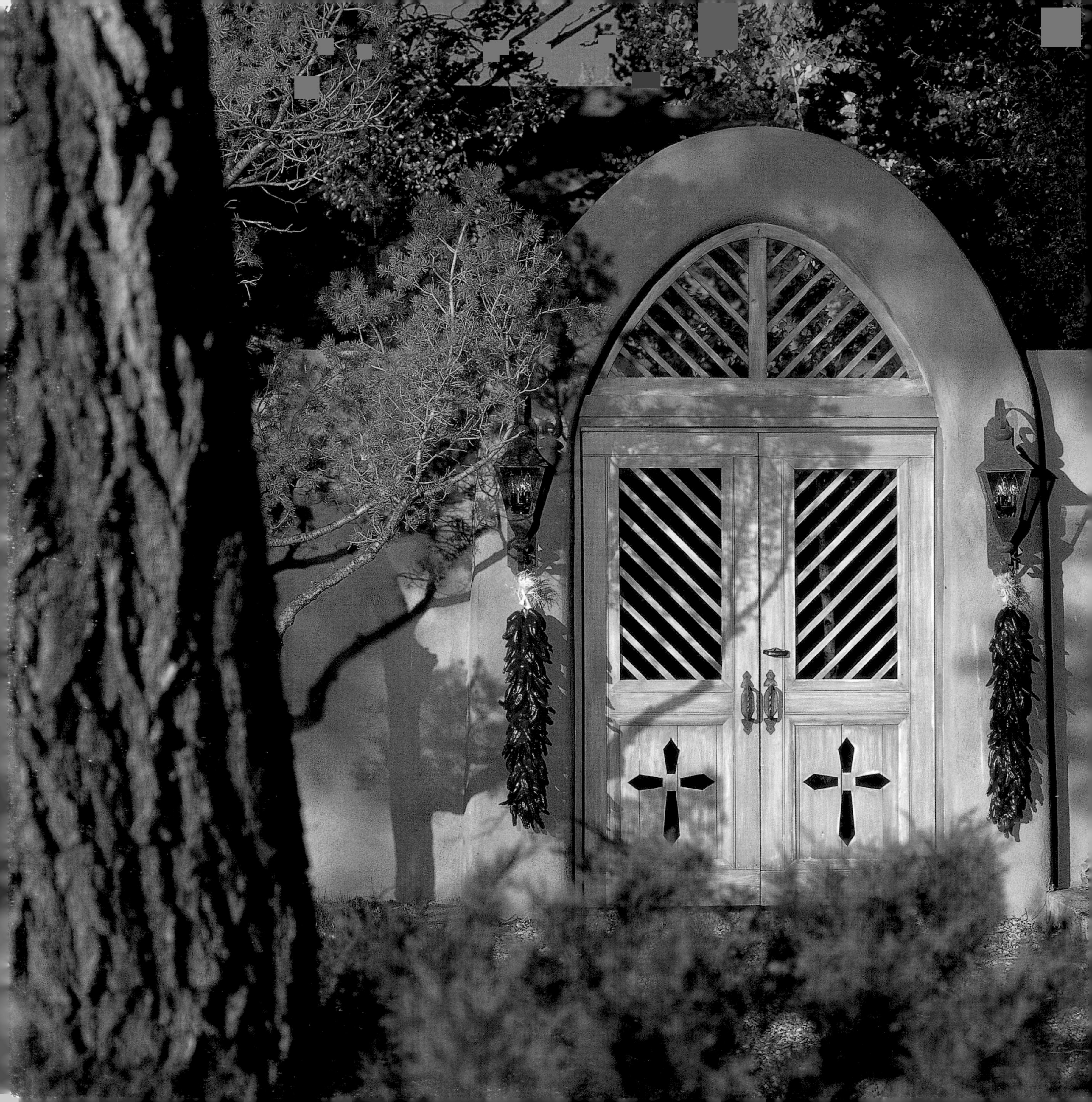

ACKNOWLEDGMENTS

H ow do we express gratitude to the Santa Fe and Taos homeowners who permitted their properties and gardens to be photographed and written about for this book? Hopefully by recording these private spaces with as much sensitivity and thoughtfulness that the owners themselves demonstrated in their creation. It has been a great privilege to have been the guests in so many remarkable houses and to have experienced the wonder and joy of living and gardening in New Mexico, clearly one of the most beautiful places in the world to call home.

We also wish to thank the Santa Fe Garden Club for allowing the use of the title "Behind Adobe Walls," the name given to the club's annual summer house and garden tours.

Finally, we want to say what a great pleasure it has been to work with editors Bill LeBlond and Sarah Putman at Chronicle Books.

Left. Entrance door to the Hulse house, Taos.

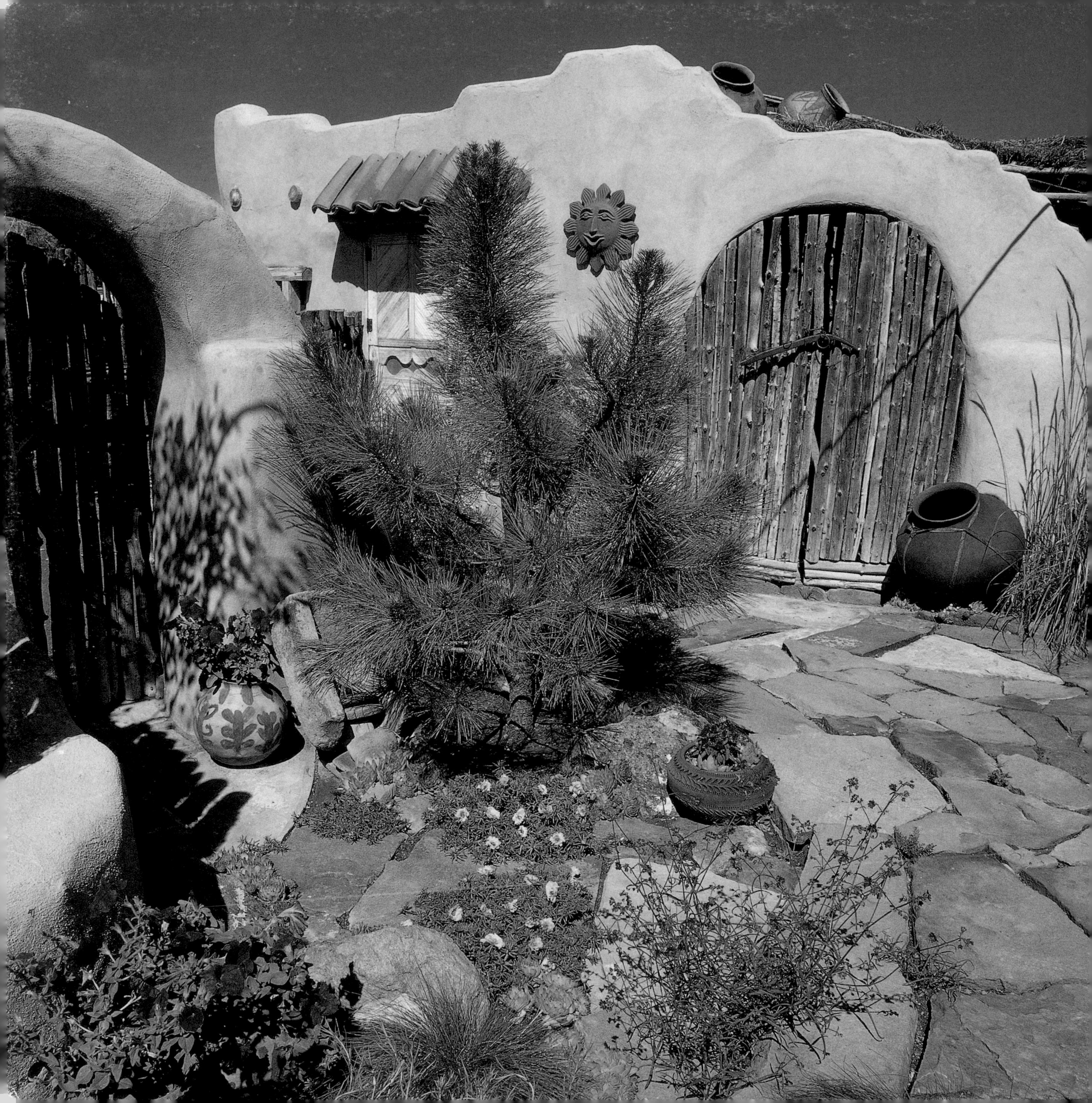

Introduction

As early as A.D. 700 people lived in and around Santa Fe and Taos, New Mexico, in the American Southwest. It has only been in the last hundred years, however, that they have done so with "style." For centuries, decisions about architecture, furnishings, color schemes, and flower gardens were luxuries that wouldn't—rather, couldn't—be thought of until the problems of harsh weather, minimal water, rampaging enemies, and insufficient food were mastered.

Coping was what counted.

Hunting, farming, and defense were the primary occupations of early cliff dwellers at present-day Bandelier and Puye outside Santa Fe. Consisting of caverns or inner rooms (*ye mokuis*) and ledges or setbacks (*te wis*), cliff dwellings reflected their inhabitants' need for survival rather than their personal taste.

By the mid-1300s, Indians along the Rio Grande had advanced their lifestyle by clustering together in multistoried "condo complexes" (as we might call them today) in more than 125 pueblos. The Taos pueblo is today one of the most historic and authentic examples.

It wasn't until the Spanish arrived in New Mexico in the late sixteenth century that settlers began to design their dwellings with a degree of individuality—albeit with minimal embellishment. The introduction and extensive use of adobe made this possible.

HOUSES...

Having learned the marvels of adobe (a technique as old as the great civilizations of Mesopotamia) from the Moors who ruled Spain in the eighth century, conquistadors brought this knowledge to the Southwest when they arrived with Coronado in 1540. While local Indians already knew about puddle adobe, which required each successive layer of clay, sand, water, and straw to dry thoroughly before the next one was applied to dwellings made of rock and lumber, what they didn't know was the art of making molded, sun-dried adobe bricks.

Adobe—whose name comes from the Arabic for "earth from which unburnt bricks are made"—became the primary construction technique of early Spanish settlers in northern New Mexico and, later, of eighteenth- and nineteenth-century Anglos who ventured west to live in Santa Fe and Taos. Weighing up to forty pounds apiece, readily produced in large quantities, quickly assembled, and easily chipped and shaped, adobe bricks—at first purely utilitarian—came to be appreciated as a kind of fourth-dimensional building material. For many modern devotees, adobe forms a spiritual connection between man and earth, by which the human need for a dwelling place is met in harmony with nature, unseparated from the landscape.

Opposite. Wessley house, Taos.

A recent house renovation in Santa Fe revealed that wildlife also appreciated the merits of adobe. Marked with hoofprints, many of the bricks had been nibbled when still fresh by deer, who probably enjoyed their nutritious straw content.

At a time in American history when Easterners didn't know much about Westerners, when English settlers—the Cabots, Randolphs, Saltonstalls, and Oglethorpes—on the Atlantic seaboard were building great Georgian country houses and governors' palaces and filling them with imported furniture, fabrics, and china, the Vigil, Valdez, Fernandez, Delgado, Prada, Lopez, and Rodriguez families in Nuevo Mexico lived in small single-family ranchos or large haciendas. With adobe walls, frequently three feet thick, boxlike rooms had ten-foot-high ceilings made of peeled logs, or *vigas*, a Spanish building tradition, and were spanned with *latillas*. The latter, borrowed from the Pueblo Indians, are saplings laid in a herringbone pattern and often painted red, blue, or green. Muslin attached to the bottom four feet of the walls prevented whitewash from smudging people's clothing. Easily expanded as families grew (and frequently willed room by room to family members), rambling adobe houses included *placitas*, or interior courtyards (a characteristically Spanish feature), and often a portal, or columned porch, across the front as well as along the sides. There, shaded from the summer sun, owners sat and gossiped. In winter, piles of piñon and juniper logs were sheltered from the snow and within easy reach to throw on roaring fires inside.

Who would have guessed that centuries later, the simplicity, authenticity, and integrity of New Mexican architecture and interior design, the so-called Santa Fe style, would entice a migration of *nouveaux arrivés* to the Land of Enchantment?

Certainly not Don Antonio Severino Martinez, whose early-nineteenth-century hacienda on the outskirts of Taos is a testimony to the endurance of adobe. The dwelling illustrates both the hardships endured by New Mexico's early pioneers as well as their daily lifestyle. A trader who prospered by bringing merchandise from Mexico City to Taos on the El Camino Real, also called the Chihuahua Trail, Martinez faced two problems as he set out to build his thirteen-room fortress: Indian raids and lack of sophisticated tools. Handmade, hand-laid adobe bricks helped to solve the construction problem. Protection was enhanced by small doors (the enemy would have to duck to enter) and the absence of exterior windows. Interior windows faced two large *placitas* where livestock and family members gathered for security.

Inside the hacienda, hard adobe floors were soaked with ox blood to give them color and sheen. Corner adobe fireplaces threw out heat in winter; twelve-candle, wooden candelabras hung from the ceilings for light. Families and their neighbors who gathered to dance the night away at a *fandango* rested and caught their breath on built-in adobe seats, called *bancos*, along the walls. Later, they fell asleep on adobe beds hollowed out in the middle, filled with corn cobs, and covered with buffalo robes.

As for furniture, there was little, since few *carpinteros*, or carpenters, lived nearby to make any. While the number of carpenters grew from two in Juan de Oñate's 1598 expedition to forty-four listed in the 1790 Spanish census, New Mexican craftsmen couldn't keep up with customer demand.

Appreciated today for its simplicity of design, highly collectible New Mexican furniture of the seventeenth through the nineteenth centuries includes *tracteros* (cupboards), *cajas* (chests), *padres* (priests' chairs), *harineros* (grain chests), *varguenos* (secretaries), and *taramitas* (footstools). Made from trees felled by ax or a two-handed Spanish bucksaw and often crude and massive, each item reveals remarkable inventiveness and personal detail. Frequently hand-painted with gesso and natural pigments, this furniture included intricately punched tin sheets, moldings, and decorative motifs by the nineteenth century.

Northern New Mexican adobe houses startled many first-time visitors. They'd never seen a city in which people lived in mud huts, each indistinguishable from the others. In 1806, Lieutenant Zebulon Pike said Santa Fe looked like a "fleet of flat-bottomed boats," while an observer in the mid-1880s reported the city had "more the appearance of a colony of brick kilns than a collection of human habitations."

One of the best descriptions of Santa Fe comes from writer Matthew C. Field, whose article appeared April 17, 1840, in the *New Orleans Times Picayune*. "Our first view of the mud-built city was from the mountain side," he wrote. "There, within half a mile … a small spot was dotted with low one story buildings, reminding us irresistibly [*sic*] of an assemblage of mole hills…. Our surprise was not a little excited to find that these mud walls could possess such strength and durability…. A very pleasing effect is produced by the grass growing on the tops of the houses, and as all the dwellings are connected, it is not uncommon to see children chasing each other the whole length of a street along the housetops."

For Santa Fe and Taos homeowners, the year 1821 was a turning point on two accounts: the independence of Mexico— and therefore New Mexico—from Spain and the opening of the Santa Fe Trail by William Bucknell. Under the Spanish, goods "Made in the U.S.A." were banned from the territory. Now, with a go-ahead from the Mexicans, American merchants flooded northern New Mexico with merchandise brought in on muleback from Franklin, Missouri: tools, utensils, fabrics, and iron nails (a real luxury). Suddenly, life in northern New Mexico began to be a little less austere. It also wasn't as wet; in the inventory of the wagons that rolled down the trail were relatively inexpensive sheets of lead and tin alloy. After years of mopping up puddles of melted snow and rain that leaked through the traditional flat roofs, homeowners soon discovered the alloy, called ternplate, that was perfect to cover pitched roofs.

Soon the population began to swell. Anglos saw New Mexico as a frontier of economic opportunity. Wagonloads of transplanted gringos rolled into Santa Fe and Taos. Before long, general stores spilling over with "imported" goods lined three sides of the plaza in Santa Fe. On the fourth side was the Governor's Palace, constructed in 1610 and the oldest public building in the United States, its doors and windows still covered with cow and buffalo skins. Time would pass before New Mexicans enjoyed all the East Coast luxuries. At a time when New Yorkers had glass windows, central heating, and horse-drawn trolley cars, Southwest pioneers were thrilled to buy a manufactured adobe brick and a squared ceiling beam from a mill yard.

The real change in architectural and decorative style in Santa Fe and Taos began in 1846, when New Mexico came under United States control. More Yankees poured over the border, and the arrival of the United States Army brought both old-timers and new settlers a greater supply of manufactured goods and skilled workers. Susan Shelby Magoffin, the first American woman to enter Santa Fe under the American flag, accompanied her husband on a trade expedition there in 1846 and carefully recorded her journey and exposure to local culture. Austerity was clearly no longer universal; visiting the home of Don Mariano Chavez, a *rico*, or wealthy man, Magoffin noticed that it was "well furnished with handsome Brussels carpets, crimson worsted curtains, with gilded rings and cornice, white-marble slab pier tables, hair and crimson worsted chairs, candelabras…[and] eight or ten gilt-framed mirrors around the wall."

In 1880, backwater New Mexico took its real leap into the nineteenth century. The railroad, and with it the "Anglo-ization" of the community, had arrived. Rolling into Las Vegas, New Mexico, in 1879, and on into Albuquerque in 1880, the Atchison, Topeka, and Santa Fe Railroad was the transportation and communication link that finally connected the area to national architectural trends. A spur line operated by the Denver and Rio Grande supplied Santa Fe with rail service in 1880 as well.

You might say, only slightly tongue-in-cheek, that Home Depot had come to New Mexico. Businesses now offered a wide inventory of building supplies. Rope & Castle, a Las Vegas, New Mexico, company advertised "Doors, Sash & Blinds, Lumber, Lath & Shingles, Moldings, Pickets, Window Glass, White Lead, Putty and Oil, Roofing Felt, Building Paper, Plaster Paris, Cement"—and, perhaps best of all, "Plumbing Fixtures."

For the next thirty years, architectural eclecticism was evident throughout Santa Fe. The St. Francis Cathedral, completed in 1886, was Romanesque Revival. The four-story Palace Hotel, 1880, was French Second Empire. The Catron Block, 1891, on the plaza, exemplified Italianate Style. Buildings sprang up in the Queen Anne style. The Moorish Revival Scottish Rite Temple, 1911, was the icing on what had become an architectural hodgepodge.

Residents were determined not to be behind the times. While turn-of-the-century Gingerbread Gothic and the crisp lines and fresh symmetry of Territorial style, introduced to New Mexico in 1851 with the construction of Fort Union (brick friezes, white columns, pedimental lintels, and wide halls) remained popular, an influx of Eastern expatriates introduced a still broader display of architectural styles. A walk through Santa Fe today reveals a smattering of early twentieth-century houses whose styles and embellishments include Greek Revival, Mission Revival, Spanish Colonial Revival, Mexican Colonial Revival, as well as Bungalow.

More remote, less populated by newcomers, and farther away from railroad lines, Taos was less susceptible to "foreign" influences. There, pueblo style architecture remained remarkably intact. Taos residents were not about to abandon their centuries-old style of adobe construction for contemporary fashion.

Original architectural roots were not to be forgotten for long in Santa Fe, however. After New Mexico became the forty-seventh state in 1912, and by the time World War I broke out, "something strange happened in Santa Fe; puebloid fever broke out," writes architectural historian John D. Morrow. "A new romanticism for the old architectural styles fostered the Spanish Pueblo Revival Style."

The movement broke out in Santa Fe's burgeoning art colony, whose members began arriving in the early 1900s. Many had come to New Mexico because they had tuberculosis. Checking into the Sunmount Sanatorium in Santa Fe, many patients who were cured stayed on. Inspired by the area's pure light, salubrious weather, and freedom of thought and expression, those in the art, writing, and poetry colonies soon recognized that something bad was happening to the rich architectural legacy that provided their new-found paradise with a distinctive character. Caught up in the nation's "back to the land" impulse, which included the Arts and Crafts movement, they organized and acted to ensure that the architectural esthetic that first drew them would remain.

Dr. Edgar Lee Hewett, an archeologist, was the group leader. Hewett helped found Santa Fe's School of American Research and was a prolific writer on Southwestern history. He tirelessly promoted the need to appreciate the area's traditional architecture. Of immediate concern was the Territorial legislature's intention in 1909 to demolish the Palace of the Governors and erect a courthouse on the plaza.

"Concerned citizens" in favor of demolition lobbied that the palace's mud construction portrayed New Mexico as backward and poor. "Concerned historians," in favor of preservation, said the adobe building exemplified New Mexico's unique Spanish heritage. Save the Palace of the Governors and turn it into a historical museum, they pleaded. To their everlasting credit, the traditionalists won.

The opening event at the restored Palace of the Governors was the New-Old Santa Fe Exhibition in 1912. Photographs and illustrations of northern New Mexico's most important monuments highlighted the area's abundance of architectural details—corbels, *latillas*, vigas, and *canales*. Artists, archaeologists, and members of the Chamber of Commerce, who astutely recognized that the architectural preservation of Santa Fe would be a tourist draw, were also on hand to answer the public's questions about the "new-old" architecture. Prizes were given to architects for their designs of buildings and houses in the traditional style; several of these designs became buildings at the University of New Mexico.

Heady with success, conservationists under historian Ralph Twitchell spearheaded the Spanish Territorial/Pueblo-style construction of the New Mexico pavilion at the 1914 Panama-California Exposition in San Diego. Designed by the Rapp Brothers—Isaac H. and William M., whose firm had been in business since 1890—it was an immediate success. So much so that New Mexican officials decided to build the Museum of Fine Arts in Santa Fe along traditional lines. Completed in 1917, the structure is an adaptation of the mission church façades of the Acoma and Laguna pueblos and contains Spanish Colonial style furniture designed by archeologist Jesse Nusbaum.

As important as the building itself was its first exhibition. Opening on November 24, 1917, it focused on painters of the Santa Fe and Taos school. The show drew national attention to the area's creative stimulus—an allure which continues today.

Public approval and pride in the restored Palace of the Governors and the newly erected museum marked an abrupt about-face in the architectural history of Santa Fe and Taos. Once again, the majority of homeowners looked into New Mexico's rich architectural past. About ninety percent of all old-house restoration and fifty percent of new-house construction between 1912 and 1917 followed the tradition of Pueblo style. The famed La Fonda Hotel in Santa Fe continued the trend in 1920, going with the flat-top adobe look.

Territorial style was not abandoned; it simply became the second-most popular regional design. An adaptation emerged, however. After World War II, Spanish Territorial style buildings traded masonry construction for a wood frame with brown stucco finish, a kind of faux adobe that has remained popular, since the price of real adobe bricks has skyrocketed.

Of all the early promoters of Santa Fe style, a description used by writers and designers as early as the 1930s, artist Carlos Vierra was among the first to put his words into works. Built in 1921 on the Old Santa Fe Trail, Vierra's large adobe house epitomized Spanish Territorial/Pueblo architecture with its two-story set-back, flat-roof design that incorporated vigas, corbels, *canales*, and a portal. The house quickly became an example of tasteful new-old house design and inspired the large numbers of Anglo newcomers who had begun to settle in Santa Fe and Taos. To those willing to build in Pueblo-revival style, Vierra sold lots he owned on Buena Vista Loma.

Certainly the best known of early New Mexican architects and preservationists was John Gaw Meem. Cured of tuberculosis in Santa Fe in the 1920s, he spent the next sixty years designing or redesigning public buildings and private dwellings in New Mexico, using both Pueblo and Spanish Colonial styles. "No man has worked more wholeheartedly than John Gaw Meem to find the graces of the past," wrote art professor Bainbridge Bunting, "recognizing the formidable forces of modern material life, to save what can be saved in order to keep history alive while respecting the best uses of modern conditions."

With a return to the past on a roll, the Santa Fe Holding Company—early real estate developers—sponsored in 1927 a contest, limited to artists and architects, "to develop ideal plans for private residences planned in true Old Santa Fe Style." Rules said that construction costs could not exceed $16,000. The winner, builder Katherine Stinson (also a pioneer aviatrix), received $250; the company used her plans for neighborhood development in Buena Vista Heights.

In 1936, The Santa Fe Building Supply Company climbed on the restoration bandwagon, creating eighteen blueprints reproduced in the book *Santa Fe Style Homes*. Written by artist Wilfred Stedman "in the interest of better building," the introduction set high standards: "… Let frugality be your guide in [choosing features] and let not a liking for quaintness dull your judgment," Stedman writes. "A house [should be] homelike, while formal and correct, lacking nothing of those qualities vital to domestic style…. Decorative schemes [should] be in strict harmony. Interiors should be bright and cheerful; only light tints and colors used, warm or cool schemes as the various rooms may require. Furnishings should be carefully chosen for utility, comfort, and appearance so they fit into the decorative scheme."

In the 1940s, the uncluttered, local-handicraft way in which pioneer New Mexicans "furnished" their houses was discovered on a national scale. Unable to import furniture and accessories from Europe during World War II, American department stores turned to the Southwest and began to promote Santa Fe style. Early settlers would have chuckled at the term. It was nothing more than a romanticizing of the pioneer Santa Fe and Taos settlers' need to make do with the area's only available furnishings, a mixture of Indian pots and blankets with Spanish rugs and furniture. Still, customers of Marshall Field & Company in Chicago were told that Santa Fe style was *the* look. In fact, model rooms in the department store included swags of chiles to spice up the color scheme.

By 1943, the Southwest decorating trend was sufficiently newsworthy that *New Mexico* magazine featured an article, "Styled in Santa Fe," in the December issue. "Oddly enough, one store suggesting Indian decoration for the summer home found visitors were so fond of the whole effect," the writer reported, "that they wanted their own homes redecorated—suburbanites, apartment-house dwellers, including penthouses. Even a bachelor wanted the scheme copied for his own quarters."

While Santa Fe had its first appointed city planning board in 1912, while concerned residents in Santa Fe and Taos in the 1920s helped preserve and maintain landmarks, and while many important buildings had been restored by private citizens, there nevertheless remained throughout the 1930s and 1940s a dire need for a local building code to preserve the towns' architectural integrity by law.

In 1957, the Historic Style Ordinance was passed in Santa Fe. Written by Oliver La Farge, author of the Pulitzer Prize–winning novel *Laughing Boy*, the ordinance dictates the proper style for architecture within the bounds of the city's historic district. Only two styles are permitted: Old Santa Fe Style, a mixed bag of Pueblo, Spanish Territorial, and Territorial Revival; and Recent Santa Fe Style, which means almost anything goes, provided that eighty percent of a building have the effect of adobe construction.

Fraught with problems, controversy, and interpretations through the years, the code has nevertheless helped preserve the past. What the code hasn't done, critics contend, is allow New Mexico's adobe architecture to strike out and make an up-to-date statement for modern Santa Fe.

Building permits aside, present-day Santa Fe and Taos are as popular as ever. Rediscovered by the media in the 1970s, written about endlessly in magazines and newspapers, both towns draw full-time and part-time homeowners from across the United States and abroad. Many buy and restore old houses, others build new ones, both in town as well as out of town.

Perhaps "led" here by inner voices, perhaps making a deliberate, rational decision to move here, most homeowners share a common decorative aesthetic. The so-called Santa Fe style continues to be popular, but in a much looser, less contrived manner.

"Expatriates" still inevitably surround themselves with sufficient New Mexican furniture, paintings, and accessories to assure them that they are no longer in Scarsdale or Santa Monica. Many new homeowners have expanded their decorating repertoire, however, to reflect a refreshing worldliness like that evident in Santa Fe and Taos in the twenties and thirties. These homeowners avoid a purely local style, mixing items from all parts of the world, including North Africa, Asia, Provence, Shaker New England, and New Mexico.

Future architectural and interior-design historians looking back on Santa Fe and Taos at the turn of the twenty-first century will see that Santa Fe style began to throw out runners in many new directions. While traditional Spanish Pueblo and Territorial styles remain almost omnipresent, particularly with "spec" houses, more and more new homeowners commission architects to design something different. While wood frame and faux-adobe stucco continue to be the usual building and exterior ingredients, straw bale and pumice construction is rapidly catching on.

With the past behind us, the present with us, the future soon to overtake us, it is the authors' hope that readers will appreciate that Santa Fe and Taos have a surprisingly wide-ranging design diversity. There may be an old Santa Fe style, yet there is increasingly a new Santa Fe style. But more important than sheet rock, nails, lamps, or paintings, there is New Mexico itself.

Why is it that people keep coming down the trail to settle in Santa Fe and Taos? Back in 1893, in his book *Land of Poco Tiempo*, anthropologist and journalist Charles Lummis wondered the same thing and gave an answer, one as valid today as then: "Sun, silence, and adobe—that is New Mexico in three words.... It is the Great American Mystery.... 'Picturesque' is a tame word for it. It is a picture, a romance, a dream, all in one."

Amen.

...AND GARDENS

In seven-thousand-foot-high Santa Fe and Taos, early settlers struggled for enough food. Battling Southwest summer heat, frequent twenty-five-mile-an-hour winds, poor alkaline soil, minimal rainfall, hailstorms, wild critters, and early September and mid-May frosts, Native Americans and Spanish conquistadors treasured any crops that survived High Country conditions. Raising flowers was out of the question; filling one's stomach was more important than filling a vase. No one in New Mexico in the seventeenth and eighteenth centuries, other than a handful of subjugated Indians who tilled the soil for mission friars, had the time or inclination to cultivate vineyards or orchards.

Gardening changed for the better after the Spanish introduced *acequias*, or irrigation ditches, many of which continue to run in northern New Mexico. Even today, farmers willingly share rationed water, governed by *parciantes*, commissions of member-shareholder landowners. The elected manager of an *acequia*, the *majordomo*, directs *acequia* members who work together to keep the ditches clean and free flowing.

While *acequias* were imperative for survival in early New Mexico, their limited water supply didn't allow farmers to plant their fields beyond the cultivation of basic crops, mostly corn.

The passing of time and the arrival of a Frenchman would make a significant horticultural difference. On August 6, 1851, Bishop Jean Baptiste Lamy rode into Santa Fe. According to historian Paul Horgan, "The weather was hot and dry. There had been an extended drought. [Lamy] entered the city amid crowds of citizens and accompanied by 8,000 Catholic Indians who animated the triumph with sham battles and dances. The cannon of Fort Marcy fired salutes. A Te Deum was sung in the parish church of Saint Francis. A state dinner followed at the house of the resident vicar, Father Ortiz. The day was crowned by a good omen: rain fell in torrents. Everything indicated a good beginning for the bishop."

Born in the Auverne, a Frenchman who liked his wine, fruit, and cheese, Lamy set about taming the soil to furnish his table with the same energy he tended his flock. Soon he was importing grapevines, fruit trees, and horse chestnut and elm trees to Santa Fe. Legend also has it that the archbishop introduced lilac bushes to New Mexico.

Lamy's green thumb was so sufficiently admired that the September 11, 1875, issue of the *New Mexican*, a Santa Fe newspaper, ran an article on the Bishop's four-acre, spring-fed garden adjacent to the St. Francis cathedral (the construction of which he initiated and oversaw throughout his lifetime).

According to the newspaper, Lamy's garden was "among the most charming spots on the backbone of the continent.... The enclosure…is set with a great variety of fruitbearing trees and bushes, with innumerable floral shrubs arranged for continuous blossoming in various colors throughout the season, thus shedding a delightful fragrance whenever and whithersoever the winding walks may entice."

In her novel *Death Comes for the Archbishop*, Willa Cather describes Lamy's last years. "This period of reflection the Archbishop spent on his little country estate, some four miles north of Santa Fe. Long before his retirement from the cares of the diocese…[he] bought these few acres in the red sandhills near the Tesuque pueblo, and set out an orchard which would be bearing when the time came for him to rest," she wrote. "He chose this place in the red hills spotted with juniper against the advice of his friends, because he believed it to be admirably suited for the growing of fruit…"

Historian Paul Horgan elaborated on the Archbishop's love affair with the land. "Lamy thought [gardening in New Mexico] was worth it…. He would say the purpose of it all was to demonstrate what could be done to bring the graces of the earth to a land largely barren, rocky, and dry."

Lamy proved his point. Gardening was, and is, possible in northern New Mexico (Zone 5 in today's horticulture vernacular).

Neither desert nor rain forest, the High Country of Santa Fe and Taos can be tamed, especially behind adobe walls. Transplanted Easterners recognized this fact. After the 1920s, they began to surround their homes with adobe walls for privacy and for the added enjoyment of growing flower beds, which flourish in interior patios.

Protected from the elements and kept warm by the heat-retaining adobe, flowers do especially well in Santa Fe and Taos when the soil is properly prepared and adequately watered, often by drip irrigation. Grateful for warm days and cool nights, gardeners successfully grow irises, roses, blue mist spirea, yarrow, lavender, coreopsis, poppies, snapdragons, daisies, columbine, day lilies, flax, and peonies. Wild grasses and wildflowers, including chamisa, Russian sage, asters, and sunflowers, grow equally well and are especially happy when the summer "monsoons" in July and August soak the earth.

The first nursery in Santa Fe, Clarendon Gardens, was begun in the 1880s by horticulturist Arthur Boyle. It sold roses, smilax, and other popular turn-of-the-century flowers. Born in England, Boyle had been a sheepherder in Australia before coming to New Mexico as an agent for English capitalists. Turning to flowers, he prospered. Later, with L. Bradford Prince, Amado Chavez, Peter Van der Veer, and Grant Rivenburg, he founded the New Mexico Horticultural Society.

Today, more than half a dozen northern New Mexico nurseries cater to the demands of Santa Fe and Taos gardeners. At Santa Fe Greenhouse alone, it isn't unusual for a thousand customers a day in the spring and summer to buy twenty thousand dollars' worth of plants and trees.

Native plants and grasses are especially fast sellers and are often the most hardy ingredients in xeriscape gardens, developed in the 1970s to cope with drought conditions. These gardens, commonly found along the front range of the Rocky Mountains, require very low maintenance, and as little as one-third the water required by more conventional gardens.

Plants that do exceedingly well in a Xeriscape garden include sand sage, butterfly bush, Apache plume, Spanish broom, lamb's ear, blue flax, penstemons (of which there are more than two hundred varieties in New Mexico), gayfeather, ice plants, and daisies. Indian rice grass and buffalo grass are also good growers.

To the astonishment of first-time visitors to the area, landscaping in Santa Fe and Taos also allows for a variety of trees, including maples, green ash, cut-leaf birch, mountain ash, pines, junipers, and aspens.

As the authors of this book, we have been invited into some of the most thoughtful and truly striking gardens in northern New Mexico. We hope readers will share our appreciation for the homeowners who have wrestled with less-than-perfect conditions, and who shared the colorful, fragrant rewards of persistence.

19

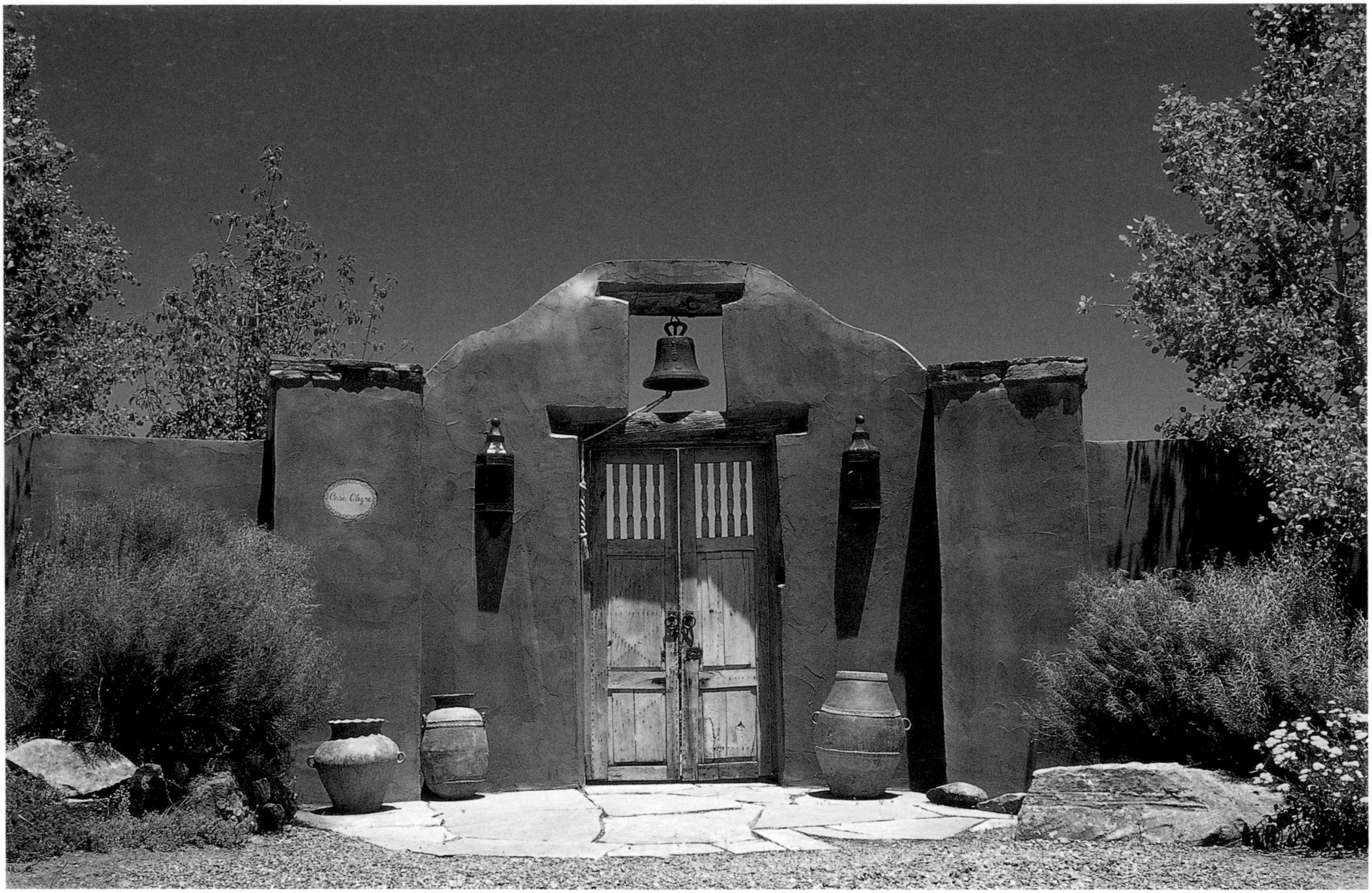
Casa Alegre

Casa Alegre

If you didn't know where Casa Alegre was, you wouldn't dream anyone lived there. Hidden in the hills outside Santa Fe, accessible only by a steep, winding dirt road, this eight-thousand-square-foot, two-story house with a pitched tin roof is wedged into a crevasse as if it had been lowered into place by helicopter. Backed up to a rock cliff behind and facing a towering mountain of piñon-covered earth, the double adobe home of interior designer Barbara Windom and poet Victor di Suvero is a very private hideaway.

Transplants from the West Coast, Barbara and Victor built where only the most athletic angels would dare to tread. Brought up in the film industry in Los Angeles, Barbara was used to houses built in canyons and on steep inclines. Victor, a Venetian, was equally undaunted by unusual building sites. Putting their house where their hearts were, the couple successfully created one of northern New Mexico's most dramatic Shangri-las.

Surrounded by a high adobe wall hiding extensive gardens and manmade streams and ponds, the house was designed and built by the legendary Betty Stewart. A Southwestern Mammy Yokum who always wore blue jeans and a cowboy hat, Stewart, who died in 1994, wasn't an architect. "She was a designer/ builder and one of the most difficult people you can imagine to work with," recalls Barbara, one of several Santa Fe home

Opposite. Bought at the Mexico City flea market, an 1840 Mexican bell welcomes guests to Casa Alegre. *Above.* On a portal, a mid-19th-century Penasco New Mexican chest with a contemporary Mexican tree-of-life.

21

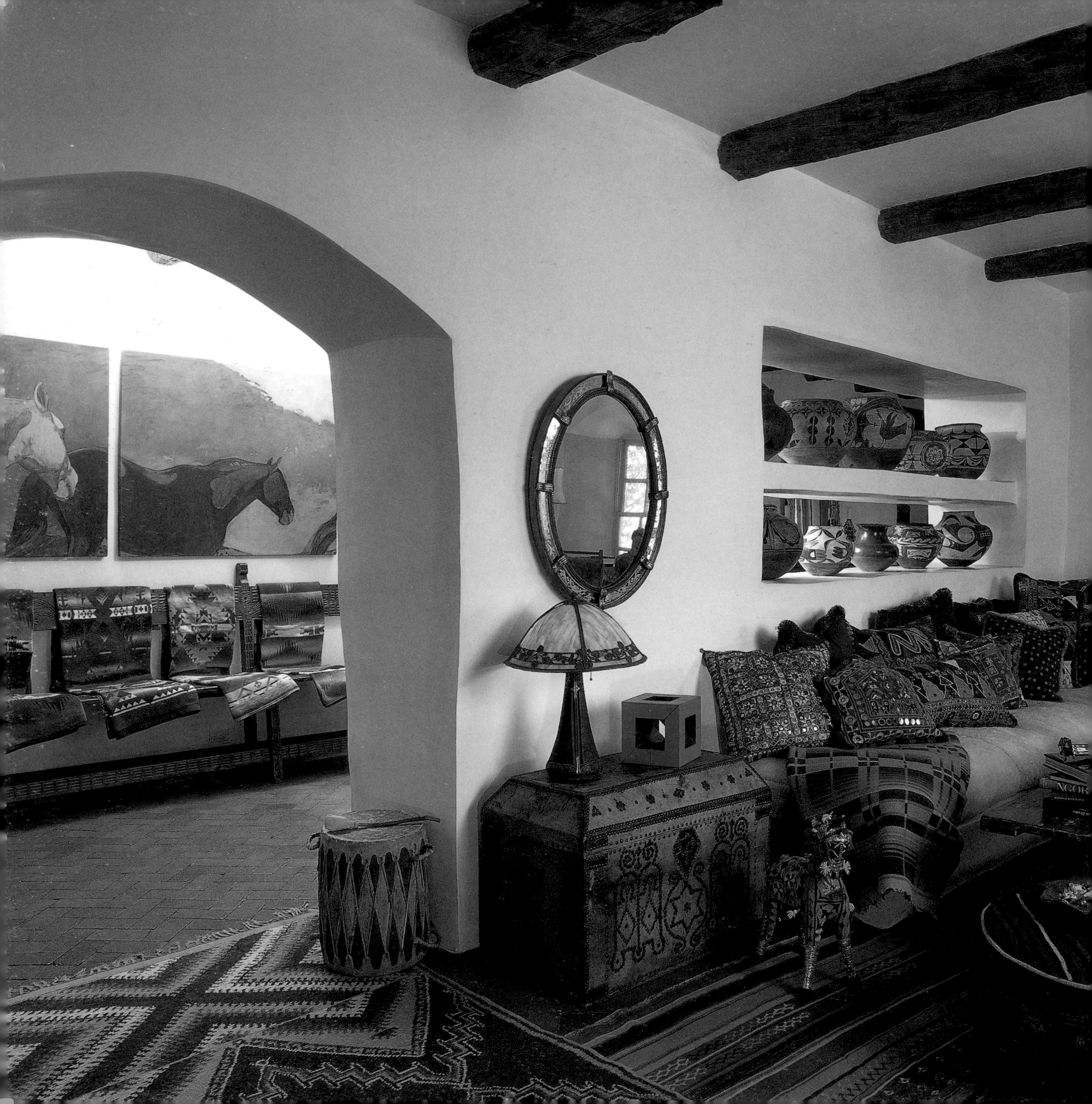

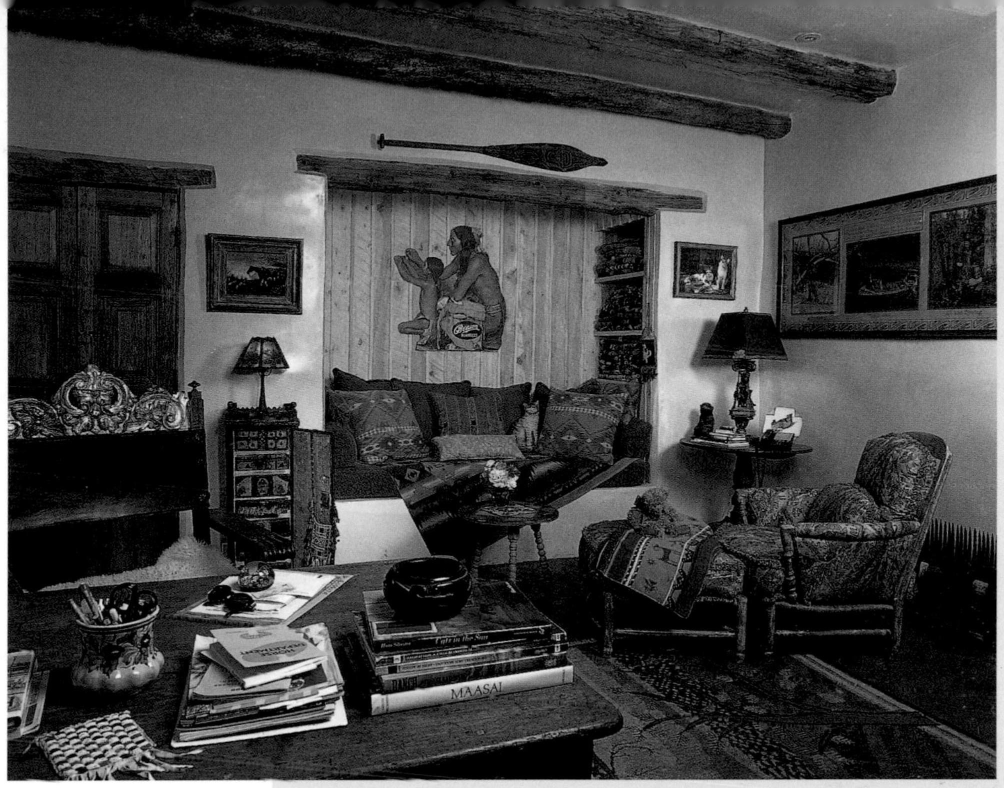
MAASAI

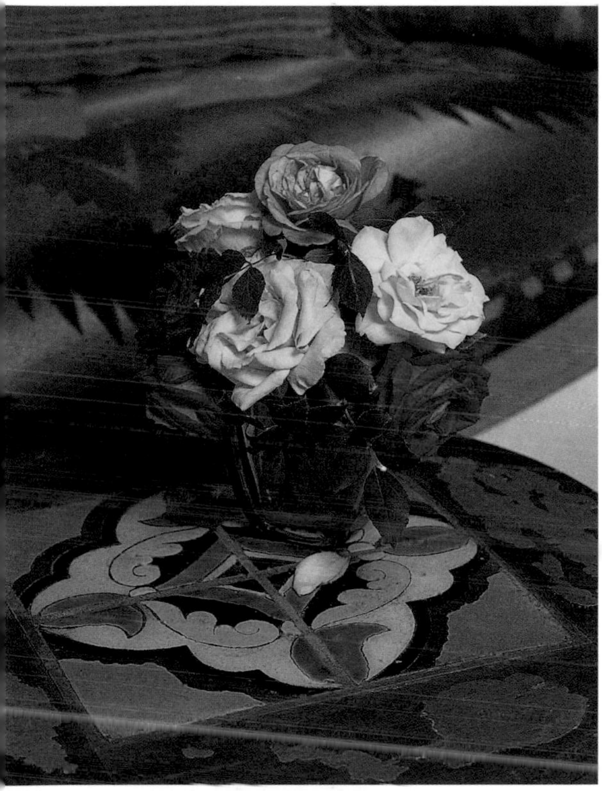

Opposite. Paintings by New Mexican artist Susan Hertel hang above a display of antique Beacon blankets in a hallway. The eclectic libary includes a Taos Indian drum, Moroccan rugs, a Venetian mirror, a Moroccan chest, an American 1930s lamp, and 1920s Pueblo pots.
Above. A table made from California Catalina tiles.
Right. In the study, a 1940s Beacon blanket sign of a Native American. Framed together, three early-20th-century photographs of Native Americans by Roland Reed.

owners who went through a love-hate relationship to live in Stewart style. "Betty couldn't read blueprints; she didn't understand why anyone wanted a closet, a kitchen, or a garage. And yet she had a magical sense of proportion, a God-given ability to position ceiling beams, wide-splayed windows, and undulating archways. She's become a legend," Barbara adds. "Her polished walls, which ripple and undulate, have a sheen like an egg shell. It was worth all the hassle."

A petite woman whose gentleness and reserve mesh beautifully with Victor's European graciousness and brio, Barbara clearly loves her house as much as she does her extensive stables. A frequent traveler to South America, she owns thirty horses, all Peruvian pasos, which she breeds and sells through her company, La Estancia Alegre.

"I grew up with horses. I showed hunters and jumpers and rode competitively all over the United States," Barbara says, settling down to talk in her enormous kitchen/dining room with its massive cathedral ceiling. Here, and throughout the

Top. The living room boasts Venetian sconces, sculpture by Degas and Diego Giacometti, and paintings by New Mexican artists William Penhallow Henderson and Joseph Bakos.

Bottom. On the portal, Spanish tile paintings hang over Mexican piñata molds of a cat and dog.

Opposite. 1920s Pueblo pots decorate shelves above a Guatemalan table with paintings by New Mexican artists W. Wood Woolsey and Joseph Sharp. The rug is Navajo. Dining room chairs are by Richard-Mulligan, Los Angeles.

house, antiques from around the world give the Windom–di Suvero property a sophistication so often lacking in Santa Fe, where style frequently turns into a cliché with little cachet. Sufficient New Mexican furniture, paintings, and accessories assure a visitor he's not in Akron. They are arranged, however, with an enticing restraint. The effect arouses curiosity rather than smothering the visitor.

Now retired, Barbara marketed her design talents to numerous clients when she ran an interior design firm in Los Angeles. "It started when someone who liked my house in Malibu asked me if I'd be their interior designer," she recalls. "I agreed, and before I knew it, I had other clients, and then more clients." Successful from the start, she made certain that any house she decorated—and she frequently juggled three or four at a time—"looked like the owner and not me. It had to be comfortable and unpretentious." Restrained grandeur was also soon recognized as a Windom trademark.

Twenty years later, she walked away from a flourishing business. She was twice divorced and burned out professionally. Fortunately, she'd met Victor, and they decided to begin new lives together. "Santa Fe was the perfect place to start over again," she says. "The thing I love about it is that no one is working the room here, like in L.A. and New York. No one in Santa Fe is hustling for a job. People are here because they choose to be here, not because there's work here.

"Building a new house," Barbara says, "really got my mind going in a new direction." Bringing a good deal of furniture from California, she drew a furniture layout and added other pieces from her relentless search for treasures in local New Mexican antique shops. Determined to sidestep a boring all-French, all-English—or all-Southwestern—house, Barbara decided Casa Alegre "would not be a do-re-mi house, a house cut from a cookie cutter."

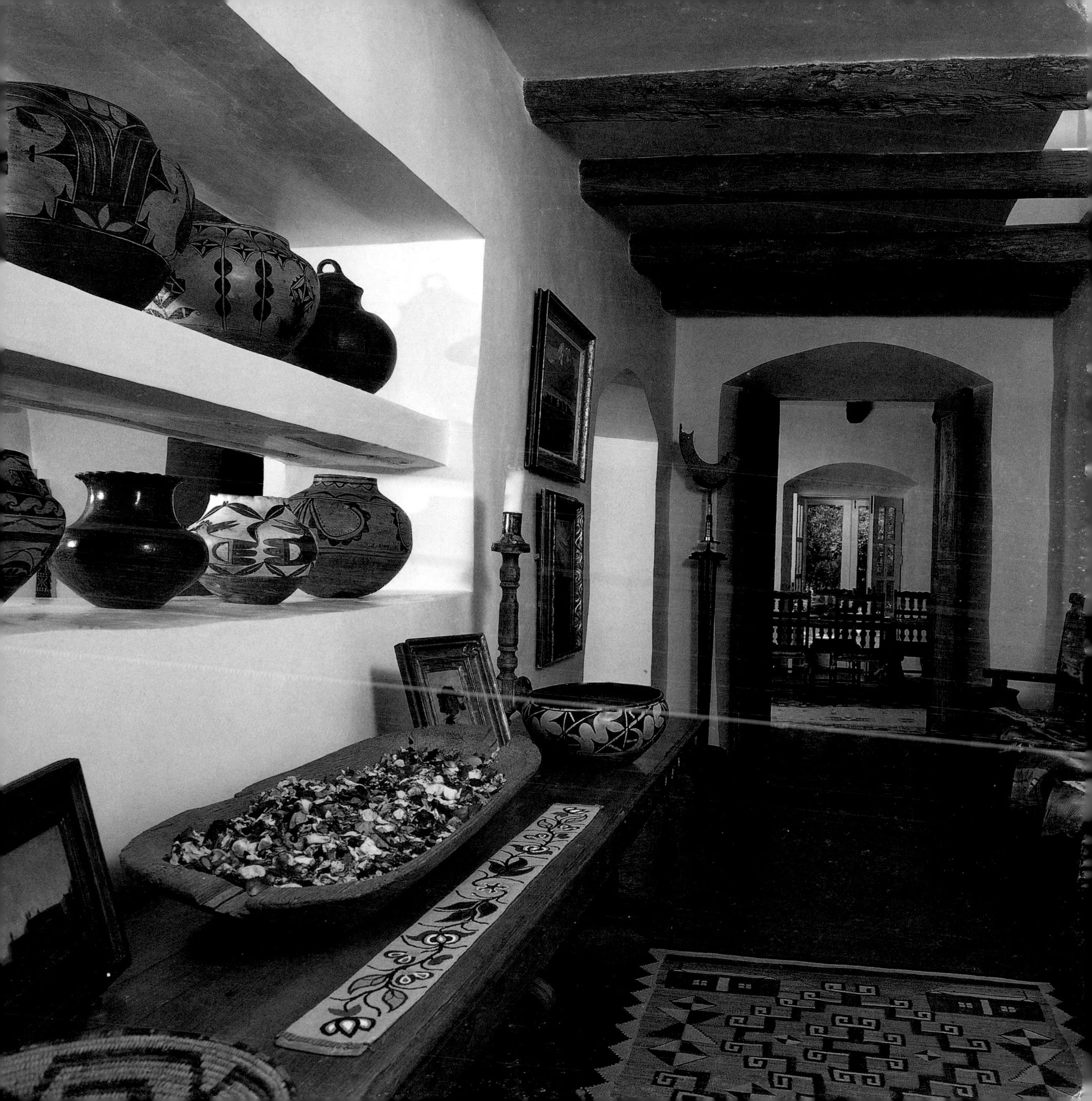

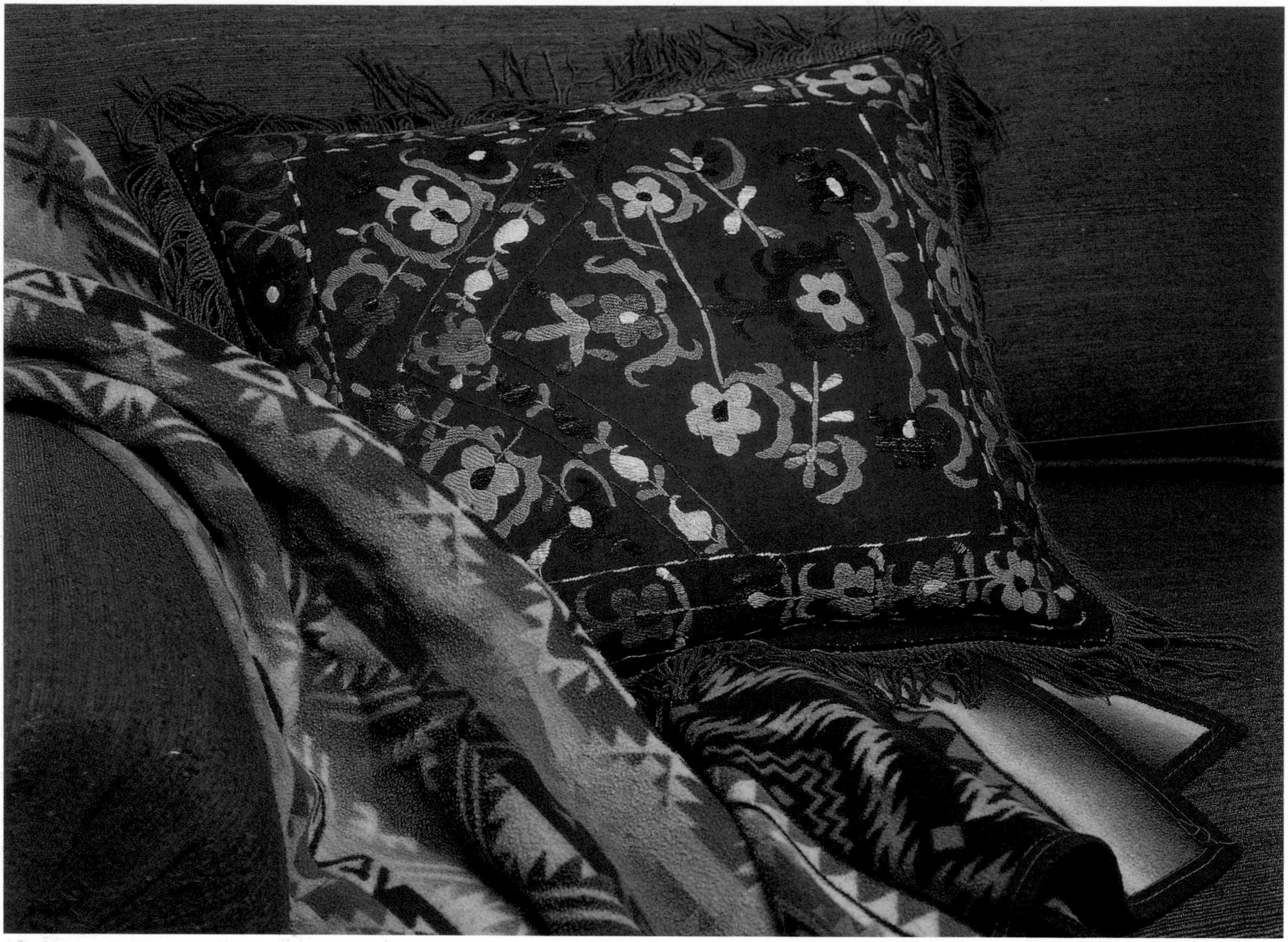

Above. A pillow covered with Indian fabric adds color to a Beacon blanket.
Right. Mexican pots sit beside a bench carved by New Mexican artist William Penhallow Henderson.
Opposite. In the bedroom, Fortuny fabric, pillows with Venetian lace, and a Beacon blanket add drama to an 18th-century Venetian settee.

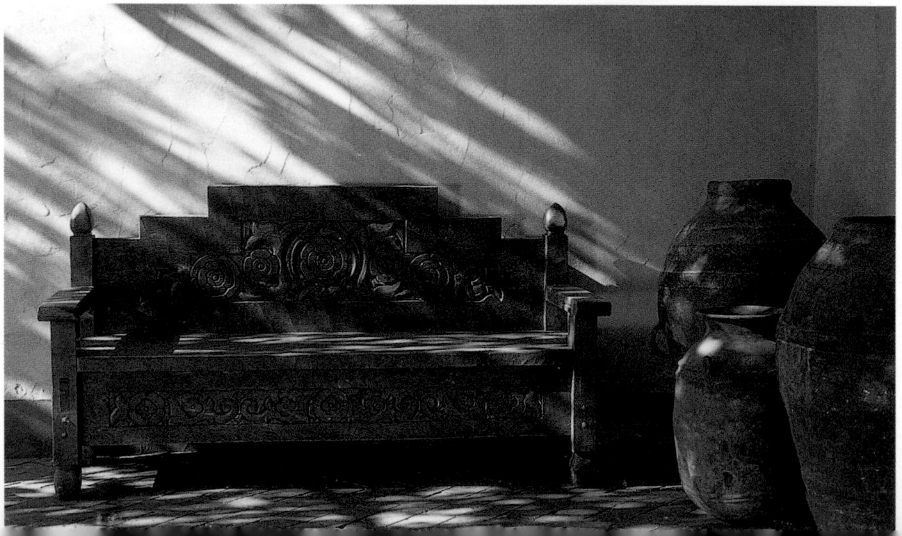

Barbara succeeded. Within each room "there's a surprise: a painting, a chest of drawers, a fabric, something the first-time visitor wouldn't expect." She also made certain the colors in the house worked. "There's got to be a natural progression," she always told her clients, and she executes her philosophy in her own house. "Colors, both on the walls and in fabrics, must pull you through a room and onto the next one. Flow is absolutely essential."

One of the first to buy Maria Martinez's now highly acclaimed black pottery from San Ildefonso pueblo, Barbara also recognized long ago the collectibility of Beacon blankets. Made in Massachusetts in the mid-nineteenth century, the hundred-percent cotton blankets were used by traders to barter with Indians. The blankets' strong colors and imaginative patterns and designs "make them wonderful to decorate with," Barbara says. Indeed, walking through her house, a visitor sees them everywhere—on the backs of chairs, on sofas, hanging on a railing, stacked up in an armoire, folded on shelves.

At the far end of the house's main hallway, the master bedroom, a veritable showroom of Fortuny fabric, takes advantage of the extraordinary vastness of the New Mexico landscape. Beyond the room's French doors, a million-dollar view of mountains, valleys, and arroyos spreads as far as the eye can see. A secluded covered terrace with old Adirondack bent-wood furniture and a white Mexican hammock is "perfect for stargazing," Victor says, pointing to a nearby hot tub the couple uses for more relaxed viewing.

Adjacent to the couple's bedroom is a bathroom suitable for a Venetian doge. Carefully placed mirrors give greater depth and monumentality to the room, which is totally covered with aquamarine tiles. "I wanted Victor to feel that he was near his beloved Adriatic," says Barbara. "After all, Santa Fe is a long way from Venice."

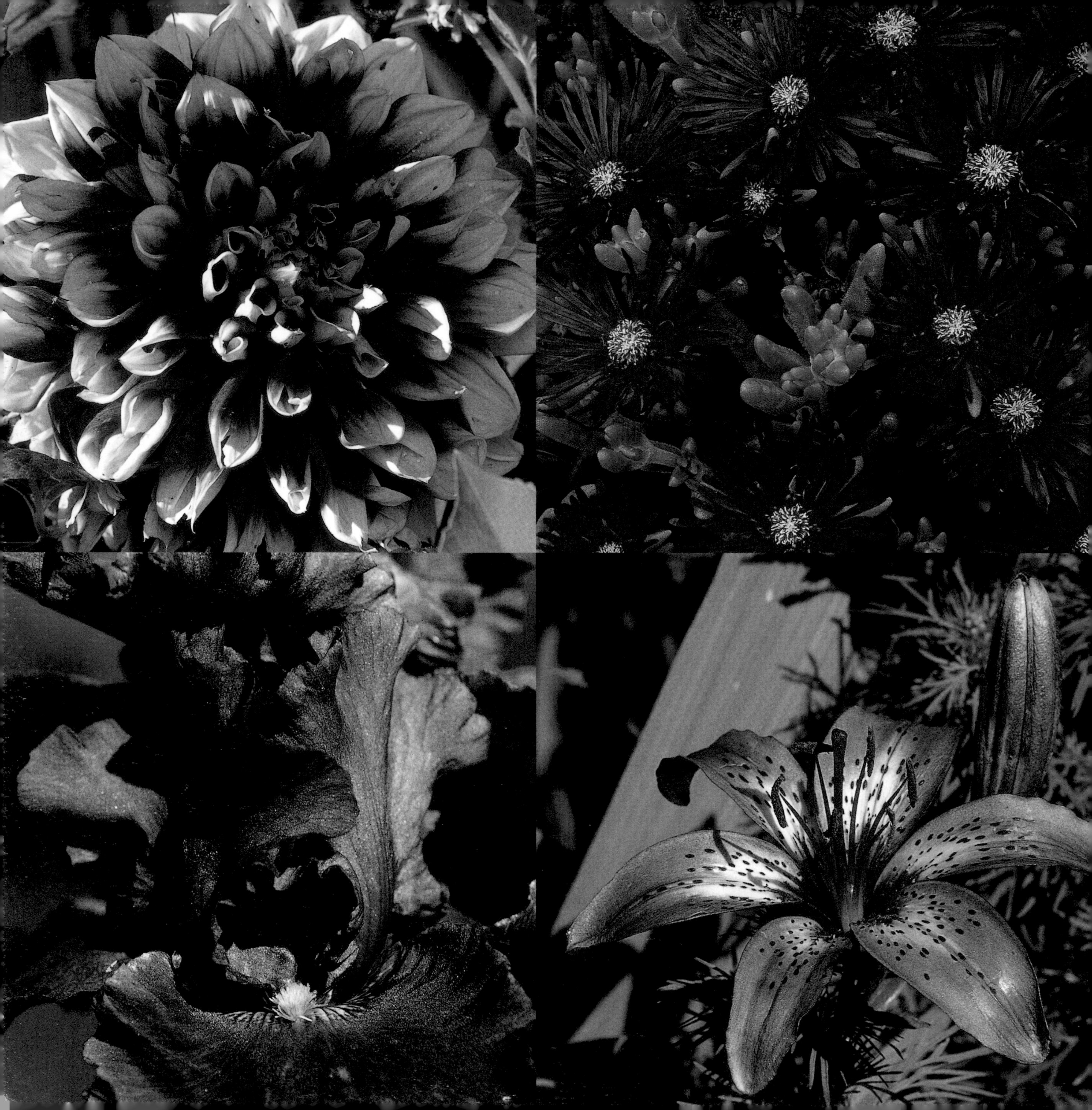

Native Son

I n Santa Fe, old-timers are hard to find. New-comers from across the nation and abroad are now in the majority. Artist Ford Ruthling is a rare bird. He's a native son, one with a paintbrush in one hand and a spade in the other. A successful artist—and a tinsmith, wood-worker, and ceramist, as well—Ford is equally well known as a gardener, one whose palette of petals is as colorful, whimsical, and compelling as his sought-after canvases.

"I grew up here on a farm. It's why I have an affinity with the soil. My grandparents had an apple orchard in Tesuque," he recalls, referring to a small, formerly Hispanic agrarian com-munity ten minutes from Santa Fe's four-hundred-year-old plaza. Today, expensive houses have replaced fields once full of corn and cattle. "I'd come home from school, change out of my 'good clothes,' and work until dark. We had to scratch in the soil to make a go of it. I don't regret a bit of it. We were a family and we had some wonderful times."

Brought up by a German mother, "Ma," the Ruthling kids were taught to say 'Madam' and 'Sir' and bow at the waist when they were introduced to someone, Ford remembers. The "someones" turned out to be many of the community's—and the nation's—leading artists: John Sloane, John Marin, George Bellows, Gus Bohman, Will Schuster, and Randall Davey. "Santa Fe was a very small community in the thirties and forties. You knew everyone," Ford says. "I was fortunate.

Opposite. Artist Ford Ruthling has one of the most spectacular gardens in Santa Fe. Terraced on three acres, it is planted with scores of different flowers, including dahlias, daisies, irises, and tiger lilies. *Above.* The bench was given to Ruthling in the 1950s by well-known local poet Witter Bynner.

29

I wanted to be an artist, and I was surrounded by people who shared my interest. They and my family encouraged me."

After serving in the Air Force, then returning to Santa Fe to become director of exhibits at the Folk Art Museum, Ford began to paint…and to sell. "I made a life-changing discovery," he confides. "I could make a living as an artist. And I could take any day off I wanted to." Ford's thirty-five year career has produced more than twelve hundred oil canvases of birds, animals, plants, landscapes and figures.

Although frequently spoken of by art critics and art lovers as a folk artist, Ford insists such a label is incorrect. "I'm a naturalist whose work looks 'folksy.' I straddle fine and folk," he says. Anxious not to paint himself into a corner, the artist purposely executes what he calls "maverick subjects": iron wall sculptures, bowls he has fired in Mexico, even bedsheet designs.

Outside his studio in his three-acre garden, Ford reveals his additional talent, an extraordinary green thumb. Three terraces surrounding his 1907 Territorial-style house off the Old Santa Fe Trail burst with plants and flowers, their variegated colors and shapes juxtaposed as only an artist could conceive.

Above. Once on top of a Tyrolean farmhouse, the 19th-century wrought iron rooster belonged to Ford Ruthling's mother. "It was on our house in Tesuque, outside Santa Fe," he says.
Above, right. Beside an old Mexican door, garden tools have been welded together by Ruthling into a wall art abstraction.
Opposite. A 19th-century Mexican nativity child peers from behind glass at viewers from a recessed crib in an old Mexican table. *Milagros,* or motifs, are attached to his clothing. The beaded African crocodile was bought at the Santa Fe flea market. Flower petals fall on Ford Ruthling's ledger.

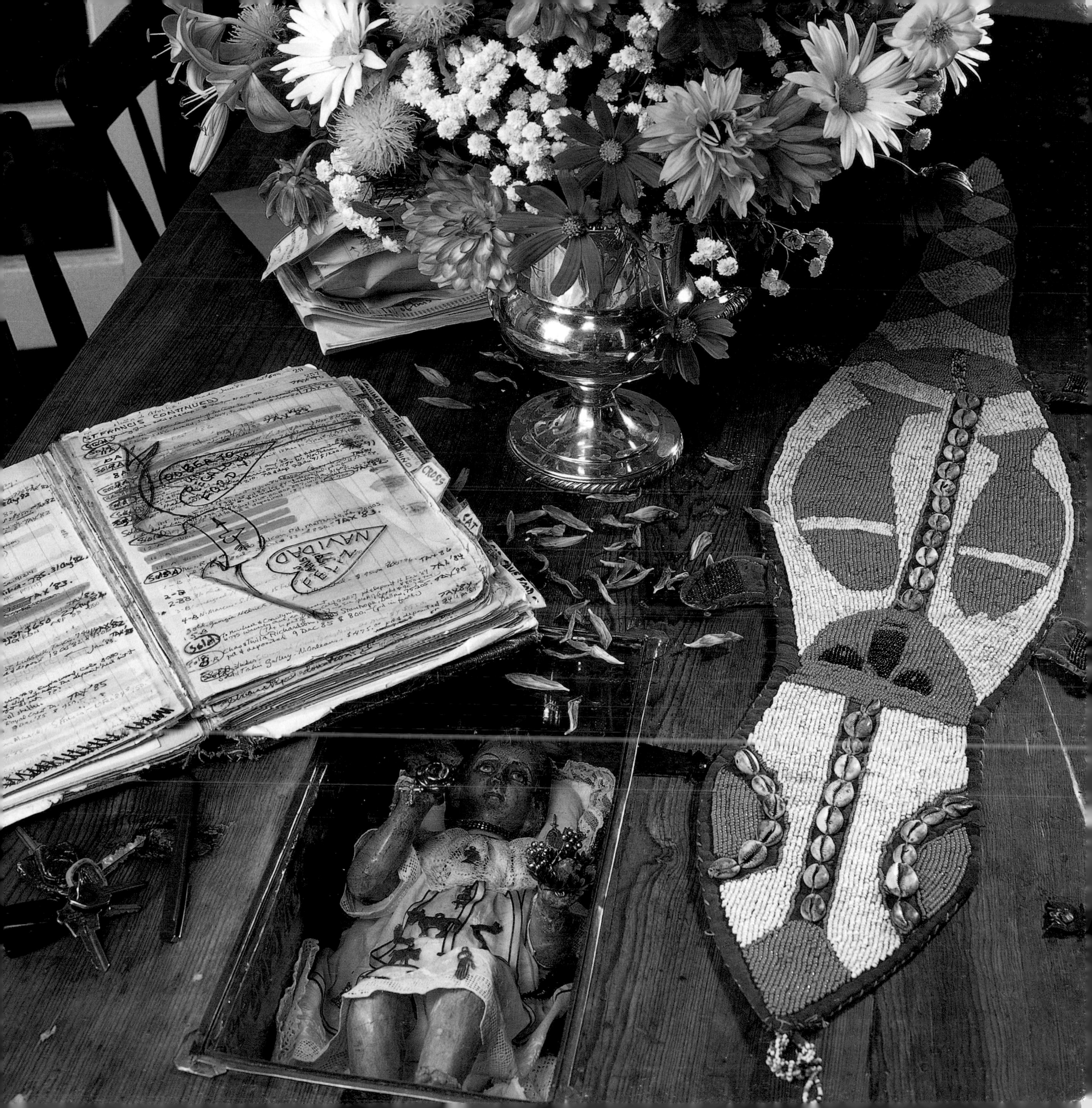
ST. FRANCIS CONTINUED
NAVIDAD
CROSS
CAT

Left, above, and opposite. His work sought by collectors and museums nationwide, Santa Fe artist Ford Ruthling divides his time between making art and gardening. Tending to three acres of riotously colored flowers interspersed with his sculpture, he says, "Gardening is therapy. It lifts my spirits. Unless, of course, I find cutworms or grasshoppers. Then I get depressed." Raccoons and pheasants are different. "I love to share my garden with them," Ford says.

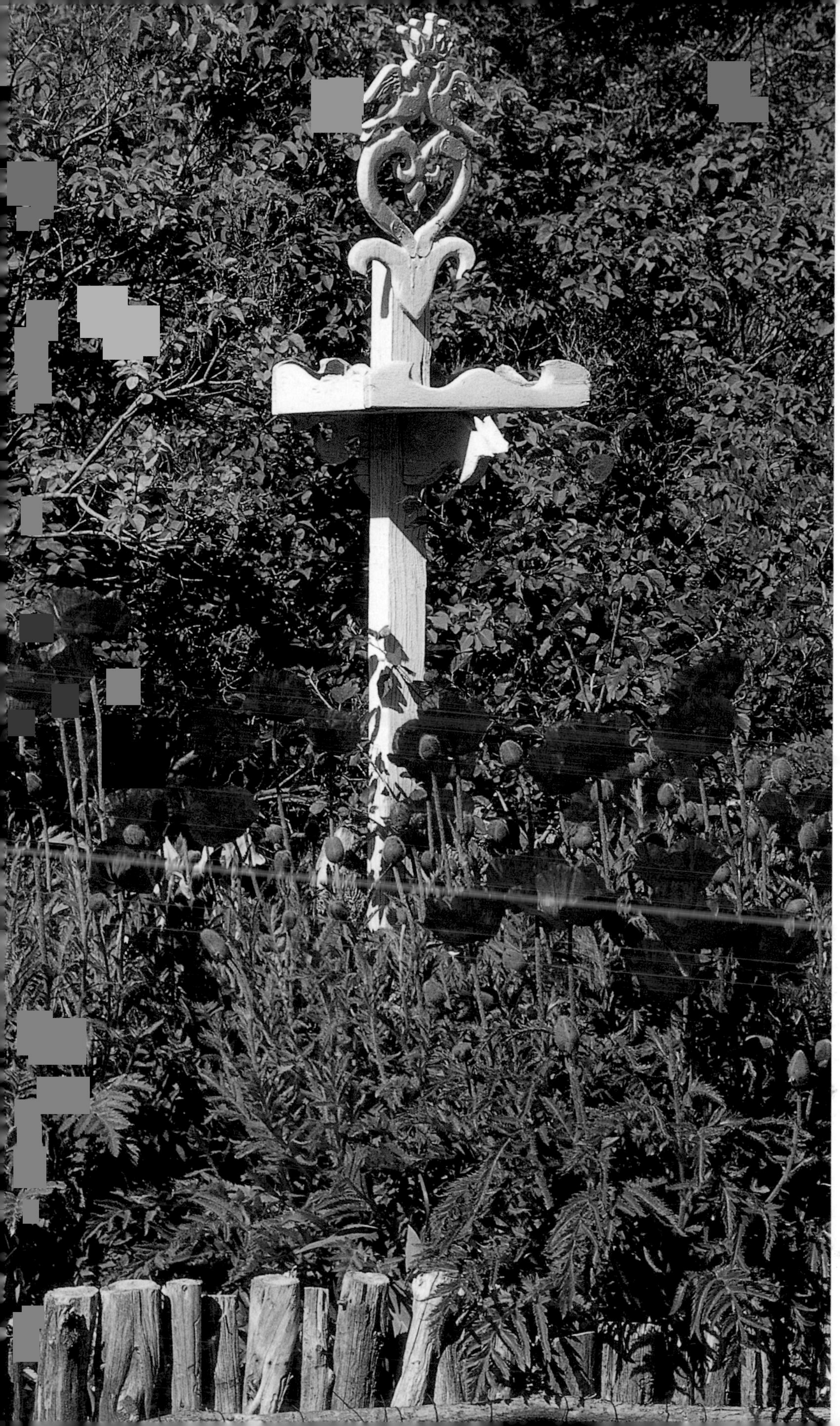

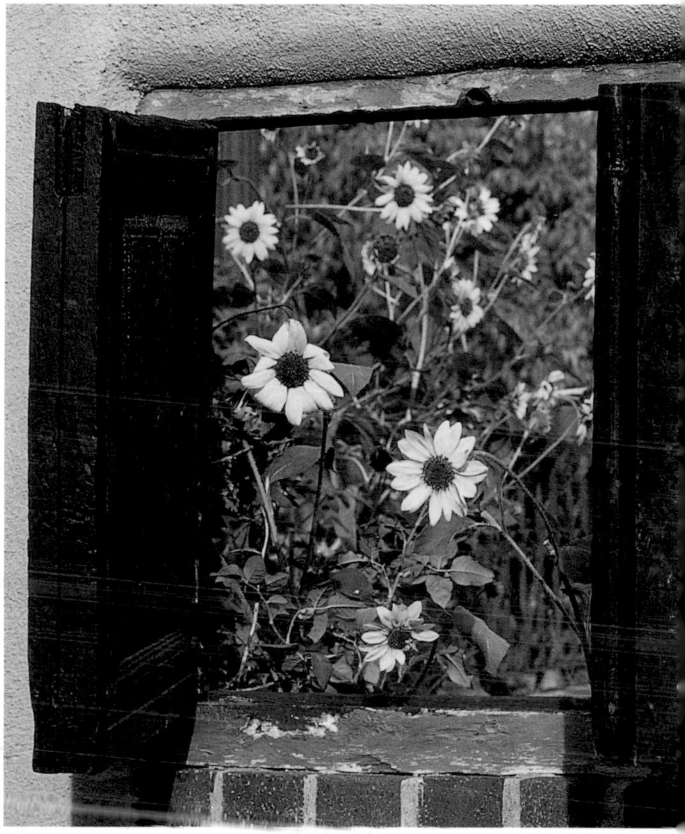

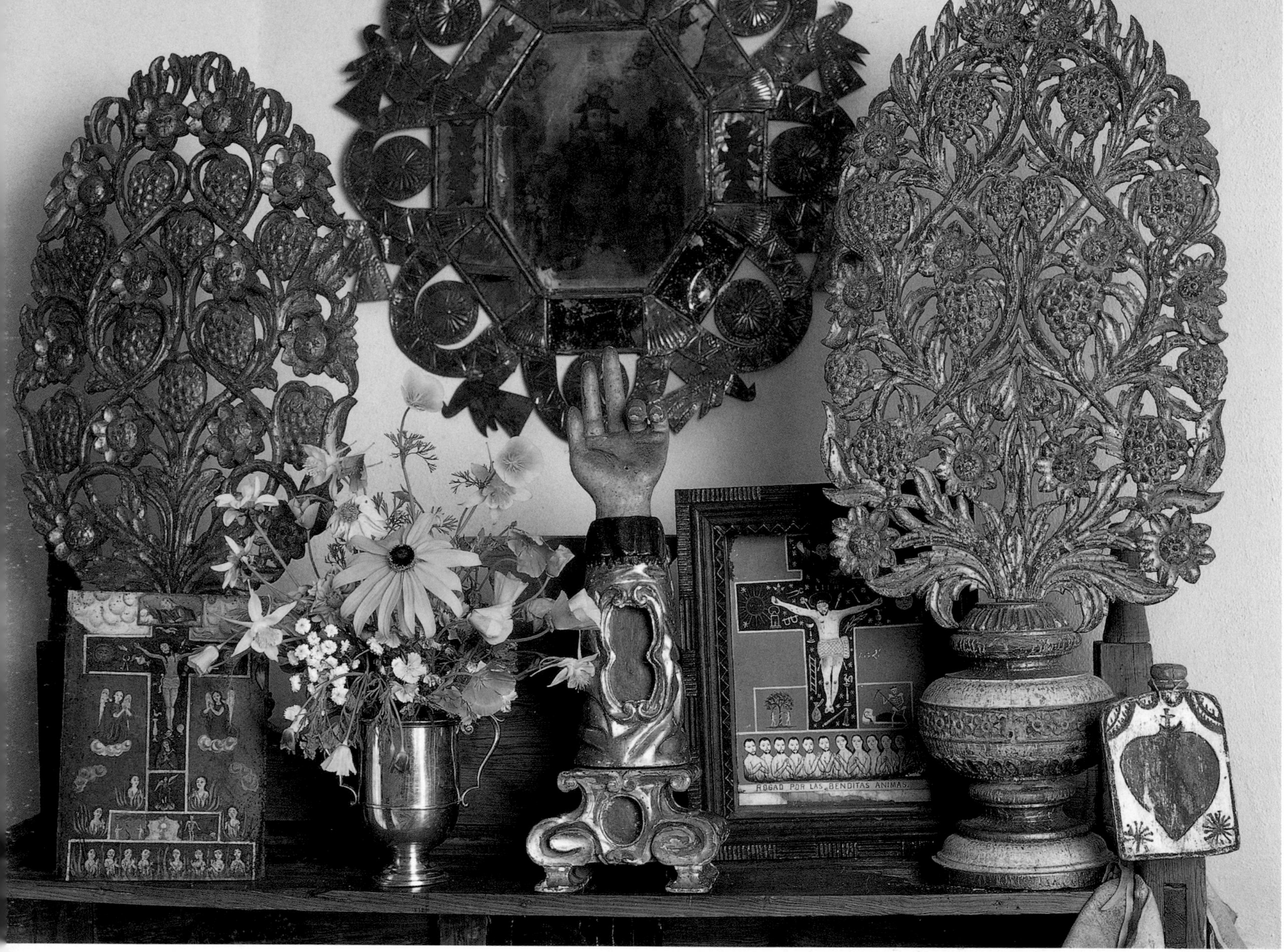
ROGAD POR LAS BENDITAS ANIMAS

Above. Eighteenth-century altarpieces from Portuguese Goa straddle a 19th-century Spanish reliquary. Santo Nino de Atoche hangs in a 19th-century New Mexican tin frame. *Opposite.* Carved out of stone, a half-moon by Ruthling hangs over the artist's acres of flower gardens.

Old wooden garden furniture, round tables with umbrellas, adobe walls with weather-beaten painted doors and windows, brick walkways: Ford's is a garden that is clearly intended to give joy to visitors.

Of the numerous varieties of flowers here, which are Ford's favorites? Poppies, delphinium, and lilies, he says. While they certainly predominate, the grounds are planted with dozens of other blooms: daisies, cosmos, marigolds, petunias, roses, and larkspur. In the spring, irises, tulips, daffodils, and lilacs abound.

"Of all the colors, white is the most important to have in a garden. It gives depth and dimension," Ford says. "It delineates the other plants and flowers."

Devoting a minimum of three hours each day to his garden, Ford sees his work as an artist and his work as a gardener as symbiotic. "To leave my studio after three or four hours' work in front of a canvas and to go out into the out-of-doors, to cut, to prune, to till, to plant—it is very therapeutic," he tells the numerous art collectors who come to his house. "My garden restores my soul and promotes creativity. I want it to be a place where others can also gain a sense of serenity and peace."

Do higher powers play a role in garden design? "Yes, in a way," Ford says. "I've learned that plants and flowers have a way of disappearing, then reappearing, often in areas of the garden where they weren't originally planted. Frequently, they are better located the second time around. I think it's a way for God to keep his hand in gardening." It's also one of the reasons Ford's garden has such originality, he believes. "I certainly don't take full credit for what you see. There's someone up there who's gardening with me."

———■———

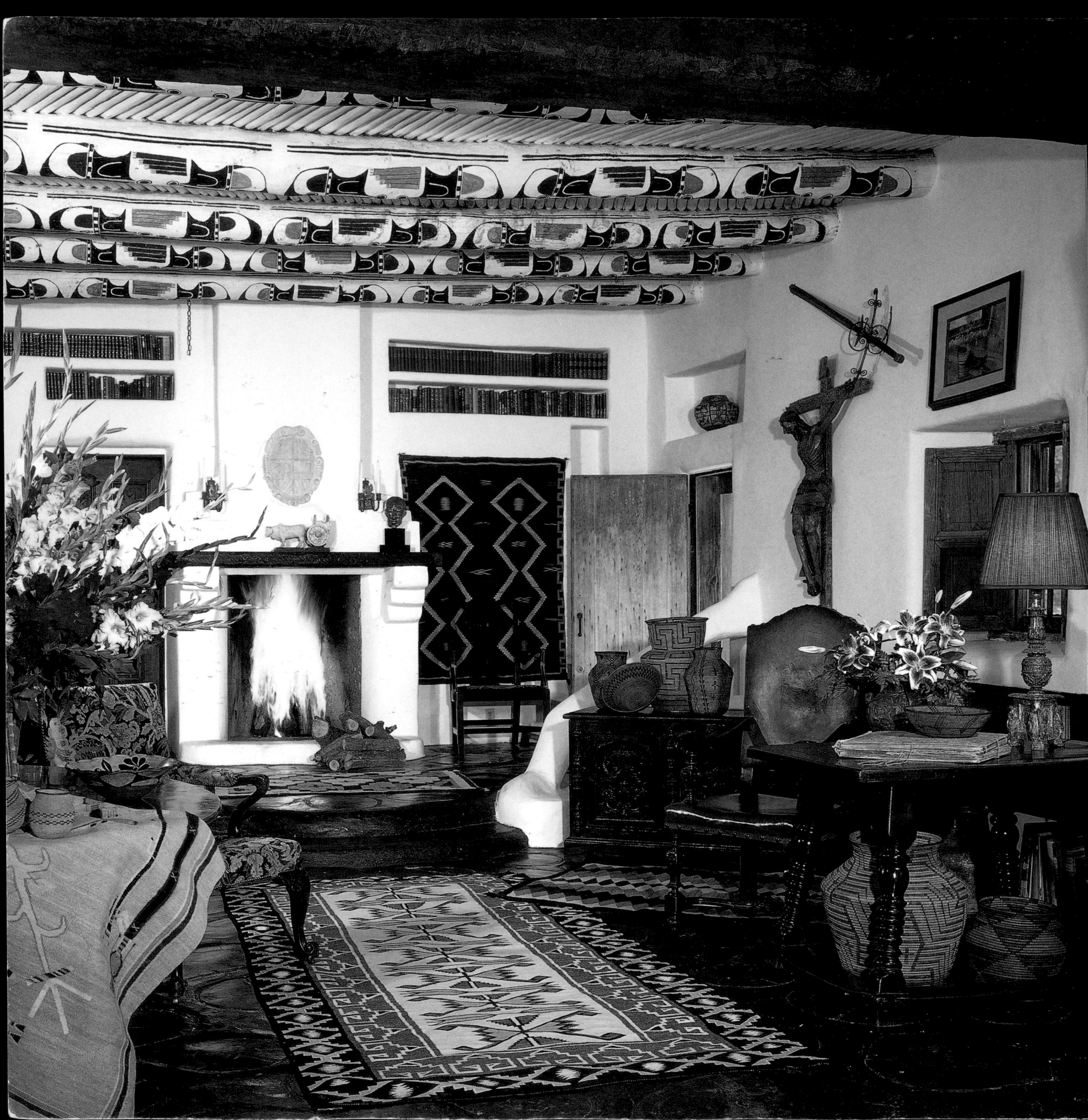

A Taos Legend

A resident of Taos in the late 1940s (and also of Beverly Hills, New York City, Virginia, Jamaica, and Austria), Millicent Rogers is a New Mexico legend.

Blessed with great beauty and wealth, an heiress to a Standard Oil fortune, Rogers was no poor little rich girl. She was a multifaceted, multitalented "hostess with the mostest." Her biographers emphasize her artistry as a fashion and jewelry designer, her talent as a raconteur and conversationalist, her commitment to the welfare of Indians, and her flair for interior design.

Rogers, who died at fifty-two in 1952, lived in Taos on a hacienda, La Manclia Farm. Today, few realize that it is still standing and that it remains remarkably close to the way she left it. Each summer Rogers's son, Arturo Ramos, and his wife, Jacqueline, (who also maintain a New York City apartment) occupy the dwelling.

"If you want to know the real MR," Jackie Ramos says, using the affectionate nickname family and friends called her mother-in-law, "you'll find her here in the library." A tall, captivating blond, former model, and internationally well-known racehorse owner, Jackie motions to the rows of books that line the enormous room's wraparound shelves. Subjects include fiction, poetry, art, history, fashion, and architecture.

Opposite. Painted with Native American symbols by artist Dorothy Brett, vigas in the living room of Millicent Rogers's hacienda are in keeping with the room's Navajo rugs, 19th-century Mexican crucifix, and Pima baskets. The bust of author Ian Fleming, a frequent houseguest, sits on the mantle.
Above. A photograph by Horst of Rogers sits beside a few pieces of the legendary international hostess's vast Navajo turquoise and silver jewelry collection.

"Here, look at the notes in the margins in this book," she says, selecting a title at random. Commentaries in Rogers's perfect penmanship run up and down the edges of the pages. "Any book she read—and she read voraciously in Italian, French, German, Greek, and Latin—she added to." The book's author clearly wasn't going to have the last word!

"MR was cleverer than most men. It is probably why she had a succession of husbands. They couldn't keep up," explains Arturo Ramos, adding that Clark Gable and Ian Fleming, neither one of whom she married, were the two men to whom his mother felt the closest. One of Rogers's three sons, the tall, handsome international businessman admits, "I never thought of MR as mother. She was a presence, but not an especially maternal one."

While the guest of actress Janet Gaynor, who had a house outside Santa Fe, Rogers fell in love with New Mexico. Six months after her visit she bought her Taos property, a seventeenth-century Spanish hacienda. Barefoot, wearing Navajo velvet skirts, white blouses, and turquoise and silver jewelry, Rogers spent the last six years of her life renovating, decorating, and adding rooms to the hacienda. "It was full of Indians. They were always painting vigas, *latillas*, and corbels, doing murals in the patio, or just camping out," recalls Arturo. "She was mad for the native culture. I would drive her all over the Southwest to Indian dances in an old World War I weapons carrier. We'd rough it and sleep in a tent." Rogers's arrival in New Mexico was a bit more luxurious, however. "She'd be met at the Lamy train station by a fleet of cars: one for her, one for the luggage, one for the servants."

Opposite, top. Taos pueblo artist Joe Swazo painted murals of a prairie fire on the hacienda's gallery walls Italian Renaissance candelabra are lit when Arturo Ramos, Millicent Rogers's son, and his wife, Jackie, entertain at night. *Opposite, bottom.* Corbels around the courtyard are decorated with Indian symbols.

Left. In the dining room of La Mancha, a Navajo Germantown rug hangs over an Italian Renaissance table. Jacobean chairs stand behind place settings of English silver and Spode china. The fireplace is one of twelve still in use in the former 17th-century fort.

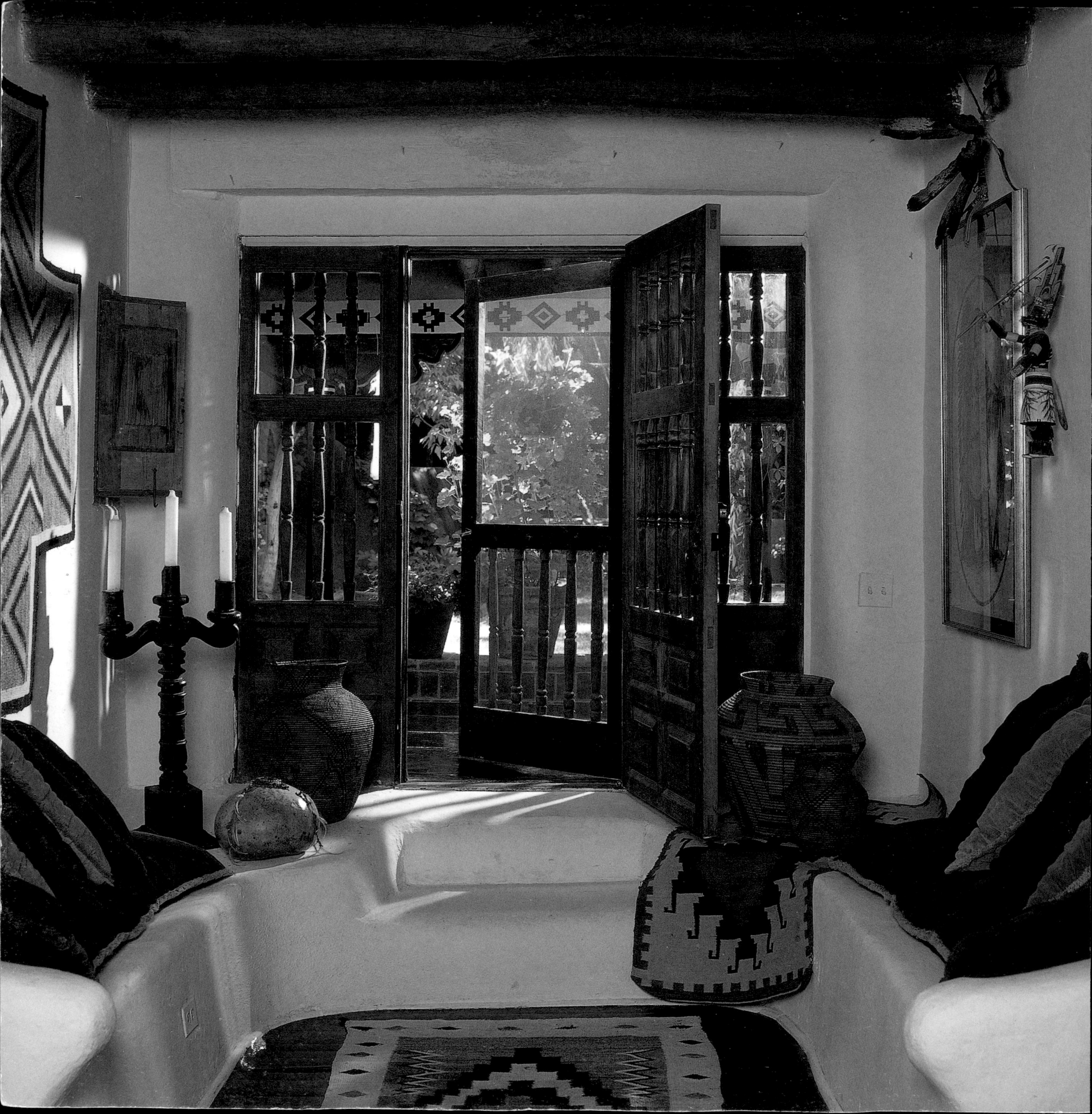

Jackie, who has kept up the family tradition of hosting a nonstop house party, frequently looks back in time as well. "I wish I'd seen the house when MR lived here. It had to have been fabulous. It was full of French Impressionist paintings, Aubusson rugs, African masks, European furniture, Indian rugs and pots. They were gone by the time Arturo and I were married."

Left in a state of shabby gentility, the property demanded a second-generation facelift. Jackie, with Arturo's blessing, took on the task. She turned someone else's house into a home of her own. Today, La Mancha Farm, a seventy-eight-acre oasis hidden behind high adobe walls and shaded by cottonwood trees, continues to have a universal—and historic Southwest—atmosphere. Every room in the house contains remarkable Indian artifacts, as well as American and European antiques.

Annotated scrapbooks from the thirties—mementos of skiing in Austria, hunting in England—are stacked up on tables, along with numerous copies of *The Blood-Horse*, Jackie's favorite magazine.

Do members of the Millicent Rogers's fan club—who come to Santa Fe to visit the nearby Millicent Rogers museum—find the house very often? "Rarely," Jackie says, gratefully. But, one day, one did—Rogers's longtime New York friend, Diana Vreeland, editor of *Vogue*. "She had been invited here often but never came when MR was alive. One day, she showed up unannounced. I was up on a ladder fixing something," Jackie remembers, "and there she was, jet-black hair, blood-red lipstick, and wearing orange slacks. I took her through the house. All she said was, 'Fabulous. Fabulous.' She'd cross her hands, with those incredible long, perfectly manicured red nails, and emit this long, drawn out, ecstatic 'Fabulous.'"

It was a reaction that MR would have enjoyed.

Opposite. Apache woven baskets, a Navajo dazzler rug, and an Italian candlestick decorate a hallway leading to the garden and swimming pool.
Top. Guests sleep under an American quilt in a 19th-century Jamaican bed. Furnishings include an English nanny's chair, a Philippine santos, and a New Mexican landscape by Oscar Berninghaus.
Bottom. A late-19th-century hand-painted Apache shaman healing skin hangs on the wall in the den. Paintings by George McChesney, Taos, hang between Apache peyote fans.

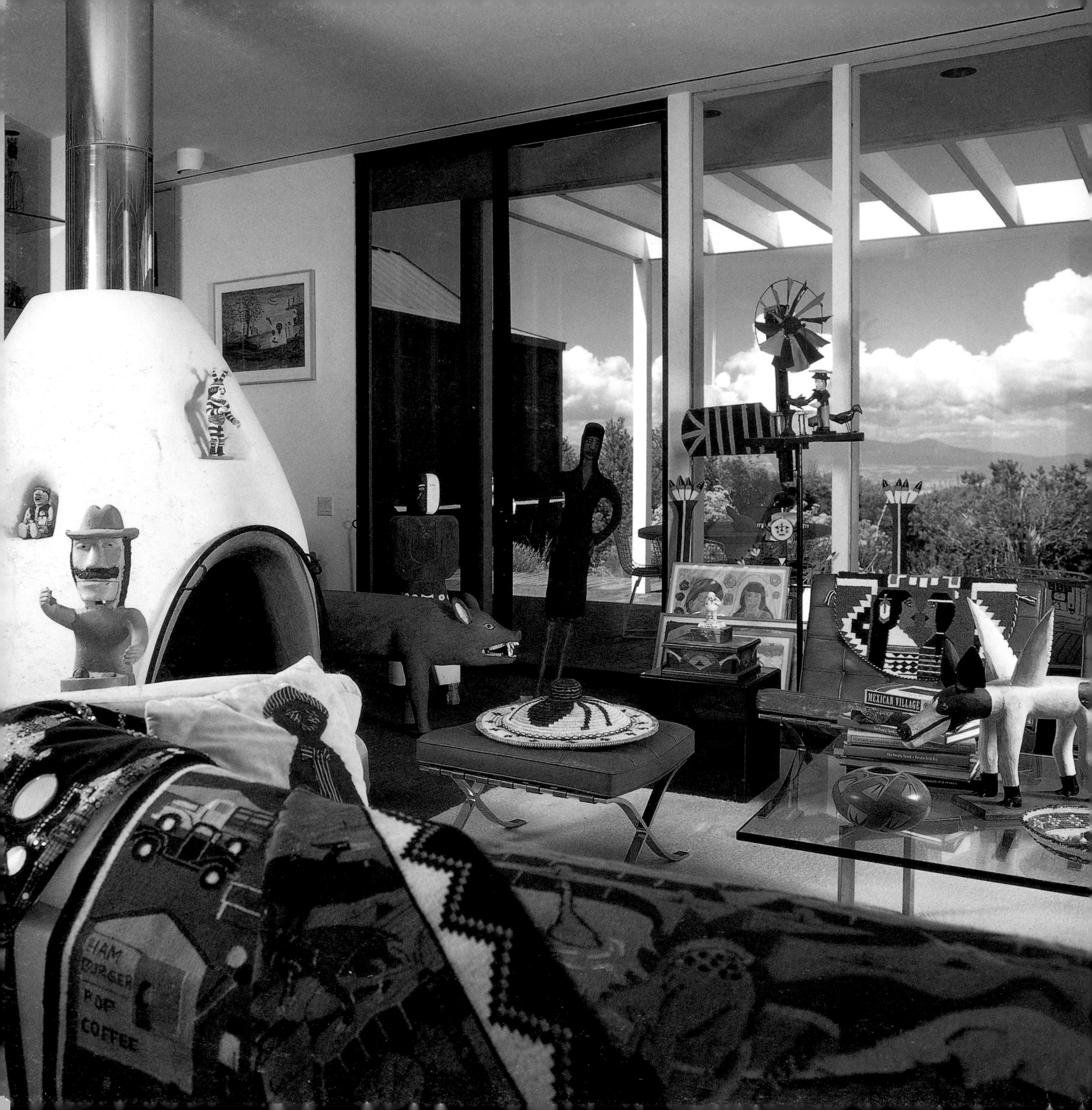
MEXICAN VILLAGE
HAM
BURGER
POP
COFFEE

The Beginning of the Trail

For centuries, settlers have considered Santa Fe to be the end of their trail. For collectors Jan and Chuck Rosenak, it became their beginning. Former lawyers in Washington, D.C., the couple moved to the Southwest in 1985, only to make frequent sorties in pursuit of contemporary American folk art. Firm believers in going to the source rather than buying from galleries, the Rosenaks are as likely to be found driving down dirt roads in Arizona on the Navajo reservation as they are to be climbing up four flights of stairs in a Brooklyn housing development. They are always on the lookout for artistic creations by untrained, often unrecognized, and frequently unschooled American artists.

Once collectors of contemporary American paintings, the couple experienced their simultaneous epiphany when they attended the 1973 Whitney Museum's Biennial Exhibition of Contemporary American Art.

Walking through the exhibit separately, they met for lunch to discuss their reactions. Both had singled out the same item: the "Expulsion of Adam & Eve from the Garden of Eden," a wood carving by Edgar Tolson, a self-taught, part-time preacher from Kentucky.

"We agreed, we had to have a Tolson," Chuck says. "From then on, we were off and running. We stopped collecting paintings and moved into folk art." Today, there are more than six

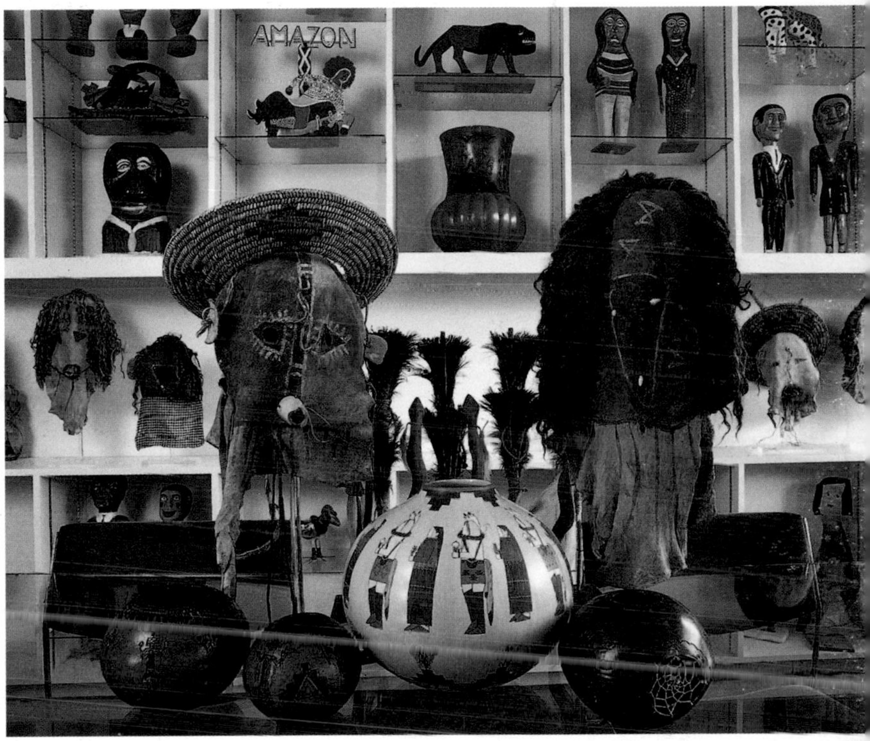
AMAZON

Opposite. Facing the Jemez mountains, the house of Jan and Chuck Rosenak contains one of the nation's great contemporary American folk art collections. In the living room are the Nutcracker and whirligig by John Vivolo; a pig, or javelina, by Leroy Archuleta; and Winged Dog by Stephen Polaha.
Above. Two Navajo *yei* masks of spirit gods guard a pot by Ida Sahmie. On the shelf is a micaceous pot by Chris McHorse.

Top. Designed by architect Hugh Newell Jacobsen, the frontier town facade of the Rosenaks' house is a backdrop for Navajo artist Delbert Buck's man and woman on horseback. Twenty years old, Buck is one of the nation's youngest folk artists.
Bottom. In winter, the Sangre de Cristo mountains are covered with snow.
Opposite. Navajo spirit figures by Robin Willeto stand in front of a painting by African-American artist Xmeah Sha Ela' ReEl. The Navajo pictorial rug is by Linda Nez.

thousand original pieces in the Rosenaks' collection, from wood carvings, sculpture, and wall hangings to fish decoys and pots. In fact, the Rosenaks have become renowned scholars in what is now recognized as a major field of art. Authors of several books on American folk art, the couple's most recent title is *Contemporary American Folk Art: A Collector's Guide* (Abbeville, New York, 1996). "There were about six collectors of contemporary American folk art when we began. Now, there are several thousand—ten of whom are very serious—with Europeans increasingly joining the ranks," Chuck says. "There are at least a hundred galleries showing the work, and more than fifty museums, including the Abby Aldrich Folk Art Museum in Williamsburg, Virginia, collecting as well. It's happened within the last ten years."

Like many Santa Feans, the couple wanted an adobe dwelling. Owners of acreage in Tesuque, about ten minutes north of Santa Fe, the Rosenaks flew famed East Coast architect Hugh Newell Jacobsen west to design their house. En route to the site, flying at an altitude of thirty-five thousand feet, Jacobsen came up with a stop-'em-dead-in-their-tracks alternative to the usual Santa Fe cliché, however. He filled out the bottom of a letter he was writing to a friend with a sketch of a Western frontier town. It was a kind of Neo-Tombstone style that would become the façade of the Rosenaks' house. The rest would be streamlined modern with no Santa Fe embellishments—no *latillas*, no *vigas*, no *nichos*—and lots and lots of space to show off the Rosenaks' ever-growing collection.

"It took a lot of convincing to get the house approved by the city's architectural review committee," Jan Rosenak recalls. "The colors of the frontier façade were especially tricky. Traditional adobe brown was all the committee knew, or would okay. Hugh did an end run. He selected historic colors that are on the Palace of the Governors. There was no disputing the colors were traditional; therefore, the committee passed them for our house, too."

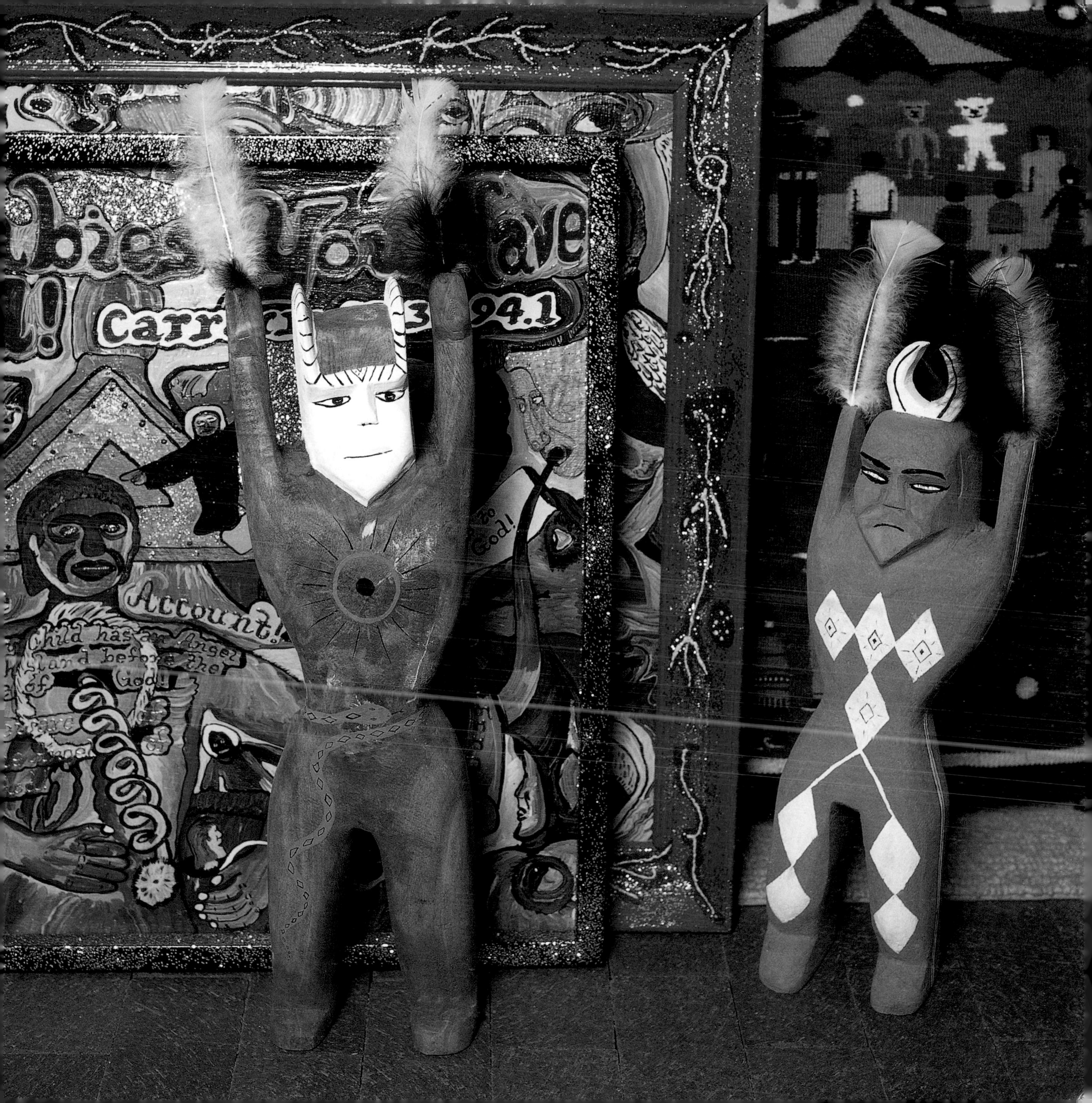

94.1
Account!
God!

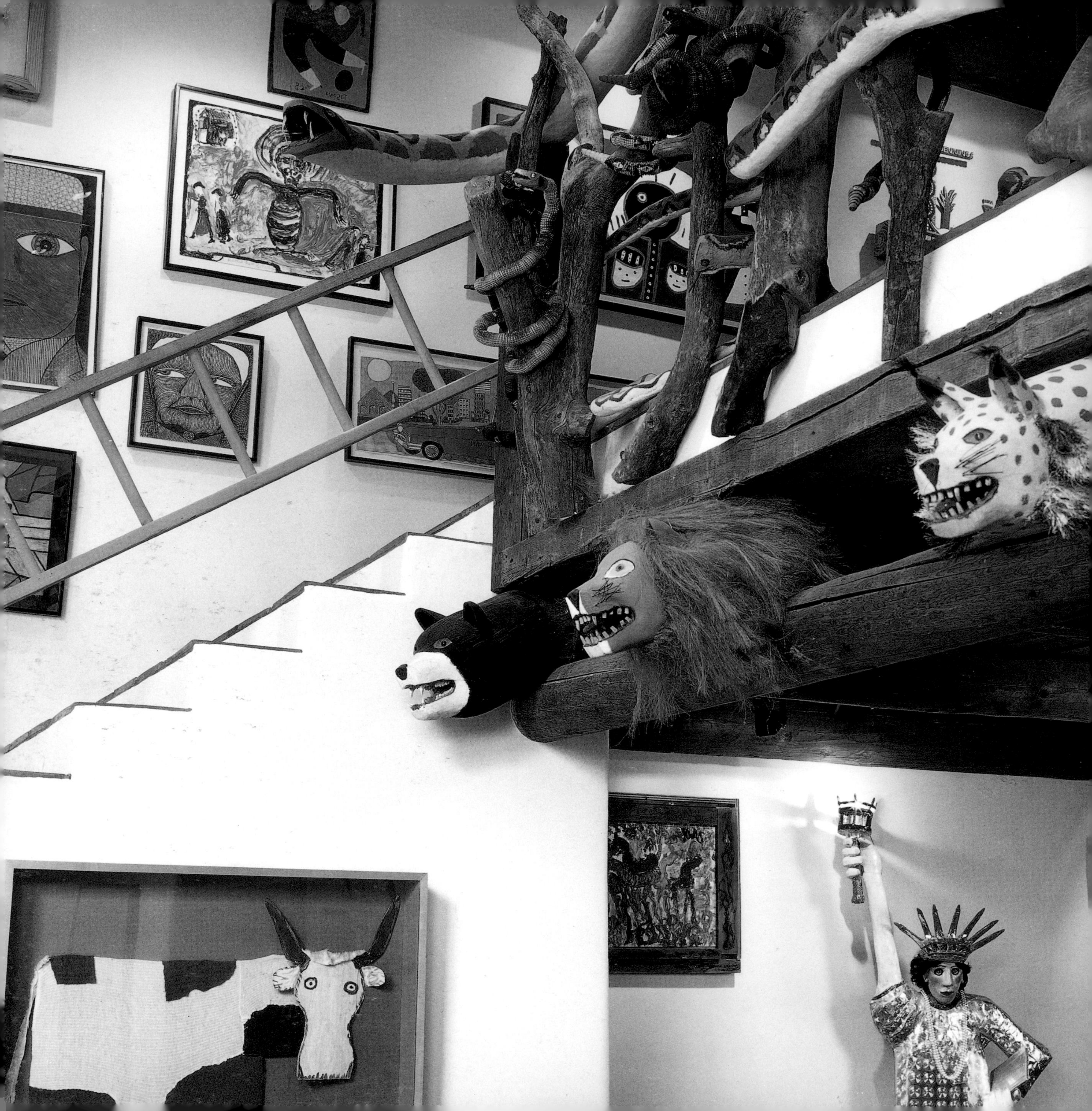

Parking their cars (that is, tying up their Chevys and Range Rovers) in the corral in front of the house, the Rosenaks' guests, many of whom are museum groups and fellow collectors, wouldn't be surprised if Belle Starr and Wyatt Earp emerged to greet them. Will they swagger out of the general store or the saloon? Instead, Chuck and Jan are there, full of enthusiasm and a wide-open willingness to share their findings with dazzled visitors. Works by America's most sought-after contemporary folk artists are on view anywhere and everywhere throughout the house—on floors, tabletops, bookshelves, and stair landings as well as on walls. Rather than arranging a staid museum-like exhibition, the Rosenaks have created a free-form display that perfectly reflects the nature of the art. Rattling off the artists' names—Howard Finster, Helen Cordero, Arthur Vigil, Mamie Deschille—the Rosenaks admit to an insatiable drive to keep adding to their amazing treasure trove, some of which is always on loan to museum exhibits—or stashed away behind doors.

"It finally got to the point where we had so much," Jan confesses, opening a closet spilling over with undisplayed art, "that we built a gallery." Also designed by Hugh Newell Jacobsen, it is an underground structure with a balcony that provides a sweeping view of the artworks eighteen feet below.

"When we began to collect in the seventies, most academics and museum directors insisted that American folk art had been produced for the most part in New England and that the artists were all dead," Chuck laughs. "We proved them wrong. There are plenty of folk artists at work today—and they are everywhere in the nation." After a visit to Chuck and Jan Rosenak, it is hard to believe, however, that those artists have anything left to sell.

Opposite. In the gallery are carved wooden animals by Hispanic Leroy Archuleta, a cow by Navajo Mamie Deschillie, and a Statue of Liberty by Puerto Rican Gregario Marzan.
Above. An armadillo by Leroy Archuleta, a snake by Miles Carpenter, and a rare late-19th-century Germantown Navajo rug with Masonic symbols.

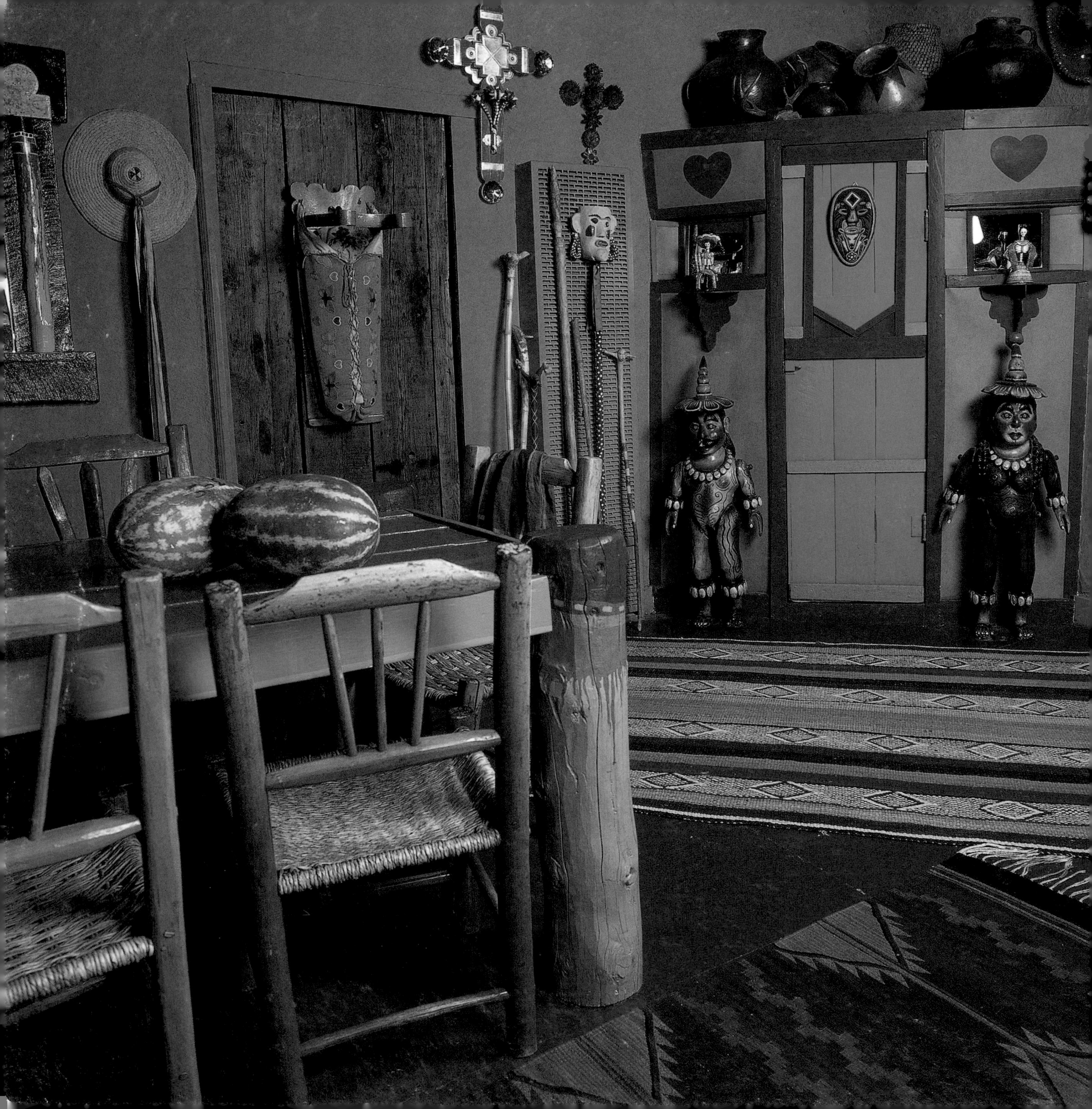

The Little House that Could

For Nona Wesley, an interior designer, furniture painter, muralist and artist, there was never any doubt that her little house in Taos *could* be made wonderful. Like the ugly duckling, it was a question of achieving a breathtaking transformation over time. A fearless visionary when it comes to a paint bucket, Nona, a raven-haired, olive-skinned beauty, has turned a nondescript, pint-sized, one-hundred-year-old adobe into a showcase of hot, dazzling colors. It is this courage and vision that draws clients, both private and corporate, to her from around the country.

"I've been in love with color since I was a teenager," Nona says. "My parents let me choose the colors for my bedroom. I selected Kelly green walls and turquoise bedspreads. I immediately realized that certain colors could have a nurturing, comforting effect on me—and others. I've been pursuing that line of spiritual design ever since."

Nona's living room/kitchen and bedroom—the only major rooms in the house—are a veritable museum of colorful ethnic folk art. Things Mexican, Guatemalan, Venezuelan, Peruvian, and Brazilian are everywhere and go together. With the exception of her northern New Mexican pieces, Nona's collection is strikingly "south of the border": beaded Huichol dolls and musical instruments, Tarahumara pots, Chiapas masks, and Peruvian rugs mingle with Zuni rattles, Hopi headdresses, and Apache baskets.

Opposite. Beneath a display of Mexican pots, two articulated ceremonial effigies from Guerrero, Mexico, stand guard in the kitchen. The chairs are from Esquinapa, Mexico.
Above. Mexican Huichol prayer arrows and a fire drum decorated with spiritual symbols.

49

Above. A Hopi headdress, *tablita*, and Zuni rattles are part of Nona Wesley's collection of Southwestern Indian artifacts.
Right. Together with fellow artist Mel Weiner, Nona designs hand-painted "Bordertown" furniture.
Opposite. A coyote fence surrounds a High Country rock garden. The Tarahamara pots were brought back from Mexico.

"If I didn't live in Taos, I'd live in Mexico. I have been there countless times on buying trips, for clients and for the stores I've owned," Nona says. "I'm astonished at the wonderful things there are to buy there. I also never cease to be amazed by the peoples' imagination and uninhibited willingness to combine colors—colors that most people wouldn't have the flair to put together. I stand there with my mouth open when I look at a row of houses in a Mexican village. They are all painted different colors. You'd think that homeowners got together, talked about what colors they were going to use, experimented, and finally made a decision. Wrong. Mexicans have a God-given, innate ability to get it right the first time when it comes to color. They throw caution to the wind."

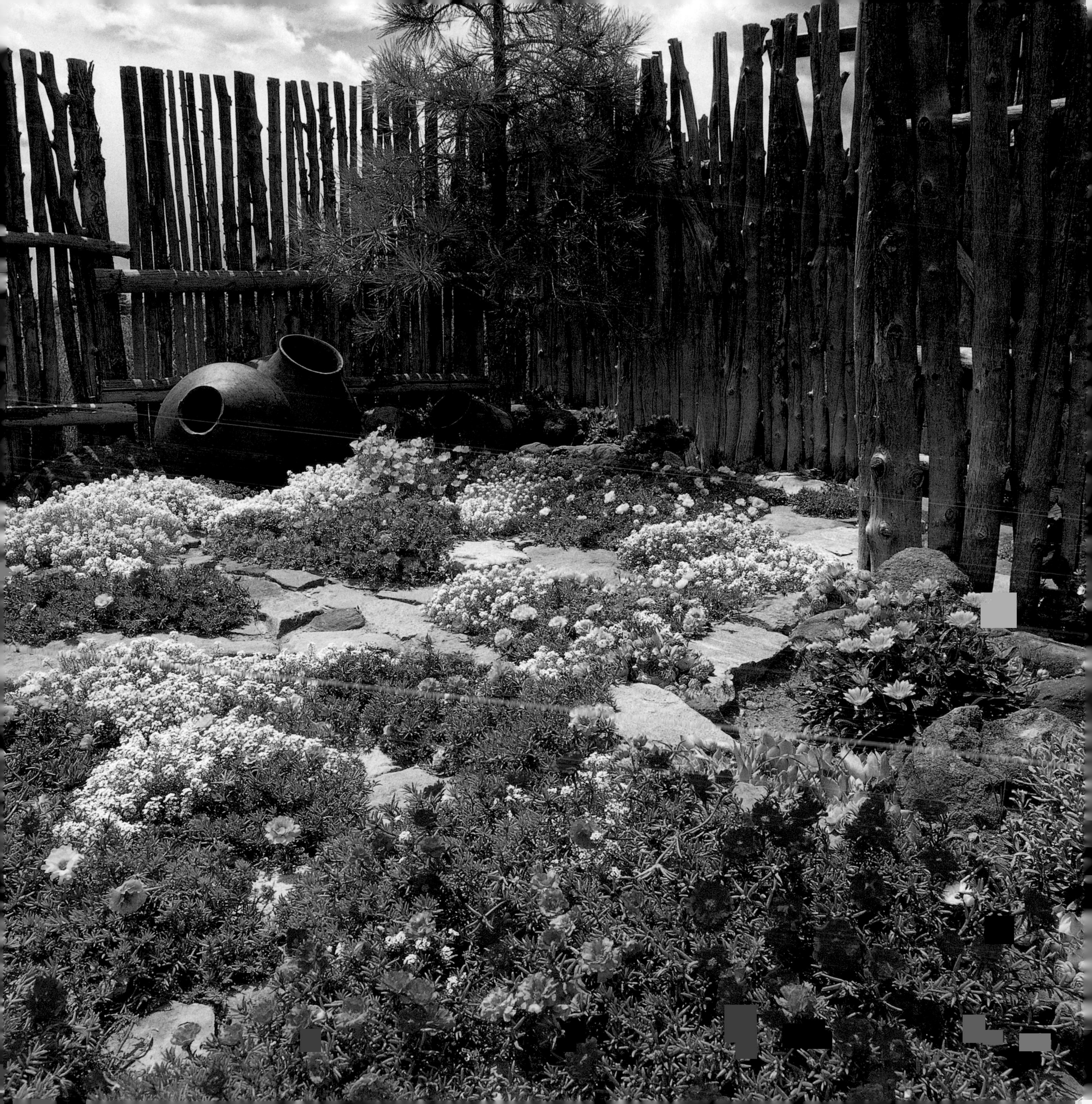

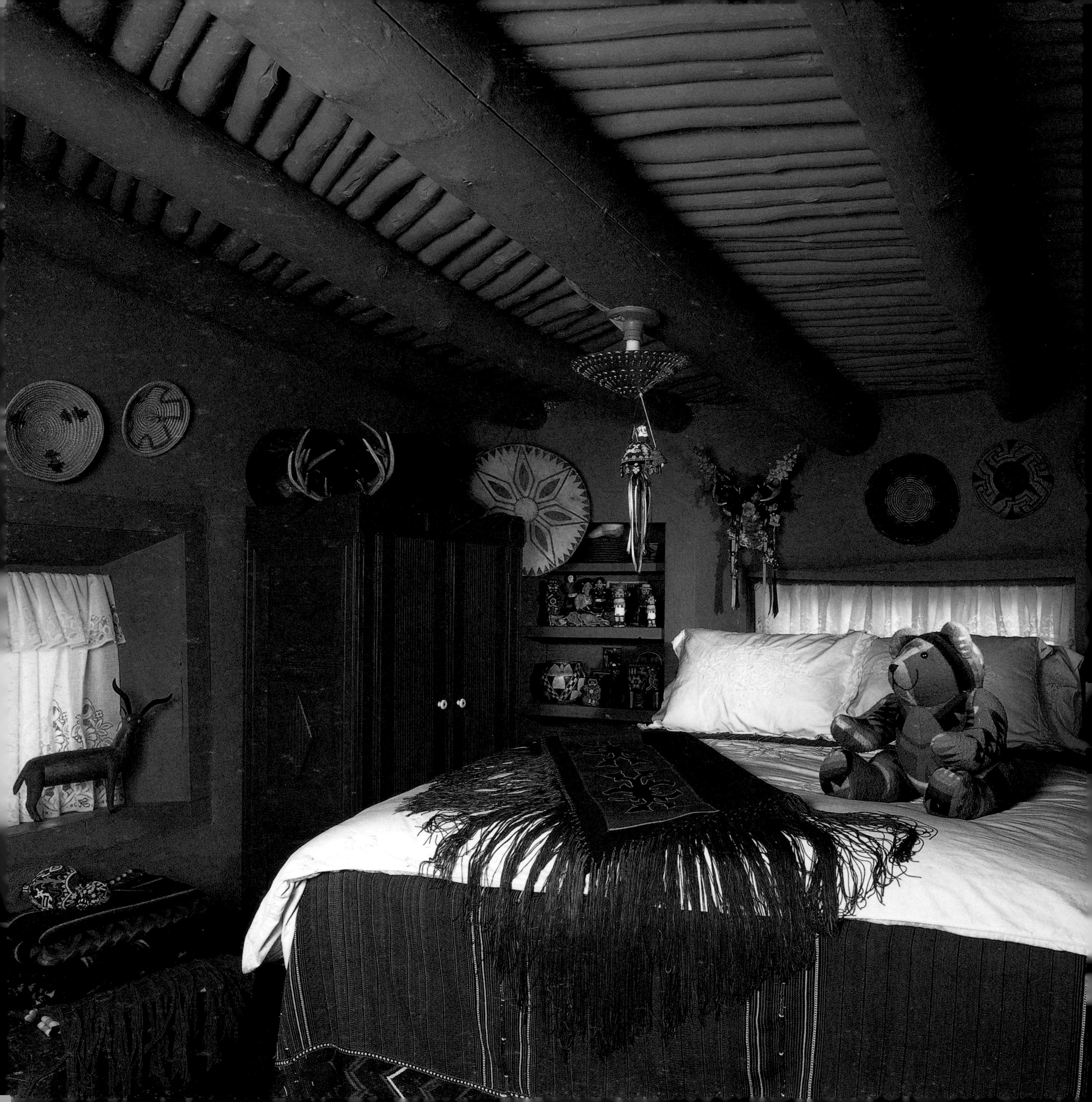

Uninhibited in her own pursuit of "energy, security, stimulation, safety, and happiness"—words she uses in conjunction with colors—Nona admits she is "smitten" by the powerful impact of color combinations. She painted her bedroom walls shrimp pink, the ceiling *latillas* clematus, or lavender, and the floor verbena, or wild orchid. A handwoven, multistriped Guatemalan bedspread, ruffled, white curtains on the windows, and numerous artifacts—on the walls, on shelves, and in corners—add to the room's intense drama. A look inside her closet reveals further color compulsion. All the plastic hangers are different colors. "I bring them back from Mexico, along with water buckets, laundry hampers, and jugs—all in flamboyant colors," Nona says.

Anxious to experiment with new color combinations—coral, deep burgundy, and turquoise; magenta, Mexican pink, and mango; ruby red, tangerine, and rain-forest green—Nona is purposely gentle when determining a client's own palette preferences. Most people, she has learned, are anxious to stay within the limits of color acceptability and are insecure about being different. "I work with people to determine their color needs. We get a color point of reference, then cross-reference it. It isn't a long, tedious process," she explains. "What we try to do is unleash emotion. It's wonderful how people open up when surrounded by the right colors for them."

Step inside Nona's own "casa colores" and it is abundantly clear that the owner has opened the door wide to allow her own genius full freedom. So much so that one wonders what wonderful colors she'd come up with if she were commissioned by God to create an entirely new rainbow.

■

Opposite. Old Apache and Pima woven baskets hang on a bedroom wall, a Oaxacan painted deer rests on a windowsill. A Navajo dance shawl lies on top of a Guatemalan bedspread.
Below. "I was inspired by Acoma pottery designs," says Nona Wesley of her wall treatment. She also painted the traditional Mexican equipale chair.

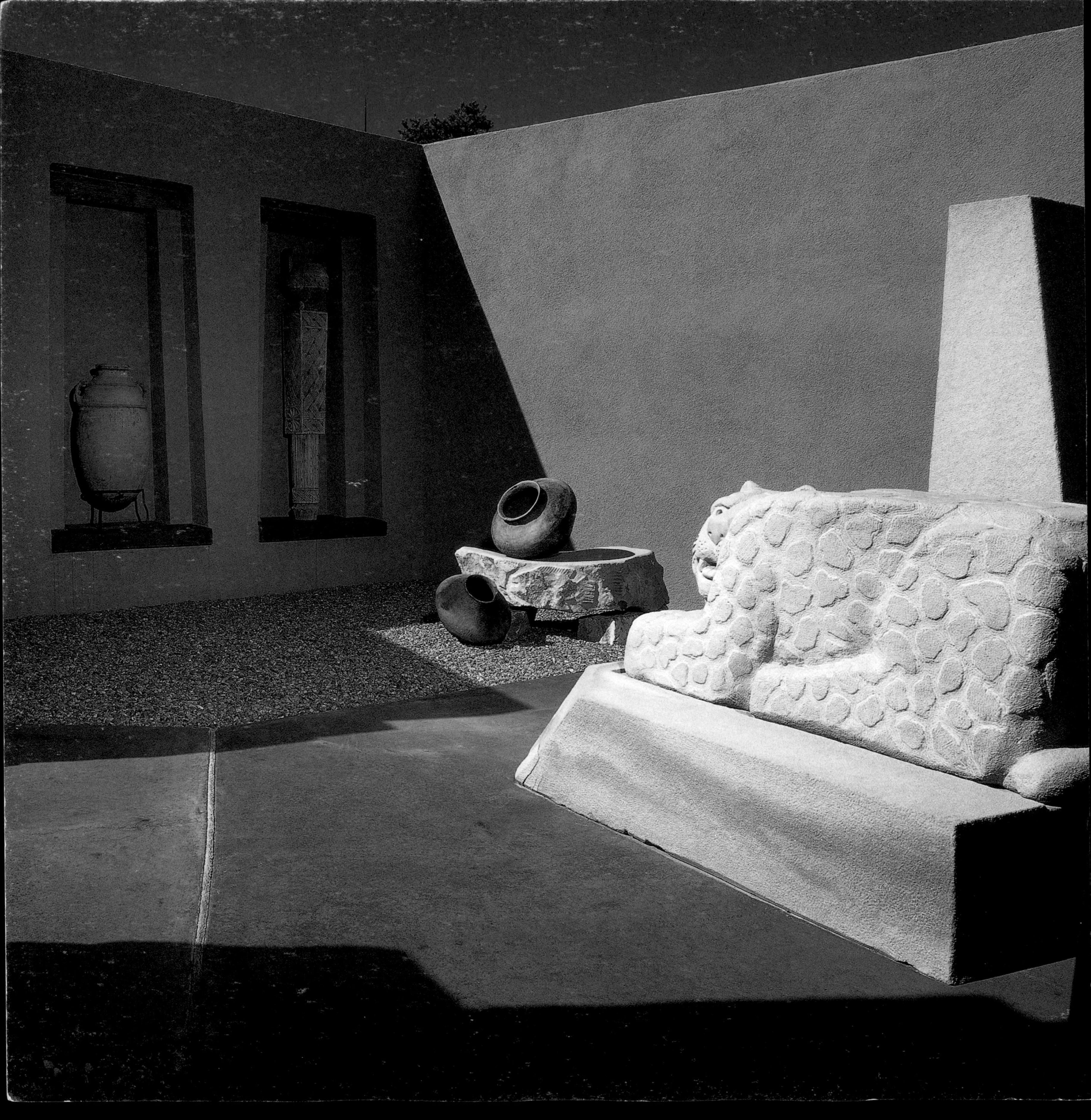

Santa Fe Mayan

At a thousand feet above the seven-thousand-foot altitude of Santa Fe, with 360-degree views of four mountain ranges, Soaring Eagle is not only the highest house in the city, it is unquestionably one of the most unusual. Surrounded by sixty-five piñon-covered acres, the Egyptian-Mayan-Incan temple-like residence, owned by Arlena and Marty Markinson and designed by Adrian Dewindt, appears suitable for the gathering of priests and priestesses. Instead, it is the dream come true of a transplanted New York couple who, like Moses, were led to the mountain top. "I was meant to live here. I was channeled for the land and for the house," Arlena, a retired psychotherapist turned ordained minister, tells awestruck visitors. Her husband, Marty, a bicoastal entertainment executive, concedes he had no part in the revelation. But Arlena did. "I didn't build the house. I envisioned it," she confides. "I wanted the house to be an expression of my being, to reflect all the cultural experiences I've had in past lives."

Stepping through a twenty-foot-high entrance portal, guests ascend a seemingly endless outside flight of stressed stairs, which dip in the middle and are made of ox blood–colored poured cement. Catching their breath, they pass through a series of pre-Columbian theme courtyards illustrating water, sky, and fire. At last, just past a stone jaguar by sculptor

Opposite. The Mayan-Incan temple style house of Arlena and Marty Markinson was designed by Adrian Dewindt. The inner court contains a stone jaguar by Doug Hyde and Tarahamara Indian pots. *Above.* Stepping through a 20-foot-high entrance gate, guests ascend an endless flight of stairs to the main house.

55

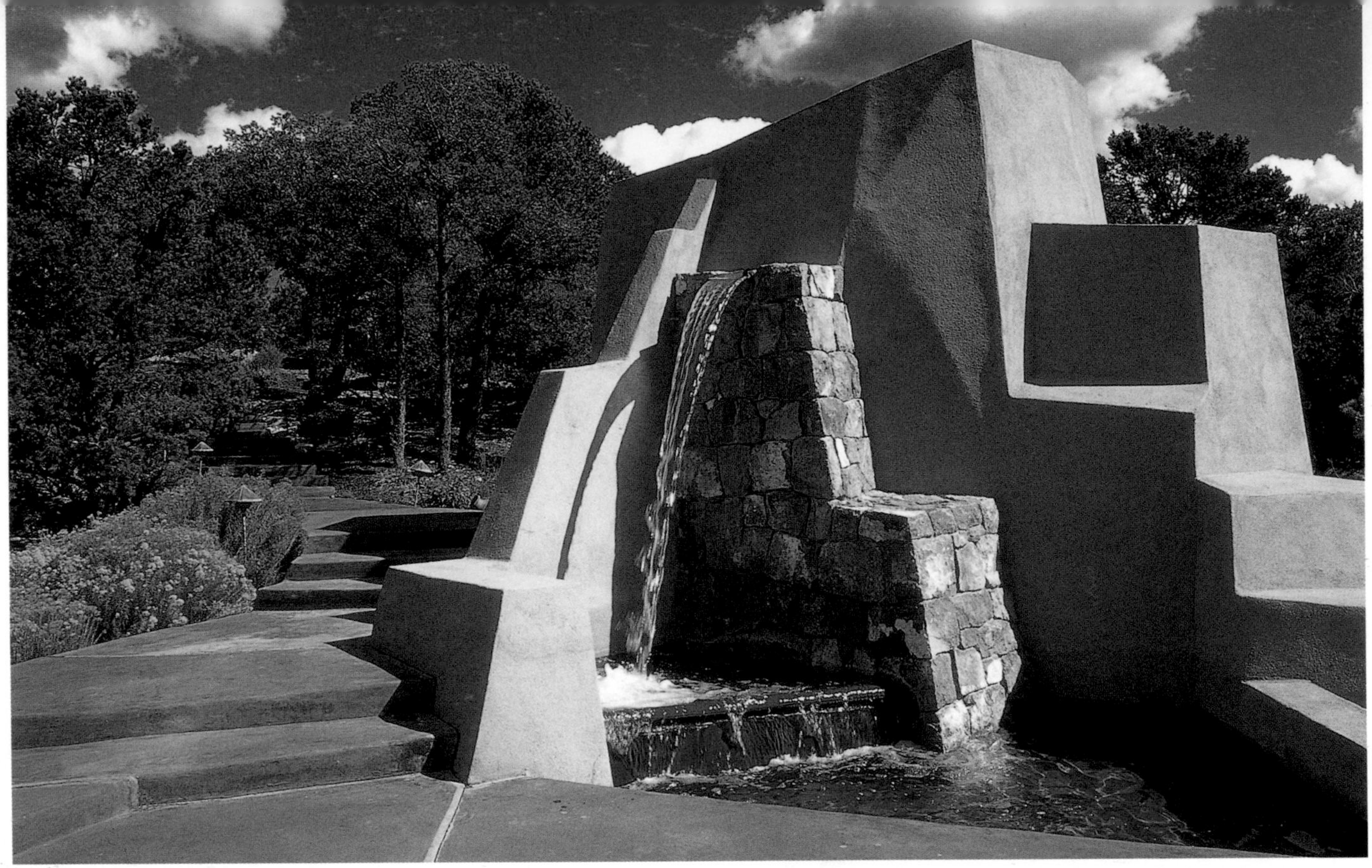

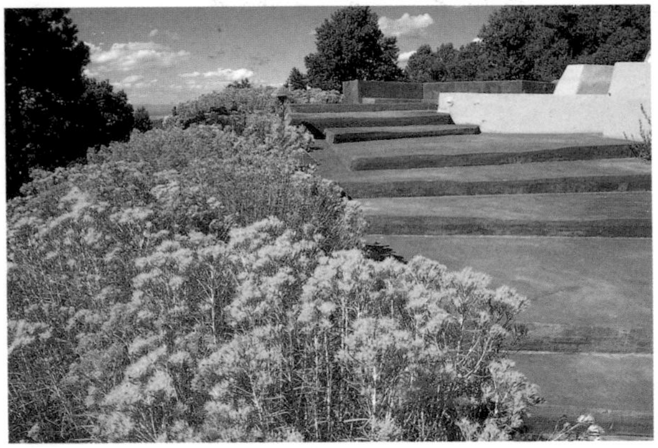

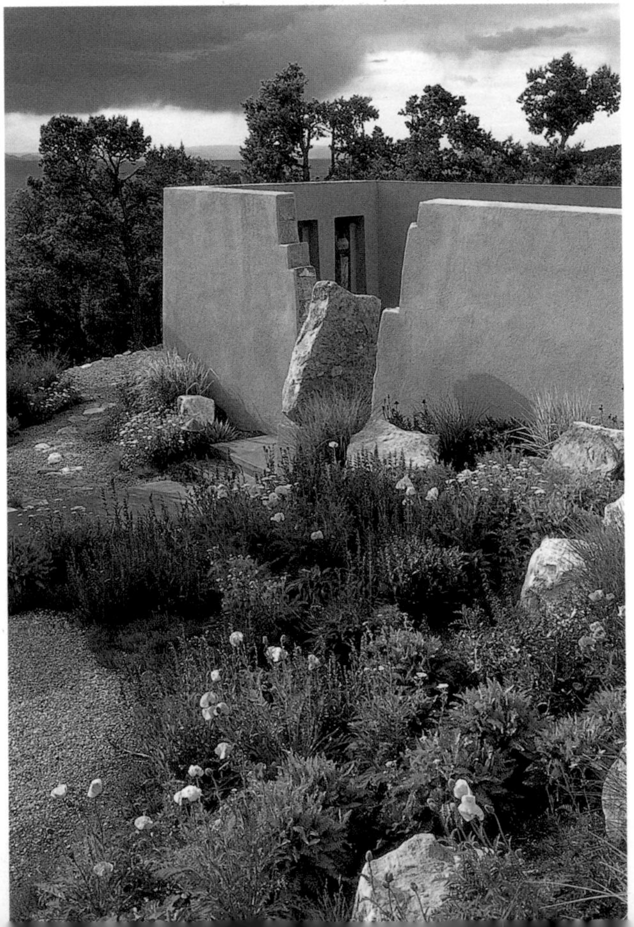

Above. Halfway up the entrance stairs, visitors catch their breaths beside a fountain of stone and adobe. The water is recycled. The hand-trawled concrete steps were stressed to appear worn and hand colored section by section.
Right. Artificial Indian ruins in the landscape add to the drama of Soaring Eagle.

Doug Hyde, appears the house's front door. Correction.
The seven-thousand-square-foot "temple's" Inca-esque grand
entrance looms ahead: a 1,250-pound, twelve-foot-high steel-
and-copper trapezoid through which any top-ranking resident of
ancient Cuzco would have been proud to pass. (Designed by
artist Larry Hall, the massive structure took ten men to install.)

Past the threshold, Soaring Eagle takes off. Guarding the
entrance foyer are two life-sized figures, a horse kachina and
a buffalo kachina, both by artist Jeff Hengesbaugh. Decorated
with buffalo skin, horse hair, and Indian artifacts—drums,
blankets, shaman beads, and fetishes—the primeval figures
cause the weak of heart to grow weaker.

Left and above. Interior designer Deena
Perry commissioned artist Larry Hall to
make the massive steel-and-copper front
doors, and Jeff Hengesbaugh to recreate
early-19th-century, life-size Hopi kachinas
for the entrance hall. A pueblo rug hangs
on the wall behind a table made from a
19th-century Pakistani wood carving.
The antique Indian headdresses, *tablitas*,
were worn for festivals and ceremonies.

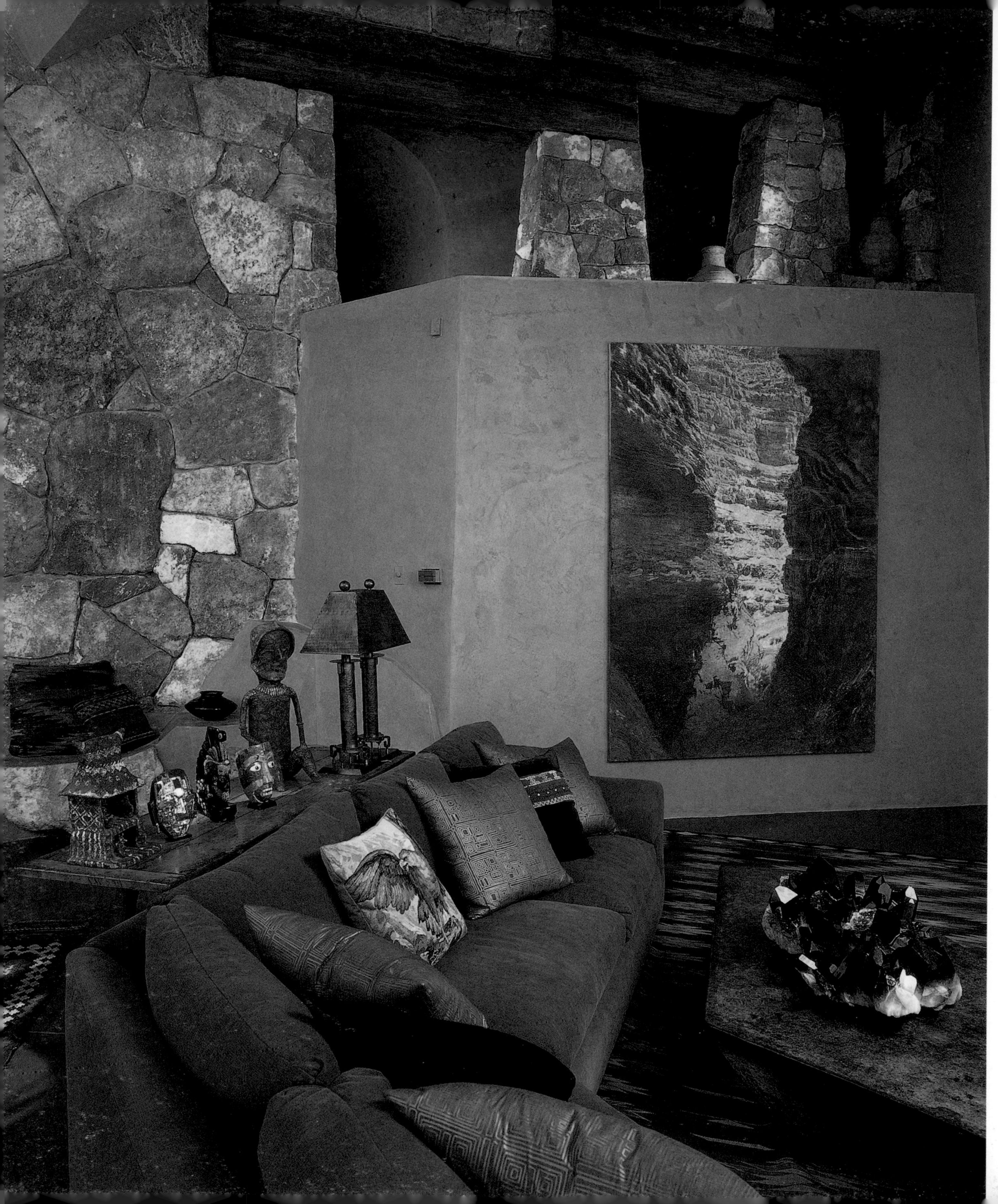

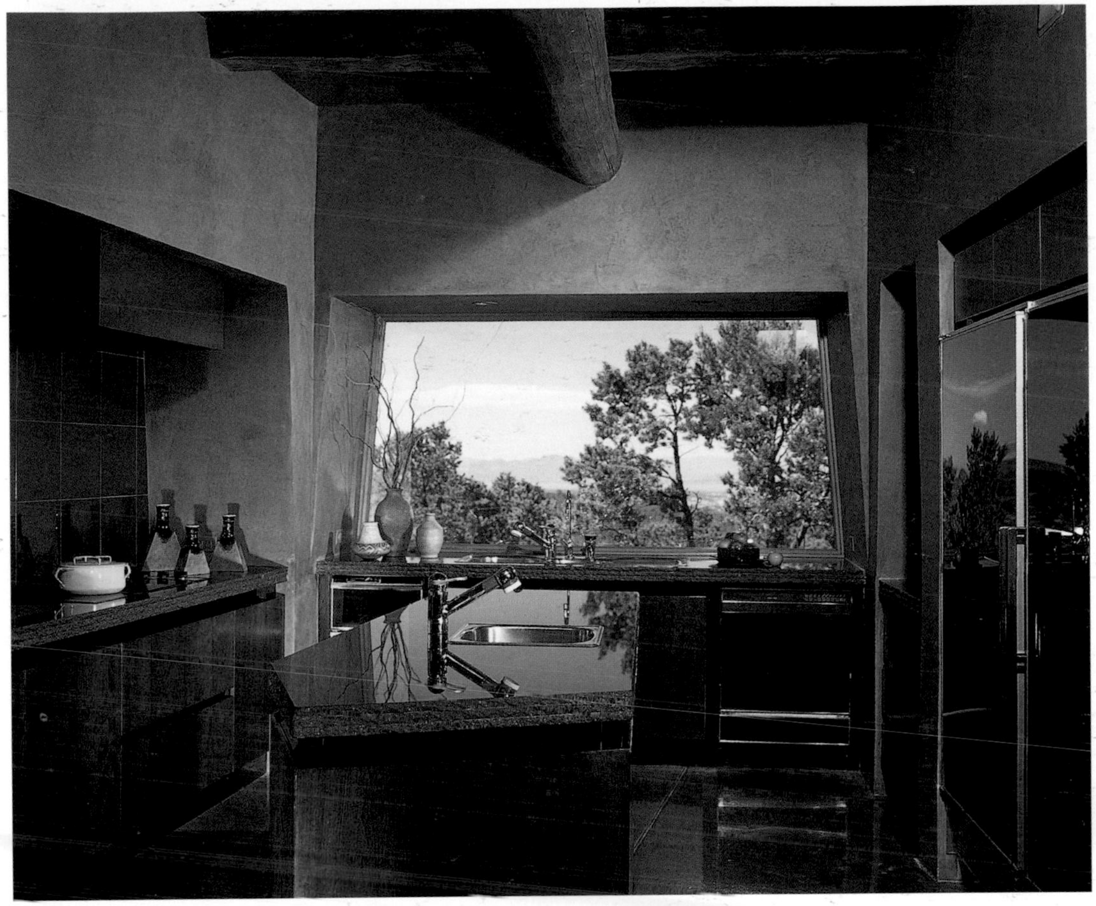

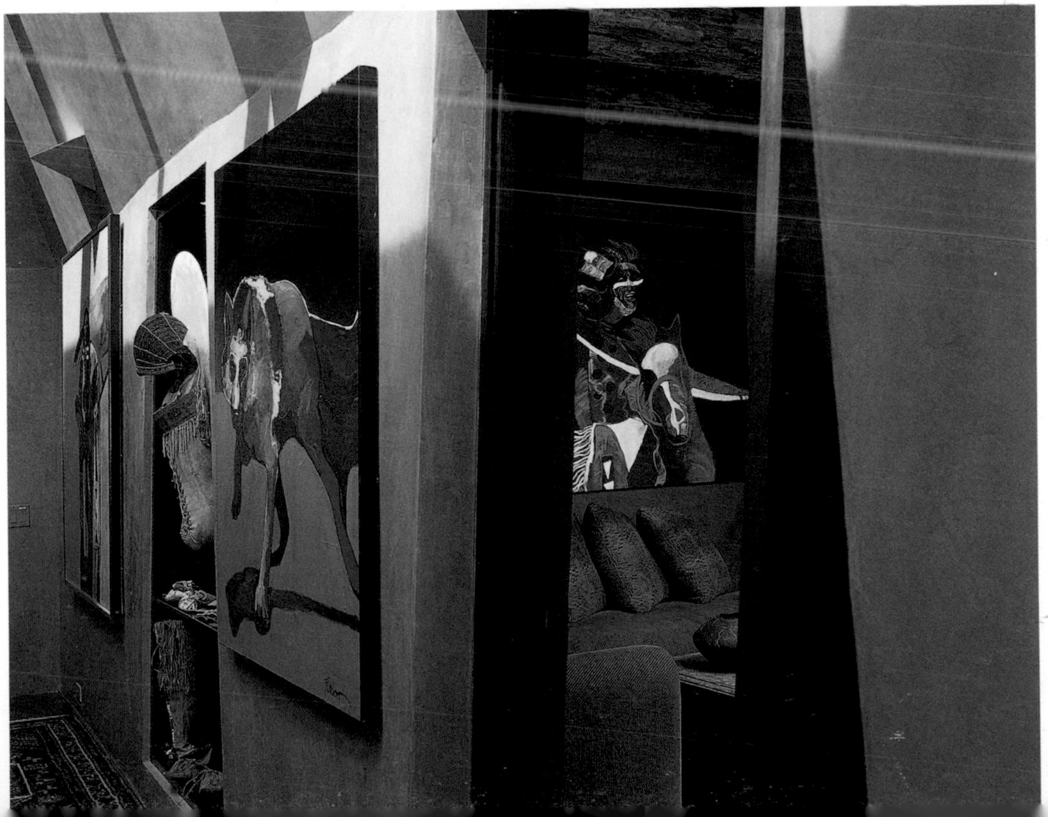

Opposite. With a 22-foot-high ceiling, the living room in Soaring Eagle has stone walls—all from the property—resembling ancient Cuzco. Peruvian artifacts are in back of a chenille sofa by Menage. On the metal coffee table, designed by Deena Perry, is a black crystal. The lamp is by Platt. The painting is by Merrill Mahaffey.
Above. Black, the neutral color throughout the house, is also the color of the granite counters in the kitchen.
Left. Paintings by John Nieto line a passageway.

Above and opposite. "There are no horizontal or vertical lines in Soaring Eagle. They're all angled," says designer Adrian Dewindt. Interior designer Deena Perry explains that pigments were put into plaster to produce wall colors, then sealed with Okkon. Terracotta, cobalt blue, black, and Venetian red were trawled into the concrete floors, then sealed with a high gloss finish.

"Arlena didn't care if anyone felt intimidated by the house and its decoration," recalls Deena Perry, the house's interior designer. To meet her client's requirements, she immersed herself in the back-to-earth colors, symbolized textiles, and bare-bones furnishings of ancient civilizations. "Arlena had vision, inspiration, and intuition. And she expected the very same from everyone who worked on the house. She frequently spoke of the need to reflect the power of the land. No other client I've had has required this connection."

Adrian Dewindt also recognized that Soaring Eagle would be a challenging commission. "Arlena spoke in metaphysical concepts, of being in harmony with the land, but never in terms of rooms. I've designed five churches, and the client never once said anything about soul, spirit, God. Arlena did all the time. Yes, the house is theatrical. But, it has great substance. There's recognizable honesty in the materials used, and in the phenomenal craftsmanship."

With twenty-two-foot-high, all-glass front windows, crystal-shaped ceilings, numerous passageways ("not hallways!" says Arlena), Soaring Eagle, like an abstract sculpture, is a profusion of angles with no horizontal or vertical lines whatsoever. Towering, raw earth-colored plaster walls combined with great expanses of intricately laid rocks, full of marine fossils, give massive form and clear definition to the house's interior space which, according to Arlena, is full of energy.

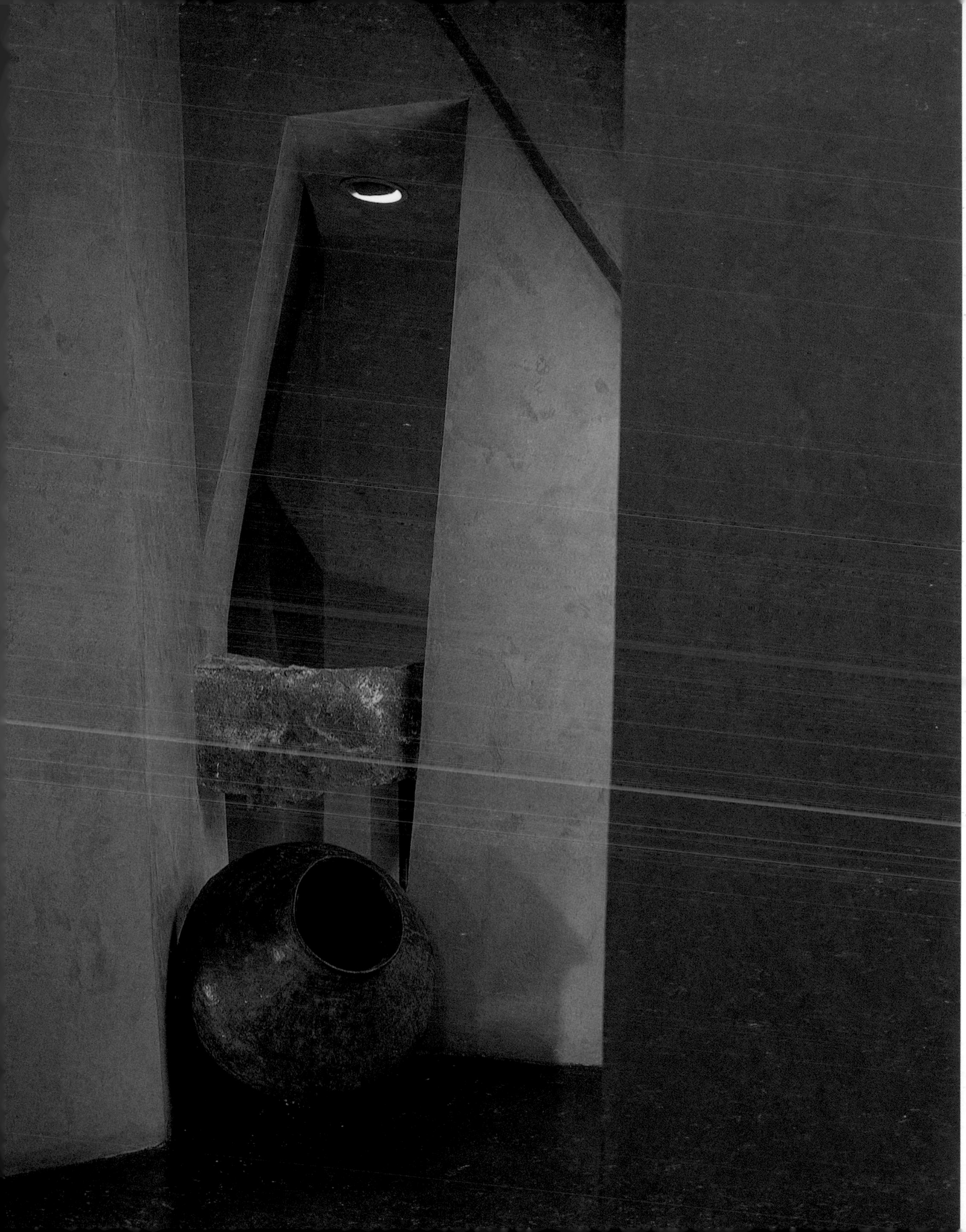

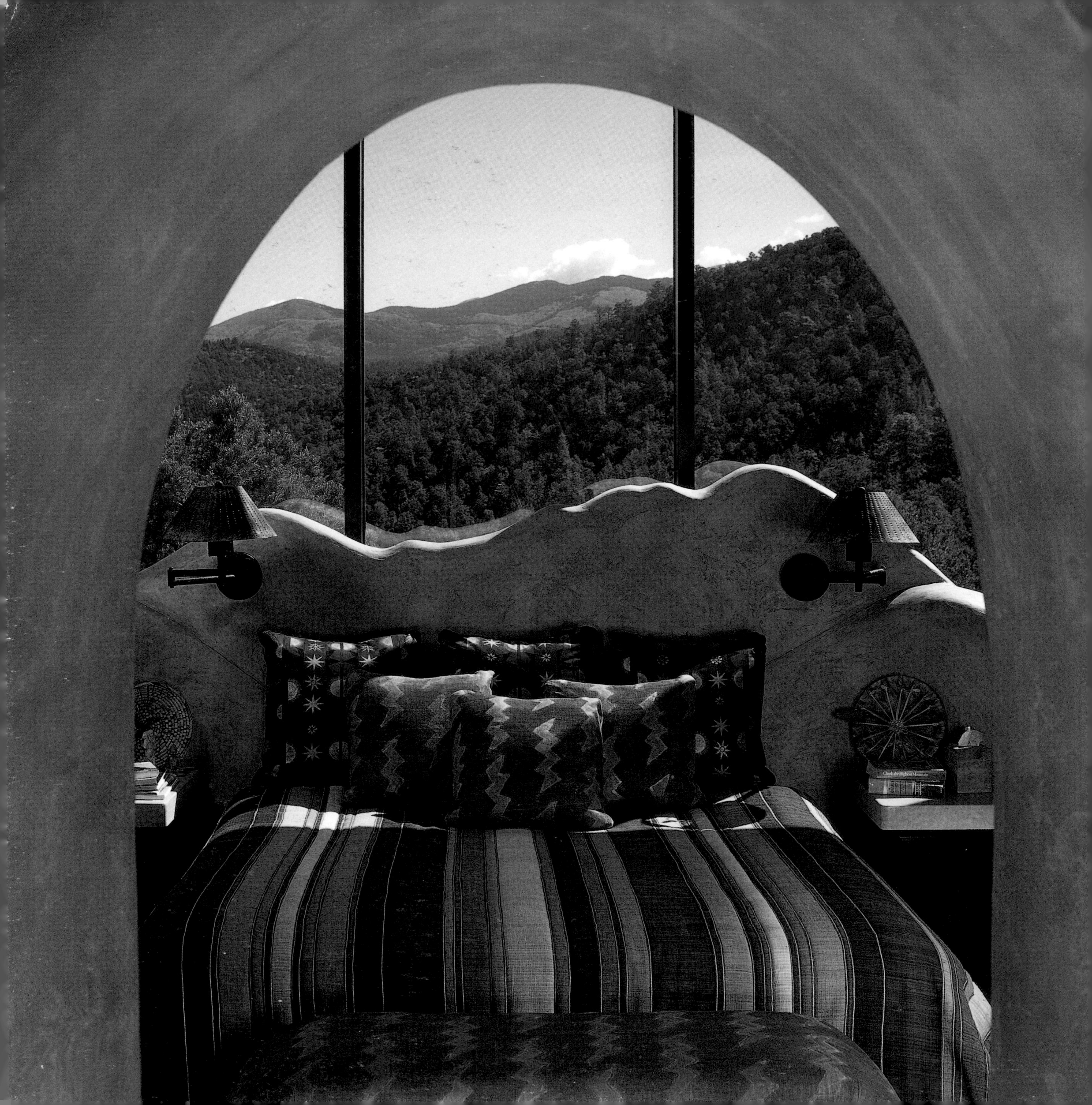

"I hired a geomancer who staked the energy lines on the land so that Adrian could design in accordance with their intersections," she points out. "It was important that there be no short circuits. We wanted to be sure that important areas of the house have low levels of energy. And that high levels have means by which to escape…which they do in the living room—up the chimney." The placement of the couple's bedroom was of special importance as well. "It has been designed to hold energy," Arlena points out. "The bed is placed so that when Marty and I go to sleep our crown chakras receive energy from Mount Baldy."

On reflection, one wonders if Mount Baldy doesn't get its energy from Arlena.

Opposite. Facing the Santa Fe ski basin and the National Forest, the Markinsons' bedroom has hand-painted fabrics by Barbara Beckman.
Left. At 8,000 feet, the living room windows look across to the Sangre de Cristo mountains and down onto Santa Fe. The room contains a Steinway piano, a coffee table made from a gear from a sugarcane mill, and an Amazonian mask.
Above. The living room fireplace is hit by a bolt of copper lightning.

63

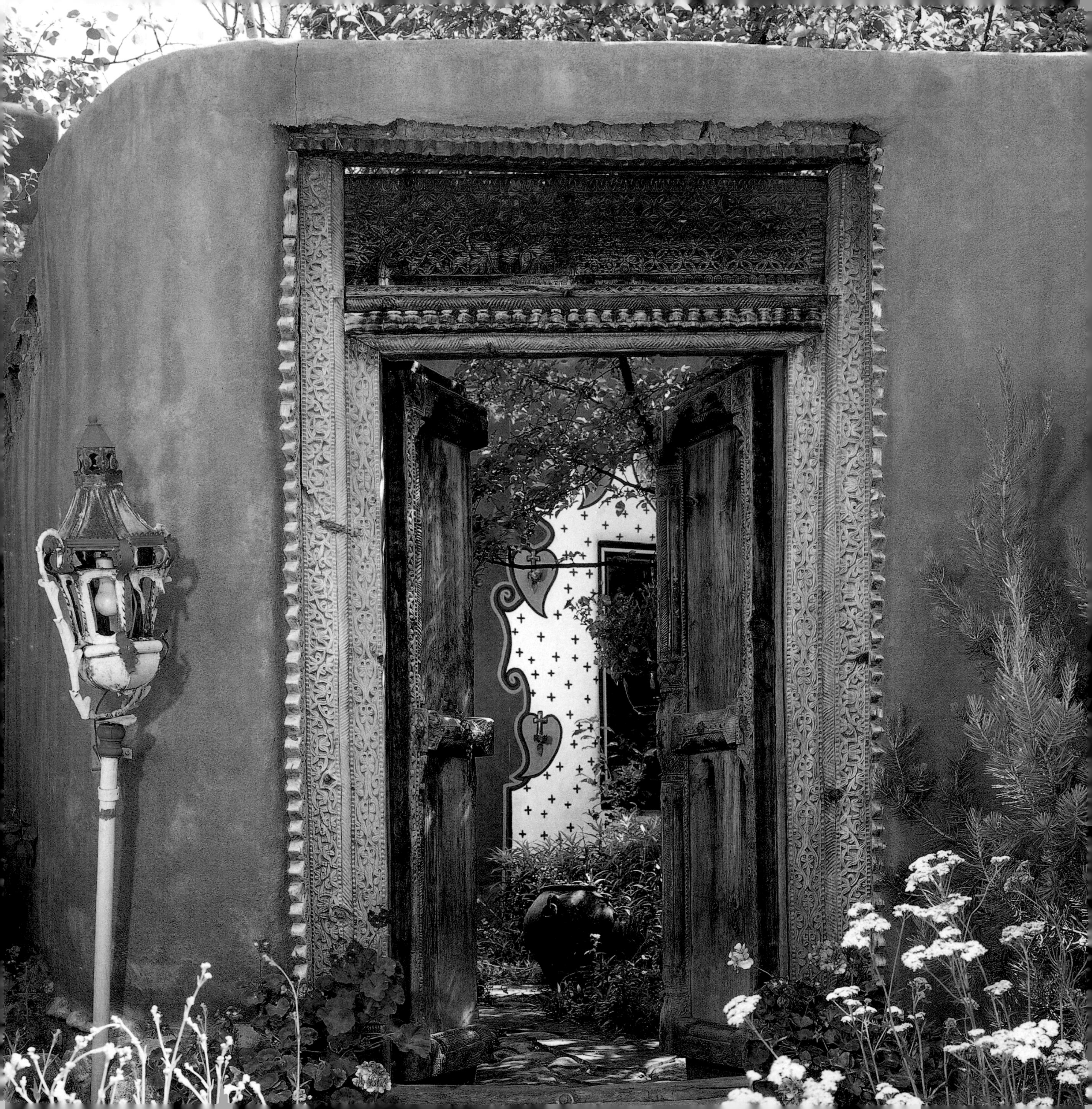

Once Upon a Time

Once upon a time, there was a Texan who lived in a large English-style mansion full of beautiful antiques and contemporary paintings. Once upon a time, there was a run-down, tiny jewel of a Santa Fe house in the Historic District that needed a loving owner. Once upon a time, the Texan bought the little house, restored it, and filled it full of whimsical, colorful furniture and accessories.

"It sounds like a fairy tale, but that's exactly what happened," explains Dallas-based interior designer Rosemari Agostini. For more than twenty-five years, she has helped her client Lupe Murchison wave a wand over numerous town houses, ranches, and homes-away-from-home, all in need of tender, loving care. She has also orchestrated numerous theme parties and special events in Texas for Lupe's hundreds of guests. "There's no challenge too difficult," she says of Lupe's willingness to tackle a tough fund-raising or design job. "Great sport, brilliantly creative, tremendous energy:" these are some of the qualities Rosemari uses to define the active Texan, who comes to Santa Fe frequently to enjoy a bit of rest and relaxation.

Located in what was until recently a centuries-old Hispanic neighborhood on Acequia Madre, the Murchison house is hidden from public view down a dirt road. After pushing open an old gate in a high adobe wall, visitors enter an oasis of flowers, trees and shrubs. Color abounds, and even more so inside the

Opposite. An old Moroccan door in an adobe wall frames a Ford Ruthling paint and tin window decoration.
Above. Additional light and air enter the walled-in garden through shuttered windows.

65

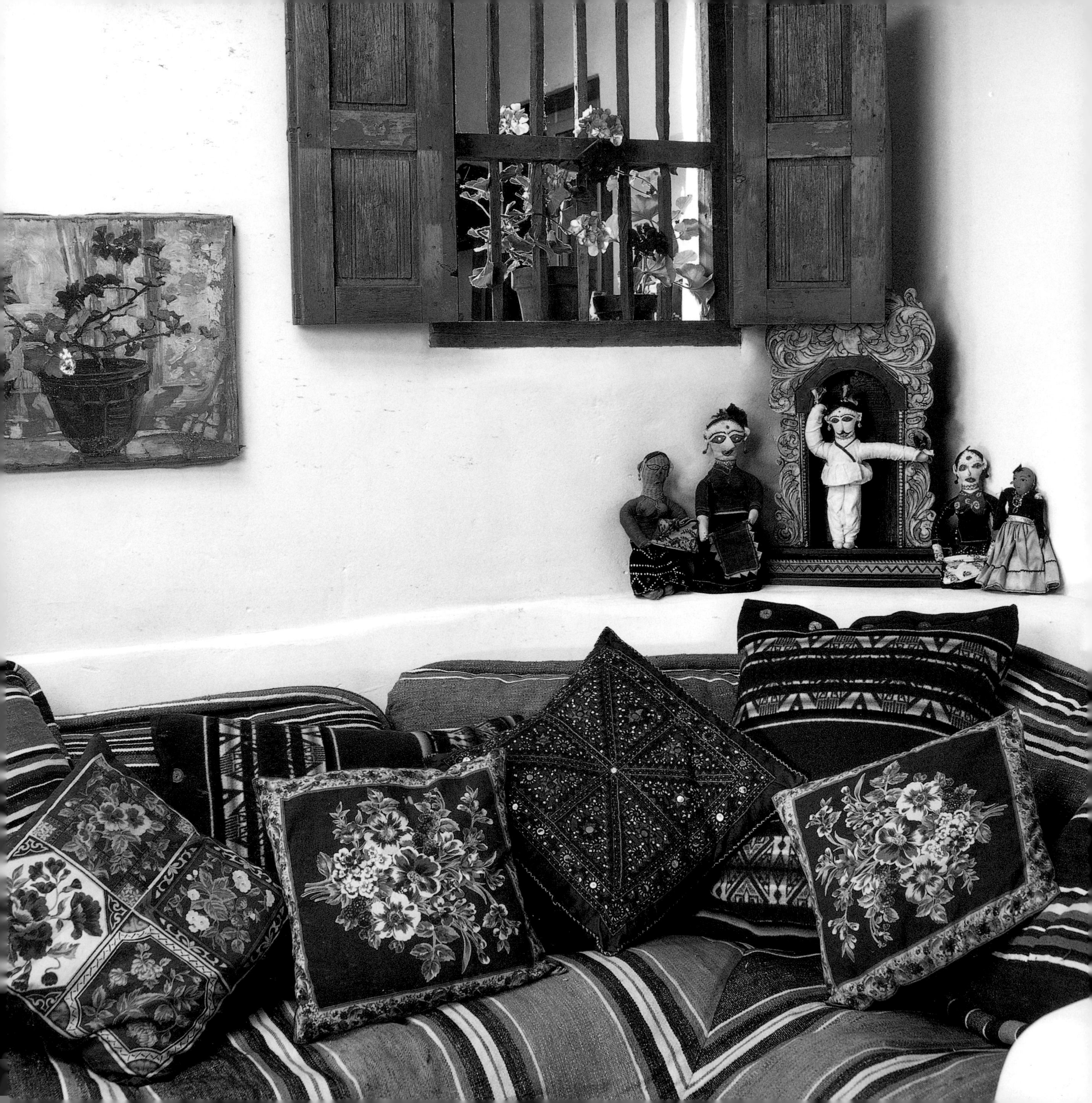

seven-room house. "We painted all the walls white to show off the large ethnic and folk art collection—New Mexican, Mexican, Native American, Guatemalan, even Pennsylvania Dutch," Rosemari says. On display almost everywhere in the house's very small rooms, the collection is so large one wonders how twenty-five dinner guests find room to sit down.

Bringing many items from Texas, Lupe and Rosemari also prowled the Santa Fe flea market and local antique shops. "We have a great artistic camaraderie. I'm always given a free hand to be creative," Rosemari says. A good example is the master bedroom: dozens of bouquets of dried roses hang from the vigas. The effect is sensual. The treatment of the walls, however, is sacred. With age-old Hispanic crucifixes, numerous paintings of Madonna and child—the room could easily be a chapel. "One can kneel down to pray, or go to bed," Rosemari says with a sly smile.

Opposite. Pillows covered with Indian fabrics, Native American and Indian dolls, and an anonymous painting give color to a living room corner.
Above. Woven Guatemalan fabric covers the dining room table. The crucifix is New Mexican, the chandelier "a junk heap find."
Left. Navajo dolls on a Beacon blanket.

67

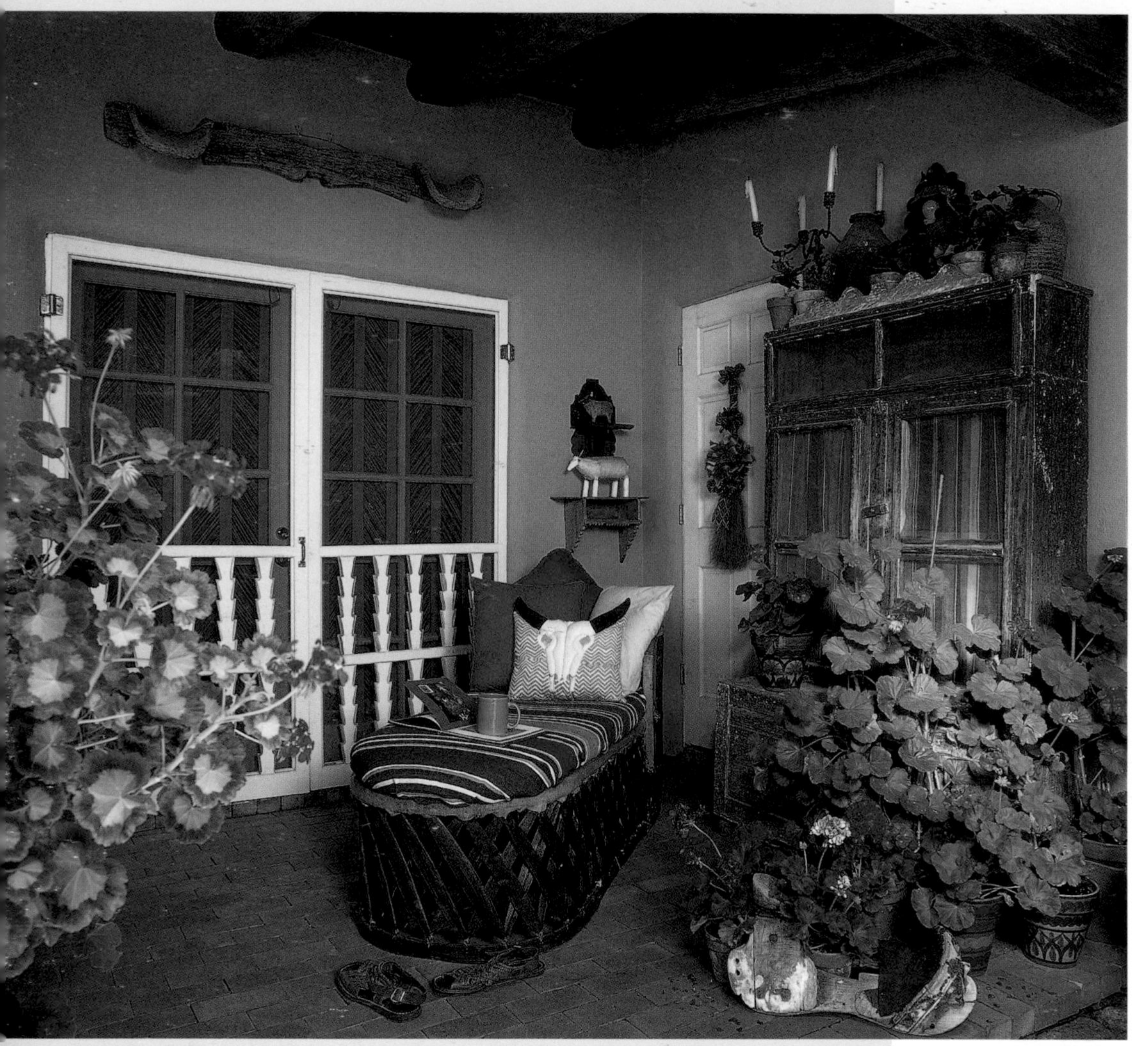

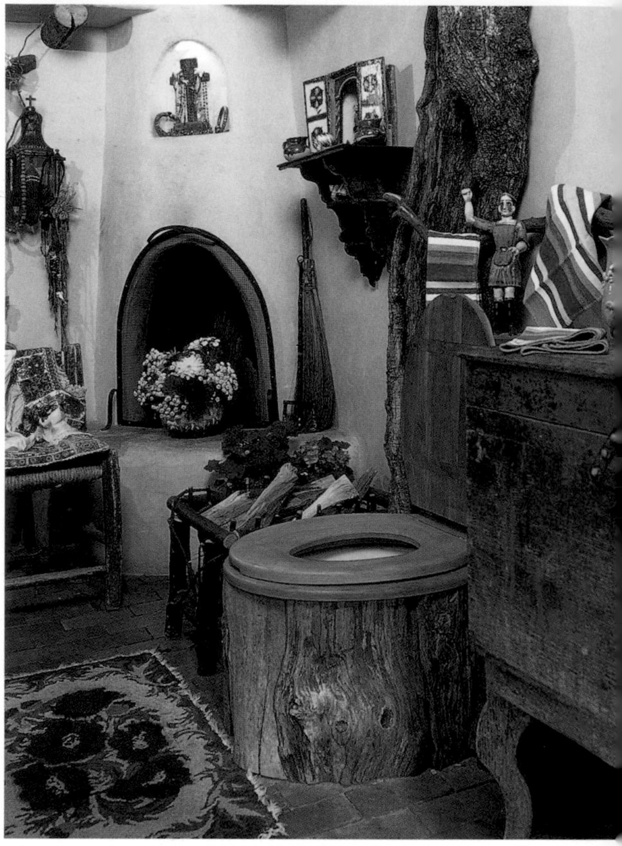

"No one who knows Lupe's house back in Texas believes she lives in such a tiny house in Santa Fe," Rosemari says. "Or that her Santa Fe house is full of so many fun, inexpensive things. Our goal was to make sure that everyone who comes here is made to feel good."

Once upon a time, a client and a decorator had a meeting of the minds, and successfully fulfilled their goal.

Left. Geraniums go into the greenhouse in winter, then help decorate the portal all summer. Custom-made New Mexican style screen doors and an antique New Mexican cupboard give regional authenticity.
Above. A custom-made commode crafted out of walnut, oak, and cypress sits beside a New Mexican chest turned into a bathroom sink. On winter days, a fireplace gives welcome warmth.
Opposite. French doors open upon a bedroom containing a Mexican folk art figure. The contemporary painting is by George Bireline.

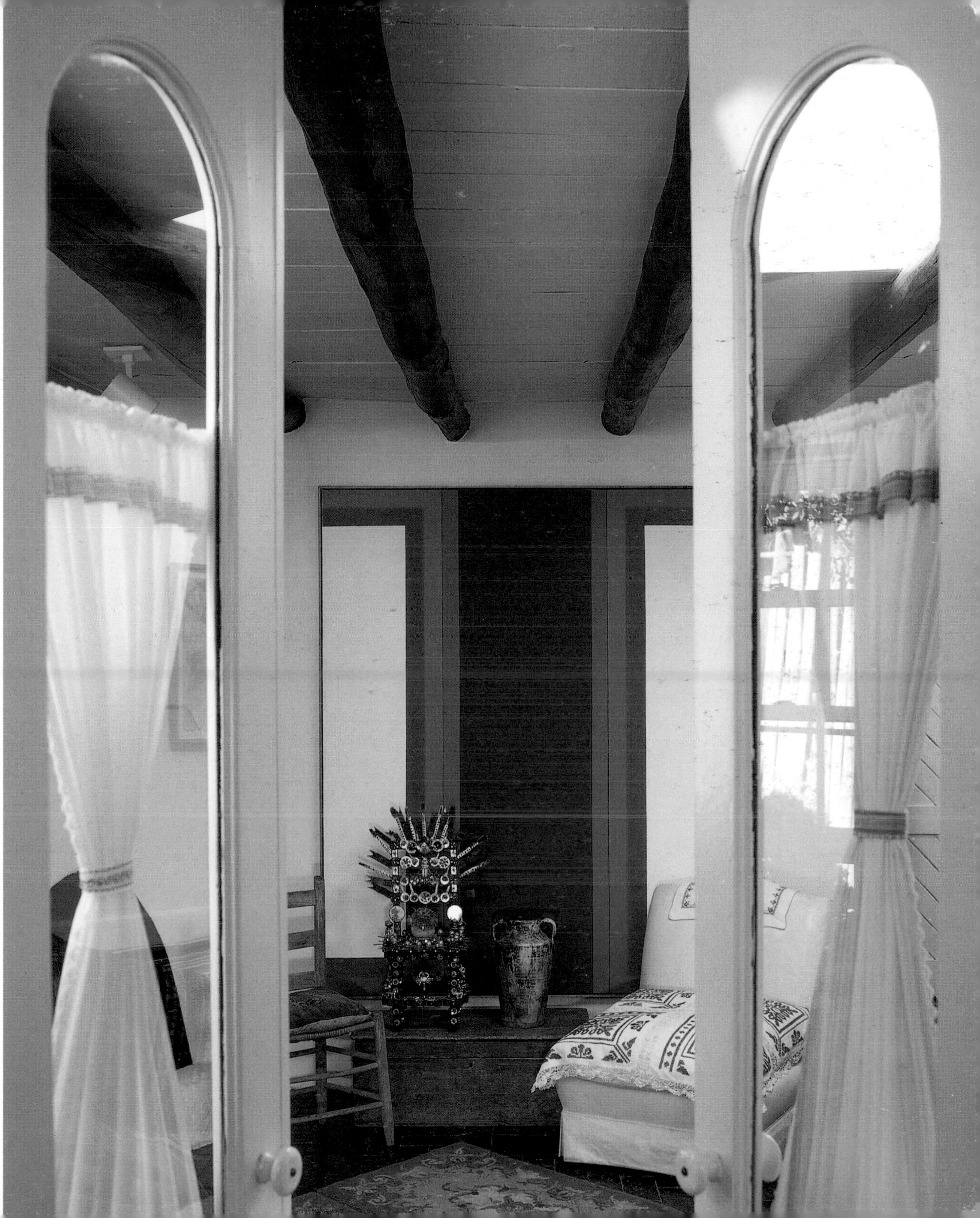

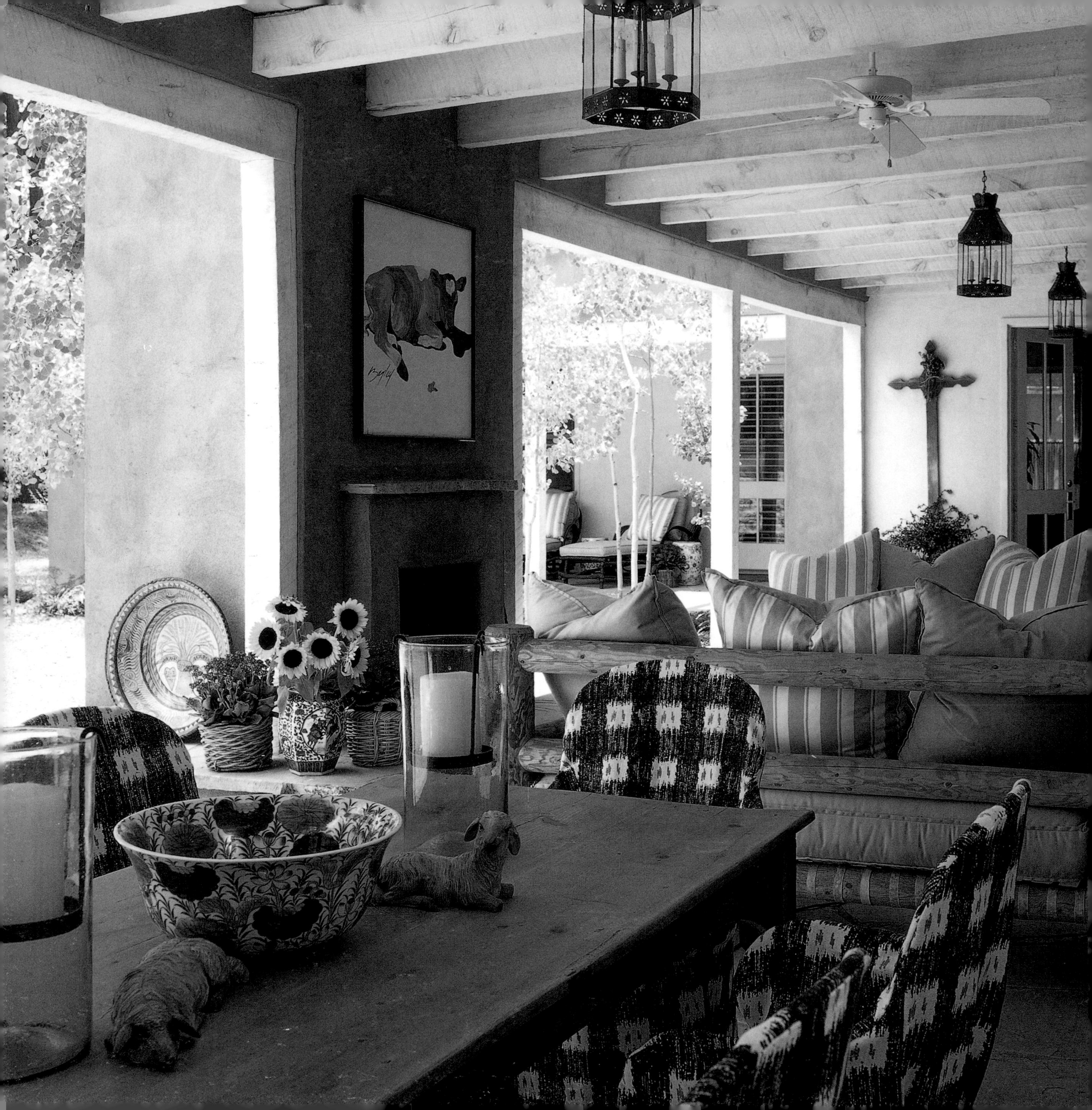

Bigger Is Better

Los Angeles interior designer Hank Milam
has the inscription on his tombstone
thought out. "'Bigger Is Better' is my choice,"
says the part-time Santa Fe resident. "Volume, dimension, weight, and proportion—these have been key elements in
my furniture and accessory selection since I started my design
firm in Laguna, California, in 1962. I prefer to have one or two
really dramatic, sizeable 'statement' pieces in a room rather than
a lot of unmemorable things. I realize that scale is a luxury. But
if impact is important, it's worth the additional cost," Hank
explains.

The designer's own Southwest showcase in Tesuque, ten
minutes from Santa Fe's plaza, dramatically reveals the aesthetic
truth of his philosophy. Designing the 4,500-square-foot house
with his wife and partner, Miram, the designer opted for over-
sized rooms and high ceilings. No wonder. The couple's collection of large pieces of antique and contemporary furniture,
eighteenth-century carved European wood sculpture, and one-
of-a-kind accessories requires architectural grandeur to be appreciated. Even numerous potted plants, including towering
bamboo, testify to the Milams' penchant for scale. "They were
trucked in from California," says Miram. A former model who
stands a striking six feet tall, she lends graceful proportion to
the grand living room, the length of which is made cozy and
less intimidating by matching fireplaces at both ends.

Opposite. "We live on the portal year-round," says
Hank Milam, a California-based interior designer
whose Santa Fe house is a frequent weekend retreat.
A painting by Don Bagley hangs over the fireplace.
Furnishings include a New Mexican cross, 19th-
century Italian crèche animals, and a Mexican table.
Above. A double row of flagstones cap the walls on
the Territorial style house.

Above. Dinner guests are joined by a life-size 19th-century carved wooden deer. It originally hung outside the entrance of an English brewery company. Plants were brought from California. A wall decoration is made from contemporary Mexican tiles.
Opposite. Twin fireplaces at each end of the Milams' living room have contemporary Spanish mirrors over them. The room's furnishings include a 19th-century Russian wooden bear, a 17th-century Italian chandelier, a 19th-century French coffee table, and late-18th-century German church angels.

Though he limits his jobs for private and corporate clients to six a year, Hank had to do some juggling to fit the building and decorating of his Santa Fe house into his schedule. He succeeded, yet now the Milams wrestle with finding time to visit the house. Whenever they can, they load their car with armloads of fresh California-grown flowers, and two dogs, and set off down the Los Angeles/Santa Fe trail.

"Santa Fe is our retreat. It is where we catch our breath," Miram says. "It is also where we have a complete change of design," Hank adds. "Our California house is 1960s Milano: black, white, and chrome. Here in Santa Fe, we've done an about-face. We wanted a more relaxed, historic feeling. If I had to define the house, I'd say it's a romanticized New Mexico farmhouse."

One of the most admired houses in Santa Fe, the Milams' dwelling captivates visitors from the moment they step through the front door onto the waxed flagstone floors. There are no carpets in the house. There are, however, blue-and-white Mexican tiles everywhere, in the kitchen, in the bathrooms, on the back of the bar, in alcoves. "It's my favorite color combination," Hank explains.

Hank also confesses to an obsession with stripping the paint off almost anything carved out of wood, which he feels looks better "in the raw." Off went the paint on a nineteenth-century French carousel horse, an eighteenth-century German Madonna, a pair of seventeenth-century Italian church columns, a nineteenth-century Russian bear, and an eighteenth-century English stag.

All very large, all very dramatically positioned, the pieces "now reveal the wonders of wood," Hank says. "I want to see the grain, the striae, and the cracks in a wood carving. I'm sufficiently into stripping that friends laugh at me and say I bleached out my dogs. Take a look at them—their hair is off-white!"

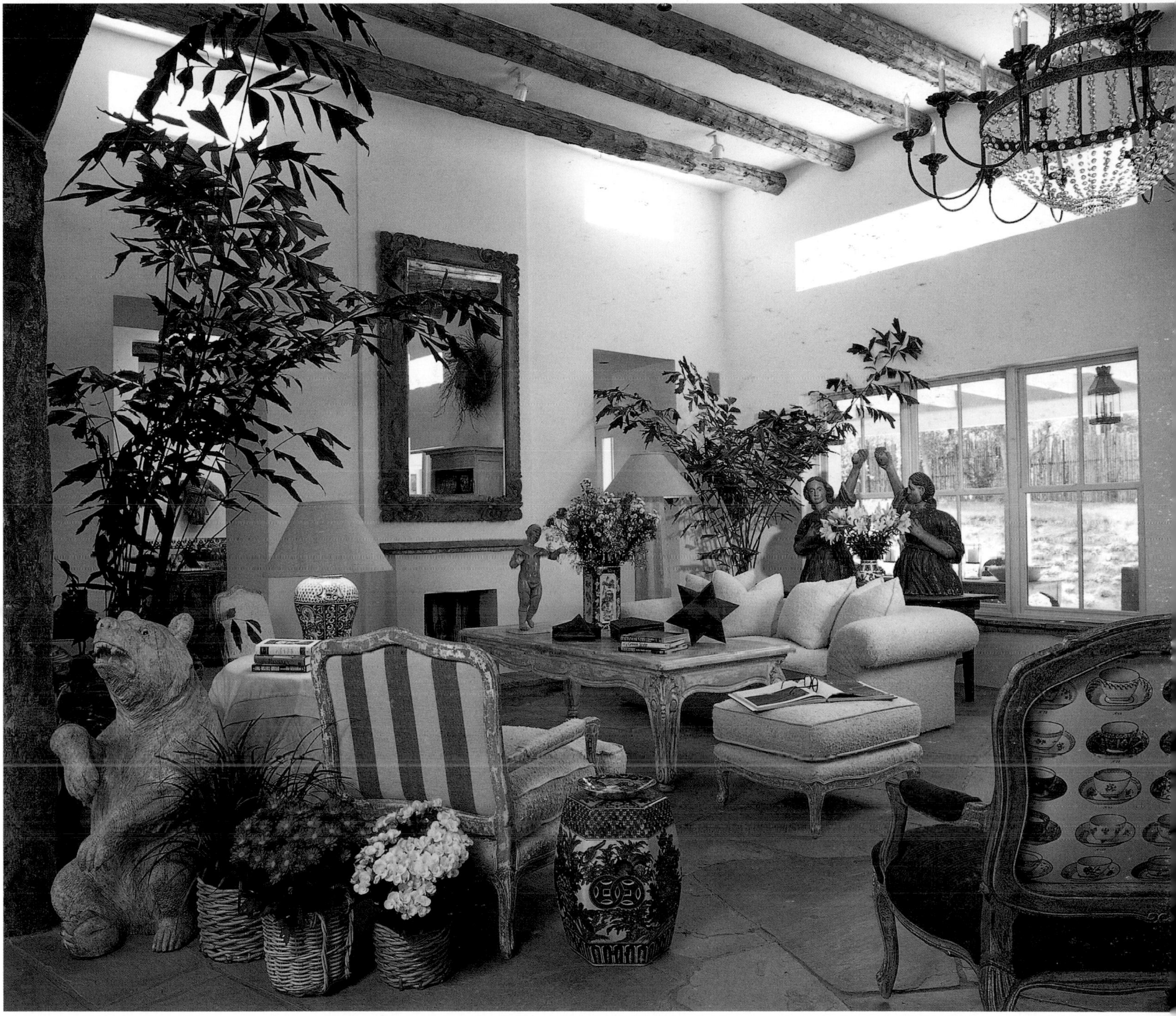

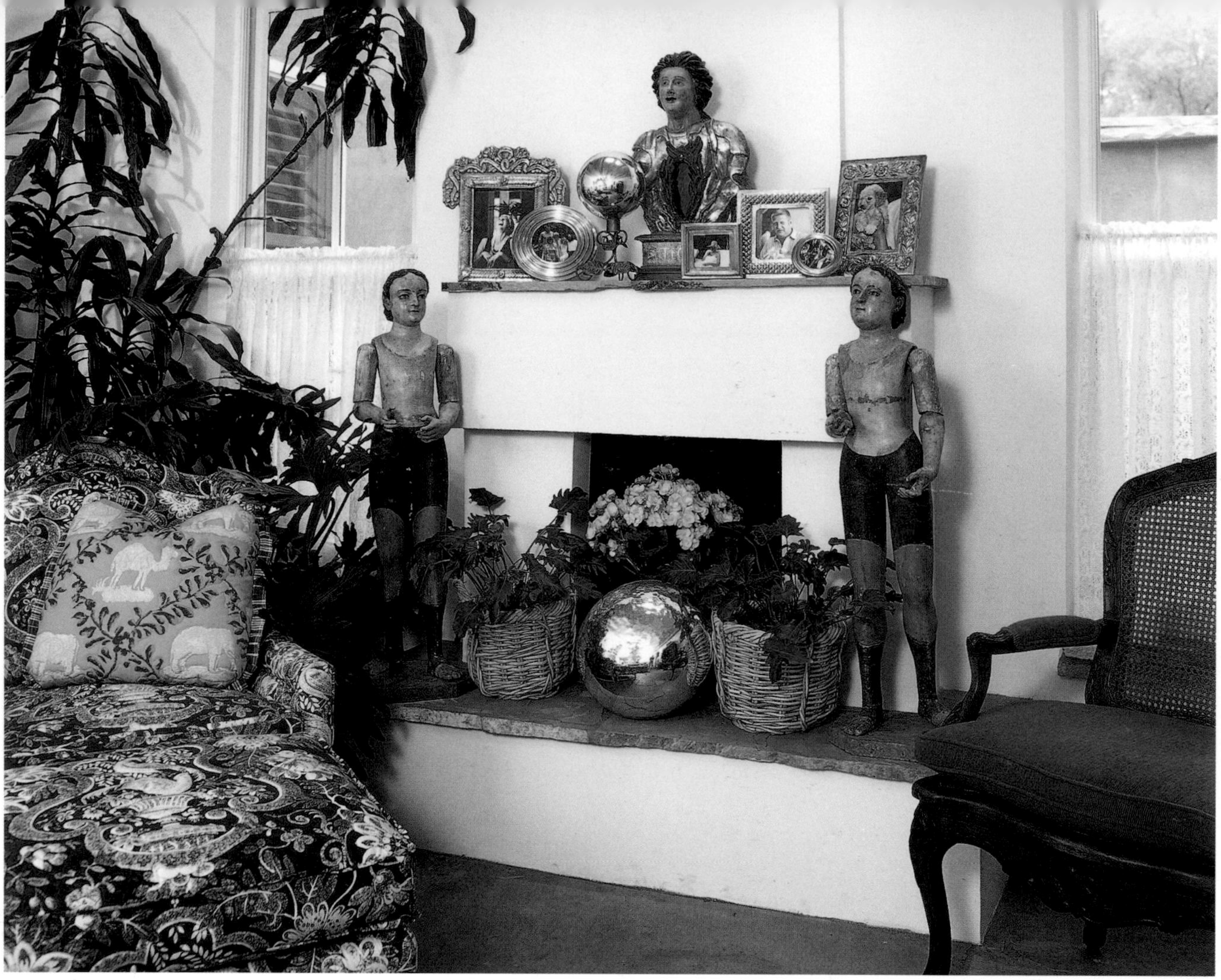

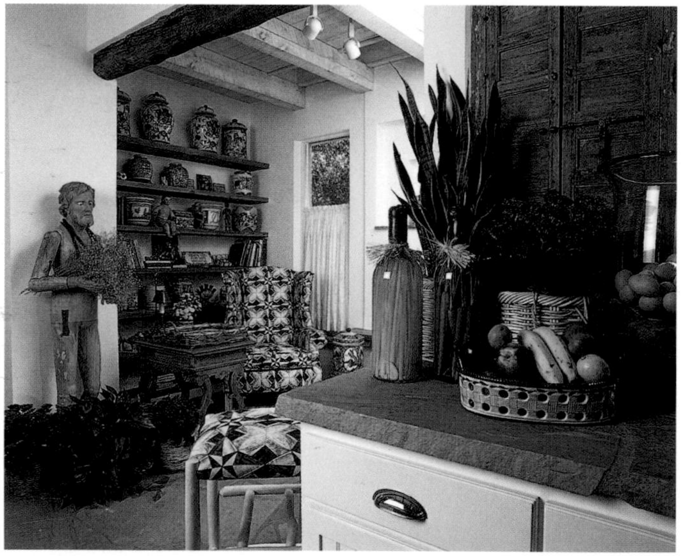

Above. A pair of early-19th-century Mexican wooden figures in a guest room. The sofa is covered with Pierre Deux fabric.
Right. Stripped and bleached, an 18th-century life-size Italian crèche figure stands in the kitchen beside shelves of blue-and-white Chinese pottery.
Opposite. In the master bedroom, a contemporary carved wooden Chinese dog lies on an 18th-century Peruvian bench.

Bringing many pieces from California, the Milams also prowl for treasures in Santa Fe antique shops, especially La Puerta, Claiborne Gallery, and Foreign Traders. "It's amazing what you find here. Some of the most exciting pieces are now coming north from South America, Peru in particular," Miram reports. When selecting fabric for the house, she followed the family color scheme. Chairs, sofas, benches, and pillows are covered in raw white silk or cotton, with blue-and-white designs—with an occasional dollop of Giverny yellow.

Asked to list the dominant ingredient in his interior design approach, Hank is quick to reply. "Implied formality," he says. "I love juxtaposing something truly fine, something very striking, with something simple, basic, and unrefined." To demonstrate, he points to an imposing seventeenth-century Italian chandelier. Hanging at one time in a church, it now occupies the vast ceiling space in the Milams' fifteen-foot-high living room. With multiple strands of crystal beads, the decidedly formal European fixture is arresting, made more so by its position, hanging from the middle of a very Southwestern ceiling of old New Mexican wooden vigas.

"Placement is critical when decorating a house," Hank adds. "It isn't what you have, it's where you display what you have that makes the difference. When things are wrong, it hurts. When things are right, it's magic."

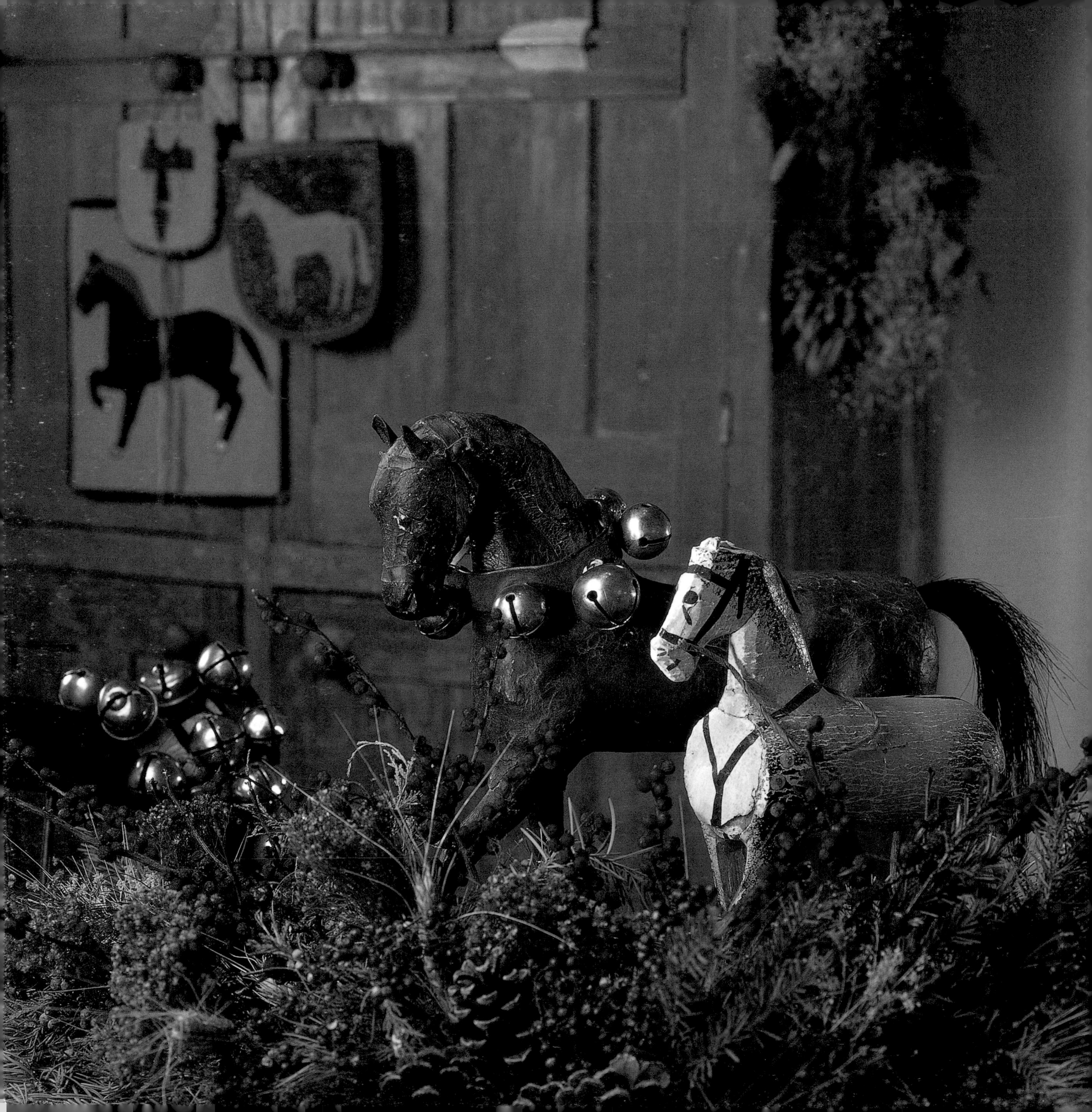

Feliz Navidad

Visions of sugarplums dance through the heads of many people at Christmas. But for Chris O'Connell, the holidays are when her equestrian fantasies are really let loose. "That's when I allow all my horses to stampede through the house," she explains to guests who marvel at her colorful yuletide corral. Stallions, mares, colts, ponies—two hundred of them, antique, brand-new, tin, bronze, leather, wood, and fabric—are in her collection. "Some of the horses go back to my childhood, when my Swedish grandparents decorated the Christmas tree with them," she explains. "Horses are the motif I use the most when I do up the house for Saint Nicholas each year."

A former Hollywood television and film executive, Chris mystified her family when she announced she was quitting her high-powered job to move to Santa Fe and open a women's apparel store. "'You're going to do what? You're going where?' That was the puzzled reaction I got when I packed up my belongings, told all my dogs and cats to jump in the car, and drove here to start a new career," explains the high-energy Chris, who says she realized she was going out on a limb.

Always fascinated by fabrics, textures, and colors, she had begun to weave and to design her own line while still in California. "I'd go home from the studio and stay up all night at the loom or the drafting board," she recalls. Before long, Chris's textile art was marketed throughout the country, at Neiman Marcus, Saks Fifth Avenue, and I. Magnin.

Opposite. At Christmas, designer Chris O'Connell decorates her living room with antique toy horses. Many are family heirlooms. She adds Yuletide arrangements of New Mexican grasses, berries, and tree boughs. A late-19th-century Scandinavian cupboard is hung with beaded Indian bags. The bells are used in Pueblo dances.
Above. Bales of hay tied with red ribbon welcome Santa's reindeer.

In 1985, she opened Spider Woman, one of Santa Fe's first retail outlets specializing in clothing, accessories, and even furniture with a Santa Fe twist. Soon, Chris found her talent featured in major magazines and newspapers and books on Santa Fe style. She had become as successful a designer as she had been a Hollywood mover and shaker.

Then one day, she sold out. Why? "I was ready to move on. I'd proved that my designs had real public appeal," says Chris. Besides, major manufacturers, including Beacon Looms, Westpoint Stevens, and Brunschwig & Fils, were anxious for her to design for them. And that's what Chris continues to do today, as well as tackling commissions in the interior design world.

Pilar, Chris's eight-year-old daughter, shares her mother's childlike enthusiasm for Christmas, joyfully evident throughout their 1,600-square-foot adobe house. Chris designed it herself in the pitched-roofed northern New Mexico style. Gathering dried grasses, pine cones, and fir boughs, she begins transforming her house into a Southwestern way station on the Santa Claus trail around December 10 each year. "I don't think Christmas should begin at Thanksgiving," she says. "It is a special time and shouldn't be merchandised to death, including in one's own home."

Using her collection of old carpenters' tool boxes, the inventive Chris fills them with colorful Christmas ribbons that stream over tables and down the sides of antique, painted armoires and cupboards, some from New Mexico, others from Scandinavia. Festive arrangements of gourds, birds' nests, and pinecones, together with cowboy boots and watering cans full of dried flowers, give the house a natural, Southwestern winter look.

"I was brought up to 'make do.' I was taught as a child that life isn't about things, lots of things. It's about people, love, and helping one another...and a few of our favorite things," she says with a good laugh. "I used to have a lot of 'things.' I'm down to about twenty household pieces today, all of which I treasure."

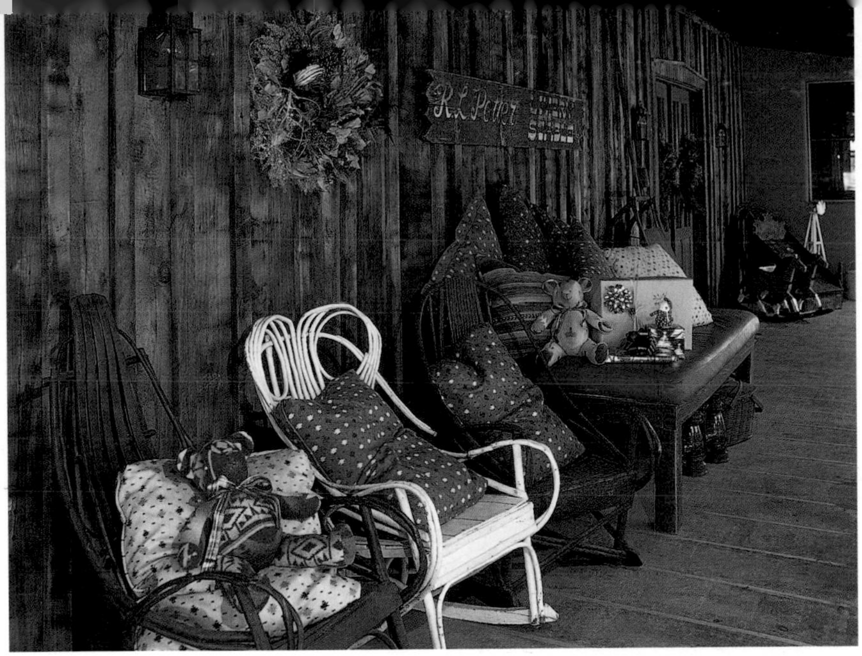

Opposite. A Navajo Germantown rug is a backdrop for a collection of Native American artifacts, including antique pueblo drums and dance wands, Hopi moccasins, and a kachina.
Left. Antique willow rockers with pillows covered in fabric designed by O'Connell for Brunsweig & Fils line a portal wall of old Montana barn siding.
Below. A contemporary folk art Santa stands against a collection of early-20th-century Mexican crosses and late-19th-century tintypes of Native Americans.

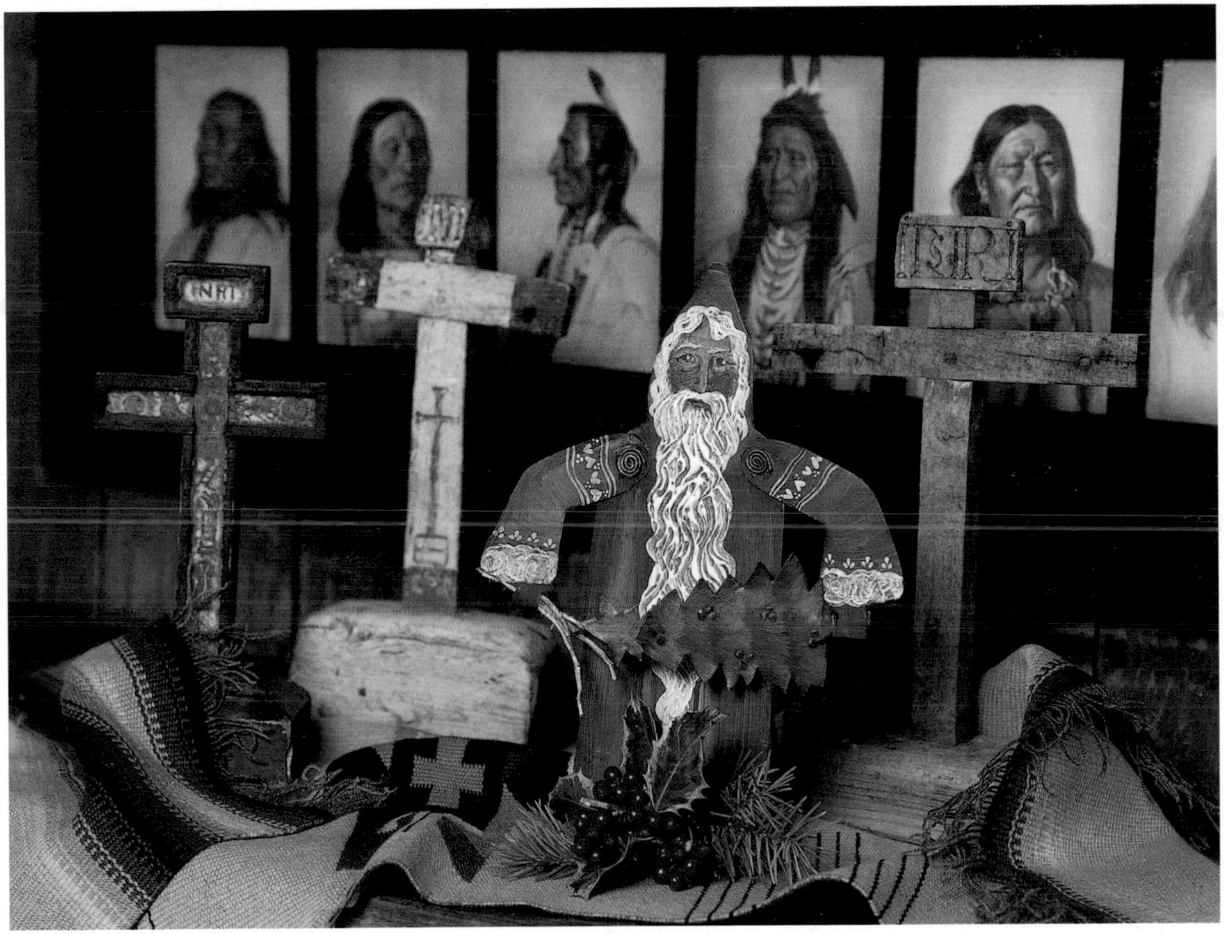

Above. A colonial Mexican bench is festooned with
pine swags containing New Mexican buffalo gourds.
Opposite. "I've collected horse ornaments for the
Christmas tree for over twenty years," says O'Connell.
Fire kindling is kept in an old tin lariat box.

The O'Connell collection, which is simply and dramatically
displayed against a neutral palette of "Always Almond" walls
and sage green, poured-concrete floors, includes an eighteenth-
century New Mexican *granero*, or grain chest; a Blackfoot back-
rest made of willow boughs; an 1880 Plateau Indian child's
beaded bonnet; an enormous Fritz Scholder aquatint of an
Indian warrior on horseback; and Indian drums, drums, and
more drums. Add to the list half a dozen oil paintings by New
Mexican artist Carol Anthony, all of which have a mystical,
Monet-like quality.

"If there is a constant thread that weaves itself through my
career, it would be my fascination with how primitive cultures,
in their efforts to create utilitarian objects for survival, have
always transformed raw materials into objects of beauty," Chris
says. "I have followed this grassroots approach to design in my
own home."

For guests, no moment of decorating truth is more warmly
apparent than Christmas in the O'Connell Santa Fe household.

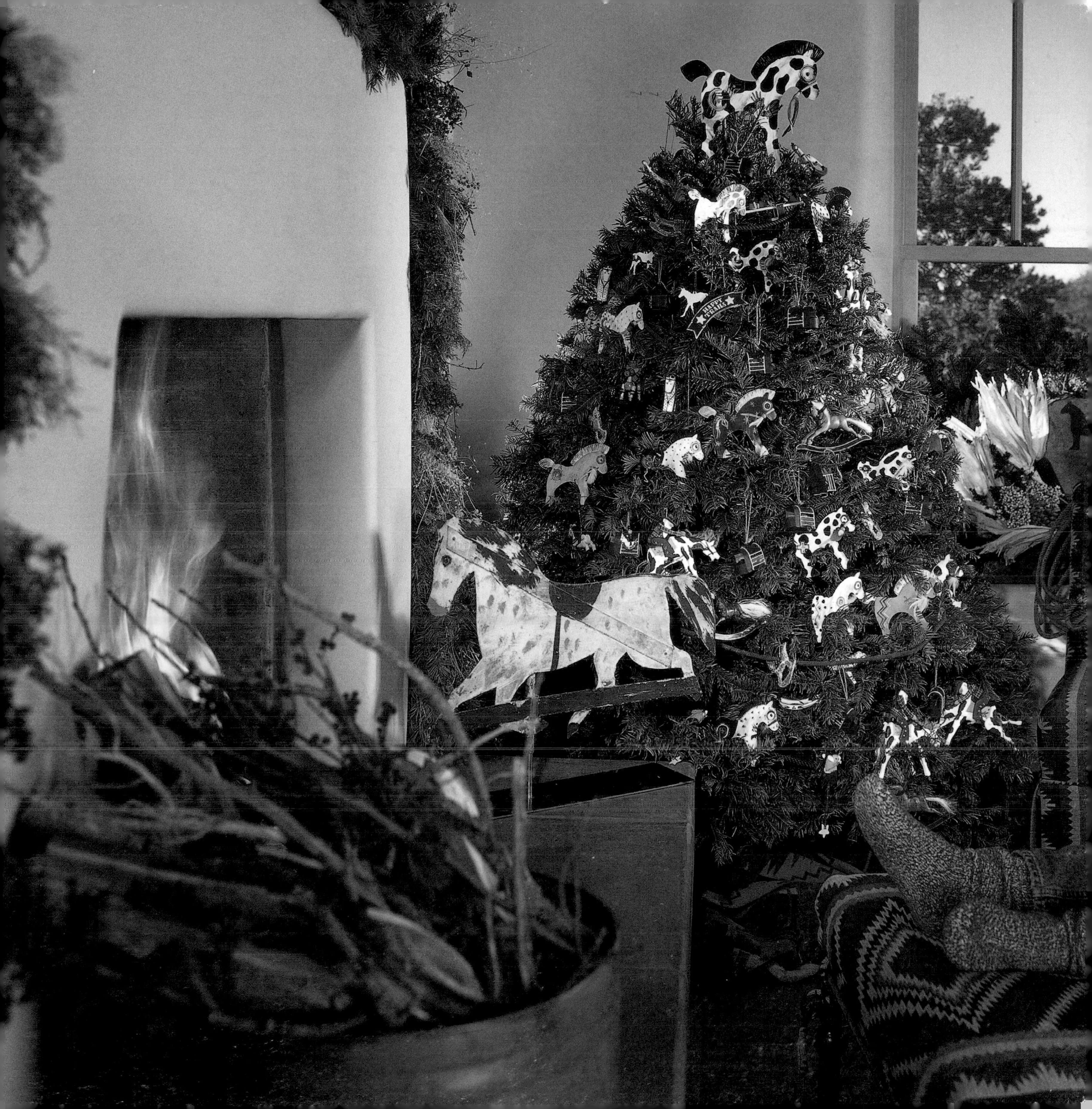
HAPPY TRAILS

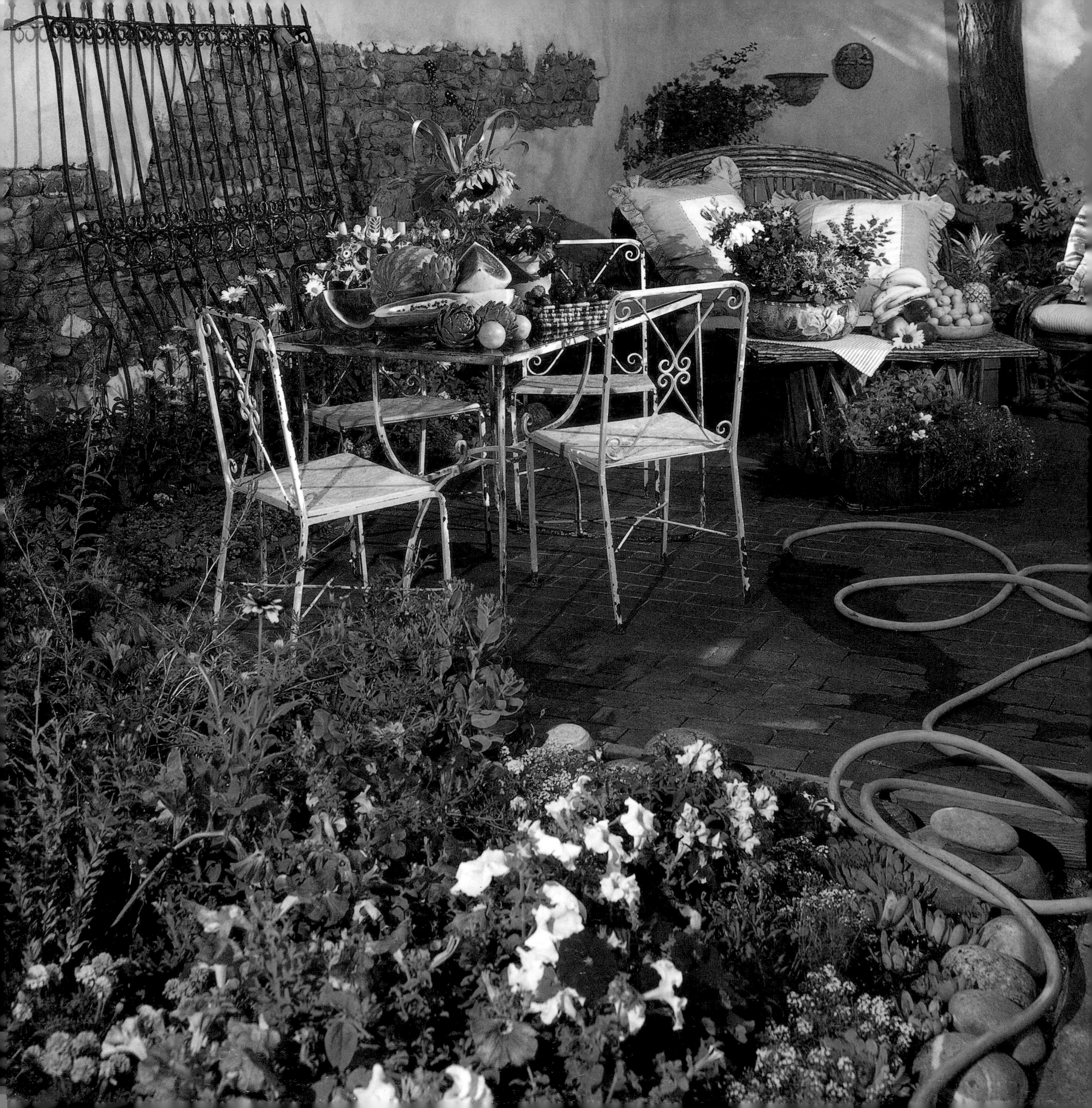

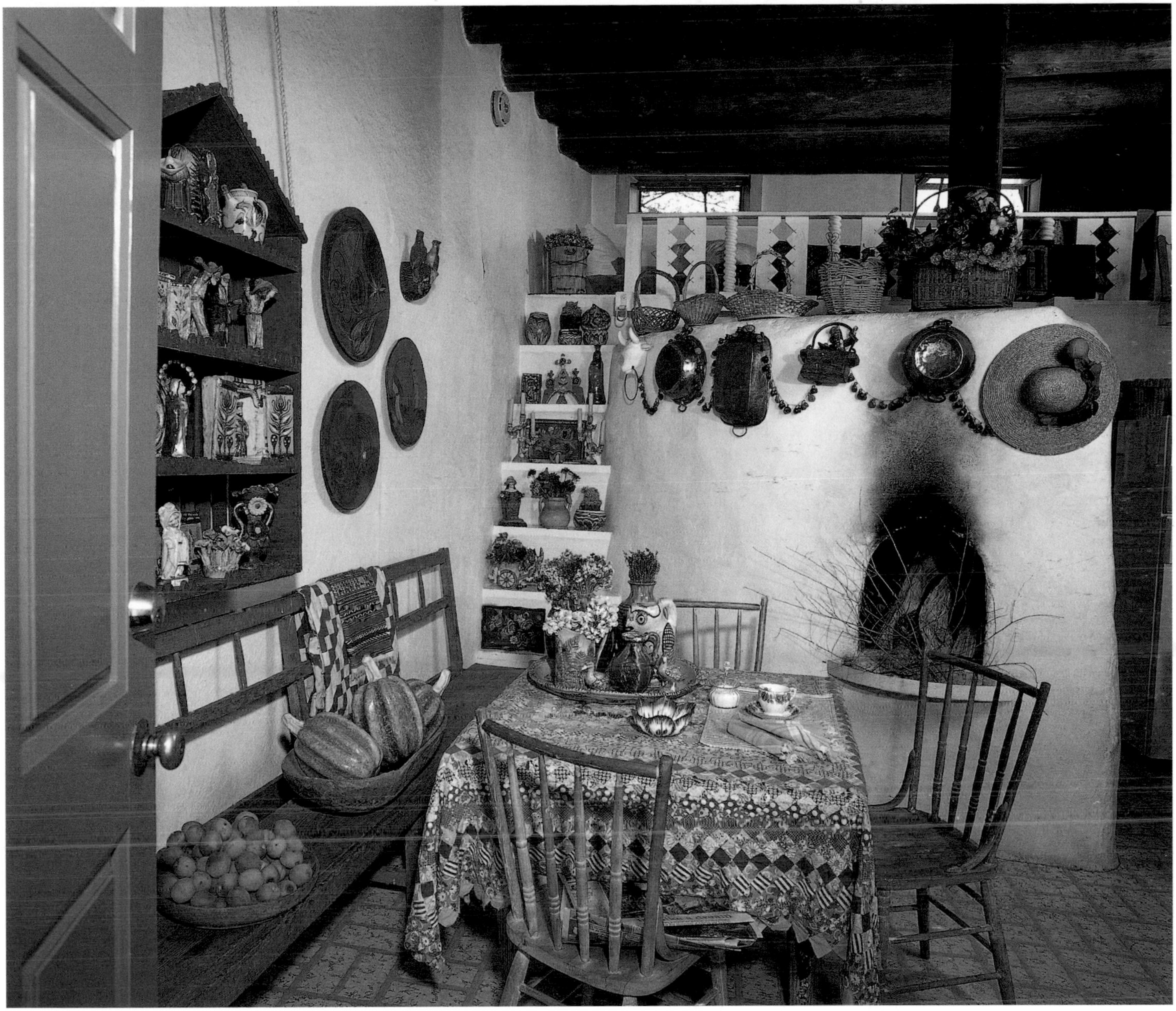

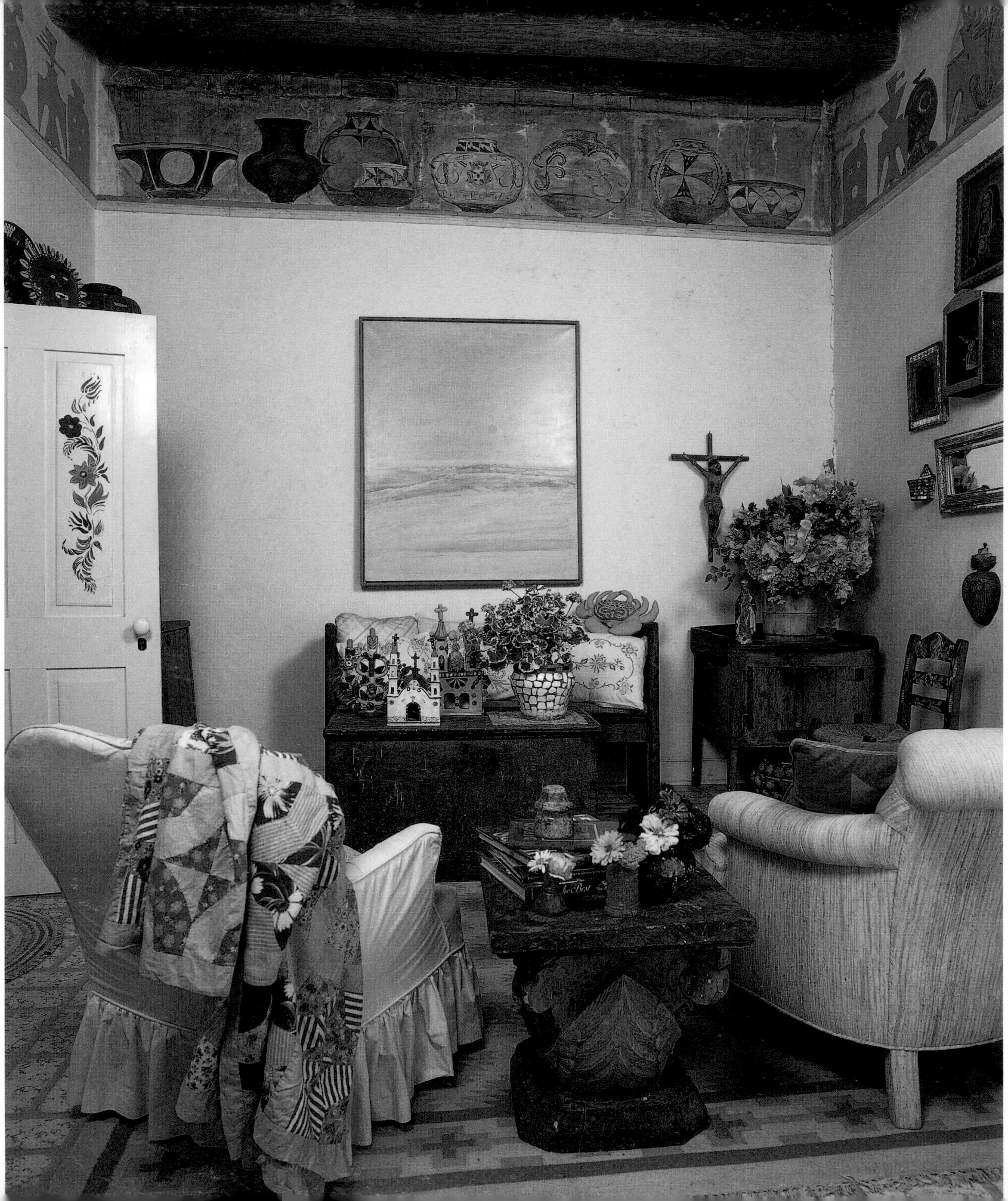

Opposite. A handkerchief-size living room contains a Filipino coffee table, a 19th-century Massachusetts wooden blanket box, and a painting by Forest Moses. "We don't know who painted the frieze of Indian pots," Diane says.
Above. Kitchen shelves display the Maloufs' collection of Mexican and South American figures, plates, and religious objects.

Be that as it may, the Malouf house reveals a thoughtful owner's imaginative eye for New Mexican and Mexican folk art. With all-white walls, it is full of colorful artifacts, such as pillows covered in faded, old floral-patterned fabrics, worn hooked rugs, and antique painted furniture. With twenty-four-inch thick adobe walls, the doll house (that is truly what it is) is blessed with one outstanding architectural feature: sixteen-foot ceilings. As if they were not dramatic enough, a hand-painted trompe l'oeil frieze of Indian pots in the living room adds a decorative bonus found in no other house in Santa Fe. "We have no idea who painted it," Diane says. "It was probably done in the fifties. There's no signature. The sad thing is, it is unfinished, which leads us to believe that the artist had to move out quickly."

The Maloufs have no intention of beating a retreat. "This house is my celebration of life," Diane confides. "We come here to get away from professional problems. There are no frills. We don't even have a fax. Frankly, it is a concession to my husband that we even have a telephone."

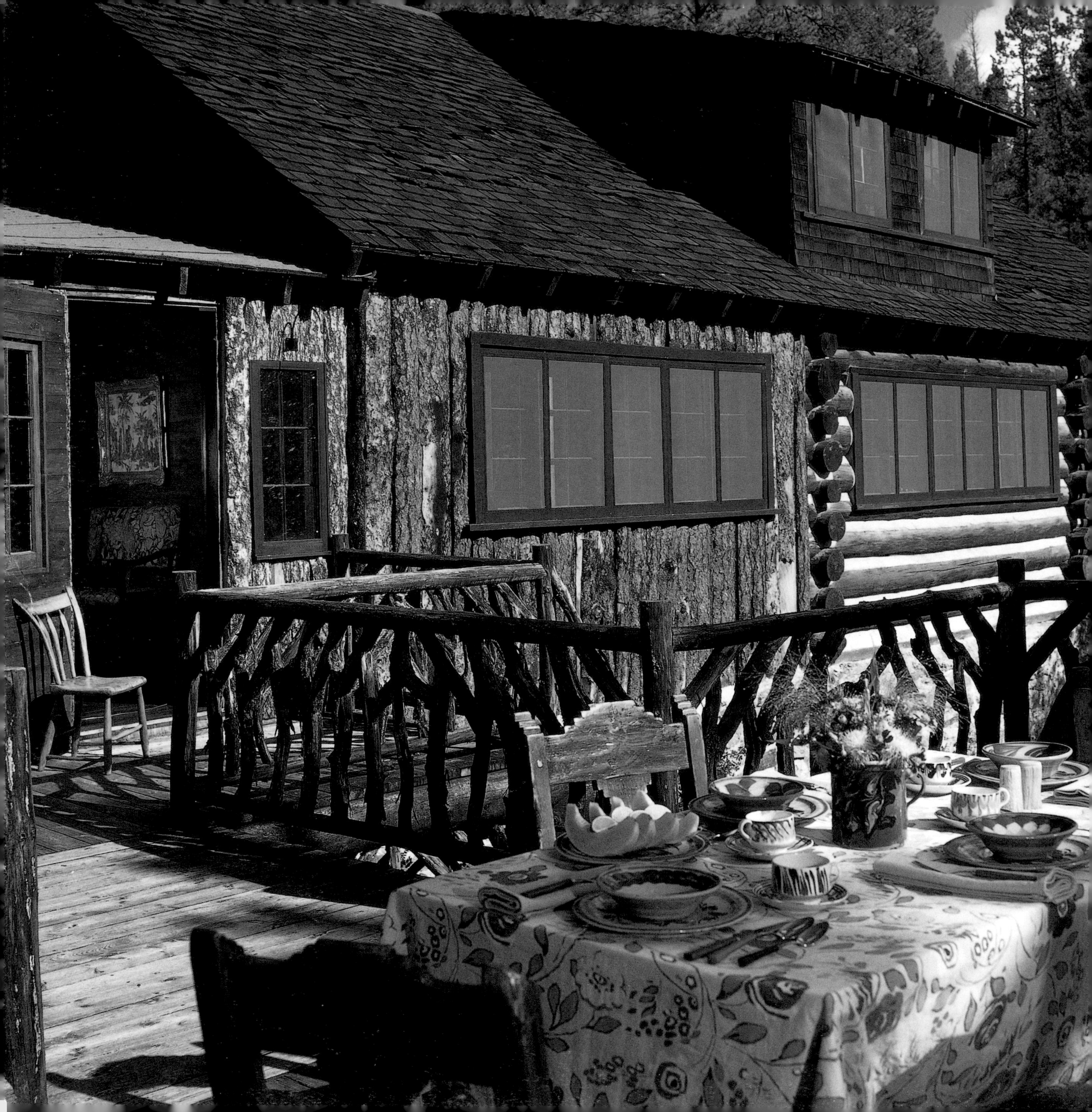

Right at Holy Ghost

You're creeping along, up a winding road through the Pecos River valley, when suddenly there's a fork. You look at the directions Chris Hill has given you, then proceed right to Tererro. (The left-hand turn would have gone to Holy Ghost Canyon.) Soon a time-worn general store appears. Old men sit in front, rocking with the boards and gossiping; just-arrived second home owners from Texas and Oklahoma rush in and out, their arms loaded with provisions. You continue to handle the turns in the road. And then you're there. Way up the mountainside, tucked into the ponderosa pines, surrounded by fields of wildflowers, and hanging over the river, an old log cabin lies camouflaged in the wilderness.

"I had a Mercedes convertible on order when I stumbled onto this property. The price was the same. I put in a bid, got the cabin, and canceled the car," Chris tells amused friends, all of whom hope for an invitation to stay overnight. "I'm from San Antonio, Texas, so to come up here to escape the summer heat back home is heaven. I light a fire even in August. It can drop down to the forties."

An architect with a house in Santa Fe as well, Chris loves the history of the area. "The town of Pecos was settled by the Spanish in 1825," he says. "The American Metals Company worked the valley in the twenties for lead, tin, and copper.

Opposite and above. Built in 1914 on the edge of the Pecos River, the log cabin of Texan Chris Hill is an hour's drive from his Santa Fe residence. "The '40s china came with the house, together with a lot of other neat stuff," he says. "The china is perfect for meals out on the deck."

Below. Turn-of-the-century Indian beaded moccasins and a bag are combined with a French folk art clock, a flea market find.

Right. The tin bathroom sink, tub, and hose faucets were "make do's" during World War II. American 1930s sconces are on contemporary pine paneling.

Opposite, top. A house gift, bear claw slippers came with a note saying "I don't want you to go barefoot."

Opposite, bottom. Rather than stoke up the woodstove, Hill frequently cooks on a vintage two-burner.

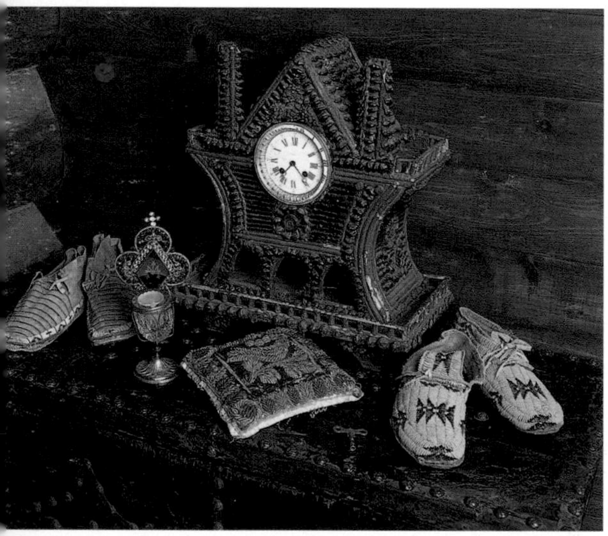

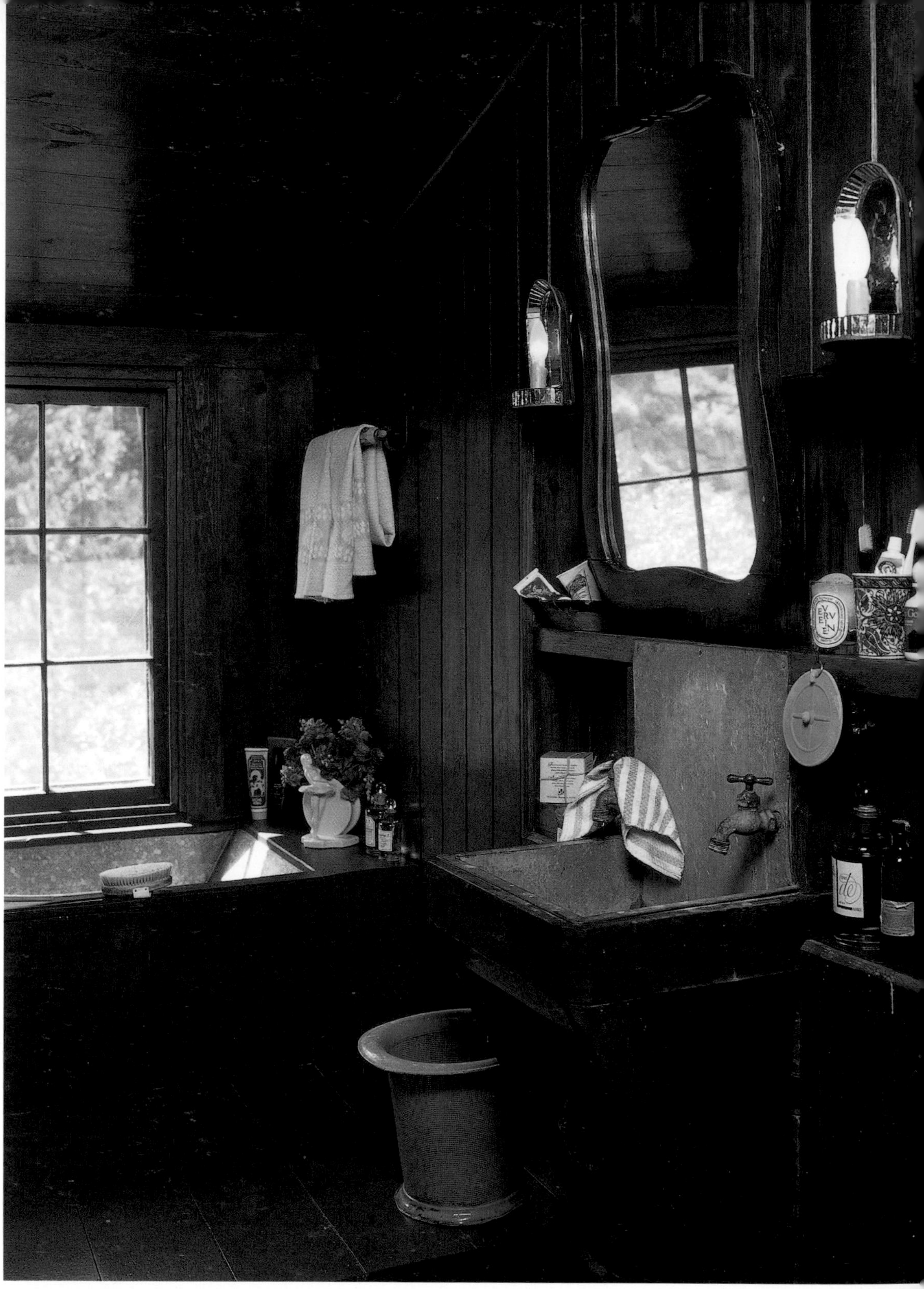

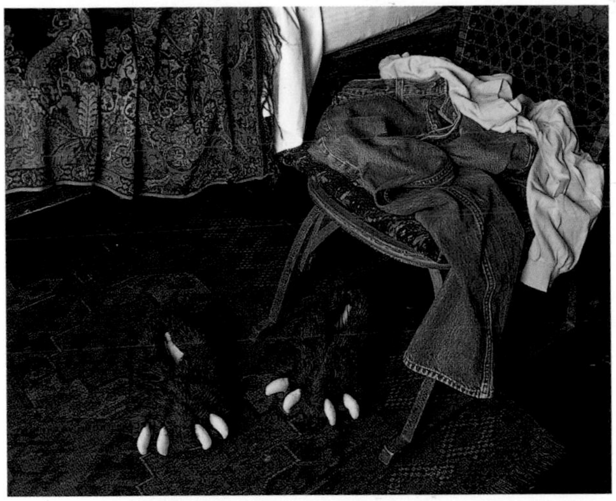

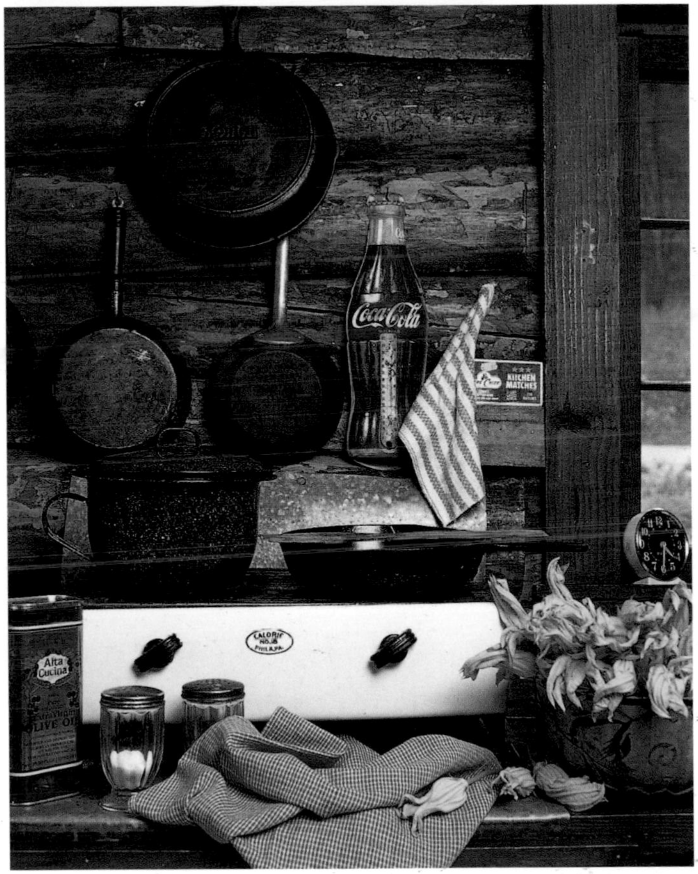
Coca-Cola
KITCHEN MATCHES

There were about fifteen hundred miners and their families living here. Now, about two hundred families come here, mostly in the summer."

With his two New Mexico properties only an hour apart, Chris, like many people in the City Different, is pleased to have an escape hatch. "It's amazing, but Santa Fe has so much going on, that I needed a place to catch my breath," he says.

Listed on the New Mexico State Register of Historic Landmarks, the cabin was built in 1914 by A. J. Connell. A designer at Tiffany's in New York City and then a forest ranger in New Mexico, Connell eventually became headmaster of the Los Alamos Boys School. With a stone base, log walls (fir, pine, blue spruce, and ponderosa) and a shingled roof, the building is decorated in what Chris calls "le style hodgepodge."

"When I consider buying something for one of my houses, the question I ask myself is, 'Why not?' Unless I come up with strong answer, I get it," Chris explains as his *modus decorati*. For the cabin, the result is country eclectic: Moroccan rugs, 1950s Mexican furniture and pottery, Taos paintings, Spanish chests of drawers, Russian icons. The mountain-man motif appears in the way of a bearskin rug. When it comes to the bathrooms, "old-fashioned" best defines the lead bathtubs and sinks. "They had new fixtures. They were awful," Chris recalls. "I tore them all out and put in period fixtures." A 1940 General Electric icebox adds to the cabin's World War II–era authenticity.

Above. Deer antlers sit on a chair built by
a New Mexican folk artist.
Right. On cool summer nights, the living
room fireplace is frequently lit.
Opposite. Arrangements of wildflowers,
"picked in the yard," fill the cabin all summer.

Fleeing to the Pecos to be out of the Santa Fe social loop,
Chris looks forward to "doing as little as possible" in the wild.
"I read, hike, fill the hummingbird feeders, and cut flowers."
Pressed to talk about his occasional parties, he confesses,
"I've had as many as thirty-five people for dinner." Eating out
on a large deck on the edge of the roaring Pecos river, guests are
startled when two halogen lights come on to give definition
to a nearby rock cliff.

"It is my one small concession to the end of the twentieth
century," Chris confesses. "Everything else about this place is
purposely old-fashioned. It's the way I want it."

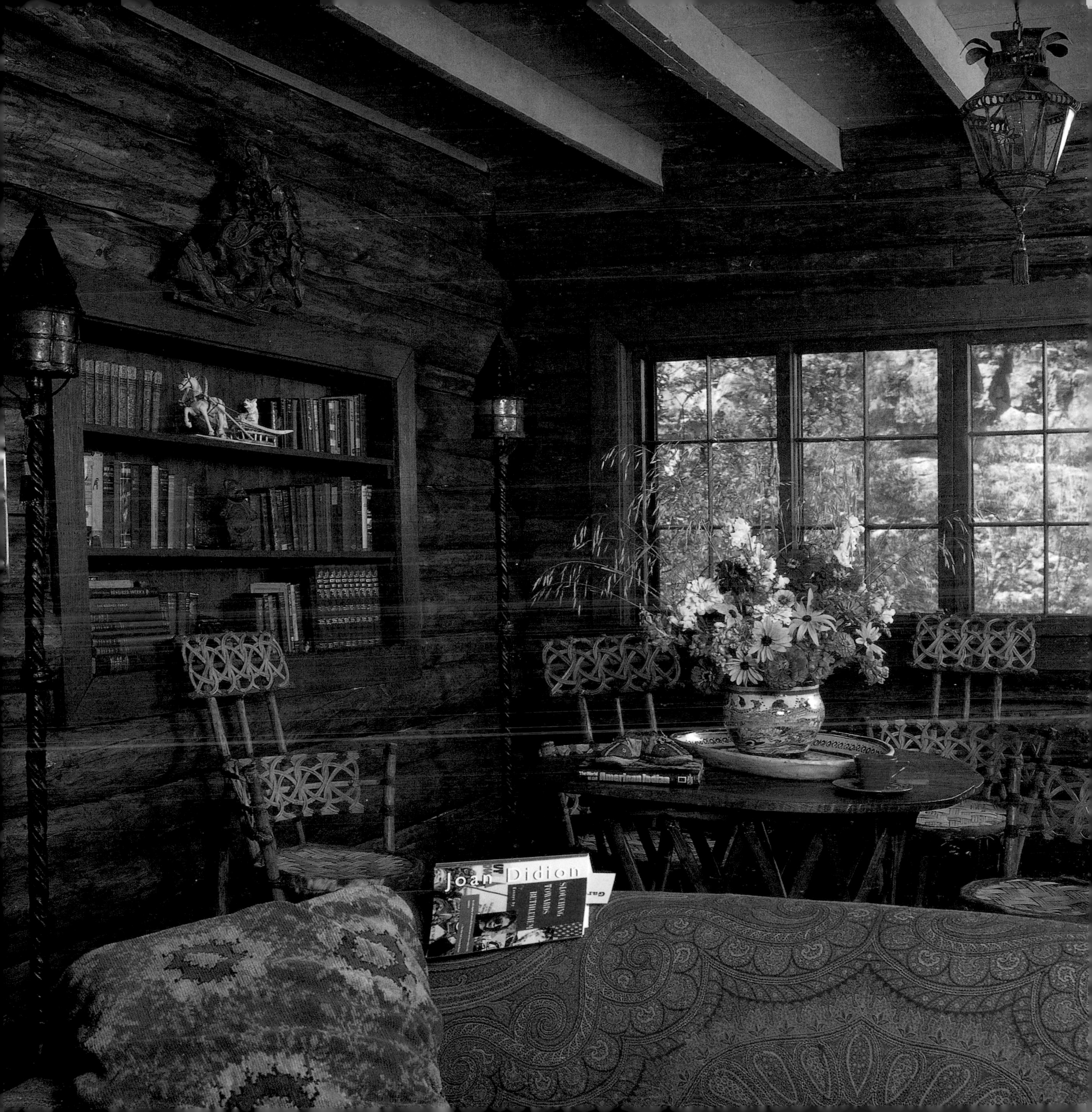
Joan Didion
SLOUCHING TOWARDS BETHLEHEM
American Indian

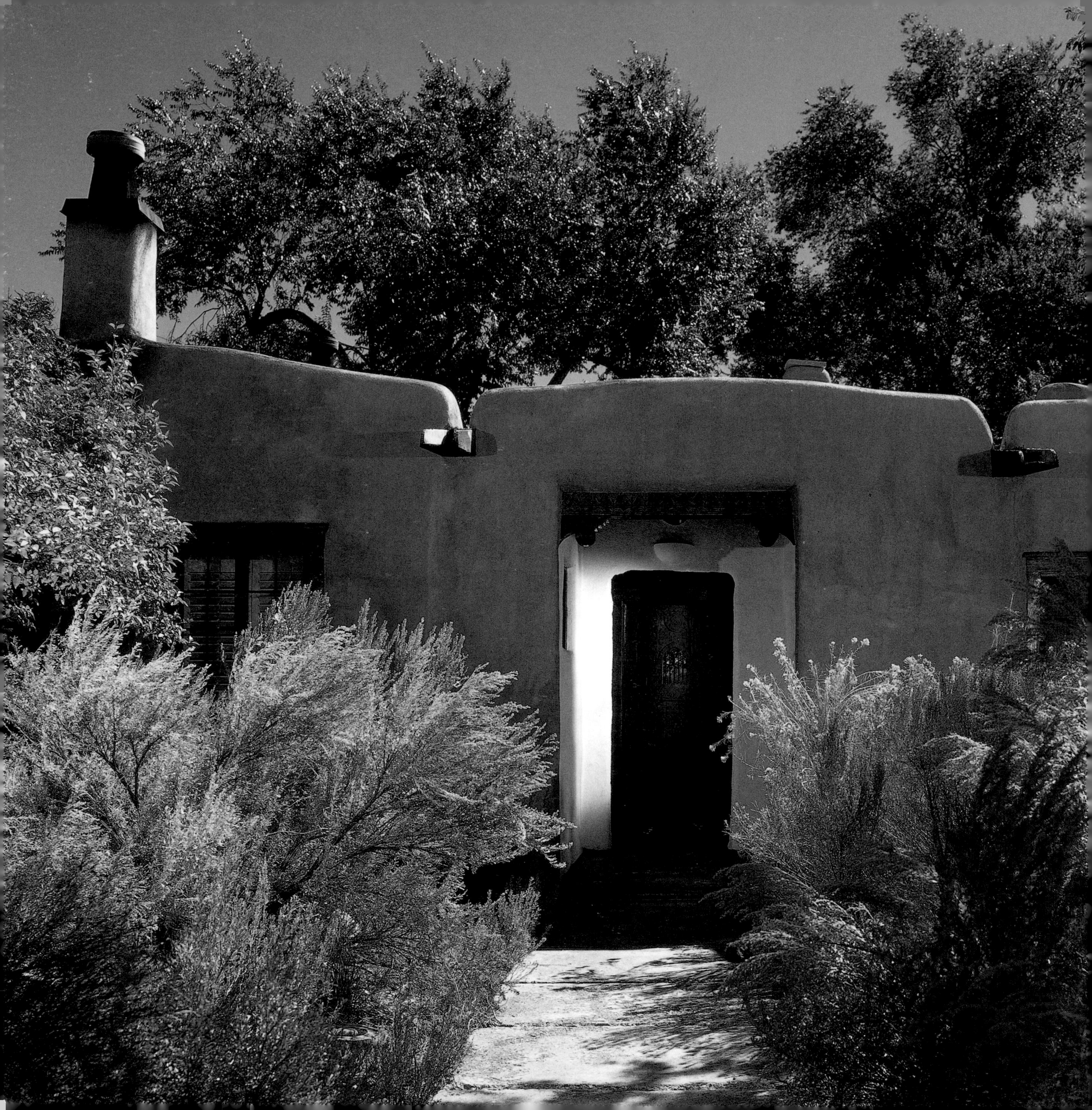

White on White

A freelance graphic designer with clients nationwide who also seek his interior design skills, David Hundley settled for two primary colors inside and outside his 150-year-old Taos house: white and blue. "White expands a room to make it look larger," he says, seated in his deceptively narrow eleven-by-thirty-foot living room. An imposing gentleman who would easily look at home in a wrestling or boxing ring, David is just in from an early-morning tennis match. "White walls also give furniture and paintings a chance to stand out, to be really seen and appreciated."

Stepping outside to a walled-in gravel courtyard with a spectacular view of the Sangre de Cristo mountains, David points to the color of the house's exterior window trim, gates, and doors. They are all blue. "Sky blue, with a bit of violet in it," he explains, looking upward to the cloudless hemisphere. The flowerless gardens with mint-colored chamisa bushes and sweet-smelling, wild sage surround the house with exactly the unprofessional, natural landscape he prefers. Peach-colored exterior adobe is the dwelling's only other color.

"I grew up in New Mexico, went to design schools in Switzerland and England, worked for advertising agencies in Chicago, taught in California, and now I've come back here to live. The pull of the Southwest won out," David says while

Opposite. The front of this 150-year-old house is planted with drought resistant chamisa and sage. Chinese elms shade the back side.
Above. Barbells stand tall in a dressing room fireplace. The tusks and 1930s gazelle skull are from Kenya. A Rio Grande blanket covers a 19th-century New Mexican chest.

95

Right. Resting on the living room mantel is a crayon by Lester Johnson, to the right a "landscape" by Joe Waldrum. The cross is 19th-century Russian, the English club chairs are reproductions. *Opposite.* The 1960s Knoll coffee table is by Florence Knoll; the Knoll wire side table by Warren Platner. The settee is a reproduction Louis XVI; the chairs reproduction Italian nineteenth century.

performing a coffee ceremony with a silver George Jensen thermos, a rose-colored English stoneware cup, and a black Chinese lacquer tray. It is symbolic of David's primary thesis that anything of good design goes together with anything else of good design. "Weeding out, narrowing down, and severe selectivity: these are key to my interior design," he makes clear when showing his house. The limited but impressive inventory of modern paintings, vintage photographs, works on paper, and antique and contemporary furniture confirm their owner's insistence that "less is better." The exception to the Hundley rule of Zen-like interior design are numerous stacks of art and design books, and a library in which no shelf has room for another title.

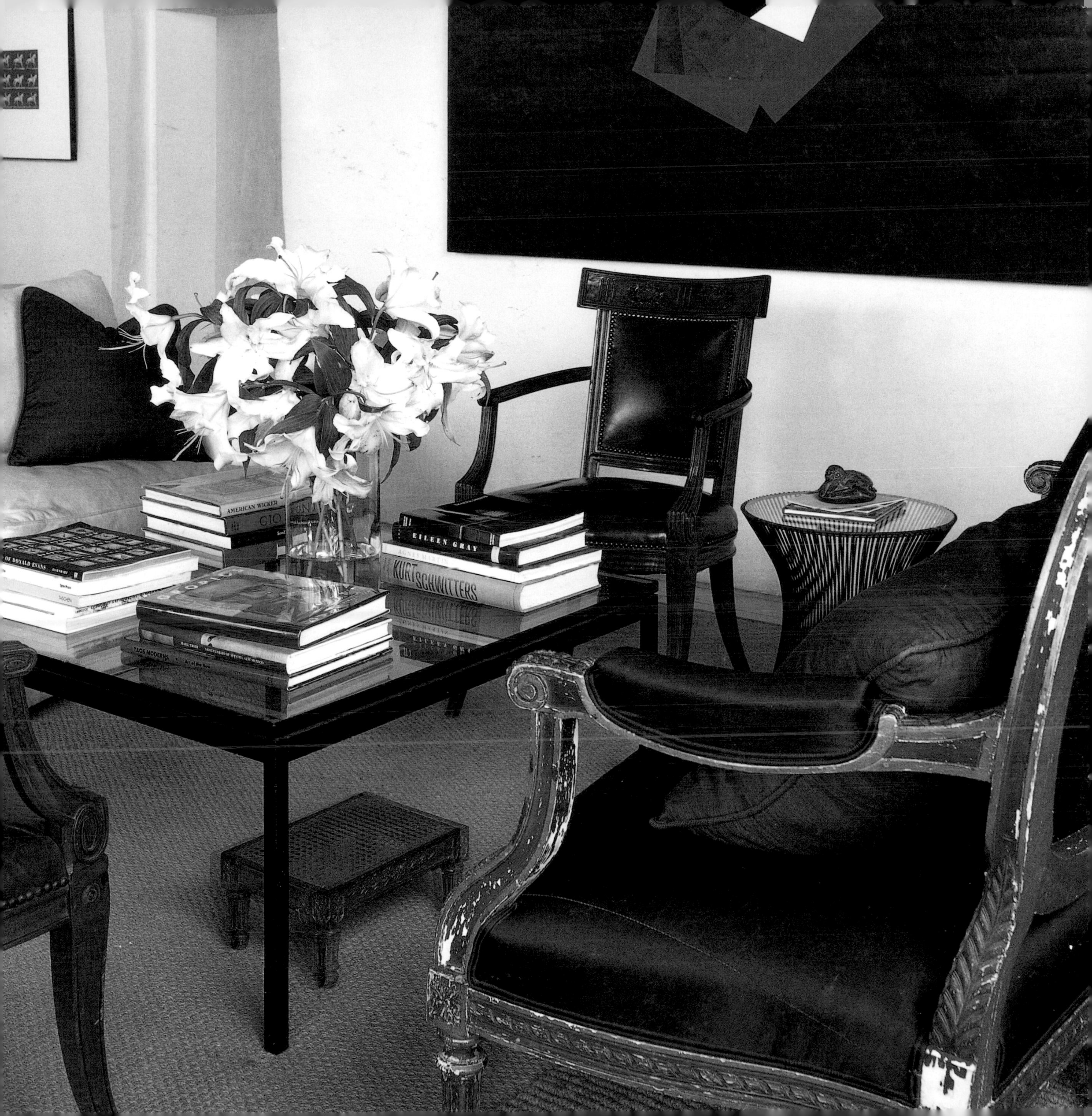
AMERICAN WICKER
EILEEN GRAY
KURT SCHWITTERS

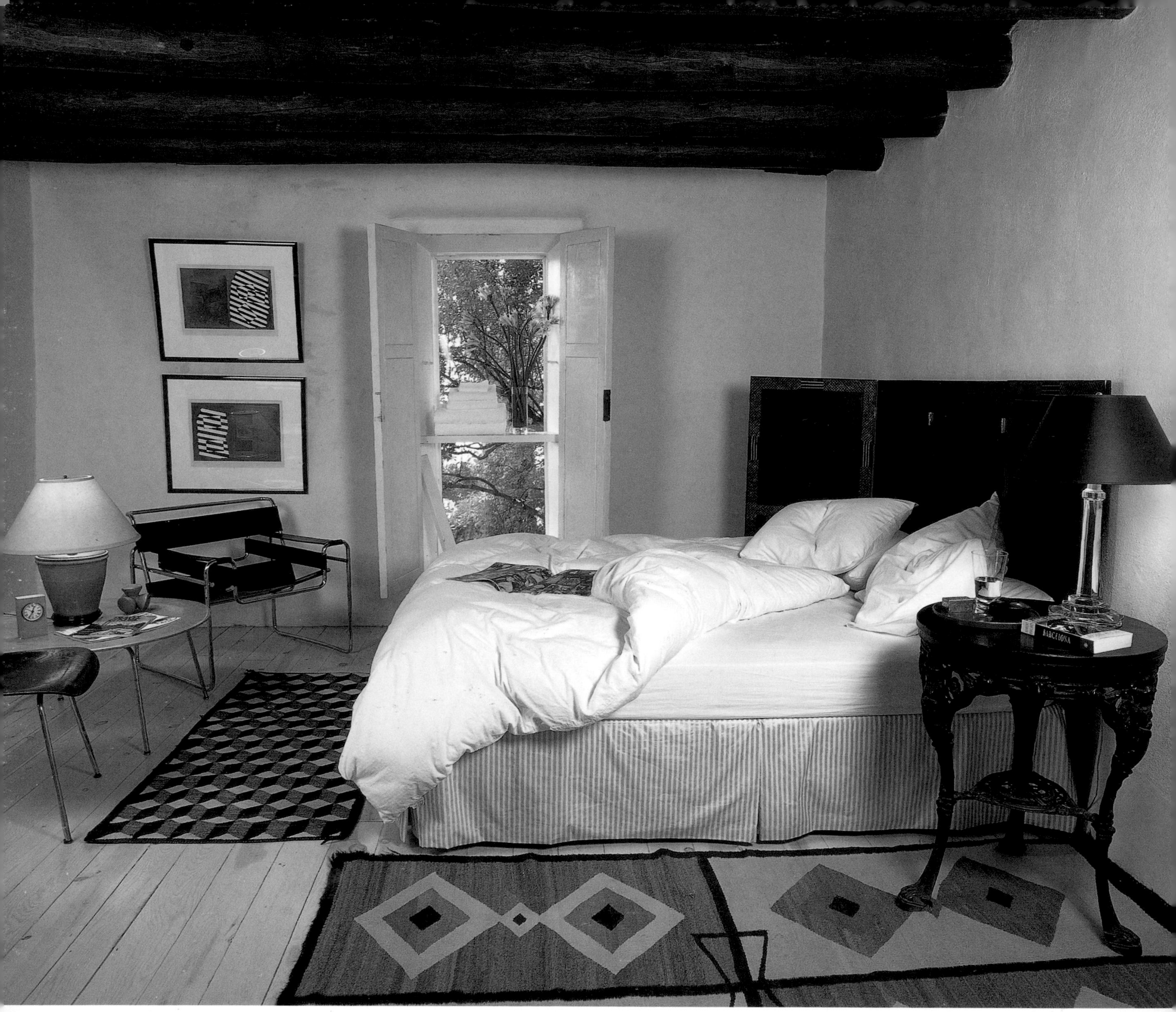
BARCELONA

"When I bought this house in 1987, it had no heat, no electricity. It had been in old Hispanic families for generations. I have many eighteenth- and nineteenth-century documents pertaining to the property. Families wouldn't leave the house to one son or daughter; they'd leave one room to a son, another room to a daughter, and so on," David explains, later pointing out that he hadn't changed anything in the house architecturally. Maintaining its numerous small rooms, undoubtedly added on as each new owner's finances allowed, he learned to duck when passing through low doorways. "Houses used to be measured by the number of vigas in a room," he says. "They'd say that a room was twenty vigas long. Everyone knew what that meant."

Today in Taos, people know what the Hundley look means as well. Streamlined. "My graphic design background taught me how to get a message across to a reader quickly and simply. Translated to interior design, a homeowner's intent must immediately be clear to a viewer as well," David strongly insists. "People find it hard to edit a room. But you have to—that is, if you want to get your interior design message across fast and effectively."

Opposite. Early 1920s Navajo rugs cover the bedroom floor. Joel Bass paintings hang over a Marcel Breuer chair. The low table is by Charles Eames; the bedside table is 19th-century English.
Above. The dining room screen and chandelier by David Hundley were inspired by traditional northern New Mexican designs. A late 1800s Navajo rug serves as a table covering.

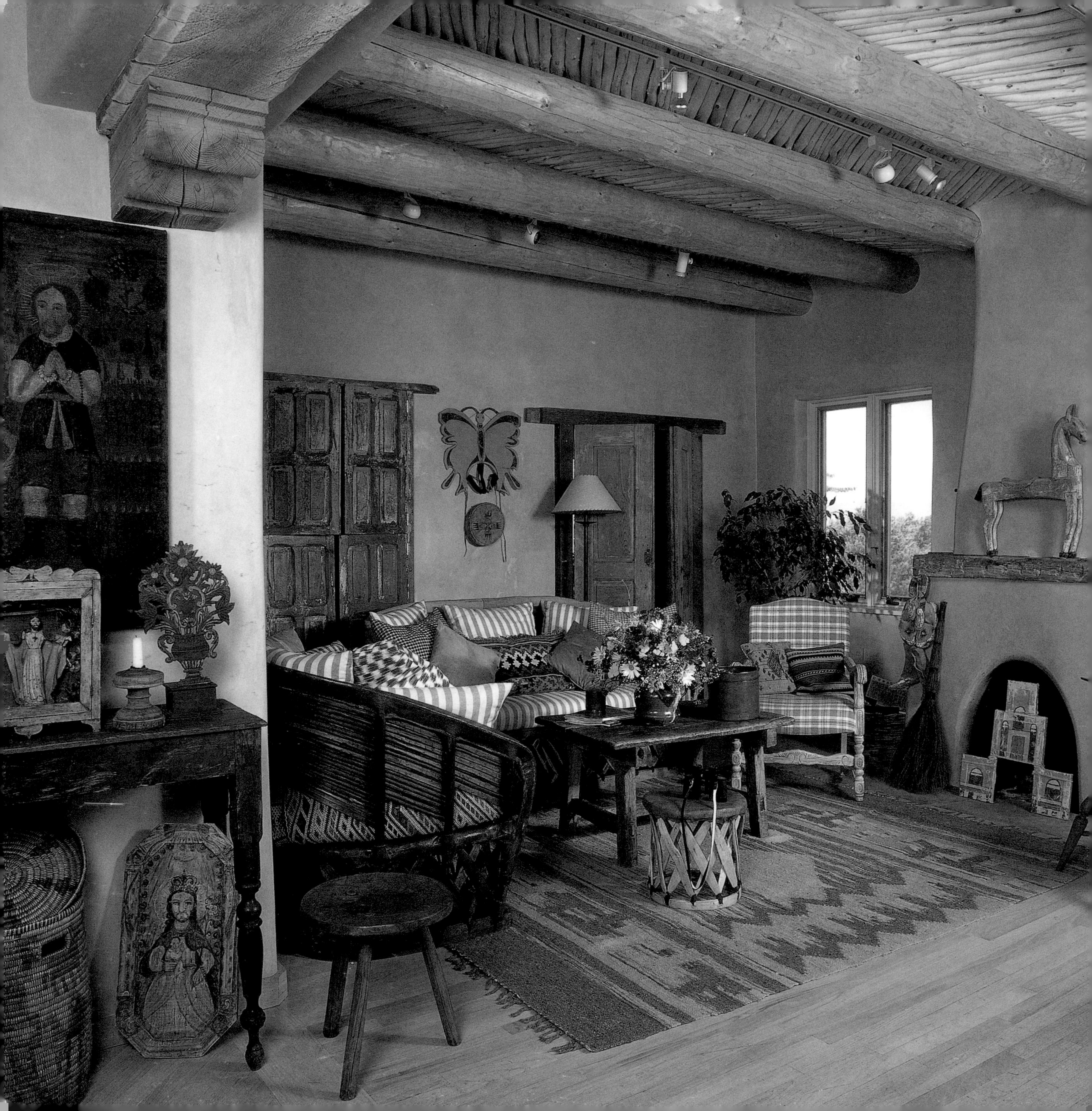

Flea Market Finds

One word describes Patty and Serge Gagaran: "pixilated." With twinkling eyes, wide-angle smiles, infectious laughs, and contagious senses of humor, the couple, both of whom are under five and a half feet tall, are on perpetual overdrive. Whether entertaining friends and family, skiing, playing tennis, or working in the garden, this husband-and-wife team does everything with remarkable flair.

Their folk art–filled Santa Fe house (they also live in Connecticut) reflects the couple's personalities. It is colorful. It is full of surprises. It is original. And "it has taken a lot of hard work," says Patty, who is the first Saturday-morning customer to work the stalls at the city's weekend flea market.

"It was never a question of money. Nothing in the house is expensive. Good taste has nothing to do with dollars and cents. Like every house I've decorated, it simply took a lot of leg work, discipline, and an eye. I went everywhere in and around Santa Fe to buy, piece by piece. I'd find something, bring it home, live with it for a while, then keep it, or return it. You know whether something is right or wrong. If it doesn't work, find something that does."

Opposite. In the sitting area off the kitchen, Patty Gagaran entertains before and after meals. The room's collection includes an early Mexican painting of San Ysidro; Hopi headdresses, *tablitas;* and a wooden horse from a Rajasthani children's carousel. *Above.* An antique New Mexican birdhouse, a Mexican cupboard, and a painting by late-19th-century St. Louis artist Henry Lewis go together in the living room.

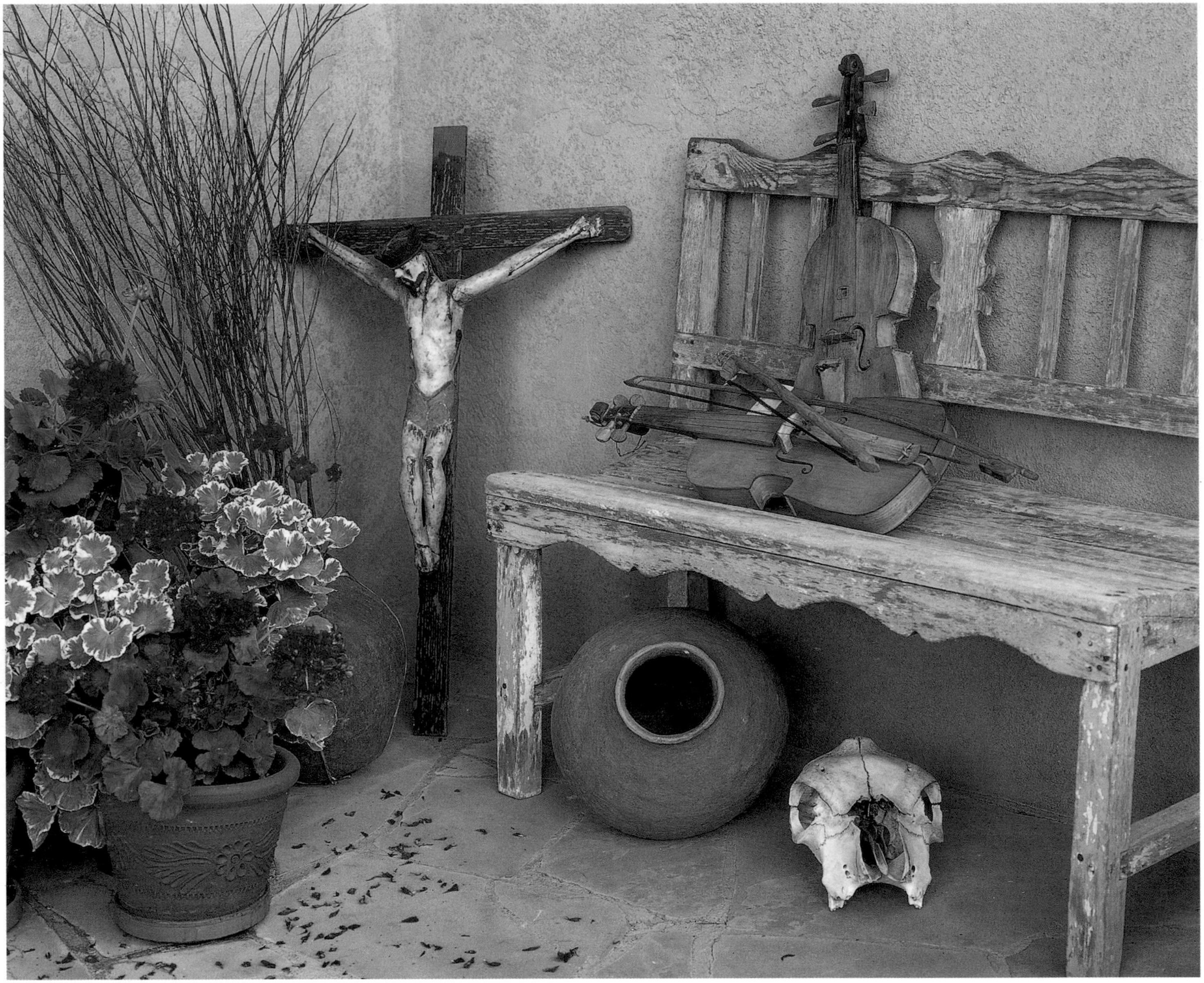

Above. In the garden, an old New Mexican crucifix rests beside a weathered bench. The vintage violins were used in fiestas. *Opposite, top.* "Serge added the gingerbread to the bottom of the front porch Territorial windows," Patty Gagaran says. *Opposite, bottom.* The guinea hens and duck on the dining room table came from Lake Victoria. The New Mexican angel "was carved by a Spaniard who worked for Native Americans."

A noted dealer who has shown often at the well-known Winter Antique Show on New York's Park Avenue, Patty deals primarily in American country, especially painted eighteenth- and nineteenth-century furniture. A source today for many collectors and museums (albeit great finds are harder and harder to find), she started out with no great expectations in the 1970s. With her historic Connecticut house spilling over with "things," she said "Oh, what the hell," and accepted a long-standing invitation from Russell Carrell to have a booth at his famous outdoor antique shows held throughout New England. Soon another friend, Martha Stewart, made an equally enticing offer. "Before Martha became famous as an author, she ran a successful catering business from her house in Westport, Connecticut. She couldn't use all the space she had, so she asked me if I would like to start an antique shop in her empty barn. I said yes. That was what really got me going as a dealer," Patty recalls. "Today, I take things from New Mexico back East to sell whenever I return."

How do two Connecticut Yankees (although Serge's family fled St. Petersburg, Russia) find their way to a second home in New Mexico? By way of a miracle, Patty insists. Growing up in St. Louis, spending summers as a child with her family in Santa Fe, she hadn't been back to the City Different in more than thirty years. Then, she returned unexpectedly one weekend after seeing a noted specialist in nearby Phoenix who said there was nothing he could do for a badly damaged eye. "When I was in Santa Fe, I went to the Santuario de Chimayo," a kind of Southwestern Lourdes. "Within days, my eye returned to normal," Patty relates with raised eyebrows and a slight smile. "I also received an answer to Serge's and my question: Where could we live in the winter after he retired as an engineer from Sikorsky? We wanted somewhere we could ski, play tennis, sit in the sun, and not vegetate intellectually and culturally. My inner voice said 'Santa Fe.' I'd come full circle."

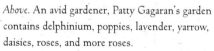

Above. An avid gardener, Patty Gagaran's garden contains delphinium, poppies, lavender, yarrow, daisies, roses, and more roses.

Right. A primitive painting of sheep was bought in Vermont. An Indonesian and a New Mexican drum stand beside a New Mexican chest in front of a Navajo rug. The Mexican santos would be dressed for festivals.

Opposite. In the master bedroom, a painting by Amos Ferguson bought in Nassau hangs over the bed built by Serge Gagaran out of tepee poles. The antique door is New Mexican. Rare Russian icons are from Serge's family.

Her desk drawer full of vintage Brownie Instamatic snapshots of her youth in Santa Fe—dirt roads; her horse, Pajamas, tied up to hitching posts on the plaza; houses made from real adobe—Patty admits she made an initial decorating mistake when she and Serge bought their house. "I sent a truckload of New England antiques out to New Mexico. And I sent it right back up Route 66 an hour after it arrived…with the same things inside," she admits with a chuckle. "Everything looked awful, so spindly and thin, so out of place. I realized that the Southwest calls for clunky Mexican, Spanish, New Mexican things, and also heavy Irish and Provençal furniture. I went right out and started to buy everything for the house locally. It took three years until the house was finished. Fortunately, I love the hunt. So, I enjoyed every minute of it."

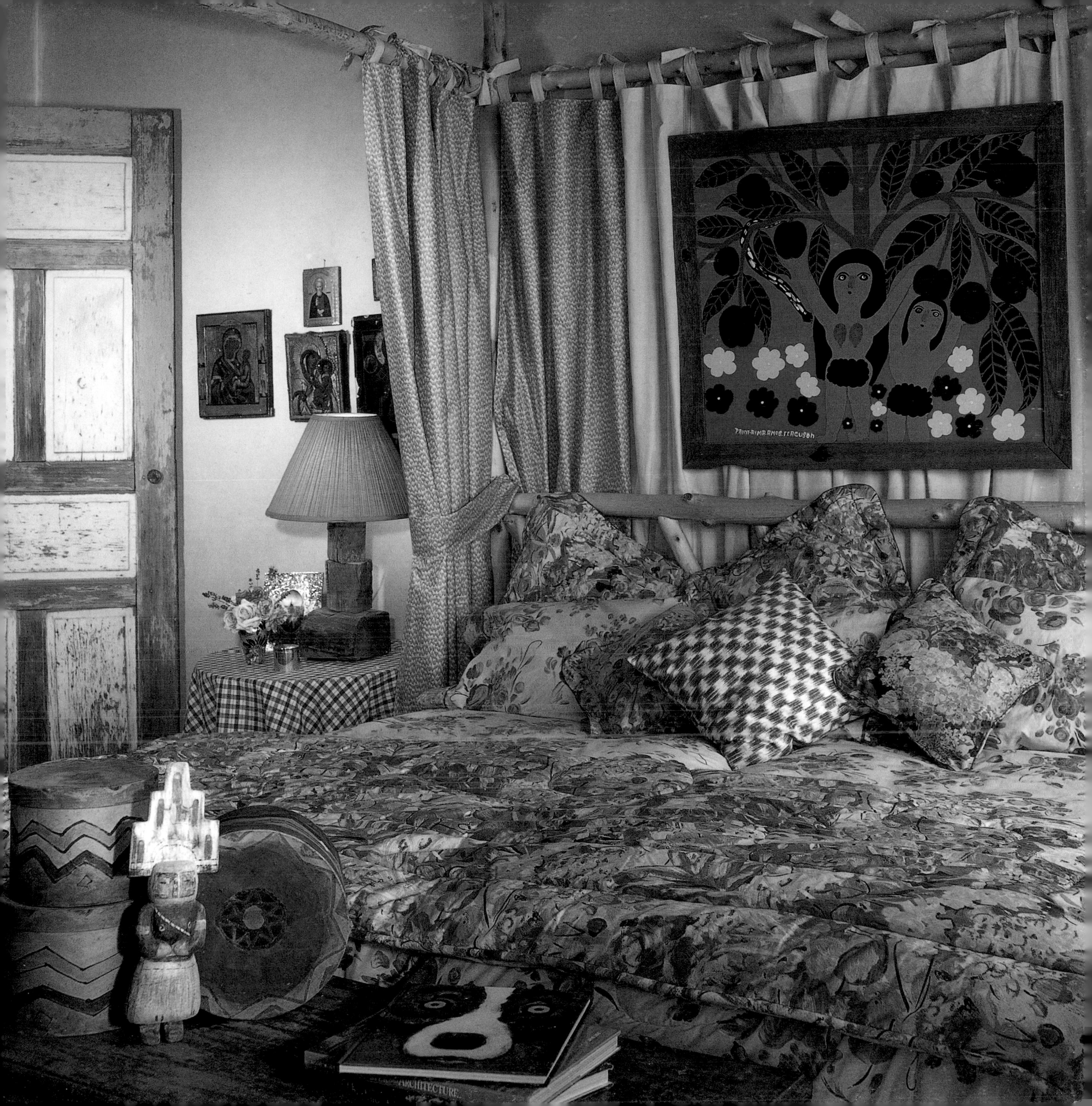
PAINT-BY MR. AMOS. FERGUSON
ARCHITECTURE

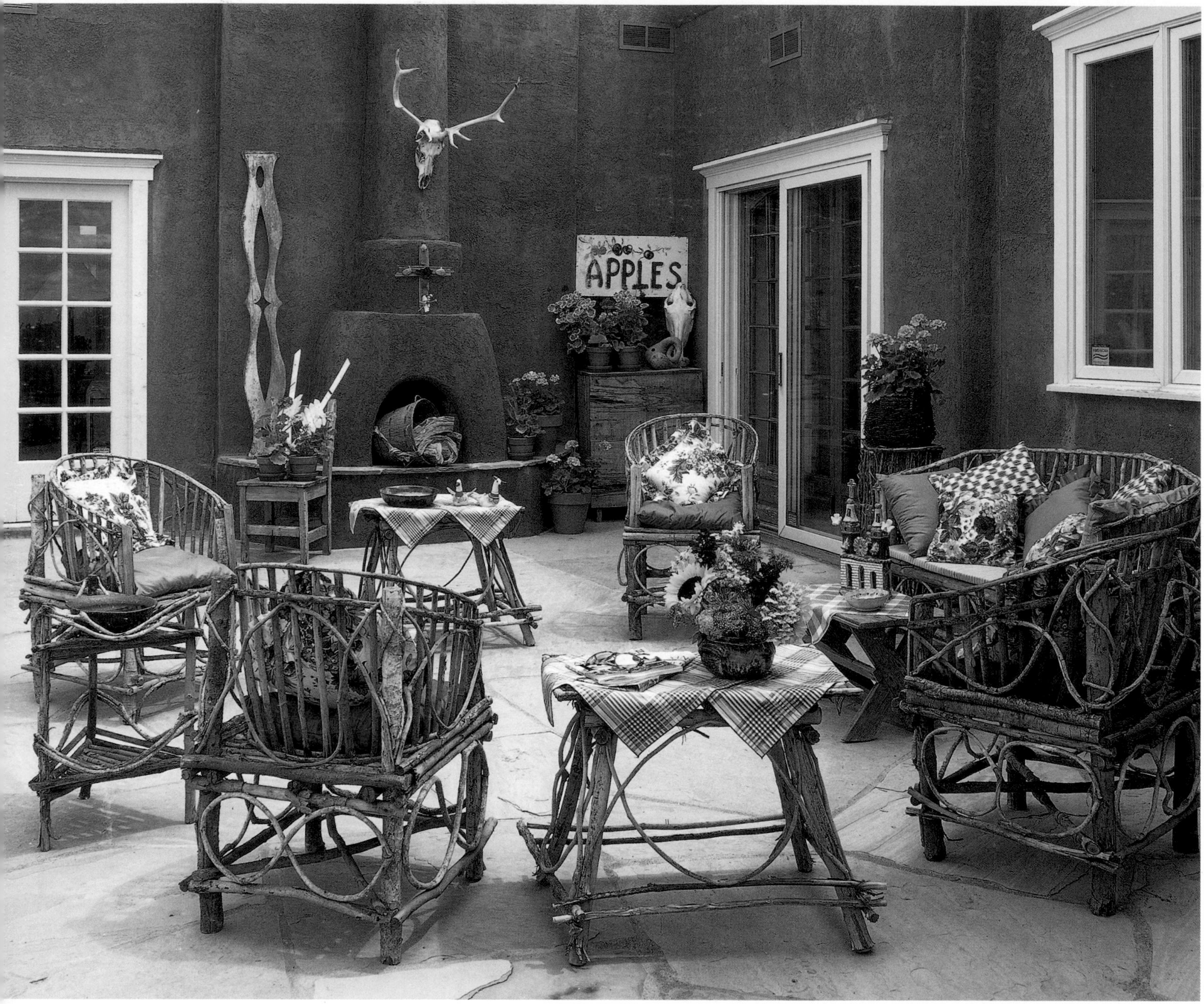
APPLES

Beginning with antique painted doors, mainly from Mexico, and kilim rugs from Turkey, Patty wanted the house to be colorful. "Not aggressive color," she says, but "definitely Southwestern colors." She needed the right background for her antique collection, which includes Native American and Tarahamara Indian painted drums, an apple orchard sign from the forties, rustic birdhouses, folk-art paintings, duck decoys, Indian woven baskets, eighteenth-century Hispanic santos, and—of course—Southwestern and New England painted furniture.

The Gagarans' outdoor terrace looks into the cloud-enshrouded Sangre de Cristo mountains through a forest of piñons and junipers. Bentwood furniture is made cozy and comfortable by massive chintz pillows. Flower beds, designed by popular Santa Fe landscape architect Tina Rousselot, explode in the summer with colorful snapdragons, hollyhocks, roses, delphiniums, and daisies.

And over it all, high up on a stake, spins a Saul Steinberg cut-out tin cat, straight from the pages of the *New Yorker* magazine. A safe distance below, a canary teasingly rotates in the wind. The cat that wants to eat the canary? Undoubtedly, and the future possibility keeps viewers entertained. The humor also reminds guests of their host and hostess's own remarkable decorative whimsy. With little expenditure and a great deal of savvy, the Gagarans have created a Santa Fe house with a lot of wit and a great deal of very personal style.

Opposite. On the patio, the twig furniture is from the Philippines; the 1940s "apple" sign from an orchard in Tesuque.
Above. New Mexican *retablos* line the wall behind an antique New Mexican painted table. The baskets are Tarahamara.

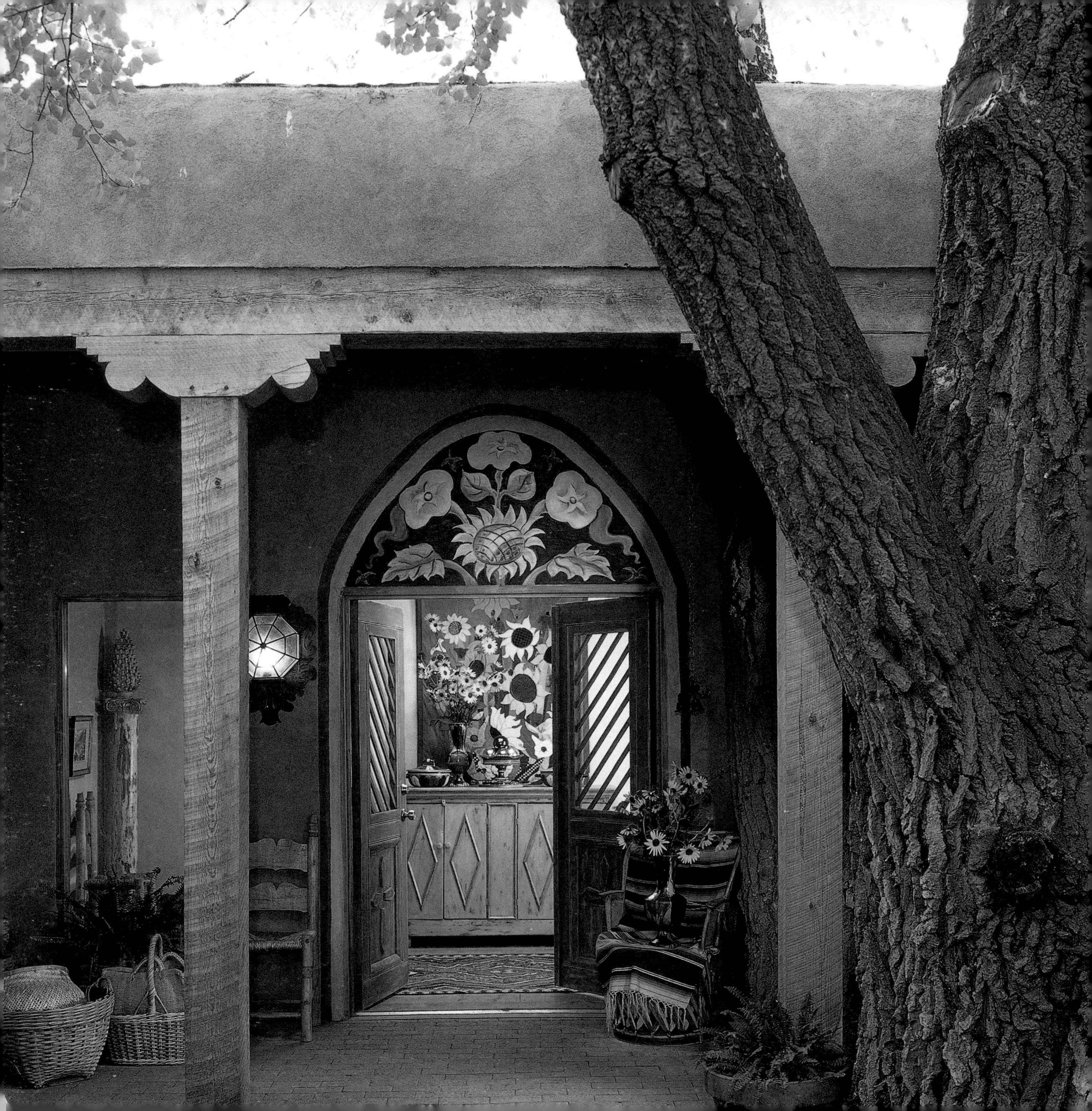

A Place in the Shade

You drive by Sandra and Max Hulse's house in Taos several times before you find it. A grove of ancient, hundred-foot-tall silver-leaf poplars hides the couple's hideaway. At a seven-thousand-foot altitude, it faces the majestic Sangre de Cristo mountains. Residents of San Angelo, Texas, the Hulses, like many northern New Mexican second-home owners, come to Taos to beat the heat in summer and to ski in winter.

"I first knew Taos in the 1930s. I came in July and August as a child. Lots of Texans did. I remember when Taos was a simple farm community. My idea of heaven was to ride the hay wagons," Sandra recalls, speaking in a soft Texan drawl. "When you'd go down to the plaza, Indians from the pueblo would be there wearing their turquoise and silver jewelry. In summer, they'd be dressed almost entirely in white. It was magical back then."

While Taos has certainly changed, the Hulses' house continues to maintain an otherworldly quality. An oasis of greenery in an otherwise desolate plain of scrub vegetation, it sits atop a vast water table. Green lawns surround the house, which is totally shaded by those fabulous trees.

Founders of a company that made appliquéd wall hangings for both residential and commercial decoration, Sandra and her husband returned to New Mexico initially by way of Santa Fe. Owners of several houses there, they moved farther north to

Opposite. The front door of Sandra and Max Hulse's Taos house was copied from a church in nearby Arroyo Seco. An artist, Sandra created the over painting and designed the wall hanging in the front hall. *Above.* For parties, candles are lit in front of St. Francis, carved in Mexico.

109

Left. In the kitchen, a display of Mexican drip pottery from the 1920s and '30s is from Oaxaca. "I bought it all in Texas. I've never found any in Mexico," Sandra says.

Above. A Mexican cupboard is lined with colorful Mexican pottery, including a baking dish in the shape of a chicken.

Opposite. The dining room wall is covered with Mexican *batas*, hand-painted trays sold to tourists. "Put a lot of them together and they look wonderful," Sandra says. "One or two look tacky." Mexican serapes cover the tables. The glass balls are from Mexican fishing nets.

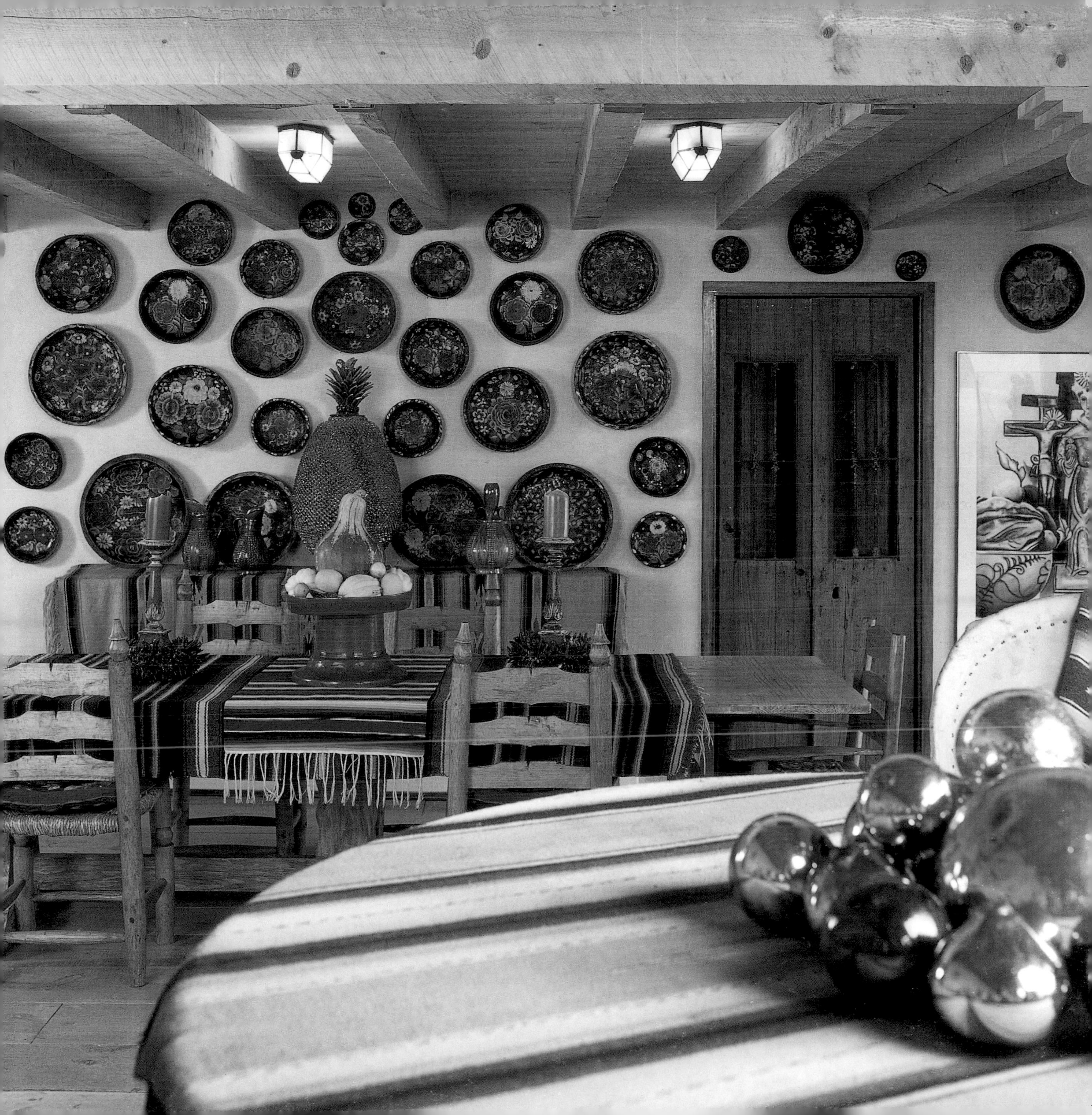

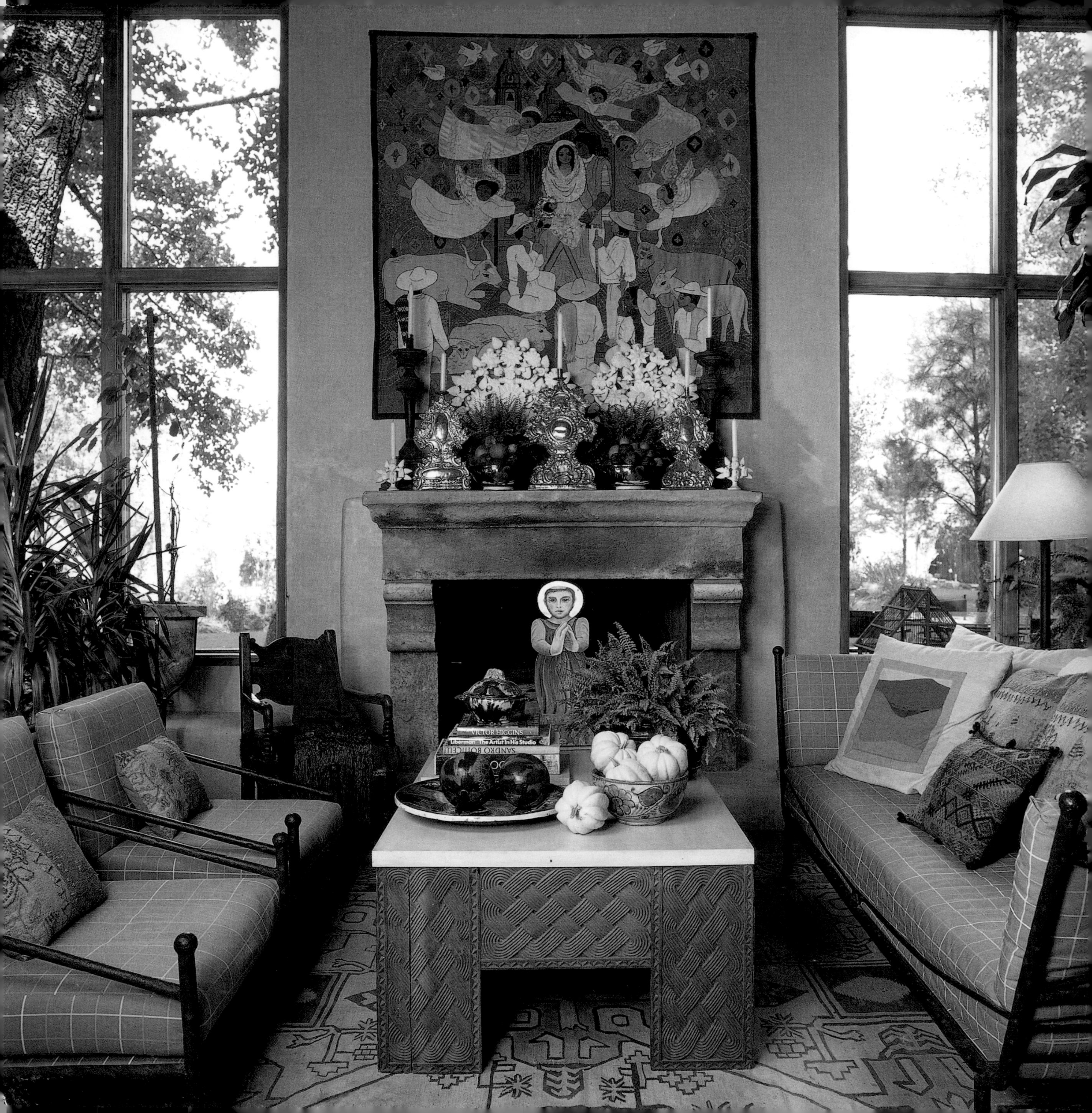
VICTOR HIGGINS
Liberman The Artist In His Studio
SANDRO BOTTICELLI

Taos when they realized they were seeing "the same friends in New Mexico we saw in Texas. Also, we wanted a quieter, less-discovered place than Santa Fe," Sandra says.

Searching Taos for a house, "we kept going by this property that had been for sale for two years. Finally, I got curious and stopped. It was a bunch of old farm buildings, including a beauty shop. It was completely unlivable as a private house," says Sandra, who figured out the solution—without an architect. Raising roofs, building connecting passageways, and making a side entrance, she turned an ugly duckling into a swan. A complex of different-sized building blocks covered with a rich pink adobe and trimmed in apple green, the Hulses' house became streamlined and modern.

The words that Sandra, who has become a painter, uses most often to describe her six-months-a-year nesting place are: "grandeur with warmth," "unintimidating," and "harmonious." A thoughtful blend of eighteenth- and nineteenth-century "around the world" antiques and a museum-quality collection of colorful, vintage Mexican pottery of the twenties, thirties, and forties makes the description accurate. Even in the house's twenty-by-twenty-five-foot living room, with its towering forty-foot-high ceiling, visitors enjoy an intimacy that a room this size normally wouldn't allow.

"A house should be a shelter, a place where one can leave the outside world and retreat inside for warmth and security," Sandra says. "I really didn't want anything to be astounding about this house. The nicest thing anyone can say after they leave is, 'It was nice. But I can't remember why.'"

Opposite. A French 18th-century mantle in the living room is decorated with Mexican, Filipino, and Spanish candelabra and candlesticks. The coffee table is Filipino. The wrought iron furniture was designed by Bruce Eicher, Los Angeles. The wall hanging and St. Francis are by Sandra Hulse.
Above. In the entrance hall, a cross by Elizabeth Steving hangs beside a 19th-century Mexican column and ceramic pineapple.

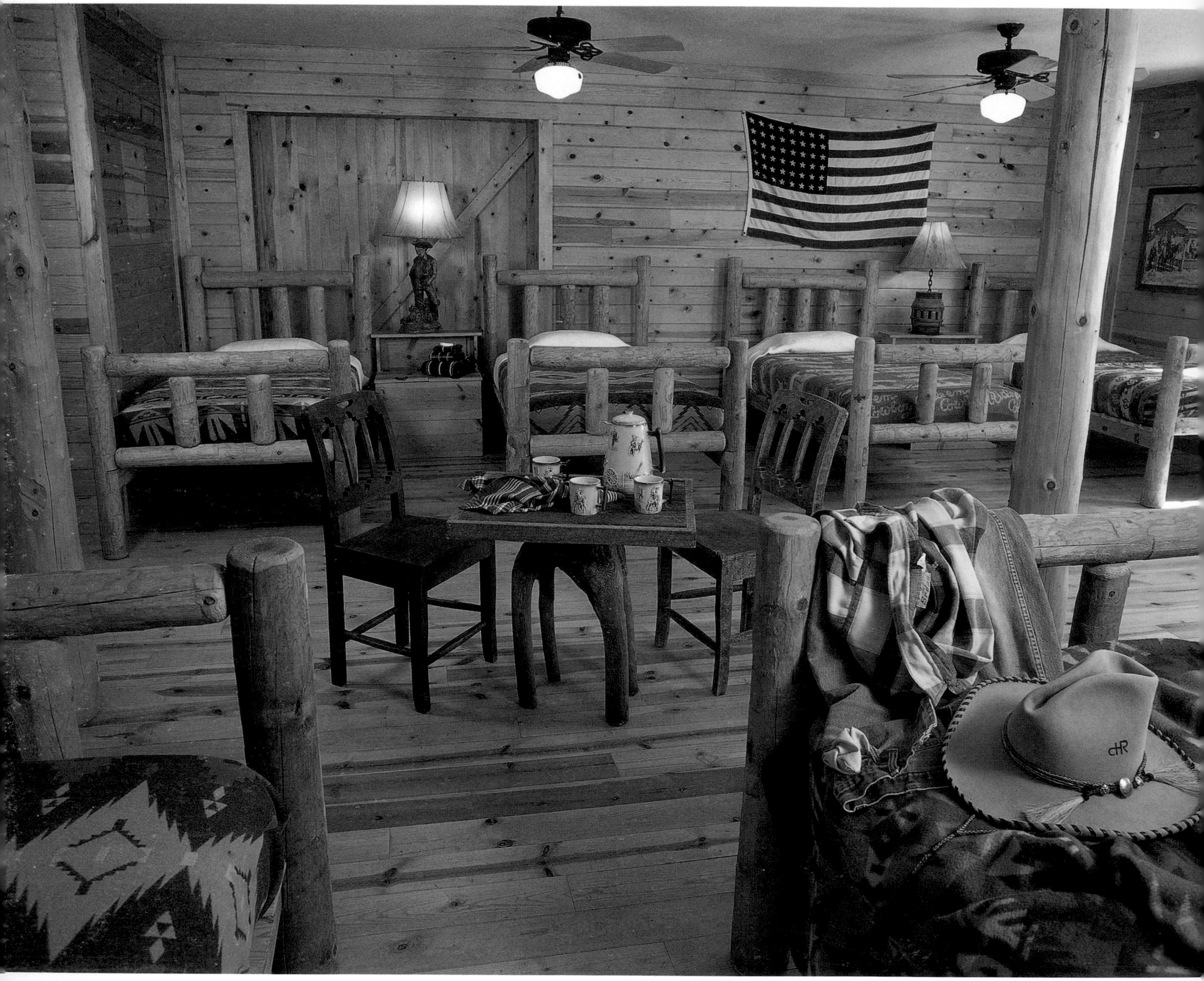

Dead Horse Ranch

The name of the 6,300-acre spread between Santa Fe and Las Vegas, New Mexico, is Dead Horse Ranch. Judging from the amount of energy that is generated on the property, Live Wire might be a more accurate description.

Owned by Houston financier Pete Coneway and his wife Lynn Coneway, the historic working ranch is a mecca for equestrians. Arriving from throughout the country and abroad, horse lovers book far ahead to enroll in one of the ranch's highly praised horsemanship clinics. A few bring their own mount; most sit in the saddle on one of the ranch's thirty-five quarter horses.

"We run the clinics. But Richard Cozad, who's been training and showing horses all his life, instructs the people who come to the clinics. There are three four-day clinics a year, and each is limited to ten people," says Lynn Coneway. A participant in every clinic, she is almost always in residence at Dead Horse, while Pete flies in on weekends. Her no-nonsense, down-to-earth business savvy has been invaluable in speeding up the ranch's four-star reputation as a training center.

"We started the clinics two years ago, in 1993, and we've filled every one," she says proudly, adding that participants are fed and housed while they are at Dead Horse. Some bed down in a bunk house, others in one of the guest houses.

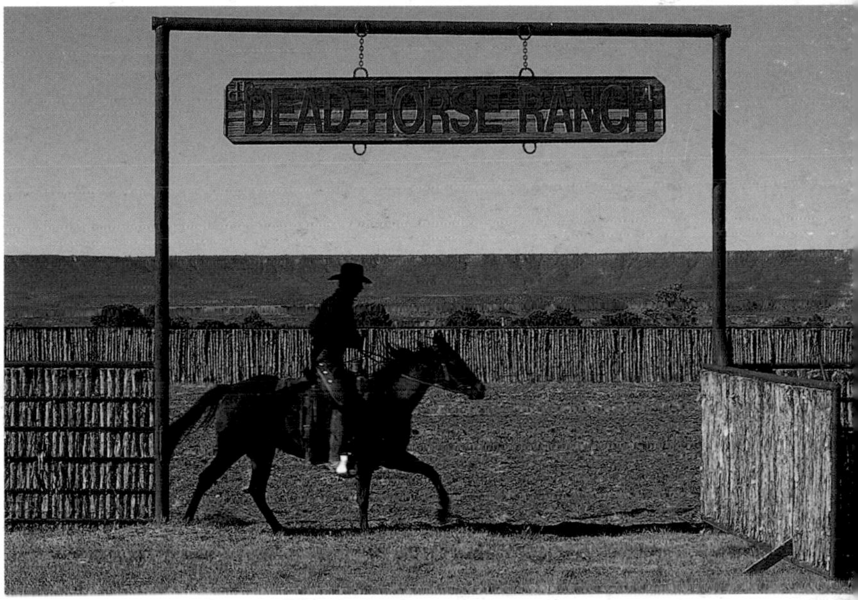
DEAD HORSE RANCH

Opposite. The bunkhouse above the barn at Dead Horse Ranch is often full with houseguests, wranglers, and participants in the ranch's equestrian clinics. Covered with Beacon blankets, the beds are made from hickory logs.

Above. Astride a quarter horse, trainer Richard Cozad welcomes guests to the 6,300-acre spread.

Top. In back of a high adobe wall, the ranch house is surrounded by an enormous lawn and towering cottonwood trees. *Bottom.* Painted on the outside by Bonnie Beebo, a tepee serves as an extra guest room.
Opposite. A Queen Ann dining room table and chairs are combined with a 1940s Navajo rug, an 1890s Truchas, New Mexico cupboard, *trastero,* and an old cross.

Walking from the ranch's barn with its long rows of horse stalls, Lynn crosses a thick green lawn scattered with a half dozen vintage, iron-wheeled Atchinson Topeka & Santa Fe luggage carts. Nearby, a colorfully decorated contemporary Indian tepee is shaded by a grove of towering cottonwoods and Russian olive trees. In the distance, past vast pasture land and low-lying hills, the horizon line is broken by towering mesas and plateaus.

Passing through a gate in a high adobe wall, Lynn enters the ranch-house compound. A low, one-story, double adobe building, Dead Horse's main house is deceptively undramatic on the outside. History reveals that what went on inside during the twenties is otherwise. One of New Mexico's most compelling unsolved murders took place here.

Falling in love with the ranch, New York socialite Emily Vanderbilt bought it, moved to the Southwest, and restored the main house (much of which remains architecturally as she left it). Vanderbilt also fell in love with Ramos Whitfield, a local, and married him. With a polo field and a guest list of New York's 400, Dead Horse was anything but backwater. It all came to a banner-headline ending, however. Emily was shot to death in bed. Ramos lived wealthily ever after.

"I've never found any photographs of the house when Vanderbilt lived here. But I envision it to be very much like the way our decorator, Susan Dupepe in Santa Fe, furnished it today," Lynn remarks. A walk through the rooms reveals that Dupepe astutely chose to combine today's popular ranch style with Native American handicrafts and English antiques, the latter coming from the Coneways' other homes.

"Lynn and I talked every day about pieces I'd found I wanted her and Pete to have in their house," says Dupepe, who bids frequently in person for her many clients at Western furniture auctions in Wyoming, Colorado, Montana, and Texas. "They wanted the house to be relaxed and fun, a place where you can put your feet up and mud won't hurt."

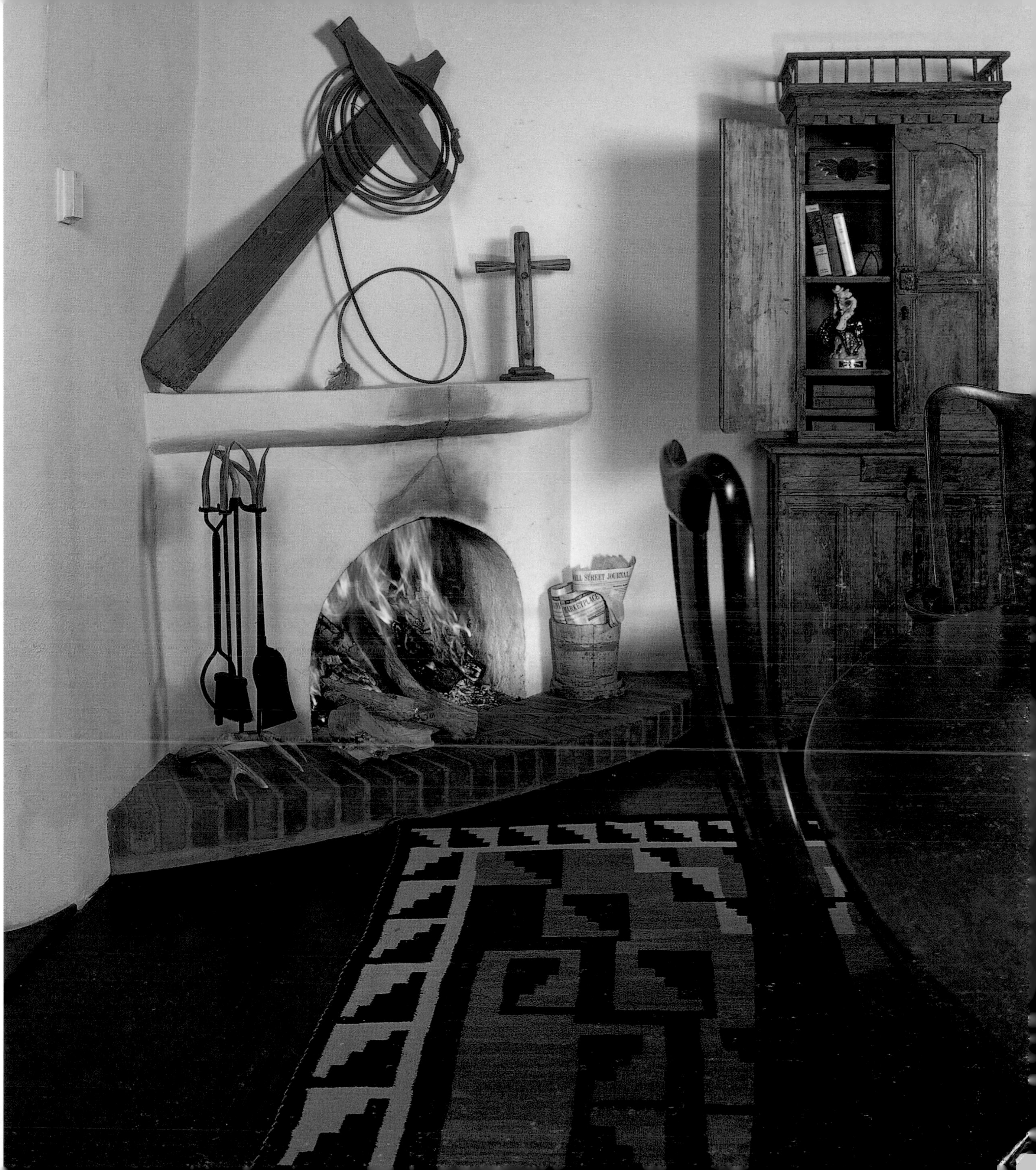
STREET JOURNAL
MARKETPLACE

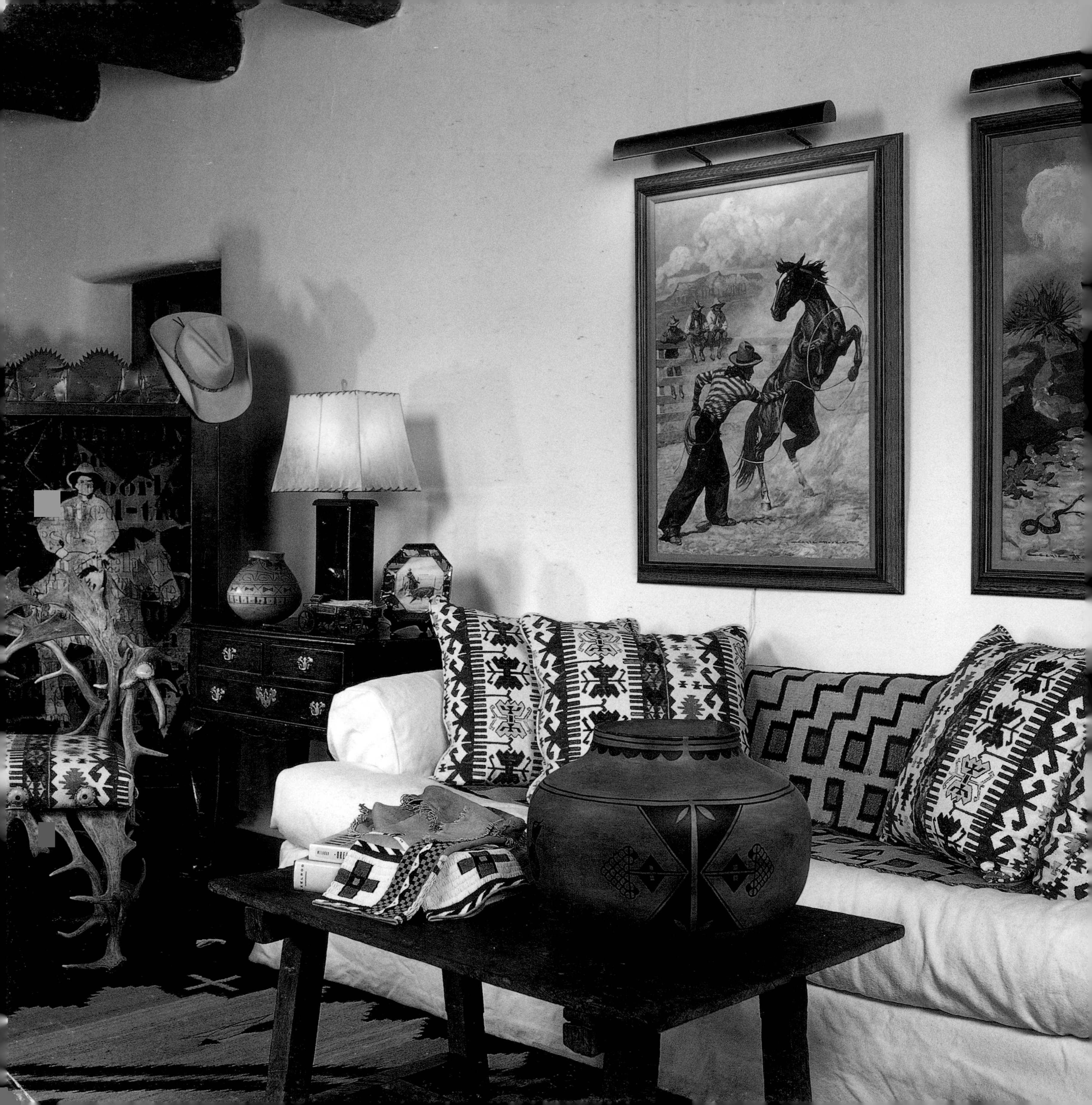

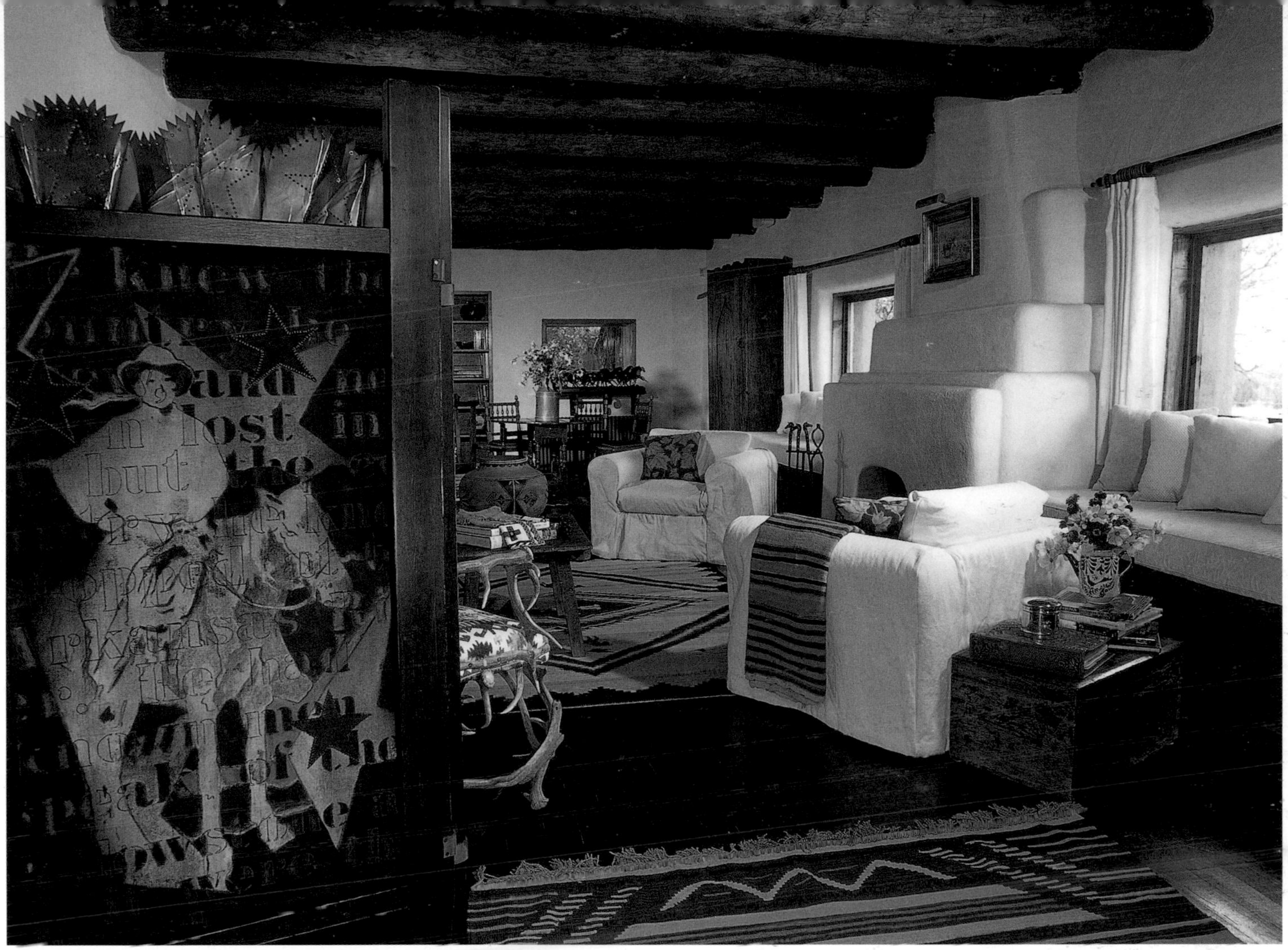

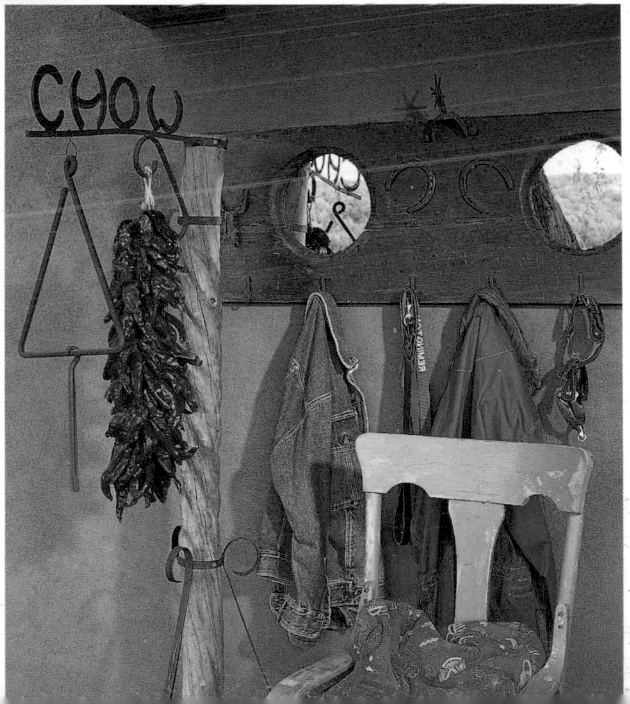
CHOW

Opposite. Magazine illustrations from the 1940s hang over a sofa in the living room of Dead Horse Ranch. An enormous Zia pot sits on an old New Mexican table beside a turn-of-the-century English horn chair. *Above.* "All the furniture is covered with white cotton material in order not to take away from the house's remarkable rugs, pottery, and art," says decorator Susan Dupepe. The screen by Venita Smithey from Houston is made from old newspaper illustrations. The rugs are Navajo. The beams are original. *Left.* At chow time, ranch owners Lynn and Pete Coneway and their friends hang up their coats in the hall and settle down for some serious eating.

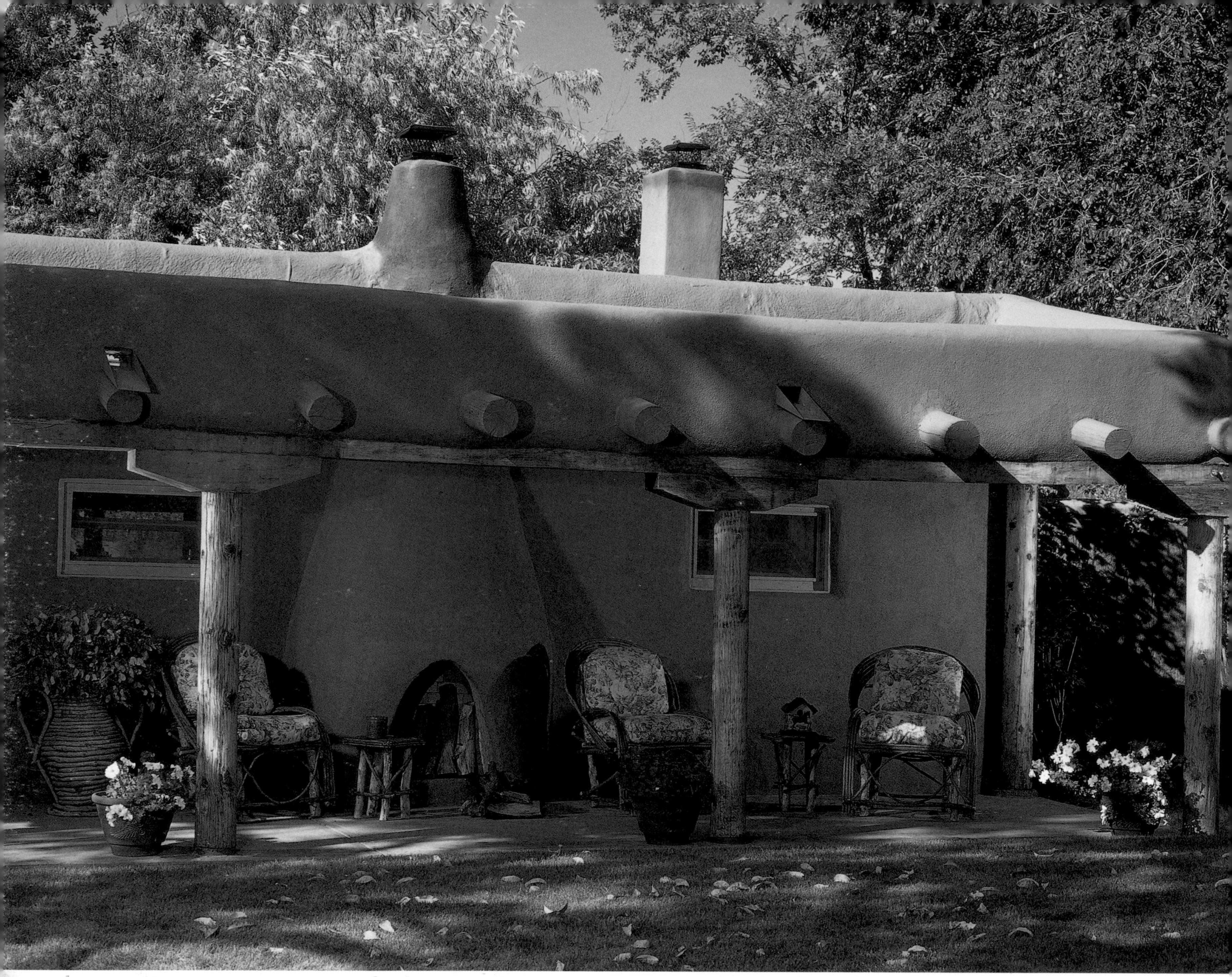

Above. After riding all day, the Coneways and their guests relax on the portal. The furniture is apple twig; the cushions are covered with printed English linen.
Opposite, top. A Jim Beam bull whiskey decanter joins a pair of antique spurs on the mantle. "The cowboy plate was made in Montana in the '40s for coffee shops," says interior designer Susan Dupepe.
Opposite, right. Made in Idaho, two studded leather chairs after Molesworth are for relaxing on the portal. On the table, a rare, highly collectible Skookum doll was made in the '40s by Pendleton to sell the company's blankets in trading posts.

Covering the house's dark-stained wooden floors with antique Navajo rugs, Dupepe complemented the couple's country English antiques with country New Mexican pieces: painted cupboards, armoires, and old tables. Western art, all bought by Pete, who has collected for many years, hangs on most of the house's chalk-white walls. Museum-quality bronze statues of horses and cattle give a further working-ranch feeling to Dead Horse. So do antique bits and bridles, which hang down from wall sconces, while handmade, commissioned tin chandeliers, with Southwestern design motifs, hang from vigas in the ceilings.

"We have a lot of people who return regularly for our clinics," Lynn reports, returning the conversation to horses, her favorite subject. "They appreciate what they learn. And they like being able to stay at Dead Horse."

As the sun sets behind the Sangre de Cristo mountains and the aroma of homemade tamales wafts out of the kitchen, it isn't hard to understand why.

■

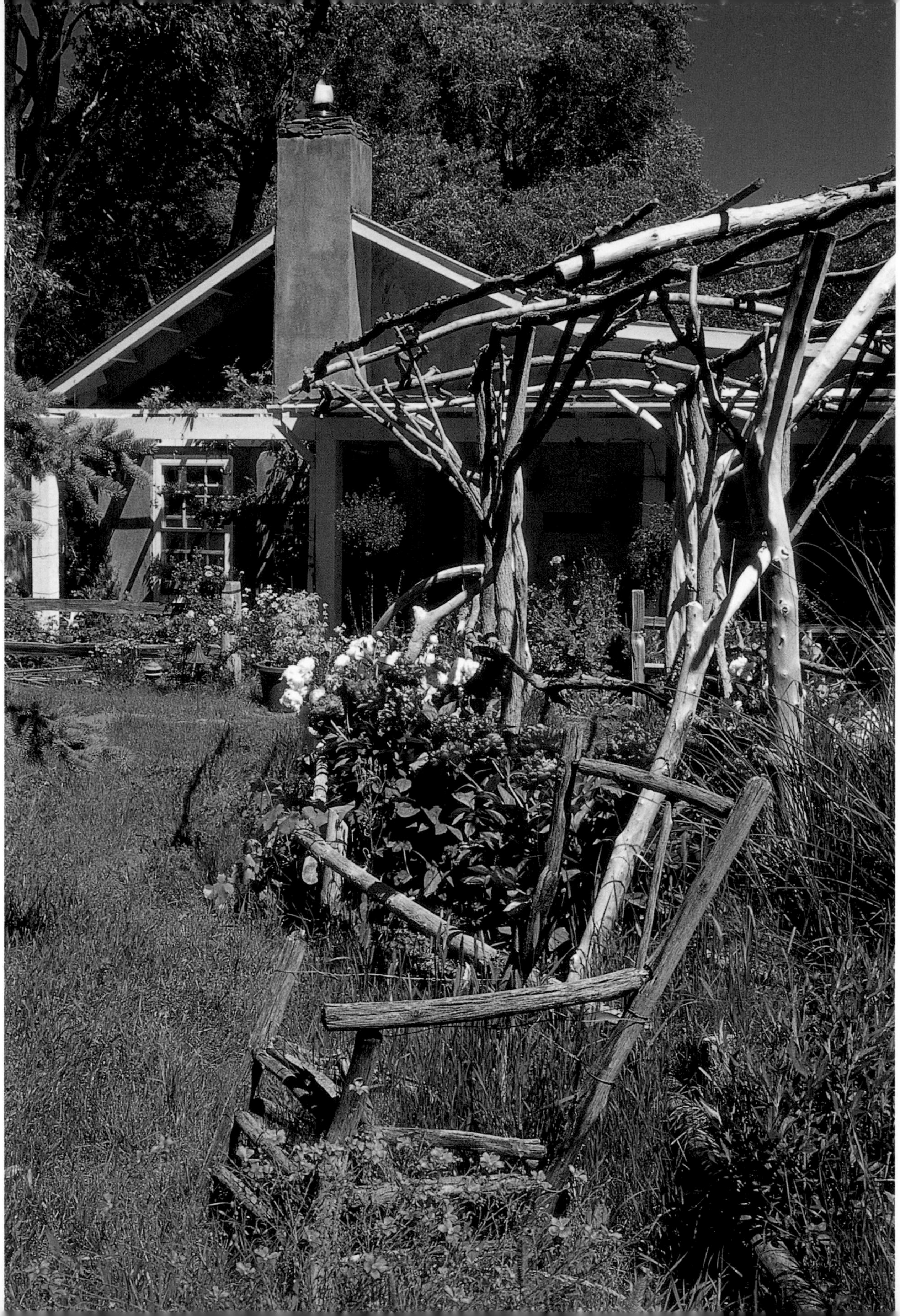

A Bit of Old England

Thank God, they didn't get Inky, Pinky, and Parley-Vous," exclaims Suzanne Crayson with relief. The night before, raccoons had banqueted on carp in a pond belonging to this enchanting Englishwoman. Her Cotswoldian oasis outside Santa Fe would make Anne Hathaway feel at home in the garden and delight Beatrix Potter with the wildlife. "Marilyn Monroe also managed to hide in the rushes," Suzanne continues, still concerned. "She has a pink heart over her right bosom and ruby-red lips. She's very seductive, but, thank heavens, she's also very smart. Still, I've got to do something to keep my fish alive. Last year, it was a bear who feasted on the honey in my hives. He comes back in the fall for the pears. Now, it's those bloody raccoons. Oh, well, what can you expect? After all, I live in the country, five minutes from the plaza."

Giving directions to her gardeners and a professional "pond man" who had come from Albuquerque to deal with the problem, Susan was in total command at Tesuque Meadow. She had learned her management skills as a "girl Friday" to the stars in Los Angeles. "I grew up in London, also in Surrey, where I positively fell in love with nature. My sister and I used to take long rambles. Then I married and moved to California thirty years ago. Show biz seemed the natural thing to go into. Being English, I was in demand as a kind of secretary-nanny to the stars."

Opposite. Hidden from view in the Tesuque valley, Susan Crayson's "cottage" is surrounded by gardens reminiscent of her native England.
Above. Papyrus and native New Mexican grasses grow beside a pond of recycled water.

Making sure her visitor has a glass of minted iced tea and a piece of cherry pie, Susan, dressed entirely in white, stretches out on a sofa, surrounded by two dogs and four cats, in her antique-filled living room. Her Mayfair accent in keeping with the English-style flower beds outside her French doors, she recalls the time she first demonstrated a green thumb. "I had an apartment in Hollywood and I loaded the terrace down with hanging baskets, dozens and dozens of them. They turned out to be a traffic hazard. Drivers would get distracted by the flowers and very often come close to having an accident."

Interested in knowing more about the World College in Las Vegas, New Mexico, Susan began to come to the state in 1982. Staying one night in the La Fonda Hotel in downtown Santa Fe, she learned there was a concert across the plaza in the auditorium of the Museum of Fine Arts. "I thought, this is for me. A small town with great music. I was ready for the move and packed up my things and moved here." A music graduate of the Royal Academy in London, Susan loves the fact that Santa Fe is a kind of Salzburg of the Southwest. She was recently chairman of the board of the Symphony Orchestra. She also delights in the notion that "almost anything that grows in England can be made to grow here, with a good deal of watering, soil enrichment, and talking to. I go around my garden regularly talking to the flowers and the trees. I tell them, 'I see you. I see you.' Just like people, everything in a garden wants to be recognized as being worthwhile. I know that everything in my garden is happy. I can feel the energy."

Living at first in Santa Fe, Susan craved the country. Buying two acres of thickly vegetated land along the Little Tesuque river in the nearby hamlet of the same name, she set to. Like a homesteader, she had to clear the land. Then she commissioned designer Betty Stewart to build an adobe farmhouse, compact and unpretentious like a Provençal *mas*. The wraparound portal, however, is a decidedly New Mexican embellishment. Later, she erected a stone guest house.

Opposite. "Susan planted bulbs right up to the first frost. She never stopped," says gardener Barbara Massey. "Any that were leftover went into wooden tubs."
Above. Strolling along paths covered with arbors, garden lovers walk through fields of columbine, poppies, irises, and peonies each spring.

"The garden is my real love," Susan confides to the numerous visitors who come to pay homage. "The truth is, I didn't know what I was doing at first. I'd sit down with a catalog and order anything. It's a sort of by-guess-and-by-God garden. Some things made it, others didn't. Today, after thirteen years, I've learned there are three main qualities to being a gardener. They are patience, caring, and wonder." She adds a further bit of instruction. "You have to be really brutal in a garden. You cannot let plants and flowers grow where they want. Like children, they need instruction."

With nary a sign of this severe discipline, flower beds both around the house and throughout the acreage strut their colors from May until the first frost, normally in early October. Against a backdrop of solid green, the spring chorus line includes tulips, lilacs, lupines, daffodils, and bleeding-hearts.

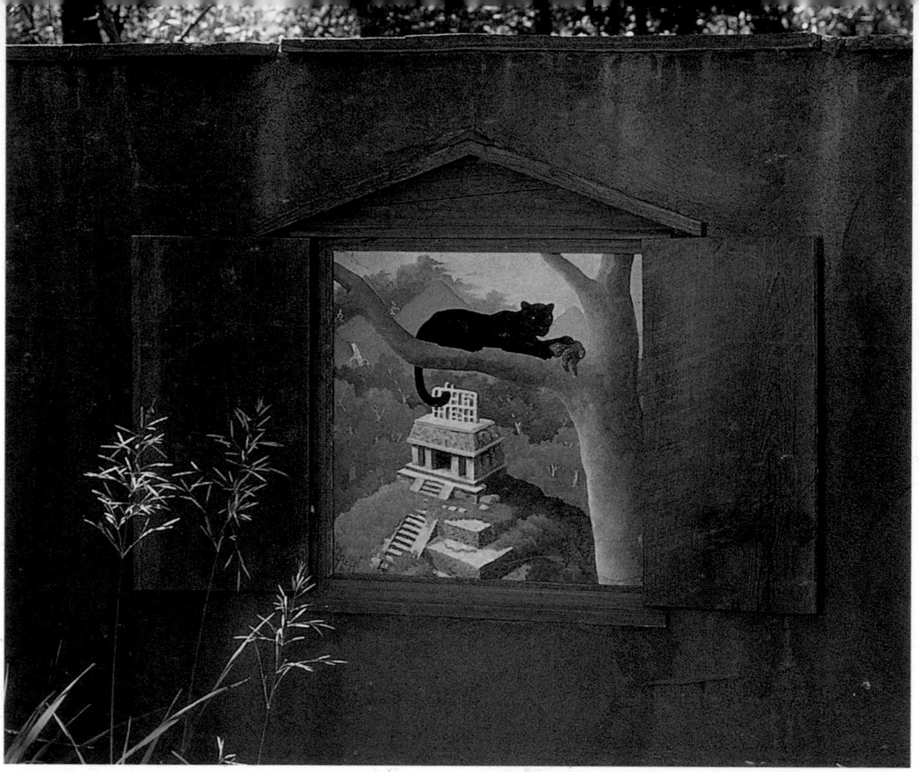

Above and right. "Sacred places" in the garden wall were painted by Walter Green to depict Crayson's favorite places in the world, including Tibet, the Caribbean, and Stonehenge. Covered by shutters in winter, they open to the world each spring.
Opposite. Oriental poppies nod their heads beneath a grove of aspen trees.

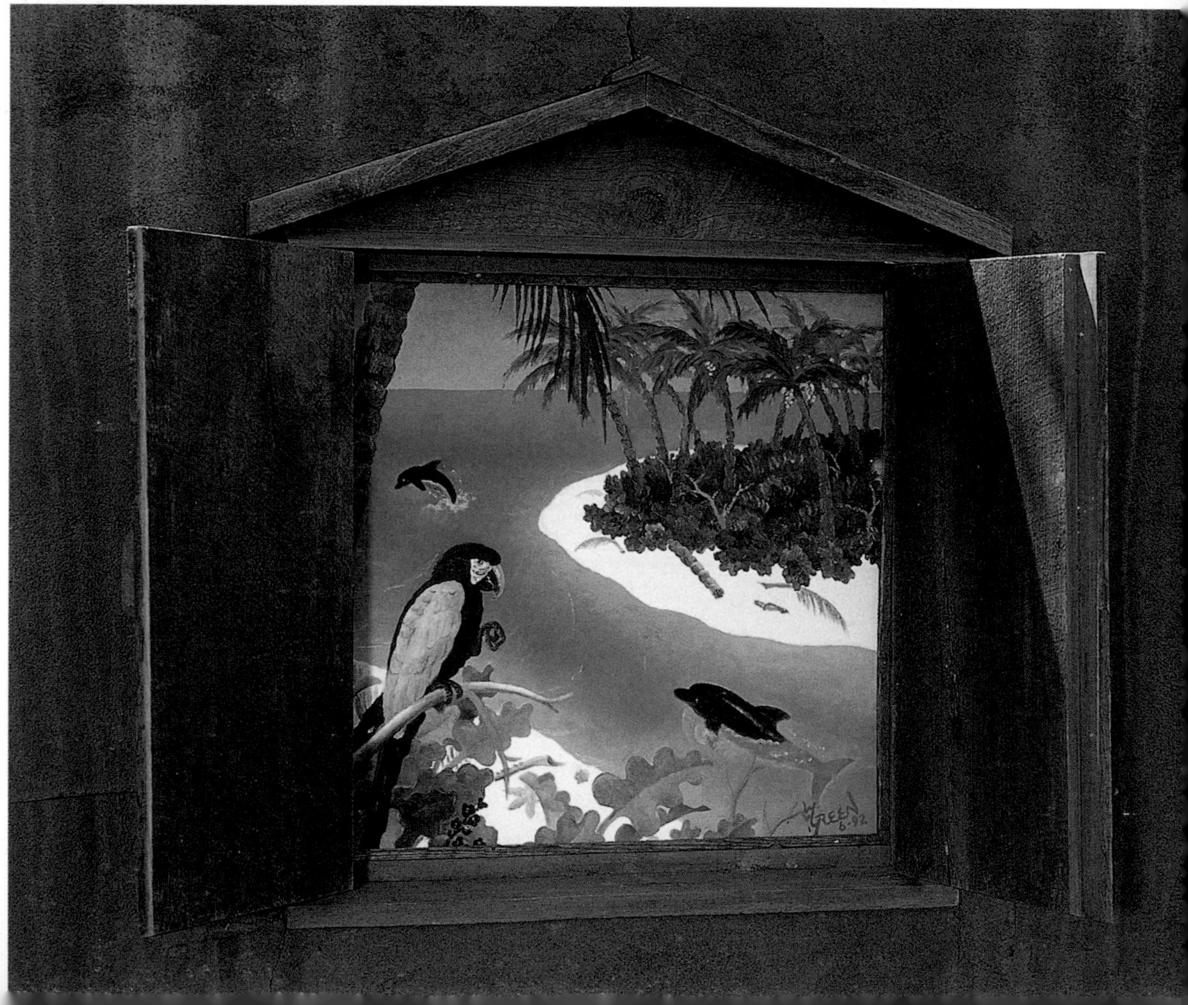

Later, Oriental poppies, iris, peonies, penstemon, delphiniums, and sweet peas bloom. Summer is "like the tropics," Susan says excitedly. "Things grow as if they've had their corsets taken off." Roses, lavender, and blue-mist spiraea, golden rod, day and Oriental lilies, and sunflowers vie for their place in the sun.

Moving out of the cool, half-lit living room into the heat of the garden, Susan has one more accomplishment she wants to share. Leading the way to an area where hedges of berries and currants provide the ingredients for "summer puds," she recalls an occurrence involving her feathered friends. "One day, I came out here and can you believe, I found a mother robin actually teaching her young how to eat my red currents. Bloody cheeky, I thought, after all I've done for them."

Continuing down her garden paths with their numerous "ins and outs"—areas for relaxing and contemplation—Susan acknowledges she is fortunate to have so many trees: mostly cottonwoods, mountain ash, and silver birch. Numerous man-made elements add further to the many delights of Tesuque Meadow. They include a Bentwood arbor, a gazebo, a bridge, stone terraces, wooden fences, delightfully weathered old chairs, benches, and tables, and birdhouses galore.

"Drones, that's what I need more of," says Susan, concluding her garden tour. "I have six beehives and plenty of queens—but it's the drones, the workers, I lack." A moment later, inside, she is on the phone, "Hello, this is Crayson here. Have you got any drones?"

A gardener's work is never done!

———■———

POSTSCRIPT

This was the last interview Suzanne Crayson gave. She died unexpectedly in August 1995. These pages are a memorial to her great love for nature and all animals, especially her dog Joey.

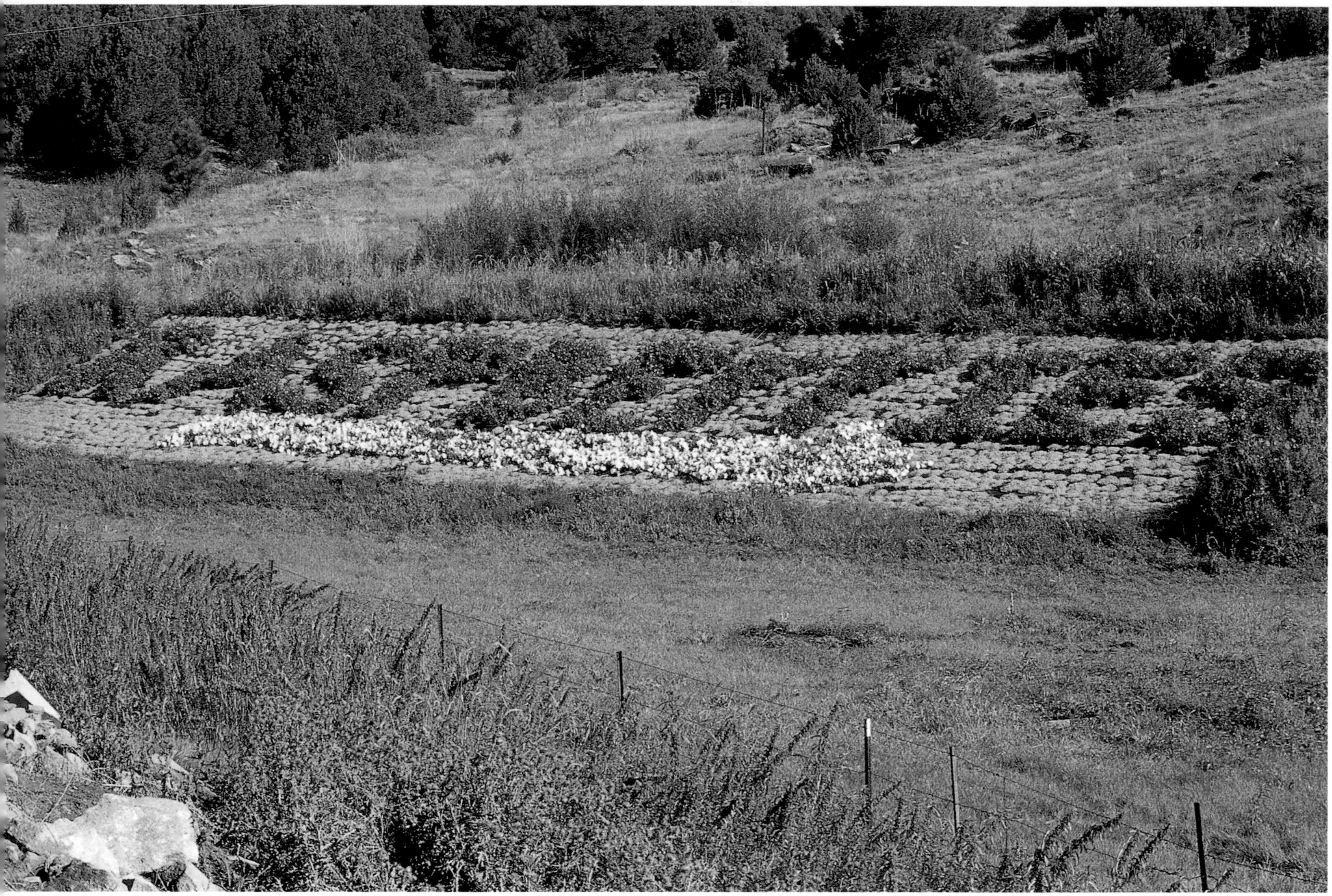

Mmm, Mmm, Good

Along the road at the Salman Ranch near Mora, New Mexico, red petunias spell out the word "raspberries" in enormous letters. The sight is sufficiently startling to make pilots of small planes bank and circle to get a better look. Motorists slam on their brakes, get out of their cars, and pinch themselves to see if it's a mirage. It seems too delicious, too sweet, too good to be true that raspberries can grow in the rugged, dry countryside between Santa Fe and Taos.

"It's no joke. We grow some of the best raspberries you've ever eaten," says Jeff Salman, third-generation owner of the ranch. "Warm days, cool nights, and drip irrigation: the combination keeps the flavor concentrated. The berries don't bloat with water as they do in rainy climates." In the late summer and early autumn, hungry berry lovers line up at the ranch store to purchase flats of the desirable fruit, which is also made into jam, vinegar, and syrup. As a bonus, they are able to enjoy a stroll through one of the most unusual flower gardens in New Mexico.

Within the tumbled-down, roofless walls of an old adobe house on the ranch, the Salmans, who also own a large nursery in Santa Fe, have laid out riotous flower beds that testify to what can be grown in northern New Mexico. The ruined building, along with the nearby restored San Rafael Mission Church and grist mill, is part of the La Cueva National Historic Site.

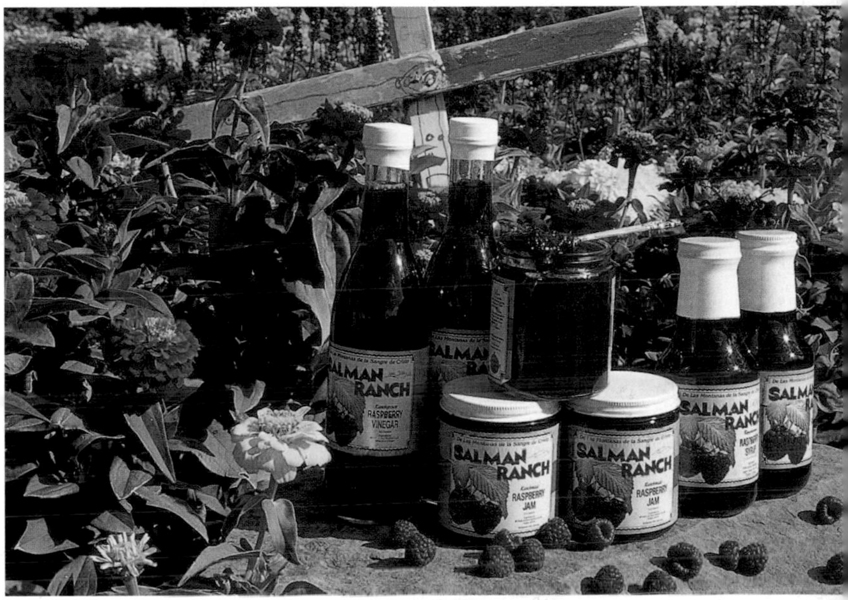
SALMAN RANCH
RASPBERRY VINEGAR
SALMAN RANCH
RASPBERRY JAM
SALMAN RANCH
RASPBERRY JAM

Opposite. Outside Mora, New Mexico, halfway between Santa Fe and Taos, the Salman Ranch spells out the word *raspberries* in red petunias.
Above. Raspberry lovers from throughout northern New Mexico stock up on the ranch's raspberry jam, vinegar, and syrup.

Where settlers in the mid-1800s struggled for survival, flowers of every color and variety are lovingly cared for today. Surrounded by adobe walls that retain warmth on nippy nights and give protection from strong winds, annuals, perennials, and wildflowers are dramatically contained in the ruins of the house's kitchen, living room, and bedrooms, as well as in an old corral. Included in the list of present-day floral inhabitants who now grow like Topsy inside the ruins are marigolds, petunias, cosmos, roses, day lilies, larkspur, delphinium, spotted gayfeather, salvia, yarrow, potentilla, gaillardia, penstemon, zinnias, Apache plume, and poppies. Additional occupants of the ruin are ornamental grasses, including Karl Foerster feather reed, hardy pampas, silky thread, and maidenhair.

"The main business of the ranch is to grow raspberries. The gardens were an afterthought," Jeff Salman says. "It's amazing, though, how many people come to see the flowers, but then leave with raspberries."

Garden appreciation has its rewards.

Left. "Warm days, cool nights, and drip irrigation keep the flavor concentrated," Jeff Salman says of his family's acres of raspberry plants.
Above and opposite. An adobe ruin outside Mora has been turned into a showcase of flowers by the Salman family, owners of a Santa Fe nursery.

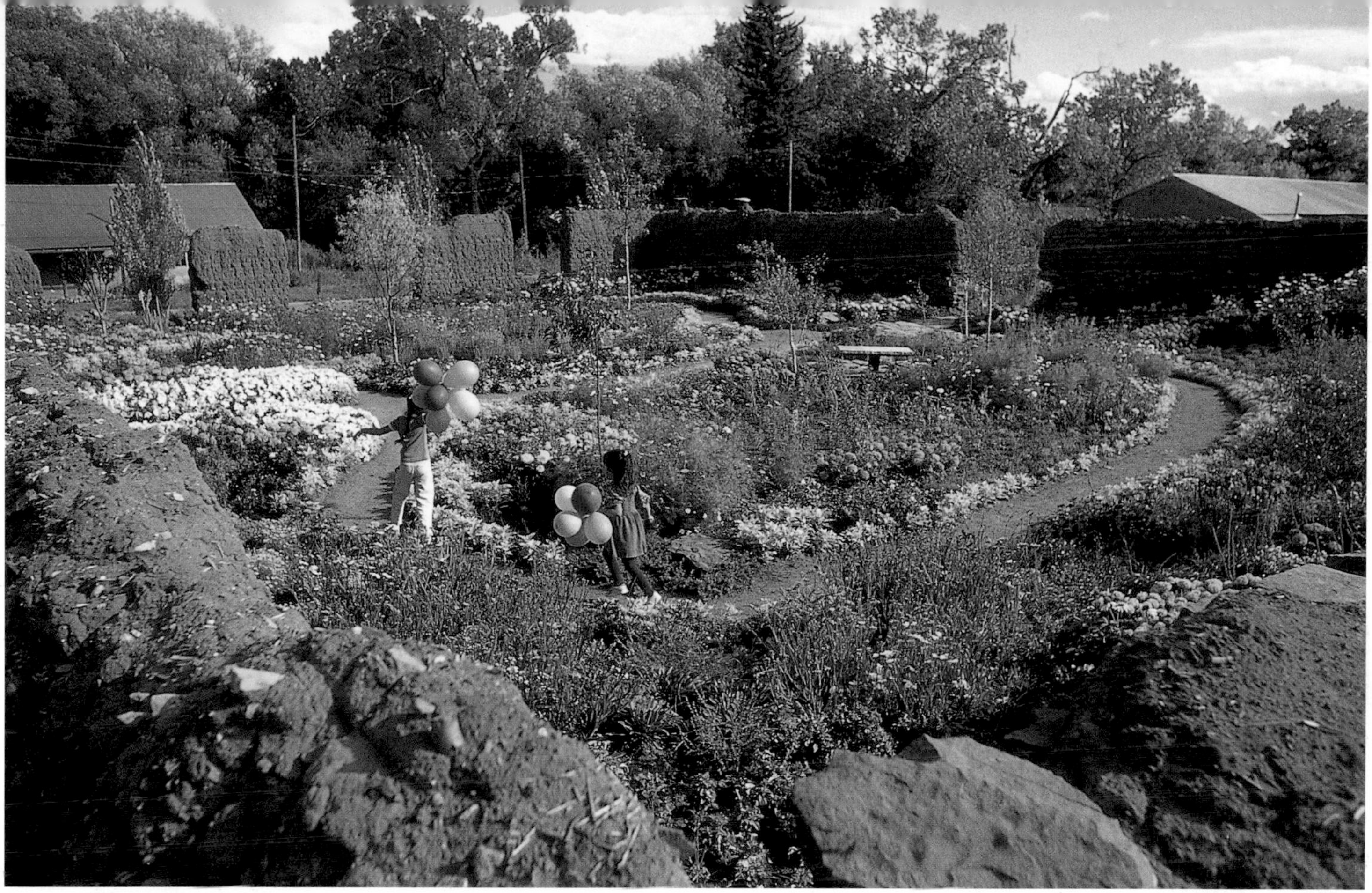

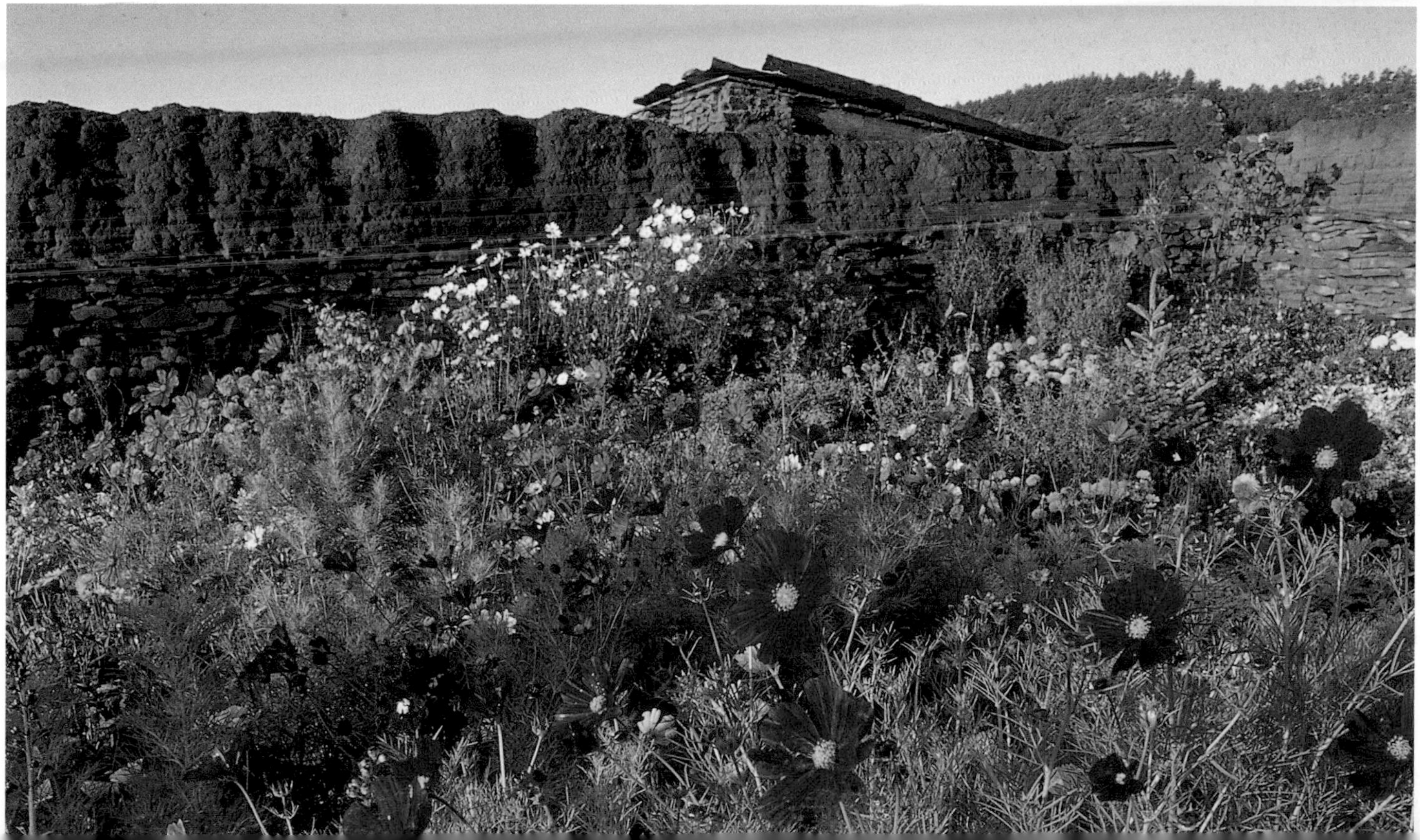

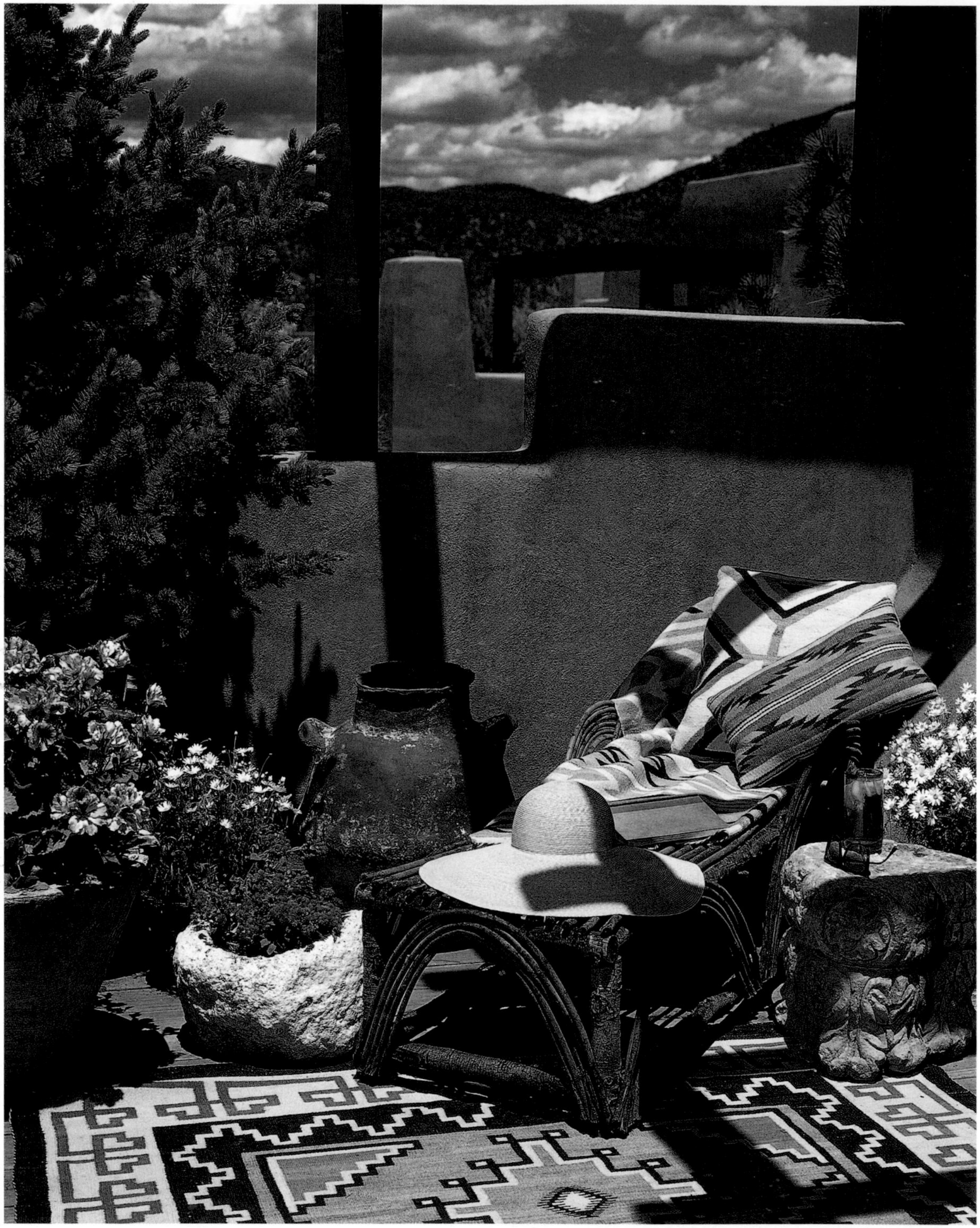

Keep It Simple

Actress Martha Hyer Wallis, the widow of film director Hal Wallis, knew exactly the lifestyle she wanted eight years ago when she moved to Santa Fe from Beverly Hills. Selling their California houses, as well as a large collection of French and English antiques and paintings, Martha scaled back her lifestyle. "My motto today is simplicity, simplicity, simplicity," she says. "Now I lead a contemplative, quiet life. I read, paint, write, and most important of all, I think."

Today, Martha is home at Los Miradores, an attractive "gated community" nestled on a plateau at the base of the Sangre de Cristo mountains, ten minutes from the Santa Fe plaza. Perfect for those anxious to avoid maintenance and security problems, Los Miradores was built by William Zechendorf, the New York City real estate mogul. Traditional adobe construction and acres of natural New Mexican landscaping have given the community character.

The thickly planted, all-green garden entrance to the Wallis property adds further to the sense of established history. "The pine trees were trucked in from Colorado," Martha says, looking out over the mini-forest of full-grown evergreens. "Huge moss rocks were lowered into place by cranes. The garden was planned so that you feel the house is in a forest glade. I wanted to feel secluded and surrounded by nature, even though I am living right in Santa Fe."

Opposite. Looking into the Sangre de Cristo mountains, the house of Martha Hyer Wallis reveals the actress's dramatic decorating style. A Navajo rug, a Mexican pot, and a Greek column join forces on the portal.
Above. Battenberg lace covers a log bed beside a Navajo rug. A Texas longhorn skull hangs on the wall.

Above. In the dining room, a painting by James Harrill of the Taos pueblo hangs beside a table covered with lacquered goatskin. Branding iron candlesticks surround rock crystals and geodes. *Opposite.* On display under a naturally shed deer antler chandelier is an antique Zuni pot, a painting by Paul Kinslow, and a sculpture by R. C. Gorman.

The streamlined architecture inside the house, together with Martha's spare decoration, provides a continuation of the peace and tranquility that she was determined to achieve in her new surroundings. "In California, I thrived on clutter. If I saw something beautiful, I bought it. I had to have it," she says. "Now, when I see something beautiful, I appreciate it, and I pass it by. It really is a new 'me.' This new-found approach translates into the way I decorated the house. I wanted it to be Southwestern, but without looking like a trading post."

All-white walls and monochromatic furniture fabrics and carpets provide a neutral background for Martha's carefully placed—and highly selective—collection of paintings, sculpture, and handicrafts, all by New Mexican artists. "I brought some things from my house in Palm Springs. But I bought most of the furniture and art for the house in Santa Fe," she says. "I'm especially fond of decorating with geologic objects, such as crystals, geodes, and fossils." Other natural accessories in the dining room include a massive chandelier made from deer antlers. ("They'd already been shed," Martha points out.) They hang over a dining room table made from lacquered goat skin. A Texas shell-stone coffee table adds a further back-to-the-earth touch to the living room.

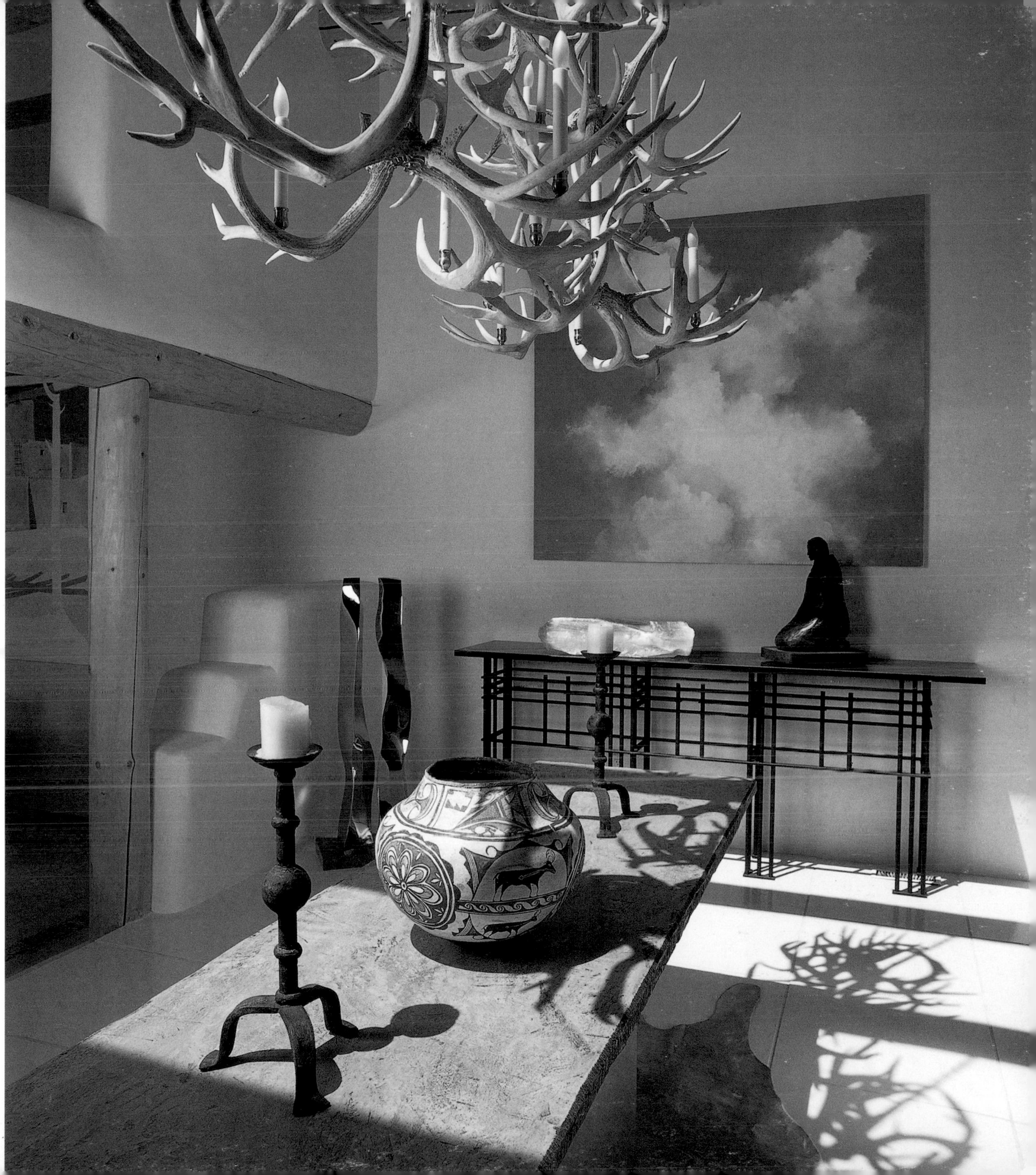

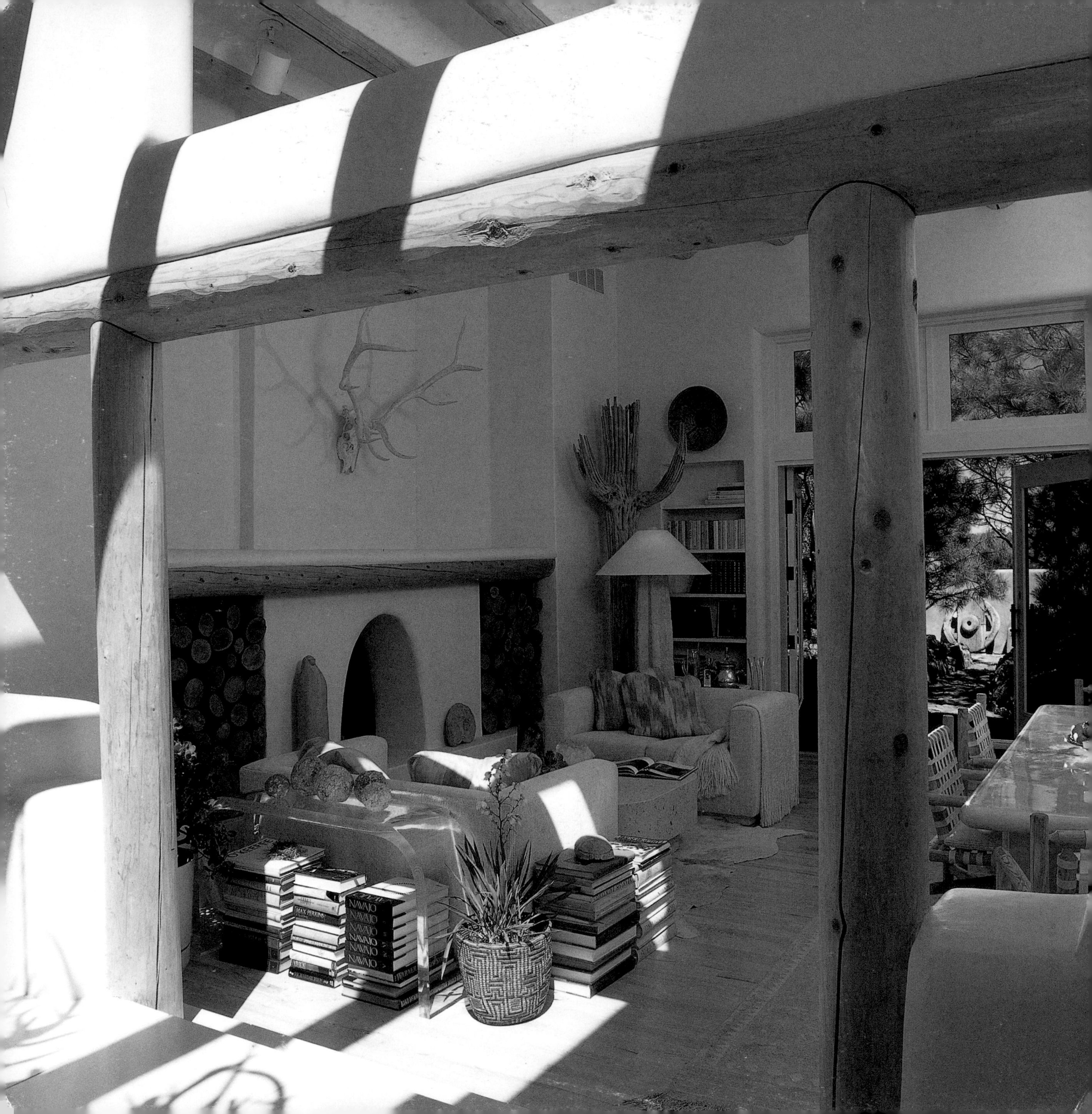
MAX PERKINS
NAVAJO
NAVAJO
NAVAJO
NAVAJO
NAVAJO
NAVAJO

Opposite. "Stacks of big books make ideal end tables," Hyer says. Four-feet-high alcoves for piñon and cedar logs also serve a decorative usefulness. The floors are oak planks.

Above. In the master bedroom, a Texas shell stone table sits beside a New Mexican cupboard, *trastero*.

Right. New Mexican twig shutters block out strong sunlight in the library. The antique muskets belonged to famed Hollywood producer Hal Wallis, Martha's deceased husband.

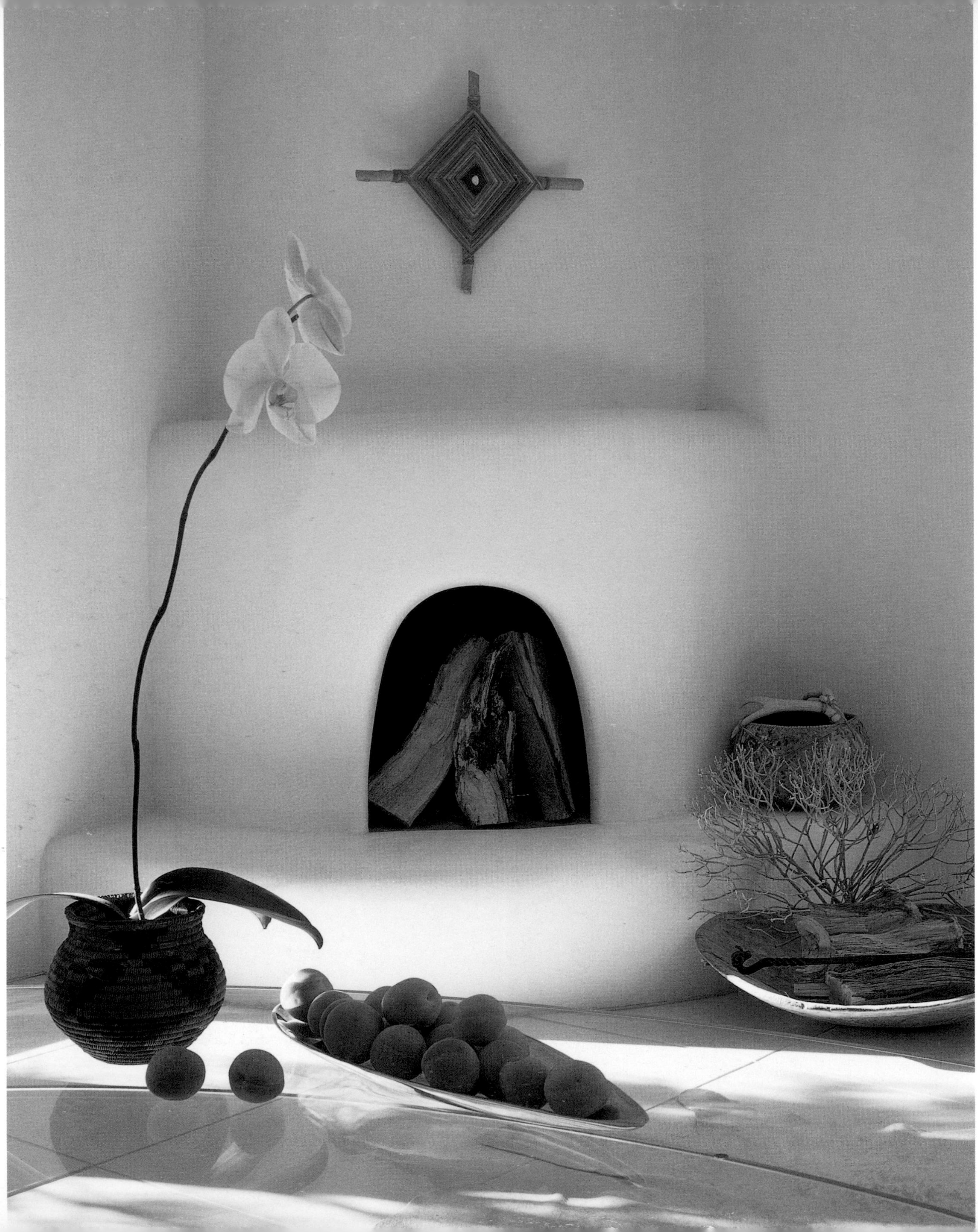

On the landing outside Martha's bedroom, a large canvas by an anonymous Blackfoot Indian chief is among the house's many examples of outstanding art. The painting's provenance is historically fascinating. "When the Great Northern Railroad began to solicit passengers, the company built hotels along the way, including one in North Dakota. A Blackfoot Indian chief was invited to paint a pictograph on a canvas that stretched across a wall in the lobby. He was delighted to accept the offer," Martha says. "His theme was a battle between the Blackfoot and another tribe." Eventually removed from the hotel, the mural was divided into several sections, each of which was offered for sale. Martha bought her portion at a Santa Fe gallery.

In her recently published biography, *Finding My Way*, Martha candidly tells of her own battle for independence, spiritual and material. She feels strongly that her success goes beyond peace of mind and is further reflected in her home's freedom from extraneous decorative elements. "I made certain the house met my need for space, for light, for solitude," she tells visitors, many of whom fail to understand her new back-to-the-basics lifestyle. "A question I am frequently asked," she says, "is 'What on earth do you do all day?' People who knew me in California, where I never stopped running, simply cannot grasp the changes that Santa Fe inspired me to make. Moving here has allowed me to live happily ever after."

———■———

Opposite. An Indian woven Eye of God looks down on an Indian woven basket and a Nambeware server full of apricots.
Above. A Mexican colonial bench sits beneath an Indian pictograph commissioned by the Great Northern Railroad. It was painted by an anonymous North Dakota Blackfoot.

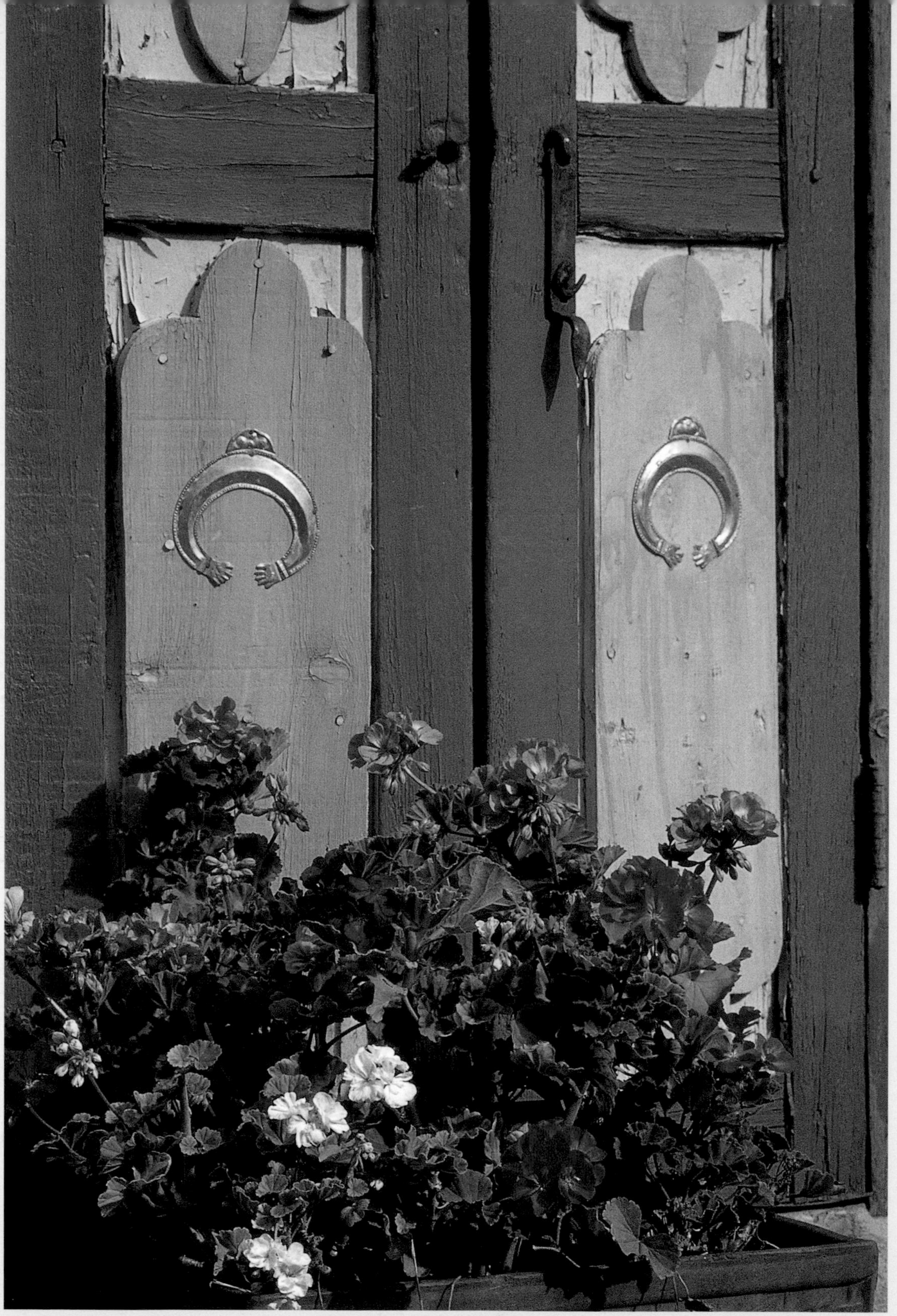

Bullock, Alice. *Mountain Villages*. Santa Fe: Sunstone Press, 1981.

Bunting, Bainbridge. *Early Architecture of New Mexico*. Albuquerque: University of New Mexico Press, 1976.

———. *John Gaw Meem: Southwestern Architect*. Albuquerque. University of New Mexico Press, 1983.

———. *Taos Adobes: Spanish Colonial and Territorial Architecture of the Taos Valley*. Santa Fe: Museum of New Mexico Press, 1964.

Burba, Nora and Paula Panich. *The Desert Southwest*. New York: Bantam Books, 1987.

Casey, Robert L. *Journey to the High Southwest*. Seattle: Pacific Search Press, 1983.

Chauvenet, Beatrice. *John Gaw Meem: Pioneer in Historic Preservation*. Santa Fe: Museum of New Mexico Press, 1985.

Horgan, Paul. *The Centuries of Santa Fe*. New York: E. P. Dutton, 1956.

Iowa, Jerome. *Ageless Adobe*. Santa Fe: Sunstone Press, 1985.

Johnson, Kathryn. *Taos Guide*. Santa Fe: Sunstone Press, 1983.

LaFarge, Oliver. *Santa Fe: Autobiography of a Southwestern Town*. Norman, Okla.: University of Oklahoma Press, 1959.

Lummis, Charles. *Land of Poco Tempo*. New York: Charles Scribner & Sons, 1893. Reprinted edition, Albuquerque: University of New Mexico Press, 1952.

Magoffin, Susan Shelby. *Down the Santa Fe Trail and into Mexico: The Diary of Susan Shelby Magoffin, 1846–47*. New Haven, Conn.: Yale University Press, 1926.

Mather, Christine. *Santa Fe Christmas*. New York: Clarkson Potter Publishers, 1993.

Mather, Christine and Sharon Woods. *Santa Fe Style*. New York: Rizzoli, 1986.

Noble, David Grant, Editor. *Santa Fe: History of an Ancient City*. Santa Fe: School of American Research, 1989.

Panich, Paula and Burba Trulsson. *Desert Southwest Gardens*. New York: Bantam Books, 1990.

Reeve, Agnesa Lufkin. *From Haciendas to Bungalows, Northern New Mexico Houses, 1850–1912*. Albuquerque: University of New Mexico Press, 1988.

Sanford, Trent Elwood. *The Architecture of the Southwest: Indian, Spanish, American*. New York: W. W. Norton, 1950.

Seth, Laurel and Sandra. *Adobe!: Homes and Interiors of Taos, Santa Fe and the Southwest*. Stamford, Conn.: Architectural Book Publishing Company, 1988.

Simmons, Marc. *New Mexico: A Bicentennial History*. New York: W. W. Norton, 1977.

Spears, Beverly. *American Adobes*. Albuquerque: University of New Mexico Press, 1986.

Taylor, Lonn, and Dessa Bokides. *Carpenters and Cabinetmakers: Furniture Making in New Mexico, 1600–1900*. Santa Fe: Museum of New Mexico Press, 1983.

Warren, Nancy Hunter. *New Mexico Style*. Santa Fe: Museum of New Mexico Press, 1986.

Weigle, Marta and Kyle Fiore. *Santa Fe & Taos: The Writer's Era, 1916–1941*. Santa Fe: Ancient City Press, 1982.

Opposite. Old New Mexican doors in a garden with contemporary squash blossom necklace design motifs.

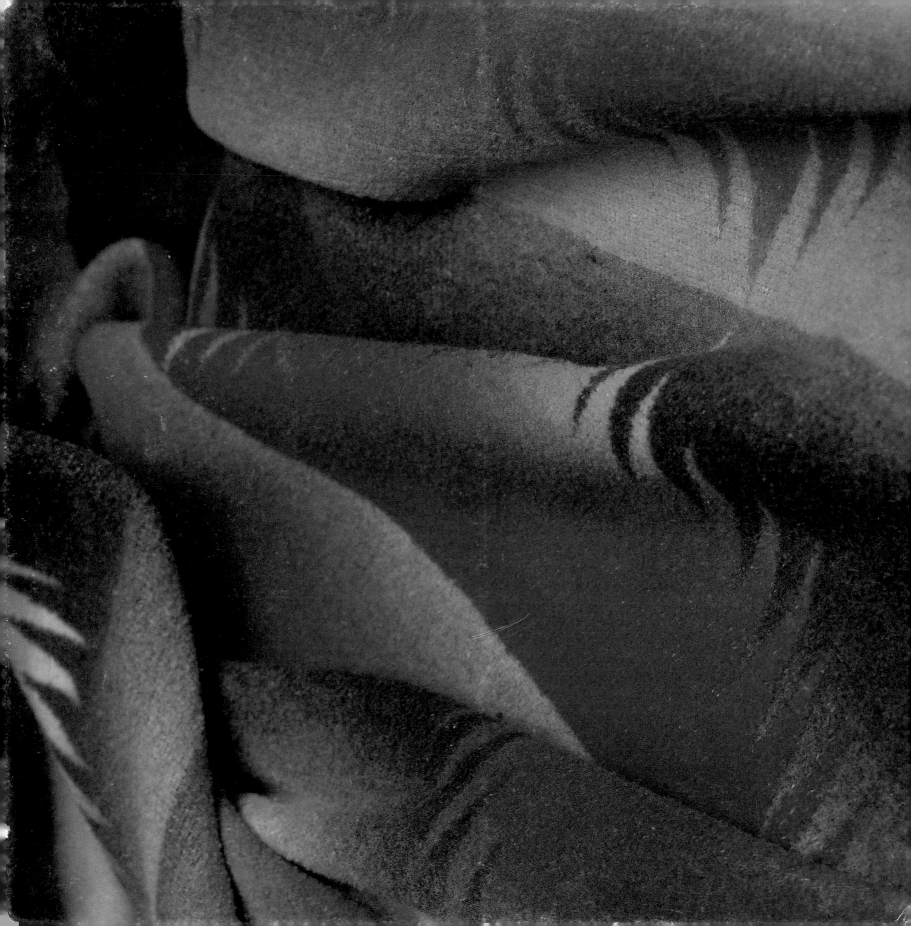